St. Michael's College

100 Years of Pucks and Prayers

St. Michael's College
100 Years of Pucks and Prayers
with a Foreword from Senator Frank Mahovlich

Kevin Shea
with Larry Colle and Paul Patskou

Fenn Publishing Company Ltd.
Bolton, Canada

St. Michael's College:
100 Years of Pucks and Prayers

A Fenn Publishing Book / First Published in 2008

All rights reserved
Copyright 2008 © St. Michael's College, Kevin Shea, Larry Cole, Paul Patskou
and Fenn Publishing Company Ltd.

All rights reserved. No part of the work covered by the copyrights herein may be reproduced or used in any form or by any means – graphic, electronic or mechanical, including photocopying, recording, taping or information storage and retrieval systems – without the prior written permission of the publisher, or, in case of photocopying or other reprographic copying, a license from Access Copyright, the Canadian Copyright Licensing Agency, One Yonge Street, Suite 1900, Toronto, Ontario, M6B 3A9.

The content, opinion and subject matter contained herein is the written expression of the author and does not reflect the opinion or ideology of the publisher, or that of the publisher's representatives.

Fenn Publishing Company Ltd.
Bolton, Ontario, Canada
www.hbfenn.com

The publisher gratefully acknowledges the support of the Canada Council for the Arts and the Ontario Arts Council for its publishing program.

We acknowledge the support of the Government of Ontario through the Ontario Media Development Corporation's Ontario Book Initiative.

We acknowledge the financial support of the Government of Canada through the Book Publishing Industry Development Program (BPIDP) for our publishing activities.

Care has been taken to trace ownership of copyright material in this book and to secure permissions. The publishers will gladly receive any information that will enable them to rectify errors or omissions.

Design: First Image
Printed and bound in Canada

Library and Archives Canada Cataloguing in Publication

Shea, Kevin, 1956-
St. Michael's College : 100 years of pucks and prayers / Kevin Shea ; with Larry Colle and Paul Patskou.

ISBN 978-1-55168-348-5

1. St. Michael's College (Toronto, Ont.)—Hockey—History. 2. Toronto St. Michael's Majors—History. 3. Hockey players—Ontario—Toronto—Biography. I. Colle, Larry II. Patskou, Paul III. Title.

GV847.75.S34S47 2008   796.962'6309713541   C2008-903671-9

Dedication

To the players, students, faculty, and fans who, through the years,
have shown true passion in proudly wearing, or cheering for,
the double blue of St. Michael's College.

Contents

	Foreword — Frank Mahovlich		8
	Introduction		9
		"Snapshot"	
Chapter 1	The School Established		11
Chapter 2	Early Hockey History	Father Henry Carr	16
Chapter 3	Touring the Eastern Seaboard	Marion Hayes	23
Chapter 4	The Debut of the Memorial Cup	Eddie Convey	26
Chapter 5	Sponsorship, and the Toronto Maple Leafs Connection		31
Chapter 6	1934 — The First Memorial Cup Championship	King Clancy	38
Chapter 7	The Thirties	Johnny Crawford	44
Chapter 8	Early 1940s — Building a Dynasty	Father Hugh Foley	49
Chapter 9	1945 — Memorial Cup Mastery	John McCormack	56
Chapter 10	Major Disappointment	Les Costello	65
Chapter 11	1947 — A Dynasty Continues	Ed Sandford	71
Chapter 12	From Feast to Famine	Leo Labine	80
Chapter 13	Rebuilding the Brand	Ed Chadwick	85
Chapter 14	The Monarchs Arrive at St. Michael's	Peanuts O'Flaherty	89
Chapter 15	The Clang of a Goalpost	Bob Schiller	94
Chapter 16	The School's Centennial	Lloyd Percival	97
Chapter 17	Heartbreak in St. Kitts	Charlie Cerre	103
Chapter 18	Leaving Their Mark	Pat Hannigan	106
Chapter 19	Toronto's Civil War: The Majors vs. the Marlies		110
Chapter 20	The Big M	Gerry Odrowski	113
Chapter 21	Keon's Coming Out Party	Cesare Maniago	116
Chapter 22	Debut of the Drapers	Pat Quinn	121
Chapter 23	Setting the Table	Arnie Brown	124
Chapter 24	The Power of Bauer	Barry MacKenzie	128
Chapter 25	The Majors Leave the OHA	Tony Fritz	143
Chapter 26	Neil McNeil and the Demise of the Metro Junior Hockey League	Jim McKenny	156
Chapter 27	Majors Redux: St. Mike's Returns to the OHL		164
Chapter 28	Trials and Tribulations	Mark Napier	169

Chapter 29	**A Season of Havoc**	*Mike Jefferson*	172
Chapter 30	**Building Towards Future Successes**	*Mark Popovic*	175
Chapter 31	**Becoming a Contender**	*Tim Brent*	178
Chapter 32	**Strength in Numbers**	*Tyler Haskins*	181
Chapter 33	**Falling Back, Springing Forward**	*The Donatis*	183
Chapter 34	**Disappointment and Change**	*Father Joe Redican*	186
Chapter 35	**The Move to Mississauga**	*Michael McGurk*	188
Chapter 36	**Buzzers — 1933 to 1961**		191
Chapter 37	**Buzzers — 1961 to Today**		205
Chapter 38	**Family Ties**		221
Chapter 39	**St. Mike's First Superstar** — Frank Rankin		230
Chapter 40	**Noble Warrior** — Reg Noble		231
Chapter 41	**First-Class Champion** — Joe Primeau		233
Chapter 42	**Kitchener-Waterloo Warrior** — Bobby Bauer		235
Chapter 43	**Talent With Intensity** — Ted Lindsay		238
Chapter 44	**A Dash of Red Mixed with Double Blue** — Red Kelly		241
Chapter 45	**Hockey's Hercules** — Tim Horton		244
Chapter 46	**The Big M Wore the Big M** — Frank Mahovlich		247
Chapter 47	**In a Class by Himself** — Dick Duff		251
Chapter 48	**Smooth-Skating St. Mike's Centre** — David Keon		253
Chapter 49	**Instilling a Dream** — Father David Bauer		256
Chapter 50	**Net Worth** — Gerry Cheevers		262
Chapter 51	**A Lifetime Devoted to Hockey** — Jim Gregory		264
Chapter 52	**Hockey's Global Ambassador** — Murray Costello		267
Chapter 53	**Conclusion**		269
	Appendix 1 — All-Time St. Michael's Majors Regular-Season Scoring		270
	Appendix 2 — St. Michael's Buzzers — All-Time Roster		281
	Appendix 3 — St. Michael's Alumni in the NHL		290
	Appendix 4 — St. Michael's Alumni Who Have Coached in the NHL		294
	Acknowledgements		295
	Bibliography		297
	Index		299

Foreword

When I was growing up in Schumacher, Ontario, I was aware of St. Michael's as a destination for hockey players, and athletes in general, because a lot of players from our town had gone there. There were Murray and Les Costello, the Hannigan brothers, and a fellow by the name of Ron Wallace. Ron wasn't Catholic, but he was a great athlete. NHL scouts from the various teams had visited our house, and when Bob Davidson of the Toronto Maple Leafs came, he sold my father on the education at St. Michael's. My father spoke with several respected men in the community — all of the managers of the mines my father worked for — and they all agreed that St. Mike's would be the best thing for me.

At the time when I was thinking of going to the school, Bill Dineen was the captain of St. Mike's. They also had Les and Dick Duff from nearby Kirkland Lake, and Jack Caffery. I remember when Father Flanagan came to the house with the Leafs' scout and he brought a school yearbook and I studied all the players on the team. Those names ring out in my mind: Caffery, Paul Knox, Jim Logan, and Kenny Linseman — I ended up finishing my career playing with his son.

St. Michael's was always very competitive, and we had an excellent reputation, one that we were all very proud of. When we went into Guelph or St. Catharines, they knew we would give them a good game. Each of us felt that we had to play hard to live up to that reputation. When I went on to play with Red Kelly, another great St. Mike's guy, it was the same feeling. There's a standard there at St. Mike's, in what we stood for and how we played, and we tried to live up to that. This is what St. Mike's was all about.

When I see alumni from the school, they are always helping each other, supporting the school, continuing the good work. My classmates have been my friends all my life — Bill Kyle, Peter Buchmann, Pat Hannigan. Both Peter and Pat have passed away, but we were friends right to the end. I still feel the same way about the school and that community of people today as I did back then. They live up to their motto, "Teach me goodness, discipline, and knowledge," and these were my experiences at St. Michael's.

Frank Mahovlich

Senator Francis William Mahovlich
St. Michael's 1953–1957

March 21, 2008

Introduction

Nestled in a neighbourhood on the edge of Toronto's downtown core sits historic St. Michael's College School. The location, just east of the corner of Bathurst Street and St. Clair Avenue West, is not the only location where the school has existed, but it is the one most fondly recalled by those interested in hockey legacies.

The school itself, having been founded in 1852, pre-dates this building. As you approach the school from Bathurst you'll see a welcoming arch, rescued by the Old Boys' Club from the school's Cherry Hill location when that building was demolished. It's a glorious reminder of the school's humble but magnificent beginnings.

The current yellow-bricked school opened in 1950. The arena, in behind the school and opened in 1960, isn't particularly impressive if you aren't aware of the talent that has, at one time or another, skated on this ice surface. No one — student, athlete, or historian — would dare speak disparagingly of the St. Michael's College School Arena.

When it comes to breeding success, it is impossible to argue with the extraordinary results attributable to St. Michael's College. In basketball, there's Duke. In football, there's Notre Dame. In hockey, there's simply no one close to St. Michael's College.

As of September 2008, a total of 184 St. Michael's College alumni have attained their boyhood dreams by skating in the National Hockey League. What's more, an astonishing 14 have achieved immortality by being inducted into the Hockey Hall of Fame. Eugene Melnyk, the current owner of the St. Michael's Majors and himself a St. Michael's alumnus, has stated: "No other school in the world can claim such impressive statistics. But even more importantly, over 6,000 students who chose to make hockey part of their experience at St. Michael's have learned the importance of leadership, discipline, adversity, and staying true to strong values."

Gary Bettman, the commissioner of the NHL, added, "St. Michael's has played an instrumental role in the growth of hockey at every level, and has enjoyed unprecedented success within the NHL. Throughout our history, St. Michael's alumni have had impact on the ice as well as in coaching and management capacities. The NHL has been fortunate to reap the benefits of the hard work that the administrators, teachers, coaches, and players at St. Michael's have contributed to this esteemed hockey tradition."

"St. Michael's College School is an example of solid academic and athletics traditions," stated Prime Minister Stephen Harper. "Its hockey program, established in 1906, has been the launching point for many young men who later have become part of Canada's splendid hockey landscape."

Father Joe Redican, principal of St. Michael's College School, is immensely proud of the school's century of involvement in hockey. "Father Henry Carr transformed St. Michael's into a modern high school when he saw that its graduates needed to be able to matriculate in order to go on to a greater range of higher studies. Hockey was introduced in 1906 as a way of furthering a well-rounded education. Hockey has provided an opportunity to learn teamwork and the value of physical activity and competition. In the process, St. Michael's has been at the very heart of Canada's hockey history."

But as remarkable as it is to revel in a 100-year hockey history rife with champions and championships, more importantly, the Basilian philosophy espoused by St. Michael's College is intertwined with the successes of the game. *Doce Me Bonitatem Et Disciplinam Et Scientiam* — "Teach me goodness, discipline, and knowledge." There simply is not an alumnus who doesn't embrace the motto of his alma mater.

If there is an underlying theme to the proud 100-year hockey history of St. Michael's College, it is the bond of friendship forged and strengthened throughout that century by players and fans alike. St. Michael's College has given students wonderful gifts — goodness, knowledge, and discipline, as well as sportsmanship — but there may be an even greater gift offered to all within the walls of the school and upon the ice of the rink. Friendship may be the greatest gift of all.

1
The School Established

Passage on the famine ship from Ireland was perilous. With little water and even less food, terrified passengers clung to whatever meagre possessions they could salvage for their trip across the icy waters of the Atlantic Ocean, not having any idea what might await them in their new, adopted homeland of Canada. Exhausted and scared, some were so hungry that they chewed on leather shoelaces for what little flavour they might be able to coax into their ravenous stomachs.

Between May and October of 1847, a total of 38,000 desperate Irish arrived in Toronto, overwhelming a city that, at that juncture, was home to just 20,000. As significant as this influx was to Toronto, it represented only a small percentage of the estimated two million refugees forced to abandon Ireland during the potato famine and put down roots in the United Kingdom, Australia, or the United States.

Many of the refugees who landed on the shore of Lake Ontario were suffering from cholera or typhus. The city constructed fever sheds at what is today the corner of Bathurst and Front streets, intended to contain the suffering Irish on their arrival. Many didn't survive, and during the summer of 1847 more than a thousand immigrants died, many undocumented, having boarded the ships in Ireland without identification of any sort. Their bodies were picked up daily and delivered to St. Paul's Basilica, home to Toronto's first Roman Catholic congregation. The summer heat demanded quick burials, so the bodies of the unnamed were interred in unmarked trenches near the church.

Michael Power was born in Halifax in 1804 and ordained as a priest at the age of 23. He was erected as Bishop of Toronto in 1841, becoming the first English-speaking bishop to be born in Canada. St. Paul's served as the seat of Toronto's first Catholic bishop until St. Michael's Cathedral was built in 1848. Visiting Ireland to observe firsthand the peril that had befallen the population, Bishop Power witnessed the mass exodus from the docks in Dublin. He wrote to his diocese in May 1847, alerting them to the impending influx of starving Irish. Upon his return to Toronto, Bishop Power immediately visited the fever sheds, ministering to the desperate immigrants. In doing so, Bishop Power was himself infected with typhus, and died on October 1, 1847. Power's kindness helped integrate the new arrivals with the Irish Catholics already established in Toronto, usurping their negative reputation for "rebellion, rum, and Rome" within a city where the Orange Lodge played such a dominant role that it would earn the nickname "The Belfast of Canada."

As a result of immigration tied to the potato famine, the Irish-born population had become the single largest ethnic group in Toronto. At that time, there were but two parishes in the city, catering to the spiritual needs of 8,000 Catholics.

Following Bishop Power's death, there was a three-year gap before his replacement, Armand-François-Marie de Charbonnel, was named. Almost immediately, the French-born bishop recognized the need for Catholic schools for the young residents of his parishes. Bishop Charbonnel reflected on his own education at the College of Annonay near Lyon, a school established by the Congregation of St. Basil, a community of priests founded in France in 1822. Bishop Charbonnel sent a letter to Pierre Tourvieille, the superior-general of the Basilians in Annonay, asking that he designate priests who could establish a boys' school in Toronto.

In 1852, the Basilians from Annonay arrived in Toronto to educate the city's young Irish Catholics.

An elaborate banquet was held to celebrate St. Michael's Allan Cup victory in 1910.

Theirs was a modest beginning: their first class consisted of just eight students in the tiny St. Mary's Lesser Seminary. The 1975–76 Program of Studies comments on the curious circumstances: "Five religious men, two of them Irish and the other three speaking no English, from a French religious community which had chosen an Asian bishop, St. Basil, as its patron, came to Anglo-Saxon Protestant Ontario at the request of the French bishop of Toronto to serve an Irish-Catholic population."

Meanwhile, under the direction of the Christian Brothers, classes commenced at St. Michael's College on Queen Street East, tied to the cathedral completed just a few years earlier by Bishop Charbonnel's predecessor, Michael Power. "This institution offers its students the advantages of a Christian education, and at the same time, a sound academic course to prepare them for a business career and the liberal professions. The number of students is limited to 50," announced the *Toronto Mirror* on August 20, 1852.

Twenty-one students enrolled at St. Michael's. Bishop Charbonnel, though disappointed that the two schools couldn't co-exist, merged them under the name of St. Michael's College on February 14, 1853. The school, now completely under the direction of the Basilian Fathers, combined education at three levels: high school, classical college and seminary. Forty-seven students, thirty of whom were boarders, moved into the Bishop's Palace on Church Street.

In 1853, John Elmsley, a church benefactor and champion of Catholic education, offered property adjacent to the University of Toronto to the Basilian Fathers on the condition that a parish church be erected as well as a college. Elmsley was 30 when he married a Roman Catholic, converted, and underwent a spiritual awakening. He readily gave his life to his adopted church and embraced the plight of the Irish famine immigrants. He stood side by side in the fever sheds with Bishop Power, both of them ignoring the risk of contagion as they helped nurse the sick and console the dying.

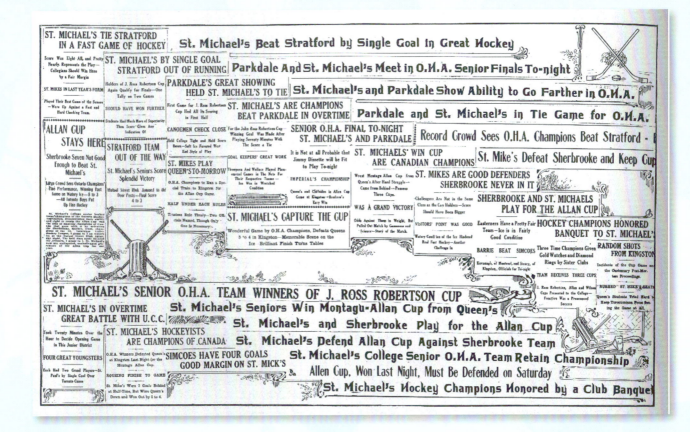

A collage of sports page headlines chronicles the Allan Cup championship won by St. Michael's College in 1910.

"Elmsley had been instrumental in pushing the Irish poor into the arms of the church as they gradually became aware that it was their only source of succour in an alien city," wrote Murray Nicholson in "John Elmsley and the Rise of Irish Catholic Social Action in Victorian Toronto." Along with Bishop Charbonnel, Elmsley realized that forceful action needed to be taken if Toronto's famine Irish were to be retained as Catholics. Elmsley had been concerned with the lack of education available for the Irish Catholic. He had often paid teachers' salaries out of his own pocket, and his decision to donate the lots at Clover Hill was his latest endeavour in serving this need.

The cornerstone for St. Michael's College and St. Basil's Church was laid on September 16, 1855. The school opened one day short of a year later with a curriculum that replicated what was being taught in Annonay, France. The attached St. Basil's was consecrated on November 16, 1856.

Bishop Charbonnel sought affiliation with the non-sectarian University of Toronto; this took place officially in March 1881, although not fully until December 1910, when St. Michael's College was declared a federated college in the Faculty of Arts and Science of U of T. Also in 1910, the College School adopted the Ontario high school curriculum.

Due almost entirely to the efforts of its Alumni Association, in 1902 a new St. Michael's College was built at the corner of Bay and Bloor. The school offered education at the prep school (grades 7 and 8) and high school as well as the university levels, and it attracted students from across North America. The school was well known for its athletic programs, and because it was known as an Irish-Catholic institution, the school's teams were tagged the "Fighting Irish of Bay Street."

Father Henry Carr, born in Oshawa, Ontario, was an alumnus of St. Michael's College and was ordained as a priest in 1905. That year, he began teaching full time at St. Michael's. He had only been ordained for ten years when he was appointed superior

THE SCHOOL ESTABLISHED

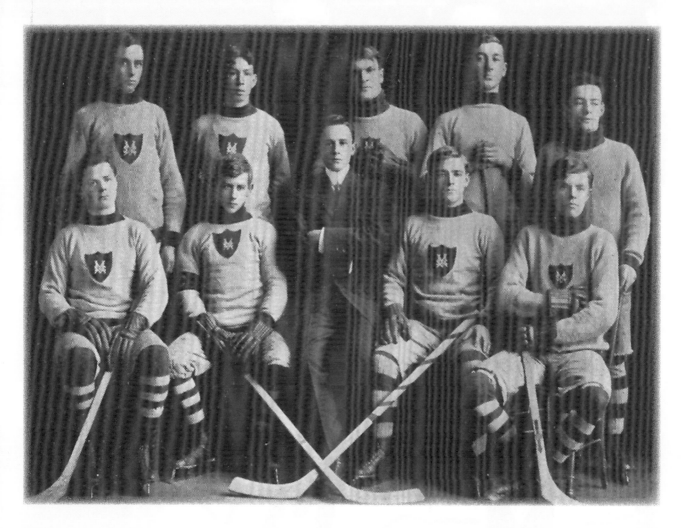

St. Michael's entry in the Ontario Hockey Association in 1911

at St. Michael's College, a position he held for 10 years. Father Carr made several very important contributions to the Toronto school. One was the realization that the traditional classical course offered by Roman Catholic high schools left students disadvantaged when they sought admission to university. Father Carr set out a broader curriculum that would better qualify graduates. But he was arguably best known for his contributions to sport; he married athletic and intellectual pursuits to offer better-rounded students to the community.

When he was appointed superior of St. Michael's College, Father Carr had ambitious plans for the school. In a letter to President Falconer in 1916, he stated that in "a comparatively short time" St Michael's College could be made "the greatest Catholic education centre in the world." Towards this goal, he set out to secure a more highly trained staff and house them in a larger school. At the time, St. Michael's was located on Bay Street, midway between Yonge and University in the midst of private homes. Father Carr planned to extend the school eastward, on land that St. Michael's either owned or had secured on a long-term lease from the city. His building program faced a serious challenge in the 1920s when the City of Toronto decided to extend Bay Street through property owned by the school. The city made a modest offer for the property it planned to expropriate; St. Michael's took the city to court; litigation gave way to arbitration, which yielded an award considered generous for the amount of land being taken, but which was inadequate to replace the Arts Building that was to be demolished to make way for Bay Street.

Later that decade, the school initiated an ambitious fundraising effort that would allow for further expansion. Although $3 million was pledged, the stock market crashed and the board of trustees decided to defer construction plans. Finally, in 1936, new classrooms and residences were completed on Queen's Park Crescent, and two years later, a refectory building was constructed on Elmsley Place. In 1939, Pope Pius XII granted St. Michael's the status of a pontifical institute, the first to be established outside of Rome.

St. Joseph's College did not move to the campus until 1926, when it obtained the Christie House, a grand residence at the northeast corner of Queen's Park Crescent and Wellesley Street West. The Loretto College residence moved into its present location on the north side of St. Mary Street in 1959.

The overcrowded high school moved from Clover Hill into a new two-storey, yellow-brick structure at 1515 Bathurst Street, close to the corner of St. Clair Avenue West, in September 1950. The high school was christened St. Michael's College School, an autonomous, private preparatory school, independent of the University of Toronto but retaining an affiliation. The new location had room for a sizeable sports field next door, and in 1956 an outdoor rink was added adjacent to the school.

From 1912 until 1931, the Junior and Senior hockey programs at St. Michael's College had been played at the Arena Gardens, also known as the Mutual Street Arena. When Conn Smythe led a consortium in building Maple Leaf Gardens in 1931, St. Mike's moved its games there. Meanwhile, the Junior 'B' Buzzers called Ted Reeve Arena in Toronto's east end, their home.

Boarders scrambled to play games of shinny on the natural ice rink at Wells Hill, across the street from their residences.

Then, on the first of July, 1960, after eighteen months of planning and construction, a new classroom building and a new arena were complete. The new St. Michael's Arena's housed all facets of the hockey program, except the Majors, who continued to play at Maple Leaf Gardens until the Junior 'A' program was discontinued after the 1961–62 season. The arena was dedicated in an emotional ceremony staged prior to a special All-Star Game on November 7, 1960. Fathers Sheedy and Conway oversaw the dedication.

In 1971, the Clover Hill location of St. Michael's College School, parts of which had existed for more than a hundred years, was demolished, but not before the Old Boys' Association salvaged the main entrance, which was re-erected as a memorial arch at the Bathurst Street location as a permanent reminder of the school's roots.

2

Early Hockey History

When Father P.J. Kelly organized the first St. Michael's hockey team in 1896, the game was still finding its balance on wobbling legs. Toronto's first recorded hockey game took place at the Granite Curling Club in February 1888, and two years later, the Ontario Hockey Association was organized, including six Toronto teams. The Toronto Junior Hockey League, which included the Granite Club, Trinity, the University of Toronto Varsitys, Upper Canada College, and the Victorias, was formed in 1893.

In a letter written to Father Mallon in the early 1940s, Father Kelly recalled with astonishing detail the history of that first team. "In 1896, a hockey team was assembled in St. Michael's and entered into a local league including Victoria, McMaster, and Knox Colleges. Though not a star team, it had considerable success. In those days of primitive sport, no substitutes were allowed and periods were the half-hour. No body pads were used, though French notebooks were allowed on shins."

One member of the team, who went on to support the game though his entire life, was Jimmy Fitzgerald, who "threw an ugly shoulder at point." Later known as J.P. Fitzgerald, he became the sports editor of the Toronto *Telegram*. A teammate was Siss Miley, who was described as an adept stickhandler "effeminate only in sobriquet."

In the early decades of the twentieth century, the Ontario Hockey Association was faced with the new threat of professional teams taking its best players. Being paid to play hockey was still an offence punishable by banishment from the OHA, but some players were paid handsomely under the table by "amateur" teams, while others were given jobs with few responsibilities with the team's sponsor. Yet, for every player that was paid to play hockey, there were thousands who simply played for the love of the sport. And for every "professional" team, there were hundreds of men and women in communities of all sizes that were more than willing to put up the money that would enable Junior, Intermediate, and Senior teams to play hockey.

An OHA rule passed in 1898 limited Junior teams to players under the age of twenty. As a result, several schools entered teams into OHA Junior competition. None reached a playoff final until 1902, when Upper Canada College defeated Stratford to take the series.

Father Henry Carr, the youngest member of the faculty at St. Michael's College, was convinced that athletics helped mould boys into men, but he also saw sport as an avenue through which St. Michael's College might become accepted on a par with other comparable schools in Toronto, such as Upper Canada College and St. Andrew's. "It was part of a philosophy of education that the Basilian Fathers have," explained Father Patrick Fulton in a CBC interview. "The motto of the school and of the Basilian Fathers is 'Teach me goodness, discipline, and knowledge.' Hockey is only one of the areas where we excel. [At the beginning of the 20th century], that was the cheapest form of entertainment they had. There was a backyard with ice and they had a few sticks and away the Basilians went. And then they said, 'We'll bring this to our students as well,' so it's always been a part of how St. Michael's grew up."

Having noted hockey's popularity increasing across the nation, Father Carr followed his appointment as athletic director of St. Michael's College in 1906 with the creation of a Prep School league, collaborating with his colleagues at Upper Canada College and St. Andrew's College. Raising the $300 for admittance to the Ontario Hockey Association took some work, but Father Carr finally found a sympathetic supporter in the superior, Father Roche, who authorized the payment.

With a squad coached by Jimmy Murphy and featuring William LaFlamme (top row, centre), the St. Michael's team won the Robertson Cup as OHA champions, then went on to collect the Allan Cup in 1910.

Although the other school teams were more experienced, St. Mike's surprised the pack by going through the season undefeated and winning the league championship. The team included captain J. McCool, star forward Jules Timmons and goaltender Clarence Doheny. They went on to face Parkdale in a series that saw the first two games end in ties before the St. Michael's Juniors won the third in overtime. They faced Stratford next, but lost; Stratford went on to the Junior championship. During that series, Charlie Rankin, the brother of future St. Michael's star Frank Rankin, was killed in a car accident near Berlin (known today as Kitchener) while returning from a game against St. Mike's.

In 1908, St. Mike's was again the champion of the Prep School group. They again faced their old rival, Stratford — this time, in the provincial final. In the first game of a two-game, total-goal series, St. Mike's Juniors won the contest, played in Toronto, by a score of 7–6. "A whole trainload of enthusiastic St. Michael's supporters went to Stratford with high hope that the victory would be repeated," wrote W.A. Hewitt in a retrospective published in a Maple Leaf Gardens program from 1937–38. "Alas and alack, something went wrong with the works, very wrong indeed, for the Midgets snowed St. Mike's under an avalanche of goals, winning the game 21 to 4 and the round 27 to 11."

Father Carr's players were now two-year veterans of Junior hockey, and three of the seven had passed the age limit to compete in the league. In 1909, Father Carr entered a team in the OHA's Senior division, using these players as the nucleus. The roster included Winnett Thompson in goal, as well as skaters Jimmy Dissette, Jerry LaFlamme, Art Lowes, Dutchy Richardson, C.E. Roche, and Jules Timmons. "There was general surprise when St. Mike's entered the Senior series with virtually the same team," Hewitt recalled. "But manager Frank Dissette and coach Jimmy Murphy had faith in their team and that confidence was justified by the final outcome."

In the OHA Senior playoffs that year, St. Mike's met the 14th Regiment from Kingston, who had won the OHA Senior championship the year before. Game One was a 12–9 victory in favour of St. Mike's, which was followed by an 11–8 win in Kingston, giving St. Michael's a 23–17 advantage in the two-game, total-goal series and the provincial Senior championship. "St. Mike's victory was wholly unexpected," commented Hewitt, "and as their chances were so lightly regarded, it made victory all the sweeter."

It was the first of many championships that St. Michael's would claim over the century.

Early Hockey History

Membership in the OHA Senior league fluctuated from year to year. The five that took the ice in 1909 were the fewest since its inception. In 1910, the circuit grew to 11 teams, despite the unprecedented demand for players created by the rise of two professional leagues, the short-lived Canadian Hockey Association and the National Hockey Association, forerunner to the National Hockey League.

Professionalism had definitely made a permanent impact on the sport. By 1908, the Stanley Cup, originally donated for the amateur hockey championship of Canada, had become the preserve of pro teams, leaving Senior amateur teams without a prize to compete for. William Northey, a sportsman from Montreal, had played a key role in the formation of the Eastern Canada Amateur Hockey Association. After three of its member clubs abandoned the league by turning pro, Northey convinced a colleague, Sir Montagu Allan, to donate a new trophy for amateur hockey. Allan, who was president of the Merchants Bank of Canada and sat on the board of Canada Steamship Lines, was also an avid sportsman, although his interests leaned more towards horses than hockey. Nevertheless, he responded to Northey's request, and the Allan Cup was born.

Like the Stanley Cup in its early days, the Allan Cup was conceived as a challenge trophy. It was initially presented to the Montreal Victorias, with the understanding that the champion of their league would defend the title against challengers. In the spring of 1908, the Ottawa Cliffsides were the first team to lay claim to the Allan Cup. Although St. Michael's were the reigning OHA Senior champions, the Cup's trustees rejected their challenge on the grounds that it had arrived too late. Queen's University of Kingston, Ontario, challenged for the trophy and won.

St. Mike's asked that their 1909 challenge be held over to 1910, but that request was also dismissed because there was no guarantee that either St. Michael's College or Queen's University would win their respective league championships the next year. Upset yet undaunted, St. Michael's paraded through the entire 1910 regular season without suffering a single defeat. The team was no longer coached by Father Carr, who chose to step aside in order to concentrate on the Prep School squad. Taking his place was Jimmy Murphy. Father Carr continued to coach the Junior team until the First World War began in 1914. At that time, he left the hockey program and exclusively coached the school's rugby (football) team.

In the 1910 OHA Senior semifinal, St. Mike's faced their old rival, Stratford. The two-game series saw the teams skate to an 8-all tie in Game One in Stratford, then St. Mike's took the second game 4–3 back in Toronto. The victory gave St. Mike's a berth in the final against Parkdale, who had edged the Toronto Argonauts to earn their spot. Game One, played before a capacity crowd, ended in a 4–4 tie. The second game saw an even greater demand for tickets, and the doors to the rink were locked well before game time.

Herb Matthews fired a goal on a Peter Spratt rebound that put St. Mike's ahead at the 25-minute mark of the first of two 30-minute periods. It appeared as though that goal would hold up as the winner, but Parkdale scored with mere minutes left in the game. "The Parkdale crowd simply went mad," reported one paper. "They shouted and cheered and threw their hats away and acted like Queen Street asylum patients on a jamboree."

Overtime was not sudden death at that time; rather, the teams played as many 10-minute periods as were necessary to decide a winner. The first overtime period was scoreless, but just seconds from the opening faceoff of the second overtime, Matthews wired a shot that was saved, but the puck rebounded directly onto the stick of captain Jerry LaFlamme, who made no mistake in putting the puck into the back of the net. That goal turned out to be the winner, eliminating Parkdale and propelling St. Mike's to a championship series against Queen's, who had defeated the Cliffsides.

A St. Mike's–Queen's final was almost better than could have been scripted. On March 16, the teams faced off in Kingston before an overly exuberant crowd. Two police officers had been appointed to guard a bank of 75 seats purchased for 50 cents each by St. Michael's supporters who arrived from Toronto by train, but in spite of the guards, Queen's students had usurped the seats. The arena manager scrambled to find enough

St. Michael's Junior entry in the Ontario Hockey Association in 1912

The Junior OHA team from St. Michael's College in 1916

seats and standing-room space for the Toronto supporters just as the puck dropped to begin the winner-take-all contest.

The first half saw Queen's take a 4–2 lead, and their commanding play did not bode well for the visitors. But in the second half, St. Mike's battled back and scored three unanswered goals, including the winner off the stick of Herb Matthews with five minutes left to play. "The wearers of the light and dark blue were all over the ice checking like wild men," recorded the school's yearbook. St. Michael's went on to win the contest, earning the title of Senior hockey champions of Canada and winners of the Allan Cup. "There, emblazoned on the annals of time, is found that unforgettable squad who went through a hectic series to capture the Senior Amateur championship of Canada."

Jerry LaFlamme was the star of that edition of the St. Michael's team. While attending dental school at the University of Toronto, LaFlamme later won a second Allan Cup championship in 1917 when he captained the Toronto Dentals. He went on to referee in the National Hockey League during the 1920s, then returned to St. Michael's to coach the team beginning in the 1933–34 season.

On March 19, St. Mike's faced a challenge for the Allan Cup from Sherbrooke, the champions of the St. Lawrence League. The game, played in Toronto, ended in an 8–3 victory for St. Michael's, allowing the school to continue their reign as champions.

The Allan Cup went through growing pains during its early life. The trophy's trustees ordered St. Mike's to defend its championship on February 20 and 22, 1911, versus the Winnipeg Victorias, even though the OHA season had not yet been completed. (Winnipeg's season had ended when they won their league championship on February 2.) The OHA pointed out that the deed of gift of the Allan Cup stated that "the Cup is to be competed for only at the end of a season, between clubs having won the championship of some recognized league or association in Canada."

St. Mike's, acting on the OHA's advice, refused to compete. After much discussion, the trustees awarded the Cup to Winnipeg. But the OHA stood firm, refusing to relinquish the trophy. As it turned out, St. Mike's did not win its own league championship in 1911. They were defeated in both semifinal games by Parkdale, who were then beaten by the Eaton Hockey Club of Toronto.

The OHA defied the Allan Cup's trustees and refused to forward the trophy to Winnipeg. As a result, there was no Allan Cup championship that season at all. Behind the scenes, lawyers worked feverishly to break the stalemate. Finally, on December 5, 1911, nine months after the Eaton Club's OHA victory, the trustees withdrew the trophy from competition, at which time the league returned the Cup. But William A. Hewitt, secretary of the OHA, refused to send the trophy to the trustees; instead, he returned it to Sir Montagu Allan, the trophy's original donor.

In the meantime, the Eaton Hockey Club and the Winnipeg Victorias both returned as champions of their respective leagues in 1912, and the two faced each other for the Allan Cup in March of that year. The Victorias easily handled the Eatons and became the Allan Cup victors.

❖

John Ross Robertson was a Toronto-born journalist who helped found the Toronto *Evening Telegram*, the voice of working-class Toronto, in 1876. In 1896, Robertson was elected to Parliament, representing the electoral district of Toronto East, but he did not run for re-election in 1900. It was in his capacity as president of the Ontario Hockey Association from 1899 to 1905 that he left his enduring hockey legacy, as he battled to protect hockey from the influence of professionalism. Robertson came forward at the annual meeting of the OHA in 1908 and announced that he was donating a trophy for the Senior series. Two years later, at the OHA's annual meeting in November 1910, he donated eponymous trophies for Intermediate and Junior hockey in Ontario.

The J. Ross Robertson Cup is still awarded in Ontario's Junior division. When Junior hockey split into two classes, Junior 'A' and 'B,' in 1933–34, the trophy was assigned to the Junior 'A' stream, and decades later, when the top level of Junior hockey was again separated into Major Junior and Provincial Junior 'A' classes, the J. Ross Robertson Cup remained with the higher tier as its championship trophy.

St. Michael's won the J. Ross Robertson Cup as champion of their Prep School Junior division in 1908–09 and 1909–10.

❖

Jack Spratt, St. Michael's hockey star of the 1910's, later joined the priesthood. He coached the Owen Sound Greys to a Memorial Cup championship in 1927.

The Eaton Athletic Association had been formed in 1910 by the T. Eaton and Company department store, which billed itself as "Canada's Greatest Store." The athletic association included a hockey team, which was equally determined to become Canada's greatest hockey team. The Eaton Hockey Club imported the best players in the area to be members of its team, among them Frank Rankin, who had led the Stratford Juniors to the OHA championship in three consecutive seasons between 1907 and 1909. He moved to Toronto in 1910 to join and serve as captain of Eaton's Senior club. The Eaton team also lured Jerry LaFlamme and Herb Matthews.

With Rankin starring at rover and leading the league in scoring (15 goals in four games), the Eaton Hockey Club won the OHA Senior championship in 1910–11. They repeated in 1911–12.

Rankin joined St. Mike's for the 1912–13 season, and again led the league in scoring, this time notching 22 goals in five games. St. Michael's went through its season without a defeat, playing against Kingston, Peterborough, and the University of Toronto. St. Mike's

The 1914 edition of St. Michael's Junior hockey team

then played four memorable games against Midland, a series won by St. Mike's. But in spite of his scoring prowess, Rankin was unable to lead his team past the Toronto Rugby and Athletic Association (TR&AA) in the OHA Senior final, a two-game, total-goal series played at the newly completed Arena Gardens (later known as the Mutual Street Arena). The teams split the games, but TR&AA prevailed by a 10–8 margin.

Rankin scored 10 goals in just two games the next season, but again, St. Mike's suffered a devastating loss at the hands of TR&AA in 1913. The rivals met again in 1914. In the first of "two stirring contests" that caught the imagination of hockey fans across the city, TR&AA won 6–5, scoring the decisive tally in the last ten seconds of play. The second game was played before 7,127 onlookers, "constituting a new record in Toronto for a hockey match, either amateur or professional," according to the OHA Rulebook of 1914. TR&AA eked out a 3–2 win to earn the championship.

As the decade progressed, St. Michael's Senior team, which had been composed solely of current students, began including alumni as part of the lineup. In 1915, the Seniors were runners-up in the provincial final for the third year in a row. This time, they faced the Toronto Victorias; St. Mike's lost Game One 2–1, tied the second contest 2–2, and lost 4–3 in the deciding game.

The school withdrew from Senior competition in 1916 due to the war. Team captain Jerry LaFlamme, by then a practising dentist in Toronto, moved over to play for the Toronto Argonauts Senior team in 1918–19.

Although St. Mike's was not represented by a Senior team during the First World War, St. Michael's did enter Midget and Juvenile teams in the Toronto Beaches Hockey League, the forerunner to the Toronto Hockey League.

While Frank Rankin was the first St. Michael's College hockey star to be inducted into the Hockey Hall of Fame, several exciting players emerged who would go on to star in the National Hockey League. In 1915–16, the most compelling player to pull on the double blue for St. Mike's Junior team was Reg Noble.

EARLY HOCKEY HISTORY

Noble joined St. Michael's after playing Junior in Collingwood. After his one season with the school, he played professionally with the Toronto Blueshirts and Montreal Canadiens of the National Hockey Association. With the formation of the NHL a year later in 1917–18, he was assigned to Toronto, where he played several years as a Blueshirt, Arena, and St. Patrick before a 1924 trade sent him to the Montreal Maroons. In 1927 he was dealt to the Detroit Cougars, who became the Falcons and ultimately the Red Wings. In 1932–33, he wrapped up his major-league career as a Maroon. In 530 games in the NHA and NHL, Noble scored 181 goals and 109 assists for 290 points, and was a member of Stanley Cup championships with the Blueshirts in 1918, the St. Pats in 1922, and the Maroons in 1926.

Father Carr elected not to ice a Junior team in the OHA in 1916–17, but they returned in 1917–18. Stan Brown joined St. Michael's as a nineteen-year-old defenceman; by the next season, he was playing Senior hockey with the Toronto Dentals from the University of Toronto. Brown earned his shingle as a dentist, yet spent part of the 1926–27 season with the New York Rangers, then a portion of 1927–28 with the Detroit Cougars. He had 10 points in 48 regular-season NHL games.

St. Michael's College had initiated its hockey program and had commanded considerable respect as a result of its Senior program. But in terms of hockey, it would enjoy its greatest successes at the Junior level, fuelled in large part by the role played by the Memorial Cup. As the First World War drew to a close, those days still lay ahead.

SNAPSHOT ▶▶ ▶▶ ▶▶ ▶▶ ▶▶ ▶▶ ▶▶ ▶▶

Father Henry Carr: The Driving Force

The increasingly important role of athletics in the program at St. Michael's College can be directly attributed to Father Henry Carr. Not only did Father Carr revolutionize the academic program, he did the same for athletics. It was his aim for the school to "break through an iron curtain that shut out St. Michael's from public competition in school sports," according to a biography, *Henry Carr: Revolutionary*.

"Henry Carr was not interested in his own reputation as a coach, though it was considered. He was convinced that athletics helped appreciably to form boys into men, and he also saw competitive sports as a contact with the public, and hence a way of getting St. Michael's accepted as a school cut in the same pattern as its neighbours in the city."

Father Carr was very earnest in his ideas. "At no other time is the true character of a boy more manifest than when he engages in a manly contest," he stated in the school's 1914 yearbook. His Basilian values were never compromised, though, as he exhibited in an article for the 1911 yearbook: "One of the greatest triumphs of a college is when it can boast that its students, though not unaccustomed to victory, can cheer with pride as their team goes down to defeat."

Father Carr could not have anticipated the enormous demands that athletics would put on students — in many cases, adversely affecting their academic pursuits. This was an issue the school often discussed through the years, culminating in the decision to withdraw from Junior 'A' hockey in 1961. "Athletics cannot perform their function properly and be a success if they do interfere [with scholastic disciplines]," Father Carr had written half a century earlier. "In my experience, I have never known a boy to fail in his classwork because of athletics."

3
Touring the Eastern Seaboard

At the conclusion of the 1910 schedule, the Allan Cup champion St. Michael's Seniors embarked on a brief tour of the United States' eastern seaboard to face teams in New York and Boston. The team included goaltender Winnett Thompson, defencemen (then called point and coverpoint) Pete Spratt and Jimmy Dissette, centre Jerry LaFlamme, rover Jack Spratt, and wingers William Richardson and Herbie Matthews. "Not only did this move encourage new fans to watch hockey, as all sport promoters know, a packed house watching a skilled performance is the best way to turn a curious observer into a novice fan," commented the *New York World*.

"Hockey as the Canucks play it bears little resemblance to the parlour game of pingpong shinny into which the game has degenerated around here," observed the *New York Times* in their December 25, 1910, edition. "The visitors are experts in all the essential requirements of the style of game that Canadian enthusiasts appreciate so well."

On December 27, St. Mike's skated out onto the ice of New York's St. Nicholas rink, experiencing artificial ice for the first time. "The only difference is that the skates do not hold as well and that it is harder to keep the puck from rolling," reported one member of the St. Mike's squad.

Spratt scored four goals in a 6–0 win over the New York Athletic Club, champions of the Amateur Hockey League of America. "He's only 17 years old but he was far superior to any of the others on the ice," enthused the *Times*. "He toyed with the rubber so skillfully that it seemed like mere play to him to get it away from the New York skaters and skim over the ice at terrific speed with the disk bouncing playfully in front of him as he ploughed through the New York team." Jerry LaFlamme and Herbie Matthews also scored for the Irish. "The St. Michael's team gave an exhibition of speedy skating and clever hockey such as is rarely seen here," added the *Times*. "The rink was well-filled for so early in the season, and the crowd was completely won over to the visitors by the clean, fast hockey they played."

The winning St. Michael's team was feted with a parade down Broadway in a procession of "puffing and snorting automobiles."

On December 29, St. Mike's took on the Boston Hockey Club, whose lineup included several Harvard graduates. The result was a 5–3 win over Boston in front of 4,000 fans, including Boston mayor John "Honey Fitz" Fitzgerald (grandfather of U.S. president John Fitzgerald Kennedy) and his children. "The Canadians showed their superiority in skating and clever stick work," noted the *New York Times*.

The contest was again filled with Jack Spratt's "wonderful rushing, dodging, and shooting," according to the *Boston Post*, which added that the game "was the largest gathering that ever watched a hockey game in this part of the country."

Spratt, incidentally, was so inspired by his teachers at St. Michael's College that he later joined the seminary, becoming just the first in a long line of excellent hockey players who passed from pucks to priesthood.

❖

The St. Michael's Seniors visited New York again in 1911, 1913, and 1915. The latter visit, which resulted in a loss to the New York–based St. Nicholas Hockey Club at their home rink, gave the Toronto team their first glimpse of Hobey Baker, who was garnering

New York newspapers covered St. Michael's barnstorming foray down the eastern seaboard in 1910. Jack Spratt shone during this series of exhibition contests.

considerable attention for his exploits on the ice in his debut season with the St. Nicholas team. Jimmy Murphy, manager of the St. Mike's team, expressed his thoughts on the American star. "Naturally, I watched Hobey Baker closely, and while I cannot admit that he is deserving of all the praise lavished on him by the New York press, I am quite free to say that he has the makings of a great hockey player," he commented in the *New York Times* on April 4, 1915. "He has natural speed that compares favorably with [Hall of Famer Frank] Rankin at his best. He has one weakness — he circles far too much. Taking the puck at his end, he circles back of the net and works across the ice two or three times on his way down. In our game, he would continually be throwing his team offside."

Baker led the American Amateur Hockey League in scoring that season with 17 goals in eight games and was named to the league's First All-Star Team. "His stickhandling is good, but not finished," continued Murphy. "I would not rate him as a better man than Harry Meeking of the Toronto Victorias, nor is he anything like as pretty a player as Dick Irvin. I consider Irvin the greatest amateur hockey player I have ever seen in action."

❖

Over the Christmas holidays of 1919–20, the club from Yale University toured southern Ontario. On December 30, they fell 10–5 to the Hamilton Tigers. On New Year's Eve, Queen's University edged them 8–6 in Kingston, while Yale rang in the new year by dumping the Brockville Hockey Club 7–4.

On January 2, 1920, Yale's barnstorming tour took them to Toronto's Arena Gardens. St. Michael's pieced together an alumni team that included Jerry LaFlamme and Tex White on defence, with Jack Spratt and Vic Dunn at forward. "White scored one goal and made many brilliant rushes, but missed many opportunities by his failure to pass the puck," scolded the *New York Times*. "LaFlamme did not take the game very seriously until the last period when he uncorked some of his old speed and was all over the ice." A Yale defenceman, Smith, scored two of his team's goals in a 3–2 victory.

Marion Hayes: The Pride of St. Michael's Women's Hockey

SNAPSHOT

Curiously, the University of St. Michael's College iced women's hockey teams in the 1920s. Marion Hayes (back row, far right) starred on this 1925 squad.

Although St. Michael's is generally regarded as an all-boys' school renowned as much for its hockey achievements as its scholastic standing, during the 1920s, when the school carried a university program aligned with the University of Toronto, the University of St. Michael's College iced a women's hockey team for several years. One of the team's stars was particularly memorable.

At the age of 94, she still did her own income taxes and housekeeping, moving the furniture to make sure her home was spotless. She was much loved by her grandchildren and great-grandchildren, all of whom she helped with their mathematics homework, since that was the subject she taught in secondary school in Cornwall. But Marion MacGillivray (nee Hayes) never told anyone in her family of her remarkable days at the University of St. Michael's College as one of the pioneers of women's hockey.

The St. Michael's women's hockey team started in 1924, when it entered women's interfaculty competition. It is only by piecing together faded yearbooks and the diaries of religious congregations that some small light is shone on this heretofore unknown part of St. Michael's hockey history. However, in December 1925, the members of the St. Michael's women's hockey team, many of whom lived in residence at St. Joseph's College, were waylaid by a smallpox quarantine that kept them confined to their residence for over a month. The carrier, it turned out, was an elderly nun who never left the residence, which confounded everyone.

The team was quite strong, and team leaders like Vera Mitchell were dismayed by the turn of events. The players were grounded just when they were supposed to playing their hockey schedule. The season was down the drain for the team.

Women's hockey recovered for the 1927 season, with Marion Hayes gracing the photos of one of her many women's athletic teams. Hayes played on the women's baseball and hockey teams until her 1928 graduation year, however, women's hockey faded from the sports scene — hindered, no doubt, by the chauvinistic attitude prevalent at the time. "Did you ever see a girls' hockey team in action? If not, you have missed one of the most amusing spectacles of your college career, unless you are a rabid hockey enthusiast, delighting only in the technique of the game," reads one entry in the St. Michael's College yearbook of 1935. "The play we offered, in conjunction with the other teams, had but occasional flashes of real hockey as when a surprisingly good pass was successful or when one of the two goals was engineered. But, if your sense of humour is a functioning appendage, you would have been amply rewarded."

Marion Hayes passed away shortly after her 94th birthday on August 31, 2001. Her daughter-in-law, Madeleine MacGillivray, said Marion never mentioned her athletic past. "She never spoke about it. All we have is a photo of her in a hockey uniform." However, Madeleine does have wonderful memories of a mother-in-law who was humble about her athletic past.

TOURING THE EASTERN SEABOARD

The Debut of the Memorial Cup

For today's fan, watching hockey in the 1910s would be a curious experience. Each team used seven players at a time, with substitutions all but nonexistent. Goaltenders, by rule, were obliged to remain on their feet at all times. Players wore little equipment — there were neither masks nor helmets — and what equipment was worn was crude and entirely unsuitable by today's standards.

The rinks themselves were usually made of natural ice, housed within an arena that more closely resembled a barn. Two on-ice officials oversaw games, using bells instead of whistles. Television and the Internet were still fantasies decades away from realization, and a concept called radio was being discussed but was still a few years away from its introduction to mass audiences.

But the game as it was played was succeeding in drawing new fans every day. Support for Junior hockey had grown to the point that, during the annual meeting of the Ontario Hockey Association in December 1918, it was agreed to establish a memorial "of some enduring character, to OHA members who have fallen on the fields of war." That memorial took the form of a trophy for the Junior hockey championship of Canada, parallel to the Allan Cup that was emblematic of Senior supremacy. Originally named the OHA Memorial Cup, the trophy is known today simply as the Memorial Cup.

Under the original format, the champions of western Canada (and winners of the Abbott Cup) faced their eastern counterparts (winners of the George T. Richardson Memorial Trophy). From 1919 to 1928, they played a two-game, total-goal series. In 1929, the format changed to a best-of-three series.

In 1934, Junior hockey was divided into Junior 'A' and Junior 'B' classes. The Memorial Cup became the Junior 'A' championship trophy; in Ontario, the Sutherland Cup was created for the provincial Junior 'B' championship, there being no national award at this level.

In 1937, the Memorial Cup series was expanded to a best-of-five format, and it became a best-of-seven series beginning in 1943. Prior to the 1971–72 season, Junior 'A' hockey was reorganized into two classes: Major Junior and Tier II or Provincial Junior 'A.' The Memorial Cup serves to this day as the Major Junior championship trophy, while Provincial Junior 'A' teams competed first for the Manitoba Centennial Trophy and then, beginning in 1995, the Royal Bank Cup.

In 1974, the Major Junior league in Ontario separated from the OHA and operated under the Ontario Major Junior Hockey League banner. In 1980, the name was simplified to the Ontario Hockey League (OHL).

Between 1972 and 1982, the Memorial Cup was contested by the champions of the three Major Junior leagues — the leagues now known as the Western Hockey League (WHL), the Ontario Hockey League (OHL), and the Quebec Major Junior Hockey League (QMJHL) — in a three-team tournament. They played a double round robin (four games apiece), with the top two teams facing off in a single-game final. That format changed in 1983 with the addition of a fourth team, which represented the city hosting the tournament. Teams play a round-robin schedule (three games each), followed by a semifinal game between the second- and third-place teams. The winner of this game proceeds to a single-game final against the first-place team.

Much of what happened during the first Memorial Cup season has been lost to history, although St. Michael's College iced a team in 1918–19 that was coached by V. Dunne and included D. Cronin, F. Halloran, O. Legge, W. McComber, Herb Munroe, G. O'Connor and W. Rocque. The first Cup champions were the team from the University of Toronto Schools (UTS), managed by Frank Selke, who would play a role in the lasting relationship between St. Michael's College and the Toronto Maple Leafs. UTS won the Prep League, then defeated a Woodstock squad and the Montreal Melvilles to earn the eastern championship. In a two-game, total-goal series against the western champs, the Regina Pats, they prevailed 29–8.

Father Bellisle's Junior team of 1920 had only two returning players, McComber and Munroe. They were joined by goaltender V. Loranger, defenceman Jack Millan, and forwards Jack Killen, Jack Lynch, and Steve Rice. "We have had a most successful year, and the prowess of the team is amply demonstrated by the fact that the majority of the players have been drafted to the Intermediate team," applauded the school's yearbook.

The school yearbook capsulized the 1920–21 season by writing, "From the goaler to the subs, every man played excellent hockey, and the team as a whole was imbued with the spirit which spurred the players to give the best that was in them." Art James starred in goal for St. Michael's, while Chris McCarnet, Jack Millan, and Joe Murphy performed well at forward. St. Michael's College played a six-game season, competing against St. Andrew's College, UTS, and Upper Canada College. St. Mike's won the Prep Group, but ended up losing to De La Salle in a two-game, total-goal series. St. Mike's took Game One and led Game Two for 57 minutes, but De La Salle responded with a late goal to tie the score. During the 10-minute overtime, De La Salle scored. The series ended with De La Salle scoring six goals to St. Michael's three. Art Gauthier played with St. Michael's in 1920–21, and after several seasons of skating with the Galt Terriers of the OHA Senior loop, he joined the Montreal Canadiens for 13 games at centre during the 1926–27 season.

Jack Millan returned to play for St. Michael's during 1921–22. The team split the six-game campaign, winning three and losing three. St. Andrew's went on to win the Prep Group.

One of the players who starred for St. Michael's College following the First World War was Larry Aurie, who came to the school from Sudbury in 1922–23. That season, St. Mike's was champion of the Prep Group, but lost to the University of Toronto Varsitys in the OHA playoff. Appearing in seven contests, Aurie led the OHA in both goals (16) and points (20) in 1922–23. He returned to Sudbury to play two more seasons of Junior, then, after a year of Senior hockey in Galt, he turned professional with the London Panthers of the Can-Pro League in 1926–27. The following season, he was a member of the Detroit Cougars of the NHL.

Although just five feet, six inches tall, he was both skilled and tough (he was nicknamed "Little Dempsey") and finished among the NHL's point leaders in 1934–35. In 1936–37, the Detroit captain tied for the league lead in goals (23). It appeared as though he would also win the scoring title, but towards the end of that season, he broke his leg and finished fourth, three points behind Sweeney Schriner. After retiring from the NHL at the conclusion of the 1937–38 season, he was named playing coach of the Red Wings' farm team in Pittsburgh, but returned to the Red Wings for one game as an emergency replacement during the 1938–39 season. He scored the winning goal in that game, the 147th and final goal of his NHL career. In 12 NHL seasons spanning 489 regular-season games, all with Detroit, Aurie also tallied 129 assists for 276 points.

By the mid-1920s, St. Michael's had become a much-desired hockey destination for promising young players.

During that era, the teams of the Junior league competed in a pre-season tournament, with the winning squad claiming the coveted Sportsmen's Patriotic Association (SPA) Trophy. In a 4–3 victory over the University of Toronto Schools during the SPA series on December 12, 1923, St. Michael's discovered that they had a new star on their hands. "Trottier at centre far outclassed any man on the ice," wrote *The Globe*. "He scored all

The Memorial Cup debuted in 1919 and today is still presented to the Canadian Hockey League's champion Junior team.

his team's goals and with his clever poke-check, stopped play after play at centre ice." Dave Trottier, a student from Pembroke, Ontario, delighted the St. Mike's fans with his terrific play. Facing the Aura Lee Juniors in the SPA tournament on December 16, Trottier again starred. "He was easily the best man on the ice and a continual thorn in [goaltender Joe] Stark's side. He broke up play after play at centre ice and several times stickhandled his way right in on Stark."

Trottier played two seasons with St. Michael's, leading the Junior squad in goals in 1923–24 (13 in six games) and assists in 1924–25. By 1925–26, he had joined the University of Toronto Grads Senior team, with whom he won the Allan Cup in 1927. The Varsity Grads were selected to represent Canada at the Olympic Games in 1928, the first time there were separate Winter and Summer Games. After practising at Toronto's newly built Varsity Arena, the team embarked by ship for St. Moritz, Switzerland. The Grads were deemed far enough ahead of the competition that they were given a bye into the medal round, where the winners of three divisions joined Canada in a three-game round-robin tournament.

Canada defeated Sweden 11–0 in its first game and then walloped Great Britain by a 14–0 score. The deciding game, played against Switzerland, saw Trottier and his teammates claim the gold medal after dusting off the host country by a score of 13–0. Trottier contributed 12 goals to his country's cause. It was the only gold medal that Canada won at the Olympic Games that year.

In April, after the Olympics, the Montreal Maroons signed Trottier for an astronomical $10,000, but Toronto argued that he was not a free agent, that he was already their property. The league sided with the Maple Leafs. By the end of November, the Maroons had purchased the lightning-quick forward from Toronto for $15,000. He played 11 seasons with the Maroons, capping his career with a season as a Detroit Red Wing in 1938–39. In 446 games, he scored 121 goals and 113 assists for 234 points.

The 1923–24 season also saw the arrival of one of the finest players ever to be affiliated with St. Michael's College. Although it was the only year that Joe Primeau would play for the Double Blue, his influence permeated the hockey program at St. Michael's right into the 1960s. Primeau starred with the team, later coached the team, and served as an advisor during some challenging years.

❖

D'Arcy Coulson was a tough-as-skate-leather defenceman for St. Mike's, who ended up scoring five goals in the six-game 1926–27 campaign. In December 1930, he was signed by the NHL's Philadelphia Quakers. Coulson played 28 games without contributing any points, but he certainly added toughness to the lineup by earning 103 minutes in penalties, the most on the team. The Quakers had an abysmal season, winning just four of their 44 games while losing 36 and tying four, for a dismal winning percentage of .136, which remained the worst in NHL history until the woeful Washington Capitals set a new standard for futility with a .131 percentage in 1974–75. The franchise suspended operations at the end of the season and never returned.

As for Coulson, he was claimed by the Montreal Canadiens in a dispersal draft after the Quakers folded, but never played another NHL game.

Another player who starred with St. Michael's Juniors in the 1920s was Rollie Conacher. The cousin of the Hall of Fame Conacher family (Lionel, Charlie, and Roy), Rollie first suited up for St. Mike's in 1923–24 and had developed into a very solid centre by 1926–27. During that season, which saw the Toronto St. Mary's team reincarnated as the Toronto Marlboros, Rollie led St. Michael's in scoring with 10 goals and 13 points. Conacher was moved to the Marlboros the next season, and he signed with the Toronto Maple Leafs in October 1928, although he never played in the National Hockey League.

Although its Junior team didn't reach the Memorial Cup final in 1927, the school did make a contribution. Jack Spratt, the outstanding scorer of those earlier St. Michael's teams, had been ordained and spent the early part of the decade at St. Thomas University in Fredericton, New Brunswick. He relocated from the Miramichi to Owen Sound, Ontario, in 1926 and became the coach of the Owen Sound Greys of the OHA's Junior

The 1927–28 St. Mike's Junior team reunited many years later, and the yearbook reporters captured the event. Front row: Charlie Cerre, Father Maurice Whelan, Leo Bruyea, Harry Doran, and Father Wilf Kehoe. Middle row: Pat Glynn, James Sullivan, Eddie Convey, and Jack Oakley. Back row: Bill Regan and Walter Dunbar.

league. Under Father Spratt, the Greys, who had won the Memorial Cup in 1924, defeated the Port Arthur West Ends to claim the Memorial Cup in 1927, making the Greys the first team to win the trophy twice.

❖

The St. Michael's Junior hockey club looked better than promising on paper prior to the 1927–28 regular season. A highly regarded trio consisting of centre Eddie Convey and wingers Charlie Cerre and Wilf Kehoe was devastating to opponents. In the six-game season, Convey scored 12 goals and led the league with six assists. "Convey's checking was à la [Frank] Nighbor, Cerre showed some smart stickhandling while Kehoe stuck to his check like a leech," according to the yearbook. "Jimmy Sullivan played defence beside Bill Regan, who brought the crowd to its feet with his famous corkscrew rush." Morrie Whelan was in goal for St. Mike's.

St. Michael's went through the season undefeated. In the playoffs, the Double Blue first met Georgetown, spanking that squad 9–3, then Belleville, who fell 11–5 to St. Mike's. Then, Toronto fans got the match they were hoping for: St. Michael's versus the Marlboros. St. Mike's lost both games (4–1 and 4–2), but "their grit and never-say-die spirit won them the applause and admiration of even the staunchest Marlboro supporters," according to the school yearbook.

Coach Joe McGahey's Juniors may have fallen short of the predictions, but the yearbook recapped their season in glowing terms: "A game, fighting team imbued with the Double Blue spirit that never says quit; a resourceful and dynamic coach who shaped a collection of comparatively inexperienced players into one of the smoothest hockey machines in Junior Hockey; the support of the biggest following any team in Toronto can claim and a consuming desire to see the Memorial Cup standing with our other trophies — this was what St. Michael's gave to Junior hockey this year."

Bill Regan, from Creighton Mines, Ontario (near Sudbury), enrolled at St. Michael's College in 1925. The big defenceman played well, but it wasn't until 1927–28 that he really blossomed. During the six-game schedule, both Regan and Eddie Convey scored 12 goals for St. Mike's. After his fourth year at the school, Regan signed with the Boston Bruins, but a trade in February 1930 saw Bill make his NHL debut with the New York Rangers in 1929–30. He played two seasons with the Rangers. In 1932–33, the Rangers loaned him to the New York Americans, with whom he completed his NHL career. His totals show five points in 67 contests.

❖

The Toronto *Mail and Empire* claimed that the 1928–29 team "possessed hockey jerseys, sticks, and ambition, but little else." Of the squad that went to the semifinals the previous season, only two — Wilf Kehoe and Leo Bruyea — returned for the 1928–29 campaign. The rookies included Jess James in goal, a superb stickhandler from western Canada named Jack Pereyma, and Joe Primeau's brother Jim.

The team didn't disappoint the pundits — they finished last — but they played a smart team game under Father Jack Spratt, the former St. Mike's star. A 1–0 win over Upper Canada College was the season highlight for the young group.

Father Spratt returned to coach St. Mike's in 1929–30, but was again faced with dismal prospects for the season. St. Michael's met UTS to begin the season, losing 2–1 in an exciting overtime contest. Astonishingly, St. Mike's won four of the remaining five games to earn a second-place finish in the league.

According to the school yearbook, second-year goaltender Jessie James's "consistent saves" were what "stamped him as the outstanding netminder of the group." Punk Holt and Jack Oakley were solid as a wall on defence, and Jimmy Primeau, with his relentless work ethic, reminded onlookers of his brother.

St. Michael's had spent a decade pursuing the dream of a Memorial Cup championship. Their chase would finally end in a celebration during the decade of the 1930s, an era that would also include a formal relationship with a National Hockey League team.

SNAPSHOT ▸▸ ▸▸ ▸▸ ▸▸ ▸▸ ▸▸ ▸▸ ▸▸   *Eddie Convey*: *A Bust In the Big Apple*

Eddie Convey had enjoyed a modest season with St. Mike's in 1926–27, but he evolved into a high-scoring centre when placed between Cerre and Kehoe in 1927–28. That year, he finished second in OHA Junior scoring. Eddie served on the first student's council at St. Michael's College that year, too, but Frank Selke lured him to the Toronto Marlboros the next season, where he played between future Hall of Famers Charlie Conacher and Harvey "Busher" Jackson on a line known by the media as the Three Musketeers. The Marlies reached the Memorial Cup final, where they met the Elmwood Millionaires from Winnipeg in a best-of-three series. It took the Marlboros just two games — a pair of 4–2 victories, the first of them in overtime — to win the championship, and Convey scored a goal in each game. It would be the first of seven Junior championships for the Marlboros.

While much of that 1928–29 Marlboros team went on to play in the NHL for the Maple Leafs (Red Horner and Alex Levinsky as well as Conacher and Jackson), Convey signed with the New York Americans, with whom he spent three seasons, collecting two points through 36 games.

Convey's struggles to score with New York are the subject of an oft-repeated story. He told his friend King Clancy, the Maple Leafs' star defenceman, that he was going to be demoted to the minors unless he started producing more goals. The mischievous Clancy enlisted teammates Charlie Conacher and goalie Lorne Chabot in trying to get Convey a goal in a contest against Toronto. The plan devised by Clancy was that if the Leafs were two or three goals ahead of the Americans, he would have Conacher miss a check on Convey, then would himself fall in trying to stop Eddie, giving the forward a clear breakaway on which to score.

Late in the game, the Leafs held a decided lead and Clancy put the plan into effect. Convey easily deked past Conacher, then skated past a clumsy Clancy. But with a clear lane on Chabot, and given a healthy percentage of open net, Eddie fired the puck high and wide.

Clancy nodded to Conacher and Chabot, indicating that Convey should get another opportunity. Sure enough, a few minutes later, Eddie flew past the "Big Bomber" and sidestepped Clancy. With even more net left open by Chabot, Convey leaned into a shot and caught Chabot in the throat. Conacher and Clancy raced over to the gasping goalie, who glared at the two and sputtered, "No more charity, guys. That guy doesn't deserve to score!"

Conacher glanced over at Clancy. "Whaddya think, King?"

"Chabot's right," Clancy replied. "Next time Convey comes down in our end, cut his legs out from under him!"

5
Sponsorship and the Toronto Maple Leafs Connection

The role played by Conn Smythe, the longtime owner and general manager of the Toronto Maple Leafs, in cementing St. Michael's reputation as a hockey hotbed cannot be overstated. Born in Toronto, Smythe was studying engineering at the University of Toronto when he led the U of T Varsitys to the 1914 OHA Junior final and a championship the following season. The coach of the team he faced in the 1915 final, Frank Selke of the Toronto St. Mary's, would later play a vital role in the future of both the Toronto Maple Leafs and St. Michael's.

After winning the Junior championship in 1915, Smythe and his teammates enlisted in Canada's war effort. After a few months, he was transferred to the 40th (Sportsmen's) Battery, where he organized a hockey team that would compete in the OHA Senior series. Smythe played one game and then devoted himself to coaching. The team didn't complete the season because they were summoned overseas in February of 1916.

Following the armistice, Smythe returned to university, coaching various teams. Having gained a reputation for having an astute eye for hockey talent, Smythe was hired in 1926 to assemble and manage the newly created New York Rangers. The players he recruited included goaltender Lorne Chabot, defenceman Ching Johnson, and forwards Frank Boucher and brothers Bill and Bun Cook. But the Rangers' ownership quarrelled with Smythe and released him just prior to the start of that first season, replacing him with Lester Patrick. Ironically, the Rangers team that Smythe put together won the Stanley Cup championship in just their second season (1927–28).

After being fired by New York, Smythe returned to Toronto and coached the University of Toronto Varsity Grads, taking them to the Allan Cup championship. The team was selected to represent Canada at the Winter Olympic Games in 1928 (as most Allan Cup champions were until the 1960s), but Smythe did not go. Instead, he put together a consortium that purchased the Toronto St. Patricks, a franchise threatening to move to Philadelphia, for $160,000. On February 14, 1927, the team was renamed the Maple Leafs, and before long, the green and white of the St. Pats gave way to blue and white uniforms.

Conn Smythe, in spite of his very strong Protestant beliefs, realized the value of St. Michael's in sourcing prospects for his Toronto Maple Leafs.

The concept of sponsorship is almost as old as the game of hockey itself. For example, in the 1890s, the Ontario Hockey Association required that each of its Senior teams sponsor a Junior squad in order to maintain a supply of reserves, either for immediate use or to replace graduating players season by season. Just over a decade later, the OHA ruled that, should a player so much as appear in a single game for a team, his rights belonged to that team until it saw fit to release him.

"Amateur hockey in Canada had organized itself in anticipation of professional hockey sponsorship," wrote John Wallner in *Athletics and Academics: St. Michael's College Withdrawal from Ontario Hockey Association Junior 'A' Competition*. "The Junior, Senior, and Intermediate classifications established a hierarchy of players and a vertical integration of teams that assisted player development and recruiting and provided a structure with which the professionals could later negotiate."

With the establishment of the National Hockey League in 1917, teams began to sponsor amateur players through a variety of agreements. By the 1930s, and continuing until the NHL's "universal" amateur draft was instituted in 1969, the National Hockey League had a virtual stranglehold on young hockey players from across Canada and, to a much lesser degree, the United States. If an NHL scout spotted a player of any age anywhere in Canada or the U.S., they would telegraph NHL headquarters in Montreal and put that player on the team's negotiation list. The player was seldom informed of this development until the NHL club chose to take the next step.

❖

Jack Adams, the innovative general manager and coach of the Detroit Red Wings from May 1928 (when the team was still known as the Cougars) until 1963, is generally credited with the idea of a farm system in professional hockey. Taking a page from Branch Rickey, who initiated a farm system while with baseball's St. Louis Cardinals in the late 1920s, Adams built a core group of players that led the Red Wings to seven consecutive first-place finishes and four Stanley Cup championships between 1948 and 1955 by employing a progressive series of minor-league team teams to feed his NHL team. The system was so successful that, almost immediately, other NHL executives followed suit.

The Toronto Maple Leafs had instituted their own rudimentary farm system in the 1920s. By 1926, they had an agreement with the Toronto Marlboros of the OHA Junior league. The Leafs provided the Marlies with Red Horner, Joe Primeau, and Carl Voss that season; in 1927–28, they added St. Mike's alumnus Rollie Conacher and his cousin Charlie, as well as Harvey Jackson and Alex Levinsky. That same season, the Maple Leafs purchased a stake in the Toronto Ravinas of the Canadian Professional Hockey League, using them to nurture Lloyd Gross, Joe Ironstone, Gerry Lowrey, George Patterson, Joe Primeau, Art Smith, and Carl Voss.

"There is anecdotal evidence that [Conn] Smythe was financing players at St. Michael's [by paying the tuition of a select group of players] even before he bought the St. Pats, but I've never come across any record of it in writing," stated Father William O'Brien, the school's archivist, in a 1997 interview with *Canadian Hockey* magazine. Indeed, no written record can be found of any formal agreement between the Maple Leafs and St. Michael's until 1954, although there is no doubt that such a relationship did exist.

The first time that the two teams were publicly aligned was in the school yearbook of 1929, which mentioned that St. Mike's players Joe Primeau and Alex (Rollie) Conacher were property of the Toronto Maple Leafs. The sponsorship agreement between the two became formalized at some point later, likely in a verbal agreement between the school's athletic director and Conn Smythe.

The earliest written agreement consists of a simple letter dated October 9, 1954, on Maple Leafs Gardens letterhead. The letter, sent to Father Flanagan by Conn Smythe, "confirmed previous arrangements" and delineated the terms of the agreement "with regard to sponsorship of St. Michael's Hockey Club for 1954–55." Maple Leaf Gardens was to pay St. Michael's College $10,000 plus "their share of the hospital tax when refunded." The Leafs were to receive 6 percent of gross gate receipts.

In return, the NHL club expected the following:
- your full co-operation in enlisting good students and good hockey players in to your school;
- that it be made known to these boys that the Maple Leaf Hockey Club is financing them and therefore, second to school spirit, they should be indoctrinated with the Maple Leaf spirit and will sign with us, with your assistance, when requested;
- you have the full rights to the student and his hockey ability when he is with St. Mike's, but we are to have full hockey rights in him if he is going to leave the College, and any monies accruing from the sale of a player should be the property of Maple Leaf Gardens.

Smythe added, "We are willing, when you act as Agent, that a fair commission be returnable because of the sale, but the thing sold is our property and should be so considered. No sale, transfer, or release should be made without the consent of Maple Leaf Gardens."

The relationship, whether signed on the dotted line or not, proved immensely beneficial to both St. Michael's and the Toronto Maple Leafs. It's impossible to overlook the irony that the world's single most productive Catholic prep school in terms of developing hockey prospects was supported financially for years by a Protestant who made no secret of his ill feelings towards those who followed the teachings of Rome. Smythe's suspicion of Roman Catholics seems rooted in his childhood. "The route to and from kindergarten was full of fear for me, because we had to pass St. Michael's College," he recalled in his memoirs. Smythe, at five years of age, was attending the Wellesley School at Bay and Wellesley streets, not far from St. Mike's. "Religion was very bitter in those days. The Knights of Columbus, Catholic, celebrated St. Patrick's Day; the Orangemen, Protestant, July 12. But those were just the *big* fighting days. All year, when Protestant and Catholic kids came together, there would be fights. We were scared to death of being attacked by the Catholics if we went the short route north past St. Michael's. In our ignorance, we sincerely believed that if we were captured by the priests, we'd never be seen alive again."

While Conn was overseas in August 1942, preparing for battle, his son Stafford took leave from the naval base in Halifax where he was training and returned to Toronto to marry his longtime girlfriend, Dorothea. What should have been a time of great happiness for the young couple was instead an act that created a rift within the Smythe family. "Conn was furious because Mom was Roman Catholic, and he never approved of Dad seeing a girl 'outside the faith,'" stated Tommy Smythe, the son of Stafford and Dorothea.

The religious issue made the wedding arrangements cumbersome, and Stafford and Dorothea were forced to make their plans in secret. As Tommy Smythe recalled: "Mom and Dad ended up having two small ceremonies — one in the vestibule of a Roman Catholic church followed by another at St. Charles United Church near the home of Conn and Irene. Although my grandfather opposed the marriage, he put his anger aside and attempted to be there to witness his son's union. Unfortunately, Conn could not obtain a furlough allowing for his arrival in Toronto on time."

When Conn finally returned home, he was greeted by a long letter from Dorothea. "Her long, handwritten prose explained that she loved my father dearly, and he loved her, and although the pressures of religion had forced them to separate in the past, their mutual love always pulled them back together. Mom assured Conn that if she and my father were blessed with children, they would be raised in a manner in which Conn would be proud. Conn eventually accepted Mom and they grew to love each other and became great friends as well."

Yet Smythe never allowed religion to stand in the way of his pursuit of hockey championships. Indeed, many claimed that St. Michael's gave the Maple Leafs an unfair advantage in the recruitment of talent. "You had every priest in Canada keeping an eye on the best hockey players in his parish with thoughts of sending them to St. Michael's," stated Father O'Brien. While every team could dangle the opportunity to play hockey in the NHL, the Toronto Maple Leafs were also able to offer an excellent Catholic education.

When St. Michael's left Junior hockey, Conn sent a letter to the principal. Even at this late date, it seems the best he could muster was a grudging admiration: "I myself, with a father born a few miles from Belfast, had always a wary eye turned toward the Catholics, but in my association with your school through your Sports Directors, and knowing the way you have treated the Protestants who have attended your school, I have gained a knowledge of your religion which, at least, has made me respect your whole organization very much."

❖

Frank Selke should be credited as a key architect in building the relationship between the Toronto Maple Leafs and St. Michael's College.

The bond between the Toronto Maple Leafs and the St. Michael's Majors was largely cemented by a sportsman named Frank Selke. Born in Berlin (now known as Kitchener), Selke moved to Toronto in 1919 and found work as an electrician at the University of Toronto Schools. While there, he coached the school's OHA Junior team, and in that first season, UTS won the first-ever Memorial Cup championship. Selke then became coach of the Toronto St. Mary's, a Junior team based out of St. Mary's Roman Catholic Church at Bathurst at Adelaide streets. Like St. Michael's, St. Mary's realized the importance of supervised athletic development for boys and entered teams in the OHA's Junior and Senior leagues.

By 1926, being involved in hockey had become too cumbersome for St. Mary's, and when the church abandoned the sport, Selke reorganized the old Marlboros. "It took money to attempt such a hazardous undertaking, and Conn Smythe was one of the first I appealed to," stated Selke in his memoir, *Behind the Cheering*. "Just as I had always been an admirer of his undoubted ability, perhaps he found something in me worthy of approval as well, for I was finally successful in selling him an interest in my team."

Selke took a year to rebuild the Marlboros, relying on his uncanny ability to detect talent — and the skills of a player he had first coached at St. Mary's in 1924–25, Joe Primeau. Smythe was so impressed that by the next season, he had offered Selke the position of manager-coach with the Toronto Ravinas. Several former NHLers, including Bobby Boucher, Bert Corbeau, and Lloyd Gross, played for the Ravinas. And so did Joe Primeau. The team was renamed the Falcons midway through the season, and, after suffering from poor attendance, played some of its home games in Brantford, Ontario. The team folded at the end of the 1927–28 season and Selke returned to the Marlboros, where he guided a team that included Charlie Conacher, Harvey Jackson, and Eddie Convey to the Memorial Cup championship over the Elmwood Millionaires in 1928–29. "One day when Conn was in a mood that was more despondent than usual, he asked me what he thought he should do about [the Maple Leafs' poor showing, missing the playoffs]," laughed Selke. "'I'll tell you how,' I said. 'Just fire the old men you have playing on your team now. Replace them with these young bucks I have with me on the Marlboros. Do that and you'll never look back!'"

Selke certainly was correct. When the Maple Leafs won the Stanley Cup in 1932, they did it with Conacher, Jackson, Primeau, Red Horner, and Alex Levinsky, all of whom had played with Selke on the Marlies.

Selke was promoted to business manager of the Leafs in September 1929. In that capacity, similar to an assistant general manager in today's game, he was involved in the day-to-day operation of the team.

Smythe, with the assistance of Selke and head scout Squib Walker, set up an entire hierarchy of feeder teams. "We had a system of sponsored teams at that time, all across the country, Junior and Senior teams that would supply us players who usually started in the minor pro leagues until they showed they belonged with the Leafs. Through those years, the backbone of the team came up through our farm system," Smythe wrote in his memoirs. St. Michael's became a valuable part of that system, as both Selke and Smythe realized that the offer of a solid (and free) Catholic private school education would serve as a terrific lure to parents who wanted their hockey-playing boys to finish high school before embarking on a career as a pro athlete. It was a benefit that no other NHL team could offer. "One attraction we had when going out to sign players of school age was the chance to offer them tuition at St. Michael's College School in Toronto, whose Junior teams were always powerful. We could go to parents in Winnipeg, Regina, Kirkland Lake, or wherever, and say, 'Look, if your boy will come into our system, we'll make sure he gets the best schooling he can handle.' To enter St. Mike's, a boy had to be a good student first, although it didn't hurt if he was a good hockey player, too. St. Mike's liked to win."

Smythe laughed when he recalled one argument he had with St. Mike's. "There was never any question of refusing a boy we sent them because of religion, although one time, that charge was made. One St. Mike's alumnus was very high on a Protestant kid from Cornwall, but the college turned him down. The alumnus came to me and claimed it was because of religion. I went to debate the matter with the priest who was in charge of admissions. He listened to my plea but when I finished, he said, 'Sorry Connie, but I've made my decision.' I've had some arguments with priests and usually when they said no, you've had it. So I rose to go. He opened the door for me. Just as I was leaving, he added what I guess was the real reason. 'Y'know Connie, he isn't much of a hockey player.'"

A very vocal critic of the relationship between the Maple Leafs and St. Michael's was Smythe's arch-enemy, Jack Adams, the coach and general manager of the Detroit Red Wings. He claimed that the arrangement made every Roman Catholic priest in Canada a scout for St. Michael's, and, in turn, the Toronto Maple Leafs.

He was absolutely right!

❖

After the Second World War, Conn Smythe's son Stafford was overseeing the family's sand and gravel business (C. Smythe for Sand), but as a good hockey player himself (he scored 21 points in 16 games for the Toronto Marlboros in 1940–41), he had a great desire to become more involved in his dad's other business, the Toronto Maple Leafs.

Stafford and his father disagreed on many things. Stafford felt that while sponsorship was working quite well in recruiting players from other parts of Ontario and the rest of Canada, the Leafs just weren't seeing much development in the Toronto area. Conn disagreed, and challenged his son to find these players the Leafs were missing.

Stafford accepted the challenge, and with the help of hockey men like Buck Houle, he set out to create a minor-hockey network in Toronto that would send players upwards to the Toronto Marlboros and, in some cases, all the way to the Toronto Maple Leafs. By the late 1940s, such a system had been set up, starting with a Pee Wee team sponsored by Shopsy's delicatessen. "We would scout all the little league teams," recalled Houle in William Houston's *Inside Maple Leaf Gardens*. "During the summer, we'd try to get them to play for Shopsy's. It was a process of elimination. The ones we missed at the Pee Wee level, we'd get at Minor Midget, or Minor Bantam or Midget. We just sifted them out. If they were any good by the time they were 16, we'd put them on the protected list for the NHL."

As the cream rose to the top, the best Junior-aged players ended up playing for either the St. Michael's Majors or the Toronto Marlboros. Houston quotes Conn Smythe as saying, "Put the dogans in the Micks' school and put the Protestants in with the Marlboros."

In 1948, Billy Harris was a 13-year-old Bantam playing hockey in Toronto's east end. In his book *The Glory Years*, Harris recalled becoming a member of the Toronto Maple Leafs organization. "During the summer of 1948, Stafford contacted my coach, Cliff Cooper, and asked him to consider coaching the Marlboro Minor Bantams. The Riverdale Mercury Pee Wee team then became the nucleus of the Marlie Minor Bantams."

Prior to a game at the Royals Curling Rink that November, Stafford introduced himself to the players. "I would like to take this opportunity to welcome you young hockey players to the Toronto Maple Leafs organization," he said. "There will be some benefits. You will receive the best coaching available. There will be lots of practice time and the [Maple Leaf] Gardens will be available for practice at least once a week. You will be admitted free of charge to any event at Maple Leaf Gardens. We will watch your progress and believe that some of you will one day play for the Toronto Maple Leafs. Good luck to all of you."

In 1949, Harris's Toronto Marlboro Minor Bantams won the Toronto Hockey League championship. In exchange for a Marlboros team jacket, each boy was instructed to sign a contract, agreeing to play for the Marlboros organization the next year. Better players made their way to the Junior 'B' Weston Dukes and then the Marlboros.

As proof of the effectiveness of Stafford Smythe's mini-network, the Toronto Marlboro Juniors won the Memorial Cup in 1955 and 1956 with a lineup of Toronto-based players who had come up through the system, including Bob Baun, Carl Brewer, Billy Harris, Al MacNeil, Harry Neale, Bob Nevin, and Bob Pulford. Several of them,

St. Michael's was the breeding ground for some of the greatest players ever to pull on a Toronto Maple Leafs sweater, including (left to right) Red Kelly, Frank Mahovlich, Tim Horton, and Dick Duff.

joined by St. Michael's alumni Dick Duff, Dave Keon, and Frank Mahovlich, formed the nucleus of the Toronto Maple Leafs dynasty in the 1960s.

As the 1960s dawned, serious discussions began to take place regarding expansion from a six-team league, which the NHL had been since 1942, to a 12-team league. One players' association had already been scuttled, but it became apparent that another would likely rear its head. And the divide between teams that were "haves" versus those that were "have nots" (Toronto, Montreal, and Detroit in the former camp, Chicago, New York, and Boston in the latter) was getting tedious for some owners. In the decade leading up to the 1967 expansion, the New York Rangers had missed the playoffs seven times, while the Boston Bruins amassed a streak of eight consecutive seasons without postseason activity.

An amateur draft was instituted by the NHL in 1963 both as a way to narrow the talent gaps between teams and to prepare for the phasing out of amateur sponsorship. The draft would involve only those players who had not yet signed contracts with NHL teams. Because sponsorship was so pervasive, relatively few top prospects were available to be drafted in the early years. Beginning in August 1966, teams were barred from adding any more players to their sponsorship lists, and by 1969 the draft was truly "universal" in scope.

Prior to the 1963 draft, the Toronto Maple Leafs zeroed in on Peter Mahovlich and Garry Monahan, two promising youngsters playing with St. Michael's Juvenile hockey team who had not yet signed an agreement giving the Leafs, or any other NHL team, an option on their services. The Leafs hoped to sign them up and assign them to their Junior 'A' affiliate, the Neil McNeil Maroons, thus removing them from the draft pool.

Both Mahovlich and Monahan refused to sign, and the Maple Leafs could only look on as the Montreal Canadiens chose Monahan first overall in the inaugural NHL draft. Detroit, with the second selection, took Mahovlich. The Leafs, selecting sixth, took Walt McKechnie from the London Junior 'B' club. In that same 1963 draft, the Leafs drafted Jim McKenny and Gerry Meehan from Neil McNeil.

The Maple Leafs similarly missed out on one of the plum selections of the 1966 draft. They had tried to secure the rights to 14-year-old Brad Park in 1962 by offering his father, Bob, a coaching position with Neil McNeil if his son played for the team. But even if Park had played with Neil McNeil, it wouldn't guarantee that his NHL rights belonged to the Leafs unless they chose to drop another player from their already crowded reserve list. They chose not to, and Brad was a free agent as a result. He joined the Toronto Marlboros in 1965–66 and that spring was selected second overall by the New York Rangers.

The end of the sponsorship era came on the heels of the demise of Junior 'A' hockey at St. Michael's. The last crop of players developed at the school included two who would find themselves involved in a pivotal deal in Leaf history. In 1964, the Maple Leafs had won back-to-back Stanley Cup championships and had their sights set on a third. The playoff success masked the fact that their defence corps of Bob Baun, Tim Horton, Carl Brewer, and Allan Stanley, spelled occasionally by Larry Hillman and Kent Douglas — a unit as good as any in NHL history — was aging. Replacements would be needed eventually. So on February 22, 1964, when general manager Punch Imlach pulled the trigger on a deal with the Rangers, chief scout Bob Davidson was horrified to learn that St. Mike's alumni Rod Seiling and Arnie Brown, two of Toronto's best defensive prospects, were bound for New York along with Dick Duff, Bob Nevin, and Bill Collins. In return, Toronto obtained veteran forwards Andy Bathgate and Don McKenney. Looking back, others view the trade with regret. "It was the end of us developing from within," commented David Keon. "We lost something as an organization," Frank Mahovlich concurred. Bob Baun summed it up: "[The Bathgate trade] ripped the heart out of the club."

Although the Leafs won the Stanley Cup in 1964, the players they acquired did not remain in the fold for long. Bathgate was traded to Detroit in May 1965 while McKenney was claimed on waivers by the Wings that June. Meanwhile, Arnie Brown enjoyed 10 NHL seasons and one in the World Hockey Association before injuries took their toll. Rod Seiling starred in 15 NHL seasons. "I would like to have stayed with the Leafs," shrugs Brown, a sentiment shared by Seiling, although both agree that they were able to break into the NHL much more quickly as New York Rangers.

6
1934 — First Memorial Cup Championship

Prior to the 1933–34 season, the Ontario Hockey Association separated its Junior division into two classes: Junior 'A' and Junior 'B.' Accordingly, St. Michael's, with a wealth of fine hockey players, competed at both levels, calling its Junior 'A' team the Majors and its Junior 'B' squad the Buzzers.

To supply the Junior teams, the hockey program at St. Michael's had developed a very efficient and convenient feeder system with teams in each age group playing in the Toronto Hockey League. The youngest students at the school, usually 14 years of age, played for the Minor Bantam squad, then progressed through Bantam, Minor Midget, Midget, and Juvenile. From there, a player matriculated to the Buzzers and, at the top of the hockey "food chain," the Majors.

The pre-season Sportsmen's Patriotic Association (SPA) tournament of 1933 saw the Majors defeat the Toronto Young Rangers in the final. But while the school and its fans got excited about prospects for the season ahead, not everyone was so pleased. "Winning the SPA Trophy in those days was equivalent to receiving the kiss of death, as far as the Memorial Cup was concerned," an article in the Maple Leaf Gardens program observed. "Few teams ever accomplished the double feat."

Jerry LaFlamme, the dynamic star of the St. Michael's championship team of 1909, returned to coach both the Junior 'A' and 'B' hockey teams in 1933. "By nature, he is reserved and quiet, but his sparkling humour and cheerful disposition are radiated in the merry twinkle of his steel-blue eyes," wrote the yearbook, now called *The Thurible*. "Hockey was Dr. LaFlamme's primary interest, having been ignited as a boy."

In the view of the yearbook, LaFlamme's success as a hockey coach was attributed to his preparation. "He teaches the game with much the same method and insistence on fundamentals as the algebra teacher does LCM [least common multiple]. The secret of his success is individual attention. Apart from the occasional talk in the dressing room, all his work is done beside the rink. He exerts a tremendous influence on the boys with whom he comes in contact. His constant and real interest in their problems, apart from hockey, has won their love and admiration. His word is law with the players and they respect the maturity and sanity of his judgment."

❖

The newly named Majors played a 12-game regular-season schedule in 1933–34. Over the course of the season they proved to be an immensely talented hockey machine. The lineup included captain Regis "Pep" Kelly and centre Don Willson, both of whom had played with the Memorial Cup champion Newmarket Redmen the previous season. Future NHL stars Bobby Bauer, Clare Drouillard, Reg Hamilton, Art Jackson, and Nick Metz were among the skaters, joined by John Acheson, Frank Bauer (Bobby's brother, who saw infrequent action), Jim Burke, and John Hamilton.

The Majors' kicked off what would turn out to be an undefeated season on December 15, with a 6–2 win over the West Toronto Nationals. Two subsequent victories were terribly lopsided. An 18–2 drubbing of the University of Toronto saw Jackson, Kelly and Drouillard each score four goals, while a 24–2 debacle featured a six-goal performance by Drouillard.

Prior to the playoffs, Father Lynch modestly acknowledged the strength of the team. "We've had other good teams before, but never got past the semifinals. I will say this, though, that this team is as good a team as we've had."

The first round of the playoffs matched St. Michael's against the Oshawa Majors. The best-of-three series began with a stutter as Oshawa led 5–3 going into the third period of Game One before Art Jackson fired two goals to tie the score. St. Mike's then took the next two games by scores of 8–2 and 10–5.

As the Majors marched to the OHA Junior 'A' title, the Buzzers won the Sutherland Cup as the Junior 'B' champions. In an unprecedented turn of events, both of LaFlamme's teams, winners of their respective divisions, met in a single-game elimination to decide the OHA Junior championship. "[Dr. LaFlamme's] affections and interest were so divided that he would not take charge of either team in the game," the 1936 edition of *The Thurible* said. "He could not keep still for a minute, but wandered all over the place, applauding the success of first one team, and then the other."

The Buzzers wore white-and-yellow sweaters specially created for the occasion. The spirited sudden-death contest, officiated by NHL stars King Clancy and Joe Primeau, drew 5,000, including 1,000 school children, to Maple Leaf Gardens. The Buzzers clung to a 2–1 lead after one period, but their "big brothers" with the Majors scored six unanswered goals in the second frame and outscored the Buzzers 5–1 in the third to cinch a 12–3 decision. "While the Preps showed plenty of the fight that marked their gallant climb to the 'B' Division title, they could not cope with the superior speed and playmaking ability of the Majors," reported *The Globe*.

Every player on the Majors, with the exception of netminder Harvey Teno, earned a point in the contest. Pep Kelly scored three goals and added two assists for the victors, while Bobby Bauer also earned a hat trick. Fourteen-year-old Gene Sheedy scored two of the Buzzers' three goals.

After eliminating the Buzzers and winning the OHA Cup, the Majors faced New Liskeard at Maple Leaf Gardens. "Can the Northerns topple the mighty Mikes?" queried *The Globe*. Several hundred fans made the trip from northern Ontario to Toronto by train to cheer on the Northern Ontario Hockey Association (NOHA) Junior champions.

Game One was a 13–3 rout for St. Mike's. Harry Frost opened the scoring for the "Liskies," but it was the first and only reason for the northern Ontario fans to cheer. "The students proved altogether too fast and clever for the Northern standard-bearers, who battled gamely in a hopeless cause," wrote *The Globe*.

Game Two turned out to be the deciding match, though it was more of a foregone conclusion. St. Michael's toppled New Liskeard 16–3, scoring 10 goals in the third period alone. Art Jackson and Johnny Acheson each scored four times in the one-sided affair. Clare Drouillard led all scorers with three goals and four assists in the game. Frank Bauer replaced Don Willson, who had broken his nose in the first contest.

The next rung on the ladder for the Majors was a pair of games at the Gardens against the Maritime champion Charlottetown Abegweits for the Richardson Trophy, symbolic of the eastern Canadian championship. St. Michael's steamrolled over the Abbies by a score of 12–2 in the opener, but lost Clare Drouillard to a severe charley horse during the contest. Frank Bauer took Drouillard's place in Game Two, a 7–2 win that gave the Majors a 19–4 advantage in the two-game, total-goal series. The victory earned the Majors the right to compete for the Canadian Junior championship.

The Memorial Cup final was a best-of-three series between the Majors and the Edmonton Athletic Club Roamers. All games were played at Shea's Amphitheatre in Winnipeg, a neutral site that boasted artificial ice.

The Majors were impressive even in their practice sessions. "Four hundred curious railbirds watched the Toronto Irish go through their paces for nearly an hour at the Amphitheatre Rink. There was scarcely a spectator who was not visibly impressed by the skill and hockey availability of the easterners," suggested the Canadian Press (CP).

Because teams relied on only one goaltender at that time, each needed to secure a second in order to scrimmage. For this purpose, St. Mike's invited Walter "Turk"

Harvey Teno backstopped the St. Mike's Juniors to the Memorial Cup in 1934. Although he played briefly with the Detroit Red Wings (November 1938), Teno was a longtime minor-league goalie. While with the AHL's Cleveland Barons in 1945–46, he tutored a young goaltender named John Kiszkan. By the next season, the prodigy had changed his name to Johnny Bower, and today, he credits Teno with helping him become an NHL-calibre goalie.

Broda of the Winnipeg Monarchs to join them. "After being blazed at from all sides during practice, Turk seemed inclined to pick St. Michael's for two straight victories," added CP.

Game One was a seemingly easy 5–0 blanking of the Roamers by St. Mike's. "The smooth-skating sharpshooting Irish from the Queen City downed the Western champions with a torrid attack in the second period, but in the first and third periods, the Edmontonians put up a better attack," reported CP. Pep Kelly led the Majors with two goals.

Game Two was much closer. Before 4,500 fans, the two teams fought for their hockey lives. In the second period, "with Bill Carse and Gordon Watt in the penalty box, Neil Colville grabbed the puck at centre ice in a brilliant effort to give Edmonton their first goal," reported CP. "Nick Metz gave chase. They bumped and Colville went through with only Harvey Teno in the St. Mike's net to beat. Metz tore after him and threw his stick to stop the goal. Both went down. Metz was chased for ten minutes and Colville drew a minor for the scuffle on the ice. Peanuts were pitched onto the ice as the fans roared and the game had to be called (briefly) while the ice was swept."

By the end of regulation time, the game was tied. "The boys from the Alberta capital never quit trying and they matched the hockey skill of the Easterners all through the eighty minutes of hockey that left every player nearly exhausted. It was their ability to finish off attacks that gave the Easterners their win." St. Mike's defeated Edmonton 6–4, but need an overtime period to do so. "The husky lads who wear the double blue of St. Michael's College in Toronto are the kings of Junior hockey in Canada," proclaimed the Canadian Press.

"There is no question that this Toronto team is one of the smoothest, high-powered machines this part of the country has seen in years and years," commented the *Toronto Telegram*. "They must be classed with the immortals of all time in the Junior class."

In a March 12, 1934 article in *The Globe*, Dr. Duke McCurry, who played with the 1920 Memorial Cup champion Toronto Canoe Club and who refereed several playoff contests during the 1934 playoffs, offered his opinion that the St. Michael's College team of 1933–34 might be the greatest OHA Junior team of all time. "St. Mike's has everything," he said. "They have been superbly coached by one of the smartest hockey men ever known. There isn't a weak man or link in the lineup. In 1920, we had only six outstanding players on the Red Ring team. St. Mike's has twice that many." McCurry cited the Kingston Frontenacs of 1911, his own Toronto Canoe Club of 1920, and St. Mike's as the three best teams he had ever witnessed.

The triumphant Majors returned to Toronto, where they were greeted by the De La Salle band and 500 supporters. They all proceeded to a breakfast reception at the King Edward Hotel. The 1933–34 season was extraordinary for the school, for while the Majors carried home the SPA Cup, the OHA Cup, the Richardson Trophy, and the Memorial Cup, the Junior 'B' Buzzers collected their own hardware that season.

As a postscript to the remarkable season, St. Michael's received a challenge from the Moncton Hawks, Allan Cup champions in 1933 and 1934. The Senior club proposed an exhibition series with St. Mike's, but the idea evaporated when the Moncton squad demanded payment. Instead, the Majors accepted a challenge from the Cities Service Oilers, the champions of Toronto's Mercantile League that year and a club of Senior calibre. The age difference proved challenging for the younger Majors, who tied the Oilers 5–5 in the first contest, but lost 6–3 and 5–4 in ensuing games. The losses, although strictly exhibition, were the first suffered by the Majors that season.

Six members of the newly crowned Memorial Cup champions immediately signed professional contracts. The entire line of Art Jackson, Pep Kelly and Nick Metz was signed by the Toronto Maple Leafs, as was defenceman Reg Hamilton. Bobby Bauer was picked up by the Boston Bruins and Clare Drouillard was signed by the Detroit Red Wings. Eight of the 12 team members eventually played in the NHL. Only substitute goaltender

St. Mike's captured the Memorial Cup in 1934. It was the first of four Junior championships the school would win, as it collected the prestigious silverware again in 1945, 1947, and 1961.

1934 — First Memorial Cup Championship

Ted McLean (one game during the regular season), Frank Bauer, Johnny Hamilton, and high-scoring Johnny Acheson failed to play at the NHL level. Acheson had come to the fore during the Memorial Cup playdowns, leading the Majors with 22 goals and 33 points in 13 contests. He enjoyed a long, fruitful Senior career that included an Allan Cup championship with the Ottawa RCAF team in 1942 and was awarded the Distinguished Flying Cross as a flight lieutenant in the air force during World War II.

Goaltender Harvey Teno was signed by the Detroit Red Wings, and when Normie Smith was suspended early in the 1938–39 season, Teno made his NHL debut. The Windsor, Ontario, native played his first NHL game on November 17, 1938 (a 7–1 win over the Montreal Canadiens), then followed with four more games that month. His career record is two wins and three losses in five NHL games.

Robert Theodore Bauer was born February 16, 1915, in Waterloo, Ontario, one of 11 sports-minded children. After playing city hockey in the Kitchener-Waterloo area, he moved to Toronto and attended St. Michael's College. As a 15-year-old in 1930–31, he starred on the Prep School squad, then graduated to what would be the Junior 'A' team for three seasons between 1931 and 1934.

Pep Kelly, Art Jackson, and Nick Metz, all members of the Memorial Cup champs, went on to play with the Maple Leafs.

After winning the Memorial Cup in 1934, Bauer played his final season of Junior with the Kitchener Greenshirts, where lifelong friendships were forged with two teammates. Joining Bauer at forward was Milt Schmidt, while Woody Dumart played defence. The three Kitchener-area lads were signed by the Boston Bruins, who placed them together on a line and sent them for seasoning to the Providence Reds of the International-American Hockey League in 1936–37. There, coach Albert "Battleship" Leduc dubbed them the Sauerkrauts because of their shared German heritage. That tag was shortened to the Kraut Line. "He said, 'All you fellows come from Kitchener-Waterloo,'" Milt Schmidt recalled. "'There's a lot of people of German descent from there. We gotta get a name for ya — the Kraut Line!' We didn't mind. It was a name that kind of stuck to us."

Bauer played his first NHL game on March 21, 1937, the Bruins' final regular-season contest of the season. In the third period, he scored his first NHL goal. In all, he appeared in 327 regular-season games over a career interrupted by the Second World War. He scored 123 goals and 137 assists for 260 points, and played on Stanley Cup championship teams in 1939 and 1941. Three times, he won the Lady Byng Trophy as the league's most gentlemanly player, and on four occasions was named to the NHL's Second All-Star Team. The 32-year-old Bauer retired after the 1946–47 season, in which he scored 30 goals in 58 games, but his playing days weren't done. He continued to suit up with the Kitchener-Waterloo Dutchmen in OHA Senior competition, and made a curious one-game comeback on March 18, 1952. That evening, the Boston Bruins retired the numbers of all three members of the Kraut Line. In his final NHL game, Bauer scored a goal and added an assist against the Chicago Black Hawks. Bauer, who died in 1964, was inducted posthumously into the Hockey Hall of Fame in 1996.

Clarence Drouillard, known as Clare to all, was signed by the Red Wings in February 1936. Like Teno, Drouillard was also from Windsor, and the two had played together with the Windsor Wanderers in 1932–33. Clare played 10 games at centre with the Red Wings in 1937–38, his only NHL games.

Following the championship with St. Mike's, Reg Hamilton signed with the Toronto Maple Leafs, joining the team during the 1935–36 season. After winning a Stanley Cup championship, his second with the Leafs, in 1945, Hamilton was traded to Chicago, where he spent two seasons with the Black Hawks. Reg Hamilton collected 108 points in 424 regular-season NHL games.

Art Jackson went straight from St. Mike's to the Maple Leafs, where he joined his Hall of Fame brother Harvey (better known as "Busher"). He spent three seasons with Toronto, joined the Boston Bruins in a trade during 1937–38, spent the next campaign with the New York Americans, and returned to the Bruins for the 1939–40 season. After winning a Stanley Cup championship with Boston in 1941, Jackson won a second with the Maple Leafs in 1945. Art played in 468 regular-season NHL games and scored 123 goals, 178 assists, and 301 points.

They called him "Pep" for his enthusiastic skating style, but he was born Regis Kelly. Like his linemates Art Jackson and Nick Metz, Kelly was signed by the Toronto Maple Leafs immediately after the St. Mike's championship in 1934. Through his eight NHL seasons, the winger played with the Maple Leafs, Chicago Black Hawks, and Brooklyn Americans, scoring 74 goals and 53 assists for 127 points in 288 regular-season games.

Imported from Wilcox, Saskatchewan, Nick Metz joined his St. Mike's linemates with the Leafs in 1934–35. He played his entire career in blue and white, including eight seasons with his younger brother Don, also a St. Mike's alumnus. In 12 seasons, Nick was part of four Stanley Cup championships (in 1942, 1945, 1947, and 1948), and collected 131 goals, 119 assists, and 250 points in 518 games.

Centre Don Willson played parts of the 1937–38 and 1938–39 seasons with the Montreal Canadiens, scoring two goals and seven assists in 22 games.

"Those rip-roaring Gaels of '34 were little short of tremendous," wrote Ed Fitkin in a Maple Leaf Gardens program. "Nothing could touch them from the time they hit the OHA league barrier until they routed Edmonton to win the Memorial Cup."

The Irish Help Clancy Lower the Boom — SNAPSHOT

On March 17, 1934, the Toronto Maple Leafs paid tribute to Francis "King" Clancy in a ceremony prior to their game against the New York Rangers. That evening, several floats were pushed out onto the ice surface, each with a St. Patrick's Day theme that reflected Clancy's proud heritage. "Whenever I think back to March 17, 1934, and how the Maple Leafs honoured me with a 'night,' I'm still amazed at the work they went to just for me," Clancy stated humbly. "They gave me the greatest tribute an individual could ever hope to get. I didn't do anything to deserve it. They must have banded together and said, 'He's an Irishman. Let's give him a night,'" Clancy chuckled.

King was dressed in a specially created green Leafs sweater that bore a shamrock on the back where his number 7 would usually be seen. A series of icons loosely associated with Clancy's Irish background were pulled onto the ice — a giant pipe containing teammate Ken Doraty; a bottle of ginger ale containing trainer Tim Daly; goaltender George Hainsworth emerged from a giant boot; Red Horner stepped out of a massive boxing glove; a huge top hat held Baldy Cotton, followed by Joe Primeau on a super-sized harp and a monstrous shamrock that held opponent Bill Cook. The Memorial Cup champion St. Michael's team emerged from a float shaped like a potato. "When my turn finally came, the lights were all turned out and, dressed in royal robes and wearing a crown, I was ushered in on a big throne pulled by Hap Day," Clancy recalled. "As the float reached the middle of the rink, I got hit in the face with a handful of soot from Day and [Charlie] Conacher. When the lights came on, I looked like Santa Claus but my face was pitch black."

Clancy was given a number of gifts, including a grandfather clock from the Maple Leafs. "This was a fantastic night to give anybody and I have wonderful memories of it. Now, what more could a man ask for than to be taken to a city's heart like I was? I always look back upon it as one of the greatest things that ever happened to me in sport."

The Maple Leafs paid tribute to King Clancy on St. Patrick's Day, 1934. The Memorial Cup champion St. Mike's team was included in the evening.

The Thirties

Hockey, like so many things in life, is cyclical, and much of the Memorial Cup championship team of 1934 was lost to graduation. Coach LaFlamme rebuilt the team using two returning players, goalie Harvey Teno and defenceman Johnny Hamilton, as the foundation. Added to the team from the Buzzers were Johnny Crawford and John "Peanuts" O'Flaherty, both of whom went on to NHL careers, as well as Chuck Corrigan, who would appear briefly in the big league.

Due in large part to the goaltending of Harvey Teno, St. Mike's made the playoffs in 1934–35 and faced Eddie Livingstone's Toronto Lions in the opening round. Game One was a 4–0 shutout for the Majors. Anxious to skate the Lions into oblivion, the Double Blue were shocked when the Lions roared back, winning 4–1 in Game Two. In the third game, the teams were deadlocked at five apiece going into overtime. Harvey Teno was struck in the face by a puck and was forced to leave the game for medical attention, but he showed great courage by returning to finish the contest. "It seemed St. Michael's burning speed cooled out a little and the Lions capitalized," reported the yearbook. "For 60 minutes, both teams struggled valiantly but still the count remained deadlocked. It was a desperate battle to escape elimination. Lions scored and the last sound of the gong from the timekeeper's bench wrote 'finis' to the exploits of the Junior 'A' team."

O'Flaherty moved to the West Toronto Nationals in 1935–36, and went on to play in the NHL for the Americans (New York in 1940–41 and Brooklyn in 1941–42), collecting six points in 21 games. After a long American Hockey League career, O'Flaherty returned to St. Michael's College as playing coach of the Monarchs of the OHA Senior league in 1950–51, doubling as coach of the Junior 'A' Majors.

After two seasons with the Majors, Corrigan went on to play with the Toronto Maple Leafs during the 1937–38 season, and joined O'Flaherty on the New York Americans in 1940–41. In 19 NHL games, the winger had four points.

For 1935–36, Tommy Dunne was brought up from the Buzzers to play goal, replacing Harvey Teno. Bus Benson also graduated from the Buzzers and led the team in goals, scoring 12 in nine games. Pat McReavy proved to be "a tireless backchecker with an ability to lay down perfect passes to his wings." He completed the season as the Majors' point leader, collecting 17. Don Metz, who had been away from St. Mike's for two years, returned, adding strength to the Majors. "Don plays right wing and is a fast skater and a clever and heady stickhandler," according to the yearbook. Metz scored nine goals and 13 points. George McNamara anchored the defence and was noted as a "clever stickhandler with a good shift when rushing, as well as very capable defensively." Making up the rest of the team were Johnny Mitchell, promoted from the Buzzers, as well as Hal Jackson, Chuck Corrigan, and Fred Hunt.

The team finished first, winning nine and losing just once, to West Toronto. The team scored 60 goals, allowing just 16. In the first round of the playoffs, the Majors met the Toronto Native Sons in a two-game, total-goal series that saw the Majors take the opening round, nine goals to six.

Next, St. Mike's met the tough West Toronto Nationals in a best-of-five series for the Big 6 title. West Toronto took the first game, 1–0. "Both teams played fast, hard hockey, with West Toronto coming through with the only goal of the game." In the second game, according to the yearbook, "the Nationals got off to a flying start and could do nothing wrong, as they skated off with a 6–1 victory." The Majors led for the better part of Game Three, but the West Nats squad scored three quick goals late in the game to secure a 6–5 decision, thus eliminating St. Mike's from further play that season.

Several of the players tutored by Dr. LaFlamme were added to the reserve lists of National Hockey League teams. "The LaFlamme-trained lad goes well in the Big Time for several reasons, chief of these is that he can play hockey, but important, too, is his acquisition of the habits of teamwork, discipline and clean living," as stated in the school yearbook.

Fred Hunt, whose nickname "Fritz" stuck with him from childhood, made his name in hockey more through his association with the American Hockey League than his Junior or NHL careers. In 1940–41, Hunt played 15 games with the New York Americans. Four seasons later, he was added to the lineup of the New York Rangers. His NHL statistics show 59 games played, in which he collected 29 points. But the speedy winger spent eight seasons in the AHL, scoring 20 or more goals on four occasions. Six of his AHL campaigns were played with the Buffalo Bisons, and Hunt would later be named general manager of that franchise. In his honour, each year, the AHL presents the Fred T. Hunt Memorial Award to the league's most sportsmanlike player.

Defenceman Harold Jackson, known as Hal in hockey circles, was signed by the Chicago Black Hawks following his single season with St. Mike's. He entered the NHL with the Hawks in 1936–37, and the next season was part of a Stanley Cup championship. After a series of trades, Jackson emerged with the Detroit Red Wings in 1940–41, playing a single game. He joined the Wings again in 1942–43 and won a second Stanley Cup with Detroit. He played the remainder of his NHL career, which ended after the 1946–47 season, with the Red Wings. In 219 regular-season games, he recorded 51 points.

Lured away to join the Northern Ontario Hockey Association's Copper Cliff Redmen following the 1935–36 season, Pat McReavy joined the Boston Bruins in 1938–39 and played parts of four seasons with them, including a Stanley Cup season in 1940–41. He was traded to Detroit in November 1941 and finished the season, and his NHL career, that year. McReavy scored five goals and 15 points in 55 NHL games.

Following his brother Nick to St. Michael's in 1935–36, Don Metz scored nine goals for the Majors during their 10-game season in 1935–36. He joined the Toronto Maple Leafs during the playoffs in 1938–39, and stayed with them for the better part of eight seasons. During his NHL career, Don won the Stanley Cup five times: 1942, 1945, 1947, 1948, and 1949. In 172 NHL games, he notched 20 goals and 35 assists for 55 points, adding 15 more points in 42 playoff contests.

❖

"Last November, Coach LaFlamme gazed upon his youthful recruits with a good deal of perplexity," wrote *The Thurible* about the 1936-37 season. "He was pretty much baffled about whether they were a team capable of attaining the heights he had in mind."

The Majors played 12 regular-season games and finished first, winning nine, losing two, and tying one for 19 points:

Gene Sheedy, an excellent sweep checker, was flanked by Fritz Hunt and Jack Inglis on the first line. Inglis came from Wilcox, Saskatchewan, the home of Nick and Don Metz. "The toughest checker in Junior hockey is a product of Father Murray's Notre Dame School," said a Maple Leaf Gardens program that season. Smith, brother of NHLers Winky and Nakina Smith, centred the second line, with Ross Hunt at right wing and Paul McNamara on left wing.

The defence comprised George McNamara, John Callahan, Bonik "Bunky" Lukasik, and Ab "Two Ton" Tonn. The Buzzers' Tommy Dunne was in net.

Inglis led the team in scoring with 16 goals and 22 points, followed by George McNamara with 19 points, including 11 goals, from his spot on the blue line. Gene Sheedy

1936–37		
TEAM	GP	Pts
St. Michael's Majors	12	19
Oshawa Majors	12	18
Toronto Young Rangers	12	17
British Consols	12	16
Toronto Varsity Blues	12	6
Toronto Lions	12	6
Toronto Native Sons	12	2

collected eight goals and five assists while Fritz Hunt and Ross Hunt each finished the season with matching records of five goals and five assists.

In the playoffs, the Toronto Young Rangers were the first opponents the Majors faced, in a best-of-three series. St. Mike's coasted to win the series, although the Young Rangers won the second game in overtime.

The league title pitted St. Mike's against the British Consols, led by Billy Taylor, the former Buzzer who topped the OHA Junior league in regular-season and playoff scoring. The Majors swept the Consols in three straight, by margins of 4–3, 5–3, and 3–1, the latter a come-from-behind win.

In the first game of the best-of-five OHA final, St. Michael's was challenged by the Stratford Midgets, a mercury-quick team. Gene Sheedy's hat trick led the Majors to a 6–2 victory in the opening contest. Stratford won Game Two by a 7–4 score at home.

Just prior to the third game, played in Stratford, a memorial service was held to honour local legend Howie Morenz. The Stratford Streak had died on March 8. With McNamara and Callahan missing from the lineup, St. Mike's still came from behind three times in the first period of Game Three, but the Majors suffered a heart-wrenching 5–4 loss.

The missing defence pair returned for Game Four. "Those hockey enthusiasts who were lucky enough to obtain a ticket for this game unanimously agree that it was the fastest, most thrilling struggle ever witnessed in Stratford," stated the school's yearbook. With the Majors leading 6–4 with 35 seconds left in regulation, Stratford scored, but it was too late as St. Michael's held on to win the game.

The deciding contest, Game Five, was played in Toronto at Maple Leaf Gardens, the Majors' home rink. A capacity crowd watched Fritz Hunt open the scoring, but Stratford stormed back with two in quick succession. George McNamara went end to end to tie the score just before the first period came to a conclusion. Stratford's goalie, Red McAtee, turned in a superb effort, but in trying to clear the puck, he accidentally knocked it into his own net. The goal seemed to break Stratford's spirit, and St. Michael's went on to win by a lopsided margin of 8–3, giving the Majors the series and the OHA Junior championship. George McNamara had three goals for the victors and Jack Inglis had two. Netminder Tommy Dunne played the game of his career to earn the win.

Next up was a series against the Northern Ontario Hockey Association (NOHA) champions, the Copper Cliff Redmen. The Redmen, who had played in Newmarket in previous seasons, were organized just prior to the 1936–37 season by coach Max Silverman, who assembled an impressive collection of talent to play in Copper Cliff, just outside Sudbury. The team played Senior hockey all year, and were bigger and stronger than the Majors.

The Majors won Game One by a 5–2 score, but despite the result they were visibly exhausted. Copper Cliff won Game Two, then, led by Pat McReavy, who had starred for St. Michael's in 1935–36, put the Majors away efficiently with a smothering 8–2 victory to take the series. Tired or not, St. Michael's was easily outmatched, and the Redmen moved on to face the Winnipeg Rangers in what the Canadian Press called "the most spectacular Junior series in history." Winnipeg ended up winning the Memorial Cup, but Pat McReavy of Copper Cliff led all playoff scorers with 36 points.

Through the playoffs, the Hunts and Sheedy each scored five goals in 6 postseason games for the Majors. Sheedy was the league's playoff scoring leader with 10 points.

"We cannot find the right words to use when we come to Dr. LaFlamme," said the yearbook. "He has built up a record and a spirit for the College that will stand for many years to come."

After a self-imposed absence from the OHA's Junior division, the Toronto Marlboros returned in 1937–38 and finished the season in first place with a flawless 12-win season, earning 24 points. Oshawa's Generals, named after their new sponsor, General Motors, came in second with 16 points. St. Michael's collected seven wins and five losses for 14 points, good for a third-place finish.

Johnny Inglis led the Majors in scoring with 14 goals and 21 points in 12 games, sixth best in the league. "Jack keeps his elbows out like a pair of aeroplane wings and is a jerky skater but he does his chore in workmanlike manner," chuckled W.A. Hewitt, longtime secretary of the Ontario Hockey Association. Inglis was described by his school's yearbook as being "as polite as they make them off the ice, but has more elbows and knees than an octopus in play and usually manages to have about half of these jabbing his opponents when in close."

Gene Sheedy picked up 15 points in his fourth season of Junior 'A' with St. Michael's. Sheedy "is certainly a hard fellow to outwit," commented a Maple Leaf Gardens program at the time, while "George McNamara is easily the class of Junior defencemen locally." McNamara scored eight goals and had 13 points, while his brother Paul scored seven times, finishing with 10 points.

Orville Smith, who would help the Oshawa Generals win Memorial Cup championships in 1939 and 1940, contributed seven points in 10 games. Guy Roach, promoted from Junior 'B,' was the hardest bodychecker on the team. "He hits them where they meet and drops them in their tracks," exclaimed the Maple Leaf Gardens program. Claude Morrison played goal that season for the Majors.

Oshawa went on to win the John Ross Robertson Trophy as OHA champions in 1937–38, the first in an extraordinary string of seven consecutive seasons participating in the league final, winning on six occasions.

1937–38					
TEAM	GP	W	L	T	Pts
Toronto Marlboros	12	12	0	0	24
Oshawa Generals	12	8	4	0	16
St. Michael's Majors	12	7	5	0	14
Toronto Young Rangers	12	6	6	0	12
Toronto Native Sons	12	5	7	0	10

❖

The OHA split its Junior 'A' league into two divisions for the 1938–39 season. St. Mike's was the class of its division, racking up 20 points. The Guelph Indians came in with a strong second-place debut. The Varsity Blues won just once and tied three in their last full season of Junior 'A' hockey. The Oshawa Generals ran away with first place overall, garnering 26 points while suffering but one loss through the 14-game campaign. The Young Rangers finished second in their division with 19 points. The woeful Toronto Lions finished last for the second season in a row, and dropped out of the league after this season.

Don Dunbar led the Majors in scoring with 21 points, but the contributions of the McNamara brothers must be noted. George, a rugged defenceman with speed, was strong both offensively and defensively. He scored 11 goals and 19 points in 14 games for the Majors, finishing sixth in the league in points. Paul, a quick-skating forward with a strong shot, played just six games for the Majors, but scored four goals. *The Thurible*, the school's yearbook, enthused, "No higher tribute can be paid to them than to say that they were loved and admired by students and faculty alike." Both brothers played with the Toronto Marlboros in 1939–40.

The Oshawa Generals, just three seasons old, had already become a dominant franchise. Sparked by the prowess of Billy Taylor, a former St. Michael's College student, the Generals again won the OHA championship, defeating the Toronto Native Sons in the league final. The Generals won the Memorial Cup as well in 1938–39.

1938–39					
TEAM	P	W	L	T	Pts
Group 1					
St. Michael's Majors	14	10	4	0	20
Guelph Indians	14	7	5	2	15
Toronto Marlboros	14	4	9	1	9
Toronto Varsity Blues	14	1	10	3	5
Group 2					
Oshawa Generals	14	13	1	0	26
Toronto Young Rangers	14	9	4	1	19
Toronto Native Sons	14	7	6	1	15
Toronto Lions	14	1	13	0	2

SNAPSHOT ▸▸ ▸▸ ▸▸ ▸▸ ▸▸ ▸▸ ▸▸ ▸▸ ▸▸ *Johnny Crawford:* Helmeted Hero

Johnny Crawford was a hockey pioneer in head protection. Although a handful of hockey players had worn helmets of some design prior to Crawford, he was one of the few to wear one regularly through his career. But this practice wasn't inspired by safety as much as vanity. While playing football at St. Mike's, the burly Crawford had lost his hair in what was believed to be an allergic reaction to the paint used on the helmet. His hair never grew back, and the self-conscious Crawford, still in his teens, wore a leather helmet to cover his bald pate.

Often known as Jack (a nickname he despised), Johnny Crawford was born in Dublin, Ontario, not far from Stratford. He was recruited by the St. Michael's hockey program to play defence, and was so effective that in October 1937 he signed as a free agent with the Boston Bruins. He played 12 seasons with the Bruins, including two Stanley Cup championships (1939 and 1941). In 1942–43, he was named to the Second All-Star Team, and in 1945–46 he was a First Team All-Star. Remembered as a sturdy, stay-at-home defenceman who delivered thundering body checks, Crawford played 548 games and scored 38 goals and 140 assists for 178 points.

Milt Schmidt, a teammate with the Bruins, remembers how funny Crawford could be. "Brimmy [netminder Frank Brimsek] always had something wrong with him. When he did, we knew we would win. He would dress and sit staring at the floor. After a while, Johnny Crawford would stand over him and yell, 'What's wrong, Brimmy?' Brimsek would look up and say, 'See spots! See spots!' We'd all crack up and it took a lot of tension out of the room."

Following his term with the Bruins, John was the playing coach of Boston's AHL farm team, the Hershey Bears. He retired at the end of the 1952 season and devoted his full-time attention to a paper product distribution company in Cape Cod he had started with his brother. Soon, Crawford became a pioneer of a different sort. He was asked to add analysis to Boston Bruins radio broadcasts, and when he accepted, he became the first former player to be involved in broadcasting NHL games.

After three seasons, Crawford returned to coaching and guided the AHL's Providence Reds to a Calder Cup championship. He continued coaching with various American League teams, including the Rochester Americans and Baltimore Clippers, until 1966. And while barking out orders from behind the bench, you can be certain that Johnny Crawford always wore a fedora to cover his bald head.

8
Early 1940s — Building a Dynasty

By the late 1930s, enthusiasm for hockey around the school had waned, and St. Michael's did not enter a team in the Junior division in either 1939–40 or 1940–41. Players who had toiled for the Majors in 1938–39 scrambled to find positions elsewhere. Not all were successful, but the McNamaras, George and Paul, landed with the Toronto Marlboros, while John Callahan found a spot with the Toronto Young Rangers. Several boys, including Neil Morrison and Gene Sheedy, found employment in Toronto's Mercantile League. Tom Somers moved north and was part of the Timmins McIntyre Miners.

The OHA's Junior loop dropped to six clubs, one of whom, the U of T Varsity Blues, did not complete the schedule. The Oshawa Generals led the field with 32 points in 18 games, followed by the Marlboros, Young Rangers, Guelph Indians, and Native Sons.

Perhaps it is because St. Mike's did not compete in the Junior 'A' division in 1939–40 that the Toronto Maple Leafs missed out on having Hall of Famer Elmer Lach join the organization. Or, maybe he simply changed his mind about Toronto. Whatever the case, Leafs owner Conn Smythe called Elmer Lach "a deserter" — not because he was dodging military service, but because Smythe felt he was pre-destined to be a Toronto Maple Leaf. "'He came east to play hockey at St. Michael's College in Toronto, a Leaf-sponsored team, and he agreed to sign with me,' Smythe will complain, 'but he deserted, went back home without saying a word to play some Senior hockey, and then returned to star for Montreal,'" wrote Douglas Hunter in *War Games*. Lach signed with the Canadiens in October 1940 after spending two Senior seasons with the Moose Jaw Millers.

Although the Majors didn't participate in the OHA in 1939–40, St. Michael's still had an extraordinary year. All five of the teams that took the ice in the school's colours won their respective groups: the Junior 'B' Buzzers, the Midgets, the Minor Midgets, the Bantams, and the Minor Bantams. In fact, the latter three teams each went through their respective seasons without suffering a loss. In their nine-game season, the Minor Midgets scored 92 goals and allowed just one. The Bantams, meanwhile, scored 48 goals while their opponents tallied just nine. The Minor Bantams were equally dominant, collecting 55 goals while allowing just four.

1940–41
For a second straight season, St. Mike's did not ice a Junior 'A' team in the OHA. The Toronto Marlboros finished first (25 points in 17 games) in what was now a five-team league, with Oshawa and Guelph — now sponsored by the Biltmore Hat company — tied for second. The Toronto Young Rangers were now sponsored by the popular Bowles Lunch restaurants, hence their new name, the Bowles Rangers. They finished fourth, while the Native Sons lost all 15 of their games and finished last.

1941–42
After a two-season hiatus, the St. Michael's Majors returned to Junior 'A' action, coached by Reverend Hugh Mallon. The team consisted primarily of players who had toiled

The captains in St. Mike's hockey program for 1940–41 congregated by the outdoor arena on St. Joseph Street. Left to right: Farrell Gallagher (Buzzers), Greg Carter (Midget), Hugh Foley (Minor Midget), Pat Powers (Bantam), and Armand Fitzgerald (Minor Bantam). The school did not ice a Junior 'A' team that year.

1941–42					
Team	GP	W	L	T	Pts
Brantford Lions	24	19	5	0	38
Oshawa Generals	24	17	7	0	34
Guelph Biltmore Mad Hatters	24	13	11	0	26
Toronto Marlboros	24	12	10	2	26
Toronto Young Rangers	24	11	11	2	24
St. Michael's Majors	24	10	14	0	20
Toronto Native Sons	—	0	24	0	0

for the Buzzers during the previous season, including Frank Bennett, George Dodd, Farrell Gallagher, Gerry Gregoire, Gerry Hickey, Bernie Lobriaco, Tommy O'Neill, Cecil Schmalz, and goaltender Jean Marois. Hugh Foley, later to return as a priest at St. Michael's, was also part of the Majors squad that season. George Rebstock came over from the Junior 'B' St. Catharines Saints, Bob Stanton had played for the Toronto Bowles Rangers and netminder Joe Cleary, who had previously competed for St. Michael's, had spent the previous season with the Marlboros, where he led the league with seven wins.

Frank Bennett was the team's scoring leader, nabbing 20 points that season, and Gerry Hickey scored a team-best 11 times. "Speedy, shifty 'Hick' was not only the most dangerous puck-carrier, but was a penalty killer and defensive bulwark due to his sweeping effective check," the yearbook noted. Tommy O'Neill was playing defence for the Majors. "Colourful, consistent Tom O'Neill — as popular with the fans as his potent fists were unpopular with the opposition," said *The Thurible*. O'Neill was the bad boy of the Majors, serving 28 minutes in penalties.

Much was expected of Farrell Gallagher, although he was unable to complete the season. "One night, Farrell Gallagher broke his leg. There were only two minutes left to play; St. Mike's were four goals down. An opposing player broke away, 'Gag' driving in hot pursuit. He caught his man but could not stop, smashing into the end boards. He was carried off the ice — out for the season. His body was lost to the team but his fighting spirit remained. His teammates picked up his flaming torch of courage and fanned that unquenchable spirit that Farrell Gallagher had enkindled in their hearts."

The Brantford Lions, in their inaugural season, surprised everyone by finishing first, collecting 38 points. The Marlboros plummeted from their first-place ranking in 1940–41. The Majors endured a disappointing return, winning 10, losing 14, and collecting 20 points. The Toronto Native Sons dropped out of the league partway through the schedule and the OHA declared all their games as forfeited losses.

The sixth-place Majors faced the fifth-place Young Rangers in what should have been an evenly matched series, but St. Michael's was eliminated by Ed Wildey's crew. The Majors of 1941–42 were "outplayed, outskated, outscored, but never out-fought," in *The Thurible*'s estimation. The yearbook called them "a team that lost but was never beaten."

1942–43

By 1942, the Second World War had escalated and discussions were being held to discuss whether hockey should continue with so many Canadian boys enlisted in military service. It was wisely decided that the sport provided a healthy diversion to the global conflict being waged. Seven teams competed in the OHA Junior 'A' league during the 1942–43 season. The Oshawa Generals finished first overall with 36 points (teams occasionally played four-point games), 10 better than second-place Brantford. The Hamilton Whizzers, new to the league, tied the Lions with 26 points but had one fewer win. Also new were the Stratford Kroehlers, sponsored by a furniture manufacturer in the small southwestern Ontario city, who cobbled together a 24-point debut. St. Mike's copped fifth place, winning nine, losing 11, and tying one for 23 points. The Marlboros sunk to a sixth-place finish, while the Toronto Young Rangers, who brought up the rear, withdrew before the season was completed and forfeited their final three games.

1942–43					
Team	GP	W	L	T	Pts
Oshawa Generals	22	17	5	0	36
Brantford Lions	22	12	10	2	26
Hamilton Whizzers	24	11	9	4	26
Stratford Kroehlers	25	7	9	9	24
St. Michael's Majors	21	9	11	1	23
Toronto Marlboros	21	8	12	1	17

The 1942–43 Majors, again under Father Mallon, had several key members return from the previous year's team, including Frank Bennett, Jean Marois, and Tommy O'Neill, all of whom eventually played in the NHL. O'Neill, who would play wing with the Toronto Maple Leafs, played defence for the Majors, and for a second straight season he led the team in penalty minutes, with 34. Gerry Hickey was the team's point leader, collecting 27. But several new faces graced the Majors in 1942–43, players who would play crucial roles on the team in the seasons ahead. Brian Lynch was recruited from the Winnipeg Rangers and was the Majors' top goal scorer with 17. Dave Bauer, not yet ready for the priesthood, served as captain of the Majors and tallied 21 points, third best on the team. Frank Dunlap joined the team from Ottawa St. Pat's. Scouts drooled over Pat Powers, the son of former Toronto St. Patricks coach Eddie Powers. Bob "Snuffy" Schnurr joined the team from the Junior 'B' Kitchener Packers.

On the final day of the regular season, the Majors and Marlboros were tied for the fifth and final playoff slot. St. Mike's snuck into the playoffs by defeating the Marlboros 6–4, but the Marlboros were only briefly eliminated. When Barrie withdrew from the playoffs, the Marlboros took their place and met their nemesis, the Majors, in the first round.

The first game was an 11–6 shellacking at the hands of the Marlboros, but St. Mike's battled back with a pair of victories, 6–2 and 7–4, to win the best-of-three series. Unfortunately, the Majors lost to Brantford in the OHA championship final, concluding their season.

Father Bill Conway's love of hockey predates his coaching success. Here's Bill Conway as a member of the 1940–41 Midget squad.

Had any of the team's members gotten into trouble during the season, they would have been well cared for legally. Tommy O'Neill, better known as "Windy," played two seasons with the Majors before joining the Toronto Maple Leafs in 1943–44. While playing with the Leafs, O'Neill continued to attend university and was given special dispensation to play strictly home games and the odd road trip when school permitted. He played 66 games over two seasons, scoring 10 goals and 22 assists, and was part of the Leafs' Stanley Cup championship won in 1945.

Frank Dunlap, also known as "Judge" when he was in law school, went on to become a district court judge in Pembroke. Like O'Neill, Dunlap played strictly home games for the Toronto Maple Leafs during 1943–44. That season, he played 15 games with the Toronto Maple Leafs while also playing 15 for St. Mike's. Frank later played professional football, suiting up for the Toronto Argonauts and Ottawa Rough Riders alongside his brother John, better known as lawyer Jake Dunlap. Both were members of the Ottawa Rough Riders squad that won the Grey Cup in 1951.

Similarly, Father Ted McLean was an outstanding hockey player before entering the seminary. Here, young 'Teddy' was already starring with the 1940–41 Bantams.

1943–44

With its membership up to 10 teams, the OHA Junior league was again divided into two divisions. In the West, the St. Catharines Falcons won top honours, followed by Galt's Kist Canadians and, in their final season, the Brantford Lions. Oshawa again topped the East, losing but three of 23 games for a 46-point first-place finish. Not far behind was St. Michael's, winning 21, losing four, and compiling 44 points.

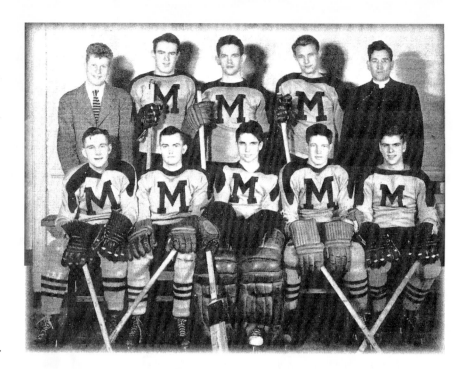

The 1942–43 edition of the Majors, coached by Father Mallon, featured Frank Dunlap and Frank Bennett (back row, second and third from left) and Windy O'Neill (front row, far left), who went on to NHL careers, and Dave Bauer (seated, second from right), who followed the calling to a life in the priesthood.

1943–44					
Team	GP	W	L	T	Pts
East					
Oshawa Generals	26	23	3	0	46
St. Michael's Majors	25	21	4	0	44
Hamilton Szabos	25	12	12	1	25
Toronto Marlboros	26	8	15	1	18
Toronto Young Rangers	25	1	23	1	3
West					
St. Catharines Falcons	26	15	9	2	32
Galt Canadians	26	15	11	0	30
Brantford Lions	25	11	13	1	23
Port Colborne Recreationists	26	10	16	0	20
Stratford Kroehlers	25	7	16	2	16

Paul McNamara, a St. Mike's alumnus, took over the coaching reins with the Majors in 1943–44. Bobby Schnurr, slight but shifty on his skates, led the Majors in scoring with 60 points. Not far behind was Joe Sadler, who had moved up from the Buzzers that season, with 55 points. The Toronto *Telegram* said of Johnny McCormack (48 points) that "a gamer kid never put on skates." *The Thurible* stated of Dave Bauer (37 points), "In all the long history of St. Michael's, none have borne the title of captain more worthily than Dave." During a contest against Galt, Bauer took a pass from behind the net, but the puck squirted away from him. Instead of attempting a backhand, "Dave switched from a left-hand shot to a right, and blasted it past Philby, the goaltender," reported the *Toronto Daily Star*.

Newcomer Ted Lindsay collected 29 points, including 22 goals. "His self-possession and aggressiveness are accentuated when his smile reveals teeth lost in action." The *Telegram* described him as "fearless on the attack."

Frank Dunlap, playing on a line with Bauer and Schnurr, picked up 25 points and, as noted, played 15 games with the Leafs. "Burly 'Biff,' with the huskiest build on the team, had a fighting Irish temper that was a constant fright to converging opponents," reported the yearbook. "Putting the puck behind the goalie gave him real boyish pleasure and he skated back with his strong Irish mug beaming unaffectedly."

Helmeted Teddy McLean was in his second season with the Majors and "packed a lightning shot and a devastating swivel-hip to upset impulsive forwards." Gus Mortson, who had come to St. Mike's with Ted Lindsay after playing the previous year with the Kirkland Lake Lakers, was introduced on defence "with a lightning rush and a thumping body check when he chose to use it." Jimmy Thomson played most of the season with the Toronto Marlboros after arriving in Toronto from Winnipeg. "The St. Mike's sweater does make a difference," chuckled the *Telegram*. "Jimmy Thomson looked ten times the better hockey player wearing the big M for the Irish."

Pat Boehmer split the goaltending duties with third-year veteran Jean Marois. Boehmer's "coolness and nonchalance had the customers slapping each other on the back when he played," said *The Thurible*. Eighteen-year-old Marois, in his final year with the Majors, was summoned to join the Maple Leafs to replace injured Benny Grant. Marois played a single game with the Leafs, winning 8–4 over the Chicago Black Hawks on

December 18, 1943. It would be 10 years before he played another NHL game. After serving in the Canadian military in 1944–45, the diminutive netminder became property of the Montreal Canadiens and toiled in the Quebec Senior Hockey League, where he was named to the league's All-Star team on three occasions. In 1953–54, while a member of the Quebec Aces, Jean was loaned to the Chicago Black Hawks and played two games (both of them Chicago losses) as an injury replacement.

McNamara's band of merry men dismissed Galt in the first round of the playoffs. Up next was Hamilton, and the Majors dumped the Szabos in the best-of-three series with wins of 5–2 and 11–5 to go with an 8–2 loss.

Finally, St. Michael's faced the Oshawa Generals for the OHA Junior 'A' championship. It would be a formidable test for the Majors, as the Generals had won six consecutive league championships and had reached the Memorial Cup final in five of the previous six seasons. "Anyone who bets on either of these teams is daffy," warned *The Globe and Mail*. "We are of the opinion that the series will go the full seven games and the final game will end in a draw!"

The series wasn't as tight as paint on a fence, but it was spectacular for the fans. The Generals edged St. Mike's 4–3 in Game One, spanked them 5–1 in Game Two, and took a commanding lead in the series with a 5–3 victory in Game Three. Resilient and undaunted, the Majors won Game Four by a 3–2 score on St. Patrick's Day, but the season was over for the Majors when Oshawa blanked them 2–0 in Game Five. "The Irish were champions without a championship," declared *The Thurible*.

Ted Lindsay shone in the playoffs, scoring a league-best 13 goals and 19 points in 12 games. John McCormack contributed 15 points and Frank Dunlap 14, while David Bauer and Bobby Schnurr each added 12 points.

So impressive were the Majors that, when the Generals were allowed to add four OHA players to their lineup for their Memorial Cup series against the Trail Smoke Eaters, they selected three of St. Michael's skaters — Dave Bauer, Ted Lindsay, and Gus Mortson — along with goaltender Jean Marois, who was added for insurance but saw no activity for the Generals. Even more remarkable is the fact that the western champions suffered injuries to Lorne De Paolis, Mark Marquess, and Frank Turik and were granted permission by the Canadian Amateur Hockey Association to add three reinforcements to their decimated lineup. They, too, chose players from the Majors, "turning the final game into something resembling a St. Mike's inter-squad match," according to *The Memorial Cup* by Richard Lapp and Alec Macaulay. The three who joined the Smoke Eaters for the fourth game of the series — played, like each of its predecessors that spring, at Maple Leaf Gardens — were John McCormack, Bobby Schnurr, and Jimmy Thomson.

The Memorial Cup was presented to the Generals on April 22, after an 11–4 victory, giving Oshawa a four-game sweep of Trail. Lindsay scored twice for the Generals, while Gus Mortson added an assist. McCormack and Schnurr each contributed a goal and an assist for Trail in a losing cause.

The 1943–44 edition of the Majors featured several future NHLers, including Frank Dunlap, Ted Lindsay, Johnny McCormack, Gus Mortson, Jimmy Thomson, and netminder Jean Marois. In addition, Dave Bauer, Gerry Gregoire, and Ted McLean answered a higher calling.

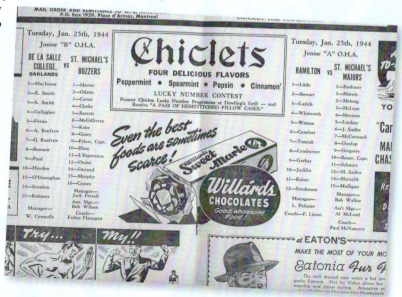

EARLY 1940s — BUILDING A DYNASTY

For Bauer, Lindsay and Mortson, it was their first Memorial Cup championship. Following the win, Bauer declared that it was great to be included with such a bunch of winners, and that perhaps next season, a few Generals would help his St. Michael's team win the national Junior championship.

Mortson and Thomson played together for much of their hockey careers, first with St. Michael's in 1943–44 and 1944–45, and then with the Toronto Maple Leafs from 1946–47 to 1950–51. Mortson was traded to the Black Hawks in September 1952, but the defence partners would have one last hurrah together in Chicago in 1957–58, after Thomson was dumped there for his role in helping organize a players' union — an initiative led by Ted Lindsay. While playing with the Leafs, Mortson and Thomson were nicknamed the Gold Dust Twins, and they contributed significantly to Stanley Cup wins in 1947, 1948, 1949, and 1951. Mortson played 13 NHL seasons with Toronto, Chicago, and Detroit, and although he contributed 198 points in 797 regular-season games, his primary role was to stop the opposing team, which he did with great efficiency, earning a First Team All-Star selection in 1950. Jim Thomson played 787 games and had 234 points, but like his partner, proved exceptional at shutting down the other team. Jim was a Second Team All-Star in 1951 and 1952.

SNAPSHOT ▶▶ ▶▶ ▶▶ ▶▶ ▶▶ ▶▶ ▶▶ ▶▶

Father Hugh Foley: The Last of the Basilians

Father Hugh Foley, the "La Salette Flash," is the last surviving member of a very special breed of St. Michael's Majors players who would become Basilian priests. A bright and thoughtful resident of the Basilian residence in Toronto, Father Foley played for the 1941–42 Majors team coached by Father Mallon. Father Foley's dad, Vincent, also attended St. Michael's around 1910. Hugh attended the school from 1937 until 1942, then went to the Basilian novitiate to study for the priesthood.

Father Foley was certainly not the only St. Mike's hockey player to follow a calling to the priesthood. Father Jack Spratt was part of the St. Michael's team that successfully toured Boston and New York City in 1911, beating the U.S. amateur champions of that era. Cardinal George Flahiff played for the 1925 entry in the Prep School group. In Phillip Wallace Platt's biography, *Gentle Eminence: A Life of Cardinal Flahiff*, the cardinal's hockey-playing prowess was described. "He rarely bodychecked; he relied on his skating skill, his speed and his stickhandling — in a word, on the art of the game rather than on the advantage of weight and size." Cardinal Flahiff became one of Canada's most beloved church leaders, championing the progressive vision of the Second Vatican Council.

Father David Bauer had a profound influence on a generation of hockey-playing students, while Father Les Costello helped initiate the Flying Fathers, a collection of hockey-playing priests who raised millions of dollars for charity. Father Ted McLean was captain of the 1945 Memorial Cup champion Majors. Father Ray Hannigan played for the 1947 Memorial Cup champion Majors. Father Ray became a priest in Montana long after his hockey career was over.

Other notable hockey-playing Basilian Fathers include Maurice Whelan, a goaltender for the 1927–28 Junior hockey team; Matthew Sheedy and Ted Flanagan, both of whom played on the 1931 Junior squad; and Gerry Gregoire, who played for two years in the early 1940s. Father Rocco Volpe toiled on the 1947–48 Buzzers along with Father Art Holmes, who also played for the 1946–47 edition. Fathers Whelan, Flanagan, and Volpe also took turns coaching the Buzzers, as did Father Mallon. Legendary coach Father Bill Conway played for the 1941–42 squad. Father Frank Orsini starred two years for the Buzzers, from 1933 until 1935.

Father Foley helped out as equipment manager of the St. Mike's Bantams in his first year. After playing with the St. Mike's Minor Bantams and Minor Midgets, Foley noticed a poster advertising tryouts with the Majors in 1941, when the team was being revived after a two-year hiatus. The 1941–42 team started out as a weak unit, but pulled together as the season progressed. "Those great teams of [Red] Kelly and [Ted] Lindsay that came after us built on what we accomplished," Father Foley says. "We were responsible for laying the foundation of the good teams that followed us."

Foley's father decided not to tell Hugh that the Boston Bruins had an interest in him. "I was mad at him, which did not happen very often. He wanted to protect me. Dad told me [about it] after I was in the seminary, although I don't think I would have changed my mind about joining the seminary."

Father Foley came from La Salette, Ontario, close to Red Kelly's hometown of Simcoe. He has fond memories of Father Henry Carr, who taught him in the seminary, calling him "one of the greatest teachers I ever had." Father Carr's vision for St. Michael's, both at the university and secondary level, "was to make it part of Toronto and to make it known academically and in sports." Father Foley later taught and coached at Windsor's Assumption College for 17 years. He remarked that Father David Bauer was innovative in his coaching — one of Father Bauer's frequent strategies was to use four defencemen to kill penalties. Father Bauer loved to rattle the cages of the Maple Leafs executives he dealt with. Apparently, he thought that Punch Imlach and Harold Ballard both needed edification, so he gave them copies of *True Humanism* by the French Catholic theologian Father Jacques Maritain. "I don't know how many pages they read," Father Foley chuckles.

Father Foley's fondest memories are of the atmosphere at the school in the 1930s and 1940s. "We had the best teachers. They really liked the kids," he says. "Their hearts were in it. Their spirits were there. The lack of supplies and facilities didn't matter because we had good teachers. I loved St. Mike's. I was so happy."

1945 — Memorial Cup Mastery

The fortunes of the St. Michael's Majors took a distinct turn for the better with the hiring of alumnus Joe Primeau, who took over as coach in 1944, replacing Paul McNamara, who was forced to retire due to illness.

The Majors enjoyed a superb season, losing only one game all year and finishing comfortably in first place. Three teams — Brantford, Hamilton, and Stratford — elected not to return for the 1944–45 season, and the league returned to a single-division format. Membership fell to six when Port Colborne dropped out after winning just one of its seven games.

Under Primeau's guidance, the Majors, who had finished second in 1943–44, snapped the unprecedented streak of the Oshawa Generals, who had landed atop the standings seven years in a row. St. Mike's had also been runners-up to Oshawa in that year's OHA final, and they were equally determined to loosen their rivals' grip on the provincial and eastern Canadian titles.

The St. Mike's squad included goaltender Pat Boehmer, who also acted as a practice goalie for the Toronto Maple Leafs. "His marvelous dexterity with both skates and glove were truly something to marvel at," suggested *The Thurible*.

The defence position was well stocked with Johnny Arundel, Ted McLean, Gus Mortson, and Jimmy Thomson. McLean had suffered a painful rugby injury during the off-season, but came to camp ready to play and was given the team's captaincy. "A little fellow with a big heart, the mighty mite always comes up with a three-star effort," stated *The Thurible*. A Maple Leaf Gardens program from that season said of Mortson, "the big lad with all the skating speed comes roaring out of his defensive area and it generally takes half the opposition to run him down, if they can." The yearbook added, "His ripping shot and flying sorties always provided the fans with an extra thrill." But *The Thurible* reserved its highest exaltations for Jimmy Thomson, who had arrived from Winnipeg in 1943 and played most of the 1943–44 season with the Toronto Marlboros before joining St. Mike's for one regular-season contest and the entire playoff series. "Able to slam a flying winger into oblivion with a booming body-thump or zip up the ice with his swinging strides, Jimmy was a real sixteen-cylinder dynamo going both ways. Jim could rush like an express train while his stickhandling and playmaking started many lantern-plays."

Coach Primeau placed Johnny Blute, John McCormack, and Joe Sadler on the first line. "[Blute's] terrific speed, heady play, determined backchecking and uncanny knack of hitting the jackpot assured him the left wing berth on the big-gun line," mentioned *The Thurible*. "Belying his appearance of a limp dishrag on skates," John McCormack was second in voting for league MVP honours. "His famed dipsy-doodle and tricky passing together with his magic sweepcheck and goal-putting ability marked him as first string centre." Joe Sadler had "a quick burst of speed that catches his checkers flat-footed, and when he comes sailing in from the starboard side and sizzles his low, hot one goalwards, there are few goaltenders able to touch it."

Les Costello—"his smooth, graceful skating added an extra dash of colour to his play,"— was placed on a line with Tod Sloan and Frank Turik. "When in possession of the rubber, [Sloan] was like a greased banana, and was always sure-fire when cruising near the nets." Turik, who was scooped from the Trail Smoke Eaters after the 1944 Memorial Cup final, showed "smooth, aggressive drive and neat playmaking."

1944–1945

TEAM	GP	W	L	T	Pts
St. Michael's Majors	19	18	1	0	36
St. Catharines Falcons	20	12	8	0	24
Galt Red Wings	20	12	8	0	24
Oshawa Generals	20	9	11	0	18
Toronto Young Rangers	19	6	13	0	12
Toronto Marlboros	20	2	18	0	4
Port Colborne Recreationists	7	1	6	0	2

Coach Joe Primeau (in cardigan, centre), looks on as one of his troops receives medical attention. Defencemen Gus Mortson and Jim Thomson (shirtless) attend to other matters.

Leo Gravelle, who spent the 1943–44 season with Port Colborne, joined the Majors in 1944–45. "His ubiquitous play, blinding speed and rifle shot made him a marked man." Bob Paul was a rugged winger who had "a tricky shift and blistering drive that nets him many important goals."

Blute and Gravelle tied for the league lead in goal scoring, both connecting 30 times. Gravelle was the league's leading point collector that season with 52. At the time, there was no trophy presented for such an accomplishment, although the Toronto Marlboro Hockey Club would remedy that during the summer by donating the Eddie Powers Memorial Trophy. Defenceman Jim Thomson led the league with 52 minutes in penalties.

Vengeance was a dish served ice cold one night early in the season when the Majors made a very loud and very clear statement by pummelling the Generals 12–1 at the Oshawa Arena. The Toronto *Telegram* boasted, "St. Michael's College Majors served due and solemn warning to Oshawa that their long reign in the throne of the Junior OHA is likely to terminate this year."

❖

After winning exhibition contests against the Windsor Spitfires and HMCS *York*, St. Mike's embarked on a remarkable season. Through 19 regular-season games, the Majors outscored their competition 183–29. St. Michael's only stumble was an 8–6 loss to against St. Catharines in unlucky game number 13, but when the final buzzer of the regular season sounded, they had compiled an outstanding record of 18 wins against that lone loss.

There were several highlights over the course of the regular season. Johnny McCormack put on a one-man clinic against Oshawa, scoring four of the Majors' goals in a 5–1 victory and checking the Generals unmercifully. In the process of whipping the Galt Red Wings 14–2 late in the schedule, Leo Gravelle scored six goals. St. Mike's clearly had the Marlboros' number all season. After defeating the Dukes 10–1 in the season opener, the Majors dumped their rivals 15–1, 14–1, and 18–2 in subsequent meetings.

❖

Stars of the 1945 Memorial Cup championship squad reunited for the annual Old Boys' contest in 1962. Left to right: Les Costello, Tod Sloan, and Fleming Mackell.

St. Mike's faced St. Catharines in the best-of-seven group semifinal. Game One saw the Falcons start off strong, holding the score at 1–1 after the first period. But St. Mike's found their game in the second on back-to-back goals by Les Costello and Bob Paul, which unravelled St. Catharines. The final score was 6–1 in favour of the Majors. "Leader for St. Mike's was large Jimmy Thomson. He rushed well, was strong on defence and broke up many plays," reported *The Globe and Mail*. "Gravelle was certainly a threat every time he moved towards Harvey Jessiman in the St. Catharines goal."

St. Mike's was caught flatfooted by the Falcons in Game Two. "Outhustled and checked dizzy," St. Mike's bowed 4–2. St. Catharines was up by four goals in the third period before Tod Sloan broke Jessiman's shutout bid. Gus Mortson also scored in the third period to make the score presentable.

The third game in the series was another high-scoring affair, with St. Mike's emerging as the victor. Coach Primeau double-shifted centre John McCormack, placing him between Bob Paul and Leo Gravelle on one unit and John Blute and Joe Sadler on another. The Majors got three goals from Paul in the 8–3 victory, while Les Costello picked up two goals and five assists. According to *The Globe*, "No one was really outstanding for St. Catharines. All tried hard but were up against a situation where their best work was not sufficient."

St. Catharines coach Rudy Pilous recruited Jack Taggart and Ron Matthews from the Oshawa Generals as military replacements, but was denied in his bid to also add Barry Sullivan. Taggart played well for the Falcons, but Matthews, a defenceman with Oshawa, was played at forward and appeared lost in that position.

St. Mike's dominated Game Four of the semifinals. "They outsped the Falcons and checked them to a standstill," reported *The Globe and Mail*. Gravelle picked up a hat trick, but it was John McCormack who was selected as the game's star by Joe Primeau. "McCormack showed his uncanny checking skill," stated *The Globe*. "He can work more magic with his stick than Toscanini." McCormack scored twice in the game, a 9–2 win over the Falcons. Jimmy Thomson and Gus Mortson were especially aggressive in halting any Falcon attacks, although Mortson hurt his shoulder in the contest.

The series was determined in Game Five, as St. Mike's mauled the St. Catharines Falcons by a 14–1 count. The game was never close, but the Majors pumped seven goals behind netminder Harvey Jessiman in the last 10 minutes of the third period. Tod Sloan earned a hat trick and added three assists. Les Costello scored a pair of goals and racked up five assists. Leo Gravelle, Joe Sadler, and Frank Turik each notched two markers.

In the OHA Junior 'A' final, St. Michael's required little effort in rolling over the Galt Red Wings. The Red Wings featured future NHLers Pete Babando, Lee Fogolin, and Marty Pavelich, as well as high-scoring Bill Curik and Win Mousseau.

The initial game of the series was a 13–4 debacle favouring the Majors. John McCormack worked his magic, finishing with five goals plus an assist. Tod Sloan contributed a hat trick. In Game Two, netminder Pat Boehmer celebrated his 19th birthday with an 8–3 St. Patrick's Day win. The Red Wings' goalie, Cec Gruhl, certainly wasn't enjoying the luck of the Irish. Jim Thomson, wearing a football helmet to protect a broken nose, scored three goals, all on shots from the blue line. High-scoring John Blute also added a hat trick. Galt suffered injuries to centre Bill Curik (a badly cut leg) and Harry Kazarian, who saw stars after a heavy collision with Frank Turik.

Game Three was an 8–2 triumph, and then the Majors completed a sweep of the series with a tidy 5–1 win — though not without some serious fisticuffs. The victory gave the Majors bragging rights to the John Ross Robertson Cup as OHA Junior 'A' champions for 1945.

Next stop was the All-Ontario final against the Porcupine Combines, champions of the Northern Ontario Hockey Association. In the opening contest, the Majors smothered the Combines 12–3. Joe Sadler and Tod Sloan scored four goals apiece, while Leo Gravelle and Les Costello each chipped in a pair. Gus Mortson and Bob Paul scored the other tallies. Leo Curik, Ray Hannigan, and Sid Smith scored for the Porcupines. Smith and his Oshawa Generals teammate Barry Sullivan had been added to the Porcupines' lineup, along with Al Dewsbury of the Toronto Young Rangers. Stu Pirie, the South Porcupine netminder, was caught by a puck that split his upper lip in the second period, but after receiving stitches, he gamely returned to the crease. St. Michael's subsequently smothered the Combines 8–6 in Game Two, then picked up another 12–3 win to easily take the best-of-five series from their NOHA challengers.

The Montreal Royals put up a respectable fight in the eastern Canadian final. The opening salvo was fired when the Royals, a team that included brothers Doug and Howie Harvey as well as Fleming Mackell, shocked the Toronto team with a 3–1 victory in Game One. It was the seventh consecutive victory for the Montreal Juniors, while St. Mike's was "tied up tighter than a 5 p.m. traffic jam" en route to only their first loss in 11 tries. Bob Paul scored the Majors' only goal of the game.

Undaunted, St. Michael's catapulted over the Royals 7–1 in Game Two. Coach Primeau had bitten his nails to the nub as the Royals scored at the 22-second mark, but the goal was called back on an offside. *The Globe* wrote: "Montreal showed little of the fire and speed that characterized their 3–1 victory in Game One. Only occasionally did their first-game brilliance show." Conversely, St. Mike's picked up goals by Johnny McCormack and Leo Gravelle in the first period, shone in the second with goals from McCormack, Gravelle, captain Ted McLean, and Joe Sadler, then added another goal from Gravelle in the third before Jim O'Connor beat Boehmer to break the Majors' shutout bid. "The winners' goals were all masterpieces. They had to be, as Howard Harvey in the Royals' nets again played marvelously," according to *The Globe and Mail*. "Blond Leo Gravelle, swishing around in

Captain Teddy McLean accepts the Memorial Cup from the OHA's William Hewitt on behalf of his triumphant teammates in 1945.

high gear every time used, led the Irish goal getters with three markers." Both Doug Harvey and Fleming Mackell were missing from the Royals' lineup in this contest.

The seesaw series took another swing in Game Three, as the Royals won 4–3 to recapture the lead in the series. "Howard Harvey was incredibly cool in the Royals' goal and refused to lose his head despite the feverish milling around him," said *The Globe*.

Bob Paul, Frank Turik, and Tod Sloan traded goals with Lyall Wiseman, Fleming Mackell, Kenny Burnett, and Cliff Malone, who netted the winning goal for Montreal. In the dying minutes of the game, Majors coach Joe Primeau used four forwards and one defenceman in an attempt to even the score.

After the Royals' John Chenier opened the scoring for Montreal in Game Four, Joe Sadler tied the score before the first period was complete. But a three-goal explosion for the Majors in the second frame made all the difference. Tod Sloan scored twice and Leo Gravelle once to put St. Mike's up by three; Les Costello drove home a third-period insurance marker to give the Majors a 5–1 victory and tie the series at two games apiece. Pat Boehmer starred in goal for St. Mike's, while Doug Harvey was outstanding on defence for the Royals.

Game Five put the St. Mike's Majors ahead in the series as they took the contest 4–3 on a late goal by Tod Sloan that proved to be the winner. The Royals, who had trailed the

Majors 3–1 going into the third, rebounded with goals by Cliff Malone and Doug Harvey before Sloan's unassisted tally saved the day. Les Costello, Bob Gray, and Ted McLean scored the other St. Mike's goals.

With Bob Paul sidelined with a broken thumb and Leo Gravelle on spot duty due to injury, St. Mike's was hard pressed to contain the battling Royals in Game Six. Pat Boehmer and his mates fended off three or four dangerous attacks from the Royals early in the first period before Tod Sloan scored just past the two-minute mark. Sloan's goal opened the floodgates, and Montreal netminder Howie Harvey was left defenceless as Sloan scored a second, followed in short order by tallies from Jimmy Thomson and Joe Sadler. But as the Majors admired their work, linemates John Chenier and Jimmy O'Connor both scored to reduce the Majors' margin.

The second period took an aggressive turn. "Elbows, high sticks and rumps were tossed around freely," noted *The Globe and Mail*. Doug Harvey played all but 45 seconds of the game, and tangled with Johnny McCormack every time the two collided. Meantime, "(Howie) Harvey and Pat Boehmer were called upon to make spectacular saves." Joe Sadler fired a backhand shot past Harvey for the only goal of the second period. In the third, Lyall Wiseman and Joe O'Connor narrowed the score for Montreal, but St. Mike's capped the game with late-period goals from Joe Sadler (his third) and Jimmy Thomson to complete the 7–4 win. The Majors collected the Richardson Trophy as eastern Canadian champions, and prepared for the school's first appearance in the Memorial Cup final since their championship in 1934.

❖

The champions of western Canada in 1945 were the Moose Jaw Canucks, coached by Roy Bentley, a former Chicago Black Hawk and brother of Hall of Famers Doug and Max. The team's star centre, Doc Couture, missed the tournament in order to stay home and write his exams. Instead, he ended up being summoned to join the parent Detroit Red Wings in their Stanley Cup final against the Maple Leafs.

The final was played at Maple Leaf Gardens. Game One was an 8–5 win for St. Michael's, before 12,420 fans. "Beaten only four times in 38 previous starts this season, Coach Primeau's class-laden collegians struck swiftly for two goals in the first eight minutes, held Moose Jaw at bay through a bristling second period and sealed the issue with three rapid-fire goals early in the third," reported the Canadian Press. "'We missed enough chances to win a dozen hockey games,' [Moose Jaw] chorused, as well as they could chorus between clenched and gnashing teeth," said *The Globe and Mail*. St. Mike's goals were scored by Les Costello, Johnny McCormack, Joe Sadler, Tod Sloan, and Frank Turik, as well as two by Gus Mortson, who was used on the wing in this game. "The former defenceman did a robust job on left wing and imparted a dash of physical strength up front that came in handy." Bert Olmstead collected the hat trick while Metro Prystai and Frank Ashworth, "a pair of Canucks with plenty of scat and scamper," added the other goals for Moose Jaw.

Moose Jaw rebounded with a 5–3 victory in the second game of the series. Roy Bentley's charges came out strong against the Majors, who "were unable to cope with Moose Jaw's close checking and lightning-quick breakaways when St. Mike's players were out of position." Prystai, Ashworth, Lou Hauck, and Mark Marquess (with two) beat Pat Boehmer, while Tod Sloan scored two and Joe Sadler the other for the losers. Johnny Blute was scratched from the Majors' lineup and Phil Samis saw infrequent action in his place.

The loss in Game Two stirred the Irish blood of the St. Mike's players, who then downed Moose Jaw 6–3 in the third contest. St. Mike's beat Canucks goalie Bev Bentley four times in the first period. John McCormack and Jimmy Thomson both netted a pair. The Canucks clawed back in the second, but the Majors responded with a tally from the stick of Sloan to stay ahead. Les Costello picked up the lone goal of the third period. "Although there was plenty of end-to-end play, checking was extremely close and brilliantly efficient," reported *The Globe*. "It was a stirring sight to see attack after attack led up, then broken up. Both sides were equally adept."

Jack Miller fired the first goal of Game Four, a Canucks tally that occurred just 35 seconds after the opening faceoff. A second Moose Jaw marker, this one scored on a fierce shot by Ralph Nattrass, "who can stop an attack with a shrug of a wide shoulder," followed midway through the period. Frank Turik, "heir to Dave Bauer's Human Fly act along the boards," scored to close out the scoring in the first period. Jim Thomson made a sensational end-to-end rush that resulted in the first goal of the second period, tying the score. Then Frank Turik went to work, scoring his second and third goals of the game. In between, Lou Hauck tallied for Moose Jaw. Although scoreless, the third period was extremely exciting. Pat Boehmer held down the fort for St. Mike's, robbing Marquess once and Bert Olmstead and Frank Ashworth twice each. Then Ashworth found himself on a breakaway, but Ted McLean dove to knock the puck away. Final score: 4–3 for the Majors, who now held a three-games-to-one lead in the series.

The Majors took the enthusiasm away from the Canucks early in Game Five, and never let their opponents back into the contest. "The Canucks knew that they were at the end of the trail very soon after the puck was dropped," reported the *Regina Leader-Post*. "They tried to break into a gallop, found that the old zip was missing and all the encouragement that 14,000 spectators provided failed to produce the spark that would make the red and white Moose Jaw flyers flame again."

Leo Gravelle potted three goals, including one on a penalty shot, to lead the Majors, with Costello, McCormack, Mortson, and Turik adding singles. Bert Olmstead and Mark Marquess replied for Moose Jaw. Tod Sloan was assessed four minors and a misconduct during the game. But with the 7–2 win on April 23, 1945, the St. Michael's Majors had captured the Memorial Cup.

The trophy was presented by W.A. Hewitt, treasurer of the Canadian Amateur Hockey Association, to Father Mallon and Joe Primeau. Students celebrated by spilling out onto Yonge Street and forming a conga line "which drew laughing police attention and caused many awakened folk to think V-E Day was being celebrated at midnight," laughed the *Toronto Daily Star*. To commemorate the championship, the school gave its students the day off on April 24.

After the game, Metro Prystai of Moose Jaw admitted, "We were beaten by a better team, although we hope they know they've been in a tough series."

Even though the Maple Leafs were competing for the Stanley Cup at the same time, the city of Toronto seemed caught up in Memorial Cup excitement. A total of 65,437 paid to attend the five games at Maple Leaf Gardens, bettering the previous record of 59,301 for a five-game series, set in 1943 when the Winnipeg Rangers faced the Oshawa Generals.

With the win, Joe Primeau captured the first jewel in a unique triple crown of hockey coaching. In 1950, he guided the Toronto Marlboro Seniors to an Allan Cup championship, and in 1951, he was behind the bench for the Toronto Maple Leafs' exciting Stanley Cup victory.

For Gus Mortson, who scored four goals in the series alternating between wing and defence, it was his second Memorial Cup championship in as many years, and his first in Majors colours (he had been an addition to the Oshawa Generals lineup in 1944). Joe Sadler had been with Trail, the Generals' opponents in 1944, and contributed significantly to his new team's championship in 1945. Sadler and John McCormack played a highly effective checking series against Moose Jaw, while the Costello-Sloan-Turik line was potent on offence. Costello scored three goals, Sloan four, and Turik five through the series. John Blute saw action in Game Five, his first of the series, as he replaced Bob Paul, who was still nursing a broken thumb. Pat Boehmer was outstanding in goal throughout the entire playoff run for St. Mike's. "Cool as a cucumber, Pat Boehmer turned in the most sensational puck-stopping displays of his career," boasted the school's yearbook.

❖

Leo Gravelle was nicknamed The Gazelle for good reason. The speedster flew up and down the rink, making plays at full speed, a skill many goal scorers never acquire. Author Stan Fischler referred to Gravelle as "one of the fastest, if not *the* fastest, skater in National Hockey League history." Gravelle played only one season with St. Michael's, but left a sizeable impression in spite of his smallish stature. He signed with the Montreal Canadiens and was in the NHL club's lineup through most of 1946–47, but was back and forth between the Canadiens and the AHL's Buffalo Bisons the next two seasons. Leo played all 70 games of the 1949–50 season, scoring 19 goals. The next season, he was swapped to Detroit and completed that season, but did not play in the NHL again. Gravelle scored 44 goals and 34 assists in 223 NHL regular-season games.

When the Boston Bruins signed Ed Sandford, they took his linemate (and cousin), too. Ed Harrison, who was so instrumental in the success of both the Buzzers and the Majors on a line with Sandford and Red Kelly, joined the Bruins in 1947–48. His best year with Boston, 1949–50, saw him play an important role on a checking line, while still scoring 14 goals and 26 points, both of which were NHL career bests for him. In November 1950, he was traded to the New York Rangers, but played just four games there before he was sent to the minors. In 194 NHL games, Ed Harrison totalled 27 goals and 24 assists for 51 points.

After starring in his native Edmonton, Alberta, Phil Samis moved to Toronto to attend St. Michael's College in 1944–45, playing defence for both the Junior 'A' Majors and the Junior 'B' Buzzers. He next spent two seasons with the Oshawa Generals, then played with the AHL Pittsburgh Hornets, the Maple Leafs' top farm team, in 1947–48. During that year's NHL playoffs, Samis was summoned to Toronto and made his first, albeit brief, NHL appearances. When the Leafs defeated Detroit 7–2 to sweep the Red Wings and collect the Stanley Cup, Phil Samis earned the right to have his name engraved on hockey's most prestigious trophy. He returned to Pittsburgh the next season and didn't climb back to the NHL until 1949–50, when he was called up as an injury replacement for two games with the Maple Leafs.

Following his hockey career, Samis went into dentistry. Dr. Phil had an outstanding career with his Montreal dental practice. "More than twenty years ago, I did extensive research on inserting microchips into the teeth of patients so it would help in identification should a disaster occur," recalled Samis. "Watching the horrors in New Orleans [caused by Hurricane Katrina], that kind of identification would have been invaluable. It's unfortunate that the idea never came to fruition."

St. Michael's celebrated championships with a banquet held at the King Edward Hotel on May 14, 1945 (it had been rescheduled because of VE Day celebrations in Toronto). Invited guests included Mayor Robert Saunders, William A. Hewitt of the CAHA, secretary Frank Smith of the Toronto Hockey League, Captain James T. Sutherland, alumni Ted Lindsay and Paul McNamara, King Clancy of the Maple Leafs, and Detroit Red Wings manager Jack Adams. Clancy, Adams, and Saunders, as well as Joe Primeau and Father Hugh Mallon, were guest speakers and paid special tribute to the Memorial Cup champion Majors, the Sutherland Cup–winning Buzzers, and the St. Michael's Midgets, who captured both the league championship and the King Clancy section of the THL. Presentations included the Memorial Cup, miniature replicas of the Memorial Cup, Memorial Cup medals, OHA Junior 'A' medals, and gold watches from the school to members of the Majors; the Sutherland Cup and OHA Junior 'B' medals to the Buzzers; and THL plaques to members of the Midgets.

SNAPSHOT ▶▶ ▶▶ ▶▶ ▶▶ ▶▶ ▶▶ ▶▶ ▶▶   *John McCormack:* "Goose" with Style

Lanky John McCormack was establishing himself as a scoring star in his hometown of Edmonton, Alberta, when scouts for the Maple Leafs took notice. "Toronto scouted me back home and invited me to a training camp. It was 1943–44. That's when they had all the wartime kids," begins McCormack. It was the Leafs' intention to have John play Junior in Toronto, to be groomed for a role on the parent team. Because there were rules concerning the number of out-of-province players an OHA team was allowed to sign, the Maple Leafs had to arrange for a transfer to get John to play for one of Toronto's Junior teams. "Mr. Hewitt — Foster's father, Billy — was head of the CAHA. He had an office in Maple Leaf Gardens and [the Leafs] could pretty much do whatever the hell they wanted," he chuckles.

"[Leafs management] mentioned it to me in Edmonton that if I made the Toronto Maple Leafs, I could go to St. Mike's. I was ecstatic about it," John says. "My mother and dad thought it was wonderful. They were very devout Catholics. It worked out just fine. I never regretted it. It was a wonderful thing and I just had fun from day one."

The 1943–44 season was John's first with the St. Michael's Majors. "We should've beaten Oshawa. We didn't quite make it, but we came awful damned close. We had a good club."

Nicknamed "Goose," McCormack played an integral role in the Memorial Cup championship of 1945. That season, he finished fourth in scoring, but his two-way play was what impressed observers. "Tod Sloan, [Les] Costello, Bobby Paul, [Leo] Gravelle, Johnny Blute — we won the Memorial Cup. Great party."

After winning the championship with St. Mike's in 1945, John turned pro with the Tulsa Oilers, the Toronto Maple Leafs' affiliate in the United States Hockey League, where he played with former Junior teammates Gus Mortson and Joe Sadler. After a year in Tulsa, he took the 1946–47 season off. "They were always looking for recruits [for the priesthood]," he explains. "I talked to some of the boys — [David] Bauer, [Ted] McLean, and Gerry Gregoire — they were all in the seminary at that time and having a good time. Frankly, I thought I had a calling, and if I did, I was delighted, and if I didn't, well, I tried."

He concluded that a life in the priesthood was not in his future and returned to hockey in 1947–48. "I came back and played with the Senior Marlboros while I went to university." John led the OHA Senior division in scoring with 77 points that season. "I went to the University of Toronto in [St. Mike's College]. I was in residence all the time. I took a general arts course — psychology, English, the whole shmear." That same season, Goose got his first taste of the NHL. On January 31, 1948, he was in the lineup as the Toronto Maple Leafs defeated the Detroit Red Wings, 3–2.

McCormack spent parts of four seasons with the Toronto Maple Leafs, but after a falling out with Conn Smythe he was relegated to the minors, where he remained until he was sold to the Montreal Canadiens in September 1951. He spent three seasons with Montreal, winning a Stanley Cup championship in 1953. The Chicago Black Hawks picked up McCormack on waivers just prior to the start of the 1954 season, which would be his final hurrah in the NHL. In 311 regular-season NHL contests, Goose scored 25 goals and 49 assists for 74 points.

"I was grateful I was exposed to St. Michael's College," he concludes. "All I have are fond memories. It was great."

10
Major Disappointment

As he prepared to lead his team into the 1945–46 season, Joe Primeau had his work cut out for him. Any time a team has reached the pinnacle, there is only one direction in which to go, and there are always plenty of people willing to assist in the inevitable tumble. What made Coach Primeau's task even harder was that he had to reconstruct a team that had graduated so many players to the professional ranks. Fortunately, the championship Buzzers squad offered a deep well of talent from which to dip.

Primeau gladly welcomed back goaltender Pat Boehmer, who debuted with the Majors in 1943–44 as the understudy to Jean Marois and had been outstanding in backstopping the Majors throughout the entire championship season in 1944–45. Backing up Boehmer was Bob DeCourcy, the Buzzers' steady netminder and a more-than-adequate substitute who would later be signed by the New York Rangers and play a single NHL game, replacing injured Charlie Rayner in a loss to Boston on November 12, 1947.

Most of the defence from 1944–45 had graduated. Jimmy Thomson moved up to the Pittsburgh Hornets of the American Hockey League, while Gus Mortson had joined the Tulsa Oilers of the United States Hockey League — both Leaf farm clubs. Defencemen John Arundel and Phil Samis moved over to the Oshawa Generals, joined by forward Bobby Gray. Arundel would play three games with the Maple Leafs in 1949–50, but would return to St. Michael's to play Senior hockey in 1950–51.

Ted McLean was back for a second season as team captain. The quietly effective leader, like his former teammate Dave Bauer, eschewed a professional hockey career to become a priest. "I had only played hockey for fun," he said some time later. "I knew I wanted to become a priest." McLean was joined on the blue line by Bob Paul, who had played with the Memorial Cup champions the previous year. Pat Powers first played with the Majors in 1942–43, and then joined the air force. He was back on defence for St. Mike's in 1945–46.

The Majors lost forwards John McCormack and Joe Sadler, which represented a blow to their offence. In 1943–44, Sadler had led all St. Mike's goal scorers with 38 and finished second on the team in points, while in 1944–45, he finished with 42 points, third best on the powerful Majors. McCormack had contributed 89 points over those two seasons, but more importantly, had proven his mettle over and over in defensive responsibilities. Coach Primeau was pleased to welcome returnees Les Costello and John Blute, but knew that the burden of replacing much of his lost production would fall on the shoulders of second-year Major Tod Sloan, a student from Falconbridge, Ontario. "He is noted for his ability to dig deep into the opponent's territory for possession of the puck and come out of a scramble with a goal or an assist," said an article in a Toronto Maple Leafs program that year. "His large number of penalties wasn't secured for merely saying 'boo' to the referee."

Sloan's linemates were Les Costello and Roy McKay, both from Timmins, making for an all–northern Ontario trio. "When the Irish opponents decide to blanket Sloan with a bit of close checking, McKay and Costello generally run wild with a flock of points."

Primeau was excited about Toronto cousins Ed Sandford and Ed Harrison, who moved up from the Buzzers. Sandford was considered a prime prospect to one day reach the NHL. "He is cool and steady, a deliberate checker and possessed with skating ability to break fast and get the play out of his own end of the rink," claimed the Toronto *Telegram*. The Eds had proven themselves especially effective on a line with Leonard Kelly, known

1945–46					
TEAM	GP	W	L	T	Pts
St. Michael's Majors	28	26	2	0	52
Galt Red Wings	28	22	6	0	44
Oshawa Generals	28	17	11	0	34
St. Catharines Falcons	28	14	14	0	28
Toronto Marlboros	28	11	16	1	23
Toronto Young Rangers	28	8	17	3	19
Barrie Flyers	28	8	18	2	18
Hamilton Lloyds	28	3	25	0	6

The St. Michael's Majors celebrate after winning the OHA championship in 1946. The squad, coached by Joe Primeau (bottom, second from left), included Red Kelly (middle, left), Fleming Mackell (back, second from left), and Les Costello (upper, right) amongst its roster.

by all as "Red." Kelly "has proved capable of handling himself in any type of going, and can carry the puck out of danger. Kelly can score goals when they are badly needed," continued the *Telegram*.

Another new face was a familiar one to anyone following the Majors. Fleming Mackell had impressed the Maple Leafs' brass so much during the series against the Montreal Royals in the spring of 1945 that he was signed to a contract and sent to St. Michael's for 1945–46.

The Majors were joined by seven teams in the OHA Junior 'A' circuit that season. The Marlboros, Young Rangers, Oshawa Generals, Galt Red Wings, and Barrie Flyers were all back, while Hamilton returned with a team called the Lloyds and a new team, the Barrie Flyers, made their debut.

The Majors finished the season in first place. The Buzzers' line of Kelly, Harrison, and Sandford made the transition seamlessly, contributing 24, 30, and 19 points respectively. But it was the Sloan-Costello-McKay line that monopolized the scoring. Les Costello collected 40 points and Roy McKay 41, but it was their centre, Tod Sloan, who led the OHA in scoring. He fired a league-best 43 goals and collected 75 points. At the conclusion of the season, Sloan was the first OHA player to be presented with the new Eddie Powers Memorial Trophy, donated by the Toronto Marlboros to honour a man who had been a fixture around local rinks throughout his life, including coaching the Toronto St. Patricks in 1924–25 and 1925–26. Sloan, whose cousin David Keon would later star at St. Michael's, also received the Red Tilson Memorial Trophy as the outstanding player in the OHA Junior 'A' league.

In the OHA final, the Majors met their arch-rivals from Oshawa, a match that pitted coaches who had once been linemates against each other. Joe Primeau of the Majors had centred Oshawa coach Charlie Conacher on the Toronto Maple Leafs' Kid Line during the 1930s. Maple Leaf Gardens was packed for each of the six games in the bitterly contested series. Oshawa went up two games to one, but the Majors found their second wind and came back with three straight wins to take the series and the John Ross Robertson Trophy. St. Michael's then swept the Montreal Junior Canadiens in three straight in the eastern final to capture the Richardson Trophy.

With the victory, St. Michael's returned to the Memorial Cup for the second consecutive year. The best-of-seven series began at Maple Leaf Gardens. This time, the Winnipeg Monarchs provided the opposition.

Winnipeg won the first game 3–2, but Toronto rallied to win the next two games by scores of 5–3 and 7–3. The Monarchs, coached by Walter Monson, a gold medal winner with Canada's hockey team at the 1932 Olympics, evened the series in Game Four, winning 4–3.

Toronto earned a 7–4 victory in Game Five, with Tod Sloan contributing five of the goals, including one on a penalty shot; the Majors now needed but one more win to become only the second team to repeat as Memorial Cup champions. But Winnipeg spoiled the plans with consecutive 4–2 victories, and the Monarchs clinched the Memorial Cup title for the third time. The game was tied at two apiece in third period, but George Robertson picked up the winner and the insurance marker to give his Monarchs the victory. "It was the seventh game, the score was tied 2–2 and some big winger came down on Ted McLean and Pat Powers on defence, gave them the old deep one, and beat Pat Boehmer with a high, hard one. There were only 30 seconds to go," recalled Les Costello in *Life After Hockey*. "Everybody was dejected. Winnipeg won out."

The hopes of the west were realized, while the ambitions of the Majors were squashed. An unprecedented 102,585 paying customers witnessed the exceptional seven-game series.

The leading scorers for the two teams — Harry Taylor of the Monarchs and Tod Sloan for the Majors — were both property of the Toronto Maple Leafs and would play together on the Stanley Cup championship team of 1949.

Tod Sloan led the OHA in every offensive category during 1945–46 — goals, assists and points. Yet, the Toronto Maple Leafs were so strong during that era that it took several years for the crafty forward to find a permanent spot in the lineup. Sloan played a single game with the Leafs in 1947–48, and split the season between the AHL Hornets and the NHL Leafs in 1948–49. It wasn't until 1950–51 that Tod joined the Leafs full time, and it was perfect timing, as he scored 31 goals and 56 points and contributed significantly to the Maple Leafs' fourth Stanley Cup win in five seasons. Sloan had a career year in 1955–56, scoring 37 goals and 66 points and earning selection to the NHL's Second All-Star Team. He played with Toronto until he was sold to the Chicago Black Hawks in June 1958. In his third and final season with Chicago, he was part of the team's Stanley Cup championship of 1961. Tod's NHL statistics show 482 points (220 goals and 262 assists) in 745 regular-season games.

SNAPSHOT ▶▶ ▶▶ ▶▶ ▶▶ ▶▶ ▶▶ ▶▶   *Les Costello: Flying Father*

Les Costello had excelled as a member of the Holman Pluggers, the outstanding Juvenile hockey team from his hometown of Timmins, Ontario. In fact, so good was the freewheeling Costello that the priests at St. Joachim's parish in nearby South Porcupine contacted their colleagues at St. Michael's, strongly suggesting that someone should take a look at the five-foot, eight-inch bulldog who could score as readily as he could scrap for the puck.

Les was signed to a C-Form by the Toronto Maple Leafs, who brought him to Toronto in 1944 to attend Grade 11 at St. Michael's College. Once on the ice, Costello immediately established himself as one of the toughest boys on the team, yet off the ice, he was disarmingly charming, attracting friends like a magnet.

The migration of hockey players from northern Ontario to Toronto started, in earnest, with Les Costello. "All of a sudden, we saw guys like Cossie [Costello] and my brothers [Gord and Ray] getting to play at St. Mike's and then they were making it onto the Leafs," recalled Pat Hannigan in *Les Costello: Canada's Flying Father*. "This really encouraged us younger guys to play and work hard."

Each year during the Easter holidays, St. Mike's held tryouts for aspiring Junior hockey players, and many boys from the Timmins area travelled down to Toronto, hoping to follow the path blazed by players like Les Costello. Pat Hannigan recalled how tough the tryouts could be. "We decided that, being from Schumacher and wanting to make the team, we were going to kick the shit out of everybody at the tryout. They thought that the guys from the north were the absolute toughest goddamned things they'd ever seen in their lives. And we were, because we didn't want to go back to work in the mines. We needed to get out of the north and the only way to do it was with our skates."

Les Costello joined the Majors in 1944–45 and contributed to the offence at better than a point-a-game clip during the regular season (19 points in 17 games). That spring, in the Memorial Cup final against Moose Jaw, Costello scored in the opening game, an 8–3 win for the Majors. He tallied again in Game Three, chipping in the winning goal. The line of Les Costello, Tod Sloan, and Fleming Mackell "is generally considered one of the all-time greats in Junior hockey," claimed the *Timmins Daily Press*.

"We had a very good team and really, I was lucky," said Costello in Michael A. Smith's *Life After Hockey*. "My big ability was that I could skate. As far as my shot was concerned, it wasn't much. I think I was a little lazy and didn't backcheck much, but I liked to take the puck and go with it."

It is no coincidence that Costello's second season with the Majors, 1945–46, saw St. Mike's again proceed to the Memorial Cup championship, although this time they lost to Winnipeg in an exciting seven-game series.

Les played a third season with the Majors and returned to the Memorial Cup final for the third consecutive spring in 1947. Playing the Moose Jaw Canucks again, the line of Costello, Mackell, and Ed Sandford "passed the disk around like a hot biscuit." In a four-game sweep, the Majors romped to their second Memorial Cup victory in three years. "Les played on one of the best Junior teams that ever existed," states Murray Costello, Les's brother. "His energy and skating abilities allowed him to meld with that team very easily. He was a key guy for them and played very well."

After turning professional with Toronto's American Hockey League affiliate, the Pittsburgh Hornets, in 1947–48, Les was promoted to the Leafs on March 20 for the playoffs. In five games, he scored twice and added two assists. The Toronto Maple Leafs won the Stanley Cup that season, and Costello had his name engraved on hockey's greatest trophy.

He spent most of the following season in Pittsburgh again, although he was called up for 15 games with the Leafs in 1948–49. "He almost forced his way onto the Leafs because he was so bloody good and so tough. They couldn't ignore him," suggested Pat Hannigan. Yet Conn Smythe bristled at the young winger's attitude. "Les treated everybody the same. He didn't defer to anybody," said Father Scully, who got to know Les Costello in the seminary. "He tangled with Conn Smythe and got shipped down to Pittsburgh. Connie didn't like this brash young player from South Porcupine."

Again in 1949–50, Les spent the season with the AHL Hornets, playing a single playoff game with the Leafs that season. "St. Mike's sold its soul to Conn Smythe," suggested Pat Hannigan in Charlie Angus's biography of Costello. "They did whatever Conn Smythe wanted. If a Protestant couldn't make the Marlies, they'd get bumped onto St. Mike's and the school would take them."

Embellishing further a disparity built along religious lines, Hannigan added, "All the Irish Catholics played in Pittsburgh and all the Protestants played in Toronto. There were many Protestant players who made the Leafs who weren't as good as the Catholics playing in Pittsburgh."

Les Costello's career numbers in the NHL belie his talent. He appeared in only 15 regular-season games, all with the Leafs. He connected for two goals, three assists, and five points. Les added two goals and two assists for four points in six playoff games.

St. Michael's College's mini-dynasty spanned three years, 1944 to 1947, and contributed a number of players who played roles in the Toronto Maple Leafs' run of four Stanley Cup titles in five seasons from 1946 to 1951. Fleming Mackell, Gus Mortson, Tod Sloan, and Jimmy Thomson were significant players, while Les Costello, John McCormack, and Rudy Migay played lesser roles. Even more astonishing is the number of players who chose to devote to their lives to the church: David Bauer and Ted McLean entered the seminary straight from St. Michael's College; John McCormack played one season of pro hockey in Tulsa, then chose the priesthood, although he left and returned to hockey; Les Costello and Ray Hannigan both played professional hockey for several years before answering the call and joining the seminary. "It was a fabulous school and the priests had a big influence on us," says John McCormack. Pat Hannigan feels it was more a reflection of the era. "These young guys were quite religious. They didn't know beans about the Bible, but their mothers brought them up to be very respectful of the church."

"I was influenced at the time by Dave Bauer," Costello told author Michael Smith. "He was the guy who wanted you to read [Etienne] Gilson and [Jacques] Maritain and all the great philosophers. He said there were a lot of things to do in life besides play hockey. At the time, I wasn't paying too much attention to him. I was thinking about what I would do in the future, wasn't real sure, so I decided to turn pro. I had finished Grade 13, so I was ready for university, but the pros wanted me, so I went to Pittsburgh."

Les wasn't enjoying the game the way he thought he should. Even though he was realizing the dream of many boys as a pro hockey player in the Toronto Maple Leafs organization, something was missing. "I had been thinking of the priesthood and decided I'd better go back to Toronto and university and give it a chance. Smythe and the guys were very surprised!"

"Les came to St. Mike's from a good solid family," stated Father David Bauer. "He and his brothers have always been concerned with other people. He had a good Catholic upbringing. I think he really came to St. Mike's to play hockey. It's possible that while there, he had his priorities changed a bit. By playing professional hockey, he got a chance to look at the world. We at St. Mike's were surprised when he quit playing hockey and attended the seminary."

Les Costello retired from hockey to join the priesthood in May 1950, still at the peak of his hockey abilities. "The game was a joy for him to play," says his brother Murray. "It was exhilaration to play, but the rest of it — the adulation, the money, even the Stanley Cup — didn't mean anything to him."

Costello earned his degree at the University of Toronto, then attended St. Augustine's Seminary for four years. "Things went so well that before I knew it, the seven years went by and I was called to the priesthood. God has a plan for everybody. They don't seem to know sometimes, but he definitely has a plan for everybody."

On May 31, 1957, Les Costello was ordained as a priest at his home parish in South Porcupine, Ontario. His selfless contributions to his community endured for close to 50 years. But Father Les didn't abandon hockey completely. When a North Bay boy lost sight in one eye during a hockey game, Father Brian McKee arranged a charity hockey contest in which a team of clerics would compete against local media celebrities. Father Les was the first priest to volunteer for the event. The game, played in North Bay in February 1963, raised $3,500. Here were the roots of the Flying Fathers, who used slapstick routines to amuse the crowd — including a confessional to which the referee sentenced "sinning" players.

Soon, requests were flooding in for further appearances, and the Flying Fathers became the Harlem Globetrotters of hockey. "The games were all scripted and choreographed," admitted Frank Quinn, the team manager. "It was all so corny, but it worked." When it came time to resurface the ice between periods, the priests insisted that it be flooded with Holy Water to give the Flying Fathers an edge with the Man Upstairs.

Through some 40 years of travelling across Canada, the Flying Fathers raised over $4 million. But then, at the age of 74, while playing with the Flying Fathers in December 2002, Father Les Costello fell and hit is head on the ice during the pre-game skate in Kincardine, Ontario. Doctors diagnosed broken ribs, but Costello failed to get better. On December 10, 2002, Father Les Costello died.

So many people wanted to say goodbye to him that the funeral had to be held in the McIntyre Arena in Timmins instead of at his beloved St. Alphonsus. In his biography of Father Costello, Charlie Angus describes the spontaneous outpouring of affection for the much-loved priest. "As they moved to take the coffin from centre ice, something unforgettable happened. There was a momentary silence, as if people didn't know what to do. Spontaneously, people began to clap. The clapping echoed throughout the arena as people wept and cheered openly."

The Schumacher street on which St. Alphonsus was located (it has since closed) was renamed Father Les Costello Drive, and a foundation to raise fund for food banks, homeless shelters, and other charities in northern Ontario was also launched in memory of Father Les.

In spite of the loss of their spiritual leader, the Flying Fathers decided to continue to play their brand of exhibition hockey games. "Father Les was the heart and soul of the team," said team manager Frank Quinn. "To lose him was tough. He made it fun, but we have to carry on, and we're still making a lot of good money for those who need it."

11
1947 — A Dynasty Continues

From the moment they pulled on their skates to prepare for the 1946–47 season, coach Joe Primeau's squad was seasoned and ready to compete. The Majors won 33 of 36 games with a dynamic lineup that included captain Ed Sandford, Les Costello, Ray Hannigan, Ed Harrison, Red Kelly, Fleming Mackell, John McLellan, Rudy Migay, and Benny Woit. During one prolific stretch, the Majors went 19 games without a loss, including eight victories in which they scored in double figures.

"Somebody at home [in Fort William, Ontario, now part of Thunder Bay] had something to do with St. Mike's," explains Woit. "They gave us a call and we went right over there, Rudy Migay and myself. They told us to go down there [to Toronto] and we went down. It was beautiful!"

While most of the boys had signed C-Forms with the Toronto Maple Leafs, Benny's rights already belonged to the Detroit Red Wings. "I signed with them when I was 15 or 16," he says. "Jack Adams was from Thunder Bay and he was the manager for Detroit."

Howie Harvey, the brother of Hall of Fame defenceman Doug, was brilliant in goal for St. Mike's, surrendering just 59 goals all season. He was equally brilliant in the classroom, where he maintained an 86% average in spite of a heavy hockey workload.

During the eastern Canadian championship series of 1945, Frank Selke, working on behalf of the Toronto Maple Leafs, had been so impressed with Howie's work with the Montreal Royals that he placed him on the Leafs' negotiation list. Another member of the team, Fleming Mackell, was also placed on Toronto's list just moments after midnight on his 16th birthday, beating the Montreal Canadiens, who intended to do the same thing, by a matter of hours.

Harvey was touted as the netminder who would one day replace Turk Broda in goal for the Toronto Maple Leafs, but severe allergies eventually forced him to leave the game he loved. Following games, Harvey's hands and face would swell considerably. During his year with the Majors, followed by two seasons with the Marlboros, Toronto's team doctors suspected that Howie was allergic to material used in his hockey equipment, but they were never able to diagnose what it was that caused such a reaction. "The gloves and the pads bothered him and he used to get pretty sick on the ice," remembers Woit. The persistent skin rash forced Howie to retire from hockey in September 1949, at just 21 years of age. "He would certainly have gone to the NHL," Benny adds. "He was as good as any of them up there."

❖

The Majors cruised to a first-place finish during the regular season. Although their offensive output (234 goals in 36 games) was impressive enough, the truly astounding statistic was found in the goals-against column. St. Mike's allowed 40 fewer goals than the second-place Generals, while ninth-place Hamilton allowed an unbelievable 313 and still didn't finish in the cellar (that dubious distinction went to the Toronto Young Rangers).

The season saw the return of the Stratford Kroehlers after a two-season hiatus, while the Windsor Spitfires made their debut.

Fleming Mackell led the league with 49 goals and 82 points. In the latter category, teammates Ed Sandford and Les Costello finished second and third, with 67 and 62 points respectively. As the top scorer in the league, Mackell was presented with the Eddie

The mid-1940s were spectacular for the powerful St. Michael's Majors. At a practice during the 1946–47 season, several stars pose with their coach. From left to right: Joe Primeau, Ed Sandford, Bob Paul, Red Kelly, Joe Williams, Les Costello, Johnny McLellan, and Fleming Mackell.

1946–47					
TEAM	GP	W	L	T	Pts
St. Michael's Majors	36	33	3	0	66
Oshawa Generals	36	28	8	0	56
Galt Red Wings	36	27	9	0	54
Stratford Kroehlers	36	22	14	0	44
Toronto Marlboros	36	20	16	0	40
Barrie Flyers	35	17	16	2	36
Windsor Spitfires	36	10	24	2	22
St. Catharines Falcons	36	7	25	4	18
Hamilton Szabos	38	6	32	0	12
Toronto Young Rangers	36	6	30	0	12

Powers Memorial Trophy, while Sandford received the Red Tilson Memorial Trophy as the outstanding player in the OHA. Les Costello combined a finishing touch with aggressive play, earning 78 penalty minutes, third in the Ontario Hockey League. Future St. Mike's and Maple Leaf teammate Phil Samis of Oshawa was second in penalties that season.

Naysayers questioned the team's ability to chase after the Memorial Cup, but Coach Primeau never wavered in his belief. "Joe claims that the Irish have a better-balanced club than the one that lost out to Winnipeg Monarchs in the Memorial Cup Finals last year," suggested the Maple Leaf Gardens program.

The Majors met the Oshawa Generals in the best-of-seven semifinal playoff series. With an 8–5 comeback victory in Game One, St. Mike's showed that they meant business against Charlie Conacher's squad. The third period was but a minute old when the line of Mackell, Costello, and Sandford combined on a beautiful passing play that resulted in a goal by Mackell. That started a six-goal spree for St. Mike's, including a hat trick by Mackell. Lou Crowdis, the Generals' goalie, "almost single-handedly held off the determined enemy attack," according to *The Globe and Mail*. He made one save with his face, which halted the game until repairs were made.

The second game ended in a lopsided 10–2 win for the Majors. "The Generals were checked dizzy and turned in their most wretched puck-passing display of the season," reported *The Globe*. Crowdis again was injured during action, this time from an errant stick from Fleming Mackell.

Hannigan, Costello, and Harrison each scored twice for the victors in a contest that was marred by a brawl in the third period. A frustrated Mackell took his anger out on Calum Mackay, who gladly reciprocated. As the two tangled, everyone, including those on the bench, joined the fray, with the exception of St. Mike's netminder Howie Harvey. A British bulldog was gingerly dropped over the boards and it raced enthusiastically from player to player, wagging its tail. "The resulting laughs were more help in quelling the fight than [referee] Farrell's best efforts," was *The Globe*'s verdict.

The rough stuff carried into Game Three. Leaf chattel Eric Pogue threatened and wrestled with Ed Harrison, and even after being whistled to the penalty box, the combatants continued their fight. The only fight that didn't really result was Oshawa's on-ice effort, which paled in a 9–4 loss. Ed Sandford scored three goals and added as many assists, while Fleming Mackell tallied twice for St. Mike's.

Although the Majors counted on finishing off the Generals in Game Four, Oshawa was having no part of their opponent's plan. If not for a late goal by Fleming Mackell, the Generals would have taken the game within regulation time, but as the buzzer went to end the third period, the teams were deadlocked at two goals apiece. Both teams enjoyed great chances in the first overtime, but Harvey for St. Mike's and Oshawa's Bill Reddoch — replacing the injured Crowdis — were sensational in goal. Then, in the second overtime, Ray Ceresino fired a weak shot towards the Majors goal that Leo Curik deflected past Howie Harvey to win the game and prolong the series for at least one more contest.

Coach Primeau cited a two-minute stint of adversity in the second period — during which Harry Psutka and Benny Woit were both in the penalty box — as the key to St. Mike's victory in Game Five. He sent Red Kelly, Fleming Mackell, and Ed Sandford over the boards to kill the penalties, which they did magnificently. Back at full strength, the Majors rebounded with three goals that period to pull away from Oshawa. Then, in the third, St. Michael's buried the Generals. "It was a rout from then on. The Irish poured in practically at their leisure," wrote the *Toronto Daily Star*. "Charlie Conacher's boys were outplayed, hurried on their passing and shooting." Final score: St. Mike's 10, Oshawa 3. The Generals packed their belongings for another season while the Majors moved on to the OHA final.

❖

The OHA final pitted St. Michael's against the Galt Red Wings in a best-of-seven series. In Game One, "they defeathered the Red Wings into abject surrender, 8–1," according to *The Globe and Mail*. Les Costello, Ray Hannigan, and Ed Harrison each scored two goals, with singles going to Red Kelly and Ed Sandford.

"A tall bundle of hockey dynamite blew Galt Red Wings' championship hopes further asunder," said *The Globe* of Game Two, in which Ed Sandford's hat trick led the way to a 4–2 victory. Pat Hannigan scored the Majors' fourth goal against Terry Sawchuk. It was a rough game in Galt. Fifteen seconds after the puck dropped, Fleming Mackell and Bill Scott were sent off for high-sticking. As soon as Scott returned, he mixed it up with Benny Woit and both players were penalized. Harry Psutka of St. Mike's duked it out with Dean McBride of the Red Wings and both earned major penalties. Red Kelly and Bob Robertson were escorted to the penalty box shortly afterwards with a matched set of roughing minors. Later in the game, Fred Glover paired off with Bob Paul in a fight. "The hard-working right winger took on just about every member of the St. Mike's squad," reported *The Globe*. "At that, he was one of the best performers for Galt."

"Galt was hopelessly disorganized," observed *The Globe*, "and their smart little goalie, Terry Sawchuk, was besieged with pucks, but magically, he kept a good percentage from moving in behind his armour." Nonetheless, St. Mike's danced to a 9–3 victory in Game Three. Les Costello netted three goals and Ed Harrison two for the victors.

The St. Michael's Majors earned their third consecutive OHA championship by winning 6–2 in Game Four. "Howard Harvey, as usual, was great in the St. Mike's nets," reported *The Globe and Mail*. "Kelly was outstanding on defence. The Irish forwards worked hard, but the big line of Sandford, Mackell and Costello was a standout." Sandford picked up a goal, Mackell added two, and Costello was held to an assist in this deciding contest.

Next on the Majors' agenda were the champions of the Northern Ontario Hockey Association, the Porcupine Combines. Game One was a debacle, resulting in a final score of 16–2 for the Majors. Three Timmins boys, who would likely have been playing with the Combines were they not attending school at St. Michael's, figured heavily in the scoring: Les Costello (two goals and three assists), Ray Hannigan (a goal and an assist), and Johnny McLellan (an assist). "The Porkies were no match for the high-flying Irish and the game evolved into a dreary spectacle," reported *The Globe and Mail*. "A good number of customers left long before the game was over."

Astonishingly, the Combines held St. Mike's to a 1–0 win in Game Two. "Porcupine were as brilliant a team last night as they were dismal Saturday when they fell 16–2 before the co-ordinated power of the Irish youngsters," admitted *The Globe*. The Majors disposed of the Porcupine Combines by a 7–3 margin in Game Three. Jack Donlevy, who had played goal for the St. Michael's Buzzers during the 1945–46 season, made many fine saves during the three-game series and was as strong as a goalie can be without defensive protection. In October 1947, he attended the Toronto Maple Leafs training camp, joined there by his opponent at the other end of the ice, Howie Harvey.

❖

After bombing South Porcupine in the All-Ontario final, St. Mike's faced the Montreal Junior Canadiens in the eastern Canadian final, outscoring them 37–4 over three games, including a scandalous 21–0 win in the final game. The Junior Canadiens dressed just 10 players, but the Majors were on a mission. "St. Mike's backchecked as assiduously when they were ahead 20–0 as they did when they were on top 10–0," reported *The Globe and Mail*. Montreal's goalie, Roy Scurrah, "kept throwing himself heroically in front of a relentless storm of rubber." Fleming Mackell picked up six goals and two assists, Ed Harrison scored four times and assisted on two others, and both Les Costello and Bob Paul had three-goal games and an equal number of assists. Howie Harvey earned an easy shutout. For the third straight year, the Majors were going to the Memorial Cup final.

After the game, a number of awards were presented to the St. Michael's team. On behalf of his team, Red Kelly accepted the John Ross Robertson Trophy, emblematic of the OHA Junior 'A' championship. Howie Harvey then skated forward to accept the James Richardson Trophy, awarded to St. Mike's as eastern Canadian champions. The Eddie Powers Trophy was presented to Fleming Mackell, the OHA's scoring champion, while captain Ed Sandford was handed the Red Tilson Memorial Trophy as the league's most valuable player.

❖

The win over Montreal set up a Memorial Cup championship between the St. Michael's Majors and the Moose Jaw Canucks for the second time in three years. The series was held in three western Canadian cities: Winnipeg, Moose Jaw, and Regina.

Game One was played in Winnipeg, and saw the Majors wallop the Canucks 12–3. "A disappointing Moose Jaw outfit held on for one brief period before the magic sticks of the eastern powerhouse went to work with a vengeance," reported Regina's *Leader-Post*. The line of Sandford, Costello, and Mackell "passed the disk around like a hot biscuit." The line collaborated on 13 points. Costello had a hat trick, Mackell picked up two goals and three assists, and Sandford contributed five assists. Meanwhile, Ed Harrison added two goals and two assists in the rout. "They're a wonderful hockey club," acknowledged Moose Jaw's coach, Kenny Doraty. "Our number was up early and I knew it."

Game Two was staged in Moose Jaw, with Toronto dumping the hometown Canucks 6–1. The Majors took a 3–0 lead by the end of the third period, with two of three from the stick of Ed Sandford. The captain picked up his third goal, one of two scored by St. Mike's in the second period. After Les Costello scored with two Canucks in the penalty box,

The 1946–47 season saw the Majors collect the John Ross Robertson Trophy, the James Richardson Trophy, and the Memorial Cup. Howie Harvey was named top netminder, Fleming Mackell led the league in scoring, and Ed Sandford was recipient of the OHA's MVP trophy.

the crowd began to chant, "We want referees," and they continued for more than four minutes. The third period saw Moose Jaw score early, but it was negated by the Majors' sixth goal, Ed Harrison's second, to complete the St. Mike's victory.

"My four-year-old son Donald could lead St. Mike's to the Memorial Cup," snickered the *Winnipeg Tribune*. "That's how competent the youthful Easterners are." The sports editor of the *Regina Leader-Post* quipped, "Only thing wrong with the Toronto Juniors is they're playing for the wrong cup. These St. Mike's would make a fair stab at winning Lord Stanley's mug!"

A crowd of 5,959 waded into the Queen City Gardens in Regina to witness Game Three. Bob Wilson of Moose Jaw scored the lone goal of the first period. St. Mike's replied with four unanswered goals in the second — Hannigan, Paul, Harrison, and Costello were the marksmen. After Wilson was called for a penalty with 1:27 remaining in the second period, fans began to toss bottles and assorted debris onto the ice. Referees Vic Lundquist of Winnipeg and Ken Mullins of Montreal ended the period and tacked the remaining time onto the third.

The Majors continued to score. Harrison completed his hat trick with two goals in the third, while Migay and Hannigan tallied the others. Then, with seven minutes left in the third period and St. Mike's ahead 8–1, Metro Prystai — who, according to *The Globe and Mail*, "is to Moose Jaw what Babe Ruth was to the Yankees" — took a slashing penalty. The fans rained bottles down on the Majors, halting the game. "The hoodlums took over

Tens of thousands of Double Blue supporters lined Toronto's Bay Street as a procession led the Majors from Union Station to City Hall. Howie Harvey and Red Kelly rode in this car.

after another Moose Jaw penalty, bringing several bottles over the boards. One Canuck and two players from the Toronto club were struck glancing blows by the missiles. The ice was cleared, but again, bottles and other odds and ends were heaved to the ice while the referees tried vainly to face off in the southeast corner of the rink," wrote the *Leader-Post*. Majors skaters Rudy Migay and Bob Paul, as well as Angus Juckes from Moose Jaw, were hit by bottles. The national anthem was played in hopes of silencing the crowd, but to no avail. Al Pickard, vice-president of the Canadian Amateur Hockey Association, then took to the public address system and announced that, should any further displays occur, the game would be called and the victory awarded to St. Michael's. No sooner had he finished his admonishment than an empty liquor bottle smashed onto the ice surface. The outburst continued and the game was summarily called with six minutes remaining in the third period. St. Mike's was awarded the win. Both teams left and made their way to their respective dressing rooms. Ken Doraty, coach of the Canucks, was nearly in tears. "Hundreds of fans, ashamed and disgusted at the stupidity of the irresponsible few, streamed away from the national final long before it was halted."

Father Mallon, manager of the Majors, immediately sent a telegram to Hanson Dowell, the president of the CAHA, which read: "Two St. Michael's players were hit by bottles thrown on ice in demonstration of uncontrolled hoodlumism unparalleled in our experience. The game was called and awarded to St. Michael's with six minutes of play remaining. Are other reasons for demanding change of venue necessary? The Memorial Cup is not worth playing for at such risk to our players."

On Monday morning, readers of the *Regina Leader-Post* were greeted with the headline: "We Hang Our Heads in Shame." The accompanying article stated, "In Brooklyn, they'd call it a rhubarb, but Regina simply branded it the most disgraceful and humiliating episode in the city's sports history. Saturday's Memorial Cup shambles gave Regina a pair of the blackest eyes you ever saw."

It appeared that a handful of "scatterbrained hoodlums" from Moose Jaw had caused the turmoil that was such an embarrassment to most in attendance. The Canadian Amateur Hockey Association issued an apology to both teams: "A repetition of bottle throwing or other illegal interference will result in the calling of the game Tuesday and awarding it to our Eastern champions. It is our responsibility as Westerners to provide satisfactory playing conditions for the Eastern representatives."

Game Four moved to Regina, where 2,186 watched as St. Mike's skated away with a 3–2 win, and the Memorial Cup. Fleming Mackell started the Majors' thoughts of championships by scoring on Bev Bentley just 38 seconds into the first period. Bob Paul put St. Mike's up by two with a goal early in the second, firing a rocket past the Moose Jaw goaltender. The Canucks scored midway through the period when Harvey Stein golfed a puck past netminder Howie Harvey. The St. Mike's goalie argued that the puck didn't cross the goal line, but the referee shook off the protest and indicated a goal.

Moose Jaw scored the tying goal at 4:40 of the third with St. Mike's two men short. St. Michael's apparent lethargy was immediately concluded, and the Majors poured on the pressure. The winning goal was a peculiar play that came from the stick of Ed Sandford at 10:37. The captain backhanded the puck towards the Moose Jaw goal. Les Costello, standing on the lip of the crease, faked a deflection that Bentley followed, but the puck never changed its course and the puck went past the netminder into the far corner of the Canucks' goal.

Canadian Amateur Hockey Association vice-president Al Pickard of Regina picked up the Memorial Cup and handed it to captain Ed Sandford, saying, "St. Michael's Majors are the greatest Junior team the east has ever had." It was the second time in three seasons that St. Michael's had skated away with Junior hockey's greatest prize. Afterwards, Les Costello fulfilled a promise he had made to his teammates prior to the series. "When we win the Memorial Cup, I'll stand on my head at centre ice," he chuckled. "Go on," said the team, almost in unison. Sure enough, after the presentation, Costello skated to centre ice, got down on all fours, and, laughing hysterically, briefly stood on his head while the Regina fans, curious at first as to what the fiery forward was doing, realized the stunt and applauded wildly.

"[The Majors] do everything like professionals," said the *Leader-Post*. "If they're not the Junior team to end all Junior teams, they'll do until a better one comes along."

Following the St. Michael's victory, coach Joe Primeau told *The Globe*, "I think the boys deserve a lot of credit for winning in four games. I figured we'd win, but that it might take six games."

The Moose Jaw Canucks clearly appreciated their opponents, too. The players streamed into the victors' dressing room following the game and suggested that they exchange sweaters. The Majors were quick to accept the proposed gesture of sportsmanship.

The Majors traversed the Canadian prairies by train, celebrating as they crossed each provincial boundary. Father Mallon, the team's manager, read aloud a telegram received by Coach Primeau from Toronto mayor Robert H. Saunders. "On behalf of the city council and citizens of Toronto, I extend hearty congratulations on the brilliant triumphs of the St. Michael's Junior hockey team in winning the Junior hockey championship of Canada."

While some players gazed out at the flat landscape outside the windows of the train, several students pulled out their books and studied for exams that would greet them on their return.

When the Majors returned triumphantly to Toronto, they were greeted with a parade and a gala reception organized by civic officials. As the players drove up Bay Street to City Hall Square, they were greeted by thousands of exuberant fans standing shoulder-to-shoulder in celebration.

"It was a great hockey club," reminisces Benny Woit. "They were all terrific guys. We went through the whole works; beat everybody." Woit and Rudy Migay left the Junior champion Majors after that season. "Rudy and I went back to Port Arthur. Our manager was pretty influential in getting us back there because that was where we were from. St. Mike's gave us a rough time about it." It turned out to be a fortuitous return for the two Lakehead boys. They had won the Memorial Cup with St. Michael's in 1947 and went on to win a second Junior championship in 1948, this time wearing the sweaters of the Port Arthur West End Bruins.

Woit joined the Detroit Red Wings for two games during the 1950–51 season and was a full-fledged member of the team by 1951–52, when the Wings captured the Stanley Cup. In fact, during Woit's four full-time seasons in Detroit, the Red Wings won the Stanley Cup championship three times — 1952, 1954, and 1955. A trade took Benny to the Chicago Black Hawks in May 1955, and he spent two seasons there. In 334 regular-season games, the versatile forward/defenceman collected 33 points.

Rudy Migay turned pro with the Maple Leafs organization and played his first games with the NHL squad in 1949–50. He spent most of the decade with the Leafs, and in 10 seasons played 418 games, scoring 59 goals and 92 assists.

Ray Hannigan was the first of three brothers to play with both the St. Michael's Majors and Toronto Maple Leafs. Arriving from Timmins in 1945, the hockey phenom scored 23 goals and 35 points for the Junior 'B' Buzzers in just eight games during 1945–46, his first season in Toronto. He was promoted to the Majors in 1946–47 and tallied 21 points in 22 games, but the Maple Leafs moved Ray to the Marlboros for his final year of Junior. By 1948–49, he was playing with the Senior Marlies, where he continued to score goals at a rapid pace. The Maple Leafs called Ray up to play in the NHL, and he made his big-league debut on February 26, 1949. He would play just three NHL games, all with Toronto and all that spring.

St. Mike's knew there was something special about Fleming Mackell when they snatched him from under the noses of the Montreal Canadiens in 1945. During his two years with the Majors, Mackell was simply terrific. Just five feet, seven inches, he was skilled, he was fast, and he was tough. The leading point-getter in the league that year had also scored a remarkable 49 goals, best in the OHA. Fleming joined the Maple Leafs for three games in 1947–48 and spent parts of four more seasons in Toronto, where he helped the team win Stanley Cup championships in 1949 and 1951. Traded to the Boston Bruins in January 1952, Mackell played there until the end of the 1959–60 season. His 665 NHL games produced 149 goals and 220 assists for 369 points. He added 63 points in 80 post-season games. Although he had every reason to be proud of his two Stanley Cup championships, he wasn't the only one in the family to hold those bragging rights. His dad, Jack Mackell, was part of Stanley Cup wins with the Ottawa Senators in 1920 and 1921.

Ed Sandford: Education Advocate

"Junior hockey was extremely popular in Ontario, and the Ontario Hockey Association's Junior 'A' league was the top of the line," recalled Ed Sandford. "If you could reach that level, you knew you had a chance to turn pro. I kept improving and finally made it to St. Michael's College. St. Mike's was renowned for its terrific hockey teams, so I considered myself in very good company."

Ed Sandford had an extraordinary hockey-playing record during his six years at St. Michael's College — he never missed being on a championship team! In 1941–42, his first year at the school, Sandford was with the Toronto Hockey League champion Minor Bantams. In 1942–43, Ed's Bantam team took the King Clancy championship. Sandford was captain of the St. Michael's Midget team that won the THL championship in 1943–44. The next year, he captained the Buzzers, winners of the OHA Junior 'B' championship. After graduating to Junior 'A,' Ed was part of the Majors team that went to the Memorial Cup final in 1945–46 and won the Cup in 1947.

"We had a wonderful team," he recalled. "By that time, I knew that pro scouts were looking at us, but I still had no thoughts of an NHL career. My first thought was about getting a good education, not that I had anything against hockey."

During the 1946–47 season, Ed scored 30 goals and 67 points in 27 games and was named the league's most valuable player. He was the leading scorer in the playoffs that spring, counting 12 goals and 24 points in nine games. "Right out of the blue, I got an offer to play for the Bruins," he told Stanley and Shirley Fischler in *Heroes and History*. "At first, I wasn't sure that I wanted to go to Boston. The idea of giving up school weighed on me. I finally decided to give the Bruins a shot, and am I ever grateful that I made that decision. It was one of the best moves of my life."

Ed spent eight seasons in Boston, playing in the NHL All-Star Game every season from 1951 to 1955. He finished eighth in scoring during the 1953–54 season, collecting 47 points, and was selected to the NHL's Second All-Star Team. Then, in June 1955, Ed was sent to the Detroit Red Wings, but after just four games, he was shipped off to Chicago for Metro Prystai. Ed retired at the end of that season, having posted 106 goals and 145 assists for 251 points during 502 regular-season NHL contests.

"If I did it over again, I would have graduated from a college or university and then turned pro," he admitted in *Heroes: Stars of Hockey's Golden Era*. "Looking back, 19 was awfully young to turn pro. You're not big enough, you're not strong enough, you haven't matured, you haven't got the poise. I saw a lot of kids go down to training camp at 16 or 17, leave school, didn't make the team and didn't go back to school. I think hockey really damaged them permanently. But that's the way the game was. The boys had to realize that and protect themselves, which they didn't do because they were so fascinated by the fact they were being scouted by a pro team." Sandford decided to change the path so many others had taken before him. "To me, hockey was just an interim [occupation]. I told everybody else to do the same, look for another career because this wouldn't last long, but not many guys did. They were never going to get old. They were going to play hockey for the rest of their lives."

12
From Feast to Famine

Wholesale changes were in store for the Majors after the 1947 Memorial Cup championship. The only returning player was backup netminder Joe Williams, who hadn't play a single game in relief of Howie Harvey during the previous season. And, as it turned out, Williams didn't make the team in 1947–48. Harvey, now overaged for Junior play, moved over to the Toronto Marlboros Senior team, where he was joined by Ray Hannigan, John McLellan, Bob Paul, and Harry Psutka.

Ed Harrison and Ed Sandford both stepped into the lineup of the NHL's Boston Bruins. Red Kelly, having worked his way through the St. Michael's Midgets, Buzzers, and Majors, graduated to the Detroit Red Wings' roster. Les Costello and Fleming Mackell, both property of the Maple Leafs, were assigned to the Pittsburgh Hornets, Toronto's American Hockey League squad. Rudy Migay and Benny Woit transferred to the Port Arthur West End Bruins of the Thunder Bay Junior league. Both Fort William–born, Migay and Woit proceeded to win their second consecutive Memorial Cup championship as members of the Bruins.

Coach Joe Primeau and his colleagues scoured the country to assemble a team, though he didn't have to look far for one of his forwards. Joe Primeau Jr., a fast-skating forward, was promoted from the Junior 'B' Buzzers and wore his father's famous number 10. Joe DeCourcy, who had enjoyed a sniff playing with the Majors while part of the Buzzers' team in 1946–47, was promoted to the 'A' club. His brother Bob had been the goaltender on the OHA championship Buzzers team of 1944–45 and had moved into the New York Rangers' farm system. Also up from the Buzzers was Brian McAllister, who "excelled in playmaking and deadly shooting," according to the school yearbook.

Ray Barry joined St. Mike's from Edmonton for his final season of Junior eligibility. While toiling with the Majors, he attended university. In 1948–49, he played for the Sherbrooke Saints, a Senior team in Quebec. The Boston Bruins signed Ray as a free agent in October 1950, and during the 1951–52 season he added three points in 18 games to the Bruins' statistics.

Bill Dunn, a former Buzzer, returned to St. Mike's after a year of Junior with the Oshawa Generals. Gord Hannigan, the younger brother of Majors star Ray, was recruited from his Schumacher home after starring with Ontario's Juvenile champions, the South Porcupine Red Wings. Hard-hitting Tim Horton, described as "the 17-year-old bruiser from Sudbury," was quickly added to the Majors roster on the advice of alumnus Charlie Cerre. "One of the best rearguards in Junior 'A,' Tim combined both hard-hitting defence work and brilliant rushing ability to become one of the best pro prospects in Junior hockey," stated *The Thurible*. Although he hadn't played hockey in two seasons, Bill McNamara was added to the lineup, the third of three McNamara brothers to play for St. Mike's. Goaltender Tom Shea and captain Jerry Fitzhenry, as well as Wally Clune, Don Oberholtzer, and Murray Valliquette, also joined the Majors for the 1947–48 season, although Oberholtzer, and Valliquette collided during a pre-season practice which resulted in the latter player suffering a fractured skull and broken nose that sidelined him for the season. In the same collision, Oberholtzer sustained a broken collarbone that kept him out of action for the early part of the campaign.

It was a long, arduous season for all involved. The St. Michael's Majors had devolved from being the elite of Junior hockey to the laughing stock of the league, finishing ninth in a 10-team circuit. It was the first time in seven years that the Majors missed the playoffs.

There were precious few bright spots in the 1947–48 lineup for coach Joe Primeau, although defenceman Tim Horton (wearing #3 in the back row) certainly stood out.

After just one season, the Hamilton Szabos exited the league. Windsor's Spitfires topped the circuit, although the Oshawa Generals gave them a run for their money all the way to the finish line. Only a horrendous season by the Young Rangers prevented St. Michael's from finishing the season in the cellar. The Majors won just six games, losing 26 over the 32-game campaign. The Young Rangers, winning but one game, had come to the end of their hockey life and folded after the season.

The Young Rangers were an interesting team. Owned by Ed Wildey, the affable Toronto sportsman, the team joined the Majors and Marlboros in using Maple Leaf Gardens as a home arena. But without an NHL sponsor, the team found it difficult to compete against the affiliates of the Original Six NHL squads. With no scouting staff to speak of, the Young Rangers had to find players left undiscovered or unchosen by the other teams, and when they did occasionally find a gem — as they did with Gordie Drillon, who went on to lead the NHL in scoring in 1937–38 — other teams would quickly arrange a transfer in exchange for an honorarium given to Wildey to assist in running his team.

Ray Barry, who was selected as the Majors' most valuable player, led the team in scoring with 37 points, while Gord Hannigan was the team's goal-scoring leader with 14. Tom Shea was strong in goal in spite of a young, often porous defence. *The Thurible* said, "He was one of the exceptional goalies in Junior 'A' hockey, and the team's low standing was no fault of his." The only league leader for St. Mike's in any category was Tim Horton, who led the OHA in penalty minutes with 137.

The 1947–48 season may very well have shaped Horton's NHL career. While playing back at home for the Copper Cliff Redmen, Tim had been a defensive defenceman with a penchant for bodychecking. But with the Majors struggling to score goals, the rookie blueliner regularly carried the puck into the offensive zone on behalf of his teammates, while continuing to "dish out heavy bodywork" in his own end of the rink. Commenting on a rare win for the Majors, *The Globe and Mail* reported: "The Irish victory was highlighted by burly Tim Horton, who took time out from his blueline bashing to fire one goal and assist on another. He climaxed a rink-long dash by rapping the puck home as he fell to the ice with the Guelph defence pair draped over his shoulders." The role of a solid defenceman with offensive prowess later identified Horton's Hall of Fame career.

1947–48					
TEAM	GP	W	L	T	Pts
Windsor Spitfires	36	29	6	1	59
Oshawa Generals	36	27	8	1	55
Barrie Flyers	36	23	13	0	46
Stratford Kroehlers	36	21	13	2	44
Galt Rockets	36	18	13	5	41
St. Catharines TeePees	36	19	13	0	38
Toronto Marlboros	32	12	17	0	30
Guelph Biltmore Mad Hatters	36	12	20	1	25
St. Michael's Majors	32	6	23	0	16
Toronto Young Rangers	31	1	30	0	2

After a dismal season in 1947–48, the Majors' core players — Wally Clune, Joe DeCourcy, Bill McNamara, Tom Shea, Tim Horton, and Gord Hannigan — returned a year later more seasoned and anxious to get back on the ice to face another campaign.

St. Michael's balked at the length of the schedule in 1948–49, and was afforded an unusual compromise. While the other eight teams played a 48-game schedule, the Majors played just 32 so that their students could attend to studies. During the last 16 games of the regular season, either the Majors or their opponents would count four points for a win.

Horton had been required to repeat Grade 12, although there was conjecture that he might have deliberately failed French in order to return to St. Mike's for another hockey season. The 18-year-old carried just three subjects that school year, each of which he had failed the previous year. Gord Hannigan returned to skate with the Majors, too, although it is believed he took but one course that year.

During 1947–48, Don Rope had played for the Winnipeg Monarchs, a strong Junior squad that Leafs owner Conn Smythe had recruited for sponsorship in 1946. Smythe was determined to have the quick-skating centre join the Toronto Marlboros, but Rope resisted. Education was important to Don and, although Protestant, he had been attending a Catholic high school in Winnipeg. Smythe shifted gears and acquiesced to the educational demand by dangling the prospect of attending St. Michael's College in front of the young man. Rope decided to move to Toronto and join the Majors. He was assigned to room with Tim Horton, another Protestant. "His build and strength stood out," reminisced Rope in *Open Ice: The Tim Horton Story*. "Tim was very modest, very laid back with the occasional burst of laughter. He loved the camaraderie of the team. He was our big star."

Two of Horton's friends from the Copper Cliff Redmen, Connie Bonhomme and Red McCarthy, joined St. Mike's that season, while Bob Sabourin, another prospect recommended by Charlie Cerre, joined the school and team from Sudbury. Willie Marshall made his Junior debut that season with the Majors, too.

Although moderately better than the previous season with 13 wins, 34 losses, and four ties, the St. Michael College Majors missed the playoffs once again.

Gord Hannigan led the Majors in scoring, firing 21 goals and collecting 34 points. Willie Marshall added 31 points and Don Rope had 29. Tim Horton again led the team in penalty minutes, sitting out 95 minutes. But Horton was undeniably the star. "When he touched the puck, everybody stood up," stated McCarthy in *Open Ice*. "He wasn't a dispsy-doodler, because half the time, he went through you, over the top of you. He was very, very exciting."

When the season ended for St. Mike's, Joe Primeau planned to have Horton and Hannigan join the Senior Marlboros for their playoffs, but this request was refused by the OHA. Instead, both boys were summoned by the Maple Leafs, who had hit a spate of injuries. "The kids tried hard, skated well but they lacked the condition and skating ability to keep up with their big brothers," determined *The Globe and Mail*. Instead, the Leafs selected former Majors Ray Hannigan and Johnny McLellan from the Senior Marlboros, while Horton, Gord Hannigan, and Don Rope practised as a forward line with the Senior Marlies. "When we practised with those guys, we put a little extra into it," admitted Rope. "They always dreaded it, especially with Tim on wing." The Marlboros were defeated by the Ottawa Senators in the eastern Canada final, while the Toronto Maple Leafs beat the Detroit Red Wings for the Stanley Cup championship.

Gord Hannigan, the speedy centre of the Majors in 1947–48 and 1948–49, was two years younger than his brother Ray, whose time at St. Mike's immediately preceded Gord's. Ray played three games with the Maple Leafs in 1948–49 and Gord followed, playing four seasons with Toronto starting with the 1952–53 season. Gord scored 60 points in 161

1948–1949					
TEAM	GP	W	L	T	Pts
Windsor Spitfires	48	34	13	1	69
Barrie Flyers	48	28	16	4	60
Oshawa Generals	48	27	18	3	57
St. Catharines TeePees	48	25	20	3	53
Stratford Kroehlers	48	25	21	2	52
Toronto Marlboros	48	20	24	4	44
Guelph Biltmore Mad Hatters	48	20	26	2	42
St. Michael's Majors	32	13	31	4	30
Galt Rockets	48	11	34	3	25

The Majors faced the Toronto Marlboros, led by George Armstrong (dark sweater, centre), in this contest from 1948-49. Goaltender Lorne Howes blocks the attempt with the Dukes' Danny Lewicki on his doorstep, hoping for a rebound.

NHL games, and after moving to Edmonton, where his older brother had lived for several years, opened a fast-food restaurant with Ray. Gord's friend, Tim Horton, got the idea of being involved in the food service industry from the brothers. A third brother, Pat, would later play with both the St. Michael's Majors and the Toronto Maple Leafs.

Defenceman Wally Clune played two seasons with the Majors, then joined the Guelph Biltmores in 1949–50. He was signed by the Montreal Canadiens in June 1953 and played five games, his only NHL experience.

Two sets of brothers starred for St. Mike's in 1948–49. Twins Mike and Neil Buchanan were joined by Norm and Ray Corcoran. Mike Buchanan played but one season with the Majors, and in 1951–52, played a game on defence with the Chicago Black Hawks. After spending that season with St. Michael's Majors, Norm Corcoran moved to the Boston Bruins' organization. He played a game with the Bruins in 1949–50, another in 1952–53, and two more during the 1954–55 season. Corcoran was part of a nine-player trade that sent Hall of Famer Terry Sawchuk from Detroit to Boston in June 1955. After but two games with Detroit, Corcoran was traded to the Chicago Black Hawks.

❖

With only four of their regulars returning for 1949–50, Father Flanagan and coach Joe Primeau set out to construct a respectable team based around captain Willie Marshall. Although Tim Horton was slated to return to St. Mike's for his final season of Junior eligibility, he reluctantly chose instead to turn pro with the Pittsburgh Hornets, Toronto's AHL franchise. Leafs owner Conn Smythe engaged in a bit of skullduggery, trying everything within his power to turn the Junior Toronto Marlboros into a Memorial Cup champion. He wanted Horton to join the Marlies, but the defenceman balked. "He didn't want to play against his old St. Mike's teammates," wrote the *Toronto Daily Star*, "and that had a bearing on his decision to turn pro." Once over the age of 18, a player who had signed a C-Form with an NHL club was no longer protected by his amateur club from being called up to play hockey professionally. Tim desperately wanted to be a Toronto Maple Leaf one day — sooner rather than later — so rather than defy the team owner, he signed a contract with Pittsburgh.

Besides the captain, other returnees to the St. Mike's Majors were Rod Roy, who was shifted from centre to defence, Connie Bonhomme, and Neil Buchanan. They were joined by newcomers Paul Alain, Bill Dineen, Joe Ingoldsby, Leo Labine, Al Marshall, Ed Plata, Jim Primeau (another of the coach's sons), Bob Sabourin, Fred Sandford, Roy Stanutz, and goaltender Lorne Howes.

The 1949–50 edition of the Majors completed their season in sixth place, making the playoffs for the first time in three seasons. Willie Marshall led the Majors in scoring

1949–50					
TEAM	GP	W	L	T	Pts
Toronto Marlboros	48	37	9	2	76
Windsor Spitfires	48	34	13	1	69
St. Catharines TeePees	48	27	17	4	58
Guelph Biltmore Mad Hatters	48	26	18	4	56
Barrie Flyers	48	21	24	3	45
St. Michael's Majors	48	19	26	3	41
Stratford Kroehlers	48	14	31	3	31
Galt Black Hawks	48	14	32	2	30
Oshawa Generals	48	12	34	2	26

with 39 goals and 27 assists for 66 points. His goal total was seventh best in the OHA that season.

As Smythe predicted, the Toronto Marlboros dominated the OHA's Junior 'A' league in 1949–50, finishing first with 76 points in 48 games.

Goalie Lorne Howes, who joined the Majors after taking the Porcupine Combines to the OHA final the previous season, was awarded the President's Trophy as the team's most valuable player.

The Majors only had a brief period of time in which to celebrate reaching the post-season. In the first round of the playoffs, St. Mike's met the Barrie Flyers, who dismissed the Majors in five games.

Willie "The Whip" Marshall is regarded as one of the greatest AHL players of all time, yet he wasn't given much of an opportunity to prove himself in the NHL. He played two games for Toronto in 1952–53, 16 in 1954–55, six in 1955–56, and nine more in 1958–59. The Kirkland Lake native scored a goal and five assists in 33 big-league games. Yet, in 20 seasons in the American Hockey League, Marshall hit the 20-goal plateau on 15 occasions, including 1955–56, when he scored 45 with the Pittsburgh Hornets and 1957–58, when he tallied 40 times with the Hershey Bears. So proficient was Marshall at scoring that in 2004 the AHL honoured him by naming its goal-scoring award the Willie Marshall Award.

SNAPSHOT ▶▶ ▶▶ ▶▶ ▶▶ ▶▶ ▶▶ ▶▶

Leo Labine: *The Lion Roared*

"I was lucky to get out of the game alive. I was a little aggressive sometimes," Labine laughed, reflecting on his career in *Heroes: Stars of Hockey's Golden Era*.

In an era when players were forced to be subservient to management, Labine wasn't afraid to speak his mind. On the ice, the gritty forward did whatever it took to win, pushing the envelope to throw opponents off their games by poking, prodding, and talking trash, and then scoring a goal. Off the ice, he showed no sign of being intimidated, either. In one series of negotiations later in his career with the Boston Bruins, a contract was slid across the desk for him to sign. He did, writing two words, and they weren't "Leo Labine"!

Recruited from Haileybury, Ontario, Leo joined the St. Michael's Majors in 1949–50 and scored 20 goals and 22 assists. But the Boston Bruins signed the young prospect and placed him on their OHA club, the Barrie Flyers, infuriating St. Mike's management, a situation further exacerbated when Hap Emms's Flyers beat the Winnipeg Monarchs for the Memorial Cup in 1951. Labine centred a formidable Flyers line with wingers Real Chevrefils and Jack White. Leo led the league's playoff scoring with 26 points in 12 games. His 36 penalty minutes also topped the OHA playoffs.

"Leo the Lion" joined the Boston Bruins for 15 games in 1951–52 and was with the Bruins until a January 1961 trade took him to Detroit. He spent parts of two seasons with the Red Wings, leaving the NHL after the 1961–62 season. Through 11 NHL seasons, Labine played 643 regular-season games in which he scored 128 goals and 193 assists for 321 points.

"I just came to play every game," he said. "When we played, other teams knew we were around!"

13
Rebuilding the Brand

It was a struggle from the opening faceoff of the 1950–51 campaign for the St. Michael's Majors, who fell back to ninth place. Joe Primeau, who had coached the Majors since 1944–45, had accepted a job coaching the Toronto Maple Leafs, whom he led to the Stanley Cup championship, won on a dramatic overtime goal by Bill Barilko. Primeau was replaced behind the St. Michael's bench by Peanuts O'Flaherty, an alumnus who was also player-coach of the Senior 'A' St. Michael's Monarchs. Bob Schiller, a rookie defenceman for St. Mike's, remembers his coach well: "He had a lot of energy but had trouble communicating with the players. He was respected for his extensive hockey background."

For the first time in three years, the OHA's Junior 'A' loop comprised 10 teams, as the Waterloo Hurricanes joined the league. The Toronto Marlboros, first-place finishers in 1949–50, held strong but, like everyone else, were surprised that the Barrie Flyers rose to first place after finishing fifth the season before. The league's elite — Barrie, Marlboros, Guelph, and Windsor — were packed tighter than commuters taking mass transit, with only 10 points separating them. St. Michael's won just 16 games, with 31 losses and seven ties for 39 points. Only the cellar-dwelling Waterloo Hurricanes, "winless and windless," had a worse season.

The Majors had lost high-scoring forward Leo Labine and goaltender Lorne Howes (who had been the Majors' MVP in 1949–50) to the Barrie Flyers, but based the squad around snipers Willie Marshall and Bill Dineen, who replaced Marshall as captain. Marshall finished the season as St. Mike's' leading scorer, collecting 29 goals and 59 points. Dineen picked up 25 goals and finished with 51 points. Other strong performances came from Jack Wheldrake, who had moved over from the Marlboros organization (49 points), Bob Sabourin (43), and first-year Major Murray Costello, a centre who was following the path his brother, Les, had blazed from South Porcupine to St. Michael's College. Murray scored 18 goals and 34 points.

The defence comprised two pairs: Neil Buchanan with Hal McNamara, and Bob Schiller — newly arrived from Assumption High School in Windsor — with Art Clune. "Neil and Hal were offensive finesse defencemen," explains Schiller. "They stickhandled and carried the puck well. The rest of us [Schiller, Clune, and spare defenceman Joe McCann] played a more physical game. I often watched Bill Barilko at Maple Leaf Gardens and was able to incorporate his hip check into my game."

But as the season got under way, the Majors posed a conundrum to those involved with the team. On paper, they seemed to have a strong, well-balanced team. Yet they weren't winning games. "It continues to be a mystery how such a talent-laden club as St. Michael's can play so poorly," wrote the *Telegram*.

The Majors started the season with Tom Battaglia in goal, but after a handful of games they were looking for assistance in net. The Toronto Marlboros were deep in goal, and went into training camp intending to start the season with Don Lockhart as their number one goalie. Don Head, John Henderson, Vic Hunt, and Ed Chadwick, all of whom had spent the previous season playing with the Weston Dukes, were also hoping to catch on with the Junior 'A' Marlies. But Lockhart hurt his knee in training camp and Chadwick got the nod to start in goal. When Lockhart returned to action, Chadwick was relegated to substitute status until Father Flanagan of St. Michael's asked permission to have Chadwick start for the Majors, replacing Battaglia. "I went to training camp with

1950–51					
TEAM	GP	W	L	T	Pts
Barrie Flyers	54	38	14	2	78
Toronto Marlboros	54	32	16	6	70
Guelph Biltmore Mad Hatters	54	31	16	7	69
Windsor Spitfires	54	32	18	4	68
Oshawa Generals	54	26	26	2	54
St. Catharines TeePees	54	23	24	7	53
Galt Black Hawks	54	21	39	4	48
Stratford Kroehlers	54	20	28	6	46
St. Michael's Majors	54	16	31	7	39
Waterloo Hurricanes	54	7	44	3	17

the Marlies. The goalie at St. Mike's at the time quit and went home. That was when I was sent to St. Mike's. It was the best thing that ever happened to me because I don't think I would have played that much with the Marlies. When I came to St. Mike's, I was the only goalie there and I played there for three years. It worked out pretty well. I don't know how I got to St. Mike's. Someone told me they bought me for a dollar."

A game against the woeful Waterloo Hurricanes seemed to be able to cure most teams' ills, and the Majors rubbed their hands in anticipation. On New Year's Day 1951, St. Mike's whacked Waterloo 12–1. Willie Marshall scored four goals, all in the third period, and three in the space of less than a minute. It was the 28th straight loss of the season for the Hurricanes.

Then, just four days later, St. Mike's received a scare when Chadwick was struck in the throat by a shot from the stick of Windsor Spitfire Chester Koneczny. Chadwick collapsed in his crease and was carried unconscious off the ice on a stretcher. While Gerry Young replaced him in net, Chadwick was examined by Windsor doctors. Windsor went on to win 6–2. Although shaken, Chadwick was not seriously injured and started the next game for the Majors.

Ironically, just three games later, Chadwick was caught in the throat again, this time by his own teammate in the pre-game warmup. Chadwick again was removed from the ice on a stretcher, but was able to watch the third period in his civilian clothes while sub-goaltender Gerry Young lost to the Waterloo Hurricanes by a score of 5–3. The win was but the second of the season for the much-maligned Hurricanes.

"The Irish, an up-and-down club that can kill you or be led to the slaughter like a lamb, depending on how they feel about it," wrote the *Telegram*. "When Chadwick is playing his best goal and Marshall and Sabourin are shooting like the snipers they are, the Majors are extremely tough." And that seemed to be the problem — St. Mike's played well when they wanted to. The *Toronto Daily Star* took a shot at leading scorer Willie Marshall, calling him "the centre who scores goals in quantity but doesn't backcheck, probably on the theory that as long as Ed Chadwick is in goal, he doesn't need to."

With inconsistency running rampant, St. Michael's Junior 'A' squad was hit by injuries in the second half of the season. Captain Bill Dineen hurt his back and missed much of the second half. Tommy Fyles, a winger on the Maple Leafs' list who had arrived from the Marlboros for the 1950–51 season, was out for a prolonged period of time, as was teammate Joe McCann.

Ed Chadwick's bad-luck streak continued, too. In a game against the Guelph Biltmores on February 27, he was knocked out when hit on the side of the face with a stick. "The kid who was the trainer came running out. I said, 'Give me smelling salts!' He tipped the smelling salts towards my nose and accidentally poured some of the crystals into my mouth. It just about killed me!"

The period was concluded and the remaining time added to the third period. "[Chadwick] could have played the third period all right, but we were pretty well beaten so I let him rest and used Gerry Young," explained coach Peanuts O'Flaherty. St. Mike's was thumped 8–2.

With a 4–0 blanking at the hands of the Oshawa Generals on March 7, the Majors were eliminated from playoff contention, ending a disappointing season. St. Mike's "was a hard-working team that clung to their opponents like leeches," according to the *Toronto Daily Star*, but simply couldn't win games.

As with any negative, it was important to take out whatever positives were possible, and they included strong leadership from Bill Dineen, great promise from young forwards Murray Costello and Bob Sabourin, solid blueline presence from Neil Buchanan, Hal McNamara, and Bob Schiller, and a solid, if oft-injured, goaltender in Ed Chadwick. "The thing that helped us most on defence was having Ed Chadwick in goal," says Bob Schiller. "He was a great goalie and gave the team a lot of confidence."

Ed Chadwick: *The Goalie Host* SNAPSHOT

Ed Chadwick was attending Toronto's Weston Collegiate when he was acquired by St. Michael's. "The first two years I played for St. Mike's [1950–51 and 1951–52], I was still going to Weston Collegiate, but I finished Grade 12 there and I needed to go to school to play for St. Mike's for a third year, so I took four subjects. By the time the season was over, I was on my way out of school."

Chadwick was a rare, if not unheard of, commodity at St. Michael's College: he was a Protestant. "My first day at St. Michael's, I was sitting in the classroom and nobody was there. I knew that the boys had all gone to Mass. The priest came in and he was all over me. He said, 'What are you doing here?' I said, 'Waiting for the class.' He said, 'You should be in the chapel.' I said, 'No, I don't have to.' He grabbed me by the neck and said, 'You're going to chapel!' Father Regan was walking by and he asked what was going on. 'Father,' the priest said, 'this boy won't go to Mass!' Father Regan said, 'He doesn't have to.' The priest asked, 'Why not?' Father Regan said, 'He's a Protestant boy.' The priest said, 'It doesn't matter. It'll do him good anyways!' So, I ended up going to Mass."

Ed has very fond memories of St. Michael's, although they don't necessarily involve the classroom. "Father Brown used to patrol the cafeteria. I loved ice cream, so when I was at school, I used to sneak back for another dish of ice cream, but he always caught me. He'd whack me across my knuckles with that big stick of his. I said, 'Father, you break my hand and I won't be able to play.' He'd say, 'Don't you steal things off my trays!' But I had a great time there."

As tough as Chadwick could be in the goal crease, he could be equally combative off the ice. He recalls his negotiations: "My first year of Junior, they paid me $5 a game. The second year I got $10 and the third year, my last year, I was holding out because I understood some of the other guys were making better money. We used to hear that the Leafs were throwing in a bit of money. So, I wouldn't sign. I was in class at the time and over the speakers comes, 'Ed Chadwick, please report to Father Regan's office.' I thought, 'Here we go!' So I went down to the office. Father Regan said, 'We've got to get this settled.' I said, 'Okay.' He said, 'We can only pay you $15 a game.' I said, 'The other guys are making more!' He said, 'Well, that's the deal,' so I went back to class. The following day, I was in class. 'Ed Chadwick, please report to Father Regan's office.' I thought, 'Here we go again!' I walked in and, uh-oh! Father Regan was there, Father Flanagan was there, a couple of other priests were there, and so was my dad. The priests were talking and said, 'Ed, we can't really afford any more than $15 a game.' My dad said, 'Ed, it's been a good spot for you,' but I said, 'Dad, I understand that but I just want to get paid what I think I'm worth.' He said, 'Let's go outside,' so we stepped out of the office and talked. We went back inside and I said, 'I'm tired of this. Whatever you've done with my dad, fine. I don't care. I'll take the $15 and run.' So I left the office.

"I went home at suppertime and my dad says, 'I'm glad you settled on that.' I said, 'Yeah, but I'm not very happy about it.' He said, 'The deal was…' and then it hit me. 'Ah-hah!' We had an interlocking schedule between Christmas and New Year's that year with the Quebec league, and they gave my dad a trip to go with us. So I said, 'If it makes you happy, Dad — fine!'

During the 1952–53 season, Ed's last with the Majors, his father and girlfriend, who later became his wife, never missed a game, home or away. "They used to take the train down to Windsor and everything," says an incredulous Ed.

"Playing with the St. Mike's Majors was the best thing that ever happened to me," admits Chadwick. "I got to play a full three years at St. Mike's. If I had still been with the Marlies, I don't know how much I would have played. That was the biggest break I ever had."

After concluding his Junior career, Ed spent a season practising with the Toronto Maple Leafs during an era when backup netminders were virtually unheard of. Chadwick was an emergency replacement for Pittsburgh Hornets netminder Gil Mayer in two games that season.

Before getting his first shot of NHL action, Ed played in Pittsburgh, Stratford, Sault Ste. Marie, Buffalo, and Winnipeg. But with an injury to Harry Lumley, Chadwick was summoned from the Winnipeg Warriors of the Western Hockey League and saw his first action on February 8, 1956, holding the powerful Canadiens to a 1–1 tie. His next game, a day later, also ended in a 1–1 tie, this time against Boston. In his third game, played February 11, Ed earned a 5–0 shutout over the New York Rangers. The next night, Ed again was in goal as his Leafs skated to a 1–1 tie with Chicago. His fifth and final game before Lumley returned from sick bay was a 1–0 blanking of the Bruins. In five games, Chadwick had surrendered but three goals.

After such an auspicious audition, it should come as no surprise that Chadwick was the Leafs' number one netminder in 1956–57, as Lumley was sent to Chicago. The Maple Leafs had struggled since their Stanley Cup win in 1951, and in spite of Chadwick's netminding, they missed the playoffs that season, as they did again in 1957–58. Ed played every game of the schedule both seasons, and posted five shutouts in 1956–57 and four in 1957–58, but times were changing. For one thing, backup netminders were gradually being introduced into the NHL, but of more drastic consequence for Ed was the 1958 arrival of Johnny Bower, an American Hockey League veteran playing with the Cleveland Barons, who was added to the Leafs' line-up in the summer's Inter-League Draft.

Chadwick's role diminished quickly as Bower's stock rose. Finally, after two seasons with Toronto's AHL affiliate in Rochester, Chadwick was traded to the Boston Bruins for Don Simmons in January 1961. Ed would see his final NHL activity in four games with the Bruins during 1961–62. Ed was traded from Boston to Detroit in 1962, then to Chicago in 1964. In 184 NHL games, Chadwick won 57 times, lost 92, and played 35 more to a tie.

14

The Monarchs Arrive at St. Michael's

The minor-pro Pacific Coast Hockey League suffered a severe blow following the 1949–50 campaign. Finding expenses too high and revenues too light, five of the 11 teams that finished that season folded. The Southern Conference, made up of the Fresno Falcons, Los Angeles Monarchs, Oakland Oaks, San Diego Skyhawks, and San Francisco Shamrocks, ceased to exist entirely, leaving players scrambling to find new hockey homes anywhere across North America in time for 1950–51. Many were absorbed into the six remaining PCHL squads, while a number found jobs on United States Hockey League (USHL) teams, but almost the entire Los Angeles Monarchs team found a most fortuitous break in Toronto.

On the eve of the new season, the OHA Senior 'A' league was in disarray. On September 2, 1950, the Kitchener-Waterloo Flying Dutchmen formally advised the Ontario Hockey Association of their withdrawal from the circuit. The issue revolved around the lack of ice time at the Waterloo Memorial Arena. The arena manager indicated that he wanted no part of a three-team Senior league with a Dutchmen team that was bound to leave after one season in favour of the new Memorial Auditorium set to open in Kitchener.

The loss of the Dutchmen would likely have doomed the Senior 'A' league, which only had entries from Toronto and Hamilton at that point. But on September 12, Kitchener-Waterloo re-entered the league with a new management group that included St. Mike's alumnus Bobby Bauer as manager and Punch Scherer, a retired defenceman who had been part of Hamilton's OHA Senior championship in 1944, as coach.

A surprise came out of left field when St. Michael's College announced that it would enter a Senior team in 1950–51. It would turn out to be the only Senior 'A' entry in the school's storied history.

The team was to be known as the Monarchs, and the nickname wasn't the only thing borrowed from the now-defunct L.A. franchise. Moving from Los Angeles to Toronto were John Arundel, Dusty Blair, Tom Fowler, Sam Kennedy, Billy McCracken, Jack "Gabby" Meldrum (the Monarchs' leader in scoring in 1949–50, with 70 points), Matt Mesich, Eddie Mulligan, Johnny Ubriaco, and Ken Watson. En route to Toronto, Watson was ordered to report to Buffalo for a medical examination for U.S. military service. St. Mike's supplemented the roster with alumnus Gord Hannigan, who had played Senior hockey with the Toronto Marlboros the previous season; goaltender Phil Hughes, a Port Arthur native who had spent the 1949–50 with the North Bay Black Hawks of the ECSHL; Harry Psutka, a St. Mike's alumnus who had most recently played with the Pittsburgh Hornets of the American Hockey League; Frank Sullivan, who had played a game with the Toronto Maple Leafs during 1949–50 but spent most of the season with the Senior Marlboros (he'd later play two more NHL games, with Chicago); AHL veteran Pat Wilson, who spent 1949–50 with the St. Louis Flyers and served as team captain; and playing coach Peanuts O'Flaherty, who was also coaching St. Mike's Junior 'A' squad.

The OHA's Senior league (or Major Series, as it was officially termed by the OHA) included the Hamilton Tigers (coached by former Boston Bruin George "Shorty" Redding), Kitchener Dutchmen (coached by Punch Scherer), Toronto Marlboros (with Flash Hollett, the former high-scoring NHL defenceman behind the bench), and the Monarchs. Both Toronto teams called Maple Leaf Gardens their home — the Marlies played Friday evenings while the Monarchs staged their home games on Saturday afternoons. All games between the two Toronto clubs were worth four points in the standings.

The Monarchs opened their season in Hamilton on October 24, while the Senior Marlboros made their season debut on October 25 against Kitchener. *The Globe and Mail* reported that Marlie coach Flash Hollett "is knee deep in coaching worries as his Toronto Marlboros try to maintain the dignity and decorum of last year's Allan Cup champions."

Games in the Senior league were fiercely competitive affairs. In a January 10 contest between St. Michael's and Hamilton, the Monarchs' Frank Sullivan, sitting out a minor penalty, was attacked by a Hamilton spectator. Sullivan retaliated by using his stick to cuff the fan in the head. Within moments, more than a hundred spectators were on the ice surface, swinging at Monarchs players. Pat Hannigan, Gord's brother, was watching the game from the stands and leapt over the boards to help even the sides. Police joined the melee and several fans were ejected. Both Sullivan and Hannigan were ejected with game misconducts. The Tigers were handed a misconduct when their coach threw a stick out onto the ice. That night, Monarchs netminder Phil Hughes was "kicking them out with gay abandon." Hamilton coach Redding said: "Hughes is carrying that team. We couldn't put the puck past him." At the other end, Child was having one of those horrific games that plague even the best athletes.

Through most of the season, the two Toronto teams were neck and neck, and a fierce rivalry ensued. On the afternoon of January 21, 1951, the Monarchs whipped the Marlies 6–1, while in Junior action, the Majors edged the Marlboros 6–4.

In early February, Harry Psutka left the Monarchs when he was invited to report to spring training by the Detroit Tigers of baseball's American League. Although he never played a major-league game with the Tigers, Psutka was an outstanding amateur baseball player in southern Ontario's Senior Intercounty League while he continued playing Senior hockey, mostly with the Kitchener Dutchmen.

Peace had yet to prevail by the time St. Mike's next returned to Hamilton. During a 4–4 tie on February 7, a fan reached over the boards and grabbed Gord Hannigan's stick, refusing to let go. A policeman stepped in and ejected the fan before trouble started. Two weeks later, during a 6–1 Hamilton romp over the Monarchs, Coach Redding of the Tigers was ejected when he jumped over the boards after Clare Shillington was boarded by St. Michael's Matt Mesich.

Although St. Michael's played exciting, winning Senior hockey, attendance at Maple Leaf Gardens was quite poor for Monarchs' games. During an informal meeting with the media, Hap Day, the assistant general manager of hockey at Maple Leaf Gardens, announced that Toronto would have just one team in the OHA Major series in 1951–52. He vowed that only the team that went the farthest in the playoffs would return. As a result, what was already a bitter rivalry became a struggle for survival between the Monarchs and Marlboros. After watching the final regular-season match-up between the Monarchs and the Marlboros, Day commented, "I have seen NHL games that were not as good." St. Mike's earned a first-place finish by edging the Marlies 2–1. Shortly afterwards, Phil Hughes, a key reason why St. Mike's finished atop the league, was awarded the Turofsky Trophy as the league's best goaltender. Ed Mulligan, who had played with Los Angeles in the PCHL, stated, "Senior hockey is just as good or better than the hockey played in the PCHL."

The playoffs saw last-place Kitchener eliminated from playoff contention, and a round-robin semifinal tournament took place between the remaining three teams. The Monarchs iced a marginally different squad to begin the post-season. Bill McCracken and Sam Kennedy were both out with injuries, so Peanuts O'Flaherty elevated Willie Marshall from the Junior 'A' Majors for the playoffs. By this point, O'Flaherty was able to concentrate his coaching attention solely on the Monarchs, as the Majors had not qualified for the playoffs.

1950–51					
Team	GP	W	L	T	Pts
St. Michael's Monarchs	33	20	10	3	58
Hamilton Tigers	40	18	19	3	43
Toronto Marlboros	32	19	12	1	42
Kitchener Dutchmen	41	11	27	3	25

The Globe and Mail brilliantly described Game One of the playoffs: "St. Michael's continued to treat their Marlboro cousins like poor relations in the Gardens, giving Flash Hollett's buckaroos the bird in the opening game of the OHA Major series round-robin. 11,297 witnesses thrilled to the robust exchange as the city rivals hammered each other all over the glacial compound." Johnny Ubriaco, who scored what would become the game-winning goal, led the way in a 5–3 win for the Monarchs, while goaltender Phil Hughes, described as "the mammoth mound of muscle," also excelled. "It became evident in the third period that the only thing Coach Peanuts O'Flaherty of the Irish could lose was his voice. His determined Double Blue–sweatered skaters had come from behind a 1–0 deficit late in the second period and were winging in high gear."

After eliminating the Marlboros, St. Mike's opened the OHA Major final at Maple Leaf Gardens on St. Patrick's Day. The Monarchs defeated Hamilton four games to one. In the fifth and final game of the best-of-seven series, Hughes blanked the Tigers 2–0 to earn his second shutout of the season. After the game, Hamilton's coach predicted, "The Monarchs should go all the way."

The St. Mike's Monarchs packed their gear and made the trek to Saskatchewan to face the Saskatoon Quakers in the Alexander Cup semifinal. The first two games in the best-of-seven series were slated for Saskatoon, with the teams moving to Toronto for games three and four. Coach O'Flaherty was confident. He was riding a team on a mission, but in addition, several of his players — Meldrum, Watson, Arundel, Fowler, and McCracken — were western Canadian boys who would be at home, more or less, competing in Saskatoon.

The Quakers were no pushovers. Reg Bentley, who played briefly in the NHL with brothers Doug and Max in Chicago, was one of the stalwarts for Saskatoon. George Senick would play with the New York Rangers in 1952–53. Chuck McCullough and Ken Hunter had both collected better than 60 points during the regular season, with Hunter leading the Western Canada Senior Hockey League in assists. Larry Zeidel had terrorized the league, leading the loop in penalty minutes.

Game One was a decisive 8–5 victory for the visiting Monarchs, with Hannigan and Kennedy each tallying twice. The second game in the series was also won by St. Mike's, this time 4–1, with Gord Hannigan again scoring two goals. Quakers coach Riley Mullen, who earlier that season had replaced former Maple Leaf Nick Metz behind the bench, was surprised at the actions of the Monarchs. "A stick isn't to break your way through the defence with," he moaned.

Peanuts O'Flaherty, who, according to *The Hockey News*, "was flying up and down the ice with all his old-time pepper," injured an ankle in Saskatoon, so he coached but did not play in Game Three. Nevertheless, his Monarchs won 4–2, with Gord Hannigan again starring, scoring the opening goal. "We were rotten," said Mullen. "That's all there is to it."

The St. Michael's Monarchs swept the series with a 9–3 win in Game Four. Gord Hannigan collected yet another goal, while McCracken and Ubriaco each added a pair. "They all played a terrific game," stated O'Flaherty.

St. Michael's advanced to face the Valleyfield Braves for the Alexander Cup, which had been newly commissioned to mark the "Major Senior" hockey championship of Canada. Valleyfield was a formidable team. Andre Corriveau was the Quebec Senior Hockey League's points leader with 89, and he finished second in goals with 34. He played three games with the Montreal Canadiens during 1953–54. Larry Kwong, who played a single game with the NHL's Rangers in 1947–48, was second in points during the regular season. Jimmy Orlando had played six seasons with the Detroit Red Wings earlier in his career. Jack Schmidt spent 1942–43 with the Boston Bruins. Rosario "Kitoute" Joannette played a couple of games with the Montreal Canadiens in 1944–45, while Jacques Deslauriers would go on to play two with Montreal in 1955–56. The Braves were coached by future Hall of Famer Toe Blake.

After breezing past the Saskatoon Quakers, the Monarchs received a rude awakening when the Valleyfield Braves emerged and outplayed them 4–1 in the series opener in Valleyfield. The Monarchs turned the tables in Game Two with a 4–1 win of their own.

The series moved to Toronto for Game Three, which ended in a 4–4 tie as neither team scored during the 10-minute overtime. The game was chippier than had been witnessed to that point. Johnny Ubriaco received a game misconduct for protesting a holding penalty, and Bill McCracken and Georges Bougie received fighting majors in the second period. St. Mike's took a 2–1 series lead with a 6–1 win over the Braves in Game Four. Dusty Blair picked up two goals in the contest.

Game Five was played in Montreal, with Valleyfield coming out on top of a 7–3 decision. The first period evolved into a free-for-all that involved players, fans and police. Monarchs coach Peanuts O'Flaherty blasted the officials and insisted that the Canadian Amateur Hockey Association appoint two new officials to replace Stan Pratt and Hap Shouldice, who had handled the entire series to that point. "Those referees are terrible," he complained. "Absolutely incompetent. Twice, my players had their sticks grabbed by spectators but Pratt and Shouldice didn't do a thing about it."

Stan Pratt was replaced by Louis Lecompte, but Hap Shouldice remained and officiated Game Six, played at Maple Leaf Gardens. A 4–1 win gave Valleyfield nine points in the series, one more than they needed, and the Braves became the inaugural winners of the Alexander Cup. The lone Monarchs goal was scored by Gord Hannigan. "It was a tough series and anybody might have won," declared Braves coach Toe Blake. "My boys played hard and well." Coach O'Flaherty offered no excuses: "There has to be a winner and there has to be a loser. The better team won, that's all."

The OHA Senior league would carry on, but without the St. Michael's Monarchs, who folded after their sole season. In fact, the league would start the 1951–52 season without any Toronto team, as the Marlboros also decided not to continue in Senior hockey, in spite of Hap Day's previous declaration. Despite the Toronto withdrawal, the league added clubs in Brantford, Owen Sound, Sarnia, and Stratford, for a total of six teams.

Consigned to history, the Monarchs would represent an interesting footnote in the story of the first 100 years of hockey at St. Michael's College. Most of the Monarchs were recruited by the Saint John Beavers of the Maritime Major Hockey League. Peanuts O'Flaherty was followed there by John Arundel, Dusty Blair, Billy McCracken, Jack Meldrum, Matt Mesich, Eddie Mulligan, Johnny Ubriaco, and Ken Watson. The Beavers finished first overall, then won the league championship over the Halifax Atlantics. The team was disbanded the following season.

Although St. Michael's hockey legacy has extended over more than a century, their one-year experiment in Senior hockey adds an interesting footnote to a fascinating franchise history.

SNAPSHOT ▸▸ ▸▸ ▸▸ ▸▸ ▸▸ ▸▸ ▸▸ ▸▸

Peanuts O'Flaherty: *A Lifetime in Hockey*

Sports and nicknames seem to be a natural match. Some sobriquets are basic and self-explanatory — for example, Leonard Kelly being tagged with "Red" or the fair-haired Pat Stapleton answering to "Whitey." Others are more descriptive of the player's style — "The Great One" for Wayne Gretzky or "The Roadrunner" for Yvan Cournoyer. Boom Boom Geoffrion and Rocket Richard were evocative enough that they are used interchangeably with each player's given name.

The best nicknames are those that completely replace the player's given name and catch your attention because they have neither rhyme nor reason — Gump Worsley, Toe Blake, Dit Clapper, Turk Broda — now *those* are nicknames! Many readers would never know that Gump's real name was Lorne, that Blake's was Hector, that Clapper's birth certificate read Aubrey, or that Broda was known to his mother as Walter.

With a name as distinguished as John Benedict O'Flaherty, it's almost sad that he was perennially known as Peanuts. While O'Flaherty was playing Prep School hockey for St. Mike's in 1933, he took a part-time job selling confections at the relatively new Maple Leaf Gardens. A journalist spotted him in the crowd hawking his treats and tagged him Peanuts. It stuck, and Peanuts O'Flaherty was the name by which he was known through his entire hockey career.

A season of Junior 'B' with St. Mike's at 15 years of age was followed by a season with the Majors in 1934–35, where Peanuts notched 10 goals in 12 games. But for 1935–36, he was lured to the West Toronto Nationals along with fellow St. Michael's alumnus Johnny Crawford. Coached by Hap Day (who was still an active NHL defenceman) and managed by Harold Ballard, both keystones in the Toronto Maple Leafs later success, the Nationals also featured the Conacher twins, Roy and Bert, as well as Red Heron and Bill Jennings. The West Toronto Nats went on to win the 1936 Memorial Cup.

Waiting his turn for an NHL career, O'Flaherty played with the Senior OHA Toronto Goodyears, competing beside Punch Imlach and Jack Draper, father of Mike, Bruce, and Dave Draper. Peanuts had to wait until he was signed by the New York Americans in October 1940, and played 10 games with the Americans, scoring four goals. The next season, 1941–42, he played 11 games, scoring a goal and an assist for the Americans, who had changed their city designation from New York to Brooklyn that season — the franchise's last, as it turned out.

Peanuts then spent the remainder of his playing career in the minor leagues, including eight successful seasons with the Pittsburgh Hornets of the American Hockey League.

O'Flaherty returned to St. Michael's to coach the Majors, but found his job description changed once he returned to the school. "Johnny O'Flaherty, when he took a position with the St. Michael's people, probably got more than he bargained for," said an article in the Maple Leaf Gardens program. "At first report, he was going to coach the Junior 'A' team. He started that job. *Alors*, along comes the new entry from his old alma mater and he got the job of coaching them, too. After that, there was naturally only one job left for him and he took it. Yes, he decided to play for the team. He's doing a good job with both clubs and everything will be just fine unless some Sunday afternoon at a Junior game, he forgets he isn't playing and leaps over the boards and tries to skate down his regular wing."

When the Monarchs folded at the end of the 1950–51 season, Peanuts moved to Saint John to serve as playing-coach of the Beavers, a Senior team in the Maritime Major Hockey League. He coached the Ottawa Senators of the Quebec Senior Hockey League in 1952–53, was playing coach of the Sault Ste. Marie Greyhounds of the Northern Ontario Hockey Association the next year, and then spent three seasons coaching (and occasionally playing) with the Senior Sudbury Wolves.

He didn't play any longer after competing in a single game with the Wolves in 1958–59, but his coaching career continued with stops all over the continent. When the Metro Junior 'A' Hockey League was formed for the 1961–62 season, Peanuts oversaw the Unionville entry, renamed Knob Hill Farms under owner Steve Stavro in 1962–63. The St. Catharines Black Hawks hired Peanuts in 1965–66, and he coached the Chicago Black Hawks affiliate for three seasons. In 1970–71, O'Flaherty coached the Rochester Americans of the AHL.

Peanuts and his wife had nine children. As chief scout of the Vancouver Canucks, O'Flaherty was a proud father when his son Gerry was claimed from the Toronto Maple Leafs in June 1972. Gerry enjoyed six productive seasons with the Canucks between 1972 and 1978. Another son, Bill, was director of player personnel for the Los Angeles Kings between 1997 and 2006, spent 2006–07 as a scout for the Pittsburgh Penguins, and joined the Florida Panthers as director of professional scouting in 2007.

On July 16, 2008, Peanuts O'Flaherty passed away. He was 90 years of age.

THE MONARCHS ARRIVE AT ST. MICHAEL'S

15

The Clang of a Goalpost

During the 1951 off-season, rumours persisted that St. Michael's College was going to withdraw from the OHA's Junior 'A' league. In addressing the rumblings, Father Flanagan commented that "as long as there are enough hockey players wanting to combine hockey with an education, the college will continue in Junior 'A' hockey." The rumours were doused when the school announced that Charlie Cerre had been hired to teach at St. Michael's as well as coach the Majors for the 1951–52 campaign. He replaced Peanuts O'Flaherty, who found coaching both the Junior and Senior teams, as well as playing for the latter, too taxing.

Cerre, a former St. Mike's hockey and football star, later attended Assumption College in Windsor, where he received his teaching certificate. For six years, he taught at Sudbury High School, also coaching the school's football team and the Frood Mines baseball team. Acting as a bird dog for St. Mike's, Cerre was instrumental in sending Tim Horton, Mike "Butch" Ratchford, and Bob Sabourin from Sudbury to St. Michael's College School.

Bob Schiller, a second-year defenceman for the Majors, comments on the team's new coach. "I thought Charlie Cerre was terrific. He was more from an advanced school of hockey. We had physical training programs, skating, passing, and breakout drills. We also had an occasional film of our game and learned a lot watching that. One of the things I really liked was the detailed breakout of individual statistics. For example, the number of stick checks versus body checks. I liked all this stuff, but some of the players did not. As the season progressed, everybody was on board. Charlie was a good leader and was always a gentleman."

After a disappointing season in 1950–51, the Majors had reason for optimism as most of the squad was returning. Only two had graduated — Willie Marshall and Hal McNamara. Father Flanagan bristled when he slyly added, "None of our players is on Boston's list, either." The Bruins had signed goaltender Lorne Howes, forward Leo Labine, and defenceman George Stanutz and moved them from St. Mike's over to the Barrie Flyers for 1950–51. With the additions of these stalwarts, the Flyers went on to win the Memorial Cup.

The Toronto Marlboros finished atop the Ontario Hockey Association's Junior 'A' circuit, winning 39, losing eight, and tying six for 84 points. The Guelph Biltmores were a scoring machine, firing a league-best 341 goals, but they finished behind the Marlies in second place. The Galt Black Hawks were third, with St. Michael's slipping into fourth place with 63 points on 30 wins against 20 losses and three ties. The Stratford Kroehlers, once a mainstay of the Junior 'A' league, dropped out after 1950–51.

"There is no doubt that they produced more heart conditions among the fans than any other team," said the school yearbook of the 1951–52 Majors. The team featured a superb lineup of young talent. Netminder Ed Chadwick was very strong, and was backed up by rookie Gerry McNamara. The defence was anchored by two Windsor-area boys, Marc Reaume and Bob Schiller. Up front, the Majors were explosive at times. Ron Wallace was the team's scoring leader with 32 goals and 65 points, followed by Bob Sabourin (31 goals and 54 points), Jim Logan (also 54 points), captain Bill Dineen (21 goals and 51 points), Butch Ratchford (46), and Murray Costello (43).

In the semifinals, St. Mike's faced St. Catharines. "Perhaps the most nerve-wracking and exciting of all was the last game of the year," wrote *The Thurible*. "The score was

1951–51					
TEAM	GP	W	L	T	Pts
Toronto Marlboros	53	39	8	6	84
Guelph Biltmore Mad Hatters	54	37	13	4	78
Galt Black Hawks	54	35	17	2	72
St. Michael's Majors	53	30	20	3	63
St. Catharines TeePees	54	30	23	1	61
Kitchener Greenshirts	54	29	22	3	61
Barrie Flyers	53	22	30	1	45
Waterloo Hurricanes	53	15	37	1	31
Windsor Spitfires	54	9	42	3	21
Oshawa Generals	54	7	41	6	20

6 to 1 for St. Catharines with only ten minutes to play in the third period. The fans were already starting to leave the Gardens when Bill Lee clicked, 6–2. Lee again, 6–3. Murray Costello, 6–4. Bill Dineen, 6–5." Bob Schiller picks up the story: "Time was running out. Bill Dineen shot one from inside the blue line. *Gong!* It hit the St. Catharines goalpost squarely and came out. Everyone in the arena heard the puck hit the post. That was it. Time was almost up." With the score still 6–5, the Majors then picked up a penalty with 2:07 to play, but it was all too much. "The bell rang for the last time on a great season for the Majors and their followers."

"We had a good team with a lot of depth in 1951–52," comments Schiller. "Bill Dineen was a great captain."

It took until February 15, 1961, for Gerry McNamara to play his first NHL game. After playing four seasons with the Majors, McNamara turned pro with the Pittsburgh Hornets in 1955–56. His career was an odyssey through such minor-league cities as Winnipeg, Sudbury, Buffalo, Cleveland, Hershey, and Rochester until the Maple Leafs summoned the Sturgeon Falls, Ontario, native to replace injured Johnny Bower. He played five games, splitting his record with two wins, two losses, and a tie. In 1970, he appeared in two more games for the Leafs. Although his NHL playing career lasted but seven games, it wouldn't be the last the Maple Leafs saw of Gerry. He was the team's general manager from September 1981 until February 1988.

Through four seasons with the Majors, Paul Knox's scoring ability improved dramatically. Although he played just two games in 1950–51, subsequent seasons resulted in totals of 12, 21, and 40 goals. While playing with the University of Toronto Blues in 1955, Knox was called up to play with the Toronto Maple Leafs for a single game on March 12 — a 2–1 loss to the New York Rangers. Paul played for Canada at the Olympic Games in 1956 and was the leading scorer, picking up 14 points as Canada earned the bronze medal.

Bob Sabourin was enjoying a terrific season with St. Mike's, his fourth with the Majors, when he was called to play for the Toronto Maple Leafs as an emergency injury replacement on March 13, 1952. That night, Montreal beat Toronto 3–1 at the Montreal Forum, and Bob got his name in the summary by getting called for a minor penalty. Through his long hockey career, it would be Sabourin's sole NHL contest.

Bob Schiller: *Skills and Thrills* ◀◀ ◀◀ ◀◀ ◀◀ ◀◀ ◀◀ ◀◀ SNAPSHOT

Like most Canadian boys of a certain vintage, Bob Schiller learned to play hockey on an outdoor rink — in his case, one built on a vacant lot next to the family home in Riverside, Ontario, a town now part of Windsor. Already one of the better players in the neighbourhood, Schiller tried out for the Assumption High School hockey team and made it, even though he was only in Grade 9. "I remember being very confident that I was going to make the team at Assumption in my freshman year, and I did," recalls Bob. "Our coach during that year [1947–48] was Father Hanrihan, and we competed in the local Windsor High School Hockey League."

By his second season, Father Ronald Cullen had taken over as coach of the Assumption hockey team. "Father Cullen was strong on discipline and was an excellent coach," states Schiller. "He knew the details of playing hockey and how to communicate it. He had a great influence on me and my game. My team play, as a result, increased significantly with his coaching."

By 1949–50, Bob was 16 years of age. He had grown and his game had improved exponentially. "The Red Wings began to notice my play, and I had many occasions to practice with the [Windsor] Spitfires [Detroit's OHA Junior affiliate] to increase my ice time," mentions Schiller. "Meanwhile, it was decided that I would play a few games

for the Detroit Hettche Spitfires [of the International Hockey League]. Hettche's was made up mainly of young guys whom the Red Wings thought had potential."

Bob had clearly been earmarked as one of Assumption's better players, and later, during that 1949–50 season, he was introduced to a gentleman who would change his life. "Father Cullen indicated that Father Flanagan, the athletic director at St Michael's College School in Toronto, was coming to Assumption for a visit. He asked if I would like to meet with Father Flanagan to discuss the possibility of going to St. Mike's to study and play hockey."

Schiller immediately agreed. "At this meeting, it was made clear by Father Flanagan that the offer to study and play hockey at St. Mike's was contingent on making the hockey team," Schiller remembers. "This did not bother me, and I felt confident that with my experience with the Assumption and the Hettche Spitfires, I could make St. Michael's Majors."

Schiller arrived in Toronto and tried out for the team. The 1950–51 season began with Bob on the blue line for the Majors. "I had been analyzing the Spitfires and the Hettche Spitfires and trying to figure out what their players were doing that I was not. I concluded I was not finishing my checks or bodychecking enough, so when I got to St Mike's in 1950–51, I was playing a much more physical game, which was necessary to compete in Junior 'A.'"

Following the 1951–52 season, Bob had completed Grade 13, but still had another year of Junior 'A' eligibility. "I had been thinking a lot about entering the priesthood," smiles Schiller. "In the fall of 1952, I entered St. Basil Novitiate in Richmond Hill, Ontario, and did not play my final year of Junior. In the summer of 1953, after reconsidering the situation, I decided to withdraw from the novitiate."

Schiller was a popular teammate while with the Majors. "A couple of times, I had 'delegations' of four or five guys who would come up to the novitiate and encourage me to leave. 'Come on, Schills. Can this joint. Your team needs you.' Of course, they were only kidding … I think! The leader: Murray Costello."

Even though his time at St. Michael's College lasted just two years, Bob very much enjoyed his time attending school and playing hockey in Toronto. "I have great memories of my days at St. Mike's, from my first day until the day that I left. The first guy I met was a student named Barry Riordan. It turns out he was from Windsor [and I later dated his sister]. I remember people saying St. Mike's was expecting me to replace Tim Horton, who had left for the pros. Whoa!! I remember travelling to Stratford for our opening game in the 1950–51 season and thinking, 'Oh boy, my first OHA Junior 'A' hockey game!' The memories were great. My roommate was Bob Sabourin. He played right wing and could really skate fast, and as the saying goes, could 'deke defencemen and goalies out of their jockstraps.' The days were divided between school classes, hockey, practice, travel for games, homework, etc. I had good grades but really had to study. The 'brain' of the hockey team was Ted Toppazzini. He always motivated us to improve our scholastic effort."

The Globe and Mail reported, "[Team manager] Father [Don] Faught was feeling quite proud of the academic achievements of hockey players Ted Toppazzini and Bob Schiller, who stood one-two in the class of 160 in the final year at St. Mike's."

Schiller attended the University of Michigan and earned a degree in engineering, but hockey was still an integral part of his life, and Bob continued to excel on the ice. During his three seasons at the university, Michigan won the NCAA championship in 1955 and 1956, and it's no coincidence that Schiller was an All-America both years. The University of Michigan's record during his three seasons at the school was 56 wins, 12 losses, and four ties. In 1981, Bob was inducted into the University of Michigan's Hall of Fame.

16
The School's Centennial

After a summer of rest, the skates were pulled out and the equipment, some of it a little more snug than remembered, pulled on. The Toronto Maple Leafs held their training camp in St. Catharines in September 1952, and Majors goaltender Ed Chadwick, along with Bob Sabourin, were invited by Leafs coach Joe Primeau to join the big squad at camp. After working out with the parent Leafs, the two returned to St. Mike's, only to be swept up in the excitement surrounding the school's centennial celebrations; among the festivities, alumni were returning for a gala dinner. "St. Mike's, who can point with pride to some of their great teams in the past, have an added impetus to win the championship this season," said *The Globe and Mail* in October 1952. "This is the 100th anniversary of the Toronto college and they would like to round it out with another Memorial Cup." Coach Charlie Cerre made no secret of the fact that he'd love nothing more to deliver a championship.

Stafford Smythe, general manager of the rival Marlboros, pointed to the Majors and said, "There is the team that could win the Memorial Cup in '53." Eleven members of the previous year's OHA semifinalist were returning, including Chadwick, defenceman Marc Reaume, and forwards Murray Costello and Bill Dineen. The Duff brothers, Dick and Les, also joined the Majors that year — Dick had graduated from the Junior 'B' Buzzers, as had Jack Caffery, considered the best Junior 'B' player in Ontario the previous season.

St. Mike's had a not-so-secret weapon at their disposal that fall. Father Don Faught, manager of that year's edition of the Majors, and the team's coach, Charlie Cerre, took great strides to make certain that the Majors had every opportunity to win the Junior championship. They secured the services of Lloyd Percival, a well-known Canadian fitness expert, to help their student athletes prepare for battle. "Percival has charts, graphs and barrels-full of statistics to prove that most athletes could improve their efficiency if they consumed more grapes, figs and raisins and eliminated frilly desserts," stated *The Globe*. "After a game, most Junior hockey players rush for the refreshment booth to stoke up on soft drinks, chocolate bars and hotdogs. St. Mike's players usually regard these tempting items longingly and settle for an apple. If St. Mike's keep on winning hockey games, the Ontario Fruit Growers Association should do a landslide business with some of the other teams."

Stafford Smythe smirked when he learned of Percival's role with the Majors. "He's been out there with a stopwatch, although what a stopwatch has to do with it, I don't know!"

Percival's employment by the Majors was controversial at the time, but proved to be just one more area in which Charlie Cerre's vision was confirmed by history. Percival's *The Hockey Handbook*, published in 1951, had been summarily dismissed by the leadership of the National Hockey League at the time. Dick Irvin, coaching the Montreal Canadiens to a Stanley Cup championship in 1952–53, his fourth Cup win as a coach, wrote off Percival's coaching notions as "the product of a three-year-old mind." The mere thought of goal setting, breath control, and using gymnastics to train was scoffed at by hockey experts in North America. But across the Atlantic Ocean, the reaction was entirely different. Anatoli Tarasov seized the contents of the book and used much of it as the foundation of one of the most amazing hockey programs ever created.

The OHA schedule saw St. Mike's open its season October 9 as the visiting team in a 7–5 win over St. Catharines. Rookie Jack Caffery scored two goals in his debut, while Les Duff scored his first Junior 'A' goal. It was the first time in five years that St. Mike's had won the opening game of the season.

The Majors opened at home as the second half of an October 12 Sunday afternoon doubleheader at Maple Leaf Gardens. Following the Marlboros game against Oshawa, the Majors faced the Windsor Spitfires. St. Mike's spanked the Spits, 10–0. Captain Bill Dineen earned a hooking penalty three seconds into the game, and followed it with a 10-minute misconduct for arguing the infraction, but the Majors had no difficulty with Windsor, who managed but 10 shots on Ed Chadwick. Murray Costello recorded a hat trick, Caffery scored in his second straight game, and Windsor native Marc Reaume also scored.

The long-standing rivalry between the Marlboros and Majors saw the results tilted very much in favour of St. Mike's in 1952–53, despite the presence of future NHL stars Billy Harris and Eric Nesterenko in the Marlboro lineup. In the first meeting of the season between the two teams, the Majors had the upper hand, winning 9–3. St. Mike's defence corps of Art Clune, Noel Price, Marc Reaume, and Ted Toppazzini "spread Marlies around like cheese," according to *The Globe and Mail*. Murray Costello netted a hat trick and rookie Jack Caffery picked up two more goals in the romp. "As far as I'm concerned, the whole team [Marlboros] is lousy," sighed Marlie GM Stafford Smythe.

The Globe and Mail acknowledged the strength of the Majors. "There doesn't appear to be a team at large capable of stopping the St. Michael's College Majors from winning the Memorial Cup. Day after day, the Majors mow down the rest of the Big Nine teams with the calculated ruthlessness of a harvesting combine."

That year's schedule included an idea introduced by Sam Pollock. The OHA's Junior 'A' teams played an interlocking schedule with the Quebec Junior Hockey League. In the first of these meetings, St. Michael's edged Henri Richard and the Montreal Royals 3–2 at Maple Leaf Gardens. Later, the Majors dumped the Quebec Citadelles, 7–2.

But as is too often the case, injuries wreaked havoc on the squad. In November, six regulars were out of the St. Mike's lineup: Costello, Dineen, Paul Knox, Paul Megaffin, Price, and Reaume. In their place, Billy Colvin, Jerry Cronin, Dick Duff, John Pascht, and Jerry Retty were called up from the Buzzers. It appeared as though Costello's absence might extend further, as the Chicago Black Hawks, who owned his rights, threatened to call the forward up for assignment to the big team by November 15. In desperation, Coach Cerre shuffled his talent further. When Dineen returned from a concussion suffered against Barrie earlier in the season, he was shifted to defence in order to replace the injured Marc Reaume. In a late-November game, Cerre had just 12 players in uniform.

While St. Michael's struggled, the Marlboros, who had more depth at their disposal, gained ground. When the rivals met in December, the Marlies prevailed 6–1. The Majors knew it was going to be a long night when, at the 59-second mark of the first period, Dave Reid passed the puck out from behind the St. Mike's goal, but it hit Chadwick's skates and dribbled back over the goal line. "A couple of months ago, there was a slight clamour to call off the Junior hockey season and give the Memorial Cup to the St. Michael's College Majors, who were running over everybody in sight, including the Marlboros," wrote *The Globe and Mail*.

Coach Charlie Cerre instituted a tough "win or else" campaign at St. Mike's. Many of the boys were assessed fines for various infractions, and Ed Chadwick was benched until he lost 10 pounds. On December 20, Gerry McNamara started in goal instead of Chadwick, and St. Mike's lost to the TeePees, 4–3, in overtime. In a rematch the next night, the Majors were up 5–0 at the end of the first period, but the kids from St. Catharines roared back for a 5–5 tie. "The Majors, panicked and bewitched, floundered in the third and blew a four-goal lead right out the window," reported *The Globe*.

With Christmas over and Ed Chadwick down to an acceptable 190 pounds, St. Michael's worked out a 5–3 win over Galt on December 27, but lost 6–2 to Kitchener the next night. Faced with a winner on paper but a losing team on the ice, coach Charlie

Cerre was taking extraordinary criticism. A tour of Quebec in early January proved to be just what the doctor ordered. On New Year's Day, the Majors trounced Trois-Rivières, 9–2, then tied the Quebec Citadelles, 2–2, before a crowd of 14,000. "Maybe things are going to get better now," sighed Father Faught. The Majors then defeated the Montreal Royals, 3–2, with several hundred St. Mike's alumni witnessing from the stands. But on January 6, a Montreal Jr. Canadiens team that included Charlie Hodge and Phil Goyette beat St. Mike's, 4–1. Before the game, Toronto's Art Clune collapsed in the hotel lobby, suffering from a severe throat infection.

Back in Ontario, a string of victories for St. Michael's followed into February, when the injury curse again visited the Majors. In a February loss to Kitchener, Ted Toppazzini separated his shoulder, removing him from the lineup for the remainder of the season. "It's an awful blow," said Father Faught. "Of all our players, we could afford to lose him least."

Then, in a bitterly contested game between the Majors and the Marlies, further disaster struck. Paul Megaffin of St. Michael's, who had just returned to the team after breaking a wrist, was checked heavily into the boards behind the St. Mike's net by Lou Bendo of the Marlboros. Bendo was called for a boarding major and was skating to the penalty box when Marc Reaume came at him, swinging. A fight broke out, and as Megaffin was getting to his feet, Marlie tough guy Gerry James arrived out of nowhere and cold-cocked Megaffin, who fell back with James on top of him and hit his head on the ice. "James was astraddle the fallen figure, throwing punches wildly, when the unconscious Megaffin suddenly went into convulsions, legs twitching sickeningly," reported *The Globe and Mail*. "The fighting stopped with the suddenness of a cannon shot. Megaffin's teeth were pried apart by [referee] Holmshaw's whistle and he was rushed from the ice on a stretcher, examined quickly by Gardens doctors, and taken to Toronto General Hospital. [Majors coach] Charlie Cerre labelled the incident one of the 'cruellest, most vicious' displays he had ever seen."

The wrath of the crowd fell on James for the balance of the game. "In some semblance of fairness to James, it seemed doubtful that he knew there was anything seriously wrong with Megaffin as he was pummelling him," stated *The Globe*. "He was simply following a time-honoured custom, unique to hockey, of continuing to punch whether or not an opponent is helplessly flat on his back."

It seems a moot point that the Majors won the contest, 3–1.

In a 7–2 win over Oshawa on February 22, goaltender Ed Chadwick took a deflected shot to the forehead at the five-minute mark of the first. He was knocked cold and cut for three stitches, then replaced by McNamara. When the Majors faced Guelph the following week, Chadwick was back in goal, but appeared gun-shy on high shots. Ron Murphy scored six goals in an 8–6 Guelph victory.

The 1952–53 season concluded with the Barrie Flyers in first place, grabbing 76 points through the 56-game campaign. Second went to the Marlboros, while St. Mike's finished third with 69 points.

The Majors had eight team members finish the season with 20 goals or better: Jack Caffery (37), Murray Costello (30), Ed Plata (29), Bill Dineen (27), Jim Logan and Mike Ratchford (23), Paul Knox (21), and Bill Lee (20). Caffery was the leading point-getter for St. Mike's, with 76.

❖

The quarterfinals pitted the Majors against the St. Catharines TeePees. They swept the series in three straight games, but lost Jim Logan in Game Two when he skidded into the end boards at full speed, breaking his leg after scoring what turned out to be the winning goal.

Next up were the Galt Black Hawks. "It will be a hard series with Galt," Father Don Faught predicted, "but if we skate all out, I think we can take them."

With Ed Chadwick winging his way to Pittsburgh to play in his first professional hockey game (he backstopped the American Hockey League Hornets to 3–1 victory over

1952–53					
TEAM	GP	W	L	T	Pts
Barrie Flyers	56	37	17	2	76
Toronto Marlboros	56	32	17	7	71
St. Michael's Majors	56	31	18	7	69
St. Catharines TeePees	56	31	20	5	67
Galt Black Hawks	56	27	26	3	57
Oshawa Generals	56	24	29	3	51
Guelph Biltmore Mad Hatters	56	22	32	2	46
Windsor Spitfires	56	16	35	5	37
Kitchener Greenshirts	56	15	38	3	33

Ed Chadwick stands ready at the edge of his crease, preparing to turn back a scoring chance.

the Providence Reds), Gerry McNamara got the start for St. Mike's in Game One, a 7–4 win in which Paul Knox connected for a hat trick in his second straight game. But Galt rebounded well, pulling out a 5–1 win with four goals against Chadwick in the third period of Game Two.

Rookie Dick Duff earned accolades in Game Three. "The wee one barged into everyone in sight, picked a fight with the biggest opponent he could find [Moe Mantha] and just generally made a nuisance of himself as St. Mike's whipped the Galt Black Hawks 6–3," reported the *Globe and Mail*. Billy Dineen scored a hat trick in the game.

Game Four was an overtime thriller that saw the Hawks inhaling oxygen on the bench in a 2–2 draw. But St. Mike's made no mistake in Game Five, firing five goals past Les Binkley in the third period to earn a 9–3 victory. Jack Caffery was the hero for the Majors, potting three goals.

St. Michael's eliminated Galt with a 6–5 win in Game Six, allowing them to face the Barrie Flyers in a best-of-nine series to decide the OHA championship.

In spite of playing their sixth game in eight days, Barrie drew first blood with a 4–1 win. Game Two saw Dick Duff lead his Majors to a 5–3 win. "A 16-year-old with three more Junior years ahead of him, this lad plays for keeps," marvelled the *Globe and Mail*. Father Faught silenced the team's critics when he boasted, "We had the legs and have had them since Lloyd Percival took over as full-time trainer in mid-January."

The Flyers took Game Three by a decisive 5–2 margin, but St. Michael's came back with a 6–4 win in Game Four. "We should award the series to St. Mike's," stated Flyers coach Hap Emms. "They've got too many thoroughbreds for us. This club [Barrie] doesn't care. I've got too many prima donnas. They think they're all stars, but there's not one on the whole club!" The Barrie lineup, by the way, featured Don Cherry, Don McKenney, Doug Mohns, Skip Teal, and Orval Tessier.

Prior to Game Five, former Majors coach Joe Primeau awarded the St. Michael's Old Boys' Trophy to Art Clune as the team's most valuable player in 1952–53. After the game, Primeau made comments on what he had observed through the game. "That little Duff seems to do everything right," he said. "He uses his body, doesn't give the puck away and has a beautiful shot. Duff is certainly a top pro prospect."

That night, the squad beat Barrie 6–4. During the contest, Flyers goaltender Bill Harrington was injured when he collided with Jack Higgins, his own defenceman. Harrington was replaced by George Cyclic, a 17-year-old Juvenile goalie. In the meantime, Barrie's coach, Hap Emms, tried to secure Charlie Hodge from the Montreal Junior Canadiens, but the request was refused by the OHA. He then tried to obtain the services of John Henderson from the eliminated Toronto Marlboros, but was rebuffed by Stafford Smythe. "I am opposed to the principle of a team receiving help from another club because of injury," said Smythe. "St. Michael's is a Maple Leaf Gardens–sponsored club. Why should we help another club to beat them? St. Michael's lost Ted Toppazzini and Jim Logan. They didn't ask for replacements."

The Barrie Flyers received permission to use Marv Edwards of the St. Catharines TeePees in goal, and in Game Six, proceeded to edge St. Mike's, 5–4. Momentum shifted, and the Flyers took Game 7 by a 6–4 margin, and won the OHA Cup, their fourth championship in six seasons, with a 4–2 win in Game Eight. "Edwards made stops that sank a brilliant, hard-skating, courageous St. Michael's College team," said *The Globe and Mail*. Ted Toppazzini, playing his first game in two months, was inserted into the St. Mike's lineup in the losing cause.

Hap Emms explained why the Flyers were able to beat the Majors: "If they had rested Bill Dineen just a little, he might have been able to lead them all the way back. But that kid, who is the greatest player in the league and the best in this series, was too tired. I don't blame Cerre. Dineen was his big wheel."

"We were in there right to the last," sighed Cerre. "Nobody thought we could do it, but that experience was too much."

Don McKenney, the Barrie captain, accepted the OHA Cup on behalf of his teammates. Ironically, he had scored the series-winning goal for the Flyers, who then went on to challenge the Quebec Citadelles for the eastern Canadian championship and a shot at the Memorial Cup.

"We came very close to getting a shot at the Memorial Cup," says Murray Costello. "That last year, Bob Schiller, a hard-hitting defenceman for us, decided to go into the seminary, and although he didn't stay there, it caused him to miss the season. Had we had one more defenceman of his calibre, it would have made the difference. We got beat out by Barrie in a long series that year and we missed out on a shot at the Memorial Cup."

Several members of the St. Michael's College Majors played their final Junior games that night: Ed Chadwick, Art Clune, Bill Dineen, Bill Lee, and Ed Plata. It would turn out to be the last game in the uniform of the Majors for Murray Costello as well.

Although the rights to most of the boys playing with the Majors belonged to the Toronto Maple Leafs, Costello was owned by the Chicago Black Hawks. "I insisted that they let me go to St. Mike's and they did," he states. "It was interesting the way the Leafs organization worked. On Sunday afternoons, we would go down to Maple Leaf Gardens for our game. The custodians at each of the pass gates were veterans and they got to know us all. All the other guys just flipped through but each time, I had to stop and show my pass because I wasn't in the Leafs chain, I was with the Chicago chain. They made me toe the mark. That was Conn Smythe doing his thing, but that was okay."

After graduating from St. Michael's College following the 1952–53 season, Murray still had a year of Junior eligibility remaining, so he was sent to play with Chicago's OHA affiliate, the Galt Black Hawks. "Having completed Grade 13, I didn't have the education thing to use as an excuse to stay at St. Mike's, so I was sent to Galt. I only played three games there before they called me up to the Black Hawks. They allowed you three games before you lost your amateur status, and they kept me for a fourth, so I turned pro and stayed with Chicago."

Murray played 40 games with Chicago in 1953–54 and was traded to Boston before the next season. Then, in January 1956, he was swapped to the Detroit Red Wings. Costello's final NHL season was 1956–57. In 162 NHL games, Murray scored 13 goals and assisted on 19 others, for a total of 32 points.

SNAPSHOT ▸▸ ▸▸ ▸▸ ▸▸ ▸▸ ▸▸ ▸▸ ▸▸   *Lloyd Percival:* A Major Influence on St. Mike's

After starring as a teenaged athletic prodigy, Lloyd Percival came to the realization that natural ability could take an athlete to a certain plateau, but that inherent athleticism could be eclipsed with proper nutrition and fitness. Beginning as a student at Whitney Public School in Toronto's Rosedale neighborhood, Lloyd excelled in baseball, boxing, cricket, football, gymnastics, hockey, tennis, and track and field. In order to advance his understanding of sport dynamics, he scoured North America — including the University of Southern California and Notre Dame — for better training ideas. By 1941, at the age of 28, Percival used his knowledge to launch a radio show called *Sports College* that introduced theories on coaching young athletes through proper fitness and diet. The program went nationwide in 1944 and ran on the CBC for 21 years.

Skeptics cast aspersions on Percival and his ideas, but he was determined to transform training practices through his methods. "It's an anomaly of Canadian sports culture that foreign athletes thrive on Percival's advice, which is almost unanimously ignored by his own country," said *The Globe and Mail.* "Lloyd Percival, in short, is a prophet without honour in his own country. He is viewed with suspicion by most Canadian sports authorities while being respected in European athletic circles."

But Percival found one believer in Charlie Cerre, the coach of the St. Michael's Majors. Cerre had read many of his books, manuals, and pamphlets, but had also admired his work with the highly successful North Toronto Red Devils Track Club. There, Percival used pioneering methods of training, including strength development and interval training that were commonplace in Europe but had yet to be accepted in Canada. It was difficult to argue with his success — the Red Devils claimed almost 6,000 track and field medals through the 1950s.

Cerre invited Percival to train the St. Michael's Majors — in so doing, earning the sneers of several on the school's faculty, as well as more vocal critics like Toronto Marlboros manager Stafford Smythe. That season, Lloyd Percival was awarded a Coronation medal by Queen Elizabeth for his contributions to Canadian fitness and sport. In 1963, he created the Fitness Institute, an athletic complex equipped with computerized fitness apparatus as well as a track, a gymnasium, and facilities in which to swim and play racquet sports. This landmark concept, so prevalent today, broke new ground by marrying science with fitness. All members would undergo a battery of tests to determine what areas needed to be improved upon. A specific training program, unique to each member, would then be established to enhance personal fitness and athletic performance.

By 1970, Percival's methods were being gradually accepted, and he was hired as a consultant to Hockey Canada, the Canadian Olympic Association and the Coaching Association of Canada.

Prior to the Summit Series of 1972, Soviet coach Anatoli Tarasov thanked Percival for introducing him to new coaching methods through *The Hockey Handbook.* Tarasov's letter praised Percival for "your wonderful book, which introduced us to the mysteries of Canadian hockey. I have read it with the enthusiasm of a schoolboy. Thank you for a hockey science which is significant to world hockey." Tarasov praised the book for allowing Soviet teams to train more intelligently and show Canada that it was not the only country in the world that could play hockey at an elite level.

Lloyd Percival's philosophies and methods continue to influence sports today, even though he died in 1974 at the age of 61. At the end of each training session with the St. Michael's Majors, Percival would recite his mantra: "Keep fit, work hard, play fair, live clean."

17
Heartbreak in St. Kitts

Changes in the OHA Junior 'A' alignment for 1953–54 included the move of the Detroit Red Wings' junior affiliate from Windsor to Hamilton, where they were known as the Tiger Cubs. And the Oshawa Generals were forced to drop out when their home rink, the Hambly Arena, was destroyed by fire. That left eight teams competing for the John Ross Robertson Cup.

The St. Catharines TeePees finished first, scoring 308 goals, 48 more than any of their competition. Barrie's Flyers had to be disappointed with their seventh-place finish after finishing first the year before. St. Michael's came in fourth.

Gerry McNamara was in goal for the Majors, with Marc Reaume (14 goals and 41 points) and Noel Price (team bad boy with 157 minutes in penalties) on defence. Forwards included 40-goal scorer Paul Knox; Dick Duff, who led the team with 75 points; 20-goal scorers Jack Caffery, Billy Colvin, Ken Gribbons, and Jim Logan; and Les Duff, who contributed scoring (55 points) and toughness (145 penalty minutes). The team was captained by Ted Toppazzini, while Charlie Cerre entered his third season as coach of the St. Michael's Majors.

On February 2, 1954, St. Michael's players were forced to deny a report that they had held a players-only meeting to discuss their frustrations with Coach Cerre, following a 5–2 loss to the Montreal Junior Canadiens. The report claimed that players complained of their coach's "poor handling of line changes and that he had not been tough enough."

A meeting had, in fact, taken place, attended by the players as well as Father Faught and trainer Lloyd Percival. "We discussed the condition of the players and went over some of our problems and that's all," insisted Father Faught. "I met with Charlie before the meeting and he knew what was to take place."

The players issued a statement that insisted "they were proud to have Charlie Cerre as a coach and would deeply resent any move to have him removed."

"After hugging bottom spot in the league standings for the first part of the 1953–54 season, the Majors climbed to the top by February," hailed the school yearbook. But at the end of the regular season, the Majors had settled into fourth place, with a record of 30 wins, 26 losses, and three ties.

They met the first-place St. Catharines Teepees in the playoff semifinals. "The tension burst a few lines of inspiration," chuckled *The Thurible*. In the eighth game of a seven-game series, both the score and the series were tied. But the TeePees scored to win the game and eliminate the Majors.

"We trailed Toronto St. Michael's by one goal late in a playoff," recalled TeePees coach Rudy Pilous in a *Globe and Mail* interview. "We pulled [netminder] Marv Edwards, even though the faceoff was in our own end. All of their players headed for the empty net." Cerre played all his men up, anticipating that they would win the faceoff and be able to control the play. Meantime, the TeePees won the faceoff and headed straight towards Gerry McNamara, past St. Mike's players who were trapped in the TeePees zone. Crushing Majors players and fans alike, Hugh Barlow of St. Catharines scored on McNamara with 28 seconds remaining in the third. With the game tied at the end of regulation, the teams treaded into overtime. Cerre and his players could only hang their heads in frustration as the TeePees scored to win the game and the series. Added Pilous, "We squeezed 4,200 people into the Garden City Rink for that game, but I've met 40,000 who said they saw it!" The TeePees went on to win the Memorial Cup in 1954.

1953–54					
TEAM	GP	W	L	T	Pts
St. Catharines TeePees	59	42	15	2	86
Toronto Marlboros	59	34	18	7	75
Hamilton Tiger Cubs	58	31	24	3	65
St. Michael's Majors	59	30	26	3	63
Kitchener Greenshirts	59	27	27	5	59
Guelph Biltmore Mad Hatters	59	26	31	2	54
Barrie Flyers	59	25	33	1	51
Galt Black Hawks	59	21	37	1	43

Paul Knox (left) and Les Duff of the Majors rejoice after putting the puck behind Marv Edwards of the St. Catharines TeePees.

Jack Caffery played his last of four seasons with the Majors in 1953–54 (he played just one game in both 1950–51 and 1951–52 while with the Buzzers), and had proven himself a terrific offensive centre, scoring 37 times in 1952–53 and 25 goals in 1953–54. While playing with the Maple Leafs' AHL farm team, the Pittsburgh Hornets, in 1954–55, he was called up to play with Toronto for three games in December, including a 2–1 loss to Chicago in his first NHL game on December 11. Jack was claimed by Boston in the 1956 Inter-League Draft and spent two seasons as a Bruin. In 57 regular-season NHL games, Caffery collected five points.

Noel Price patrolled the Majors' blue line for four seasons, beginning with the 1952–53 campaign, and played his first NHL game with Toronto on October 23, 1957, when the Leafs were shut out 3–0 by Gump Worsley and the New York Rangers. His next NHL games came with the Leafs during the following season. Noel later spent parts of two seasons with the Rangers, joined Detroit for part of 1961–62, and surfaced again in the NHL with the Montreal Canadiens in 1965–66, taking part in a Stanley Cup championship. Expansion gave Noel new possibilities, and he joined the Pittsburgh Penguins in their inaugural season. Price concluded his career with four seasons with the fledgling Atlanta Flames, retiring after the 1975–76 season. In 14 NHL seasons, Noel played 499 games and recorded 128 points.

Charlie Cerre: *Tic-Tac-Tician* — SNAPSHOT

Charlie Cerre, a speedy, smooth-skating centre, played with St. Michael's while he attended the school from 1926 to 1928. Most observers believed that Charlie would graduate to the NHL with his teammate Eddie Convey. But when a scout from the Chicago Black Hawks showed up at his family's home in Toronto's east end, Charlie's mother sent the scout away, stating that her son was going to be a priest and had no interest in playing professional hockey.

After graduating from St. Michael's College in 1932, Charlie did follow the path predicted by his mother, attending the seminary at Assumption College in Windsor. But after three years, he realized that a life in the priesthood wasn't for him.

Cerre earned his teaching degree in 1943, but, finding no jobs, moved to Sudbury and worked in the Inco nickel mine, also playing and coaching the company's baseball team. Never forgetting his roots, Cerre visited St. Mike's every time he was in Toronto, and formed a northern Ontario chapter of the St. Michael's Old Boys Association. He eventually secured a position teaching mathematics and physical education at Sudbury High School, and also coached the football and hockey teams. Maintaining his contacts at St. Mike's, Cerre was dogged in his efforts to have the school bring one of his football players into the fold to play hockey. His persistence paid huge dividends for the school, as Tim Horton was one of the few bright lights for the Majors during his two-year stint at the school, beginning in 1947–48.

After several years in northern Ontario, Cerre was asked to teach at St. Michael's in 1951, doubling as coach of the Junior 'A' Majors. Known for his fanatical attention to statistics as much as he was for his conservative business suits and argyle socks, "He kept everything on paper and some of his plays and drills were works of art," his son Paul recalled fondly. "They were almost scientific." In what can now be regarded as nothing short of revolutionary, Cerre also brought in renowned fitness expert Lloyd Percival to work with his players.

Charlie Cerre coached the St. Michael's College Majors from 1951 to 1955, then relinquished his coaching duties in order to concentrate solely on teaching. He stayed at St. Michael's College until 1958, then moved to Alderwood Collegiate, where he taught until his retirement in 1975.

Cerre was inducted into the Order of St. Michael's by St. Michael's College School on November 12, 1999. The Order of St. Michael's was founded to honour alumni and friends who have demonstrated and promoted the values of St. Michael's College School — goodness, discipline and knowledge — in their lives. Charlie Cerre's lifelong dedication to the Lord continued until October 5, 2002, when he died peacefully at the age of 93.

18
Leaving Their Mark

The St. Catharines TeePees and Guelph Biltmores tied for first place in the OHA in 1954–55, both earning 66 points on 32 wins, 15 losses and two ties. The standoff was broken by goals scored, with the TeePees having netted a league-best 260 to the Biltmores' 211. Third place went to the Toronto Marlboros, guided by their new coach, former goaltending great Turk Broda. St. Mike's took fourth with 56 points on 26 wins, 19 losses, and four ties.

The Majors were paced by the Duff brothers in 1954–55. Both of them feisty wingers from Kirkland Lake, Dick led the Majors in scoring with 33 goals and 20 assists for 53 points in 1954–55, good for fifth place in the league, while sitting out 113 minutes in penalties. His older brother Les, the team captain, finished second on the team in scoring, accumulating 51 points on 13 goals and 38 assists. He served 112 penalty minutes. Billy Colvin also enjoyed a strong 51-point season. Brian Anderson benefited from the Duffs' playmaking and earned 30 points. Frank Mahovlich played just half the season, but contributed 12 goals and 23 points in his 25 games. Gerry McNamara was a rock in goal for the Majors.

McNamara was recruited from Sturgeon Falls, Ontario, to play hockey at St. Michael's. He was a backup netminder to Ed Chadwick in 1951–52 and 1952–53, playing five games in the first season and 10 in the next. After serving his apprenticeship, McNamara took over as the principal goaltender in 1953–54 and in 1954–55.

Goaltending jobs were scarce in the National Hockey League during the 1950s. NHL teams were only required to carry one goalie at that time, and with only six teams, none of the six jobs were about to be relinquished readily. While Gerry waited his turn, he played with a plethora of teams in a variety of leagues: Pittsburgh, Hershey, Buffalo, Cleveland, and Rochester in the American league, Winnipeg and Portland in the Western league, Sudbury of the Eastern Professional Hockey League, Charlotte of the Eastern Hockey League, and North York, the Marlies, and Orillia in the OHA's Senior loop. Through the many moves, McNamara played five games for the Toronto Maple Leafs in 1960–61 and two in 1969–70. His NHL record is seven games played with two wins, two losses, and a tie.

After retiring as a player in 1973, he took a scouting position with the Maple Leafs, and was instrumental in securing Borje Salming from Sweden. By 1981–82, McNamara had been promoted to general manager of the Toronto Maple Leafs and stayed in the position until he was relieved of his duties in February 1988. It was a dark era for the Toronto Maple Leafs. Owner Harold Ballard was at his most cantankerous, and as good a GM as McNamara might have been, his power was usurped by the eccentric owner, and the team suffered for it on the ice.

Although third-place finishers in 1954–55, the Toronto Marlboros were on a tear in the post-season and not only beat the defending Memorial Cup champions, the TeePees, for the OHA championship, but proceeded to collect the Memorial Cup themselves.

❖

"Behind the constellation of stars stood these two men, respected, admired and loved by each and every player on the team." So said *The Thurible* about Father John Crowley, the Majors' new coach, and alumnus Joe Primeau, coach of the 1945 and '47 championship teams who had been recruited as an advisor to Father Crowley. The moves came as a result of the resignation, prior to the commencement of the 1955–56 season, of coach

1954–55

TEAM	GP	W	L	T	Pts
St. Catharines TeePees	49	32	15	2	66
Guelph Biltmore Mad Hatters	49	32	15	2	66
Toronto Marlboros	49	29	17	3	61
St. Michael's Majors	49	26	19	4	56
Hamilton Tiger Cubs	49	21	23	5	47
Galt Black Hawks	49	18	25	6	42
Barrie Flyers	49	18	31	0	36
Kitchener Canucks	49	8	39	2	18

The 1954–55 squad featured future Toronto Maple Leafs GM Gerry McNamara in goal (seated, far left), as well as brothers Dick and Les Duff (top row, far left) and Frank Mahovlich (top row, fourth from left).

Charlie Cerre. Father Crowley was familiar with the Majors, having served as team manager under Cerre the previous season and having been associated with the club for nine years.

Owing to the withdrawal of the Galt Black Hawks, the OHA Junior 'A' league was made up of seven teams this season, and St. Catharines placed first, with 59 points, while St. Mike's came in fifth with 47.

Pat Hannigan led the team in scoring with 69 points, giving him a third-place finish in the league's scoring race. His 38 goals were second best in the league. Frank Mahovlich finished ninth in the league with 24 goals and added 26 assists. Other notable Majors included Lou Angotti, Reg Fleming, Dick Mattiussi, Bob Pallante, Noel Price, and captain Bob Watt. Goaltending was split between Bob Savage and Tom Kelly, supplemented for two games by Don Keenan.

The Majors met the Guelph Biltmore Mad Hatters in the first round of the playoffs, with St. Mike's upsetting the heavily favoured Biltmores. Up next were the Barrie Flyers. Feeling that St. Mike's could be beaten by simply stopping Frank Mahovlich, Barrie coach Hap Emms shadowed the Majors' star with Gord Loveday. The strategy was effective, and St. Michael's lost the series to the Flyers.

Lou Angotti would take a circuitous route to the National Hockey League. He played three seasons with the Majors, beginning with the 1955–56 season, and bucked tradition by attending Michigan Tech University. During his four seasons at the U.S. college, Lou shone. He was a Western Collegiate Hockey Association All-Star in 1961 and 1962, and made the NCAA West's First All-America Team in 1962 as well. Angotti had long been coveted by the Maple Leafs, but they grew impatient and traded him to the New York Rangers in June 1964. He debuted in the NHL that fall. In January 1966, he was traded

1955–56					
TEAM	GP	W	L	T	Pts
St. Catharines TeePees	48	28	17	3	59
Kitchener Canucks	48	26	21	1	53
Guelph Biltmore Mad Hatters	48	25	20	3	53
Toronto Marlboros	48	23	21	4	50
St. Michael's Majors	48	22	23	3	47
Barrie Flyers	48	20	25	3	43
Hamilton Tiger Cubs	48	13	30	5	31

This close-knit group of teammates in 1955–56 included Gene Ubriaco (back row, far left), Lou Angotti (back row, third from left), Pat Hannigan (back row, second from right), Dick Mattiussi (middle row, far left), Noel Price (middle row, second from left), Reg Fleming (middle row, second from right), and Frank Mahovlich (front row, second from right).

to Chicago and was claimed by the Philadelphia Flyers in the 1967 Expansion Draft. One year in Philadelphia was followed by a season in Pittsburgh, then a return to the Black Hawks, where he remained for four seasons. His final NHL action was with the St. Louis Blues in 1973–74. He joined the Chicago Cougars of the World Hockey Association the following season. Lou collected 289 points through 653 regular-season games. He added seven points in 26 WHA contests. Following his playing career, Angotti coached the St. Louis Blues for parts of two seasons (1973–74 and 1974–75) and coached the Pittsburgh Penguins in 1983–84.

Reg Fleming arrived at St. Michael's College after playing two seasons with the Montreal Junior Canadiens. Playing defence, Fleming contributed nine points, as well as 93 minutes in penalties, in his sole season with the Majors before he returned to Quebec, playing for the Shawinigan Cataracts. He joined the Montreal Canadiens for three games in 1959–60, but was traded to the Chicago Black Hawks in June 1960. It was perfect timing for Reg — he added toughness to the lineup as the Hawks surprised the hockey world and won the Stanley Cup in 1960–61. After four seasons in Chicago, Fleming was traded to Boston. In 1965–66, he led the NHL in penalties in a season split between the Bruins and the New York Rangers. In 1969–70, it was on to the Philadelphia Flyers, and then to the Buffalo Sabres for their inaugural season in 1970–71. He later spent two seasons with the Chicago Cougars of the WHA. In 749 regular-season NHL games, Fleming earned 240 points, while also serving 1,468 minutes in penalties. While in the WHA, Fleming added 82 points in 119 games, and was called for 144 penalty minutes.

Pat Hannigan: The Refugee's Hero

SNAPSHOT

Like so many St. Mike's hockey players before him, Pat Hannigan felt a spiritual calling. In his case, it came later in life.

After he starred in Junior, Leaf owner Conn Smythe tried to get Pat to sign a contract with the team, but the young forward refused. Smythe, angered beyond belief, flew Pat's father to Toronto from Timmins in order to persuade the senior Hannigan that his "idiot son" should sign the contract. Mr. Hannigan stood bolt upright, looked Smythe in the eye, and stated, "I didn't raise any idiot sons," then left the office.

Ultimately, Pat signed with the Leafs, and after he did, he made his NHL debut on December 17, 1959, in an 8–2 loss to the Montreal Canadiens. It was the only game he would play for Toronto. Hannigan was traded to the New York Rangers with Johnny Wilson for Eddie Shack in November 1960, then traversed the continent pursuing his hockey dreams through minor-league teams in Baltimore, Portland, and Buffalo. His rights were traded from Detroit to Chicago, but he never cracked their NHL lineups. In the 1967 Expansion Draft, Pat's rights were secured by the Philadelphia Flyers and he played two seasons there before again traipsing through the minors, from Buffalo to Vancouver and, finally, to Phoenix.

Pat scored 30 goals and 39 assists in 182 regular-season NHL games. After retiring from hockey as a player, Hannigan provided colour commentary on Buffalo Sabres telecasts while working in the telephone industry from Fort Erie.

Then, in 1985, Pat Hannigan experienced an epiphany of sorts. It came while he was on a trip to Nicaragua with Development and Peace, a development organization of the Catholic Church of Canada, where he witnessed extreme poverty. Pat helped organize Casa El Norte, a haven for refugees, in Fort Erie. The Peace Bridge in that town is one of the largest points of entry for those refugees seeking asylum in Canada, and Casa El Norte serves as a welcome haven while claimants locate more permanent housing.

As Pat's health deteriorated, his fortitude grew as he forged friendships with refugees from all around the world, helping in any manner humanly possible. According to friends, he never missed a St. Michael's reunion, and he always insisted on wearing his Majors jacket. Pat's faith never wavered as he overcame heart surgery and kidney ailments. On December 11, 2007, he succumbed to a rare intestinal infection. He was 71 years of age.

19
Toronto's Civil War: The Majors vs. The Marlies

Between the mid-1940s and the early 1960s, you would be hard pressed to find a rivalry as intense as the one that existed between the St. Michael's Majors and Toronto Marlboros.

The rivalry was based partly in the fact that both teams played in the same city and both were often competitive at the same time. The Majors reached the OHA final in 1944, '45, '46, '47, '53, '59, '60, '61, and '62, winning the league championship in 1945, '46, '47, and '61 and extending those victories to Memorial Cup championships in 1945, 1947, and 1961. The Marlboros reached the league final in 1949, '51, '55, '56, and '58, winning the John Ross Robertson Trophy as OHA champions in 1955, '56, and '58 and taking the Memorial Cup in 1955 and '56.

But there was more to the rivalry than that — a deeper, more sinister rationale. While most National Hockey League teams sponsored one Junior team in the Ontario Hockey Association, the Toronto Maple Leafs had two, the Majors and the Marlboros, and both played their home games under the nose of Leafs brass at Maple Leaf Gardens. And for that reason, every single player on either team shared one goal: to wear the blue and white of the Toronto Maple Leafs.

With jobs in the NHL so scarce, and a substantial crop of minor-pro players already in the Toronto farm system, members of the two Junior squads looked upon their counterparts on the other team with suspicion. Will *I* be the one who makes the parent squad, they wondered, or will *he*?

Although there were exceptions, in general terms the differences between the two teams boiled down to religion and scholastics. "It seemed that a lot of players on the Marlies had given up on school or were working, so that seemed to be the delineation," comments Brian Conacher. "It gave the Leafs an option to place those that wanted to remain in school at St. Mike's, and those who didn't generally played on the Marlies. [Marlboros] Sonny Osborne and Jim Murchie were in university. And Dave Dryden was already a teacher. I didn't go to St. Mike's because I was already going to Upper Canada College."

Geography also played a role: many of the Marlies hailed from Toronto and the vicinity, while for prospects recruited from northern Ontario or western Canada, it was only logical to place them in the boarding-school environment of St. Michael's College. And during this 15-year period, the Leafs were finding a great deal of fine talent in northern Ontario, including Les, Murray, and Jack Costello; Dick and Les Duff; Gord, Ray, and Pat Hannigan; Tim Horton; David Keon (from Noranda, Quebec, not far from the mining country of northern Ontario); Frank and Pete Mahovlich; and many others.

Murray Costello recalls the bitter rivalry between the two teams. "The games against the Marlies were always tough. We always felt at St. Mike's that the intelligent guys who wanted to go to school went to St. Mike's and the grinders and guys who played tough went with the Marlies. The games were knock-down, drag 'em out battles each time. There was that kind of competition to be noticed by the Leaf brass."

Dave Keon agrees: "Everybody was hoping they ultimately were going to get the chance to play with the Leafs. They wanted to show who was going to play the best and

The storied rivalry between the St. Michael's Majors and the Toronto Marlboros, both Junior affiliates of the Toronto Maple Leafs, continued until St. Michael's excused itself from Junior hockey. Here, Ron Stewart of the Marlboros prepares to unload on Ed Chadwick of the Majors. The two were teammates with the Maple Leafs through Chadwick's entire five-season stay in Toronto.

maybe try to impress enough so they had the chance to go to the next level. It was pretty heated."

Brian Conacher continues the thread. "Number one, most of those players were aspiring to play for the Toronto Maple Leafs. Their goal and objective was the same. The games between the Marlies and St. Michael's Majors were often on a Friday night at Maple Leaf Gardens, and they were the most competitive games of the whole season. Both teams wanted to impress the Leafs."

Arnie Brown straddled the line of the rivalry, playing for the Majors in 1959–60 and 1960–61, then joining the Marlboros in 1961–62. "The competition was hot. They were tough games. The Marlies had Turk Broda as the coach. Turk was one of those guys that wanted you to run over everybody. If you're going to beat them on the rink, you're going to beat them in the alley. Father Bauer's form of hockey was a more strategic and skilled game, but you had to have some guys who stood up or you'd get run right out of the rink. That was part of my role. I was always ready to do that."

Readers must remember that Toronto was a profoundly different city in this period than today. In 1950, the boundaries of Toronto encompassed a territory one-eighth the size of the present-day "megacity." According to a 1951 census, 73 percent of the residents of Toronto and its suburbs were ethnically British, and 72 percent reported that they were Protestant. Prevailing attitudes existed in Orange Toronto, and men like Conn Smythe did little to erase the divisions.

"The Marlie guys were mostly guys from Toronto who started in minor hockey there, and those teams were all run by the Leafs back then," explains Dick Duff, noting that most of the Marlboros' players were Protestant. "We [at St. Mike's] were the 'Micks.' In those days, there was still a lot of Catholic-Protestant rivalry in Toronto, in Montreal,

Frank Mahovlich, Carl Brewer, and Dave Keon of the Maple Leafs chat with St. Mike's star Gary Dineen while Father Rocco Volpe looks on.

and other places. The people who didn't like St. Mike's didn't necessarily not like them because of the colour of their uniform, but we all grew through that."

While it is convenient to look upon the Marlboros as being the Maple Leafs' Protestant team in junior hockey, with St. Michael's as the Catholic squad, there were notable exceptions. Tim Horton, for example, was Protestant, yet he attended St. Mike's in addition to playing for the Majors. The same is true of goaltender Ed Chadwick. Meanwhile, a devout Catholic such as Carl Brewer was a Marlboro.

The loyalty that evolved from attending St. Michael's College formed an intense camaraderie amongst alumni. "The guys from St. Mike's who played in the pros afterward had a common bond," recalls Dick Duff, "and sometimes we'd break up practices with the Leafs a bit by having the St. Mike's guys scrimmage against the Marlie guys."

In his autobiography, *Lowering the Boom*, Bobby Baun discussed the rivalry: "For those of us Marlies in [the Leafs training camp in 1955], there was the novelty of skating with real NHLers, but there was something else that took even more getting used to: the presence of St. Michael's Majors. We'd played against them in the OHA as if they were our mortal enemies. Now, we would have to get along as teammates. I noticed [that there] was a real animosity between the St. Michael's graduates and the players who'd come up through the Marlboros. It wasn't unexpected ... We fought frequently and viciously, to the point that our practices were tougher than most games. I always had a running battle with Dick Duff, and I know I took my chances with his brother Les. I may have even mixed it up with both of them at the same time."

For his part, Duff made certain that he kept his allegiance prominent. When the Leafs won the Stanley Cup in 1962 and '63, he says, the Majors alumni on the team "sang the St. Mike's song on the bus and on the plane and every other place we could so we could let people know where we came from. It meant a lot to us."

20
The Big M

Led by team captain Frank Mahovlich, who finished first in the OHA with 52 goals, and teammate Bobby Boucher, who collected 41 for a fifth-place finish in the scoring race, the Majors had little trouble generating offence during 1956–57. Mahovlich finished the season with 88 points, good for third best in the OHA, while Boucher finished fourth with 74. Despite the pyrotechnics, St. Michael's finished the regular season well back, in fourth place. The Guelph Biltmores led the OHA, finishing with 77 points, followed by the Marlboros at 73 points. The Peterborough TPTs (short for Toronto-Peterborough Transport), formerly the Kitchener Canucks franchise, brought up the rear with 23 points.

The team featured many players who went on to the NHL, including Lou Angotti, Jack Martin, Dick Mattiussi, Gerry Odrowski, Darryl Sly, and Gene Ubriaco. David Keon proved that he was indeed the future of the franchise, scoring a goal and three assists in the four games he played with the Majors after being promoted from the Buzzers during that season. Bob Savage was in goal for the Majors, although Gerry Cheevers was introduced to Junior 'A' play with a single game that season.

The league was dominated by three players throughout the season: Mahovlich of the Majors and Eddie Shack and Bill Sweeney of the Biltmores. Sweeney finished the season with 106 points and Shack with 104 to Mahovlich's 88. Mahovlich trumped the Mad Hatter duo by scoring 52 goals. Sweeney scored 49 and Shack 47. Although Sweeney took the Eddie Powers Trophy as the league's scoring leader, it was Frank Mahovlich who was selected as the league's outstanding player, earning the Red Tilson Memorial Trophy.

Gerry Odrowski had been recruited for St. Michael's from Trout Creek, just south of North Bay, Ontario. The promising left winger had his season curtailed in January 1957. "I ended up with appendicitis," he shrugs. "The thing ruptured and I ended up in the hospital for five days or more. When I got to the hospital on the Sunday night, the doctors came in and had had a few 'Pepsis' and things didn't work out too well. I woke up with a drain in me and I guess I was lucky to come off that [operating] table!"

Odrowski was fortunate to have teammates who cared so deeply. "Frank Mahovlich, Dick Mattiussi, Gene Ubriaco, and Jack McMaster used to borrow the priest's car to come down to see me," he relates with a laugh. "They'd only stay about five minutes and out the door they'd go, because they had the car for the evening. It was good to see them, but away they'd go!"

The camaraderie among the players was strong. "It was an unbelievable environment," Mike Draper says. "St. Mike's had hockey players coming in from all over the country, and a lot of the fellows I played Junior with are still very good friends of mine." From that 1956–57 squad, a group of men remain fast friends in spite of five decades having gone by. "Jack McMaster, Louie Angotti, Jack Martin, Bob McKnight, who was as good a Junior player as I've ever seen, Tom Micallef, Bobby Pallante, Gene Ubriaco. The friendships have continued through the years," smiles Draper. "They're all just wonderful human beings."

After finishing first in the regular-season standings, Guelph went on to win the John Ross Robertson Trophy as OHA champions, but were beaten by the Ottawa-Hull Canadiens for the Richardson Trophy as eastern Canadian champs. Ottawa-Hull was coached by Sam Pollock with Scotty Bowman as the assistant coach.

1956–57					
TEAM	GP	W	L	T	Pts
Guelph Biltmore Mad Hatters	52	37	12	3	77
Toronto Marlboros	52	35	14	3	73
St. Catharines TeePees	52	25	25	2	52
St. Michael's Majors	52	23	24	5	51
Hamilton Tiger Cubs	52	24	26	2	50
Barrie Flyers	52	13	37	2	28
Peterborough TPT Petes	52	11	40	1	23

Frank Mahovlich, captain of the 1956–57 version of the St. Michael's Majors, led the league with 52 goals.

Although the season could be described as little more than disappointing, much-loved Father Crowley, the team's coach, was described in the school yearbook as "quiet, yet forceful, cool and calm, yet resolute and courageous." *The Thurible* noted that Father Crowley and Joe Primeau "instilled such a love of clean play, such a spirit of raw courage, such a flaming surge of St. Mike's fight into the boys that St. Michael's points with pride to the Majors of '56–57, a team that lost on occasions but was never beaten."

The Mahovlich mailbox overflowed with correspondence from NHL teams eager to have the big winger join their organization.

Ode To Odrowski: *Gerry Odrowski*

SNAPSHOT

Former Maple Leafs defenceman Bucko McDonald can be thanked for helping send Bobby Orr to the National Hockey League, but the legendary Boston blueliner is not the only hockey prospect nurtured by the barrel-chested McDonald.

Gerry Odrowski was playing public-school hockey in Trout Creek, Ontario, when he caught the eye of McDonald. "He took me down to Sundridge, which was about 60 miles away, and had me playing Intermediate 'B' with the older fellows on the Sundridge Beavers [in 1955–56]," recalls Odrowski. "If we went on a road trip, I'd stay at his house overnight, and then he'd take me to school in the morning. Bucko was like a father to me."

McDonald maintained ties with the Maple Leafs and his former teammate, Bob Davidson, who by then was Toronto's chief scout. "Bob Davidson came up to talk to me at my parents' house when I was 18," continues Gerry. "They got me to sign a C-Form, I got a hundred bucks for it, and I went down to Toronto for a couple of tryouts. That was an eye-opener because it was the first time I was in Maple Leaf Gardens. I was a big Leafs fan. We had no TV then, so that's who we got on the radio."

After signing with the Toronto Maple Leafs, Odrowski was sent to St. Michael's College, where he played left wing for the Majors in 1956–57. "I was in Grade 12. I didn't like school that much but it was a way to get my education and start my hockey career. Back in those days, nobody had anything. Before the open-air rink was ready in December, we used to skate on the creeks and sometimes fall in, and skate on the fields where the water laying there had frozen over. And we'd walk to these places and then put our skates on. By the time we got ready to go home, our feet were so cold we'd have to go home and put them in the old wood stove."

In his only season with St. Mike's, Gerry collected one assist, and when he arrived for training camp prior to the 1957–58 season, St. Mike's suggested Gerry play Junior 'B' with the Buzzers. "I said, 'I don't know. That's going backwards,'" he says. "Bucko was up in Sault Ste. Marie with a Senior 'A' team at the time. They were in Kitchener for a game and Bucko said, 'Come on over and play for me.' I said, 'How can I do that?' He said, 'Don't worry about anything! Get on the bus and get over here.'"

Gerry arrived and played left wing for the Sault Ste. Marie Greyhounds of the Northern Ontario Hockey Association, but shortly afterwards, McDonald suggested Odrowski convert to defence, a move Bucko would also later make with a young prospect named Orr. "After I left St. Mike's, that was the end of my C-Form. Toronto didn't renew it," says Gerry. "But when I was up in the Soo, Pep Kelly from North Bay was watching me. He got hold of Detroit and said, 'You should be watching him.' After the first year, I went to Detroit's training camp and thought, 'These guys don't play any better than I do or skate any faster.' I thought I had a chance to make the team."

After two years in the Soo, Gerry turned professional with the Sudbury Wolves of the Eastern Professional Hockey League (EPHL) and was named the league's top defenceman. By 1960–61, he was a member of the Detroit Red Wings, and that season went to the Stanley Cup final against the Chicago Black Hawks. After two seasons with the Red Wings, Odrowski was traded to the Boston Bruins and spent the next several seasons plying his trade in the minors. But with NHL expansion in 1967, Gerry got a second break and became a member of the Oakland Seals. He played with the St. Louis Blues in 1971–72, then spent four seasons in the World Hockey Association, playing with the Los Angeles Sharks, Phoenix Roadrunners, Winnipeg Jets, and Minnesota Fighting Saints before retiring following the 1975–76 season.

"When I went to St. Mike's, we used to go to Mass every morning," Gerry recalls fondly. "I helped the priests as an altar boy. That really stuck with me. It made a better person out of me."

21
Keon's Coming-Out Party

1957–58					
Team	GP	W	L	T	Pts
St. Catharines TeePees	52	32	14	6	70
Hamilton Tiger Cubs	52	27	18	7	61
St. Michael's Majors	52	23	22	7	53
Toronto Marlboros	52	21	21	10	52
Peterborough TPT Petes	52	21	25	6	48
Barrie Flyers	51	18	29	4	40
Guelph Biltmore Mad Hatters	52	13	34	5	31

David Keon was recruited by the Toronto Maple Leafs, who again used the promise of a Roman Catholic education at St. Michael's College as bait to secure his services.

In one of the more stunning slides in Junior 'A' history, the Guelph Biltmores — league champions in 1956–57 — plummeted like a broken elevator, falling from first to worst in 1957–58. St. Catharines finished first, while St. Mike's edged out the Marlboros for third place.

Surprisingly, it was the fourth-place Toronto Marlboros who emerged as league champions, but more remarkably, it was the Ottawa-Hull Canadiens, a Junior team without a league, that went on to collect the Memorial Cup. The squad, coached by Scotty Bowman, played a ragtag schedule of games against OHA Junior 'A' teams, Senior teams, and some minor pro teams, and even though they did not participate in the OHA playoffs, they earned the right to challenge the Junior 'A' champions (the Marlboros) for the eastern Canadian championship. It was the second year in a row that the Junior Canadiens competed for the Memorial Cup.

St. Michael's welcomed Bob Goldham as coach in 1957–58, replacing Father Crowley. Goldham had spent 12 years in the NHL, and was acknowledged as one of the finest defencemen of his era. After a sniff of Junior 'A' play the year before, David Keon was promoted to the Majors and proceeded to lead the team in scoring. His 23 goals tied him with Lou Angotti, but the slick-skating centre earned 50 points to Angotti's 42. Others making impressive offensive contributions were Jack Costello (40 points), Darryl Sly (39), and Gene Ubriaco (37). Bob McKnight captained the Majors that season. The Brothers Draper all played with the Majors as well. Older sibling Mike was a regular with the team, but twins Bruce and Dave saw their first Junior 'A' action, each playing two games.

Popular Gene Ubriaco spent four seasons with the Majors, and provided offensive punch to the team. After scoring just twice in limited duty in 1954–55, he put up seasons of 26, 22, and 19 goals. The Toronto Maple Leafs owned Ubriaco's rights, but the Sault Ste. Marie native didn't fit their plans, so in September 1963 he was traded to the Hershey Bears of the AHL, along with the rights to Bruce Draper, in exchange for Les Duff. Ubriaco became a leading scorer for the Bears, as well as one of the many fine players who never got their shot in the NHL until the expansion of 1967. The Pittsburgh Penguins leapt at Ubriaco, and in 1967–68 he responded

Coach Bob Goldham (seated third from left) was assisted by two Hall of Famers – manager Father David Bauer (fifth from left) and trainer Jim Gregory (back row, second from right). Netminder Cesare Maniago relied on Dave Keon (seated, far left), captain Bob McKnight (seated, second from right), Lou Angotti (middle row, far left), Jack Costello (middle row, fourth from left) and Mike Draper (back row, third from left), among others.

with an 18-goal season. In January 1969, he was swapped to the Oakland Seals, and by December of that year he had been traded again, arriving in Chicago, where he finished his NHL career after that season. Gene contributed 74 points in 177 games in the NHL.

Newly imported Cesare Maniago carried the bulk of the goaltending workload in 1957–58, winning 21, losing 19, and tying seven games. For a second season in a row, Gerry Cheevers made a single Junior 'A' appearance, as he spent most of the season with the Buzzers.

Keon learned valuable life lessons at the school, but on the ice, he learned to play an effective two-way game, which greatly benefited his Hall of Fame NHL career.

SNAPSHOT ▶▶▶▶▶▶▶▶▶▶

Cesare Maniago: *Hail Cesare!*

The lanky boy who tended goal for the Majors for two seasons at the end of the 1950s followed a surprising path to St. Michael's College from his home in British Columbia. "Trail is a one-industry town," he begins. "The Cominco Mine was a smelter, and in its heyday employed about 5,000 people. My dad was one of them. One day, the assistant manager, Pete McIntyre, sent word out that he wanted to talk to my dad. My father never got called to the office and figured he was going to lose his job. When he nervously went to the office to see McIntyre, my dad was asked, 'What plans does your son have in hockey?'

"My dad came home and was smiling cheek to cheek. Unknown to us, McIntyre was a personal friend of Conn Smythe's — they'd been in the war together. He phoned Smythe and was told, 'Tell him he's got his choice. He can go to the Marlboros or St. Mike's.' Well, my choice was St. Mike's. We were a good Roman Catholic family. It was a done deal within a week."

Maniago moved to Toronto and began attending the school in 1956–57, but wasn't allowed to play hockey that first year. "In those years, the Ontario Hockey Association only allowed one transfer, and they chose Dave Rimstad [a defenceman from Vancouver] for that one particular year. So all I did was practise with the Majors," explains Cesare.

Although not able to play regular-season games, Maniago still was able to impress Father Crowley, the Majors' coach. "I guess I opened up a few eyes in my first year being the practice goalie," Cesare shrugs.

By 1957–58, Bob Goldham was the newly appointed coach of the St. Michael's Majors, but Maniago's hockey career was jeopardized one day early in the season. "I was called to Maple Leaf Gardens," Cesare recalls with some rancour. "Hap Day was the [Maple Leafs'] general manager, Bob Davidson was the chief scout, and King Clancy was assistant manager, and they tried to get me to sign a C-Form. With it, you were signing your life away to one particular club. I was really hesitant. They sat me in the chair and gave me a real going-over. They said things like, 'Couldn't your parents use a hundred dollars?' I said, 'Sure, my parents could use the money.' And they'd say, 'Then why won't you sign it?'

"King Clancy, who had a son named Terry [who later played for both St. Mike's and the Leafs], said, 'I've got a boy, and if he could sign with the Toronto Maple Leafs for $100, he wouldn't hesitate!' They went on and on and on. Finally, they said, 'Sign or we're sending you back home.' They had me in tears."

Distraught, Cesare returned to school and searched out Father Bauer. "I was really concerned. I told him the story and he got redder and redder. He was fuming. While I'm in the office, he phones down to Maple Leaf Gardens and talks to Hap Day. He says, 'You met with Cesare Maniago and tried to get him to sign a C-Form. He was reluctant to do so and you threatened to send him back home to Trail. Is that correct?' Hap Day said, 'Yes, that's correct.' Father Bauer said, 'I'm telling you right now, if you try to pull a stunt like that on any of our players again, the relationship between St. Michael's College and the Toronto Maple Leafs will be over. Goodbye.' *Click.* That was it!

"Father Bauer said, 'You're not going anywhere. You're staying here at St. Mike's, even if we have to pay for it.' To this day, I idolize Father Bauer. He was just phenomenal."

Although the Majors hadn't won a Memorial Cup championship since 1947, and finished in the middle of the OHA Junior 'A' pack during both of Maniago's seasons with the Majors, an incredible camaraderie developed between teammates. "Those were some great times," says Cesare, sporting a broad smile. "The teammates were superb. I love them all."

Cesare laughs as he recalls a story involving the team. "After one of those doubleheaders that we used to play every weekend, four of us went to George's Spaghetti House [a popular restaurant and jazz club Toronto hockey players often frequented]. There was Les Kozak, Jack Costello, Davey Keon, and myself. We all ordered the spaghetti and meatballs. At that time, Keon looked at one of the shakers filled with hot red peppers and asked, 'What's that?'

"I said, 'Crushed peanuts. You pour them on your ice cream.' He takes a mouthful of ice cream and about half a minute later, his mouth was just on fire! He was giving me the evil eye and calling me every name in the book. We were just rolling in our seats." Cesare chuckles at the memory. "Even today, when I see Davey, without saying a word, I know what's going through his mind."

Another time, the same characters decided to take a road trip of a different kind. "Dave Keon, Jack Costello, and myself decided to play hooky one Friday afternoon. We went down to the track to place some $2 bets. Darned if we don't run into Father Flanagan and Father Wilson! They turn around, see us, and their jaws drop! We see them and our jaws drop! Father Flanagan comes up to us and says, 'Okay, that's it! You say nothing and we'll say nothing!'

"There was some hard work at St. Mike's, but there were some real fun times," Maniago concludes.

It was a frequent concern, expressed both by players and faculty, that it was almost overwhelming to play Junior 'A' hockey while maintaining good grades at school. "Some teachers, most of them were priests at the time, were sympathetic if we played in Hamilton or St. Catharines and didn't get home until 2:00 or 2:30 in the morning. They might let us miss our first class," he says. "But there were some teachers that weren't like that at all."

Cesare played two seasons of goal for the St. Michael's Majors. In 1957–58, he appeared in 48 games, winning 21, losing 19, and tying seven. He led the OHA with two shutouts. The next season, he won 15, lost 22, and tied five in 42 appearances, and again led the league in shutouts — this time with four. In both seasons, Maniago took the Majors to the playoffs.

"In my last year, I had the opportunity to go to college at Michigan Tech in Houghton, Michigan," explains Cesare. "Before I left, Father Bauer said, 'If you decide that you don't want to go to school, and you want to try to be a professional hockey player, give it two years. If you haven't made the NHL by then, call it a day and concentrate on your education.'" Maniago was ready to accept the scholarship being offered when he got a call from the Toronto Maple Leafs. "They wanted to sign me to a pro contract. What they wanted to do was have me be the practice goalie with Johnny Bower, because at that time, teams only had the one goalie.

"I really wanted to get into competition, so I told Punch Imlach that. He said, 'Okay, fine. We can't sign you to a full contract, but come down to camp.' As it turned out, I ended up playing Senior in the Ontario Hockey League. I think I played with every team in the league." During that 1959–60 season, Cesare tended goal for the Kitchener-Waterloo Dutchmen, the Windsor Bulldogs, Belleville McFarlands, and Chatham Maroons. "I ended up in Chatham and we won the Allan Cup. That was the first step towards improving my chances of turning pro."

The following season, 1960–61, Maniago signed with the Maple Leafs and reported to Spokane of the Western Hockey League. "I did fairly well there," he says. "I could see some progression along the way, and that is when I made up my mind to follow a pro career, although I did take two college courses a year during the off-season. I gave up on that because I progressed rapidly [in hockey] after that."

During the 1960–61 season, Cesare was summoned by Toronto and played his first NHL game on February 25, 1961, a 3–1 win over the Detroit Red Wings. He played seven games for the Maple Leafs during that stretch, then added two more starts during the playoffs when Bower was injured. In the Intra-League Draft of

June 1961, Maniago was claimed by the Montreal Canadiens, and stayed with the organization for four years. He moved to the New York Rangers in a June 1965 trade, and then, in the 1967 Expansion Draft, was selected by the Minnesota North Stars, where he earned the right to be a number one netminder.

For nine seasons, Cesare added legitimacy to a fledgling North Stars squad. He was swapped to Vancouver in August 1976, for netminder Gary Smith. Maniago played two seasons at home with the Canucks before retiring at the conclusion of the 1977–78 campaign. Cesare won 190 games, lost 257, and tied 97 in 568 regular-season NHL games, and posted 30 shutouts during those 15 seasons.

Cesare Maniago appreciated the foundation afforded by St. Michael's College. "If there was anything that I learned from St. Mike's, it was discipline," he says. "Preparing yourself for school, preparing yourself for whatever comes your way as you go on in life, to be humble and to be truthful to people, no matter how much it might hurt." Cesare pauses for a moment, reflecting on an era some 50 years in the past. "Again, I look at Father Bauer. He was an ideal type of individual. You just wanted to live your life by the things he said. He taught us to go with the flow, that you're going to have your ups and downs, and he put it in an example several times. He'd say, 'You may have a down time, but you just have to think that 90 percent of the population is worse off than you are.' I respected that, and I've tried to carry that through my life. I've taught my kids the same thing."

22
Debut of the Drapers

St. Mike's slipped from third to fourth in 1958–59, but tipped their hand as to what the future held. The seeds of the school's next Memorial Cup championship had been sown and were taking root. Tied for the team scoring lead were Jack Costello, brother of Les and Murray, and a young man named Bruce Draper, who was in his first full season of Junior 'A' hockey. Costello scored 25 goals and 24 assists for 49 points, while Draper tallied 24 times and added 25 helpers for the same point total.

David Keon enjoyed a strong season of 45 points, while Cesare Maniago was the principal netminder. Captain Darryl Sly showed great leadership. Besides Bruce Draper, his brother Dave had a strong season, as did Jack Cole, Paul Jackson, Larry Keenan, Terry O'Malley, and sub-goaltender Gerry Cheevers.

The St. Catharines TeePees finished first for a second straight season in 1958–59, but there were surprises throughout the campaign. One was the disappointing result recorded by the Tiger Cubs of Hamilton, who dropped like a stone from second place in 1957–58 to the basement.

The Peterborough Petes were quite a story. The team, which had moved from Kitchener to Peterborough just three years before, finished last in 1956–57 under coach Baldy McKay, jumped to fifth place under former Leaf great Ted Kennedy, and came in second for new coach Scotty Bowman in 1958–59. The Petes eliminated the Barrie Flyers, Guelph Biltmores, and St. Michael's Majors to capture the John Ross Robertson Trophy. The Petes trailed the series three games to one, with one tie, against the Majors, but rebounded to win the series. They then earned the Richardson Trophy as eastern Canadian champions after beating the Ottawa-Hull Junior Canadiens, a team Bowman had been affiliated with for several years.

1958–59					
TEAM	GP	W	L	T	Pts
St. Catharines TeePees	54	40	11	3	84
Peterborough TPT Petes	54	29	20	5	63
Guelph Biltmore Mad Hatters	54	23	18	13	59
St. Michael's Majors	48	19	24	5	51
Barrie Flyers	54	21	27	6	48
Toronto Marlboros	54	19	27	8	46
Hamilton Tiger Cubs	54	11	35	8	30

Darryl Sly was a versatile player who seemed as comfortable playing forward as he was on defence, although he would go to the National Hockey League as a blueliner. After three years playing for the Majors, including captaining the squad in 1958–59 while he was attending teacher's college, Sly joined the Kitchener-Waterloo Dutchmen on the advice of Father Bauer, keeping his amateur status in spite of the Toronto Maple Leafs' attempts to sign him. When the Whitby Dunlops declined the opportunity to represent Canada at the 1960 Olympic Games, the Dutchmen, with St. Mike's alumnus Bobby Bauer as coach, took the offer and went on to win a silver medal. In 1960–61, while teaching in Elmira, Ontario, Darryl was invited to join the Trail Smoke Eaters, the team that represented Canada at the World Championship in Switzerland. He took a three-month leave of absence and returned home with a gold medal. After the final game, a 5–1 victory over the Soviets, Sly told a reporter, "I'm bushed, but I am about the happiest guy in the world." Darryl was signed by the Maple Leafs and spent seven years with the organization, winning the Calder Cup as AHL champions with the Rochester Americans three times in succession. During that time, Darryl was called up to the Leafs for two games in December 1965 and 17 more in 1967–68. He later joined the Minnesota North Stars and the Vancouver Canucks, wrapping up his NHL career with three points in 79 games.

Dave and Bruce Draper, along with linemate Larry Keenan (right), would lead the Majors to the Memorial Cup in 1960–61. Leafs coach Punch Imlach called Bruce and Larry two of the best Junior players he had seen.

Born in Dauphin, Manitoba, Les Kozak was playing forward in the Saskatchewan Junior Hockey League when he was imported to Toronto as a Leaf prospect. He played one game with the Junior 'A' Marlboros in 1956–57, but was transferred to St. Michael's the following year, where he embarked on a very good three-season Junior career with the Majors. Coach Bob Goldham admitted, "I rated Kozak over Dave Keon when I coached them at St. Mike's." Les left hockey to join the priesthood in 1960–61, but returned to the game in 1961–62, playing most of the season with the Rochester Americans, Toronto's AHL affiliate, although he played 12 games with the Leafs, scoring one goal. When Les was returned to the minors, he suffered a fractured skull and retired. Kozak went on to earn his doctorate and worked on the origins of genetic disease.

One lingering question is why Larry Keenan was never able to crack the Toronto Maple Leafs' lineup. Called "one of the best Juniors I've ever seen" by Punch Imlach, Larry was a proficient scorer with the Majors. In 1958–59, he scored 17 goals, 21 in 1959–60, and 31 in 1960–61. In winning the Memorial Cup in the spring of 1961, Keenan was phenomenal, leading all playoff scorers in goals (24) and points (37) in 20 games. Larry turned pro with the Leafs organization in 1961–62, spending most of the season with Rochester, but was called up to play with the Maple Leafs on February 18 and 21, 1962. These would be the only games he ever played for Toronto. Keenan waited five years for a return engagement. Left unprotected in the 1967 Expansion Draft, Larry was picked by the St. Louis Blues. He spent 1967–68 to 1969–70 with the Blues and proved to be a proficient checking forward. Early in the 1970–71 season, he was dealt to the Buffalo Sabres. A year later, Larry packed his bags for the Philadelphia Flyers, where he finished his NHL career at the end of the 1971–72 season. Keenan's NHL career consisted of 233 regular-season games, in which he scored 38 times and assisted on 64 more for 102 points.

The Mighty Quinn: *Pat Quinn* SNAPSHOT

One player St. Mike's would dearly have loved to have had playing for the Majors was Pat Quinn, a strapping six-foot, three-inch defenceman who briefly attended the school.

After graduating from Grade 8, Pat felt the calling to be a priest. On a trial basis, the Hamilton native visited a seminary in Niagara Falls. The priests took vows of poverty, chastity, and obedience. "I wasn't sure that I was ready for that kind of commitment," admits Quinn. "Plus I would have had to give up sports, and I wasn't prepared to do that at that point." Instead, Father Cox, a local priest, contacted St. Michael's College on the young man's behalf. "I got a scholarship to go to school at St. Michael's."

Pat recalls his introduction to St. Mike's. "The day I walked in, Father Higgins grabbed me to play football. I was a pretty good ballplayer at the time." But Quinn's heart was set on playing hockey. "In those days, because I'd played for a team in Hamilton, my rights as an amateur belonged to the Detroit Red Wings," explains Pat.

Having had Frank Mahovlich "stolen" from him by the Toronto Maple Leafs, Red Wings general manager Jack Adams was not in any sort of conciliatory mood to accommodate anyone or anything associated with the Leafs. "I wanted to play hockey for St. Mike's, but because Detroit owned my rights, they wouldn't let me. They told me that if I was going to play Junior, I'd play for Hamilton [Tiger Cubs]," shrugs Pat."

After three months at St. Michael's, Quinn returned home and, later in the 1958–59 season, joined the Hamilton Tiger Cubs. "Going to St. Mike's was an adventure because I had a chance to go to a wonderful school. I was blocked from playing hockey, but they would have allowed me to stay on a scholarship to play football."

Pat spent four seasons playing Junior with Hamilton, including part of the 1961–62 season that saw the team, renamed the Red Wings, win the Memorial Cup. He was part of a Junior championship with the Edmonton Oil Kings in 1962–63. After moving from the Detroit organization to Montreal, over to St. Louis and then to Toronto, Pat Quinn finally played his first NHL game on November 27, 1968, a 3–3 tie between Toronto and the Pittsburgh Penguins.

Following his playing career, Quinn joined the coaching ranks, and in 1980, while with the Philadelphia Flyers, was awarded the Jack Adams Trophy as NHL coach of the year.

Pat Quinn was unable to play hockey at St. Mike's, but during his brief stay, he starred on the school's football team (wearing #28).

23
Setting the Table

If the season was unspectacular — another fourth-place finish, with 52 points, up just one from the previous campaign — their second-year centre, David Keon, was anything but. His 33 goals were seventh best in the OHA, his 38 assists placed him sixth, and the 71-point total put Keon seventh in the league in 1959–60.

Meanwhile, the Marlboros, who finished a disappointing sixth in 1958–59, scrambled to capture first place, pushing a strong St. Catharines team back to runner-up status.

Larry Keenan's 41 points were second best among the Majors, and Bruce Draper finished third on the team, collecting 38 points. Both players would explode during the following season. Gerry Cheevers and Dave Dryden shared goaltending duties for St. Mike's. While Cheevers was being fast-tracked to become the Toronto Maple Leafs' goaltender of the future, Dryden put up some very good numbers, too. He played 12 games for the Majors in 1959–60 and 18 during the 1961 Memorial Cup campaign, but was moved over to the Toronto Marlboros in 1961–62, when both St. Mike's and the Marlies joined a short-lived Toronto Junior league. While playing with the Marlboros, Dryden was loaned to the New York Rangers on February 3, 1962, to replace injured Gump Worsley. It would be several seasons before Dave played in the NHL again, but when he did, he enjoyed a long, successful career. In 203 regular-season appearances with the Chicago Black Hawks, Buffalo Sabres, and Edmonton Oilers, Dryden won 66, lost 76, and tied 31 games. He also played 242 games with the Chicago Cougars and Alberta Oilers of the World Hockey Association, winning 112, losing 113, and tying 10.

1959–60

TEAM	GP	W	L	T	Pts
Toronto Marlboros	48	28	17	3	59
St. Catharines TeePees	48	25	19	4	54
Barrie Flyers	48	24	18	6	54
St. Michael's Majors	48	23	19	6	52
Peterborough TPT Petes	48	22	23	3	47
Guelph Biltmore Mad Hatters	48	19	21	8	46
Hamilton Tiger Cubs	48	10	34	4	24

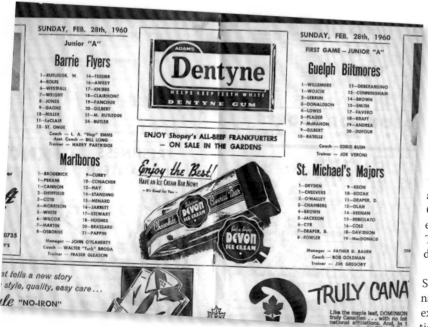

In the autumn of 1959, the St. Catharines TeePees were off to such a horrific start (one win in 12 games) that coach Max Kaminsky offered to resign. General manager Rudy Pilous refused to accept his coach's resignation, and the team's fortunes turned around to such an extent that the TeePees finished the season in second place.

In the first round of the playoffs, St. Catharines met the Guelph Biltmores, who included future NHL greats Rod Gilbert and Jean Ratelle. The TeePees, led by Ray Cullen's three winning goals during the series, eliminated Guelph in five games. In Round Two, the TeePees met the Peterborough Petes, disposing of them in six games.

In the OHA final, St. Catharines met St. Michael's, who featured Garden City native Gerry Cheevers in net. The series was extremely close, with two games finishing in ties, but in Game Six, Ray Cullen once again scored the winning goal and the TeePees won the OHA Junior 'A' Championship. Besides Cullen, the team featured Roger Crozier, Vic Hadfield, Chico Maki, Doug Robinson, and Pat Stapleton. The John Ross Robertson Cup was presented to the TeePees for the second time in six years. They went on to face the Edmonton Oil Kings, winning the series in five games to capture the Memorial Cup for the second time in six years.

Arnie Brown: *Colourful Character* ◂◂ ◂◂ ◂◂ ◂◂ ◂◂ ◂◂ ◂◂ SNAPSHOT

Although his birth certificate reads "Oshawa, Ontario," Arnie Brown very proudly calls the town of Apsley his hometown. "It's about 40 miles north of Peterborough, and my mom anddad ran a general store there," he says.

Arnie began skating at the age of five, and started playing hockey shortly afterwards. "I came through this small-town minor system, and in 1956 [when Arnie was just 14], I ended up playing with a local Senior team. We won the East Peterborough Hockey League championship that year. After the final game, which we played at the old Civic Arena in Peterborough because we needed artificial ice, a fellow came wandering down to the dressing room and said to me, 'There's some people upstairs who'd like to see you.' After I got cleaned up, I went upstairs and saw two guys sitting in a car in the parking lot. One guy rolled down the window and said, 'Are you Arnie Brown?' I said, 'Yep.' He said, 'Would you mind getting into the back of the car? We want to talk to you for a minute.'"

Today, no teenager would ever climb into a car with strangers, but it wouldn't have been so unusual in the 1950s. "They introduced themselves as Mr. Davidson and Mr. Marks. Bob Davidson was the chief scout of the Leafs and Jack Marks was the manager of the Marlboros," Brown explains. "They asked, 'Would you be interested in coming to Toronto to play hockey?' I said, 'Yeah, I would be.' I was 15 at the time and playing against industrial-league guys 25 years old who were working at the [Canadian General Electric] factory in Peterborough. Mr. Davidson said, 'We'd be really interested in you coming to Toronto and we'll give you a call in the summer to make arrangements.'

"I forgot all about it, but then I got this call in the middle of the summer from Bob Davidson. He said, 'I'd like to come up to see you.' We had lunch and he talked to my parents. I said, 'I really would like to go to school.' He said, 'Well, we're tied up with the Marlboros, but we also have a relationship with St. Michael's College. Let me see if I can get you into St. Mike's.'"

Although the Browns are Protestant, Davidson called back and confirmed that he had secured a scholarship for Arnie at St. Mike's. "He asked me if I had signed anything previously. Well, after we won the championship in that EPHL, there was a Junior 'B' team in Peterborough called Stoneys, a used car dealership. They wanted me to play in the playoffs after my team had finished so I played one game and I signed a contract. I told Mr. Davidson I'd signed this thing that I never really had thought about. He said, 'Well, you're going to have to get them to give you your release, and if they won't give you your release, there's not much hope.'"

Arnie called the coach of the Stoneys, but was surprised to find out that there was a wrinkle. "He said, 'We'd really like you to come to the Red Wings' training camp in Hamilton.' By that time, I'd received a letter from Jack Adams that invited me to try out for Detroit, but after a long conversation, I told him I'd really like to go to Toronto, so he gave me my release. He didn't have to [be so gracious, but he was]. Off I went to Toronto in the fall of 1957."

At the time, anyone who wanted to could try out for the Buzzers, St. Mike's Junior 'B' hockey team. "I put my name on a list," Brown recalls. "A priest by the name of Father Conway was the coach that year. I played football for him early that year.

Pat Quinn was there at the same time. We were down at Maple Leaf Gardens. After the first Buzzers practice, you went to the bulletin board to find out whether you were still on the list or not. First practice, my name wasn't on the list — I was devastated. I was all broken up because one of the things Mr. Davidson had said was that I had to make the Junior 'B' team to stay at the school. Davidson comes down and sees me in the stands and says, 'What's the matter with you?' I said, 'I just got cut from the Buzzers after the first practice.' He said, 'You're kidding!' I said, 'First practice, a lot of guys on the ice, I didn't get much of a chance.' He said, 'Don't be upset. Let me see what I can do about that.' The next week, I was out with the Midget team because I'd been cut by the Buzzers. Mr. Davidson saw me and walked over and said, 'Everything's going to be all right. You're going to stay here.'"

Arnie played his first year at St. Mike's with the Midget team. "That year, I broke my ankle trying to touch a puck for icing and the other guy pushed my skates out, so I missed most of that year."

As part of the Buzzers squad in 1958–59, Arnie learned a great deal from his coach. "Father Conway made you feel good all the time. In the dressing room, he always made up speeches. He was really good for kids. He was never really a guy you could get close to, but I really respected him."

Arnie spent his season with the Buzzers improving his game and doing whatever was required of him. "I fought my way through that year, but I got through it," he admits. "But at the end of the year, we played a couple of exhibition games against the Majors and I did pretty well, so the next year, the fall of '59, I was with the Majors."

The team looked quite strong. Coach Bob Goldham had a number of key players on that team. "We had Paul Jackson, Larry Keenan, Les Kozak, Terry O'Malley, and Gino Rebellato, but the main one was Dave Keon."

The 1960–61 season was a special year for Brown and St. Mike's. "That year, Father Bauer coached. We had a good team, but by the end of the year, it looked like we had a chance to go all the way." The team rolled over its opponents, and in a tough series, defeated the Edmonton Oil Kings in Edmonton for the Memorial Cup.

That spring, St. Mike's was in the throes of withdrawing from Junior 'A' hockey. "There was a real difference of opinion between priests as to whether it was going to be an academic establishment or whether it was going to be a hockey establishment," Arnie remembers. "The only way the priests said they'd support hockey was if they stopped all the travelling around the other OHA cities." As a result, the Metro Junior 'A' Hockey League was formed.

"Father Bauer was realizing this was happening and was looking to go elsewhere," says Brown. "Father Bauer was a guy who taught technical checking, technical skating. He was a great skater himself. He was not a violent man in the sense of hard-hitting hockey. He wanted to see pure hockey. He had a vision that the only way to get that was the Olympic route. He was recruiting guys that summer to go with him to UBC [the University of British Columbia, which hosted the forerunner to Father Bauer's Canadian National Team]. He came to me, and I remember going up to Bayfield, Ontario, and spending three days with him, talking to me about joining the team. After listening to him, I said, 'Sorry, Father. I don't know whether I'm making the right or the wrong decision, but I want to play pro.'"

His decision made, Arnie met Father Bauer in Toronto. "He said, 'Come on with me. We're going down to Maple Leaf Gardens.'" After driving to the arena, Father Bauer told Arnie to stay in the car while he went to see Leafs GM Punch Imlach. "He came back down and said, 'You've signed a two-year contract with Mr. Imlach. You'll get $5,500 in the minors and $8,000 if you make the big team. The second year, you'll get $6,000 and $8,500,'" offers Brown. "This was basically illegal. I still had a year of Junior left, but I was all happy about this.

"The Leafs were training in Peterborough [in September 1961], and that was just down the road from me. I went through training camp but didn't have high expectations that I was going to make it, but they took me out west on their pre-season exhibition tour. I was right there, and the day before the [1961–62] season started, I was still with the team. We had a light skate before the first game and Imlach came over to me and said, 'I want you to go back and play Junior.' I said, 'Okay.' So I went back up to St. Mike's and went in to see Father Sheedy, who was the principal. School was going to start the next day. I said, 'Mr. Imlach wants me to play another year of Junior. I'm interested in playing pro but if I'm going to play Junior, I'd like to go to St. Mike's.' He said, 'That's fine. We'll get this thing worked out, Arnie.' I said, 'Mr. Imlach would like me to go to practice whenever they're in town if I can work it around my schedule at school.' He said, 'I don't think that'll be a problem.'"

Brown was boarding with a friend's family and got a call at eight o'clock the next morning. "It was Father Sheedy and he said, 'You can't come back to school.' I was devastated. They wouldn't let me play for St. Mike's because I wanted to practise with the Leafs. I ended up not going to school that year and playing for the Marlboros." Brown did get called up to play two games with the Leafs. On October 28, 1961, he played his first NHL contest, helping Toronto beat the Rangers 5–1 at Maple Leaf Gardens. He played a second game on November 1 against the Canadiens, but missed much of the season to injury. "Dougie Jarrett ran me into the boards at Maple Leaf Gardens and I separated my shoulder," he sighs.

As the Maple Leafs won the Stanley Cup three years consecutively from 1962 through 1964, Toronto's management made few changes. In the fall of 1962, Brown attended the Leafs' training camp again. "It looked like I had a shot at making the team," he says. "The last practice before the season started, Imlach comes up to me and says, 'I want you to go to Denver.'" At the time, Denver was a lower-level Leaf farm team in the Western Hockey League. "I had played in Rochester before [three games during 1961–62], and if I wasn't going to go the Leafs, I wanted to go to Rochester," Brown continues. "He said, 'Let me think about it,' and so at 10 o'clock the next night, Mr. Imlach said, 'You're going to go to Rochester this year.'"

Arnie admits, "That might have been the kiss of death, quite frankly. I don't think Mr. Imlach ever forgot that I'd asked to go to Rochester. The next fall, the same thing happened again. It was my second year in Rochester and Mr. Imlach had brought me up twice during those two years. It was nothing significant, but I got on the ice a few times. In 1964, he was in a real dilemma. The Leafs had really gone downhill in January and it didn't even look like they'd make the playoffs. He was really upset with some of his veterans, so he made the trade that sent myself, Rod Seiling, Bob Nevin, Dick Duff, and Billy Collins to the New York Rangers for Andy Bathgate and Don McKenney." The Maple Leafs went on to win the Stanley Cup in 1963–64. "I went on to the Rangers and spent seven years there," states Arnie. "I would like to have stayed with the Leafs."

Brown was a full-time member of the Rangers' blueline crew by the start of the 1964–65 season. In 1970–71, he was traded to Detroit. Arnie briefly played with both the New York Islanders and Atlanta Flames, then concluded his career with a season in the WHA, starting with Michigan in 1974–75, moving with the franchise to Baltimore, then joining the Vancouver Blazers when the previous franchise folded. In 681 regular-season NHL games, Arnie scored 44 times and collected 185 points. He added 60 WHA contests, picking up eight more points.

Arnie reflects back with great fondness on his time at St. Michael's College. "I had a very, very positive experience going through St. Mike's. Your life changes. You have to take it in context. I'm 15 years old, coming out of a small town in rural Ontario, going to the big city where I've never been before. My mother is driving me up to the yellow gates of the old school and I'm going in there. It was some kind of experience! Not only that, but I hadn't really been exposed to the Catholic religion at all. They treated me so well. It didn't matter that I was a Protestant going to a Catholic school. It was very positive for me and it opened my mind unbelievably."

24

The Power of Bauer

Wholesale coaching changes seemed to be the order of the day after the 1959–60 season. Four of the seven teams in the OHA Junior 'A' loop placed new faces behind the bench, including Eddie Bush in Hamilton, Jerry Brown with the Marlboros, and Emile Francis with Guelph. There were changes at St. Mike's, too, as Bob Goldham resigned as coach of the Majors. "Due to the pressure of business, I won't be with St. Mike's next season," he stated. A former NHL defenceman, Goldham was working in sales for a Toronto building products firm.

With the 1960–61 season just over a month away, St. Michael's had yet to find a replacement for Goldham. Father David Bauer, the manager of the Majors, had scoured the industry and, although several names had been rumoured, including that of former Marlboros coach Turk Broda, it fell to Bauer to assume, on a temporary basis, the dual role of manager and coach of the St. Michael's College Majors.

Meanwhile, the Hamilton Tiger Cubs took on a new name, the Red Wings, that reflected their affiliation with their parent club in Detroit, while Guelph adopted the Royals moniker, leaving behind the Biltmore Mad Hatters brand. The 48-game schedule saw the Royals take first place in the OHA, dominating with 30 wins against just nine losses and nine ties for 69 points, 11 more than second-place St. Mike's, who earned their 58 points on 26 wins, 16 losses, and six ties.

Individually, the Majors excelled. St. Mike's leading scorer, Bruce Draper, collected 44 goals, second best in the league, and 77 points, which placed him fourth. He was also awarded the Max Kaminsky Trophy for combining gentlemanly conduct with on-ice excellence, egding Jean Ratelle. Larry Keenan finished with 31 goals, ninth best in the league, and 69 points, which placed him seventh. During the course of the 1960–61 season, Maple Leafs coach Punch Imlach announced that Bruce Draper and Larry Keenan were the two best Junior players he had seen that season. "I didn't see anyone better," he declared. "They should be good enough to give the big boys a run for their money [when they are invited to training camp with the Leafs in the fall of 1961], and if they can put some of them out of a job, it's there for them. I hope they do."

Although Father Bauer was blessed with several players who were gifted offensively, he came from a long line of St. Michael's coaches who operated on the theory that defence wins hockey games. Bob Goldham, the previous coach of the Majors, was a firm believer that the team that made the fewest mistakes usually won. Father Bauer was equally adamant that, if you check diligently, especially in the other team's territory, the goals will come.

Keenan and Draper played on the Majors' top line, but were also regarded as the two best checking forwards with St. Mike's in 1960–61. Along with linemate Bruce Draper, Dave's twin brother, "all three take turns spearheading a pattern to break up an opposition play before they develop," in the words of *The Globe*. "From these forays often comes a surprise score that takes the wind out of an enemy's sail."

Another pleasant surprise for the Majors was the play of Andre Champagne. "He had no right to make the team, but he and another boy, Paul Conlin, showed so much determination and desire that Father Bauer kept them on the club for that alone," recalls Jim Gregory. Champagne and Conlin became a very effective penalty-killing unit for the team that season. At the conclusion of the season, Terry O'Malley, the team captain, was selected as the team's most valuable player.

1960–61

TEAM	GP	W	L	T	Pts
Guelph Royals	48	30	9	9	69
St. Michael's Majors	48	26	16	6	58
Hamilton Red Wings	48	22	19	7	51
Niagara Falls Flyers	48	22	21	5	49
St. Catharines TeePees	48	18	24	6	42
Peterborough TPT Petes	48	16	24	8	40
Toronto Marlboros	48	9	30	9	27

Family bloodlines coursed through the St. Michael's Majors in 1961. Team members Terry Clancy, Bob Davidson, Wayne Mosdell, Gary Smith, and Barry Watson all had fathers who had played in the NHL. Terry's father, King Clancy, played 16 NHL seasons split between Ottawa and Toronto. Bob Davidson Sr. captained the 1945 Toronto Maple Leafs team that won the Stanley Cup. Wayne Mosdell's dad, Kenny, started his career with the Brooklyn Americans, followed by 14 years as a member of the Montreal Canadiens and a year in Chicago. Des Smith, father of Gary, spent five years in the NHL and wore the sweaters of the Montreal Maroons, Montreal Canadiens, Chicago Black Hawks and Boston Bruins during his career. The 14-season NHL career of Harry Watson, Barry's father, included stops in Brooklyn, Detroit, Toronto, and Chicago. To add one more name, Wally Stanowski Jr. also had a tryout with the team but spent the season with the Buzzers. His dad was the whirling dervish who enjoyed an NHL career with Toronto and New York.

"I left home at an early age, 15 years old, and I can remember my dad taking me to Toronto and introducing me to a priest at St. Mike's," Gary Smith recalled in *Life After Hockey* by Michael Smith. "The priest said, 'What are you here for?' I said, 'I'm here to play hockey.' I wasn't there to go to school. I was there to play hockey. As far as going to school was concerned, I didn't have much use for it, which it turns out now was unfortunate."

During the 1959–60 season, Gerry Cheevers had been the league's premier netminder, leading the OHA with five shutouts as well as a goals-against average of 3.08. But Cheevers, who was also an outstanding forward for the St. Catharines Junior Athletics lacrosse team, had harboured a secret desire to play a few shifts at wing for St. Michael's. "I want to attend university in the United States on a hockey scholarship when I'm through with Junior and I think I'd have a better chance if I could play both goal and forward," he said at the time.

"I was never a guy who was too interested in getting in goal for a practice, and Father David Bauer used to get mad at me all the time," laughed Cheevers. "I said, 'It's just not worth getting hurt in there.' He told me, 'I'm going to show you what it's like outside one of these days,' and I said, 'Yeah, yeah.'"

Father Bauer made good on that threat. Cheevers was set to graduate after that season, and understudy Dave Dryden was being groomed for the number one job, but he needed to gain some experience. At one point, the team was beset with injuries, so, less than an hour before a contest against the rival Marlboros, Father Bauer asked Gerry if he was ready to play forward. With Dave Dryden in goal, Cheevers played left wing "like a kid with a new Christmas toy" as St. Michael's and the Marlies skated to a 2–2 tie.

That season, Gerry Cheevers played eight games at forward. "I could always skate. I was just missing the instinct of knowing what to do with the puck," he admitted. "I was never so happy to get back in goal. A lot of guys were trying to get even for wayward sticks in the crease!"

Nevertheless, Cheevers recorded an assist and 12 penalty minutes. When he was inducted into the Hockey Hall of Fame in 1985, it was Father David Bauer who introduced him.

❖

March 8 was opening night of the 1960–61 playoffs, a quarterfinal contest pitting two saints against one another — St. Michael's versus St. Catharines. A blinding snowstorm raged over the Niagara region, turning a 90-minute trip into a three-hour ordeal. The Majors arrived just 10 minutes before game time, but as *The Globe and Mail* remarked, "Even the wintry blasts failed to cool off the hottest team in the league."

St. Catharines, the reigning Memorial Cup champions, opened the series with a 3–1 victory. Larry Keenan was the only Major to beat acrobatic goaltender Roger Crozier.

In spite of nagging injuries to Arnie Brown (foot) and Bruce Draper (arm), the Majors shut out St. Catharines 3–0 in Game Two. Gus Bodnar, the fourth coach for St. Catharines that season, following Max Kaminsky, Vic Teal, and Phil Vitale, ripped into his team for their lack of effort.

"Burlesque is back — sponsored by the executives, coaches and officials of the Ontario Hockey League's Junior 'A' council," sneered *The Globe and Mail* after Game Three. A crowd of 7,254 paid to see a thrilling game that, according to the record books, didn't take place.

St. Michael's had a 4–3 lead over the TeePees in the third game of the quarterfinals when the clock struck six. Referee Jack Clancy refused to drop the puck, as there was a 6 p.m. curfew on Sunday games. Even though there were only 10 seconds left to play, OHA rules called for the game to be voided and played again in its entirety. The TeePees, aware of the rules and the curfew, and playing shorthanded with almost no chance of tying the game, stalled for time on the orders of their coach.

The delays began three minutes after the opening faceoff, when netminder Roger Crozier twisted his knee and took seven minutes to ready himself for action. Jack Cole of St. Mike's was driven into the end boards by St. Catharines' Doug Jarrett, who earned a five-minute major for charging. Cole was carried off the ice and taken to the hospital, where he was diagnosed with a concussion.

As six o'clock neared, Jarrett flipped the puck over the boards on four occasions. Murray Hall spent two minutes conferring at the bench with Coach Bodnar when he was penalized for high-sticking at 18:15.

The St. Catharines executives sported Cheshire-cat grins when the game was called, while Father David Bauer fumed. "If they take this game away from us, I'll have to give it a lot of consideration. I am quite disturbed and upset over the manner in which the third period was conducted. All the referee had to do was drop the puck when they started stalling! I was always under the impression that when a team deliberately stalled, the referee could give a penalty for delaying the game."

Referee Clancy stated that he had been unaware of any stalling tactics. "I just tried to get the game in." He added, "The two injuries held the game up."

The sequence of games became quite unusual at this point. Game Three, which had to be replayed, was rescheduled for March 17. Therefore, Game Four, played at the appointed time on March 14, was actually played *before* Game Three, as was the fifth game of the series!

In that fourth game, played in St. Catharines, St. Michael's reacquired its lead in the series with a 4–1 win. By the end of the first period, the Majors were up 2–0 on goals by Bruce Draper and Terry O'Malley. Draper engineered the Majors' third goal "with a dazzling display of speed and skating finesse to control the puck for almost a minute." Draper then fired the puck across the crease, and Terry Clancy tipped it past Crozier. Larry Keenan later scored an insurance goal. St. Mike's played the last six minutes of the game shorthanded, yet, the TeePees were unable to mount a significant scoring play.

The Majors followed up that triumph by trouncing St. Catharines 8–2. "It could have been 18–2 but for a spirited youngster in the Garden City goal," said *The Globe and Mail*. The Majors fired 49 shots at Crozier, while the TeePees managed but 13 at Cheevers. Bruce Draper fired 14 of those shots himself, although only one ended up on the scoresheet. Larry Keenan scored twice for the victors. "The midget minder for the TeePees had to be the individual star of the game," reported *The Globe*. "He made fantastic stops in every period. Crozier was a lonely man, unsupported and unprotected by a team missing five men from its Memorial Cup lineup of last year."

Coach Gus Bodnar stated, "We might as well not play if they play as they did tonight."

A St. Patrick's celebration should have been the order of the day for the St. Michael's Majors on March 17, but, facing elimination, the TeePees were given a pep talk by owner Rudy Pilous, the coach of the Chicago Black Hawks at that time, and the inspiration paid dividends. In the spirit of the day, it was Terry Clancy who opened the scoring just past the three-minute mark, but that was the only tally for the Majors on the night. Ray Cullen, Doug Robinson, and John Brenneman scored the first three goals for St. Kitts.

The Globe described St. Catharines' fourth goal as an unusual tally, to say the least. "As Ray Cullen broke into the clear, he was checked by two players at centre ice and lost his stick. While they stopped to watch, he proceeded to kick the puck all the way to the goal, and Cheevers went down to smother his attempt to kick it in. If Cheevers had let it go, the goal wouldn't have counted, but he stopped it, lost control and Robinson bounced in to bat it in the goal." It was now 4–1 for the TeePees.

Brenneman scored his second goal of the night early in the third. Realizing the game was out of reach, Father David Bauer rested his stalwarts and inserted younger players. A line of Gary Dineen, Rod Seiling, and Mike Corbett played well. Nevertheless, when the final siren had sounded, the final score showed St. Catharines with a 6–1 victory.

"I can't believe the heart has gone out of this team because the one with the biggest heart, Barry MacKenzie, is in the hospital," said Father Bauer. MacKenzie had suffered a deep gash to his leg during the game. Meanwhile, St. Catharines coach Gus Bodnar was jubilant. "I knew we'd do it," he stated. "On the way over in the bus, the boys had the spirit. We could take it all yet!"

But it turned out to be St. Mike's who clinched the quarterfinal, dumping the defending champions, 4–1.

With St. Catharines two men short early in the game, the Majors capitalized, pounding in two quick goals. Paul Conlin's attempt beat Crozier, but clanged off the post, bouncing back to Sonny Osborne, who made no mistake and banged it home. Just over a minute later, Arnie Brown fired a shot from the point that eluded a maze of players in front of TeePees netminder Roger Crozier, finding its way into the back of the net to put St. Mike's up 2–0 before the five-minute mark.

Howie Kellough scored for St. Catharines midway through the first, but that was all she wrote for the TeePees. Osborne scored his second of the game late in the first period, flipping a shot into the TeePees' zone from close to centre ice. The shot was going wide, but as Roger Crozier stuck his stick out to steer the puck into the corner, it deflected between his legs and entered the goal.

After Bruce Draper was stymied by Crozier on two breakaways and linemate Larry Keenan on five, the two paired up for a final goal in the third period, scored by Keenan, that extinguished any hope the TeePees may have entertained of repeating as Memorial Cup champions.

❖

St. Michael's next met the Hamilton Red Wings in the OHA semifinals. Larry Keenan scored three times and Bruce Draper twice to lead St. Mike's to an easy 6–2 win in the opening game. Jim McKendry, a Junior 'B' player, replaced the injured Barry MacKenzie on the blue line.

"Larry Keenan personally supervised the most wanton destruction wreaked on the Hamilton Red Wings hockey team this season as he scored his second hat trick in a row to lead St. Michael's College Majors to a 6–1 playoff victory," reported *The Globe and Mail*. Larry Jeffrey drew four minors for his stickwork, which aided the Majors' cause. "Coach Sid Abel and several Detroit Red Wings, lodged in Hamilton during their series with the Toronto Maple Leafs, watched the Junior Wings. Abel was impressed with Bob Dillabough and the defence pair of Larry Ziliotto and Ron Harris, the three bright spots in an otherwise dull evening for the hosts."

Testy and tested, the Red Wings clawed their way back into the series with a 4–3 win in Game Three. The opening goal was scored by Hamilton midway through the second period. John Miszuk, holding a broken stick, kicked the puck out to Dillabough, who fired the puck past Cheevers. Miszuk celebrated, still holding his broken stick. Instead of a penalty, the Red Wings were up 1–0! Miszuk was originally credited with the goal, but the official scorer altered it to credit Dillabough. Twenty-six seconds later, Jeffrey fired a shot past Cheevers that put Hamilton up 2–0.

In the second period, Hamilton defenceman Bob Wall let a shot go from the point that Gerry Cheevers caught, but the goal judge ruled that the puck slid over the line and the goal was counted. Cheevers was flabbergasted with the ruling.

Dave Draper scored twice late in the third period to make the score respectable. Larry Keenan earned assists on all three Majors goals.

The St. Michael's win over Hamilton in Game Four was overshadowed by a near tragedy involving Bruce Draper. Moments after scoring the Majors' fifth goal with a wraparound past Hamilton's Buddy Blom, Bruce was charged into the boards and suffered a severe concussion. Bruce's twin brother, Dave, was first on the scene, and when he realized Bruce was in convulsions, he raced to the bench to get assistance. Dr. Hank Wren, an intern at St. Joseph's Hospital in Toronto, leapt over the boards, followed closely by Jim Gregory, trainer for St. Mike's. Gregory pulled Draper's tongue out of his throat, and although he was unable to hold the tongue because of the convulsions, Dr. Wren was able to insert a plastic tube between his teeth and administered a sedative to calm Draper. The quick thinking of Jim Gregory and Dr. Wren is credited with saving Bruce Draper's life. Draper was taken by car to St. Joseph's, and was reported in satisfactory condition. A noticeable pall hung over the crowd following the player's exit.

Larry Jeffrey had exited the penalty box just seconds before the goal was scored. He had served a spearing penalty for an incident with Cheevers. Still angered, he ran Draper heavily into the boards and was given a major for charging. After serving his penalty, Jeffrey was engaged in retribution from Arnie Brown with seconds to go in the game.

It was an unfortunate turn of fate for the Majors, who won the contest by a convincing 5–1 score. Larry Jeffrey had been playing on the edge throughout the series and had been Hamilton's best player that game, in fact, scoring the Red Wings' only goal.

Game Five was filled with emotions of every sort, even prior to the opening face-off. "A fantastic, frenetic finish, probably never duplicated in playoff hockey, pulled the Hamilton Red Wings from the playoff precipice as they fought St. Michael's College to a 3–3 tie at Maple Leaf Gardens last night," said *The Globe and Mail*.

Andre Champagne drew two spearing minors, one exacted on Larry Jeffrey and the other on Bob Wall, as he skated to the bench. When play resumed, the scoreboard didn't indicate the two minors to Champagne, drawing the ire of Hamilton's coach, Eddie Bush. After his tirade halted the game, the referee assessed a bench minor against Hamilton. Then Larry Jeffrey drew a penalty, eliminating the Red Wings' man advantage.

But Bush went berserk when Dave Draper slashed John Miszuk but drew no penalty. Bush tossed a stick onto the ice and was summarily ejected. While leaving the playing area, Bush threw another stick javelin-style towards the officials. With the dismissal of their coach, Red Wings captain Neil Forth and trainer Harvey Meisenheimer commanded the team, and did a masterful job. With more than three minutes remaining, they pulled the goalie and, in spite of the gamble, Hamilton scored two goals with the extra attacker to tie the score.

"It was very weak officiating," fumed Bush as he commented after the contest. "I guess St. Mike's can't do any wrong!"

Hamilton absolutely outplayed St. Mike's in Game Six, winning 5–1 to extend the series to a seventh and deciding game. The Majors, seemingly more intent on exacting retribution than winning, created a steady parade to the penalty box, allowing Hamilton to get back into the series. While Bruce Draper continued his rehabilitation, Andre Champagne joined him in sick bay with an injured shoulder. Barry MacKenzie returned to the lineup for St. Michael's and Eddie Bush was back behind the bench for Hamilton after his ejection in the previous game.

During Game Six, a Majors fan threw an eel out onto the ice, provoking loud guffaws from the crowd. The creature had a sign affixed to it, with a message addressed to Coach Bush and winger Larry Jeffrey: "We give a meal of an ugly eel to a couple of heels."

The series came down to the seventh and deciding game. At the beginning of the second period, with the Majors trailing 3–0, there was an astonishing development. After spending five days in the hospital recuperating from a severe concussion, Bruce Draper skated out for the second period wearing a helmet, earning a standing ovation from the 8,189 fans in attendance. "Father Bauer pulled a strategic move," recalls Barry MacKenzie. "We were trying to get back into the series. Bruce was not supposed to return, and he came out and it was quite inspirational." Although Draper had been cleared to play just prior to the opening face-off of the game, Father Bauer decided not to dress him as a precaution. But after falling behind three goals, the Majors' coach realized he needed the help and told Bruce to get dressed. St. Mike's tied the game by scoring three times in the second, added a fourth just 17 seconds into the third period and added an insurance goal later in the final stanza to earn a 5–3 win.

"Bruce Draper gave us something that no one else has been able to give this team, including myself," said Father David Bauer. "He gave us the psychological lift we needed."

Hamilton coach Eddie Bush and three members of his defence crew made a point of going over to the St. Michael's bench to congratulate Father Bauer. That was followed by the two teams shaking hands at centre ice. Bruce Draper and Gerry Cheevers earned most of the accolades from the defeated Wings.

"It was great hockey! I would say it was even tougher than going out to the Memorial Cup," beams Barry MacKenzie.

❖

The OHA Junior 'A' final began April 5, 1961, and pitted the St. Michael's Majors against the first-place Guelph Royals. In spite of a 10-day layoff and the loss of scoring star Rod Gilbert to back surgery, the Royals opened the series with a 6–4 victory. "I was very pleased but I still had to use the centres on double shift to offset the absence of Gilbert," mentioned Guelph's coach, Emile Francis.

During Game Two, a 2–1 Guelph win, Royals captain Al LeBrun was taken to the hospital with a serious hip injury when he tripped over some debris on the ice during the second period and crashed into the boards at full speed. A fan was escorted out of the building for throwing the garbage onto the ice surface. Fans had been throwing hairpins onto the ice earlier, and the second period took more than an hour to complete between clearing the debris from the ice, the injury to LeBrun, and two scraps between Paul Jackson of St. Mike's and Billy Taylor Jr. of the Royals. Mike McMahon and Jean Ratelle scored for the Royals, with Terry O'Malley countering for the Majors. Father David Bauer waited until the third period to use Bruce Draper. Gerry Cheevers and Dennis Jordan were both spectacular in net.

After playing tentatively in two games, Bruce Draper returned to his usual form in Game Three. He scored three goals, including the game-winner, to lead the Majors to a 6–3 win over the Royals. The line of Larry Keenan with Bruce and Dave Draper was a potent trio for the Majors. Bruce was twice cut in the mouth from high sticks during this game, but soldiered on.

Guelph manager Jack Humphreys left the bench to argue an unsportsmanlike-conduct penalty to Bob Plager with referee Hugh McLean at the penalty bench, and was removed by police on the referee's orders. After the game, Humphreys demanded that neither McLean nor penalty timekeeper Jack Hewitt be assigned to any further games in that series. Humphreys believed the two officials were biased in favour of St. Mike's. During this game, Guelph had received two misconducts and a game misconduct, and when he approached the officials to protest the severe treatment he believed his team was receiving, the police were summoned.

As Game Four slipped away from the Royals, their aggressiveness grew to match their frustration. "It was obvious what they were trying to do," said Father Bauer, shaking his head. "I was obliged to bench five or six of my star players before they were hurt." After Bob Plager drew a five-minute major for slashing Larry Keenan across the ankle at the 57-second mark of the second period, Father Bauer anchored Keenan and the Drapers to the bench so they would not be further targeted by the Royals. The final score was St. Mike's 5, Guelph 1.

With the series tied at two wins apiece, the teams skated to a 3-all tie in Game Five. "The helmeted Draper sparked the rally as he plucked the puck out of a scramble and lifted it over a sprawling Jordan at 14:32," reported *The Globe*. The Royals saw their blue line decimated. With LeBrun not back to full speed and Reg Whaley out with a pulled hamstring, Guelph coach Emile Francis could only sigh as Mike McMahon injured his knee.

Larry Keenan had six shots on goal during Game Six. He scored on four and Guelph goaltender Dennis Jordan made great saves on the other two. Two of Keenan's goals were scored on the power play. It was that kind of night for the 19-year-old Keenan, who had scored 23 goals in 19 playoff games. The game concluded with a 7–4 score in favour of the Majors. "We're in trouble now," stated Emile Francis, Guelph's coach. At the end of the second period, the score was 4–3 for the Majors, but "the Royals were hardly a match for the swift Irish forwards who skated faster and checked harder than they have during the entire series."

The second consecutive playoff series had gone to a seventh and deciding game for St. Michael's College. The Majors eliminated the Guelph Royals with a 4–1 win to clinch the John Ross Robertson Trophy as OHA Junior 'A' champions and earned themselves a berth in the eastern Canadian final against the Moncton Beavers. Jack Cole scored twice for St. Michael's, with Larry Keenan and Andre Champagne adding singles. Jean Ratelle replied for the Royals. Cole had a third goal waved off when the referee ruled that he was in the crease.

OHA president Ken MacMillan presented the Robertson Trophy to St. Mike's while a busload of Majors supporters formed a rhumba line on the ice. So disgruntled were the Royals and their supporters that the arena manager turned off the ammonia in the freezing pipes and prepared the rink for a sportsman's show that was to open the next day. Puddles of water were already appearing on the ice before the Majors made their exit from the ice surface.

"We had a team that was not picked to win the OHA Junior 'A' championship," stated Paul Conlin. "The Guelph Royals had a powerhouse that year with Jean Ratelle, Rod Gilbert, and Bob Cunningham up front." Gilbert led the league in points with 103, including a league-best 54 goals. Ratelle finished second in scoring with 101 points and Cunningham was third with 86 points. "They had Bob Plager and Al LeBrun on defence and Dennis Jordan was in net," Conlin continues. "Emile 'The Cat' Francis was their coach. They were picked by everyone to go on and they did win the league, but we were able to beat them in the finals. A lot of it had to do with Father Bauer, his coaching and his ability to motivate players and get the very best out of them. And we had Gerry Cheevers in net and that helped a lot, too."

❖

St. Michael's demolished the Moncton Beavers 11–2 in the opening game of the eastern Canadian final. "With ridiculous ease, the Majors won the first game of an Eastern Canada best-of-five final from a team which was just four hours off a plane, heavy with food and missing two of its better players," according to *The Globe and Mail*. The Beavers were without Bernie Keating and John Lordon, who were left behind to write their exams at the University of New Brunswick, but both were back in the lineup for game two.

The much smaller Beavers ran into penalty trouble early. Phillip Doiron, who had led the league in scoring during the regular season, and netminder Emery "The Cat" Cormier were both whistled off before the 10-minute mark of the game. In that same time, the Majors had scored three times. The Beavers never recovered. In the third period, St. Michael's pumped seven goals past Cormier. Paul Conlin, Larry Keenan, and Billy MacMillan each scored twice, while Andre Champagne had a goal and four assists. Moncton's coach Ron Gaudet was astonished at his team's terrible showing: "We didn't play well at all." Gaudet, who was also a regional scout for the Boston Bruins, had Harold Cotton, Boston's head scout, at the game to take a look at his brother Oscar Gaudet, who had led the New Brunswick Junior Hockey League in goal-scoring during the regular season.

St. Mike's was so confident of a win in the eastern Canada series that trainer/manager Jim Gregory had already booked flights and hotels for the team in Edmonton on the following Monday morning.

In spite of the final score, a 6–2 win for St. Mike's in Game Two, Emery Cormier was very good in the Beavers' net. Gerry Cheevers was strong for St. Mike's, too, including a play where he raced a Moncton player for a loose puck at the Majors' blue line. In the process of thwarting the Beaver, Cheevers lost his stick, raced back into the crease, and made a sensational stop on Oscar Gaudet.

The referees were quite lax on rough play. Disturbed by his team's overconfidence, Father Bauer planned a punishing practice for the team. "We can't play like that against Edmonton," he huffed. "We're going to get back to fundamentals or I'll know the reason."

St. Michael's crushed the Moncton Beavers 11–2 in Game Three. Moncton opened the scoring, but St. Mike's opened the floodgates after that. Andre Champagne scored four goals and added an assist. Paul Jackson and Sonny Osborne each scored a goal and four assists, while Larry Keenan had three assists before resting his sore hip for the remainder of the game.

Father Bauer briefly benched Arnie Brown, Paul Jackson, and Terry O'Malley for poor efforts in their own end, but sent them out in the third as a forward unit. He left them on the ice for close to six minutes, but although they scored once during that time, they were exhausted by the time they had returned to the bench.

CAHA official Lionel Fleury presented the Richardson Trophy to captain Terry O'Malley. Tommy Smith, a 13-year-old befriended at St. Joseph's Hospital by several team members, was pushed to centre ice in his wheelchair to share the excitement of the presentation with his new friends.

❖

The Memorial Cup championship series of 1961 saw the St. Michael's College Majors challenge the Edmonton Oil Kings. The Majors entered the tournament missing some key personnel. Stan "Sonny" Osborne, a forward who had scored 19 goals split between the Marlies and the Majors in the regular season, stayed behind to write his exams at the University of Toronto. Pete Noakes would miss the trip so that he could continue attending classes at Ryerson Institute of Technology. Netminder Dave Dryden, who was a first-year teacher in Etobicoke, would only play if an emergency arose with Gerry Cheevers. In an unusual practice that prevailed in Junior hockey at the time, teams were able to add eligible players from other junior teams to their list. Father Bauer added two goalkeepers — Roger Crozier of the St. Catharines TeePees (who, at the time, was serving as backup goaltender for the Sault Ste. Marie Thunderbirds of the Eastern Professional Hockey League in their final series against Hull) and Bob Perani of the Junior 'B' Weston Dukes. Perani's brother Paul was the statistician for the Majors that season.

The Majors were given an enthusiastic send-off at the school before being driven to Malton Airport for their flight to Edmonton. It was the first time that Edmonton would host the Memorial Cup championship. Flying west along with the Majors were a number of alumni, including John Arundel, the Hannigan boys (Gord, Pat, and Ray), and John McCormack.

While in Edmonton, all St. Michael's players and alumni attended Holy Mass each morning in the motel, with Father Bauer employing a portable altar supplied by the Archbishop of Edmonton.

"Playoff records seem to give the edge to the Oil Kings, trying to bring Edmonton its first national Junior championship in five attempts," predicted *The Globe and Mail*. Edmonton eliminated the Lethbridge Native Sons, Trail Smoke Eaters, Regina Pats, and Winnipeg Rangers to earn the right to play for the Memorial Cup, winning 16 of 19 games along the way. "They'll have to be good, real good, to knock us off if all the Kings play the kind of hockey they're capable of," stated Edmonton coach, Buster Brayshaw.

Whooping it up in their dressing room, the Majors celebrate their George T. Richardson Memorial Trophy victory as 1961's Eastern Canada Junior champions. Tommy Smith, a 13-year-old befriended by several team members while visiting Toronto's St. Joseph Hospital, revels in the win with his heroes.

Buster Brayshaw named three supplementary players as well, adding Bryan Hextall of the Brandon Wheat Kings and Dave Richardson and Ken Stephenson of the Winnipeg Braves. Richardson was doing double duty, having been called to join the Winnipeg Maroons as they competed in Galt for the Allan Cup, Senior hockey's championship trophy. Plans called for him to fly west later in the week. Brayshaw would start the Junior championship series with his own team, choosing not to dress his supplementary players for Game One.

Game One, played in front of 6,674 fans on April 25, saw both teams start tentatively, feeling out their opponent, before St. Mike's took the lead in the second period on a low 40-foot drive from Bruce Draper. Larry Keenan made Oil Kings blueliner Larry Hale look silly on the second goal, pulling the puck away from the Edmonton defender, pushing the puck through his legs, then circling past him to get a clear shot and a goal on Paul Sexsmith.

Early in the third, Andre Champagne lobbed the puck into the Oil Kings' end. The puck took two wild bounces and squirted over the shoulder of a bewildered Sexsmith. A fourth goal came midway through the third off the stick of Dave Draper, who converted his own rebound past the sprawled netminder.

Arnie Brown rocked Owen Mailley of the Oil Kings when the Edmonton forward was caught with his head down while skating out of his own end and was thundered to the ice with a clean check that left him on the ice for several minutes before he left, missing the rest of the contest. "It was a tough series and we were getting beat up pretty bad," remembers Brown. "I had a hip pointer and in the last game, they froze my hip."

St. Mike's blanked the Oil Kings 4–0, with Cheevers posting the shutout. Father Bauer was impressed with Edmonton's netminder, Paul Sexsmith. "He's all they said he was," the coach remarked. "I thought it should have been 3–0 by the end of the first period, but for him!"

The Globe called it "a typical sample of the Irish blanket coverage." The Majors "made very few mistakes and when they did, Cheevers performed in spectacular style."

With St. Michael's alumnus Joe Primeau in the crowd looking on, Game Two was far more wide open than the tight-checking opening game. Edmonton bolstered their lineup by inserting Bryan Hextall and Ken Stephenson, and both played an outstanding game for the Oil Kings. Duncan MacDonald replaced Billy MacMillan in the St. Mike's lineup.

In the first period, Terry Clancy opened the scoring for the Majors. Paul Conlin netted one at the 25-second mark of the second before Edmonton bounced back to score their only goal in the game, a Tom Burgess deflection on the lip of the crease, midway through the second period. Larry Keenan and Andre Champagne then added goals before the end of the second period. Keenan's goal was magnificent. Reaching out to corral a Bruce Draper outlet pass, Larry was knocked to the ice by Don Chiz, but as he flew through the air in a swan dive, he pulled Sexsmith out of the goal and put a lacrosse-type shot into the Edmonton goal. Terry Clancy then scored his second of the game for St. Mike's.

Gerry Cheevers "gave Oil King shooters the jitters with his antics, his glamorous glove and splendid pad saves," said *The Globe and Mail*. Cheevers came within 6:35 of a second consecutive shutout before Tom Burgess scored late in the third period, but it was a moot point as the Majors prevailed 4–1. "We couldn't beat that Cheevers," sighed Edmonton coach Buster Brayshaw. "The kid was uncanny. He pulled off a couple of saves bordering the impossible!" The win gave St. Mike's a 2–0 lead in the series.

Sonny Osborne flew into Edmonton from Toronto and joined the Majors squad for Game Three. He made quite a difference at both ends of the rink, too. During a scramble to the right of Edmonton goalie Paul Sexsmith, Osborne flipped the puck into the Oil Kings' goal from 10 feet out. Moments before, from almost an identical spot, Osborne had been robbed by the big Edmonton goalie, who got his body up enough to have the shot bounce off his shoulder. At the other end of the ice, Larry Hale had the puck in front of an empty net, but Osborne came out of nowhere to block the attempt as Gerry Cheevers looked on helplessly from a pile-up some 15 feet away.

Midway through the second period, with Arnie Brown and Terry O'Malley in the penalty box, Bryan Hextall picked up a drop pass and fired a rocket just off the ice from 45 feet out that just caught the inside of the post. Shortly afterwards, referee Charlie Knox was prone on the ice for several minutes. Fans booed and tossed debris on the ice, delaying the game even further and seemingly cooling off the hometown Oil Kings. When play resumed, Sonny Osborne sprinted into the Edmonton end to prevent an icing call, beat Stephenson and Wayne Muloin to the puck, and outmanoeuvred goaltender Sexsmith, who had also skated out to beat Osborne to the disk. Sonny spotted Keenan alone in front of the net and got the puck to him for an easy goal, his 30th of the playoffs.

Before the two-minute mark of the third period, Sonny Osborne scored twice to complete his hat trick. For his second goal, he took a pass from Bruce Draper and backhanded it past Sexsmith. Sixty-one seconds later, Jack Cole fed Osborne a breakaway pass that the sniper converted for his third goal. Osborne, easily the star of the contest, also added an assist.

"We had a couple of players hurt so Sonny had finished his exams and flew out," Father Bauer recalled. "They [Edmonton] couldn't believe it! This guy hadn't skated for a week and he scored the first three goals. It was a bit of an accident, but in Edmonton, they thought we just had these players coming out of the wall."

With the 4–2 victory, the Majors put a stranglehold on the series with an almost insurmountable 3–0 lead in the best-of-seven series.

With their backs against the wall, the Edmonton Oil Kings battled back in Game Four, edging the Majors 5–4 to stave off elimination. There was no scoring in the first period, but plenty of action. Just 49 seconds after the puck was dropped, hard-hitting

Tom Burgess collided with Gerry Cheevers, forcing the St. Mike's netminder to retire to the dressing room for bruised ribs and cuts to his face, delaying the game for more than 10 minutes. Burgess was charged with interference on the play. Cheevers returned and played spectacularly, finishing the game and, in the process, stealing several sure-fire goals from the sticks of the Oil Kings.

At 1:15 of the second, Burgess lofted a pass in front of Cheevers' net, but the puck struck Terry O'Malley's stick and caromed into the net for a power-play goal. The tally ignited Edmonton, who got goals from Dave Richardson and Larry Lund late in the period.

A resurgence by the Majors in the third saw Terry Clancy and Paul Conlin close the gap, but the Oil Kings connected for their fourth and fifth goals to put the game out of reach. In spite of markers from Larry Keenan and Bruce Draper late in the third period, the buzzer ended with the score Edmonton 5, Toronto 4.

"From the coach out, they wanted to win more than we did," stated Father Bauer. "If we repeat this kind of game, who knows what might happen?" Coach Brayshaw added, "We looked a bit more like the old Oil Kings and if we carry on this way, St. Mike's are in for a good series."

In the fifth game, Edmonton doubled the Majors 4–2. Bruce Draper scored the opening goal, knocking down a flip pass from his brother Dave and stuffing it under Sexsmith. Dennis Kassian of Edmonton tied things up later in the period. With Roger Galipeau serving a holding minor, Larry Lund fired a shot that struck a defenceman's stick and deflected into the net past Cheevers. Kassian scored a second goal late in the first period, snapping a shot past Cheevers.

Billy MacMillan scored in the second, a period dominated by St. Mike's, but Edmonton barred the door and kept the Majors to the single goal. Dave Richardson's third-period marker helped Edmonton change the tempo of the game, and the Oil Kings held on to win.

Edmonton's coach, Buster Brayshaw, commented that "[goaltender] Sexsmith is our meal ticket. If he's hot, we just might force the series to seven games." Father Bauer agreed, admitting he was most impressed by the five-foot, 11-inch, Winnipeg-born netminder. "He handled everything we could throw at him, although we had some defensive lapses."

Father Bauer employed an integral piece of strategy prior to Game Six, played on May 5. The coach took the team away for some solitude, where the excitement and stress of hockey were temporarily replaced with boating, quoits, and baseball. The drastic change of pace worked wonders, and following Game Six, *The Globe and Mail*'s headline shouted, ST. MIKE'S THUMP KINGS TO CAPTURE MEMORIAL CUP.

Up three games to two, the Majors doubled the Kings 4–2 in a rough-and-tumble contest to take the series four games to two and collect the team's record-setting fourth Memorial Cup championship.

In the first period, Jack Cole opened the scoring for St. Mike's, tapping in the rebound of an Arnie Brown shot. Bryan Hextall tied the score in the second, shoving the puck under Bruce Draper, who slid into the crease to assist Cheevers after the St. Mike's goalie had made two stops. Consecutive second-period goals by Bruce Draper, who fired a 30-footer past Sexsmith, and Paul Conlin, who scored the eventual winner when he fired a drop pass from Andre Champagne past the Oil Kings netminder, put the Majors up 3–1. Champagne scored an insurance marker in the third, and Edmonton's Larry Lund made it closer with a late marker, but it was too little too late for the Oil Kings and St. Mike's held on to collect Junior hockey's top trophy. Seventeen-year-old Andre Champagne led all playoff scorers with 21 points in nine games played.

Paul Conlin reflects on a triumphant season. "I was invited to the Majors' camp and managed to hang on with them that year, and what a great year it was. When we were on our way out to Edmonton for the finals, that was the first time I was ever on an airplane."

Father Bauer's zeal to assist his players in believing they could achieve great things, not just on the ice surfaces, but in their futures, was an uncompromising benefit to the

Father Ted McLean, captain of the 1945 edition of the Majors, presents Terry O'Malley with the school's most valuable player trophy.

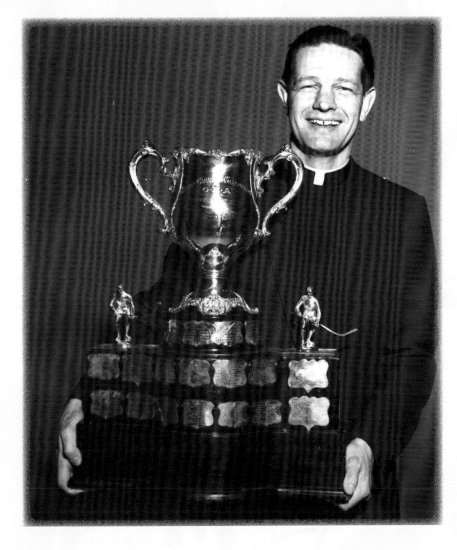

Father David Bauer holds the Memorial Cup, captured as Junior champions by his 1960–61 Majors.

players. He told them that, win or lose, they were the greatest group of boys he had ever had the honour of knowing. "We don't just respect him," said one player, "we love him for everything that he has done for us!"

Following the game, Father Bauer was informed that Max Kaminsky had died. Kaminsky had coached the St. Catharines Teepees to the Memorial Cup championship in 1960 and had succumbed to cancer earlier that day. Father Bauer offered a special service for the soul of a man known as a friend and fine coach.

With a fourth Memorial Cup championship, the St. Michael's Majors held the record for most Junior championships by one franchise, an honour they retained until the Toronto Marlboros (a team made up of several former St. Mike's players, including Andre Champagne) tied the record with their 1964 win, then eclipsed it with a championship in 1967. The Marlboros now have seven Memorial Cup championships. St. Michael's and the Oshawa Generals are next, both with four.

Even then, rumours were rampant that St. Michael's College would pull out of the OHA and that this Memorial Cup–winning game was the school's last contest. *The Globe* called the victory their "Junior 'A' Farewell."

❖

THE POWER OF BAUER

The 1960–61 St. Michael's Majors, the franchise's last Memorial Cup champions. Father Bauer called the team "the greatest group of boys, taken as a team, that I have encountered in my life."

There was a melancholy tone to an interview in which Father David Bauer reflected on the 1960–61 St. Michael's Majors. "Repeatedly, I have said that the 1960–61 edition of the Majors is the greatest group of boys, taken as a team, that I have encountered in my life.

"I am told that we have had teams which completely outclassed their opposition as in the case of the '34, '45, and '47 teams. To glory in the truth of this statement adds luster and strength to our illustrious tradition. However, I honestly doubt that any team ever wanted to win for St. Michael's as badly as the 1960–61 Majors. To win any one game or any one series, each boy had to measure up to his maximum potential. This took effort, real effort, an effort that each boy produced for every big game. Never did I lose confidence in the belief that we would win the OHA title. As for the Memorial Cup, I was not as certain. I knew that the series would be played entirely in the west against a strong Western team, strengthened by an additional three all-star players.

"Often it has been said that you cannot beat a team that will not be beaten. In my opinion, it is for this reason that they are the junior champions of Canada today.

"Who will ever forget the courage displayed by Bruce Draper when he took to the ice in that never-to-be-forgotten game in which we came back from a 3–0 deficit to eliminate a stubborn and somewhat crude and cruel team from Hamilton?

"How can we ever forget the most magnificent goal scored by Larry Keenan in that third game in Edmonton? Knocked down twice after fighting his way in from the blue line, from a prostrate position with number 9 of the opposition sitting on his back, he scored.

"How can we forget Jack Cole scoring his two goals against the Guelph Royals in the final game of that series? He had just returned to the lineup after sustaining a serious neck and head injury in the St. Catharines series. The same Jack Cole scored one goal and assisted in two others, and this aided us in winning the Memorial Cup. In a previous game, he had been checked across the mouth resulting in the loss of two teeth, and worse still, the loss of two night's sleep.

"To continue, certainly nothing can be more memorable than the two key body checks handed out by our team guardian, Roger Galipeau. It happened on the night that we finally eliminated St. Catharines Teepees. It seemed that they imagined that we might be less effective if their club employed the use of their bodies to slow us down in the first period. Within 10 seconds of time and 10 feet of space, 'Big Rog' put the game on ice by two of the most skillfully executed body checks that we have ever seen. The first of these went to the leader who led their legitimate assault resulting in Jack Cole being taken to the hospital. The second went to the biggest player on their team. Barry MacKenzie handed out a similar check to the Hamilton player who had removed Bruce Draper from the scene of action.

"I cannot fail to mention the many tremendous saves executed by our genial goaltender [Gerry Cheevers]. In my opinion, he made two almost impossible saves in the last game on the night that we won the Memorial Cup.

"Two key men in our organization, which helped us from one series to the next, are the persons of Terry O'Malley and Paul Jackson. Without their driving desire, coupled by the keen sense of humour possessed by both boys, the Majors could not be the champions that they are today. I started with these two boys as defencemen in bantam hockey some years ago. Along with Bruce and Dave Draper and Gerry Cheevers, they became the nucleus around which this year's team was built.

"Certainly this team had a great respect for statistics. However, important as these records are, we used them sparingly, Instead, we heeded more the intangibles — the spirit of Peter Noakes, Dave Dryden, or Dunc MacDonald, the tremendous contribution of Jim Gregory, our trainer and assistant manager, the loyalty and hard work offered by [secretary] Jim Holleran, [trainer] Norm Mackie, and [student manager] Ricky Noonan. To no lesser degree, the deep concern of [team doctors] Dr. Knowlton and Dr. Wren, the inspiration and leadership of Mr. Joe Primeau [team president], the co-operation of interested but not interfering parents rightly concerned about their boys and their all-round welfare, the support from our administration at the school, our students, our Old Boys, and all those who followed our progress and success through the year's campaign. These are the things that make a team great. This is why we are the Memorial Cup champions!"

❖

Ten thousand fans lined Bay Street and crowded into City Hall Square to fete the champions, both the Majors and the Buzzers. The Majors, led by the school's marching band, rode in convertible sports cars, carrying the Memorial Cup. Father Conway, coach of the Buzzers, sat with Father Bauer in the lead car.

The teams were greeted by Toronto Mayor Nathan Phillips on the steps to City Hall. Father Bauer presented the mayor with a Stetson cowboy hat (which each team member also proudly wore that day) and a hockey stick. Father Bauer then spoke on behalf of the Majors, followed by Father Conway in similar fashion for the Buzzers.

Barry MacKenzie: *Major Captain* — SNAPSHOT

It appeared that Barry MacKenzie's hockey path was set out in front of him, but a bigger foe than he had ever faced changed destiny for the top prospect. "When I was a young buck, I had tuberculosis, so I was told I couldn't play hockey," he explains. "I had played for the Weston Dukes (the Toronto Maple Leafs' Junior 'B' team) before I went into the sanitarium, and while I was in there I signed a C-Form with the Leafs. When I got out of the sanitarium, they told me I could only play high school hockey for Weston Collegiate. But after high school hockey finished, the Weston Dukes wanted me to play for them in the playoffs, so I did and I guess I had a strong playoff. Over the summer, I got a call from Father Bauer. Talk about something changing your whole life! He asked me if I'd like to play for St. Mike's. I did that instead of playing for the Marlies."

Big, strong, and solid, MacKenzie had a tough choice to contemplate, but the opportunity presented by St. Michael's College gave the Majors the edge. "I always had in the back of my mind that I wanted an education, and St. Mike's was more known for that than the Marlies were. I think also the fact that Father Bauer was the coach compared to Turk Broda, who was coaching the Marlies, just seemed to be a better fit for me."

With expectations running high, Barry looked forward to a great season with St. Mike's. "In my first exhibition game, I played centre between Larry Keenan and Bruce Draper," he recalls. "When I played with the Weston Dukes, I kept hurting my knee. I'd block a shot and I'd hurt my knee. I guess I had torn ligaments, so in my first exhibition game, I just had a brush against my knee and I was out until February 14." As a result, MacKenzie played but nine games that season, scoring once and assisting on four others. Yet, in the playoffs, the captain's presence inspired his teammates.

After a second season with the Majors, this time in the Metro Toronto Junior Hockey League, Barry followed his mentor to Canada's west coast. "Father Bauer talked about his dream of the National Team and I was a bit of an idealist, too, and I guess that's why I headed out to [the University of British Columbia] with him."

Barry was joined by fellow St. Mike's players Terry Clancy, Paul Conlin, Gary Dineen, Terry O'Malley, and Rod Seiling, each of whom eschewed a professional career, or at least put those plans on hold, in order to compete for their country with Father Bauer. "When you're surrounded by a community of teachers like the Basilians, you know that there is a bigger purpose to life than just hockey, and you really start to appreciate that there's more to life than chasing a puck around a rink. I was a Protestant, still am a Protestant, but yet I'd sometimes end up serving Mass with Father Bauer. But even from the point of view of those of us [with the Majors in 1961] who were Protestants, there was still a spiritual dimension for all of us on the team. Whatever your faith was, Father Bauer believed, 'Whatever you want to be, be!'"

MacKenzie stayed with the National Team program even after the Toronto Maple Leafs, who held his NHL rights, sold him to the expansion Minnesota North Stars in June 1967. He turned pro with the Minnesota organization in 1968–69, playing in six games with the NHL North Stars. "I more than likely could have had a longer career there, but because of Father Bauer's influence, I guess I was too much of an individual and there's no doubt I didn't really hit it off with Wren Blair. My career came to an abrupt halt with them."

But that wasn't the end of Father Bauer's influence on Barry and his career. "Father Bauer ended up recommending me to Sudbury, where I was coach of their Junior team," Barry says. "When I finished there, he recommended that I go over to Japan, and then after that, he recommended that I go to Notre Dame [College in Wilcox, Saskatchewan]. My wife used to joke that once Father Bauer died, what was going to happen to my career?"

Father David Bauer had a great impact on so many, but arguably, none more than Barry MacKenzie. "He was a great friend as far as I was concerned. He had tremendous insight. He challenged people to be the best that they could be. He used to say, 'God has given you gifts, but it's your responsibility to use those gifts to the maximum.'"

25

The Majors Leave the OHA

What began as a rumour was confirmed as fact shortly after the St. Michael's Majors won the Memorial Cup in 1961. At the conclusion of that school year, the principal of St. Michael's College School, Reverend Matthew Sheedy, issued a statement that the school intended to withdraw from Junior 'A' competition: "The OHA program as it is now constituted, with its long and demanding schedule, with its lengthy and drawn-out playoff arrangements, militates against effective school work. This sometimes results in failure in school or a lack of interest in academic achievements. Efforts to bring about an appreciable change seem to have met with no success. We feel that we have no recourse but to withdraw from the Junior 'A' program."

Father William O'Brien added confirmation of the not-so-silent whispers when he wrote, "The Majors are retiring as Canadian Junior hockey champions. Though Junior 'A' hockey will never be the same without St. Michael's, any thinking person knows that when and if a sport interferes with the cause of education, then the sport must be de-emphasized. Hockey has been a part of St. Michael's for many, many years, but these days, hockey is less of a sport and more of a business all the time.

"The decision of the school authorities is quite understandable. St. Michael's is first, last and always, a school for the education of young men. It is not a hockey factory, nor was it ever intended to be. A school team is at a disadvantage in such a situation. And students rarely can do justice to their studies, especially when they are constantly recovering from one game and preparing for the next."

❖

The 1957 edition of the St. Michael's College School's yearbook, *The Tower*, confirmed the school's insistence on merging scholastics with sport. "Sports will help the athlete, by the spirit of competition, to face greater obstacles than those on the athletic field. It helps him to develop certain powers given to him by Almighty God and brought out by his instructors."

But a tug-of-war had quietly evolved within the faculty of St. Michael's. One camp believed that sport, specifically hockey, had taken on too large a role in the school and was smothering academics. Others pointed to the original doctrine of the Basilian Fathers and felt that athletics were at the core of the school's mandate.

On May 5, *The Globe and Mail* further expanded on reasons for the exit. "Even the most rabid of supporters of hockey in the religious order have determined that students must not be forced to participate in long schedules. In particular, the series against Hamilton and Guelph in which officials feel there were deliberate attempts made to injure Majors' stars, has contributed to the withdrawal, which also was threatened a year ago. The college will refuse to put up with adverse publicity which it has received from members of the OHA Junior Council, particularly in the past two years." There had been not-so-quiet whispers around the league that St. Mike's was not wanted. One reason for the sniping was that the school's presence in the league gave the Toronto Maple Leafs an unfair advantage in attracting young prospects to their chain. The promise of a high-quality, free education certainly gave the Leafs inordinate influence over potential players and their parents.

"This was not a hasty decision," said Father David Bauer. "That idea had been bandied about for years. St. Mike's had left the Major ranks once before — around 1940. I came

Rod Seiling was a high-scoring forward converted to defence during his time at St. Mike's. It was on the blue line that he starred in the National Hockey League.

to St. Michael's in '41 and Junior 'A' hockey had just been re-established." Father Bauer was correct. St. Michael's did not participate in Junior 'A' hockey in either 1939–40 or 1940–41.

Father Bauer further expounded "Our General Council had talked about this for a long time and they talked to me about it. I suggested that some of our relationships may have been damaged a little bit if we left in a way that would sever our connection so abruptly. Hard feelings would arise from the league. St. Michael's representatives were always trying to cut down on the violence, cut down on the length of schedules, cut down on the materialism of the whole thing. We regretted very much leaving for that reason because we knew that this is a major recreational institution in this country."

Father Bauer had himself sent a letter to Maple Leafs founder Conn Smythe warning in part that "sooner or later, they [St. Mike's] will see fit to discontinue in the Junior 'A' series because of its growing professionalism, its long schedule and rough play, which so often results in unfavourable publicity — difficult for the educational institution to handle gracefully."

Father Bauer continued: "The 1961 season, I think we played 98 games! At that level and at that pressure, if you really look over the whole history of it, it's amazing the number of boys who did it and survived academically or came back at it from another route. A number of those fellows have gone on to universities. You've got Billy MacMillan, Jack Cole, Roger Galipeau, Terry Clancy, Barry McKenzie, Sonny Osborne, Peter Noakes, Brian Walsh, Paul Conlin, Dave Dryden, Terry O'Malley. It was amazing what could be done even with those difficult circumstances."

Smythe was quite perturbed to receive formal notice that St. Michael's College had pulled itself out of the league. "I feel that something has gone out of the Canadian way of life with this decision," he wrote in a letter to Father Matthew Sheedy on June 6, 1961. "Not because this affects us at the Maple Leaf Gardens in a material way, [but] because St. Mike's have always been very good friends to us over the years. It is true that there have been stupid things done in amateur athletics, but sports are something like world affairs — you cannot fold up and say you won't play. If our country persists in downgrading the natural tendency of our youth to enjoy and take part in the athletic games which have been developed in the British Empire for so long, then it won't be too many generations before this country becomes a narrow-minded, small satellite for some other state which has not as fine a program."

Father Sheedy quickly fired off a response to Smythe. "Our associations with you and Maple Leaf Gardens have always been most gratifying and conducted on the highest possible level. Working together as we have in the past, we have done a great deal for God, for youth and for Canada. St. Michael's has no intention of 'folding up and saying it won't play.' We realize fully the part we have to play in the education of our Canadian youth. We feel that it is unjust however to ask a group of guys to carry a full-time academic load of studies and at the same time play hockey from November to May. Father Bauer has repeatedly sought a reasonable schedule from the Junior 'A' Council. They have not only ignored him but have insisted that the schedule be lengthened to 60 games per season and that the playoffs be conducted on a 5/9 basis [best-of-nine series]. We feel that we are fighting a battle for sanity in sports. Does St. Michael's stand alone in the battle for reasonableness? Only time will tell!"

It should be no surprise that Harold Ballard, co-owner of the Leafs as well as the archrival Toronto Marlboros, would weigh in on the St. Michael's decision. "The league will miss St. Mike's more than the school will miss [the league]. The team has always been a credit to the league and to the Canadian Amateur Hockey Association," he said. "I don't blame a fine person like Father Bauer not wanting to be humiliated by a few nitwits who have criticized and ridiculed him and the school. I think the OHA should make some concessions."

Hap Emms, owner and coach of the Niagara Falls Flyers, was far less conciliatory. "We've done enough for them in the last 10 years, including four-point games," he told *The Telegram* on June 7, 1961. "Their main complaint is too many games, yet they have gone on exhibition tours and went out west to play in the Memorial Cup. They played more games this year than any other team!"

In a March 1960 issue of *The Hockey News*, an "unnamed but reliable source" had stated that the Toronto Maple Leafs were prepared to transfer the St. Michael's franchise to Kitchener, but only on the condition that players be accepted as students at St. Jerome's College.

There was one other idea, and although not ideal for St. Michael's, it was a compromise that had to be considered. "We had a meeting with Mr. [Stafford] Smythe and Mr. [Bob] Davidson, who were in charge of the amateur program for the Maple Leafs in those days. We discussed forming what would be the Metro Junior 'A' League," recalls Jim Gregory, who is today the NHL's senior vice-president, but who at the time was the trainer/manager of the St. Michael's Majors under his mentor, Father Bauer.

The Maple Leafs, prompted by the potential loss of St. Michael's participation, proposed a new league with a reduced schedule and made up solely of Toronto-area teams. "We'll try to make it an amateur game again," stated Toronto Maple Leafs co-owner Stafford Smythe. Father David Bauer, who had already announced that he was leaving St. Michael's to assume a post with St. Mark's University in Vancouver, commented that St. Mike's was open to considering entering a team in the newly formed league. "I am empowered to say that we are not averse to entering a team in such a league if it is formed," he said. "It will be a tremendous league; important in the development of character of future boys."

❖

The Toronto Metro Junior 'A' League splintered off from the Ontario Hockey Association's Junior 'A' loop beginning with the 1961–62 season. The new league included both Leaf affiliates, the Majors and the Marlboros, as well as the Brampton 7-Ups, Unionville Seaforths, and Whitby Mohawks. The latter three had played at the Junior 'B' level in 1960–61. The five-team league would play a 30-game regular-season schedule, and as Jim Gregory points out: "The players did not travel. They played all their games in what we call today the GTA [Greater Toronto Area]."

The OHA, meanwhile, soldiered on without its two important Toronto franchises. In 1961–62, the league was made up of the Guelph Royals, Hamilton Red Wings, Montreal Junior Canadiens, Niagara Falls Flyers, Peterborough Petes, and St. Catharines TeePees.

The St. Michael's team that started the 1961–62 campaign was almost entirely different than the team that won the Memorial Cup the previous spring. First off, coach Father David Bauer had left for British Columbia to assemble a national team for Canada. Bauer was replaced by Father Ted Flanagan, who was ably assisted by manager Jim Gregory.

Ten players were lost to age restrictions, including Gerry Cheevers, Bruce Draper, Paul Jackson, Larry Keenan, and Duncan MacDonald, who had graduated to the American Hockey League. An exodus to the University of Michigan included overagers Jack Cole, Dave Draper, and Roger Galipeau. Arnie Brown, Dave Dryden, and Dunc MacDonald were moved over to the Marlies, while Peter Noakes was placed on the Brampton 7-Ups squad.

Andre Champagne, Terry Clancy, Paul Conlin, Mike Corbett, Gary Dineen, Billy MacMillan, Tom Polanic, and high-scoring Rod Seiling, who had yet to be converted to a defenceman, were holdovers from the previous season and provided a foundation, while the remainder of the roster was liberally filled with such players as goaltender Gary Smith, defenceman Jim McKendry, and forwards Mike Walton and Tony Fritz. "We've a lot of places to fill," Father Flanagan shrugged. "Lost a hatful of good players. We have only five full-time returnees and everybody else is a rookie. Some will develop and some will be a bust."

The Marlboros, coached by goaltending great Turk Broda, featured future NHL stars Arnie Brown, Brian Conacher, Ron Ellis, Gary Jarrett, Brit Selby, and netminder Dave Dryden.

Father Ted Flanagan had big shoes to fill as he replaced Father Bauer as coach of the St. Michael's Majors in 1961–62.

Outside of the Marlboros and St. Mike's players, there were but a handful of players of note. The goaltender for the Brampton 7-Ups was Ken Broderick, who later played for Canada at the 1964 and 1968 Olympics and enjoyed a career that straddled both the NHL and WHA. One Brampton teammate was Brian Bradley, who spent three seasons in the World Hockey Association. Wayne Carleton, who had been labeled a "can't-miss" prospect during his Junior career, played part of that first season with Unionville, then was traded to the Marlies. Unionville was also home to Barry Watson and coach Cliff Simpson, who had had a cup of coffee in the NHL as a player with the Detroit Red Wings. Whitby was led by Bill Collins, who went on to play 10 NHL seasons, Billy Smith, who spent several years in the American Hockey League, and goalkeeper Bob Perani, who played a handful of seasons in the AHL and International Hockey League.

Pundits harrumphed, wondering why the Leafs would bother. It was believed that the league wouldn't be a major drawing card in the communities that housed teams and would hurt the remaining OHA Junior 'A' teams, who always found Toronto teams to be a strong draw at the box office. And, it was predicted, it would irreparably damage Junior 'B' hockey in the Toronto area, pulling the best talent out to fill the rosters of the new league. Some insiders were scratching their heads, believing that the Metro Junior 'A' league was also destined to be an expensive venture for the NHL Leafs. "We hope it doesn't go too high, but if it costs in the neighbourhood of $10,000 to $20,000 a year, it will be nothing compared to the development of players, the league and the boys' education," said Stafford Smythe.

"The league is regarded in some quarters as merely a practice loop for St. Mike's and the Marlies," stated the *Toronto Star*. Brian Conacher, a member of the Toronto Marlboros that season, says, "Even as a young player, our perception was that it didn't have quite the panache that being a member of the OHA did." But Rod Seiling recalls how good the two former OHA teams were. "St. Mike's and the Marlies were as competitive and as strong as we would have been if we had been playing in the OHA. The Leafs didn't adjust their scouting formula during the duration of the Metro Junior 'A' League."

"We played a number of games against Major Junior teams," Barry MacKenzie comments. "It was really quite different. The team we had was a pretty good team. We only had five guys back with the Majors, but much of the team came from the Buzzers. They had finished off the last season with 26 straight victories with Dineen, Seiling, and Corbett. But it was a lot different than playing in the OHA, there's no doubt about that."

❖

The St. Michael's Majors opened the 1961–62 season on Hallowe'en, visiting what *The Globe* called "the unpractised but impeccably dressed Seaforths" in Unionville, spanking their hosts 10–3. Terry Clancy equalled his entire output of the previous Junior season with two goals in the third period. The Majors next played their home opener against the Marlboros. Facing former teammate Dave Dryden in goal, they dumped the Marlies 5–2 in a game described by *The Globe and Mail* as "a scorcher all the way. The sticks were high, the elbows up and the bodychecking stiff."

The Marlboros handed St. Mike's their first loss of the season on November 24, when Dryden earned a 4–0 shutout against his former mates. The game counted for four points in the standings. Not to be outdone, St. Michael's netminder Gary Smith picked up a shutout in the next game, blanking Whitby, 6–0. The line of Seiling, Corbett, and Dineen accounted for 10 points during the contest. That line picked up 12 more points in a 5–3 win over Unionville on November 28. The game was held up for several minutes after a tussle in front of the Seaforths' net between Rod Seiling and Unionville's Doug Kelcher saw the latter lose a contact lens. In spite of the efforts of both teams to find it, the lens was not found.

With Father Flanagan suffering from the flu, Jim Gregory coached the Majors to a 7–2 triumph over Unionville on December 10. Cliff Simpson, the Seaforths' coach, commented to *The Globe and Mail*, "There isn't a team in the league that can skate with St. Mike's."

The school enjoyed a bit of fun in mid-December as the Old Boys challenged the current Majors in an exhibition contest, with proceeds contributed to a scholarship fund. The Old Boys included Ed Harrison, Johnny McCormack, a reunion of the line of Les Costello, Fleming Mackell, and Tod Sloan from the 1947 Memorial Cup champions, Jimmy Thomson and Gus Mortson together again on the blue line, and, surprisingly, several current Leafs of that time. Dick Duff, Tim Horton, Red Kelly, and Frank Mahovlich participated, although Dave Keon was threatened with a $150 fine by coach Punch Imlach if he played, so he was simply a spectator.

Maurice Richard was the referee, and King Clancy his linesman. "The Old Boys taught the young whippersnappers a lesson," joked *The Globe and Mail* about the 6–2 win for the Old Boys. "The old ones substituted heads for legs, played yoyo with the puck at times and occasionally knocked the youngsters down when they got too obstreperous." A total of $3,500 was raised for the St. Michael's Scholarship and Bursary Fund.

With alumnus Dave Draper looking on, home from the University of Michigan, St. Mike's edged Whitby 1–0 in a December 15 contest *The Globe* described as having "as much interest as students would have in a trigonometry test." Two nights later, Guelph took revenge on the team that eliminated them in the Memorial Cup playoffs the previous spring, dumping St. Mike's 7–2 in an exhibition game.

With Ken Broderick shining in goal, the Brampton 7-Ups shocked the Majors 5–2 on December 21. *The Globe and Mail* described the game as "a triumph of the good little underdog guys with hustle, harry and hotfoot toppling bustle, burly and bungle." St. Mike's lost a second straight league game on the 23rd when Whitby edged them 5–4. The Majors were without Paul Conlin, Tony Fritz, Bill MacMillan, Emile Therien, and netminder Gary Smith, all of whom had gone home for the Christmas holidays. Bill McNabb played goal for St. Mike's, as he did the next afternoon when the Majors edged Brampton, 4–3.

The Majors, the class of the Metro Junior 'A' League, rang out 1961 with a New Year's Eve exhibition game against the best team in the Ontario Hockey Association, the Montreal Junior Canadiens. With future stars Andre Boudrias and Jacques Laperriere in the lineup, the Junior Canadiens skated to a three-all tie with St. Mike's.

The next day featured a loss to Whitby, but an even bigger setback when star forward Rod Seiling injured his leg. Father Flanagan and Jim Gregory moved Jim McKendry up to forward from his blueline post to temporarily replace Seiling, and the defenceman responded by scoring four goals in a 6–1 win over Brampton on January 7. Wayne Mosdell was inserted into the lineup on defence. Unfortunately, McKendry's heroics were short-lived, as he suffered a concussion in a January 14 exhibition contest against the Niagara Falls Flyers.

As good as the Majors were, with their finesse and fine netminding, the boys were not about to back down from a skirmish. During a 6–3 win over Whitby on January 21, two policemen were required to break up a fight in the penalty box. Bob Wright, Whitby's enforcer, was grabbed when he challenged the constables while standing on the penalty bench. Wright was in the penalty box after he and Mike Corbett from St. Mike's had been sent off for roughing. The Majors' Andre Champagne earned a misconduct when he was caught throwing a haymaker at a Whitby player while sitting on the bench.

St. Michael's racked up win after win and dominated the league. But a 12-game unbeaten streak came to an end in a contest against the arch-rival Marlboros on February 25. "For speed, finesse and punishment, the Majors/Marlies match was unequalled this season," reported the *Globe and Mail* of the 5–4 Marlies' win. Incidentally, Turk Broda, coach of the Toronto Marlboros, was recovering from cataract surgery and was replaced behind the bench by manager Jack White.

St. Mike's finished a dominant first in the Metro Junior 'A' League, with a record of 25 wins against seven losses and a tie for 55 points. The Marlboros completed the season second with 44 points, while Whitby (30), Brampton (26), and Unionville (25) were well behind the leaders.

Mike Walton was just 16 years old when he joined the Majors in 1961–62. He went on to an outstanding NHL career.

1961–62

METRO JUNIOR 'A'

TEAM	GP	W	L	T	Pts
St. Michael's Majors	33	25	7	1	55
Toronto Marlboros	33	18	9	6	44
Whitby Mohawks	36	14	20	2	30
Brampton 7-Ups	36	11	21	4	26
Unionville Seaforths	36	10	21	5	25

OHA JUNIOR 'A'

TEAM	GP	W	L	T	Pts
Montreal Jr. Canadiens	50	34	11	5	73
Hamilton Red Wings	50	32	12	6	70
St. Catharines TeePees	50	19	23	8	46
Niagara Falls Flyers	50	16	23	11	43
Guelph Royals	50	18	26	6	42
Peterborough Petes	50	9	33	8	26

Meanwhile, the Montreal Junior Canadiens, having joined the OHA from the Quebec Junior Hockey League, were the cream of the more established loop.

Gary Dineen was the Metro Junior 'A' league's scoring leader with 61 points, including a league-best 35 assists, earning him the Joseph Cooper Memorial Trophy. Gary Jarrett of the Marlboros was runner-up with 55 points. Jarrett's 28 goals tied him with Bill Smith of the Whitby Mohawks for the league lead. Mike Corbett of the Majors tallied 52 points, while Rod Seiling contributed 24 goals and 50 points. St. Michael's goaltender Gary Smith was selected as recipient of the Turk Broda Trophy as the league's best netminder.

Gary Smith earned a living in the National Hockey League over 14 seasons, acquiring the nickname "Suitcase" in the process. After making his debut with the Toronto Maple Leafs in 1965–66, he would call the following NHL cities home: Oakland, Chicago, Vancouver, Minnesota, Washington, and Winnipeg. In 532 NHL appearances, Smith won 173, lost 261, and tied 74. He also played two seasons in the WHA, one with Indianapolis and one with Winnipeg, recording seven wins, 13 losses, and a tie in 22 games. Gary also played in the minors in Rochester, Tulsa, Victoria, Hershey, and Fort Worth. After all those years stacking and packing the pads, he laughed as he recalled 1979–80, his final year before retiring. "We were short players because of injuries, but had three goaltenders. I dressed and played forward one shift. It was one of the highlights of my career!"

❖

St. Michael's faced the Whitby Mohawks in the semifinals. The underdog Mohawks shocked the Majors with a decisive 4–1 win in the opening contest, played in Whitby. Paul Conlin had just returned after being out for six weeks, while Andre Champagne, Jim Cullen, and Barry MacKenzie were missing from the Majors' lineup.

Just prior to the start of the playoffs, Champagne had been rushed to the hospital with a collapsed lung, and treatment and time were required before Andre could join the team again.

St. Mike's rebounded with an 8–2 shellacking in Game Two. "You had to be one of the 1,588 present to believe this weird display," announced *The Globe and Mail*. In spite of a hat trick by Billy MacMillan and Mike Walton's goal on a penalty shot in the second, the story was more about the fights. There were 124 minutes in penalties in the third period alone. On a delayed penalty to Bill Collins of Whitby, St. Michael's netminder Gary Smith took off down the ice, got involved in the play, swung at the puck, and missed and ended up in a heap in Bob Perani's crease. That triggered a brawl in the third period that saw Wayne Mosdell throwing punches with Len Bobbie, Billy MacMillan scrapping with Bob Tripp, Emile Therien facing off against Julian Kowalski, and the netminders, Gary Smith and Bob Perani, exchanging blows. After the officials got the melee calmed, another broke out at 19:45, just before the final buzzer. Tom Polanic of the Majors dragged Julian Kowalski down the ice and administered a nasty beating that left the Whitby player's face smeared with blood.

After the contest, 11 players were fined $10 each for their participation in the ugly brawls. Terry Clancy, Ray Dupont, MacMillan, Polanic, and Smith were all fined for St. Mike's, while Whitby's Len Bobbie, Chick Carnegie, Collins, Brian Fletcher, Perani and Pete Shearer also received fines.

Although the play settled down in Game Three, a 3–1 win for St. Mike's, the animosity still existed. Terry Clancy scrapped with Whitby goaltender Bob Perani, and left him with a two-stitch cut to the eye.

With the score tied 3–3 going into the third period of Game Four, the Majors kicked down the door and scored three unanswered goals to double Whitby 6–3 and take a three-games-to-one lead in the best-of-seven semifinal. A crowd double the Whitby Arena's capacity of 941 watched the exciting game. Mike Corbett and Terry Clancy each scored a pair.

It was fitting that a trumpeter blew "The Last Post" during the dying moments of the fifth and final game of the semifinal between St. Michael's and Whitby. Missing Andre Champagne with a collapsed lung and Rod Seiling with mononucleosis, both out for the remainder of the playoffs, St. Mike's decimated Whitby with an 11–2 win to eliminate the Mohawks.

In spite of allowing 11 goals, Bob Perani was Whitby's best player. Coach Ivan Davie admitted, "They were superb tonight. I don't think anyone could have beaten them."

The Majors next faced the Toronto Marlboros in a best-of-seven series, the winner of the series to receive the Father Bill Conway Memorial Trophy as Metro Junior 'A' champions. The Majors came out flat and handed the Marlies a 4–1 win. "We just played a bad game," shrugged Father Flanagan.

With Terry Clancy, Paul Conlin, and Billy MacMillan shadowing the Marlies' big line of Gary Jarrett, Duncan MacDonald, and Gary Milroy, St. Mike's came back with a 7–3 win in Game Two. The game wasn't without its animosity. MacMillan and Jarrett fought in the first period. When Jarrett later poked at a puck smothered under Gary Smith's glove, Smith raced out of his crease and began throwing punches at Jarrett. Both received majors.

The Marlies exacted revenge on St. Mike's in Game Three, returning with an 8–3 win. Gary Jarrett of the Marlies went without a penalty for the first time that season, and his prominence on the ice paid dividends for the Marlies. Four of the team's goals were scored while shorthanded.

Three was an unlucky number for St. Mike's in Game Four of their series with the Marlies. Three goals in three minutes in the third period buried the Majors, with the final score 5–2. St. Michael's bounced back in Game Five, dumping the Marlboros 5–1. Mike Corbett had a goal and two assists to fuel the comeback.

Game Six saw St. Mike's romp back, in spite of missing three of their best scorers. Champagne and Seiling were still out recovering while MacMillan was nursing a twisted back. Paul Conlin picked up the slack, scoring twice and checking diligently as the 5–2 result evened the series at three games apiece, setting the stage for the decisive seventh game.

It took a bitterly contested seven-game series, but the St. Michael's College Majors won the inaugural Metro Junior 'A' Championship on April 3, 1962, dumping the Marlies 3–1. Early in the game, Frank Ridley of the Marlies fired a shot that hit Gary Smith on the arm and ricocheted into the top corner of the net. Angry, Smith grabbed the puck and threw it to the ice in disgust. But both the referee and goal judge ruled "No goal." The Marlies stormed the officials, to no avail. Later, Barry MacDonald broke into the clear on a breakaway but was hauled down from the side by Ridley. The referee pointed to centre ice, and Father Flanagan selected Paul Conlin to take the penalty shot. Marlies coach Turk Broda was so incensed, he first flung a stick out onto the ice, then whipped his fedora onto the playing surface and was summarily ejected. Conlin, who scored in the first period, got in too close to goalie Dave Dryden and lost the handle on the puck, which trickled harmlessly into the corner. Barry MacDonald scored what would be the winning goal midway through the third, and Corbett added a shorthanded empty net insurance marker in the dying seconds.

While leaning down talking to one of his players, an errant shot from the stick of Ron Ellis caught Father Flanagan on the forehead and took 10 stitches to close.

After the game, Oshawa Generals coach Matt Leyden presented St. Michael's captain Barry MacKenzie with the Father Bill Conway Trophy as league champions. "It is fitting that this team, with so many of Father Bill's players on it, should be the first winners," said Leyden in his presentation.

❖

The next step for the reigning MJHL champions was to face the Ontario Hockey Association champion Hamilton Red Wings in the All-Ontario final.

St. Michael's feared disaster when netminder Gary Smith pulled his groin just two minutes into the game. Although not seriously hurt, Coach Flanagan decided it was better to risk losing the game with a rookie netminder than to risk losing their all-star for the remainder of the playoffs. Bill McNabb, a 17-year-old rookie goaltender whose only Junior 'A' experience was stepping into the crease to replace Smith during the Christmas vacation,

Jim Gregory went from being a stickboy for the Majors to a spot in the Hockey Hall of Fame. Gregory credits his time at St. Michael's for contributing to much of his success.

was put in to replace the injured Smith. In the series opener he emerged as the hero, earning an important playoff shutout.

The Majors did everything they could to assist the young goalie, sliding in front of shots and thwarting every potential Marlies scoring chance en route to a 2–0 victory. "It was a dull and boring affair as St. Michael's polished their checking patterns, clung to checks like leeches and waited for breaks," wrote *The Globe and Mail*. Defenceman Ray Dupont scored the winning goal late in the second period. The 1–0 score held up until there were seconds left in the contest. With goaltender Buddy Blom on the bench for an extra attacker, Billy MacMillan outraced Bob Wall to a loose puck deep in the Red Wings end and tucked it into the empty net to cement the game with just three seconds left to play.

The Red Wings stormed back in Game Two, earning a well-deserved 5–1 decision over the Majors, who had Gary Smith back in goal, although he seemed off his game. Hamilton outshot and out-thought St. Mike's, forcing the Majors to scramble. The Red Wings led 5–0 until Mike Walton broke Blom's shutout bid late in the game. Hamilton's sniper, Paul Henderson, suffered a concussion early in the second period after being checked by Jim McKendry, and it was determined he'd likely miss several games.

The Red Wings went up two games to one after a 5–0 whitewash in Game Three. The game got out of hand with Hamilton up 4–0 in the second period and coach Eddie Bush deciding to rest his stars and play his lesser lights in the third period. The Hamilton fans chanted "Junior 'B'! Junior 'B'!" through much of the third period. During an altercation in the second period, a fan threw a smoke bomb onto the ice. Shortly afterwards, another threw a dead hand grenade, complete with handle and intact pin, onto the ice.

The Majors endured their worst loss of the entire season in Game Four, being whipped 10–3. "The Irish deserved a beating," reported *The Globe and Mail*. Even Hamilton goaltender Buddy Blom got into the act. During a delayed penalty, Blom raced down the ice, took a pass in front of the net, and fired a shot that Gary Smith kicked out. He tried again a few minutes later, but was unable to get into the play before St. Michael's regained possession and the whistle blew. "Our goalie played better forward than some of their forwards," chuckled Eddie Bush, Hamilton's coach. The third period was marred by a fight that began in the stands and worked its way down, continuing in the form of scraps between the Red Wings and Majors.

Hamilton captain Howie Menard accepted the John Ross Robertson Trophy from OHA president Lloyd Pollock after his Red Wings defeated St. Michael's College 5–3 in Game Five to clinch the All-Ontario championship, Hamilton's first. Gary Smith, out with a pulled groin, was replaced again by McNabb. In desperation, Father Flanagan moved defenceman Ray Dupont to the number one line with Gary Dineen and Rod Seiling, replacing Mike Corbett. The coach also shortened his bench, rolling two lines and four defenceman, but even that tactic had little effect on the results of the game.

Pit Martin and Lowell MacDonald scored two goals apiece for Hamilton. Rod Seiling scored two in a losing cause for the Majors.

"Experience tells," Father Flanagan said after the game. "You have to have those age-limit players with the few extra tricks. They [Hamilton] were the better team." Hamilton went on to capture the Memorial Cup, defeating the Edmonton Oil Kings four games to one.

Ten members of that ill-fated St. Michael's Majors team, the last to wear the school's iconic double blue until the franchise's return to the Ontario Hockey League in 1997–98, went on to join the fraternity of NHL players. Joining Andre Champagne, Barry MacKenzie, Billy MacMillan, Rod Seiling, and Gary Smith were Terry Clancy, Mike Corbett, Gary Dineen, Tom Polanic, and Mike Walton.

Surrounded by jubilant teammates, captain Barry MacKenzie accepted the Father Bill Conway Trophy as champion of the Metro Junior Hockey League.

Clancy spent two seasons with the Majors, then competed for the Canadian team that placed fourth in the 1964 Olympics. Signed by the Toronto Maple Leafs after the Winter Games, Clancy was plucked from the Leafs' roster by the Oakland Seals in the 1967 Expansion Draft and played seven games for the Seals in their inaugural season. He was sold back to Toronto in May 1968 and spent parts of three seasons with the Maple Leafs. In his NHL career, Terry Clancy scored six goals and six assists in 93 games.

The line of Mike Corbett, Gary Dineen, and Rod Seiling tore through Metro Junior Hockey League competition. Corbett worked his way through hockey's minor leagues until 1968, when he played two playoff games for the Los Angeles Kings, picking up an assist. Gary Dineen, meanwhile, followed Father Bauer's dream for a Canadian national team and played for his country in both the 1964 and 1968 Olympic Winter Games. Gary's rights were sold by the Maple Leafs to the Minnesota North Stars, and he joined former teammate Barry MacKenzie on the sophomore NHL squad in 1968–69, playing four games and earning an assist. Dineen later turned to instruction, and oversaw a highly successful Junior hockey program in New England.

NHL expansion gave many fine hockey players an opportunity to play the game at its highest level. Such was the case with Tom Polanic. The big defenceman graduated from the University of Michigan after his years at St. Mike's. It would take until 1969–70 for him to reach the NHL, with the Minnesota North Stars. In 19 games over two seasons, Tom collected two points.

Just 16 when he first played for the Majors, Mike Walton, the enigmatic son of former Montreal Canadien Bobby Walton (four games in 1943–44), was a prodigious goal scorer throughout his career. He entered the NHL with the Toronto Maple Leafs in 1965–66,

THE MAJORS LEAVE THE OHA

The 1961–62 St. Michael's Majors were the final edition of the Junior squad until the franchise's return to Junior action in 1997–98.

and the next season was a member of the team as they hoisted the Stanley Cup. In each of his three full-time seasons with Toronto, Walton scored 20 or more goals. He was traded to the Boston Bruins in February 1971, and the next season, a campaign in which he scored 28 goals, Mike was again on a Stanley Cup champion. Three seasons with the WHA's Minnesota Fighting Saints (he was the league's leading scorer with 117 points in 1973–74) interrupted an NHL career that also took Walton to Vancouver, St. Louis, back to Boston, and Chicago. Walton's NHL career resulted in 201 goals and 247 assists for 448 points in 588 regular-season games, while his WHA statistics show 136 goals, 145 assists, and 281 points in 211 games.

After a single season in the Metro Junior 'A' Hockey League, St. Michael's College realized that it was merely a bandage for the bigger problem as they saw it, which was that the demands of hockey on players' time, the travel, the pressure, and the costs were infringing on proper educational commitments. The league, though a valiant attempt to placate the school, had not satisfied the faculty, and St. Michael's College decided to abandon Junior 'A' hockey.

On December 18, 1960, in an interview with the *Globe and Mail*, Harold Ballard and Stafford Smythe, owners of the Toronto Maple Leafs, accused the Ontario Department of Education of "putting so much stress on education that the very existence of Junior 'A'

hockey was threatened," But, in fact, the game was evolving, and players were beginning to realize the importance of education.

After playing Junior hockey in Canada, including a Memorial Cup final appearance with the Regina Pats in 1955, Bill Hay, a big, talented Saskatchewan-born boy, made the decision to attend Colorado College in the U.S. He was named to the Western Collegiate Hockey Association's First All-Star Team and the NCAA's First All-America Team in both 1957 and 1958, and led the league in scoring in his final year. His success paved the way for his entry into the NHL with the Chicago Black Hawks, where Hay was the recipient of the Calder Trophy as rookie of the year in 1960. Hay's emergence opened the doors for other boys, who realized that playing Junior hockey in Canada was not the only path that led to the NHL.

Although Conn Smythe of the Toronto Maple Leafs grumbled that you couldn't serve two masters by playing professional hockey and attending school, a surprising number of Leafs did just that, including Carl Brewer, Dick Duff, Billy Harris, Bob Nevin, and Bob Pulford. "After I turned pro, I attended night school and went to McMaster [University in Hamilton, Ontario] in the summer until I got my degree," explained Pulford. "I don't buy the argument that hockey prevents a boy from continuing his education. More players are coming out of the American schools all the time." It took the Leaf forward seven years of off-time study, but in 1963, he earned his bachelor's degree, majoring in economics and history.

No longer was the carrot dangled by NHL teams the sole attraction for quality hockey players, and in the late 1950s and 1960s, even those who did sign C-Forms committing them to NHL teams realized that the foundation offered by education was an important component — and possible safety net — for players looking beyond the game.

Tony Fritz: Hockey Visionary — SNAPSHOT

Tony Fritz grew up in Allan, Saskatchewan, a town of a thousand people about 35 miles southeast of Saskatoon and 13 miles from Floral, the hometown of Gordie Howe. "My dad was a farmer," Tony explains. "When I was a little kid, I went to school in a horse and buggy in the summer and a sleigh in the winter."

Looking to advance his hockey career, Tony attended high school in North Battleford for Grade 11. "I wanted to play hockey at a higher level and I was thinking about the priesthood at the time." But the 16-year-old forward had a sensational season. "I was the leading scorer," recalls Tony. "It was a Senior men's league. The Maple Leafs and the Bruins came after me. The Bruins wanted me to go to Estevan and play for them there and Toronto wanted me to go to St. Mike's. It was a no-brainer for my parents. The Bruins weren't much interested in me going to school anymore, but St. Mike's was run by priests and I would be at a boarding school. We chose St. Mike's."

The young man boarded a train in Allan and ended his journey at Union Station in downtown Toronto. Shy and nervous, Tony had never seen a big, busy city like Toronto. "I got in a cab and went to Bathurst and St. Clair and there was St. Michael's." Fritz worked hard with hopes of making a team. "They had the Majors and the Buzzers, and I didn't really know the difference between them. I just knew that

On February 12, 1963, St. Michael's College staged a fundraiser for Tony Fritz, whose promising career was abruptly ended by an on-ice injury during the 1962 playoffs. Tony and his father flank King Clancy prior to the exhibition contest between Neil McNeil and Hamilton.

I had to work harder than anyone else because I didn't have the background that some of the boys did. There was Jimmy Keon and Mike Walton and all these young guys. It was really exciting! And when I made it, I thought that was great — I was the only guy who had not played Junior 'B'. Andre Champagne, Paul Conlin and Barry MacKenzie were the leaders of that team. Once I made that team, they were the ones that really helped me. They were the guys that made me feel like I was accepted."

For any aspiring NHL player, playing in Maple Leaf Gardens every Sunday in front of 10,000 people would be a thrill. "I was on Cloud 9!" Tony laughs. "The benches at Maple Leaf Gardens were right on the corridor and people would walk back and forth. One Sunday afternoon, a guy tapped me on the shoulder. I turned around and it was Gordie Howe! He said, 'I hear you're from western Canada,' and I said, 'Yeah.' He said, 'You go get 'em, boy!' The guy I idolized!"

Yet, in spite of a heady season in which the Majors won the league championship, Fritz's career took a different path. "There was about 10 minutes left in the fifth and final game of the playoffs against Hamilton. I was killing a penalty and had the puck at the top of the circle. I went to turn and shoot it out of our zone. Wayne Rivers tried to lift my stick and missed. The blade came right up into my eye. I was wearing contact lenses at the time. Instinctively, you reach up, and I saw blood running down my glove. I thought, 'I got hit,' so I headed for the trainer on the bench. What I was told is that as I got near the bench, I started skating in a circle. Maybe I was in a concussion state. The guys grabbed me and took me downstairs to the infirmary. I walked down the stairs covering my eye, and there was a nurse standing down there. She collapsed when she saw me. I thought, 'Damn, this is worse than I thought.'

"I got onto the table and they were pulling out pieces of my contact lens. It felt like there was gravel in my eye. They bandaged my eye up, put me in an ambulance, and headed to the best eye doctor around. Then I found out how serious it was. In today's world, they likely could have saved the eye. Hope springs eternal, so I was thinking, 'Once I'm out of the hospital, everything will be fine.' Little did I realize that it hemorrhaged so much on the inside that the doctors couldn't see in to determine what was going on. Eventually, when the swelling went down, the retina collapsed and fell off. They didn't have the equipment back then to laser it back up, so I became blind in that eye. At the beginning, I could see a little bit of light but as time went on, it went black."

After being released from the hospital, Tony went back to school. "It was spring and I was a baseball player. I could hardly wait to get outside and play catch. What I didn't understand was how the depth perception had changed. I reached out to catch the baseball and it hit me in the chest. I was also an altar boy, and when I went to light the candles before Mass with the long taper, I couldn't get the candle lit because I couldn't tell where the wick was. I don't have any problems anymore because I've learned to adjust."

As Tony adjusted to life with one eye, he discovered that he had a difficult time accepting the accident. "The biggest adjustment was mental," he admits. "It was my dream to play in the NHL. It was only later that I learned that I was considered one of the top five prospects in Canada at that time. And then, Mike Walton signed with the World Hockey Association for a million bucks. I just had to laugh. We always were out there competing and I was told I was considered a better player."

St. Michael's held a special fundraising exhibition game for Tony on February 12, 1963. That day, the Neil McNeil Maroons were pitted against the Hamilton Red Wings. Seven hundred St. Michael's College students, as well as most of the faculty, were bused to Maple Leaf Gardens to honour the alumnus whose promising hockey career had been cut short. A strong contingent from Neil McNeil also attended. Besides receiving the proceeds from the game, whose paid attendance was 3,400, Fritz was presented with an action shot of himself, a dozen shirts, and a complete wardrobe from Toronto Maple Leafs executive King Clancy. The Maroons shut out Hamilton

3–0. "The greatest thing was for my dad to go there with me. He was part of the ceremony," says Tony. "He was devastated when I got hurt. For him to be there was really special. One of the biggest treats was that I got my picture taken with Davey Keon, King Clancy, and Dickie Duff. Those are memories that will never go away." The next day, another benefit was held on Tony's behalf. This was a contest between the St. Michael's Arena Senior All-Stars and the faculty. Fittingly, with Tony refereeing the game, the teachers won the game 7–5. "I didn't get much money, but it did help pay for my education when I went to teacher's college."

After passing Grade 12 at St. Michael's, Fritz returned home to Saskatchewan. "I didn't realize it at the time, but I was depressed," he admits. "I had no idea what I wanted to do with my life. My goal was gone and I was floundering. I decided I'd go to school and be a teacher."

But during that year, Tony found his love of hockey hadn't waned, in spite of the accident. "I missed hockey, so I coached the local high school team. That was interesting, so I called back to the Leafs. At that time, Bob Davidson was the head scout and Punch Imlach was the coach. I said, 'Guys, if anything comes up, I want to get back into hockey somehow, some way.' They said they'd let me know if anything came up. I didn't really expect much."

But little did anyone know that the father of a student attending a private school with an outdoor artificial ice rink in Milwaukee needed someone to run their program, and just happened to be at Maple Leaf Gardens in Toronto during a business trip. "He ran into Davidson and Imlach and said, 'We've got a hockey program but we need a coach. Have you got anybody that you could recommend?' One of them says, 'There's this young guy out in western Canada and he wants to get back into hockey. You should call him.'"

The gentleman called Fritz and asked him to go to Milwaukee to discuss the position. "It was a beautiful school with excellent facilities. They offered me the position and I thought, 'What the hell do I have to lose?'" Tony accepted the position at University School and built the high school's hockey program into a powerhouse. While there, Fritz earned both his bachelor's and master's degrees in education from the University of Wisconsin–Milwaukee.

After 14 years in Milwaukee, Fritz decided he wanted to coach at the college level. After applying at a number of colleges, Tony accepted a position at Lake Forest University in Lake Forest, Illinois, in 1978. He led the Foresters to the championship of the American Collegiate Hockey Association in 1986–87 and earned coach-of-the-year honours in 2003–04. The winningest coach in Lake Forest sports history was elected to the Illinois Hockey Hall of Fame as a builder in 2007.

"Attending St. Mike's changed who I was and where I was going," reflects Fritz. "It took me out of a confined, rural area and introduced me to the big, bright world out there. After my accident, by getting through it with the help of the school and my family, by the grace of God, enabled me to run into the right people. It took me to Milwaukee. I never dreamed of being a teacher or a coach and it gave me my career. In retrospect, as much as I dreamed of an NHL career, I've been able to do so much more with my life. I missed having that NHL career, but this has turned out better than if I had been a player. Who knows what might have been, but I can look back and know I've made a difference in somebody's life. I've been able to give back. I always say I have two families — my immediate family and my players. My goal at the school is twofold. Sure, I want to win, but I want my players to become better people because they knew me.

"St. Mike's really was an outstanding experience," Fritz concludes. "Being quality people was ingrained in our value system. We all bought in, from the way we dressed to the way we handled ourselves. It taught us humility and gave us an understanding of where we came from."

26

Neil McNeil and the Demise of the Metro Junior Hockey League

For the first time in more than 20 years, St. Michael's College was not represented by a Junior 'A' hockey team. It was just one of many changes that occurred within the Metro Junior 'A' Hockey League as it prepared for its second season. The Neil McNeil Maroons replaced the Majors, while Knob Hill Farms replaced the Unionville Seaforths, the Whitby Mohawks changed their name to the Dunlops, and the Oshawa Generals returned to Junior action for the first time since the conclusion of the 1952–53 season.

After considering several options, including St. Jerome's College in Kitchener, Jim Gregory moved the Majors program to Neil McNeil High School. Founded in 1958 by the Spiritan Fathers and named for the Archbishop of Toronto between 1912 and 1934, the school straddles the former border between Scarborough and Toronto. "We were looking for a program that would give the parents an option to ensure their kids were going to be able to go to school," Gregory explains. As the Majors had done, the newly named Maroons played their home games at Maple Leaf Gardens.

Gregory explains the inclusion of the Oshawa franchise. "When the league was originally discussed, it was going to be all players who were brought there by the Toronto Maple Leafs organization. The sponsorship rule was still in effect. Wren Blair, who was working with the Boston Bruins, talked to us about putting in a team from Boston. He said it would be 20 [fewer] players Toronto would have to provide and it would be a more competitive team."

Blair's idea was grounded in sound fact: since the Montreal Canadiens sponsored both the Montreal Junior Canadiens and the Peterborough Petes in the OHA Junior 'A' league and the Toronto Maple Leafs had sponsored both the Marlboros and the St. Michael's Majors, why shouldn't Boston have two Junior teams? Boston was already sponsoring Hap Emms's Niagara Falls Flyers.

In his autobiography, *The Bird*, Wren Blair quoted Boston general manager as saying, "Hap will never agree to splitting the Junior hockey talent between Niagara Falls and Oshawa." "To hell with Hap," Blair replied. "We'll enter the Generals in the new Metro Junior 'A' Hockey League Stafford Smythe has put together."

Many of the Generals players were taken straight out of Midget, with the hope that they would grow together as a team through their four years of Junior eligibility. Fourteen-year-old Bobby Orr was a key component, as were future Bruins teammates Ron Buchanan and Wayne Cashman.

Although St. Michael's no longer had a team, its influence was still being felt throughout the league. Alumnus Johnny McCormack was coach of the Brampton 7-Ups. Peanuts O'Flaherty was behind the bench of the Knob Hill Farms team.

At Neil McNeil, coach Jim Gregory had Gary Smith in goal, a defence that included Ray Dupont, Jim McKendry, and Wayne Mosdell from the Majors as well as "an impressive newcomer to the Irish defence, Jim McKenny of Ottawa, a 15-year-old who is not out of his class in Junior 'A' company." At forward, Mike Corrigan, Mike Walton, and Mike Corbett formed one line; Mike Doran, Rod Seiling, and Gary Dineen a second; and Jimmy Keon played on a third line with Billy MacMillan and Paul Conlin. Gerry Meehan was later added to the team.

❖

Fans were staying away from Metro Junior 'A' games in droves. Opening night in Whitby saw the hometown Dunlops face the new Neil McNeil Maroons before only 703 fans. The final score of the opening game of the 1962–63 season was 7–2 for Neil McNeil.

The day before the season opened, Andre Champagne got his stick caught in the boards and the butt-end jammed him in the chest. He was taken to the hospital and the initial diagnosis was that he had a collapsed lung, an ailment that had forced him to miss much of the previous spring's playoffs. But upon further examination, doctors revealed that neither diagnosis was correct — Andre had blisters on his right lung and required surgery. The forward lost 16 pounds and two lower ribs, but returned to lineup three weeks after lying on the operating-room table. When the Maple Leafs were hit with injuries to Frank Mahovlich and Eddie Shack in February 1963, Champagne was called up to the NHL squad and played his first and only NHL games with Toronto, on February 23 and 27.

Neil McNeil finished 19 points ahead of the second-place Marlboros for first place. "St. Mike's and the Marlies were head and shoulders above everybody else," said Peanuts O'Flaherty, coach of the Knob Hill Farms team. "The others didn't have a chance. Our guy [goaltender Dave Kelly] is pretty well bombarded every night, and always has to make a bunch of good saves."

In the OHA Junior 'A' league, it was business as usual, with the exception of the St. Catharines TeePees changing their name to the Black Hawks in order to reflect their working agreement with the NHL franchise in Chicago. The two leagues played a handful of interlocking games during their season, and at the conclusion of the season, the champions of both leagues competed for the John Ross Robertson Trophy as OHA champion.

In *The Globe and Mail* on October 26, 1962, Oshawa manager Wren Blair announced that he had signed a 14-year-old public school student named Bobby Orr to an A-Form and the youngster would make his debut on November 9. "The youngster is touted as the finest defence prospect in junior hockey and has six years of junior ahead of him. He will play only on weekends because he'll stay home to attend school." In fact, Orr made his Junior debut a week ahead of schedule, against Neil McNeil on November 2. "A tow-headed tyro, 14 years old and only 133 pounds, played defence for Oshawa Generals in the Ontario Hockey Association's Metro Junior 'A' Hockey League," wrote *The Globe*, which observed that he "didn't look out of place among the bigger, stronger, but no smarter teenagers." The Generals lost 8–2 to the Maroons that afternoon.

Even with the much-heralded Orr in the game, only 545 fans attended the November 11 contest that saw Neil McNeil dump Oshawa, 4–1. The game was played at the Port Credit Arena because the Ice Follies were taking place at Maple Leaf Gardens.

The Maroons were on a winning streak when the league took a respite for an exhibition game between the Metro Junior 'A' All-Stars and the Russian Selects on November 23. The Russians were in the midst of a nine-game Canadian tour while the Canadian all-star team was comprised of Metro Junior 'A' players, including Neil McNeil's Mike Corbett, Gary Dineen, Ray Dupont, Billy MacMillan, Barry MacKenzie, Jim McKendry, and Rod Seiling, plus six players from the University of British Columbia. These six were part of the Canadian national team being assembled by Father David Bauer in order to represent their country at the 1964 Olympic Winter Games.

The Russians, far superior to the opposition, shut out their opponents 6–0 in front of a crowd of 11,725 at Maple Leaf Gardens. "Their checking, passing, skating and puck control made for a domination of the game and they received a fine hand from the crowd," wrote *The Globe and Mail*. Father Bauer said, "I think I was most impressed by their alertness" and called the Russian squad "a tremendous hockey club."

Back into their regular season, Neil McNeil walloped Whitby 13–2 on November 27, but were stopped in their winning tracks by Brampton a week later, losing 3–2 to the 7-Ups. Following several more victories, the Maroons faced Knob Hill Farms with 305 in attendance, including Maple Leaf executives Punch Imlach and King Clancy. "We teach these guys so much and take them to training camp, but most of them forget their lessons

1962–63

METRO Jr. 'A'

TEAM	GP	W	L	T	Pts
Neil McNeil Maroons	40	33	4	3	69
Toronto Marlboros	40	22	12	6	50
Knob Hill Farms	40	14	20	6	34
Whitby Dunlops	40	11	21	8	30
Oshawa Generals	40	12	23	5	29
Brampton 7-Ups	40	12	24	4	28

JUNIOR 'A'

TEAM	GP	W	L	T	Pts
Niagara Falls Flyers	50	31	12	7	69
Montreal Jr. Canadiens	50	27	14	9	63
Peterborough Petes	50	21	18	11	53
Hamilton Red Wings	50	21	21	8	50
St. Catharines Black Hawks	50	15	24	11	41
Guelph Royals	50	9	35	6	24

once they get on the ice," said Imlach, shaking his head. The game ended in a one-all tie.

With Rod Seiling summoned to join Sudbury of the Eastern Professional Hockey League for a few games, Gerry Meehan made his Junior debut in a 7–0 win over the Marlboros on December 23. The Maroons, missing 11 regulars for the Christmas holiday, still managed to ice a team that easily handled the Whitby Dunlops. Coach Jim Gregory elevated players from St. Mike's Juvenile team to fill out the roster.

Following January victories of 12–1 versus Brampton, 11–4 and 10–4 against Oshawa, and 8–0 facing Whitby, Gregory was concerned. "We're winning too easily," he mused. Netminder Smith suffered an ankle injury late in the month, but his replacement, Bill Henderson, was a more than able replacement, backstopping the Maroons to three wins and a tie and allowing just 11 goals while his teammates potted 30.

On February 17, *The Globe and Mail* wrote, "The Whitby Dunlops will derive as much pleasure out of meeting league-leading Neil McNeil Maroons tonight as a great white hunter would out of confronting a 40-foot boa constrictor equipped only with a thermos of coffee." The prophecy was correct. Neil McNeil had no trouble defeating the Dunlops, unleashing an 11–4 spanking that clinched a first-place finish. Gary Smith, his foot in a cast, watched as his understudy performed admirably in goal.

The next night, in what was a meaningless game for the Maroons, Neil McNeil faced Oshawa at the Bowmanville Arena. The idea was to attract attention in that market, as Oshawa was waiting for its own arena to be rebuilt and intended to play its home games in Bowmanville during the 1963–64 season. A capacity crowd of 1,100 watched as the Maroons doubled the Generals, 10–5. Mike Corbett collected four goals in the game, with Mike Doran, Billy MacMillan, and Rod Seiling each connecting twice. Generals rookie Bobby Orr arrived from Parry Sound in time to play the third period and sparked his teammates, who scored four goals, including two scored just five seconds apart.

Neil McNeil, who had steamrolled over the league all season, experienced their first defeat in 17 games when the Marlboros stopped them, 8–5, on February 24. The Maroons were missing Andre Champagne, who had been called up to the Toronto Maple Leafs, and Rod Seiling, who was summoned by the Leafs' AHL affiliate, the Rochester Americans. The defeat was a short-lived sting, as Neil McNeil finished off the regular season with three straight wins, including a 7–6 win over the Marlies in the final game of the regular season. In that game, Gary Dineen picked up three goals and two assists to give him the scoring championship. He collected 32 goals and a league-best 63 assists to finish with 95 points, and won the Joseph Cooper Memorial Trophy as the league's top scorer for the second consecutive season. Linemates Mike Corbett (94 points) and Rod Seiling (77) were second and third in scoring. Bobby Orr, by the way, collected 21 points as a 14-year-old phenom.

The Neil McNeil Maroons earned 69 points on 33 wins, four losses, and three ties. The Marlboros were second with 50 points, Knob Hill Farms third at 34 points, and the Whitby Dunlops snuck into fourth with 30 points. Oshawa and Brampton missed the playoffs.

❖

Neil McNeil opened the playoffs against Knob Hill Farms in the semifinals. With Gary Smith back in goal, and the addition of Steve Monteith from the University of Toronto, the Maroons swept the series in four games, outscoring their opponents 30–11. Monteith surprised with five goals, including a hat trick in Game Two. Next up was the league championship series against the Marlboros.

Game One finished with the Maroons dumping the Marlies, 9–6. Gary Dineen and Mike Walton both recorded three-goal games. The Marlboros used Dave Kelly, who had spent the season with Knob Hill Farms, in goal in place of Gerry Desjardins. "Whenever Corbett, Dineen and MacMillan were on the ice, they completely dominated the play, providing Dave Kelly with isometric fits," mentioned *The Globe and Mail*. Steve Monteith, who had played but one regular-season game before sliding into Neil McNeil's playoff picture, was cut for four stitches near his right eye after a high stick from Brit Selby. He had been cut for five stitches in that same area in the last game against Whitby. Monteith skated out wearing a helmet and was joined by teammates Mike Corbett and Mike Corrigan.

The Maroons easily handled the Marlies in Game Two. Paul Conlin, with a pair of goals, and Gary Dineen, with a goal and three assists, were the scoring heroes in this contest. Jim McKenny, who had been benched for the opening game in the series and been replaced by forward Rod Seiling, entered this game in the second period, set up a goal by Conlin, and played solid defence. Seiling, back on the forward line, earned two assists in less than 20 seconds on his first shift of the second period.

With their backs against the wall, the Marlboros dumped Neil McNeil 5–2 in Game Three of the league final. The win wasn't the only thing that was stolen. The Maroons' dressing room was broken into and several players had money stolen from their wallets. It was the third time their dressing room had been looted that season.

It appeared as though the fate of the Metro Junior Hockey League was sealed on March 27, 1963, when only 900 spectators bothered to attend Game Four of the league final. The game finished with the Maroons edging the Marlies 9–7, and *The Globe* said Neil McNeil won "simply because they didn't play as poorly as their heavier crosstown rivals." The slim crowd witnessed "a strange mixture of spasmodic, wide-open hockey intermingled with sloppy passing, poor clearing and indecisive goaltending." Mike Doran, Jim McKenny, and Rod Seiling each scored twice for Neil McNeil. Rookie Steve Monteith found himself so devoted to studying for his exams at the University of Toronto that he chose not to continue as a member of the Maroons. He had proven himself admirably, scoring six goals and seven assists in seven playoff contests. Monteith would later join Father David Bauer's Canadian national hockey team, winning a bronze medal at the 1968 Olympic Games.

The headline in the sports section of *The Globe and Mail* on Wednesday, April 3, announced, "Maroons Blast Dukes 6–2, Take Metro Junior Honors." The night before, a sloppy affair with five of the eight goals scored on the power play, the Maroons had handcuffed the Marlboros. Gary Dineen and Billy MacMillan each scored two goals, with Andre Champagne and Mike Doran adding singles.

With the victory, the Neil McNeil Maroons captured the Father Conway Memorial Trophy. Most of the players were part of the team at St. Michael's when the Majors won the trophy the previous season.

❖

The All-Ontario final pitted the Maroons against the Niagara Falls Flyers. Game One saw the Flyers jump out to a series lead by way of a 4–1 win. Niagara Falls scored two quick goals in the first period to set the tone of the game. After Paul Conlin and Wayne Maxner exchanged goals early in the second period, "it was the chippiest, longest, dreariest and sloppiest match that any of the 6,037 had seen all year," according to *The Globe and Mail*. Captain Andre Champagne had a difficult game, earning five of the Maroons' 13 minor penalties. The first two Flyer goals came with Champagne looking on from the penalty box. Flyers coach Bill Long shrugged and said, "I've never seen Neil McNeil play like that all season."

The Flyers scored four goals in the final stanza to win Game Two by a 5–4 score and take a 2–0 lead in the series. The Maroons' Gary Smith turned in an outstanding performance behind a defence that sported more holes than Swiss cheese, an appearance made all the more remarkable given that Smith left with a twisted knee in the second period. He returned to play after a 10-minute respite. But in the third, the Maroons

The Neil McNeil Maroons gather around coach Jim Gregory to accept the Father Conway Memorial Trophy as champions of the Metro Junior league in 1962–63.

stopped skating and stopped the physical play that had marked their game. Within a little more than two minutes in the last half of the third, Terry Crisp scored twice and Gary Dornhoefer added a single for the Flyers. It was the second goal of the game for the feisty Dornhoefer. Jim Keon, Corbett, MacMillan, and Champagne scored for the Maroons.

Neil McNeil battled back into contention in Game Three with a 4–1 win. Gary Smith "was Horatio at the bridge for the rest of the period until his own teammates started to click." In the third period, Mike Walton scored twice on George Gardner to lead the way for the Maroons.

In spite of the goal-scoring heroics of Niagara Falls' Wayne Maxner, who scored all three of the Flyers' goals, the Maroons won Game Four by a 4–3 margin, with a late goal by Mike Corbett giving Neil McNeil the win. Five minutes into the third period, Gary Smith was knocked out in a collision with teammate Ray Dupont and the game was halted for over 10 minutes to allow the cobwebs to clear from Smith's head. "After he was hurt in the final period, Smith returned to the net still groggy. Lining up for a few practice shots, [Smith] grinned weakly when referee Frank Slota reminded him to put on his gloves." Nevertheless, Smith came up huge in the waning minutes of the game when the Flyers pushed for the tying goal. Fans threw debris onto the ice, which further delayed resumption of the game. With just over a minute left in the game, Maroons defenceman Jim McKendry was speared in the groin, earning a major penalty for the Flyers' Gary Harmer.

Game Five was a goal-scoring clinic put on by the Flyers, featuring Ron Schock, who scored two of Niagara Falls' goals in a 5–1 victory over the Maroons on April 17. Game six started 35 minutes late, as the Maroons' bus was involved in a collision west of St. Catharines, then wouldn't start when police had cleared the accident scene. Just two minutes after the opening faceoff, goaltender Gary Smith suffered a five-stitch gash that held the game up a further 12 minutes. It was one concern after another for Neil McNeil. McKendry and Corbett missed the last two periods due to injuries. It really was a moot point, though, as Terry Crisp, Gary Dornhoefer, and Wayne Maxner led the Niagara Falls Flyers to a convincing 9–3 win to clinch the series. It was the first OHA Junior 'A' championship for the Flyers since moving to Niagara Falls from Barrie.

Disheartened, the Neil McNeil Maroons skated off the ice for the final time, watching as the Flyers celebrated their victory. Niagara Falls went on to play the Espanola Eagles of the Northern Ontario Hockey Association (NOHA) for the eastern Canadian championship.

The late spring of 1963 saw the introduction of the National Hockey League's Amateur Draft.

Garry Monahan and Peter Mahovlich, both members of St. Michael's Juvenile team, were chosen first and second overall. Monahan, just 16 years old at the time, was the first-ever player selected, a choice of the Montreal Canadiens. Mahovlich went to the Detroit Red Wings with the second-overall pick. The Neil McNeil Maroons had two players chosen, both by the Toronto Maple Leafs. Jim McKenny was the 17th selection while Gerry Meehan went 21st. Only five of the 21 players selected in that first amateur draft ever played in the NHL — a reflection on how efficiently the Junior sponsorship system had mined amateur hockey for talent. Besides Monahan, Mahovlich, McKenny, and Meehan, only Walt McKechnie, a member of London's Junior 'B' team, skated in the NHL. He was the sixth-overall selection, also taken by the Toronto Maple Leafs.

❖

The Metro Junior 'A' Hockey League was clearly in trouble. The quality of play was poor and fans seemed to avoid games like the plague. Stafford Smythe had earlier intimated that the end of the Metro league was nearing. He stated that there had originally been two reasons to break away from the OHA Junior 'A' loop, but those reasons no longer existed. One was to keep St. Michael's College in Junior 'A' hockey, but the school had withdrawn anyway. The second was to allow players to get an education while playing a reduced hockey schedule.

Smythe went to the OHA with a proposal: the Maple Leafs would not only re-enter the Toronto Marlboros in the OHA Junior 'A' loop, but a second team based in London, using the best players from Neil McNeil, Knob Hill Farms, and the Brampton 7-Ups. In addition, the Oshawa Generals asked to be readmitted to the OHA after a 10-season absence.

The OHA agreed to take Oshawa and the Marlboros, but rejected the London proposal. Stafford Smythe was infuriated. "They're forcing us to squeeze all our talent into one team. How stupid can they get? We'll have the strongest junior club in Canada. Nothing in this league will touch us. We'll win the Memorial Cup, too. That's not a prediction, that's a statement of fact." Hap Emms, the general manager of both the Oshawa Generals and the Niagara Falls Flyers, just shook his head. "If I had a chance to pick the best players from four clubs, I think I might come up with a winner, too."

"Well, what did he expect?" said the *Toronto Star*. "A few years earlier, Smythe had picked up his pucks and walked out of the league, taking the Marlboros and St. Mike's with him. His avowed purpose was to operate more economically and to develop more hockey players by having more teams. He organized the Metro League, which was pretty much a Gardens house circuit."

"At training camp for the Marlboros, we combined the best players from Neil McNeil and the Marlboros and put them into the OHA Junior 'A' League. That was just an awesome team," remembers Jim Gregory, reflecting on the 1963–64 Toronto Marlboros.

Ron Ellis was one member of that Marlboro team. "Jim Gregory did a wonderful job coaching us that season. He joined the Marlies from Neil McNeil, as did Andre Champagne, Gary Dineen, Jim McKenny, Gerry Meehan, Rod Seiling, Gary Smith, and Mike Walton. Jim didn't let us rest on our laurels. He instilled in us a desire to always improve. Jimmy did a wonderful job when you look at that team and realize how many talented players went on to NHL careers. We had a powerhouse and won the Memorial Cup that season."

Another member of that Memorial Cup-winning Marlboros team was Rod Seiling, who had been filtered through the St. Michael's' pipeline.

Seiling was a high-scoring forward in Elmira, his hometown, when scouts began to notice his progress. "I was courted by a variety of NHL teams," Rod recounts. "Back then, there was no draft. I had been a Leafs fan and, along with my parents, met with them and other NHL teams and decided that I wanted to join the Toronto Maple Leafs. They

Jim McKendry was a premier defenceman during the two-year span of the Metro Junior league.

offered me the opportunity to go to the Marlboros and attend Upper Canada College, or go to St. Michael's, and I chose St. Michael's because I thought it was a better opportunity for me to combine my education with hockey. Also, I had the opportunity there to live off campus rather than boarding, which I would have had to do at Upper Canada College."

Education was becoming more and more important to players, and Rod was no exception. "From the earliest days at home, the rule in our house was that if you didn't pass, you didn't play hockey. After I left home, I'm not sure, if my marks weren't there, whether my parents would have invoked that rule or not; I suspect they would have. But I didn't find school too challenging. I still worked at it, but I also wanted to get an education. I was driven to that due to the fact that even though I wanted to be an NHL hockey player, there was no guarantee that I was going to be one, so I did need an education. Even after I made the NHL, I went to summer school every year and got my degree."

While playing with the Buzzers and, in 1961–62 with the Majors, Rod had been part of an explosively offensive line and a league leader in scoring, but made his name in the National Hockey League as a defenceman. "I had played defence off and on through the years as the need arose," he explains. "The year they combined everything into the Marlboros [1963–64], I went to Jim Gregory, who was coaching that year, and said, 'You and I both know that we have a lot of forwards but we're a little short on defence. You're going to end up moving me back there before the year's over anyway, so why don't we start the year there? Heck, I can always move up if the need arises.' I was moved back to defence and stayed there."

When St. Michael's College withdrew from Junior 'A' hockey, it left players like Seiling in a bind. "I certainly wasn't a happy camper, to say the least, about the school's decision to get out of hockey. I had chosen to go to St. Mike's because of the ability to combine school and hockey in one location. For the school to drop the hockey program wasn't music to my ears. The Leafs moved the team to Neil McNeil and ended up putting us in school at Neil McNeil, which was fine. They tried to replicate what they had before, and at the same time they created the Metro Junior league, which was ill-fated, but it worked to some degree. I was fortunate; I boarded with Bobby Baun's parents, so it worked out very well for me personally in many ways. I had a good home life and it wasn't too far from school. But we didn't have a rink next door anymore, and it was a trek to Maple Leaf Gardens each day for practice, but you learn to live with that. It was an attempt by the Leafs to do something that, in hindsight, didn't work out very well."

Rod played his first NHL game, a 4–3 win over the Rangers, on March 2, 1963. A trade sent him to the New York Rangers in February 1964. His dream of playing for the Toronto Maple Leafs had come to an end after one game (although he did rejoin the Leafs in November 1974 for two seasons). Seiling was a big part of the nucleus that helped return the Rangers franchise to respectability after years of missing the playoffs. He would later play one game with the Washington Capitals, the Leafs again, the St. Louis Blues, and the Atlanta Flames in a career that included 979 games, 62 goals, and 269 assists for 331 points. The highlight of Rod's professional career might easily be the Canada–Soviet Union Summit Series of 1972. "My career as a pro athlete taught me a lot about life and about people, and certainly the Team Canada experience was a great plus for me."

Rod had experiences at St. Michael's College that were equally impactful. "The person who had the greatest influence on me, although he died early on, was Father Conway. And someone else who meant a lot to me was one of my teammates when I first went to St. Mike's, Jimmy McKendry. I spent a lot of time at his home. Between the McKendrys and Father Conway, they became my de facto parents to a degree, being away from home at the age of 15."

Jim McKenny: Candid on Camera

Following his retirement from hockey, Jim McKenny has been a mainstay as a knowledgeable and candid broadcaster on Toronto's CITY-TV.

"I didn't know much about St. Mike's because I never went there," admits McKenny, a prospect with the Neil McNeil Maroons in 1962–63 who went on to a National Hockey League career. "I went to Neil McNeil in the middle of September [1962]. I wanted to get out of the house, so it took me about two weeks to convince my mother to let me go. My old man was away in Laos with the Peace Corps."

Before the Amateur Draft was instituted, most of the players on the St. Michael's Majors and, subsequently, the Neil McNeil Maroons, were the property of the Toronto Maple Leafs. "I would gladly have signed [a C-Form] with the Leafs, but I never got the chance. I would have, because you got a hundred bucks for that. They stiffed me on that," he laughs.

"I was Protestant, but [the fact that it was a Roman Catholic school] was the big selling point for the Leafs as they'd always get you your education when you left home," explains McKenny. "I didn't get much school. I wasn't into school anyway. I hated it."

While most players found it hectic juggling a busy hockey schedule at the same time as a solid school curriculum, McKenny shrugs and explains why he didn't find the school year cumbersome. "It wouldn't have been that difficult [to carry the school workload as well as the hockey schedule] if I would have gone, but I never even showed up," he shrugs. "They used to strap you there, too, if you were late for school or anything. Father McCarthy used to strap about 25 or 30 guys, so I figured if you were going to get the strap anyway, you might as well come three days late. You were going to get the same thing! So if I was late, I'd just go to Greenwood [Racetrack]. Five stops on the streetcar from the school!"

Although not yet signed to Toronto, Jim regularly got the opportunity to practise with the Maple Leafs. "Whenever I got kicked out of school, which was quite often, I had to practise with the Leafs to keep me out of trouble," smirks McKenny. "They used to practise at the Tam O'Shanter rink up in Scarborough because it was close to where Punch [Imlach] lived. The place was a hole." That rink was destroyed by fire in the early 1970s.

In 1962–63, Jim McKenny played 37 games on defence with Neil McNeil, scoring 5 goals and 12 assists for 17 points. In the Amateur Draft of 1963, the first such draft, he was chosen by Toronto with the 17th pick overall. With the Metro Junior A Hockey League folding, Jim was absorbed into a powerful Toronto Marlboros squad that went on to win the Memorial Cup in 1964.

In his third and final season with the Marlboros, McKenny turned pro, playing a game with Rochester and two games with the Leafs (February 26 and 27, 1966) before he joined Tulsa of the CPHL for the 1966 playoffs. In 1968, Jim was a member of the Calder Cup–winning Rochester Americans of the AHL. After parts of several seasons spent bouncing between the Maple Leafs' various minor-league affiliates, McKenny joined the team full-time in 1969–70 and played nine seasons in Toronto. In May 1978, Jim was traded to the North Stars and completed his NHL career after one season in Minnesota. He collected 329 points (82 goals and 247 assists) during 604 regular-season NHL contests.

"Neil McNeil didn't really do anything to ready me for my later life," admits the personable broadcaster. "I was there to play hockey. I wasn't there to get an education."

27

Majors Redux:
St. Mike's Returns to the OHL

In the years that followed the 1962 decision to discontinue Junior 'A' hockey at St. Michael's College, the topic of resurrecting the franchise came up from time to time. And for several weeks in the spring of 1980, it looked as though Major Junior hockey was going to return to St. Mike's, when the Ontario Major Junior Hockey League (OMJHL) gave its cautious approval for a school-sponsored team to rejoin the league after an 18-year absence.

Rumours persisted that Reg Quinn, the Toronto-based owner of the Niagara Falls Flyers, would move his franchise to St. Michael's College for the 1980–81 season. "From a business point of view, the people [of Niagara Falls] showed me they weren't ready to support this team," Quinn shrugged. Newspaper stories at that time reported that Quinn was prepared to outright hand the team over to St. Mike's, but would be retained as the team's coach and general manager.

Sherry Bassin, chairman of the OMJHL board, went public, stating, "If St. Mike's is willing to follow the rules of our constitution to the letter, then I'm sure it could develop into a quality franchise that we would be happy to have."

But there were two stumbling blocks. One was the drafting of Midget-aged players. "If we get into the OMJHL, we'd like to be able to protect players in our school and organization," stated Father Norman Fitzpatrick, principal of St. Michael's College School at the time. St. Mike's had hoped that players below the Midget draft age and enrolled at St. Michael's College School could stay at the school, progressing right up to the Major Junior level when age and talent allowed, without concern that hockey-playing students might be plucked away by other teams in the Midget draft. But that same logic concerned many of the OMJHL governors, who saw it simply as a way for St. Mike's to protect players and have them bypass the provincial draft. "We would want all the players on our team to attend our school, too," said Father Fitzpatrick. "What we want in our organization is Catholic kids who want to go to Catholic schools." The league commissioner, David Branch, shook his head. "The Midget priority selection is a tremendous asset for our league. I can't see that being changed for anyone, be it St. Mike's or any other team."

The other stumbling block was territorial rights. Harold Ballard, the owner of the Toronto Marlboros, would have to waive his 80-kilometre territorial right before the Niagara Falls franchise could move to St. Mike's. Ballard stated that he would approve the transfer. "The Marlboros haven't exactly been getting sellouts and I'm not about to allow another team within 50 miles of here unless it's operated by St. Mike's." Ballard was well aware that a renewed rivalry between St. Mike's and his Marlies could do wonders for fan interest in Major Junior hockey in Toronto, and would increase revenue to both clubs.

"The situation is like this," explained Frank Bonello, the general manager of the Toronto Marlboros. "We don't want another Major Junior team in this city. However, if it's run by St. Michael's College in the fashion of years ago, this would be permissible." Bonello, Ballard, and the Marlies executives insisted that the franchise be sold outright to St. Mike's.

This initial faceoff signalled the return of the St. Michael's Majors to the OHL. The Majors took to the ice for an exhibition game in Guelph against the Storm.

Quinn addressed the concerns: "It's my intention to let St. Mike's operate the club. No decision has been made as far as what role I will play, if any [insiders insisted that Quinn would stay on as coach and manager]. As for the players going to school, they will all go to school, but maybe not to St. Mike's."

If all concerns were satisfied, the move from Niagara Falls to St. Michael's College would require the support of nine of the 12 OMJHL governors. But the results were surprising to all parties involved: they voted eight to three against the transfer, with one abstention. "I am stunned," a shocked Quinn told *The Globe and Mail*. "They gave no reason whatsoever for rejecting the proposal."

After courting bids from several other cities, team owner Reg Quinn finally announced that the Flyers would remain in Niagara Falls, with the promise of major renovations to the Niagara Falls Memorial Arena and the mayor's pledge that there would be 1,000 season tickets sold before the start of the new season. Paul Gauthier, who had coached the St. Michael's Buzzers in 1979–80, was named the team's head coach.

The Flyers remained in Niagara Falls until 1982, when they moved to North Bay and became the Centennials. That franchise has since become the Saginaw Spirit.

Fifteen years after that false start, the idea resurfaced. In 1995, the discussions grew more serious, involving Father Thomas Mohan, the president and principal of St. Michael's College School, and Dennis Mills, an alumnus who was the sitting member of Parliament for the Toronto riding of Broadview-Greenwood.

Mills remembers the scenario clearly. "There had been a development issue where essentially St. Mike's had lost the corner property, lost the laneway coming in off St. Clair, and had lost the entire parking lot of the arena because of that development agreement, and through Father Mohan's leadership, and I assisted him, we were able to get a resolution where we were able to recapture that land so that the integrity of the school's ability to function could stay intact."

He reflects back on how the seed of returning to the OHL was planted. "It was a Friday night and I was sitting with Father Tom in the little kitchen in the monastery at the school. I said to Father, 'I believe that one of the things that has happened with St. Michael's College School is the lack of real public presence of the institution in the whole city, the whole province, and the whole country. When I was younger, St. Mike's had a very, very high profile. I said jokingly, 'You know what we should do, Father? We should bring back the Majors!' He looked at me and said, 'Oh, I don't think we could ever do

Cardinal Emmett Carter, then the spiritual leader of Canada's largest English-speaking diocese, honoured the Toronto St. Michael's Majors franchise by conducting the ceremonial puckdrop to signal the team's return to Major Junior hockey. Cardinal Carter is flanked by Father Thomas Mohan, the school's president, and Dennis Mills. The faceoff between the captains of the Peterborough Petes and Toronto St. Michael's Majors preceded the first regular-season contest for St. Mike's since 1961.

that.' And I said, 'Today, the OHL has a different attitude and respect towards education.' David Branch, who was leading the league at that time, and the other governors had a real renewed sensitivity to not just high school education, but also they had what they call schoolboy packages for OHL players so that they could get some of their funding for Canadian universities, depending on the number of years that they played in the OHL. I was explaining all this to Father Mohan, and I knew this because my son [future NHLer Craig Mills] was the captain of the Belleville Bulls.

"The Basilian Fathers did a beautiful thing for me and my son at the end of every season with Belleville. He was allowed to come back and finish up his year at St. Mike's. He was able to graduate from St. Mike's, as I did.

"I met up with Father Mohan again in the middle of January and he said, 'When am I going to get that proposal to bring the Majors back to St. Mike's?' I said, 'What are you talking about, Father? I didn't think you were interested.' He said, 'I think we should get some alumni together and we should have a discussion. You should make a presentation and see if there's any merit in it.'"

Father Mohan pulled together a collection of alumni to discuss the possibility, while Mills contacted Jim Rooney, a St. Michael's alumnus who was then president of the Guelph Storm. "We came together one night in the old library at St. Mike's, and I gave a short preamble and Jim Rooney gave the presentation as a St. Mike's alumnus about his experience as a high school principal and also as a president of the Guelph Storm. He had all the statistics — attendance and marks and this and that for the last three years of the Guelph Storm. He essentially reaffirmed what I had said to Father Mohan about this OHL commitment to education.

"From that moment, there was a consensus of the room that we pursue it providing the franchise fee, which was at that time $1.5 million, was not funded by the school but funded by outsiders," continues Mills. "I then had conditional support from St. Michael's to try to put a franchise bid together. The conditional support I had from the Basilians was raising $2.5 million from outsiders. My very first stop was to Steven Hudson," says Mills. Hudson was the president and CEO of Newcourt Credit Group, which was one of the largest asset finance companies in Canada. "My second stop was to Reg Quinn, and Reg brought Roy Foss to the deal." Roy Foss was a St. Mike's alumnus who owned and operated a very successful General Motors dealership.

"The next stop was to Eugene McBurney." McBurney was involved with Griffiths, McBurney and Partners, a company that was involved in investment banking and underwriting institutional equity sales. "Next was to Andy Papadakos, who is a leader in the Greek community." Papadakos was involved with Domepark and had been involved with the Toronto Blue Jays' now-defunct farm team in St. Catharines. "Our final stop was to Bill Smith," recalls Mills. Smith was already retired at the time of the visit, after successfully operating Seeburn Metal Products, but had been involved in hockey in the Orillia area and brought valuable experience to the table. The founding directors of the St. Michael's Majors going into the 1997–98 season included Foss, Hudson, McBurney, Papadakos, Quinn, and Smith, and also included Daniel Jauernig, senior vice-president of Newcourt, William, McCutcheon, a chartered accountant; Peter Nichol, manager of Listowel Golf and Country Club; and Ross Tyrell, owner of Akinai Canada. "Those men knew what we were doing in terms of good sportsmanship, religion, academics, and playing the game," says Father Mohan. "They wanted to promote that, which was a marvellous thing. These men were able to put their money forward to support an opportunity to make hockey back into a sport and have it played."

Majors alumni celebrate the return of St. Michael's to the OHL. From left to right: Rod Seiling, Gerry Meehan, Mike Walton, Frank Mahovlich, Dick Duff, Terry Clancy, and Mike Boland.

Able to secure 10 investors at $250,000 apiece, Mills and his team then approached veteran broadcaster Bob McCown of Toronto radio station CJCL (The Fan 590) about contributing his talent and expertise to the project. "We sat in a restaurant and I said, 'Here's the plan. I can't do it without you,'" recalls Mills. "I had known Bob from my previous life as a member of Parliament in Ottawa. Bob said, 'I love it. We're on it.' Bob McCown became our voice of the Majors, rallying support so that when we presented to the league governors, they would be supportive of us."

The OHL's governors approved the franchise bid and on August 15, 1996, the Toronto St. Michael's Majors were admitted to the league as an expansion franchise. In spite of the team name, players would not be required to attend St. Michael's College School, although they were encouraged to do so. And, to fall in line with all the other OHL teams, St. Mike's would participate in the annual priority selection draft (a.k.a. the Midget draft) in order to stock the team — a major difference from 35 years before, when team members were simply recruited from the student body.

Mills was named president and governor of the Toronto St. Michael's Majors, a role he held for the first two and a half years of the team's new existence. Gerry Meehan, a St. Michael's alumnus, was hired as Vice-President, Director of Hockey Operations. "We had a great team. [General manager] Gerry Meehan, [head coach] Mark Napier, and [assistant coach] Michael Futa did a fantastic job in putting the hockey infrastructure together, and the record will show that for a new franchise in our first period, we were respectable," Mills states.

"The one who deserves most of the praise for bringing the team back would be Dennis Mills," stated Father Mohan. "He did most of the negotiating for the team to get back on the ice again."

Although Napier, a former star with both the NHL and WHA, started the season as head coach of the Majors, that was not originally part of the plan. "I had applied for the assistant coaching job because I owned a business at the time," explains Mark. "I talked to Gerry Meehan, who was the GM. Some things fell through with the person they were looking to hire [Mike Pelino], and he called me and asked if I'd consider the head coaching job. I thought about it for two seconds and said, 'Sure!'"

With the new Majors's season approaching, the excitement began to build. "Being a Toronto boy growing up, I knew the history of the St. Mike's–Toronto Marlies rivalry from years before," says Napier. "I didn't know all the history until I actually got there, but I found out pretty quickly that there was great tradition around St. Mike's."

Mills recalls the most important reason for returning Major Junior hockey to St. Michael's. "We didn't do this just because we liked hockey. We did it because we saw St. Michael's Majors as an instrument of bringing witness to the tradition, the values of all the Basilians, of all the lay teachers and of all the students who had gone before us, and whose value system we wanted to stamp, not just in the city presence, but in the national presence. When you're in the Canadian Hockey League, you're on television, you're on radio, you're in print locally and nationally, so it was an example of us showing some Catholic witness. If you take a look at the jersey of the St. Michael's Majors when we returned to the league, we made sure that the crest that was on our blazers was part of the front of the hockey jersey — 'Teach me goodness, knowledge, and discipline.'"

Father Tom Mohan concurred. "We were interested in making sure that the youth of the Toronto area would see good hockey and good sportsmanship, and that we'd be able to promote that. We wanted our players to be people who could play hockey well and not just defeat somebody else. We wanted to make sure that there was going to be a good relationship between hockey and academics."

Although there was an attempt to ensure that players on the team would attend St. Michael's College School, that idea was shelved when it was realized that it was not a realistic goal in the hockey world of the 1990s. But Father Mohan insisted that the team have a good moral tone. "We had regular Masses with them and there were exercises before games," he stated. "We were starting off with pretty high ideals, but it's obviously not the same Ontario as it was in the 1960s."

Once the Toronto St. Michael's Majors had been approved by the Ontario Hockey League board of governors, there was the matter of filling the roster of a team that would report to training camp on August 26, 1997. First, St. Mike's took part in an expansion draft on June 5, then an entry draft of Midget-aged players two days later, and finally the Canadian Hockey League Import Draft. They came away with 43 players.

In the expansion draft, the Majors claimed Vladimir Antipov, Windsor Spitfires; Chris Biagini, Belleville Bulls; Jason Cannon, Barrie Colts; Clarke Duncanson, Peterborough Petes; Steve Gallace, Owen Sound Platers; Mike Kosterewa, Kingston Frontenacs; Frank Kucher, Soo Greyhounds; Jay Leach, Ottawa 67's; Chad Mehlenbacher, Erie Otters; Gerald Moriarty, Sudbury Wolves; Sean Murphy, London Knights; Andrew Plumley, Oshawa Generals; Ryan Robichaud, Guelph Storm; Marcin Snita, Sarnia Sting; Rob Stanfield, Kitchener Rangers; Anthony Terzo, Plymouth Whalers; and Troy Turyk, North Bay Centennials.

In the entry draft, held June 7 at Maple Leaf Gardens, St. Mike's selected Charlie Stephens, Leamington Jr. 'B'; Jason Crain, St. Thomas Jr. 'B'; Ryan Walsh, Cumberland Jr. 'A'; Corey Batten, Quinte Jr. 'A'; Kenny Corupe, Burlington Jr. 'A'; Chris Cava, Elmira Jr. 'B'; Patrick Papageorge, Ajax Jr. 'A'; Brian Simpson, Kanata Valley Jr. 'A'; Matthew House, Streetsville Jr. 'A'; Darcy King, Stouffville Jr. 'A'; Erik Adams, Thunder Bay Midget; Michael Glumac, St. Michael's Jr. 'A'; Andrew Gibson, Peterborough Jr. 'A'; Scott McKenzie, Stoney Creek Midget; John Vis, North Bay Midget; Trent Baumgarten, Gloucester Jr. 'A'; Spencer Fowler, Ernestown Jr. 'B'; Doug Wilkey, Midland Jr. 'C'; Jason Southwell, Toronto Marlboros Midget; Trevor Wolfe, Michigan Nationals Midget; Joe Byles, York Simcoe Midget; Jeff Murphy, Gananoque Jr. 'B'; Jim Caruso, Culver High School; and Greg Kealey, Kemptville Jr. 'B'.

Finally, all three Major Junior hockey leagues (the Western, the Ontario, and the Quebec Major Junior league) participated in a draft of European Junior-age players. With their first pick, the third selection overall, the Majors selected Jan Sulc from the Czech Republic, and with their second selection, the 51st overall, they chose Ari Katavisto from Finland.

The formalities complete, the stage was now set for the OHL's newest — yet, at the same time, most storied — team to don their familiar double-blue sweaters and take to the ice.

28

Trials and Tribulations

The addition of the Toronto St. Michael's Majors brought the membership of the Ontario Hockey League to 18 teams and marked the return of Major Junior hockey to Toronto — the Marlboros having moved to Hamilton after the 1988–89 season and then to Guelph in 1991. The Majors were placed in the league's East Division, along with the Belleville Bulls, Kingston Frontenacs, Oshawa Generals, Ottawa 67's, the and Peterborough Petes.

After thirty-five years without Major Junior hockey, expansion brought the St. Michael's Majors back into the fold on Friday, September 19, 1997. The familiar double-blue 'M' made its return to the OHL against the Guelph Storm that night, as the team lost its season opener 4–2 on the road.

Two days later, the echo of pucks against the boards of St. Michael's College School Arena sounded wonderful to fans, both old and new. Following a simple ceremony and the playing of "O Canada," the Majors faced off against the Petes before a crowd of 2,004 that included Bobby Orr, Mike Keenan, and alumnus Fleming Mackell. "In a delightful bandbox of a rink that has been lovingly renovated so as to be a wonderful venue for hockey, the St. Mike's Majors not only upset the Peterborough Petes 5–2 in their home opener, but also rewarded their most devoted backers with the first real indication that this thing might actually work," said the *Toronto Star*. "Clearly, the hope is not to bring back an era gone by. The hope is to take an old idea and do it better."

"We're an expansion team, but if we work hard and play hard, we can compete with any team in the league and we proved that today," remarked Majors coach Mark Napier. He added, "We have 18 guys from 18 different teams and it may take a while to gel. It all came together today."

Napier recalled some sage advice delivered by Frank Mahovlich, the Hall of Famer who had once played at St. Michael's. "He told me that there will always be highs and lows and that you have to go with them," said Napier. "You can't get so high that you feel like you can't ever experience the lows again — you will. We've got win number one, now we have 64 more games to go."

The Guelph Storm finished first overall, just a point ahead of the 67's, who led the East. The Storm went on to win the OHL championship, cradling the John Ross Robertson Trophy at the end of a successful campaign. It was no surprise to anyone that St. Michael's, with a record of 15 wins, 41 losses, nine ties, and one overtime loss finished at the bottom of the East Division and tied for last place overall with the North Bay Centennials, who went 15–41–6–4.

"Acquiring Bujar Amidovski from Kingston was probably the highlight of that first year," remarks Mark Napier. "Kingston had decided to go the younger route and he was our overaged goalie." Amidovski was certainly noticed within the OHL. Despite winning just 12 games in 48 appearances, Bujar had a surprising goals-against average of 3.40, and the Majors ended up a respectable 11th in the league in goals against (versus 18th in scoring, with just 154 goals). Amidovski was named OHL Goaltender of the Year and won the Leo Lalonde Memorial Trophy as the best overage player in the league. He signed as a free agent with the Philadelphia Flyers organization in 1999, then was signed by the Carolina Hurricanes in 2000, although he did not get the opportunity to play in the NHL. "The opportunity that we afforded him allowed him to go on and at least have a shot," continues Napier. "I think if he had stayed in Kingston, he wouldn't have

1997–98

TEAM	GP	W	L	T	OTL	PTS
EAST DIVISION						
Ottawa 67's	66	40	16	9	1	90
Belleville Bulls	66	41	19	3	3	88
Kingston Frontenacs	66	35	26	4	1	75
Oshawa Generals	66	26	29	8	3	63
Peterborough Petes	66	20	35	10	1	51
Toronto St. Michael's Majors	66	15	41	9	1	40
CENTRAL DIVISION						
Guelph Storm	66	42	17	6	1	91
Barrie Colts	66	38	22	5	1	82
Kitchener Rangers	66	27	25	10	4	68
Sudbury Wolves	66	25	27	7	7	64
Owen Sound Platers	66	27	31	5	3	62
North Bay Centennials	66	15	41	6	4	40
WEST DIVISION						
London Knights	66	40	21	5	0	85
Plymouth Whalers	66	37	19	7	3	84
Sarnia Sting	66	32	18	13	3	80
Erie Otters	66	33	25	5	3	74
Soo Greyhounds	66	20	36	7	3	50
Windsor Spitfires	66	19	39	5	3	46

Coach Mark Napier (in jacket and tie) scans the scoreboard as his team members assemble by the bench.

had any shot. For me, that was our biggest accomplishment and my greatest thrill that first year."

Steve Zoryk, who had come to the Majors from the Ottawa 67's, was the team's captain and leading scorer that season, collecting 34 goals and 27 assists for 61 points. Anthony Terzo picked up 20 goals and 20 assists. Mike Jefferson, who changed his name to Mike Danton in 2002, came over to the Majors from Sarnia in a trade midway through that season and put up 10 points in 18 games for the Majors.

Charlie Stephens, a big centre, was with St. Mike's for parts of two seasons, including 1997–98. The first-overall pick in the OHL Entry Draft in 1997, Stephens collected 30 points for the Majors. Selected by the Washington Capitals in the second round of the 1999 NHL Entry Draft, Stephens did not sign with Washington and went back into the draft in 2001, when he was selected in the sixth round by the Colorado Avalanche. He joined the Avalanche in 2002–03, and played eight games over two seasons, collecting two assists.

Mark Napier: Pains and Gains

SNAPSHOT

Mark Napier was a sensation as a player. After a 66-goal, 130-point season for the Memorial Cup champion Toronto Marlboros in 1974–75, he was scooped up by the Toronto Toros of the World Hockey Association, who signed him as an underage free agent (he was not drafted by an NHL team until 1977, when the Montreal Canadiens took him 10th overall). Playing beside such heroes as Frank Mahovlich and Paul Henderson, Napier was named the WHA's rookie of the year with a sensational season of 43 goals and 93 points. The franchise moved to Birmingham, Alabama, a year later, and the "Baby Bull" potted 60 goals in 1976–77 and 33 in 1977–78.

Napier moved to the NHL with the Montreal Canadiens in 1978–79 and added 31 points to a potent offence that helped win a Stanley Cup championship for Montreal that season. While with the Canadiens, Mark enjoyed a 35-goal season, followed by back-to-back 40-goal campaigns in 1981–82 and 1982–83.

He was traded to the Minnesota North Stars and, a year later, to the Edmonton Oilers, where he was part of a second Stanley Cup victory in 1985. His NHL career ended in 1988–89 after three seasons with the Buffalo Sabres. Napier earned 254 points (136 goals and 118 assists) in 237 WHA games, and 541 points in 767 NHL games, including 235 goals and 306 assists.

Napier was a partner in Elite Cresting when he applied for a position as assistant coach with the newly revived Majors, but he ended up as head coach, with Mike Futa and Rod Seiling as his assistants.

"It wasn't easy the first few years," he admits. "The main problem that I had was that every player who played on the St. Mike's Majors either had to go to the school if they were high school–aged or had to have some kind of continuing education. There were definitely some kids that we could not draft because scholastically, they would not survive at St. Mike's and it wouldn't be fair to draft them, either. We did draft a couple of kids in the first couple of years and either had to trade them away or move them somehow because it just wasn't working for them. It wasn't fair to the kid and it wasn't working for the team, and it turned into a distraction. So it was very difficult at the start to find the right combination and to find the type of person we needed."

Mark felt that he had the formula right and was making headway. "We were getting to a place where we had a real good feeling for what we needed for the team to win, what kind of person we needed for the team. I thought we proved that it could work and that we were moving in the right direction, but it certainly was tough the first few years. When Father Zorzi came in, he wanted to go in a different direction and that was the end of me."

Although sports of all types are important to the fabric of St. Mike's, Mark realized the importance of hockey to the school. "Hockey, with the arena right at the school, probably appealed to and benefited the majority of student athletes," he says, adding, "I believe St. Mike's has also had a tremendous affect on hockey. Not just at the Major 'A' level and the prominent players that went on to the NHL, but also at the levels below."

Among the students who benefited from the hockey program at St. Michael's College School was Napier's son, Matt. "The really nice thing for me was that my son went to school there the three years I was there. Most mornings, I would drive him to school, but he'd have to take the subway home because we were practising. It was a really nice time for me and it really showed me what the school could do because when Matt ended up going to the University of Toronto, he was just so well prepared.

"Father Mohan treated me so well and really, really cared about the kids. He is a fabulous human being and I have nothing but love for the man."

29
A Season of Havoc

1998–99						
TEAM	GP	W	L	T	OTL	PTS
EASTERN CONFERENCE						
Central Division						
Barrie Colts	68	49	12	6	1	105
Sudbury Wolves	68	25	35	8	0	58
North Bay Centennials	68	22	39	6	1	51
Toronto St. Michael's Majors	68	20	40	6	2	48
Mississauga IceDogs	68	4	56	3	5	11
East Division						
Ottawa 67's	68	48	13	7	0	103
Belleville Bulls	68	39	21	7	1	86
Oshawa Generals	68	39	22	5	2	85
Peterborough Petes	68	40	24	2	2	84
Kingston Frontenacs	68	22	40	4	2	50
WESTERN CONFERENCE						
Midwest Division						
Guelph Storm	68	44	21	2	1	91
Owen Sound Attack	68	39	22	5	2	85
Erie Otters	68	31	33	4	0	66
Kitchener Rangers	68	23	38	6	1	53
Brampton Battalion	68	8	55	3	2	21
West Division						
Plymouth Whalers	68	51	11	4	2	108
Sarnia Sting	68	37	24	6	1	81
London Knights	68	34	27	4	3	75
Soo Greyhounds	68	31	27	8	2	72
Windsor Spitfires	68	23	33	6	6	58

The 1998–99 season brought two new teams, both of them within a short drive of the Majors' home: the Brampton Battalion and the Mississauga IceDogs. At 20 teams, the Ontario Hockey League reorganized itself into a quartet of five-team divisions, and the Majors ended up in the Central. With 20 wins, 40 losses, six ties, and a pair of overtime losses, the Majors placed 18th in the expanded league, spared from the basement by Brampton and Mississauga.

Powerful teams in Plymouth, Barrie, and Ottawa paced the league, but it was the Belleville Bulls, second in the East Division, who captured the league championship.

Mark Napier returned as coach of the Majors, assisted by Mike Futa and Mark Osborne. But after 14 games, Napier was promoted to general manager, and Futa assumed the coaching reins for the rest of the schedule.

Second-year player Charlie Stephens was dealt to the Guelph Storm seven games into the season, but the most noteworthy trade of the year came on January 11, 1999, when, amid great turmoil, the Majors sent their captain, Sheldon Keefe, along with Mike Jefferson, Ryan Barnes, and Shawn Cation to the Barrie Colts. In return, St. Michael's received Darryl Bootland, Keith Delaney, Adam DeLeeuw, and Brad Pierce. Keefe and Jefferson went on to outstanding, if flawed, Junior careers. In the meantime, DeLeeuw was named the new captain of the team.

Bootland scored 30 goals during his rookie season in the OHL, split between Barrie and St. Mike's. The trade turned out to be a blessing in disguise for the young forward. "My time at St. Mike's changed my whole outlook on life," he admits. "Until I got traded to the Majors, I never knew a thing about the Bible. Sundays changed. Every Sunday, one of the Fathers would talk to us before games and teach us a little and inspire us for the game. It opened my eyes to a whole new world. I thank the Lord for giving me a chance to play for the Majors. It was the best time of my life!" Darryl holds the team records for most career goals (109) and points (234).

Ryan Barnes endured a tempestuous season in 1998–99. Traded to St. Mike's from Sudbury early in the campaign, Barnes was one of the players later dealt to Barrie. Adjusting to the systems of three different teams would be challenging enough, yet the big, tough winger still managed to score 29 goals and had 57 points, as well as racking up an almost incomprehensible 399 minutes in penalties — 215 in 31 games with the Majors alone. Barnes was selected by the Detroit Red Wings in the 1998 NHL Entry Draft, and in 2003–04 he played his only two NHL games.

The 1998–99 season saw the debut of defenceman Mark Popovic, who could hit and contribute defensively. Although it would be difficult most games to ascertain that the future looked bright, Popovic stood out as a cornerstone of future teams. Second-year Major Kenny Corupe was the team's best point-getter, with 55.

With Bujar Amidovski having turned pro, four netminders made appearances with the Majors in 1998–99. Dwayne Bateman, Corey Batten, Patrick Dovigi, and Jeff Thomson all saw more rubber than roadkill on Highway 401 through the course of a challenging season.

Mike Jefferson: *Wasted Youth*   SNAPSHOT

Through a glorious century of hockey, St. Michael's College has had few incidents that were noteworthy for their negative nature. Unfortunately, the 1998–99 season saw just such a situation, and although the team dealt with it quickly and efficiently, it had lasting repercussions that ended sadly with an alumnus of the Majors behind bars, his promising NHL career shattered, after he fell under the influence of a troubled agent.

Mike Jefferson was born in Brampton, Ontario, and showed great hockey prowess from a young age. In 1991, his parents were approached by David Frost, who asked whether Mike might like to play for the Toronto Young Nationals, his Atom team in the Metro Toronto Hockey League. The Jeffersons agreed, but grew wary when Frost became their son's agent and began to wield a growing influence over Mike, both on and off the ice. Teammates included hotshot forward Sheldon Keefe and Joe Goodenow, the son of Bob Goodenow, executive director of the National Hockey League Players' Association (NHLPA) at the time. After being caught forging the signature of the team's general manager, Frost was banned from coaching in the MTHL. But rather than skulking away in shame, Frost took Jefferson and Keefe, as well as Ryan Barnes and Shawn Cation, his "Brampton Boys," to the Quinte Hawks, a Junior 'A' club based in Deseronto, Ontario. There, the four players and Frost lived together in a hotel room. Frost was later suspended from the Hawks for allegedly punching one of his players on the bench, in full view of horrified spectators. He was later suspended indefinitely by the Ontario Hockey Association and the MTHL for incidents on and off the ice.

In spite of the commotion within the team, the Quinte Hawks had a remarkable number of players selected by OHL teams in the 1997 draft. Among them, Barnes was chosen by the Sudbury Wolves, Jefferson by Sarnia, Keefe by Plymouth, and Cation by Oshawa.

Frost orchestrated the acquisition of all four of the Brampton Boys (also tagged by the media as the Quinte Four) by the Majors. Jefferson was acquired from Sarnia midway through the 1997–98 season, Cation was secured from Oshawa prior to the start of the 1998–99 season, Keefe had yet to play in the OHL and also joined before the season opener, and Barnes came over from Sudbury in an early-season trade.

A tempestuous era came to an end for the St. Michael's Majors on January 11, 1999, as the team traded the entire Quinte Four to the Barrie Colts. In return, the Majors received Darryl Bootland, Keith Delaney, Adam DeLeeuw, and Brad Pierce. There is little doubt that neither the team nor the school had any desire to tolerate David Frost any longer, and refused to accept the influence Frost had over these players, in spite of their abundant talent.

It was a difficult decision for the Majors to make. At the time of the trade, Keefe had 74 points in 38 games, Jefferson had 40 in 27 contests, Cation 30 points in 36, and Ryan Barnes 25 points in 31 games. Keefe, a rookie, concluded the season by finishing third in the OHL scoring derby, accumulating 116 points, (51 goals and 65 assists). He also received the Emms Family Award as the league's rookie of the year.

The Barrie Colts finished first in the Central Division in 1998–99, collecting 104 points, good for second place overall behind Plymouth. After beating Kingston in the first round of the playoffs, they were eliminated by Oshawa in the Eastern Conference semifinals. Meanwhile, St. Mike's finished fourth in their division and third from the bottom overall.

Although his Junior career was tempestuous and controversial, there was no denying Mike Jefferson's talent, and he was selected by the New Jersey Devils in the fifth round of the 2000 NHL Entry Draft.

What had started as a player-coach relationship between Jefferson and Frost quickly got out of hand. Frost had assumed what some have called a Svengali-like hold over Jefferson, and as Mike was preparing for his NHL career, Frost was certified by the NHLPA as a player agent, in spite of his previous hockey troubles.

Although he spent most of the 2000–01 season with New Jersey's American league farm team, the Albany River Rats, he was summoned and played his first two NHL games with the Devils that season. But he crossed Devils GM Lou Lamoriello when he refused to report to Albany for 2001–02, and was suspended for the entire season.

During the summer of 2002, Mike Jefferson legally changed his surname to Danton, because he wanted to distance himself from his parents. He chose Danton because it was the name of a boy he'd met at a summer camp and he thought it "sounded cool."

Danton spent the early part of the 2002–03 season with the Devils, and played 17 games, scoring two goals. But when New Jersey wanted to return him to Albany in December 2002, Danton refused the demotion and went so far as to serve the Devils with legal papers, asking to be released from the team. While his teammates celebrated a Stanley Cup championship in the spring of 2003, Danton sat at home.

Wishing to rid themselves of the quarrelsome Danton, the Devils unloaded him to St. Louis along with a third-round draft pick in exchange for the Blues' third-round pick in June 2003. Seeking a fresh start, Danton spent the season in St. Louis as a checking forward with some offensive flair. He scored seven goals and five assists in 68 games in 2003–04.

The Blues faced the San Jose Sharks in the opening round of the 2004 playoffs, but were eliminated in five games. Danton, who played in all five games, scored a goal in the fourth game, a 4–3 loss. On April 16, hours after St. Louis's season had come to an end, Mike Danton was arrested and charged with conspiracy to commit murder. In July 2004, he entered into a plea agreement to a murder-for-hire conspiracy to kill his agent, David Frost. The hitman turned out to be a police dispatcher. Frost, by the way, denies that he was ever the intended target. In fact, taped conversations from jail just a week after the arrest confirmed that Frost was still speaking with Danton, coaching him on how to deal with law enforcement officials, attorneys, and psychologists.

Danton was sentenced to seven and a half years in a federal prison at Fort Dix, New Jersey, with no opportunity for parole. His request to transfer to a Canadian prison was rejected by the U.S. Justice Department in March 2006. Because he did not testify, the motive for offering $10,000 to kill Frost remains a mystery. When he is eventually released from prison, Danton will be extradited to Canada, and it is unlikely that he would be allowed to cross the border back into the United States, seriously jeopardizing any chance to resuscitate his NHL career. He was just 24 years old at the time of his arrest.

David Frost resigned as a player agent in December 2005 after the NHLPA launched an investigation into his certification. In August 2006, he was charged by the Ontario Provincial Police for crimes alleged to have occurred between 1995 and 2001 relating to his time coaching the Quinte Hawks. And even though he was banned from two separate Ontario hockey organizations, Frost still remained involved in hockey, scouting for the Pembroke Lumber Kings, a Central Junior 'A' Hockey League team. At the time of the arrest, the Lumber Kings were owned by two of Frost's Brampton Boys, Mike Danton and Sheldon Keefe. Frost continued to be involved with the team until the conclusion of the 2005–06 season. Keefe remains owner, as well as general manager and coach, of the Lumber Kings. Shawn Cation is an assistant coach.

30 Building Towards Future Successes

Although they missed the playoffs for the third consecutive season and slipped from 48 points to 42 in 1999–2000, there were signs that the seeds planted over the preceding two years were about to bear fruit.

Mike Futa continued as coach, and Adam DeLeeuw was again the captain of the squad. A bit of salt was rubbed into the wound created by the trade of the Quinte Four to Barrie, as ex-Major Sheldon Keefe won the OHL scoring race with 121 points, while Mike Jefferson was 10th, with 87. Both contributed to the Barrie Colts' emergence as OHL champions in 1999–2000. But DeLeeuw was contributing his veteran presence and grinding style to the team, while Keith Delaney, another of the four Colts received in the exchange, led the Majors in scoring with 62 points, including 24 goals. Darryl Bootland was developing into a substantial contributor, finishing third on the team in points with 54 and tying with Delaney with a team-best 24 tallies. Defenceman Brad Pierce was with the Majors for much of the first half of the season, before being included in a deal with North Bay. Ryan Walsh picked up 21 goals and Kenny Corupe had 22 to help pace St. Mike's. Mark Popovic was developing great confidence, and contributed 11 goals and 29 assists from the blue line.

Another bright spot quickly emerging as the future of the team's success arrived in 1999–2000. Goaltender Peter Budaj stepped in to share crease duties with Dwayne Bateman and showed flashes of brilliance.

Year four saw the Majors take a quantum leap forward to an 80-point season and a second-place finish in their division in 2000–01 (just one point behind the division-leading Sudbury Wolves). Much of the credit belonged to new coach Dave Cameron, an NHL veteran of three seasons who was hired as coach and director of hockey operations on August 28, 2000. Cameron had already built an impressive coaching resume, leading Summerside to two provincial Junior 'A' championships, coaching Detroit and Port Huron in the Colonial Hockey League, guiding the Soo Greyhounds for two seasons (1997–98 and 1998–99) and serving as an assistant coach with the St. John's Maple Leafs in 1999–2000.

Ryan Walsh was top scorer for St. Mike's with 71 points. Darryl Bootland led the Majors with 32 goals and contributed 65 points. Frantisek Lukes, newly arrived from the Czech Republic, chipped in with a strong season of 23 goals, 33 assists and 56 points.

Mark Popovic, in his third season wearing the double blue, earned 42 points from the blue line and was the captain of the team. In June 2001, Popovic was selected 35th overall by the Mighty Ducks of Anaheim in the NHL Entry Draft — to date, the highest a Majors player had been selected in the draft. Future NHLers Tim Brent, Drew Fata, and Kevin Klein contributed 28, 20, and 19 points respectively.

The goaltending tandem of Andy Chiodo and Peter Budaj was outstanding. At the conclusion of the season, Chiodo was awarded the Dinty Moore Award as the first-year goaltender with the best goals-against average. Andy allowed just 86 goals in 38

1999–2000						
TEAM	GP	W	L	T	OTL	PTS
EASTERN CONFERENCE						
Central Division						
Barrie Colts	68	43	18	6	1	93
Sudbury Wolves	68	39	23	5	1	84
North Bay Centennials	68	24	35	6	3	57
Toronto St. Michael's Majors	68	18	44	2	4	42
Mississauga IceDogs	68	9	56	1	2	21
East Division						
Ottawa 67's	68	43	20	4	1	91
Belleville Bulls	68	44	22	2	0	90
Kingston Frontenacs	68	38	22	5	3	84
Peterborough Petes	68	34	26	7	1	76
Oshawa Generals	68	32	30	4	2	70
WESTERN CONFERENCE						
Midwest Division						
Erie Otters	68	33	28	4	3	73
Kitchener Rangers	68	28	30	6	4	66
Brampton Battalion	68	25	28	1	4	65
Guelph Storm	68	29	34	4	1	63
Owen Sound Attack	68	21	35	6	6	54
West Division						
Plymouth Whalers	68	45	18	4	1	95
Soo Greyhounds	68	37	20	6	5	85
Sarnia Sting	68	33	27	8	0	74
Windsor Spitfires	68	35	30	2	1	73
London Knights	68	22	36	7	3	54

2000–2001

TEAM	GP	W	L	T	OTL	PTS
EASTERN CONFERENCE						
Central Division						
Sudbury Wolves	68	35	22	8	3	81
Toronto St. Michael's Majors	68	35	23	8	2	80
North Bay Centennials	68	32	28	6	2	72
Barrie Colts	68	29	28	7	4	69
Mississauga IceDogs	68	3	56	7	2	15
East Division						
Belleville Bulls	68	37	23	5	3	82
Ottawa 67's	68	33	21	0	4	80
Peterborough Petes	68	30	28	8	2	70
Kingston Frontenacs	68	28	28	1	1	68
Oshawa Generals	68	20	36	7	5	52
WESTERN CONFERENCE						
Midwest Division						
Erie Otters	68	45	11	0	2	102
Guelph Storm	68	34	23	9	2	79
Brampton Battalion	68	33	22	9	4	79
Owen Sound Attack	68	31	27	7	3	72
Kitchener Rangers	68	26	36	6	0	58
West Division						
Plymouth Whalers	68	43	15	5	5	96
Windsor Spitfires	68	34	22	8	4	80
Sarnia Sting	68	28	31	7	2	65
London Knights	68	26	34	5	3	60
Soo Greyhounds	68	23	38	4	3	53

Alumnus Eugene Melnyk bought the Majors from the school in 2001.

games and had an average of 2.49 through the regular season. Peter Budaj, a sophomore, platooned with Chiodo and played 37 games, earning a goals-against average of 2.86.

The Majors faced Peterborough in the Eastern Conference quarterfinals and prevailed four games to three. St. Mike's then upset Sudbury, four games to three, in the conference semifinal. But the Ottawa 67's were too much for the Majors, smothering Toronto in four straight games in the conference final. The 67's went on to win the J. Ross Robertson Trophy as OHL champions.

The close of the 2000–01 season marked the end of an era in St. Michael's hockey history. Father Mohan stepped down as principal of St. Michael's College School, to be replaced by Father Daniel Zorzi, while Dennis Mills relinquished his role as president and governor of the Majors. Although Mills remained on the team's board, there were some vacancies created when other directors made the decision to leave. To fill one of these spots, Mills approached a St. Mike's alumnus who had done exceptionally well in the pharmaceutical industry. As president and chief executive officer of Biovail Corporation, Eugene Melnyk was considered one of Canada's wealthiest entrepreneurs. Dennis Mills says, "I called Eugene and said, 'Would you like to come in and buy some of these shares from people who want to leave?' He said, 'If I come in, I'd rather own it all.'"

The seed of an idea thus took root. Paying an undisclosed amount of money, Melnyk purchased the Majors, a sale that was approved by the OHL's board on August 29, 2001. "Being a St. Michael's alumnus and growing up in the Toronto area, I have a passion for both the school and the great game of hockey," stated Melnyk in a press release at the time. "To become owner of the storied Toronto St. Michael's Majors Hockey Club franchise and be part of what I feel is the premier development league in the world, the Ontario Hockey League, is an extremely rewarding and exciting day for myself."

"We are very relieved to finally close the sale after a very long process," Father Zorzi added. "We are also very excited to have Eugene Melnyk, a St. Michael's alumnus, taking over this team. Eugene is a successful businessman and a great hockey fan, and with those things working together, I predict success for the Majors' future."

"The other directors felt that they had carried the baton for a significant part of the St. Mike's journey," recalls Dennis Mills. "They had been involved for four years and then Eugene Melnyk took over the team in total."

Melnyk agreed that the Majors hockey club would retain its association with the school, and would continue to play its home games at the St. Michael's College School Arena.

But for Dennis Mills, the story had a sad ending. "The original purpose for St. Michael's College School to bring back the Majors was to show and remind people of St. Michael's College School and the Basilian Fathers and their commitment to Catholic education in Canada over the last 150 years. The notion that the team was going to leave the school, and the intellectual property of the team, the Majors, is departing as well, I find that to be sad," Mills suggests. "There's new leadership and that's terrific. I just think that there could have been, might have been, should have been, a way to make the St. Michael's Majors work, and if the Basilian Fathers and the executive of the school were to say, 'We're gone,' the name of the Majors should stay [with the school]. Could someone actually come along and call a team the Thornhill Buzzers? Could someone come along and call a team the Riverdale Kerry Blues? These are names that are part of the fabric of the school!

"When I first went to St. Mike's in the early '60s, the Basilian Fathers were like my family," states Mills. "I know those educators — not just the Basilian Fathers but the lay teachers, men like Jack Fenn, Danny Prendergast, etc. They are, in my mind, family. I don't think there's a day in my life that goes by where their impact on my thought process doesn't impact the way I may approach a business issue, a personal issue, the way I interact with people."

Mark Popovic: Blueline Brilliance — SNAPSHOT

If there is any consolation in a team finishing poorly, it is that they receive a higher position in the draft. In 1998, St. Michael's chose fourth in the OHL draft, and scored a six-foot, two-inch defenceman from Stoney Creek, Ontario.

"When I was 15, I was trying to decide between the college scholarship route or if I wanted to pursue the OHL," explains Popovic. "When I looked at my options, I was going to be a high pick in the OHL draft and St. Mike's was picking fourth, so it was pretty much a no-brainer between me and my parents. We really wanted to go there."

Mark had several meetings with Mark Napier and Mike Futa, the coaches during the Majors' inaugural season. "I really related to them. I ended up writing letters to the other teams and asked them politely not to draft me because I had decided I wanted to go to St. Mike's. Right or wrong, it was a decision me and my family made because you couldn't beat the combination of the school, the tradition, living in Toronto, having access to the University of Toronto after graduating — it was a bunch of factors me and my family felt were really important, so it was predetermined before the draft."

The culture at St. Michael's College School took a little bit of getting used to. "I'm from Stoney Creek and went to high school in Hamilton. I went to a regular Catholic school, boys and girls, so it was a little bit of a shock to go to St. Mike's when I had to wear a tie, I had to wear short hair, I had to shave every day. I was excited about it, but it was a complete shock for me. I was there for two years, but I was fast-tracked."

Mark already knew about St. Michael's legacy to some degree, but it really struck home once he was drafted. "I ended at the [Maple Leaf] Gardens and met Red Kelly and Dickie Duff," he beams. "These are legendary guys from that school. Just to be part of that tradition was something very important."

Popovic debuted that fall, and stood out in a positive way as a rookie in 1998–99. Scouts very much liked his skating, he could carry the puck very well, and he had a booming shot from the point. But while there were still lessons to learn, Mark was given plenty of opportunity. "It wasn't a great team those early years, so I jumped in and played a lot of minutes. Over my four years in the OHL, I probably played as many minutes as anybody. Right away, I was in every situation — power play, the penalty kill — I got to learn and be given opportunities, and that's all you can ask for when you go to Junior."

To lose on a fairly consistent basis is tough on anyone's confidence, but Mark endured and grew along with the franchise. "The first two years were kind of rough with the wins and losses and we didn't make the playoffs, but we were a young team and it was a good learning experience," he admits. "You always learn from those years when you're losing. You hate to lose, and you want to learn how to win. My last two years there we went to the third round of the playoffs, the conference final."

Through four seasons with the Toronto St. Michael's Majors, Popovic collected 155 points in 247 games. Twice, he was named the team's outstanding defenceman and outstanding player, and he served as captain in 2000–01 and 2001–02. By playing so well at St. Mike's, other opportunities arose for the big stud defenceman. "I got the chance to go to the World Juniors twice and won a silver and a bronze. At the under-18 [tournament], we won the gold. Those are the most memorable times of my hockey career, pulling on that Canada jersey."

Drafted in the second round of the 2001 Entry Draft by the Mighty Ducks of Anaheim, Mark made his debut on January 2, 2003, against the Buffalo Sabres, but was returned to the AHL afterwards. He was traded to the Atlanta Thrashers for Kip Brennan in August 2005, and is being given a good deal of ice time with the Thrashers. "For me, making the NHL is the way you want to go. I'm still up and down."

Popovic regards his time at St. Michael's College School and the Majors as the steady foundation on which he built his professional career and prepared himself for life. "The community, once you're part of it, is unbelievable.... The old motto, 'Teach me goodness, teach me discipline, teach me knowledge,' is something that's ingrained in you once you go there, and you live with that motto for the rest of your life."

31

Becoming a Contender

2001–02 TEAM	GP	W	L	T	OTL	PTS
EASTERN CONFERENCE						
Central Division						
Toronto St. Michael's Majors	68	40	19	8	1	89
Barrie Colts	68	38	19	9	2	87
Sudbury Wolves	68	25	33	5	5	60
North Bay Centennials	68	18	37	8	5	49
Mississauga IceDogs	68	11	47	6	4	32
East Division						
Belleville Bulls	68	37	23	5	3	82
Ottawa 67's	68	33	21	10	4	80
Peterborough Petes	68	30	28	8	2	70
Oshawa Generals	68	28	28	11	1	68
Kingston Frontenacs	68	20	36	7	5	52
WESTERN CONFERENCE						
Midwest Division						
Erie Otters	68	41	22	4	1	87
Guelph Storm	68	37	23	7	1	82
Kitchener Rangers	68	35	22	10	1	81
Owen Sound Attack	68	24	31	10	3	61
Brampton Battalion	68	26	35	5	2	59
West Division						
Plymouth Whalers	68	39	15	12	2	92
Soo Greyhounds	68	38	20	10	0	86
Windsor Spitfires	68	33	24	6	5	77
Sarnia Sting	68	27	29	5	7	66
London Knights	68	24	27	10	7	65

After five years of dreaming, building, and improving, the St. Michael's Majors completed the 2001-02 season in first place in the Central Division, edging the Barrie Colts by two points. The Majors finished second overall in the Ontario Hockey League, just behind the Plymouth Whalers.

Darryl Bootland was among the players who shone for Dave Cameron's team in 2001–02. Through four seasons with the Majors, growing his game and confidence each year, Bootland grew his offensive totals, from 30 goals in 1998-99, 24 in 1999-2000, and 32 in 2000–01 to 41 in 2001–02 — 10th best in the league. His point totals also grew, from 47 as a rookie, to 54, 65, and then 97 in 2001–02, seventh best in the OHL. Bootland was drafted by the Colorado Avalanche in 2000, but signed with the Detroit Red Wings as a free agent in 2003 and was introduced to the NHL in that 2003–04 season.

Second to Bootland in both goals and points for the Majors was Matt Ellis, who fired 38 goals and had 89 points in his fourth season with St. Michael's. Signed to the Detroit Red Wings in 2002, Matt joined the big club in 2006–07 for 16 games. After starting the season with the Wings in 2007–08, he was waived and picked up by the Los Angeles Kings.

Other future NHL players who contributed to St. Michael's success in 2001–02 were Tim Brent (59 points), captain Mark Popovic (41 points), Drew Fata (28), Kevin Klein (27), and Darryl Boyce (21), as well as the terrific duo of Peter Budaj and Andy Chiodo in goal.

Brimming with confidence, the Majors quickly eliminated the North Bay Centennials in four straight games. Wily Brian Kilrea, coach of the Ottawa 67's, had his team ready and gave the Majors a good fight, but were defeated in a seven-game series. But for a second consecutive spring, the Majors were unable to make it past the third round, upset by the Barrie Colts four games to none to end the season.

The goaltending tandem of Budaj and Chiodo was a major contributor to the success of the Majors. Peter Budaj joined the Toronto St. Michael's Majors from Slovakia prior to the 1999–2000 season and spent three stellar seasons with the squad. He completed his Junior career in 2001–02 with a season in which he played 42 games, winning 26, losing nine, and tying five, with a sterling goals-against average of 2.29 and a save percentage of .922.

Through his three seasons with the Majors, Budaj compiled a record of 49 wins, 36 losses, nine ties, and three overtime losses, as well as six shutouts, in 113 regular-season appearances. In 23 postseason games, he racked up 11 wins (including two shutouts) versus 10 losses.

Peter was drafted by the Colorado Avalanche in the second round of the 2002 NHL Entry Draft. After three seasons with the AHL's Hershey Bears, Budaj joined the Colorado Avalanche in 2005–06.

A devout Christian, Budaj espoused the virtues held so fervently by the school. "My parents brought me up with Jesus Christ as my saviour," mentions Peter. "I grew up as a Christian and try to live a Christian life. Many people think that being a Christian is not good because you cannot do some stuff that other people can. I do a lot of things I am not happy with, but I try to do the best I can."

The Majors were blessed with one of the finest goaltending tandems in Junior hockey with Peter Budaj and Andy Chiodo sharing duties in 2000–01 and 2001–02. They contributed significantly to the team's first-place finish in 2002

Not shy at proclaiming his faith, the netminder has an image of Ned Flanders, the God-fearing neighbour of *The Simpsons*, painted on his mask. "One day I walked in the room and he [Terry Geer, equipment manager of the Colorado Avalanche at the time] said, 'Oh, you're like Ned,' and he started calling me that," explains Budaj. "That was my first year [with Colorado], when I didn't have my mask painted yet. At first, I wanted to do something with my nationality, a Slovakian flag or something. I decided to go with this, and I really like." Covering both ideas, the mask depicts a well-muscled Flanders holding the Slovakian flag.

Tim Brent: *Draft Pick Heaven-Sent* — SNAPSHOT

One of the finest players to emerge from the latter-day incarnation of the Majors has been Tim Brent. Brent is unusual in that he straddled the seasons between the era the school owned the team and the period after it was sold to outside interests.

"I played my OHL draft year in my hometown for the Cambridge WinterHawks Junior 'B' team," Tim starts. "I had a pretty tough decision as a 15- or 16-year-old in whether I was going to play in the Ontario Hockey League or go to school at Indiana State of the NCAA. Education was something that was very valued in my family."

Brent didn't know a great deal about St. Mike's College School at the time he was first approached by the Majors in 2000. "I was contacted by them, filled out an information sheet, and got to go down and visit the school and the rink with [coach] Mark Osborne and [general manager] Mark Napier. I was very surprised in the fact that it was an Ontario Hockey League team that prided itself not only on how they played on the ice but on their education. It was very interesting and seemed like it was a good fit for me."

Just prior to the OHL draft, Tim was contacted by the team and informed that if he was available when St. Mike's had their pick, second overall in the draft, they were

Ryan Walsh of the Majors takes a faceoff. Behind him, banners commemorating St. Mike's hockey history hang from the rafters of St. Michael's College School Arena.

going to select him — *if* they could be assured that he would attend the school. "It was a pretty easy decision for me," smiles Brent.

One of the things that had most influenced Tim's decision was the school's legacy. "You can't help but notice when walking into the St. Michael's Arena the massive Wall of Fame they have. Some of the names that are on that wall are in the Hockey Hall of Fame and have had just unbelievable careers. That was definitely something I talked about the whole ride home back to Cambridge from Toronto," he admits. "The character of that arena was something I'll never forget."

But following the draft, the young prospect was blindsided by one of the realities of hockey. "The people who drafted me [Napier and Osborne] were let go two weeks before training camp. Dave Cameron [coach] and Bob Jones [assistant coach] then took over. If anyone had an influence on the way I play the game now, it'd be those two guys," Tim states. "I learned to be a professional at St. Mike's before I was even a professional."

Although the Majors were sold, Brent remained on his path, both on the rink and in the classroom. "I still attended the school for my final three years of high school. And the friendships I made there and the experiences that I got are things I'll definitely never forget."

Tim found the St. Michael's College School experience fully rewarding. "It was a very demanding school. The guys who come out of there are more ready for the real world or university experience than any other school I can think of. I came from the public school system in a small town, and the St. Mike's private school was an eye-opener for me, but something I thought a lot about before I chose it so it was something that meant a lot to me when I got there."

Although there were many mentors — some of them colleagues on the ice and others instructors at the school — Tim found one particular teacher who gave him invaluable lessons outside the classroom. "The principal of the school, Mr. Sheridan, was my English teacher the first two years I was there and I have to give him big-time kudos for teaching me time-management skills," says Brent. "We sat down after school a few days a week and made a plan for the upcoming week on what I had to do. There was time allotted on the bus trip to do a book report or some other kind of homework, especially if it was a long trip, like to Sudbury. Other hockey teams wouldn't have to worry about school as much when they were on the road as St. Mike's did."

In 2002, Tim Brent was chosen by the Mighty Ducks of Anaheim in the second round, 37th overall, in the NHL Entry Draft. Still unsigned, he went back into the draft in 2004 after leading St. Mike's in scoring by posting a 26-goal, 67-point campaign and earning the honour of representing Canada in the World Junior Championship. Anaheim again chose Tim, this time in the third round, and after turning professional with the Cincinnati Mighty Ducks of the AHL in 2004–05, Brent debuted in the NHL in 2006–07 during the Anaheim Ducks' Stanley Cup championship season.

Long remembered as one of the finest representatives of the St. Michael's Majors in their modern era, Tim Brent had 78 goals, 142 assists, and 220 points during 238 regular-season OHL games, all with St. Mike's. In 69 playoff contests, Tim scored 20 goals and added 50 assists for 70 postseason points.

32
Strength in Numbers

With the move of the North Bay Centennials to Saginaw, Michigan, the Ontario Hockey League realigned its divisions in 2002–03. The newly named Spirit moved out of the Central Division and into the West, while London moved to the Midwest and Brampton took North Bay's old place in the Central. The Battalion promptly won the division title, edging out the Toronto St. Michael's Majors by two points, 78–76.

The Majors faced Belleville's Bulls in the Eastern Conference quarterfinals and defeated them in a close seven-game series. They then met the Battalion, and what should have been a long, tough series was wrapped up surprisingly quickly, with the Majors skating away with the series, four games to one.

Toronto's Majors then faced the Ottawa 67's, Brian Kilrea's well-tutored squad, who finished first in the East Division. It was the Majors' third straight appearance in the conference final. St. Mike's put up a valiant battle, winning the first two games, including a shutout by Andy Chiodo in Game One, but the 67's battled back and won the series in seven games. Ottawa went on to face the Kitchener Rangers for the OHL championship, but were turned aside by the powerful Rangers, who went on to win the Memorial Cup in 2003.

A 2001 draft pick of the Phoenix Coyotes, Frantisek Lukes arrived in Canada from the Czech Republic and was in his third season with the Majors in 2002–03. Lukes led the team in goals (27), assists (46), and points (73). Several others caught the eye of NHL scouts, including Tim Brent (66 points), Kevin Klein (44), Shane O'Brien (42 points, in a season split between Kingston and Toronto), Darryl Boyce (37), Drew Fata (38 points, 19 with the Frontenacs and 19 with the Majors), and Andy Chiodo, who, in his third season with the team, was named the OHL's goaltender of the year. He posted a 26–18–6 record with a 3.01 goals-against average and a .915 save percentage. Chiodo had been drafted by the New York Islanders in the 2001 NHL Entry Draft, but when they couldn't come to terms, he went back into the draft in 2003 and was plucked by the Pittsburgh Penguins. Chiodo made his NHL debut with the Penguins in 2003–04, one of many Penguins goalies that season — the others were Jean-Sebastien Aubin, Martin Brochu, Sebastien Caron, and Marc-Andre Fleury. In eight appearances, Chiodo won three, lost four, and tied one.

Shane O'Brien played just half a season with the Majors in 2002–03, coming over from the Kingston Frontenacs. An imposing figure on the blue line, O'Brien was drafted by the Mighty Ducks of Anaheim in 2003 and entered the NHL with the Ducks in 2006–07, although he was dealt to the Tampa Bay Lightning before he was able to get his name engraved on the Stanley Cup.

❖

Continuing a successful run, the Toronto St. Michael's Majors finished first in the Central Division in 2003-04, earning their second division title since the team's 1997 reawakening. Indeed, they paced the entire Eastern Conference with 38 wins, 21 losses, seven ties, and two overtime losses for 85 points, nine more than in 2002–03 and two better than the Mississauga IceDogs, who served notice that they were no longer the laughingstock of the league.

2002–2003

TEAM	GP	W	L	T	TL	PTS
EASTERN CONFERENCE						
Central Division						
Brampton Battalion	68	34	24	6	4	78
Toronto St. Michael's Majors	68	32	24	7	5	76
Barrie Colts	68	29	26	4	9	71
Mississauga IceDogs	68	23	31	1	3	60
Sudbury Wolves	68	16	46	4	2	38
East Division						
Ottawa 67's	68	44	14	7	3	98
Peterborough Petes	68	32	22	1	3	78
Belleville Bulls	68	33	27	6	2	74
Oshawa Generals	68	34	30	2	2	72
Kingston Frontenacs	68	25	37	2	4	56
WESTERN CONFERENCE						
Midwest Division						
Kitchener Rangers	68	46	14	5	3	100
London Knights	68	31	27	7	3	72
Guelph Storm	68	29	28	9	2	69
Owen Sound Attack	68	27	30	7	4	65
Erie Otters	68	24	35	6	3	57
West Division						
Plymouth Whalers	68	43	14	9	2	97
Sarnia Sting	68	41	19	7	1	90
Windsor Spitfires	68	37	25	5	1	80
Soo Greyhounds	68	26	33	6	3	61
Saginaw Spirit	68	11	45	5	7	34

2003–2004 TEAM	GP	W	L	T	OTL	PTS
EASTERN CONFERENCE						
Central Division						
Toronto St. Michael's Majors	68	38	21	7	2	85
Mississauga IceDogs	68	36	21	7	4	83
Barrie Colts	68	31	21	12	4	78
Brampton Battalion	68	25	32	9	2	61
Sudbury Wolves	68	25	32	6	5	61
East Division						
Ottawa 67's	68	29	26	9	4	71
Kingston Frontenacs	68	30	28	7	3	70
Oshawa Generals	68	30	29	8	1	69
Peterborough Petes	68	22	40	3	3	50
Belleville Bulls	68	15	44	8	1	39
WESTERN CONFERENCE						
Midwest Division						
London Knights	68	53	11	2	2	102
Guelph Storm	68	49	14	5	0	03
Kitchener Rangers	68	34	26	6	2	76
Owen Sound Attack	68	30	27	7	4	71
Erie Otters	68	29	26	6	7	71
West Division						
Sarnia Sting	68	37	23	4	4	82
Plymouth Whalers	68	32	24	9	3	76
Windsor Spitfires	68	27	30	3	8	65
Soo Greyhounds	68	30	34	3	1	64
Saginaw Spirit	68	16	45	3	4	39

The Majors' leading scorer was Tim Brent, who scored 26 goals and 67 points in his fourth season with St. Michael's. A gifted leader, Brent was the team captain for a second season, and also led the Majors in playoff scoring with 17 points in 18 games.

The squad featured several other future NHLers: Darryl Boyce, who went on to play and study at the University of New Brunswick, made his debut with the Toronto Maple Leafs in 2007–08; Cal Clutterbuck also made his first NHL appearances in 2007–08 with the Minnesota Wild; Kevin Klein wore a Nashville Predators jersey into battle in 2005–06; and Nathan McIver played his first NHL contest with the Vancouver Canucks in 2006–07.

Other players who enjoyed strong seasons with the Majors in 2003–04 were Sal Peralta (56 points), Cory Vitarelli (29 goals), and netminder Justin Peters. Scott Lehman was awarded the OHL's Bobby Smith Trophy, presented to the player who best combines academic excellence with a high level of play on the ice.

The Majors, under head coach Dave Cameron, were not a team to be pushed around. Seven players spent more than 100 minutes in the penalty box: Scott Lehman (189), Nathan McIver (183), Ted Perry (137), Cal Clutterbuck (112), Colin Power (111), Darryl Boyce (110), and Tim Brent (105).

The first-place Majors faced the eighth-ranked Sudbury Wolves in the conference quarterfinals and had a tougher time than expected, but eliminated the Wolves with a 5–2 win in Game Seven at home. They then romped over Brampton, four games to one, including two shutouts, to reach the Eastern Conference final for the fourth consecutive spring.

The series against the IceDogs was as hard fought as any that season, and Mississauga emerged with the victory, defeating the Majors in six games. Justin Peters earned his fourth shutout of the post-season during this series, although the Majors were twice shut out themselves. The IceDogs lost to the Guelph Storm in a four-game sweep for the John Ross Robertson Cup.

SNAPSHOT ▶▶ ▶▶ ▶▶ ▶▶ ▶▶ ▶▶ ▶▶ ▶▶

Tyler Haskins: *Captain Fantastic*

Tyler Haskins joined the Majors from the Guelph Storm early in the 2003–04 season, and went on to score 17 goals for St. Mike's that season. Although a native of Madison, Ohio, Haskins quickly learned about the legacy of his new team. "It's pretty special," he recounted. "We had a sign in our weight room that said, 'St. Mike's breeds NHL champions.'"

In the 2004 NHL Entry Draft, Tyler was chosen by the Detroit Red Wings in the fifth round, and attended training camp that fall. "It was a great experience — maybe a once-in-a-lifetime experience — to be there with those guys. Playing with Steve Yzerman, a guy I grew up watching, was unbelievable. And just to be with an NHL team that's on top of their game was a great experience."

Haskins played three seasons with the Toronto St. Michael's Majors, scoring 53 goals and 148 points. In his final season, 2005–06, he enjoyed his finest offensive season, scoring 24 goals and 75 points, and added a more physical element to his game. He was also named captain of the team. "It's a lot of responsibility to lead the team, so it was nice to be chosen," he says. "It was a goal of mine since I got to the OHL. When I was a 16-year-old rookie in Guelph, I always looked up to our captain."

Haskins, who attended Humber College while living in Toronto and never attended St. Michael's College School, drew parallels between playing with the Storm and playing with the Majors. "Playing in the OHL is usually so much confined to being a hockey player, but at St. Mike's, it's really a different experience. The school is right there and it's a great school. Even for those not going there, there is a high regard for character and leadership and those kinds of things that go along with being a St. Mike's Major."

33
Falling Back, Springing Forward

After four seasons at the helm of the Toronto St. Michael's Majors, each of which was capped by an appearance in the Eastern Conference final, Dave Cameron was promoted within Eugene Melnyk's hockey organization, becoming head coach of the Ottawa Senators' American Hockey League team, the Binghamton Senators, in 2004–05. Hired to replace the popular and successful Cameron was Bud Stefanski. Like so many of the great St. Michael's players through the decades, Stefanski was from South Porcupine, Ontario, and after starring with the Oshawa Generals, he played a single NHL game with the New York Rangers in 1977–78. Stefanski had been coach of the Barrie Colts for four seasons before joining the Majors.

A considerable challenge lay before him. Much of the core of the Majors team had graduated to other levels of hockey, and the team stumbled badly, finishing in the Central Division cellar with just 67 points. Still, that result was good enough for eighth in the conference and a berth in the playoffs.

Playing his fourth and final season as a Major, Darryl Boyce led the team in scoring with 50 points (15 goals, 35 assists). Tyler Donati, who came to the Majors in a trade with Oshawa, finished with 43 points. Cory Vitarelli was the top goal scorer, potting 19 for St. Mike's. The team was tough again in 2004–05, with six players topping the 100-penalty-minute mark: Scott Lehman (189), captain Nathan McIver (160), Boyce (152), Ryan Wilson (149), Colin Power (123), and Dale Good (106).

Playing assertive, demonstrative hockey, the lowly Majors thumped the first-place Mississauga IceDogs four games to one in the conference quarterfinal. But the Peterborough Petes brought St. Mike's back down to earth in the semifinal, winning by a similar four games to one, although it took overtime in three consecutive contests to decide a winner.

Meanwhile, the London Knights, on the strength of an unprecedented 120-point season and a 31-game unbeaten streak, had little trouble winning both the Robertson Trophy and the Memorial Cup.

Darryl Boyce had a circuitous, but interesting, path to the NHL. After four seasons with the St. Michael's Majors, where he scored 54 goals, 91 assists, and 145 regular-season points between 2001–02 and 2004–05, Darryl went undrafted by the NHL (despite having attended rookie camp in 2003 with the Columbus Blue Jackets and in 2005 with the Carolina Hurricanes). Although the Toronto Maple Leafs offered Boyce a minor-league contract, he decided to forgo his NHL dream (at least temporarily) and instead attend the University of New Brunswick.

"I knew I wanted to be an NHL player, but I also knew if I was going to make that dream come true, I was going to have to do it differently than everybody else because I was not a typical 'go to Junior, get drafted, play in the American league, then go to the NHL' type of player," Boyce explained to *The Hockey News*. In two seasons (2005–06 and 2006–07) with the Varsity Reds, he collected 65 points in 53 games, was named Atlantic University Sport rookie of the year in his first season, and was a key member of the UNB national championship team in his second.

Darryl never gave up on his dream of playing in the NHL. Prior to the 2007–08 season, he signed a two-year AHL contract with the Maple Leafs and started the season with the Toronto Marlies. The parent Leafs liked what they saw in the native of Prince

2004–05						
TEAM	GP	W	L	T	OTL	PTS
EASTERN CONFERENCE						
Central Division						
Mississauga IceDogs	68	34	21	12	1	81
Barrie Colts	68	33	23	9	3	78
Brampton Battalion	68	33	24	9	2	77
Sudbury Wolves	68	32	23	6	7	77
Toronto St. Michael's Majors	68	29	30	6	3	67
East Division						
Peterborough Petes	68	34	21	9	4	81
Ottawa 67's	68	34	26	7	1	76
Belleville Bulls	68	29	29	6	4	68
Kingston Frontenacs	68	28	33	4	3	63
Oshawa Generals	68	15	48	3	2	35
WESTERN CONFERENCE						
Midwest Division						
London Knights	68	59	7	2	0	120
Owen Sound Attack	68	40	18	7	3	90
Kitchener Rangers	68	35	20	9	4	83
Erie Otters	68	31	26	6	5	73
Guelph Storm	68	23	34	10	1	57
West Division						
Soo Greyhounds	68	33	25	9	1	76
Plymouth Whalers	68	30	29	6	3	69
Windsor Spitfires	68	26	29	6	7	65
Saginaw Spirit	68	18	42	4	4	44
Sarnia Sting	68	16	41	6	5	43

The brain trust of the Toronto St. Michael's Majors gathers on draft day to set the course for the future.

2005–06						
TEAM	GP	W	L	OTL	SL	PTS
EASTERN CONFERENCE						
Central Division						
Brampton Battalion	68	44	21	1	2	91
Barrie Colts	68	43	21	1	3	90
Sudbury Wolves	68	34	28	1	5	74
Toronto St. Michael's Majors	68	32	26	6	4	74
Mississauga IceDogs	68	21	40	5	2	49
East Division						
Peterborough Petes	68	47	16	2	3	99
Kingston Frontenacs	68	37	24	4	3	81
Belleville Bulls	68	32	28	5	3	72
Ottawa 67's	68	29	31	5	3	66
Oshawa Generals	68	18	45	4	1	41
WESTERN CONFERENCE						
Midwest Division						
London Knights	68	49	15	1	3	102
Kitchener Rangers	68	47	19	1	1	96
Guelph Storm	68	40	24	1	3	84
Owen Sound Attack	68	32	29	4	3	71
Erie Otters	68	26	35	4	3	59
West Division						
Plymouth Whalers	68	35	28	1	4	75
Saginaw Gears	68	36	30	2	0	74
Windsor Spitfires	68	32	29	3	4	71
Soo Greyhounds	68	29	31	3	5	66
Sarnia Sting	68	17	46	2	3	39

Edward Island, and on New Year's Eve 2007, they signed Boyce to a two-way NHL contract. When Alexei Ponikarovsky was put out of the lineup with a shoulder injury in January, Boyce was summoned by the big club. "I was called and told to come to the airport and that I'd definitely be in the lineup the next day," he explained.

Darryl played in his first NHL game on January 24, 2008, against the Washington Capitals. But on his fifth shift, Boyce was injured, ironically suffering the same shoulder injury that allowed him to make his NHL debut. "I was skating as fast as I could and I went to hit him [Washington's Tom Poti]. The back of his ankle caught my skate and I went flying into the boards at full speed." Boyce had suffered a separated left shoulder. "At first, I thought it might just be a sore shoulder, but when I went to move it, there was nothing. I couldn't lift it."

Darryl refused to allow the dream to dissolve. "I feel I have to be a little more patient with myself out there," he said in an interview with the *Summerside Journal-Pioneer*. "Sometimes, I can be my own worst enemy, and that's just what happened. I was trying too hard and trying to impress people too much and ended up hurting myself."

Speaking to the significance of his attending St. Michael's College School, Darryl added, "My time at St. Mike's has been the foundation for me on and off the ice. "The school provided me with a great education that helped me achieve academic all-Canadian honours with a 3.5 GPA (grade point average), while hockey gave me all the tools to become a pro hockey player, where I suited up in my very first NHL game as a member of the Toronto Maple Leafs."

Respectability was the goal of the Toronto St. Michael's Majors and second-year coach Bud Stefanski in 2005–06, and they achieved exactly that, with a 74-point, fourth-place finish in the Ontario Hockey League's Central Division.

The leading scorer for the Majors for 2005–06 was Justin Donati, who finished sixth in the league with 109 points (46 goals and 63 assists). Justin's twin brother, Tyler, had 72 points. Other prime contributors were Cory Vitarelli (78), team captain Tyler Haskins (75), Ryan Wilson (61), and Scott Lehman (55).

Wayne Savage and Justin Peters split the goaltending duties.

St. Mike's was paired with the Barrie Colts in the conference quarterfinal, but fell four games to none. The Peterborough Petes went on to capture the J. Ross Robertson Trophy as OHL champs.

Tyler and Justin Donati: Twin Terrors on Ice ◀◀ ◀◀ ◀◀ ◀◀ ◀◀ ◀◀ ◀◀ SNAPSHOT

In 2005-06, their sole full season with the Majors, the brothers combined for 181 scoring points. Tyler (middle row, third from right) contributed 72 points and Justin (middle row, fourth from right) added 109.

The story of twins starring at St. Mike's harks back to the Majors' last Memorial Cup championship, when twins Bruce and Dave Draper played integral roles with the team.

Tyler and Justin Donati, born in Oakville, Ontario, seven minutes apart on October 17, 1986 [Tyler is the elder], joined the Oshawa Generals together in 2003–04. Both offensively gifted, Tyler scored 20 goals and 56 points for the Generals while Justin chipped in with 15 goals and 30 points.

On January 8, 2005, the Donatis were traded from Oshawa to St. Mike's, with Cal Clutterbuck going the other way. The twins had respectable seasons — Tyler scored 21 goals and 43 points and Justin 12 and 39. Once they had settled into their surroundings in 2005–06, they both exploded offensively. Tyler potted 36 goals and 36 assists for 72 points, while Justin finished with 46 goals and 63 assists for 109 points, the seventh-best total in the league.

The Majors weren't the only beneficiary of the boys' offensive prowess. While they were still playing in Oshawa, the Donatis' mother, Corinne, was diagnosed with cancer. The Majors devised a promotion called "Donati Points for Cancer." For each point either of the twins collected, $10 would be donated to Toronto's Princess Margaret Hospital to aid in battling ovarian cancer. Majors owner Eugene Melnyk vowed to match whatever total was raised through the fund's campaign. "As long as I'm helping the team, I'm helping my mom, too," said Justin at the time. Their total of 181 points meant that the Donati Points for Cancer Fund earned $1,810, doubled to $3,620 by Melnyk's contribution.

In June 2006, the brothers were split up for the first time in their hockey careers. The Majors traded Tyler to the Belleville Bulls, receiving Scott Baker and a draft pick in exchange. Tyler's overage season saw him post a season of 54 goals (third best in the OHL) and 75 assists for 129 points, making him the fourth-highest scorer in 2006–07. He was selected to the league's Second All-Star Team. "It sucked to get split up, but it was something we had to do if we wanted to make our hockey careers better," shrugged Tyler.

At the trade deadline in January 2007, Justin was sent by St. Mike's to the Sudbury Wolves for Jesse Messier and Justin Vaive. His combined scoring totals for the season were 47 goals and 44 assists for 91 points, and he helped the Wolves capture the Eastern Conference championship in 2006–07.

Justin joined the University of Prince Edward Island Panthers in February 2008, a team that could provide the basis for a Majors alumni association. The lineup boasted Justin's former linemate Cory Vitarelli, as well as Connor Cameron, Craig Foster, Tyson Gimblett, Kyle Spurr, and Tom Waugh.

Disappointment and Change

2006–07						
TEAM	GP	W	L	OTL	SL	PTS
EASTERN CONFERENCE						
Central Division						
Barrie Colts	68	48	19	0	1	97
Mississauga IceDogs	68	43	21	0	4	90
Sudbury Wolves	68	29	30	3	6	67
Brampton Battalion	68	27	36	1	4	59
Toronto St. Michael's Majors	68	20	41	4	3	47
East Division						
Belleville Bulls	68	39	24	0	5	83
Oshawa Generals	68	31	29	3	5	70
Kingston Frontenacs	68	31	30	5	2	69
Ottawa 67's	68	30	34	0	4	64
Peterborough Petes	68	24	39	1	4	53
WESTERN CONFERENCE						
Midwest Division						
London Knights	68	50	14	1	3	104
Kitchener Rangers	68	47	17	1	3	98
Guelph Storm	68	33	23	3	9	78
Owen Sound Attack	68	31	30	3	4	69
Erie Otters	68	15	50	1	2	33
West Division						
Plymouth Whalers	68	49	14	2	3	103
Saginaw Gears	68	44	21	0	3	91
Soo Greyhounds	68	37	23	1	7	82
Sarnia Sting	68	34	24	5	5	78
Windsor Spitfires	68	18	43	2	5	43

After taking a step forward in 2005–06, the Majors' momentum was thrust in the opposite direction in 2006–07, as they slipped to fifth in the Central Division and dropped 27 points in the standings. For the first time since 1999–2000, there would be no postseason play for Toronto St. Michael's.

Several players enjoyed strong seasons for St. Mike's, but the team lacked that individual who could score seemingly at will. Matt Caria was the team's most productive player, combining 33 goals and 42 assists for 75 points. New arrival Kaspars Daugavins, with skills that boded well for the future, finished second on the team with 60 points. Michael Haley scored 30 goals and finished with 54 points, while Mike Pelech racked up 47 points and Jason Cassidy generated 24 goals and 41 points.

At the end of the disappointing season, Coach Stefanski was reassigned and told that he would not be coaching the team in 2007–08.

❖

On Sunday afternoon, March 18, 2007, the Toronto St. Michael's Majors played host to the Belleville Bulls in the season finale. The 1,417 fans at St. Michael's College School Arena witnessed a seesaw battle that was deadlocked at 5–5 after 60 minutes. At 3:49 of overtime, Shawn Matthias scored to give the Bulls the win, and thus ended a chapter in the history of Junior hockey at St. Michael's, and in the city of Toronto. When the Majors took the ice to begin the 2007–08 season, it would be in a new home.

It was the end of an era. On March 18, 2007, the St. Michael's Majors played their final game at the venerable St. Michael's College School Arena. Changes were well underway that would see the team relocate to Mississauga.

Father Joe Redican: Leader of Men
SNAPSHOT

Father Joe Redican, C.S.B., joined St. Michael's College School as president in July 2005. An alumnus, he was the fourth generation in his family to attend the school, following his great-grandfather, his grandfather, his father, and his uncles.

Although he was never much of a skater — and as a result, never played the game — Father Redican was a hockey fan, and he clearly remembers attending Majors games and, after the Majors folded, going to Maple Leaf Gardens to watch the Toronto Marlboros.

The relationship between the school and the Majors is different than when he was a boy, but still, "There's a sense of school pride in the Majors. And then there's the Buzzers. They're not owned by the school, either, but about 20 of the Buzzers are at the school and some of the team's coaching staff is also part of the teaching staff." Father Redican explained that the school has other teams as well, while students play on various teams around the city.

Father Redican acknowledges and accepts that, with the Majors now playing their home games in Mississauga, the dynamic between the team and the school has changed. "Our arena is not big enough to accommodate an OHL team. We understood all along that there needed to be a larger venue for them," he states. "We don't have the space to put in the kind of facility they need and the parking that would be required for that size of facility. I know it was explored, but it really wasn't a viable option.

"The relationship is a bit more distant, but there are good connections and they still use the St. Mike's Majors' name," he adds. Nor does he worry about losing a prime tenant for the school's arena, either. "Being in the centre of the city, we have no trouble selling the ice to teams."

The dream of resuming the St. Michael's Majors program the way it was when the team left the OHA in 1962 was somewhat unrealistic, states the school's president. "It isn't the 1950s, and the whole reality of that level of hockey has changed dramatically over the last 20 or 30 years," he says. "The original vision was to try and recapture something that happened 40 years ago, and although I think it was laudable, I don't think it was very practical. St. Mike's is very much an academically elite school. We really don't have programs other than those leading to university. You don't necessarily have to be a great scholar to be a good hockey player, so it would sometimes be a difficult fit. I know the few kids that are there now are pretty serious students and have post-secondary plans, so that's a really good fit."

Having said that, Father Redican talks about how the school is currently connected to the Majors, besides just the name. "One of our priests does some [English as a second language instruction for] the kids who are brought in from other countries [to play hockey for the Majors], and a couple of our staff help to counsel other kids who are trying to do the beginning of university if they've already graduated from high school. We assist with additional services and I expect that will continue."

35
The Move to Mississauga

Dave Cameron (far left), who would go on to great success as coach of the Majors, is shown at the media conference announcing his initial hiring. Father Zorzi (beside Cameron) makes the announcement. Cameron returned for a second stint coaching the Majors in 2007–08.

On June 5, 2007, the official announcement was made: the Ontario Hockey League's board of governors had given its approval, and the Majors were moving to Mississauga for the upcoming season. The franchise, which would continue to carry a connection to St. Michael's College School, was to be known as the Mississauga St. Michael's Majors.

It was the final move in a sometimes-tangled chain of events.

The Majors had just completed their 10th season back in the OHL. Since their return, the team had called both Maple Leaf Gardens and St. Michael's College School Arena home, "… and as many of you know, it is an arena rich with hockey history where many of the game's greatest players once played," wrote team owner, Eugene Melnyk. "What many of you don't know is that when I purchased the Majors in 2001, I committed to the OHL that I would find a larger, modern arena for the team — a venue that was more in keeping with the many larger OHL venues that have been built across Ontario. Since then, I have been on a five-year quest searching across the Greater Toronto Area for a place to build that new arena. In the end, there simply were no financially viable options. I purchased the Mississauga IceDogs as part of a broader plan that will eventually see the Majors relocate to Mississauga's Hershey Centre."

That deal closed in July 2006, as Capital Sports Properties, the umbrella firm for Melnyk's sports empire, purchased the IceDogs from auto parts magnate Mario Forgione. That gave Melnyk two OHL franchises — one more than he was allowed, or cared, to own. The goal then became to find a buyer for the IceDogs who would move the team so that the Majors could move into the Hershey Centre in Mississauga.

At first, it appeared that that buyer would be Tom Bitove, who had designs on a move to Niagara Falls. But he was unable to come to an agreement with the city council, which concluded that the citizens simply couldn't afford to build a new, 5,000-seat arena suitable for OHL hockey. Attention then shifted to North Bay, where Moe Mantha Jr., a former NHL player, made a pitch for the IceDogs, but he discovered that his group was simply being used by the IceDogs to court other suitors. Finally, Capital Sports found a buyer in Bill Burke, an Aurora, Ontario, businessman, who made a conditional purchase, predicated on the ability to find a place to transplant the franchise.

On April 23, 2007, after a last-ditch attempt to attract Niagara Falls, Burke and Capital Sports confirmed that the IceDogs would move to St. Catharines, where they had taken out a five-year lease on the Jack Gatecliff Arena. That rink, opened in 1938 as the Garden City Arena, is certainly no stranger to OHL action, having been home to the Falcons from 1943 to 1947, the TeePees from 1947 to 1962, and the Black Hawks from 1962 to 1976. The City of St. Catharines agreed to spend $250,000 to build offices within the area for the IceDogs, as well as to build a new dressing room for the team and improve the dressing room for the Junior 'B' Falcons.

"It wasn't a difficult decision for council," stated St. Catharines mayor Brian McMullan. "We recognize how significant getting an OHL team is for a city."

For the fans and players of the St. Michael's Majors, it was a bittersweet moment. The opportunity to play in a larger, more modern rink was exciting, but it was sad to leave the venerable arena at Bathurst and St. Clair.

St. Michael's College School Arena was conceived in 1955 by Father Ted Flanagan. The rink, designed by McNamara Engineering, consists of a "three-pinned arch" made up of nine laminated timber arches fabricated from British Columbia fir. The highest point above ice level is 45 feet. The ice surface itself measures a cozy 185 feet by 80 feet. The arena seats approximately 1,000 fans, with standing room allowing another 500 to witness games.

Father Flanagan's dream became reality with the ceremonial faceoff that took place prior to an Old Boys' hockey game on November 7, 1960. That first game saw Ed Chadwick and Gerry McNamara suit up in goal for the Old Boys, who drew on the talents of other NHL (and St. Mike's) alumni, including Jack Caffery, Father Les Costello, Bill Dineen, Dick and Les Duff, Reg Fleming, Pat Hannigan, Tim Horton, Red Kelly, Dave Keon, Ted Lindsay, Frank Mahovlich, Dick Mattiussi, Rudy Migay, Gus Mortson, Tod Sloan, and Gene Ubriaco. Father Ted Flanagan and Joe Primeau coached the Old Boys.

The alumni lined up against the 1961 Memorial Cup–winning Majors, with Gerry Cheevers and Dave Dryden in goal and skaters Arnie Brown, Andre Champagne, Terry Clancy, Jack Cole, Paul Conlin, Bruce and Dave Draper, Roger Galipeau, Paul Jackson, Larry Keenan, Duncan MacDonald, Billy MacMillan, Peter Noakes, Terry O'Malley, and Tom Polanic in uniform. The champs were supplemented with older alumni, including Bob McKnight, Don Rope and Darryl Sly. Father David Bauer, Father O'Leary, and Father Bill Conway coached this squad, with Jim Gregory returning as the team's trainer.

Since that inaugural game, the arena has undergone several wholesale alterations. In 1979, the north and west ends were developed, two dressing rooms were added, a handicapped washroom was installed, and a snack bar was created. In anticipation of the Majors' return to the OHL in 1997, the arena's refrigeration plant was upgraded, a new sound system was added, a new four-sided clock installed at centre ice, new dasher boards with higher glass installed, and the roof replaced.

The cost of renovating or rebuilding the current location adjacent to the school would have been prohibitively expensive. Eugene Melnyk tried to purchase the abandoned Maple Leaf Gardens from Maple Leaf Sports and Entertainment and restore it as a home for his Majors. The idea was sound — it would extend the life of the grand old hockey emporium and harked back to the glory days when the Majors played their home games at the corner of Carlton and Church. But MLSE spurned the idea. The idea of competition didn't sit well with the arena's owners, who ultimately sold the Gardens to Loblaw Companies.

When the federal government promised to build the National Sports Institute at the former Downsview air force base, Melnyk committed to underwriting a portion of the cost and promised that the Majors would be the principal tenant of the facility, but that plan never saw the light of day.

Instead, Eugene Melnyk relocated his team to the Hershey Centre in Mississauga. "It was very important to me to keep the tradition of St. Michael's alive because it's a tradition of excellence, and that's what we're trying to do here," stated Eugene Melnyk in a *Toronto Sun* interview. "We'll get really involved in the community here in Mississauga for a long, long time."

Although many mourned the departure from the "old barn at St. Mike's," hockey fans followed the Majors to their new home on October 5, 2007, when 2,570 attended the home opener of the Mississauga St. Michael's Majors at the Hershey Centre. The game ended in a shootout loss to the Windsor Spitfires.

Dave Cameron returned to the Majors, as coach and general manager, for the 2007–08 season. A veteran of 168 NHL games with the Colorado Rockies and New Jersey Devils, Cameron had been behind the bench for the Majors from 2000–01 through 2003–04. In 2004–05, he guided the Binghamton Senators of the American Hockey League to an East Division championship.

"Dave's return to the Majors reiterates our commitment to doing everything we can to build a solid hockey organization both on and off the ice," stated Eugene Melnyk in a team press release.

2007–08						
TEAM	GP	W	L	OTL	SL	PTS
EASTERN CONFERENCE						
Central Division						
Brampton Battalion	68	42	22	1	3	88
Niagara IceDogs	68	42	25	0	1	85
Mississauga St. Michael's Majors	68	31	32	2	1	67
Barrie Colts	68	28	34	3	1	62
Sudbury Wolves	68	17	46	2	3	39
East Division						
Belleville Bulls	68	48	14	4	2	102
Oshawa Generals	68	38	17	6	7	89
Ottawa 67's	68	29	34	2	3	63
Peterborough Petes	68	28	36	1	3	60
Kingston Frontenacs	68	25	41	0	2	52
WESTERN CONFERENCE						
Midwest Division						
Kitchener Rangers	68	53	11	1	3	110
London Knights	68	38	24	4	2	82
Guelph Storm	68	34	25	5	4	77
Owen Sound Attack	68	20	41	2	5	47
Erie Otters	68	18	46	2	2	40
West Division						
Soo Greyhounds	68	44	18	2	4	94
Windsor Spitfires	68	41	15	7	5	94
Sarnia Sting	68	37	29	2	0	76
Saginaw Spirit	68	33	25	8	2	76

The Majors were rejuvenated in their new digs, improving by 18 points to 65, lifting them to third place in the Central Division. The team's scoring star in 2007–08 was Kaspars Daugavins, a young Russian sniper. St. Mike's selected him with their pick in the 2006 CHL Import Draft, and he didn't disappoint. Kaspars finished second in scoring for the Majors in 2006–07, and led the team with 40 goals and 34 assists for 74 points in 2007–08. It was not the first time Coach Cameron had enjoyed Daugavins talent, either — Kaspars was Ottawa's third pick in the 2006 NHL Entry Draft, and he played 11 games for Binghamton in 2006–07.

Strong contributions also came from Michael Pelech (49 points), captain Jesse Messier (43 points), Casey Cizikas (41), and Cameron Gaunce (40 points).

Always a team with strong marketing ideas, on February 13, 2008, the Majors held a clever fundraiser called "Paint the Rink Pink." To raise awareness and proceeds for the Canadian Breast Cancer Foundation, the ice at the Hershey Centre was painted pink, the team wore special pink jerseys, and the on-ice officials were decked out in pink as well. Mississauga mayor Hazel McCallion was joined by TV personality Don Cherry, OHL commissioner David Branch, and legendary Toronto Maple Leafs netminder Johnny Bower for the promotion, which surrounded St. Mike's game against the Guelph Storm.

In a twist of irony, St. Mike's met the Niagara IceDogs, as the team was now known, in the first round of the OHL playoffs. It was the third time in five seasons that the rivals had met in the playoffs. Niagara was anxious to return to the Hershey Centre and prove a point, and they swept the series.

SNAPSHOT

Michael McGurk: Leaving His Marks

Born in Hamilton, just down the highway from the Majors' new home in Mississauga, Michael McGurk became a member of St. Mike's as a fourth-round draft pick in 2005 and joined the club that fall. In 2006–07, the steady defenceman pulled off a juggling act that would make circus performers shake their heads in amazement. "Being part of the Majors hockey team has taught me many great skills," Michael says. "With the heavy school schedule and hockey schedule, I quickly learned great time-management skills, as I played every game in 2006–07 and still obtained an 82% average." But it wasn't strictly a constant diet of packing books along with hockey equipment. "The team and school also helped me mature and grow as a young man. I was away from my family and friends, but with the help of the team, my new family, and the school, I was able to succeed."

Michael attended St. Michael's College School for one year, but the experience will stay with him forever. "I gained an abundance of great abilities and met a great group of friends," he confirms. "The school's motto, 'Teach me goodness, discipline, and knowledge,' is really instilled into the students. There were many men I met at school — students and teachers — who were great individuals and helped me to adapt to my new school and city. School allowed me to meet many great contacts and friends who I will continue to stay in contact with, even though we are no longer in the same cities."

A quality individual with a strong work ethic, Michael was very proud to be named an alternate captain of the Majors in 2007–08. "With the great opportunity I was given, going to St. Michael's College School and playing for the St. Michael's Majors, I have gained great life experiences." He adds, "I think, with the help of school and the Majors, I became a more independent, confident, intelligent young man. The St. Michael's community played a major role in my development and I am very grateful for the opportunity."

36
The Buzzers — 1933–1961

While the Majors are predominant in the history of St. Mike's hockey, St. Michael's College School has also been ably represented by their "little brothers" the Buzzers, a team whose distinguished heritage stretches back across three-quarters of a century.

❖

With hockey gaining rapidly in popularity, there was a surplus of Junior-aged players in Ontario, so the Ontario Hockey Association made the decision to split the junior level into two classes: Junior 'A' and Junior 'B.'

The naming of St. Michael's two Junior teams appears to have been as much a media invention as a carefully crafted marketing exercise. The Majors were, candidly, the more prominent of the squads, garnering more attention and box-office revenue. The Buzzers, meanwhile, seem simply to have employed the letter B from Junior 'B' and chosen a name that would show energy and spirit.

In a curious twist, after winning the Sutherland Cup as OHA Junior 'B' champions in 1933–34, beating Preston two games to none, the Buzzers faced the Majors for the John Ross Robertson Trophy and the OHA Junior championship. Dr. Jerry LaFlamme coached both squads, but whether it was from anxiety or a need to avoid showing any bias, he delegated the duties to others. The Buzzers were badly outmatched by the Majors, and fell to the Junior 'A' team that went on to win the Memorial Cup.

The Buzzers roster included future NHLers Johnny Crawford, Peanuts O'Flaherty, and Carl Smith.

Carl "Winky" Smith, a native of Cache Bay, Ontario, came from a family of hockey players. Older brother Dalton, known as Nakina, played with the Detroit Red Wings in 1943–44. Winky didn't have his brother's size — he stood just five feet, five inches tall and weighed but 150 pounds, while Nakina was 5 foot 11 and 160 pounds — but he excelled at hockey nevertheless. In fact, Winky played with his brother on that Red Wing team in 1943–44, scoring a goal and an assist in seven games. It was the only NHL season for either brother. A third Smith brother, Orville, would later play for St. Michael's College and, although he never reached the NHL, would enjoy a long minor-pro career.

The Buzzers, coached by Dr. LaFlamme, finished first at the conclusion of the 1934–35 regular season, becoming the Prep School champions over Jarvis Collegiate and the University of Toronto Schools. They swept through the preliminary playoff round before eliminating the Niagara Falls Cataracts in the semifinals. The Buzzers then met the Barrie Colts. The Colts doubled the Buzzers 6–3 in the opening contest, but St. Michael's won Game Two. In a reason lost to time, it was decided to play another two-game, total-goal round. Barrie won 4–3 in Game One, but the Buzzers' dream of coming back was squashed when they were dumped 7–1 to lose the series.

Future NHLers Pat McReavy and 15-year-old Billy Taylor were on the Buzzers' roster in 1934–35.

The Buzzers completed the eight-game 1935-36 season with six wins, a defeat and one tie, finishing first in their league.

This year's team included goaltender Tom McLean, with defencemen Ab Tonn and Bill Stukus, who later played football for the Grey Cup champion Toronto Argonauts alongside his brothers Annis and Frank. Billy Taylor, a second-year Buzzer, played on a

Prior to the Ontario Hockey Association's split that created Junior 'A' and 'B' streams and the subsequent debut of the Junior 'B' St. Michael's Buzzers, the team participated in the OHA's Prep School league.

line with Paul McNamara and another returnee, Bunky Lukasic. Taylor scored a league-best nine goals and was the leading point collector with 18 in seven games.

The team easily outscored Bracebridge in a two-game, total-goal semifinal. The Buzzers then beat Barrie in a second such series. Kingston was up next, and the Buzzers dumped them. Then, to complete the sweep, St. Mike's defeated Guelph two games to one in a best-of-three Sutherland Cup final. Billy Taylor ran roughshod over the competition through the playoffs, scoring 27 goals and 34 points in 11 games.

Billy Taylor was an incomparable Junior, arguably one of the best in hockey's history. As a youngster wearing a miniature Toronto Maple Leafs sweater, "Billy the Kid" entertained Maple Leafs fans at the Arena Gardens with between-periods skating and stickhandling demonstrations. He led the OHA Prep Group in scoring in 1935–36, led the Toronto Mercantile Hockey League in scoring while playing with the British Consols in 1936–37, then joined the Oshawa Generals for two seasons in which they won back-to-back OHA championships as well as a Memorial Cup title in 1939 — and Taylor led the league in scoring that season. Just five foot nine and 150 pounds, the talented youngster was eagerly promoted to the Toronto Maple Leafs in 1939–40.

In the National Hockey League, Taylor never quite lived up to the success predicted for him. He was a solid, if unspectacular, pro who played five seasons in Toronto, including a Stanley Cup victory in 1942, and was then traded to the Detroit Red Wings for 1946–47. The Wings dealt him to Boston prior to the 1947–48 campaign, but late in the season he was again traded, this time to the New York Rangers. After two games, his career came to a spectacular, if not crashing, halt. Taylor and former teammate Don Gallinger were suspended for life by the NHL for gambling infractions. Although the suspension was lifted in 1970, by then, Taylor was 51 years old. After his reinstatement, he worked briefly as a scout, first with the Philadelphia Flyers and then with the Washington Capitals. Taylor played six NHL seasons, scored 87 goals and assisted on 180 others for a total of 267 points.

After a four-year absence, the Buzzers returned to OHA Junior 'B' play in 1939–40. Father Carter had taken over the coaching reins and constructed the team around St. Michael's city-champion Midget team from the previous year. Joe Cleary was in goal

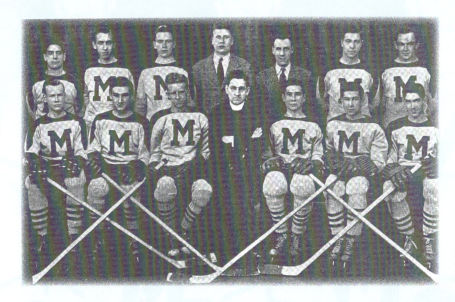

"Long-legged Bill Conway (seated, far left), who never failed to give the fans a flare of fisticuffs," clearly said a period-full of Hail Marys before commencing his career as beloved Father Bill Conway, the same man who later coached these same Buzzers.

for the Buzzers and was selected captain that year, showing what *The Thurible* referred to "fight, coolness, and aggressiveness from his position." He played for the Marlboros in 1940–41, but returned to St. Mike's to play with the Majors in 1941–42.

This season introduced several players who would become long-standing Buzzers, including Frank Bennett, Farrell Gallagher, netminder Jean Marois, and Ernie Midghall. Bennett later played seven games with the Detroit Red Wings in 1943–44. Bruising defenceman Bill Doyle led the team in scoring with six goals and four assists in six games, the third-best point total in the league. He also compiled 20 penalty minutes, second-highest total of the season.

The Buzzers went to the OHA Junior 'B' final against Upper Canada College. The teams had split the regular season, but in post-season play, UCC outclassed St. Mike's.

Father Mallon replaced Father Carter as coach of the 1940–41 edition of the St. Michael's Buzzers and built his team around the six returning players: captain Farrell Gallagher, Rudy Desilets, Lloyd Coburn, Ernie Midghall, Frank Bennett, and Bill Callahan. Goaltender Jean Marois had played one game for the Buzzers the previous season and returned as the principal netminder in 1940–41.

Playing in the Prep School circuit, the St. Michael's Buzzers were led by Gallagher, who collected six goals and four assists through the six-game season to lead the team in scoring. Marois provided outstanding netminding, a skill that would lead him to a brief NHL career. Future NHLer Tommy O'Neill was a rookie with the Buzzers that year.

In the first round of the playoffs, the Buzzers defeated UCC to win the OHA Junior 'B' Prep School championship. After a three-and-a-half-week layoff during which they waited to learn who their opponent would be, the Buzzers met St. Catharines in a two-game, total-goal series. St. Mike's lost the first game 8–3, but returned to Toronto with "every supporter on hand, the band was inspiring, the cheering magnificent and the game filled with excitement," as the Buzzers rallied and took the second contest 7–6, with Cecil Schmalz scoring five times. Nevertheless, St. Catharines led in goals, 14–10, and took the Sutherland Cup.

Tommy O'Neill, tagged with the nickname "Windy" for his penchant for talking, was a talented musician who had already registered several compositions by the time he pulled on a Buzzers' sweater. The defenceman, who would win a Stanley Cup with the Toronto Maple Leafs in 1945 as a winger, later became a popular Toronto-area lawyer and one of Leaf coach Punch Imlach's confidants.

Father Mallon found himself surrounded by a fresh-faced group of rookies to compete in the Junior 'B' Prep School division in 1941–42.

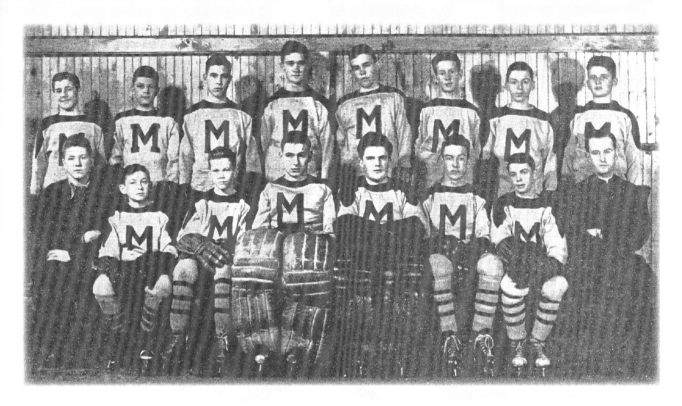

The leading scorer of the 1947–48 edition of the Buzzers was Rocco Volpe, seen in the back row, far left, while playing with the 1944–45 Bantam team at St. Mike's.

Goalie Jean Marois was returning for a third season, although he was promoted to the Majors after just two games and replaced by Joe Irvine, whose "smooth style, steady playing, almost impossible saves and, above all, the confidence his teammates placed in him, clearly proved that he more than merited the position."

The Midghall brothers — Ernie, Gerry, and Ray — dominated the lineup, while Frank Imonti was the team's leading scorer through the regular season with six goals and 11 points in eight games. Bill Conway was a welcome addition who added an edge to the team by leading them in penalty minutes with 12. Conway "never failed to give the fans a flare of fisticuffs," according to *The Thurible*. Bill Conway's lingering effect on the Buzzers wouldn't be fully felt until he had entered the priesthood and returned to St. Michael's, where Father Bill coached the Buzzers for four seasons, including an OHA championship in 1961 just prior to his death.

Father Maurice Whelan took on the coaching duties of the Buzzers in 1942–43, and for the second year in a row the team predominantly featured newcomers to Junior 'B' hockey. Joe Marzalik was appointed captain and responded with seven goals and a league-best 16 assists for 23 points, which won him the scoring championship. Joe Sadler's 16 points put him in sixth place in the league.

Competing against their longtime Prep School rivals, the Buzzers again had to reinvent themselves in 1943–44. Gerry Hector took over in goal, and the team was led offensively by John Blute, whose eight goals and two assists gave him 10 points, good for fifth in the league's scoring parade. Captain Paul Pelow was seventh, accounting for three goals and six assists for nine points.

The Buzzers missed the playoffs, but late in the season, the team's new coach, Father Ted Flanagan, promoted a line from the St. Michael's Midget team. Ed Harrison, George Scholes, and Warren Winslow looked as though they had been playing Junior 'B' hockey all season, foreshadowing highly successful Junior careers.

Father Flanagan would coach the Buzzers for 14 seasons, giving way to Father Conway in 1957–58.

The Midgets, also coached by Father Flanagan, won the league championship, winning 34 games and losing just one, scoring 356 goals while allowing only 38. The Midgets featured future NHL stars Ed Harrison, Ed Sandford and Leonard "Red" Kelly.

Unlike many boys who had received scholarships for their hockey prowess, Kelly took a different route to get to St. Michael's. "My father and my grandfather both went to St. Mike's. My dad knew some of the priests, so he got me into St. Mike's," Red explains. "I went in late, I didn't go in until October — had to help get the crops in. They accepted me, and I waited on tables there to help pay the way through."

"We knew Red's father, Lawrence, had played for St. Michael's in earlier days [1915]," said Father Mallon, "and he showed enough promise in his build, his disposition, and ability with the stick to be closely watched." But for Red, joining the St. Michael's hockey team was easier said than done. "I tried out for the 'A' team, and I was cut after one practice. I tried out for the 'B' team, and I was cut after one practice. I tried out for the Midget team, and I was cut after one practice," he laughs. "Now, I'm out in the backyard in the open-air rink, playing with some of the teachers — they were going through to be priests — and one of them was an assistant to Father Flanagan, who was coaching the Midget team. After [I played] against him out there, he went to Father Flanagan and told him, 'You'd better take another look at this guy.' They brought me back and I made the team on the third line."

Several members of Father Flanagan's Midget team graduated to the Buzzers for 1944–45, and did so in spectacular style. Ed Harrison, Red Kelly, Ed Sandford, George Scholes, and Warren Winslow all joined the team, laying the foundation for what was arguably the finest Buzzers team of all time.

Unfortunately, the remarkable exploits of the Buzzers were, in many ways, overshadowed by the 1944–45 edition of the St. Michael's Majors, who won the Memorial Cup championship.

From the first game of the season, pundits recognized that the Buzzers were a team to be reckoned with. Through 11 regular-season games, the team went undefeated. "[Ed] Sandford's free style of skating, his deceptive shot and ability to put the puck in the net; the fight displayed by fiery 'Red' Kelly, a nifty stickhandler and a very fast skater, combined with the high scoring Ed Harrison, equal in every respect to his brilliant linemates, formed the league's highest scoring line," enthused *The Thurible*. Ed Bury, George Scholes, and Warren Winslow formed a potent second unit. "Time and time again, Bury's quick sweeping strides and his clever stickhandling combined with dogged determination, would put the puck in the net," said the yearbook. "George Scholes, a smart skater, was a constant threat to the opposition. Winslow displayed the old St. Mike's fight from the opening faceoff to the last whistle of every game."

The defence included Paul Dopp, Pat Gravelle, Bill McNamara (younger brother of alumni George and Paul), Pete "Moose" McParland (the team's bad boy, earning 26 penalty minutes, third-highest total in the league), Bob Rafferty, and Phil Samis, "an exceptionally fast skater who thrived when the going got tough."

In goal, the Buzzers boasted the terrific tandem of Gerry Hector and Bob DeCourcy. "Gerry Hector possessed all the qualities that go to make a capable goaltender," mentioned *The Thurible*. The veteran enjoyed a superb season, earning two shutouts and allowing just five goals in five games. Meanwhile, "DeCourcy's keen eyes combined with a fast moving body and quick thinking saved the day many a time for the Irish," said the yearbook.

Five members of the team finished within the league's top 10 scorers. Harrison won the scoring championship with 30 points, Kelly finished second with 28 and Sandford had 23 points, sixth best in the league. Just behind Sandford in seventh was George Scholes with 20 points, while defenceman Phil Samis, who spent part of the season with the Majors, still finished with 17 points, ninth in the league.

The Buzzers began their quest for the Sutherland Cup with a two-game, total-goal triumph over the Oshawa Bees.

Next in line was a similar two-game series against the Mecca Athletic Club, a Toronto Hockey League (THL) Junior squad. St. Mike's won the first game 16–5, but in the second game, the Mecca AC shocked the Buzzers by handing them a 2–1 defeat. In spite of that victory, the Mecca AC lost the series, outscored 17–7.

Game One of a two-game, total-goal series between St. Michael's College and the Niagara Falls Cataracts resulted in an 8–4 decision for the Buzzers. Game Two was a debacle, with St. Mike's whipping the Cataracts 22–4. "[Cataracts goaltender Doug] Porter almost developed lumbago bending down picking the puck out of his net, while the goal judge almost wore the red light out," chuckled the *Toronto Daily Star*. Red Kelly led the scoring parade with five goals and four assists, with Ed Bury also scoring five but assisting on three. Ed Sandford contributed four goals and five assists and Ed Harrison enjoyed a three-goal game.

The Buzzers won the Sutherland Cup by sweeping the best-of-five championship series against the Stratford Kroehler B's. The results were 4–0, 9–3, and 9–1.

Ed Bury led all goal scorers through the playoffs with 17, while George Scholes had 26 points, best of the playoffs.

As a feeder team for the Majors, the Buzzers could never rest on their laurels for long. Their tremendous success meant that much of their 1945 championship team graduated to the Majors for 1945–46. The only constants, other than Father Flanagan behind the bench, were Pete McParland and George Scholes. Both boys performed admirably, recording 14 and 21 points respectively. The surprise came by way of Tom Selby, who finished second in league scoring with 34 points. Other notable players were Joe Primeau Jr. and two boys from the Timmins area: Ray Hannigan, from Schumacher, was new to the school, while John McLellan was down from South Porcupine. Hannigan would play three games for the Toronto Maple Leafs in 1948–49, while McLellan played two during the 1951–52 schedule. He is better remembered for having coached the Maple Leafs for four seasons, beginning in 1969–70.

In 1946-47, Father Flanagan hoped that lightning might strike twice. In 1945, both the Majors and Buzzers won their respective championships, and the coach would have loved nothing more than another double. Regrettably, it wasn't in the cards. While the Majors took the Memorial Cup championship as Junior 'A' champions, the Buzzers were relegated to also-ran status. Bob Heathcott led the scoring with 14 points, followed by Joe DeCourcy, Brian McAllister, and Joe Primeau Jr., each with 10.

Again, Father Flanagan was faced with moulding a group of youngsters into a cohesive, competitive force. Jack Corcoran and Jim Imonti were the only experienced players returning to the Buzzers in 1947–48. Leading scorer Rocco "Rocky" Volpe potted a team-best eight goals and 13 points, putting him fourth in the league. Following his ordination, Father Volpe would return to the Buzzers as coach for four seasons, beginning in 1961–62. Bill McDonagh completed the season with nine points, ninth best in the league. McDonagh made his NHL debut with the New York Rangers in 1949–50 and played four scoreless games.

Riding solid goaltending from Dennis Mooney, the Buzzers surprised fans by reaching the OHA Junior 'B' final, where they faced Hamilton Aerovox, but dropped the best-of-five series in three straight games to conclude their season.

For the third season in a row, one of Joe Primeau's offspring was a Buzzer. Jim Primeau followed brothers Joe and Bill into the St. Michael's lineup in 1948-49. Bob Sabourin, scouted in Sudbury by Charlie Cerre, also joined the Buzzers and promptly tied for the team lead in scoring with a count of 14 points. Sabourin would play a single game for the Toronto Maple Leafs during the 1951–52 campaign. Tying Sabourin for the team scoring lead was Rod Ray, whose 14 points included a team-high nine goals. Fred Sandford potted eight goals and counted 12 points.

Joe Ingoldsby, Rod Roy, Bob Sabourin and Fred Sandford graduated to the Majors for the 1949–50 season. Gerry Young starred in goal. Gord Harrison and Bill Lee tied for the team lead in points with 20, fifth best in the OHA Junior 'B' circuit. Joe Michilson and Don Peart, both returnees, fired 10 goals each to lead the Buzzers. Future NHLer Tom McCarthy joined the team in 1949–50. He became a Detroit Red Wing in 1956–57 and

Father Flanagan's Buzzers of 1953–54 introduced Frank Mahovlich to St. Michael's hockey (back row, third from left). Joining Frank from Timmins were Pat Hannigan and Pete Buchmann (middle row, third and fourth from left).

played three seasons there, followed by a fourth with the Boston Bruins in 1960–61. In 60 NHL contests, McCarthy picked up eight goals and nine assists for 17 points.

The Buzzers came out on top in their first round, best-of-three playoff series, but were stopped dead in their tracks by the high-flying Weston Dukes. "What they lacked in hockey power, they made up in fight and courage," wrote *The Thurible*.

As evidence of the high turnover rate that marked the Buzzers in this era, Farrell Crook became the team's sixth netminder in as many seasons when he skated into the crease for the start of the 1950–51 season. Defensive assistance came in the form of Marc Reaume, a rangy defenceman brought in from Windsor. Reaume would play four seasons at St. Mike's before getting the call to join the Maple Leafs during the 1954–55 season. In one of the NHL's more celebrated trades, Reaume was shipped to Detroit for fellow St. Michael's alumnus Red Kelly on February 10, 1960. Marc later spent part of 1963–64 with the Montreal Canadiens, then seemed destined to play out his career in the minors. But with Vancouver joining the NHL in 1970, Reaume's rights were secured by the Canucks, and he was enjoying his renewed NHL career when a car accident on January 24, 1971, put an end to his playing career. "I had a broken leg, broken wrist, my head hit the top of the car and put me out for three or four days, but not one cut," recalls Reaume. He collected 51 points during 344 regular-season NHL games.

Also playing on the Buzzers in 1950–51 were captain Gord Harrison and future NHLers Jack Caffery, Paul Knox, and Tom McCarthy. Kingston native Ken Linseman, father of 1984 Stanley Cup champion Ken Linseman, also debuted with the Buzzers.

The newly created line of rookie Dick Duff, Ken Linseman, and captain Jack Caffery starred for the Buzzers in 1951–52. In fact, Caffery set a new Junior 'B' scoring record.

Caffery was an outstanding athlete. After graduating from St. Michael's in 1953–54, he turned pro with the Toronto Maple Leafs organization, joining the AHL Pittsburgh Hornets in 1954–55 and making his debut with the Leafs on December 11, 1954. After a trade to the Bruins, Jack played two seasons in Boston (1956–57 and 1957–58), then

Stymied in their pursuit of the Ontario Junior 'B' championship, this talented Buzzers team included captain David Keon (front row, third from left), Dave and Bruce Draper (front row, fifth and sixth from left respectively), Gerry Cheevers (front row, far right) and Terry O'Malley (back row, second player from left).

pursued a baseball career. Caffery spent four years playing professional ball in the Milwaukee Braves organization beginning in 1959.

Duff, who was brought to St. Michael's from Kirkland Lake, was joined by another rookie who would go on to an NHL career. Charlie Burns, a Detroit native, was signed as a free agent by his hometown Red Wings in 1958 and debuted in the NHL that season. Boston picked up Burns in the 1959 Inter-League Draft and Charlie spent four seasons in a Bruins uniform. After a few seasons in the minors, his NHL career was revived when he was plucked by Oakland in the NHL Expansion Draft in 1967. He spent 1967–68 with the Seals, 1968–69 with the Pittsburgh Penguins, then finished his NHL career with four seasons as a Minnesota North Star. In 749 regular-season games, Burns collected 304 points. Interestingly, Burns was the NHL's last playing coach, a role he held with the North Stars.

The Buzzers defeated Brampton in six games during the semifinals, including three games decided in overtime, but in the OHA Junior 'B' final the Buzzers fell to the Weston Dukes.

Buzzers captain Dick Duff finished second in league scoring in 1952–53, playing on a line with Billy Colvin and Ken Linseman. The team, playing its home games at Leaside Gardens, finished in fourth place.

The Buzzers faced Weston in the semifinals, losing the first two games but winning the third. Nevertheless, the Dukes took the series four games to two.

The much-anticipated debut of Frank Mahovlich in 1953–54 proved to be well worth the wait as the young native of Schumacher, Ontario, coveted by every one of the NHL's six teams, joined St. Michael's. "The Leafs catered to me in that they brought up a couple of other players from my team back home," recalls Mahovlich. "Pat Hannigan was my roommate the first year, and Pete Buchmann came down, too. You're 14 years old, it's very difficult to adjust, but that made it more comfortable." The phenom played left wing on a high-scoring line with Buchmann and Hannigan that season.

Pat was the third Hannigan from northern Ontario to attend St. Michael's, and all three starred for the Buzzers and Majors before finding their way to the NHL. Pat became the third Hannigan brother to play for the Toronto Maple Leafs when he suited up as an injury replacement on December 17, 1959. He was traded to the Rangers and spent 1959–60 and 1960–61 in New York. Pat spent five seasons in the minors before expansion gave him a second chance at NHL employment, and the veteran spent two seasons as a Philadelphia Flyer. In all, Pat recorded 30 goals and 39 assists for 69 points in 182 NHL contests.

Captain Jack Dockeray and goalie Tommy Green were also strong for the Buzzers under coach Father Flanagan, but the injury-plagued Buzzers fell to the Weston Dukes for a third consecutive season.

Incidentally, Howie Young played for the St. Michael's Major Midgets in 1953–54, before moving on to play Junior 'A', first with the Kitchener Canucks and then with the Hamilton Tiger Cubs. They called him "Wild Thing" for good reason, as the troubled Young started in the Leaf organization and was moved frequently after debuting with the Detroit Red Wings in 1960–61. He played for Chicago, back to Detroit, back to Chicago, and joined the Vancouver Canucks in their inaugural season. After several years in the minors, Young popped up in the WHA with Phoenix and Winnipeg. In 336 NHL games over eight seasons, Howie collected 74 points. He added 42 points in the WHA. While playing with the Western Hockey League's Los Angeles Blades in 1964, Young tried his hand at acting, landing a role in the 1965 Frank Sinatra film *None but the Brave*. Following his retirement from hockey, Howie pursued further film roles. He appeared in the 1989 mini-series *Lonesome Dove* and had a part in *Young Guns II* the next year. In 1997, Howie Young made his final film appearance in *Last Stand at Saber River*, a TV movie starring Tom Selleck.

It was with great pride that Father Flanagan saw the Majors stocked with graduates of the Buzzers in 1954–55 — 15-year-old Frank Mahovlich, Pete Buchmann, Billy Colvin, Jack Dockeray, Dick Duff, Pat Hannigan, Ken Linseman, and goalie Tommy Kelly.

Continual rebuilding was definitely the norm for the Buzzers, and besides captain Frank Howarth, Father Flanagan loaded up with promising youngsters like Pete and Tom Bourke, Paul O'Neill, and John Selby.

The Thurible outlined the highlights of a disappointing season for the Buzzers in 1955–56. "The forwards were sparked by Jack McMaster, closely followed by captain Peter Bourke, Jim Sonoski, Steve Bochen and Tony Cusinato. Al Hinnegan was one of the top scorers by the season's end. Merv McNamara and Bob Keegan were the most efficient checkers, while D'Arcy Bird was one of the hardest diggers." The team also introduced a defence corps made up of Mike Draper, Bob Pallante, John Selby, Frank Sullivan, and Tom White. Don Jackson played goal, with Don Keenan among several goaltenders to see Junior 'B' action that season.

Keenan is the answer to one of the great hockey trivia questions. On March 7, 1959, in the days before backup goaltenders, Boston Bruins netminder Harry Lumley was forced to miss that night's game against the Maple Leafs. Boston asked Toronto if they could supply a goalie for the game. Keenan, who was attending St. Mike's and occasionally served as the Leafs' practice goalie, was recruited and played admirably in his only NHL game — he was named the game's third star even though Boston lost 4–1 to Toronto.

In 1955–56, Father Flanagan's Buzzers missed the playoffs for just the first time since the initiation of Junior 'B' competition, although the standings weren't decided until the final game of the season.

The Metro Junior 'B' Hockey League was created prior to the 1956–57 season, and consisted of teams in the Greater Toronto Area: the Dixie Beehives (who changed their names from the Rockets in order to better align themselves with the Junior 'A' Dixie Beehives), Lakeshore Bruins, Woodbridge Dodgers, Weston Dukes, Leaside Rangers, Brampton Regents, and St. Michael's Buzzers.

The league eventually grew beyond the borders of Greater Toronto, and in 1991 it assumed the Junior 'A' designation. In 1998 it was absorbed by the Ontario Provincial Junior 'A' Hockey League (OPJHL).

The Buzzers' 1956–57 season began slowly, owing to inexperience, according to Father Flanagan, but the team came on as the season progressed.

"The Buzzers have created a lot of interest with the fans with their Draper line," began the *Toronto Daily Star* on January 17, 1957. "Twins Dave and Bruce have been joined by older brother Mike, and it is likely the first time in the east that three brothers will play as a forward unit in organized hockey."

Mike Draper, the eldest of the trio, recalls, "I was 18 months older than the twins. I started the 1957–58 season with the Majors, but I wasn't playing very much, so I went to Father Flanagan, who was running the team that year, and I said, 'If I'm not going to play, I'd much rather go back and play Junior 'B'.' I had played both forward and defence, and in the first game, Father Flanagan put me on left wing with Bruce and Dave. That was the first time we all played together on one team. It was great. Bruce could skate and make plays, I could skate, and I had to look after them every once in a while. They were younger and smaller than I was."

In late January 1957, goaltender Gerry Cheevers was unable to play because of illness. With no backup goalie available, Cheevers was replaced in goal by Pat Flannery, a forward.

Although they occupied the basement for part of the season, on February 8, Dave Keon scored the first three goals of the game in a 4–1 win over the Dixie Beehives, putting the Buzzers in the playoffs.

Keon, captain of the Buzzers that season, also enjoyed an extraordinary seven-goal game on December 20, 1956, as he paced the Buzzers to a 10–0 victory over the Lakeshore Bruins. The young centre was a prodigious talent and went into the final regular-season game with 15 goals and 23 assists, tying him for the scoring lead with Larry Kendall of Brampton. Keon scored five goals in his game, but Kendall picked up six assists the next night to rob the young forward of the scoring championship.

In the first round of the playoffs, St. Mike's eliminated the Brampton Regents, who had lost only five times in the entire regular season.

The Buzzers next met the Dixie Beehives for the inaugural championship of the Metro Junior 'B' league. The series opened at Ted Reeve Arena, with the largest crowd to watch a Junior 'B' game all season witnessing a 4–2 Buzzers win.

Jack Martin fired a hat trick as the Buzzers dumped Dixie 6–4 in Game Two. The Beehives' goalie, Denis DeJordy, was so disgusted with the play of his teammates that in the third period, he came out of his crease and stickhandled the puck over the blue line.

Dixie took Game Three, edging St. Mike's 4–3. Game Four, a 5–2 Beehives win, ended in a 20-minute brouhaha at the final buzzer. A high-sticking brawl between Dixie's Fred Greenbridge and St. Mike's Mike Draper resulted in a deep gash to Draper's skull, and he was rushed to the hospital. Both players were subsequently dealt fighting majors, misconducts, and game misconducts. As the clock ticked off the final seconds, players from both benches swung at each other, drawing fans onto the ice surface as well. Police were called to assist the coaches in restoring order.

The Buzzers beat the Dixie Beehives 5–2 in Game Seven on March 30 to win the league championship. Mike Draper returned and scored twice. Following the contest, captain Keon was presented with the championship trophy, the G.W. Wild Trophy.

But with that victory, the Buzzers' season came to a sudden halt. "We have examinations coming up next week and it wouldn't be fair to take the boys away from their studies for trips to Peterborough," announced Father Flanagan, adding, "Dixie will make a fine representative of the league."

Mike Draper recalls the words cutting through the team like a knife. "We had a great team. We won the title on Friday night at Ted Reeve and went to school on Monday morning to find out that that had been our last game. They pulled us out of the finals and Dixie went on and won. To play so long and so hard, and then to have the rug pulled out from under you, was very, very difficult."

Beehives manager Howard Pallett initially declined the opportunity: "Even if we should win the title, it would be a hollow victory. I don't feel like putting my club into debt when I have to go into the Ontario playoffs via the back door."

"No one can tell me that this was a last-minute decision," thundered OHA president Frank Buckland. "Normally, if a team is going to default a game, we need three days' notice. This is the ultimate in poor sportsmanship and the Buzzers deserve to be suspended."

Father Flanagan noted that he had informed Metro Junior 'B' officials the previous week that his team would not continue in the playoffs. "I thought they would pass along the information to OHA authorities," he said. "I thought we did the right thing in notifying our league officials."

In the meantime, Buckland worked to convince the Dixie Beehives to play the Peterborough Stoneys for the OHA Junior 'B' semifinal. Dixie's manager reluctantly agreed. "We are doing this to save face for our league, which has been held up to ridicule by hockey fans throughout Ontario. We still don't feel we should take a financial gamble when we honestly didn't earn the right to go further."

Discussing the Metro Junior 'B' championship, Pallett added, "I feel that the right thing would be to make the cup a dead issue. We don't want it because we didn't win it, but they [St. Mike's] don't deserve it, either!"

The Beehives went on to defeat the Stoneys, who had been idle for almost a month, but were subsequently defeated by the Sarnia Legionnaires for the Sutherland Cup.

From that Buzzers team, Jack Martin played one game in the NHL, on November 27, 1960, as an injury replacement for the Maple Leafs in a 2–0 loss to Detroit. The game is well remembered by Martin as his only game with the Leafs, but others will better recall it as the game in which Gordie Howe collected his 1,000th point, becoming the first NHL player to achieve that milestone.

The Draper twins arrived back on the St. Michael's scene for the 1957–58 season. Gerry Cheevers returned to play goal, while the newcomers included Larry Keenan, Terry O'Malley, and Gene Rebellato. Each of them would be selected for the league's All-Star Game, played on February 4 at Ravina Gardens. Prior to the game, five trophies were presented, each donated by NHL teams. Boston's head scout, Harold Cotton, presented the league's rookie of the year trophy to Larry Keenan. Gene Rebellato of the Buzzers was awarded the Detroit Red Wings Trophy as the league's most valuable player. Barry Ashbee of the Lakeshore Bruins won the Chicago Black Hawks Trophy as the best defenceman; Jimmy Cannon of the Weston Dukes was named the league's best goaltender and recipient of the Toronto Maple Leafs Trophy; and Larry Kendall of the Brampton 7-Ups took home the New York Rangers Trophy as the league's leading scorer for the second year in a row.

St. Mike's faced the fourth-place Dixie Beehives in the league's semifinal. The Beehives took the series four games to two, eliminating the Buzzers from further competition.

Father Conway took over from Father Flanagan as coach of the Buzzers in 1957–58 and inherited an outstanding club that included returning stars Gerry Cheevers in goal, Bruce and Dave Draper, Dave Keon, Larry Keenan, Terry O'Malley, Gene Rebellato, and Don Young. Bruce Draper received the team's most valuable player award in a special presentation from Maurice Richard.

Although much of the team moved up to the Junior 'A' Majors for 1958–59, early indications hinted that the Buzzers would have a contending squad. Father Conway placed much faith in the forward line of Pat Baldwin (one of two returnees), Roger Felesko, and Harvey Turnbull. George Olah, a second-year Buzzer, was appointed captain.

Arnie Brown, who had played Midget the year before, moved up to Junior 'B' in 1958–59 and got serious about his hockey. "Brown is the lad who showed up as a 15-year-

Among the student athletes receiving awards in 1958–59 were hockey stars Bruce Draper (third from left), Gary Smith (standing behind student fourth from left), Gary Dineen (fifth from left) and Terry O'Malley (second from right).

old butterball at St. Michael's College and was told either to reduce weight or forget about hockey," commented the *Toronto Star* in 1957. The talented defenceman was sent to fitness pioneer Lloyd Percival, who helped him drop 37 pounds from his five-foot, 11-inch frame. "My dad owns a general store in Apsley," Brown told the *Star*. "My trouble was I couldn't pass the potato chips, candies, cakes, or ice cream without tasting."

Billy MacMillan, who would later enjoy both playing and coaching careers in the NHL, debuted with the Buzzers that year, as did goaltender Gary Smith, not yet tagged with the nickname "Suitcase." Roger Galipeau, who would be a key component in the Majors Memorial Cup championship in 1961, arrived from Sturgeon Falls to attend St. Michael's and play hockey.

After making the playoffs, the Buzzers met the Aurora Tigers in the league semifinals, but the final minutes of the first game took a nasty turn. With St. Mike's down 9–3, tempers flared, and Arnie Brown and Tom Chasczewski found willing adversaries with whom to tangle. Brown, Chasczewski, and Aurora's Gord Sampson and Bob Sheffield were banished to the dressing room. Three days later, with the series now moved to Ted Reeve Arena, police had to be called to quell an uprising among the fans. Several fights broke out in the stands between the two camps during the second period. Buzzers coach Father Bill Conway was subjected to verbal abuse by Aurora fans. The Buzzers won this contest 4–1.

Aurora went on to win the series, but lost to the Sarnia Legionnaires in the Sutherland Cup final.

"Buzzers, coached by Father Bill Conway, are rated very highly because of their well-distributed strength," declared the *Toronto Daily Star*. "They have a good goaltender in

Gary Smith, a powerful defence headed by Tom Polanic and Jim McKendry and a potent first line composed of Gary Dineen, Rod Seiling and Mike Corbett."

Expectations were running exceedingly high before the first puck of the 1960–61 season had been dropped. And the Buzzers delivered. At the conclusion of the 28-game regular season, they finished in first place, monopolized most of the team and individual awards, and had their top line finish first, second and third in league scoring. Gary Dineen took the lead with 65 points, including a league-best 32 goals, while Rod Seiling collected 55 and Mike Corbett 53. Dineen, the team captain, was also named the Metro Junior 'B' Hockey League's rookie of the year. Goaltender Gary Smith earned the award for the lowest goals-against average, 2.57.

The Buzzers opened their playoff series against Brampton and handily disposed of the 7-Ups. In a parallel series, the Weston Dukes eliminated the Unionville Jets, setting the scene for a matchup between the two longtime rivals, both connected to the Toronto Maple Leafs.

St. Mike's took Game One of the best-of five series by a 7–2 margin, following with a 5-1 win in Game Two. Seiling netted a hat trick, and for a second straight game, Dineen scored twice.

With Leafs owner Conn Smythe and former Leafs Turk Broda and Wally Stanowski looking on, the Weston Dukes opened the scoring just 45 seconds into Game Three, but the Buzzers came back with five unanswered goals and took a commanding lead of three games to none.

Weston attempted to salvage the series in Game Four, benching a few regulars and inserting some members of the Marlboros' Midget team into the lineup, but the effort was for naught. The Buzzers won 5–3, claiming the Metro Junior 'B' championship.

The Buzzers next met the Peterborough Canucks, a Montreal Canadiens affiliate, in the best-of-seven OHA Junior 'B' semifinal, sweeping their opponent in four straight games.

St. Mike's then met the Owen Sound Greys. In Game One, the Greys were up 2–0 in the first period before Gary Dineen scored just prior to the period's end. When Emile Therien scored early in the second, the St. Mike's faithful celebrated by tossing programs and other debris onto the ice surface. Corbett scored late in the third and Dineen added an empty-net marker to give the Buzzers a 4–2 victory. "I'd have a real problem on my hands if this weren't a smart, hard-working hockey club," said Father Bill Conway, acknowledging how easy it would be for his team to be overconfident. "I was lucky tonight because the Greys had us behind the eight ball and my guys realized, without being told, that they had to buckle down." The *Star* commented on the team's demeanour: "The Buzzers are confident but not overconfident, relaxed but not complacent. They've got class and they know it. They have enough power and finesse to have qualified for the OHA Junior 'A' series this winter."

The Buzzers came from behind to win again in Game Two. Down 2–1, the Buzzers scored three goals in under two minutes late in the second period to go ahead, and proceeded to win 5–2.

The Buzzers won 3–0 in the third game of the series. Within the first 13 minutes of the game, each member of the Dineen-Corbett-Seiling line had scored a goal. The Buzzers completely dominated the play, with rangy netminder Gary Smith tested only on a handful of occasions, including a breakaway by Arlen Bloomfield. Smith calmly slid out and blocked the shot. The *Toronto Star* acknowledged the fine work of Jim McKendry of the Buzzers, who "used his pokechecking style to thwart the Greys' attackers."

Owen Sound took an early 1–0 lead in Game Four, but St. Mike's rebounded with two goals of their own by the end of the second period. The Greys tied the score late in the third, but the resilient Buzzers followed with goals at 16:55 and again at 18:20, to seal their victory and the OHA Junior 'B' championship.

The Buzzers had won 16 consecutive playoff games as they steamrolled over all competition. In fact, the Buzzers ended the 1960–61 campaign with an unbeaten streak of 28 wins and a tie. The line of Dineen, Seiling and Corbett accounted for 48 of the

In September 1961, mere months after guiding his Buzzers to a Sutherland Cup championship, Father William Conway passed away, leaving behind an immense legacy.

Buzzers' 84 post-season goals. Meanwhile, opponents were only able to score 28 times on Smith.

It was the first Junior 'B' championship for the Buzzers since 1945. In both 1945 and 1961, teams from St. Mike's won both the Sutherland and Memorial cups.

As Ken McMillan, the OHA's immediate past president, presented captain Gary Dineen with the Sutherland Cup, his teammates surrounded him: Gary Smith and substitute goaltender Girard Albert; Ray Dupont, Jim McKendry, Tom Polanic, and Wally Stanowski on defence; and forwards Kevin Burkett, Paul Cassidy, Mike Corbett, Bill Crawford, Barry Jacks, Mike McLellan, Matt Oreskovich, Mike Savage, Rod Seiling, Paul Sinclair, Peter Speyer, Emile Therien, and Mike Webb.

The Memorial Cup–winning Majors were feted with a parade up Bay Street, from Union Station to City Hall Square, where they were met by the championship Buzzers team. Buzzers coach Father Conway sat with Father Bauer in the lead car of the parade. Toronto Mayor Nathan Phillips welcomed both teams on the steps of City Hall. Father Bauer offered plaudits to his team, the school, and the city of Toronto for the outstanding support afforded the Majors. Then, Father Conway addressed the assembled thousands: "This edition of the Buzzers was a great team with excellent players and a fine team spirit. To coach such a team is indeed a privilege, and the coach of this year's Buzzers is grateful for that privilege."

Father William Conway, the school's director of athletics, never got the opportunity to see another hockey season. He died following a sudden illness on September 7, 1961, at the age of 36. His loss was deeply mourned by all those who had experienced the depth of his affections, but none more than his hockey family. "The person who impacted on me most at St. Mike's was Father Conway," states Rod Seiling, a successful hockey player who parlayed his experiences into success in the business world. "St. Mike's, and especially Father Conway, gave me a sound grounding in what it takes to be a good human, to be a good Christian, to be a good person. The lessons that I learned, the discipline that was taught, have carried me through the successes that I have had, whether they be in hockey, in my business life or in my relationships. They started at home and were reinforced by what I learned at St. Mike's."

The 1960–61 hockey season was arguably the finest in the history of St. Michael's College. Besides championships at the Junior 'A' and 'B' levels, the St. Michael's Bantams won the Toronto Hockey League's 'B' Division championship. Gerry Meehan, captain of the squad, scored 91 goals through the season, flanked by Michael Grant and future NHL winger Garry Monahan. Bill Allan, a football player, who had never played goal before, developed quickly and backstopped the team to the championship.

Other noted St. Michael's' alumni that year included Mike Walton, who played on the school's THL Major Midget squad, and future member of Parliament Dennis Mills and actor Michael Ontkean of *Slapshot* fame, who both played with the Minor Midgets.

37
The Buzzers — 1961 to Today

The loss of Father Conway was insurmountable, but Father Rocco Volpe, a former Buzzer himself, took on the responsibility of coaching St. Michael's Junior 'B' entry in 1961.

After graduating from St. Michael's College School in 1948, he was ordained to the priesthood in 1957. With the exception of one year spent at Michael Power High School, Father Volpe became a fixture at St. Michael's. Perhaps other than his love of Italian (he founded the school's Italian Club and the Italian Drama Society), his greatest secular love was sports. Father Volpe served as the school's director of athletics, and he coached football as well as hockey. Father Volpe coached the Buzzers from 1961–62 to 1964–65, then again for the 1967–68 season. In 2004, he received the Order of St. Michael in recognition of his profound impact as a priest, teacher, coach and mentor. He passed away on July 25, 2007, having just celebrated his 77th birthday.

Although St. Mike's had decided to pull out of OHA Junior 'A' play, they agreed to compete in the Metro Toronto Junior Hockey League, having been granted concessions — a shorter schedule and greatly reduced travel — by the league's sponsors, the Toronto Maple Leafs. As a result, the Sutherland Cup–winning team lost virtually the entire lineup to the Majors, including goaltender Gary Smith, defenceman Jim McKendry, and the All-Star line of Mike Corbett, Gary Dineen, and Rod Seiling.

The Buzzers found a good goaltender in Bob Dunn and recruited skaters Mike Corrigan, Rocky Delvecchio, Barry MacDonald, Wayne Mosdell, and captain Mike Webb.

Corrigan, a smallish winger, spent the 1961–62 with the Buzzers and was part of the Leaf organization until he was claimed by the Los Angeles Kings in the 1967 Expansion Draft. Making his NHL debut with five games for L.A. during the 1967–68 campaign, Corrigan earned 347 points in 594 regular-season NHL games, playing with the Kings, the Vancouver Canucks, and the Pittsburgh Penguins.

The Junior 'A' Majors disbanded for good after the 1961–62 season, though several members of the team who were still eligible for Junior moved to the Neil McNeil Maroons. The end of the NHL's sponsorship system was also on the horizon, and these developments were to have a profound effect on hockey at St. Michael's College School. No longer would a player be placed in the St. Michael's hockey program for nurturing by the Toronto Maple Leafs. And no longer would appropriately talented players be able to climb through the ranks, from Bantam to Midget to Juvenile to Junior 'B' and then to Junior 'A.'

Many talented players would continue to make their way to the corner of St. Clair and Bathurst, but rather than using the Buzzers as a stepping-stone to Junior 'A,' their goal in future seasons would often be to land a scholarship at a U.S. college, where they could ply their trade in competitive leagues and have their education paid for. In time, playing at a U.S. college would also become recognized as a viable alternative route to the NHL.

The 1962–63 edition of the Buzzers featured a sturdy youngster from Barrie, Ontario, named Garry Monahan, who was captain of the team. He and Peter Mahovlich, who was playing for St. Michael's Juvenile squad, were the first players selected in the NHL's first Amateur Draft in the spring of 1963.

Monahan scored 116 goals and assisted on 169 more for 285 points during 748 NHL contests over 12 seasons. He started his career with Montreal in 1967–68 and also played with Detroit, Los Angeles, Toronto, and Vancouver.

Mike Webb captained the Buzzers in 1961–62.

Perennially in the shadow of his brother Frank, eight years his senior, Peter Mahovlich was an excellent player in his own right. The Detroit Red Wings introduced "The Little M" to the NHL with three games in 1965–66. He played parts of four seasons in Detroit, then, following the 1969–70 campaign, was traded to the Montreal Canadiens — interestingly, in exchange for Garry Monahan. During nine seasons with the Canadiens, he contributed to four Stanley Cup victories (and played with his brother, "The Big M," on the first two). Pete also played for Pittsburgh and concluded his career back where it started — with the Red Wings. He collected 773 points (288 goals and 485 assists) in 884 regular-season NHL games, and added 30 goals and 42 assists for 72 points in 88 playoff games.

Although Gerry Meehan spent 1962–63 with the Neil McNeil Maroons, he has played a critical role in Toronto St. Michael's Majors history. When the Majors returned to Junior hockey, Meehan served as their vice-president and director of hockey operations. As a player, Gerry joined the Toronto Maple Leafs in 1968–69, but was traded to the Philadelphia Flyers late in his rookie season. He went on to play with Buffalo, Vancouver, Atlanta, and Washington, in addition to two games with the Cincinnati Stingers of the WHA in 1978–79. His NHL playing career comprised 670 games, in which he scored 180 goals and added 243 assists for 423 points. Gerry graduated from law school in 1982 and joined the Buffalo Sabres' management team two years later. After Scotty Bowman stepped down from the general manager's position during the 1986–87, Meehan was named to replace him, and stayed in that role until 1994.

With the demise of the Metro Junior 'A' league, some familiar names entered the Metro Junior 'B' fold in 1963–64: the Brampton 7-Ups, Neil McNeil Maroons, and Whitby Dunlops. Also in the league were the Etobicoke Indians, Markham Seal-A-Wax (later to be known as the Waxers), North York Leafs, and the Buzzers.

Garry Monahan played his final season with St. Mike's, and by 1964–65 he was playing with the Peterborough Petes, one of Montreal's Junior affiliates. The team captain was second-year Buzzer Joe Brady.

Andy Culligan played well for St. Mike's in 1964-65, his second season of Junior 'B,' and that summer, the Buzzers captain was chosen by the Chicago Black Hawks with the second-overall pick in the Amateur Draft. Several other players returned to Father Volpe's team that season, including John Bear, Licio Cengarle, Brian Dunn, Bill McNeill and Frank Micallef. Newcomer Grant Cole impressed in goal for the Buzzers.

Gerry Marlborough assumed the coaching reins in 1965–66, and was fortunate to have a number of returning players on which to build a foundation. The Buzzers relied heavily on captain Bill McNeill and returning goaltender Grant Cole, a Calgary native, who commanded the Detroit Red Wings' fourth pick in the 1966 Amateur Draft. The Fullan boys, Larry and Rick, starred in their first year of Junior 'B.' Larry would go on to play four games with the Washington Capitals in 1974–75.

After a one-year hiatus, St. Michael's returned to the Metro Junior 'B' Hockey League for the 1967–68 season. A familiar face was behind the bench as Father Volpe took on the coaching chores. He had a fine team, with Grant Cole returning for another season in net, returning Buzzer defenceman Ed Zuccato as captain and Larry Fullan starring at forward and selected to the OHA's Junior 'B' First All-Star Team. Newcomer Mike Boland, a forward, was picked up by the World Hockey Association's Ottawa Nationals in 1972. The NHL's Philadelphia Flyers signed Mike in September 1973, and during the 1974–75 season, he played his only two NHL games. Peter Sullivan was drafted by the Montreal Canadiens after explosive seasons with the Oshawa Generals. He found his way to the NHL by passing through the World Hockey Association. "Silky" was signed by the Winnipeg Jets in 1975 and put up seasons of 32, 31, 16, and 46 goals in the rebel league. When the Jets franchise was absorbed into the NHL in 1979–80, Sullivan stayed with the Jets and played two seasons of NHL hockey. In the WHA, Peter earned 295 points in 313 games; in the NHL, it was 82 points in 126 games.

Vic Sluce, a former Junior 'B' forward in Scarborough, Ontario, was hired as coach of the Buzzers in 1968–69 and would spend four seasons behind the bench. He appointed Phil Branston, a second-year Buzzer, as captain.

Coach Sluce had a couple of familiar names in his lineup in 1969–70. Returnee Steve Mitchell was appointed captain, while Paul Cerre was the son of former St. Mike's Majors coach Charlie Cerre. But as the season progressed, the name Dave Gardner emerged more and more spectacularly. Dave finished the campaign with 54 goals, making him the first OHA Junior 'B' player to hit that plateau. Including 42 assists, Gardner finished with an incredible total of 96 points, earning him the honour of St. Michael's Athlete of the Year. Dave was drafted in the first round, eighth overall, by the Montreal Canadiens in 1972. In 350 NHL games, played with Montreal, St. Louis, California, Cleveland, and Philadelphia, Gardner scored 75 goals and 114 assists for 189 points.

The 1970-71 edition of the Buzzers finished fifth in the Metro Junior 'B' Hockey League, winning 24, losing 15, and tying five. Paul Wieczorek was named captain of the squad.

A young defenceman from Kitchener joined the team this season. Dave Maloney went on to play Junior 'A' back home with the Rangers, and in 1974, he was drafted in the first round of the NHL Entry Draft by the New York Rangers. In his 11th season as a Ranger, he was traded to the Buffalo Sabres, and after completing the year, he retired in 1985. Over 657 regular-season NHL games, Maloney scored 71 goals and had 246 assists for 317 points.

Gord Cowan, a second-year Buzzer, captained the St. Mike's Junior 'B' team under Vic Sluce, who returned for his fourth and final season behind the bench in 1971–72. The team endured some struggles, and finished 10th in the 12-team league, compiling a record of 13 wins, 25 losses, and six ties. The Markham Waxers won both the league championship and the Sutherland Cup.

Playing on the Midget team for St. Mike's that season was Mike Kaszycki, whose 226-game NHL career included stops with the New York Islanders, Washington Capitals and Toronto Maple Leafs between 1977–78 and 1982–83. In that span, he collected 122 points.

A wave of change swept over Junior hockey prior to the 1972–73 season. What had been known as Junior 'A' hockey was now designated as Major Junior 'A' (later shortened to Major Junior), while a number of Junior 'B' teams lobbied the OHA to be promoted to Provincial, or Tier II, Junior 'A.' Of the teams in the Metro Junior 'B' loop, only the Buzzers and the Markham Waxers remained. They were joined by half a dozen new teams, stretching from Peterborough to Bramalea.

The Buzzers soldiered on amongst their new rivals, but finished a dismal 10th in the 10-team Metro Junior 'B' Hockey League. Under newly appointed coach Les Duff, they won just eight games, losing 21, and tying five. Greg Reeves captained the squad in 1972–73. The Toronto Nationals captured the league championship.

If Les Duff's impression of his team was less than joyous during his first season with the Buzzers, he had great reason to smile in 1973–74. Paul Gardner, whose brother Dave had set scoring benchmarks, was a walk-on at camp and proceeded to demolish scoring records, collecting 87 goals and 44 assists for 131 points in 44 games. Paul was named the Metro Junior 'B' league's most valuable player that season.

Duff chose Joe Haffey, a second-year vet, as captain. Also playing with the Buzzers that season was Dwight Schofield. The Massachusetts-born defenceman made his NHL debut with the Detroit Red Wings in 1976–77, but didn't return to the league until he joined the Montreal Canadiens during the 1982–83 season. Schofield also played for St. Louis, Washington, Pittsburgh, and Winnipeg, getting into 211 NHL games and earning 30 points before retiring at the conclusion of the 1987–88 season.

Mike Draper replaced Les Duff as coach of the Buzzers in 1974–75. The team featured captain John Stornik as well as a couple of players, Billy Carroll and Mike Gillis, who both went on to fine pro careers. Gillis was selected by the Colorado Rockies in the Amateur Draft of 1978. During his third season with the Rockies, he was traded to Boston, and in six NHL seasons, he scored 33 goals and 76 points in 246 games. Following a successful career as a player agent, Gillis assumed the role of general manager of the Vancouver Canucks during the summer of 2008. Gillis talked with CBC Radio about the impact the school had on his life: "It's unbelievable that when you go anywhere in Canada and even parts of the U.S., if you mention you went to St. Mike's, everybody recognizes it."

There were a number of superlatives for coach Mike Draper in 1975–76. His goaltending tandem of Randy Maxwell and Rick Wilson had the league's lowest goals-against average. Captain Loris Muzzatti was named to the Central Division All-Star Team, as were Frank McCarthy and Billy Carroll. Carroll scored 21 goals and 39 assists and was named the league's most valuable player. He went on to a high-scoring Junior career with the London Knights. In 1979, the New York Islanders chose Carroll in the NHL Entry Draft. His timing couldn't have been better. Joining the reigning Stanley Cup champions in 1980–81, Billy was part of three more championships with the Islanders. In October 1984, he joined another dynasty when he was plucked from the waiver wire by the Edmonton Oilers. Billy earned his fourth Stanley Cup ring in 1984–85. A 1985 trade sent Carroll to the Detroit Red Wings, where he ended his NHL career following the 1986–87 season, but not before compiling 84 points in 322 regular-season contests. He added 18 points in NHL playoff action.

In his third and final season behind the bench, Mike Draper led the Buzzers to a record of 16 wins, 14 losses, and six ties, good for fourth place in the Central Division of the Metro Junior 'B' league in 1976–77. The Seneca Nationals, featuring Wayne Gretzky and Paul Coffey, won the league championship.

Peter Rajtek captained the Buzzers, included 20-goal scorer Pat Graham. Selected by Pittsburgh in the fifth round of the 1980 NHL Entry Draft, Graham debuted as a Penguin in 1981–82. Pittsburgh traded Pat to the Toronto Maple Leafs in the summer of 1983. His three seasons in the NHL resulted in 103 games played, in which he collected 28 points.

Father Joe Brady coached the Buzzers in 1977–78, guiding the squad to a strong first-place Central Division finish with 25 wins against 10 losses and a tie. Mike McCarron, who would later own the team, was solid in goal for St. Mike's. Dan Haffey wore the "C" for the Buzzers in 1977–78. In the Metro Junior 'B' final, the Buzzers were beaten by the Oshawa Legionaires.

Dan Batten was entering his third season with the Buzzers when he was named captain under new coach George Volpe in 1978–79. Greg Britz enjoyed a strong season, scoring 26 goals and 26 assists. After attending St. Mike's, Greg played for Harvard and was picked up as a free agent by the Toronto Maple Leafs in November 1983. He played seven games over two seasons for the Leafs, and another game with the Hartford Whalers in 1986–87. Britz was held pointless in his eight-game NHL career.

Although he played but two games for St. Mike's in 1978–79, Craig Muni, a big defenceman, clicked for two goals and three assists for the Buzzers. Muni was drafted by Toronto in the second round of the 1980 Entry Draft, and debuted with three NHL games in 1981–82 while still competing with the Junior Windsor Spitfires. After four seasons spent playing infrequently with the Leafs, he was scooped up by the Edmonton Oilers. During his seven seasons with the Oilers, Craig sipped champagne from the Stanley Cup three times — 1987, 1988, and 1990. Through 819 games that also included stops in Chicago, Buffalo, Winnipeg, Pittsburgh, and Dallas, Muni recorded 147 points.

Signed by the Los Angeles Kings in 1981, defenceman Howard Scruton earned four assists in his four NHL games as a member of the Kings in 1982–83.

At six foot four and 215 pounds, Mike Stothers presented an imposing figure on the Buzzers' blue line. Drafted in the first round in 1980 by the Philadelphia Flyers, Stothers toiled in the AHL until 1984–85, when he played one game with the Flyers. During his fourth partial season with Philadelphia, Mike was traded to the Maple Leafs, where in 1987–88 he played his final NHL season. In 30 NHL games, Mike Stothers collected two points.

Ken Strong has his name forever linked with Darryl Sittler. Drafted by Philadelphia in 1981, he was traded to the Toronto Maple Leafs for their captain in January 1982, and collected four points in 15 games over three seasons in Toronto.

Rick Zombo was also a member of the Buzzers that year. An Illinois boy, Rick was drafted by the Red Wings in 1981 and debuted in red and white during the 1984–85 season. Three games into the 1991–92 campaign, Detroit sent Zombo to St. Louis. He completed his NHL career with a season with the Boston Bruins in 1995–96. The defenceman played 652 games in 12 NHL seasons, contributing 154 points.

The Buzzers finished second, just two points behind Bramalea, in the Central Division in 1978–79. Reaching the Metro Junior 'B' final, they faced the Oshawa Legionaires for a second consecutive season. The Oshawa squad, coached by Mike Keenan and starring Dale Hawerchuk, eliminated St. Mike's for a second straight spring.

Led by four future NHL stars, the Buzzers finished first in the Metro Junior Hockey League in 1979–80. Gord Dineen scored 11 goals and 24 assists for 35 points, Paul Gillis had 20 goals and 36 assists for 56 points, Scott McLellan had 43 goals and 48 assists for 91 points, and Tony Tanti scored 31 times, adding 27 assists for 58 points as the Buzzers turned in a record of 28 wins, nine losses, and five ties. Mike Pikul captained the team, which was coached by Paul Gauthier. The Belleville Bobcats went on to win both the league championship and the Sutherland Cup as Ontario Junior champions.

The Dineen family is legendary in St. Michael's College circles. Bill, the hockey patriarch, starred with the Majors in the 1950s, while three sons, Peter, Gord, and Kevin, also attended the school. Gord was chosen by the New York Islanders in the 1981 NHL Entry Draft and made his first appearance during the 1982–83 season. In 1987–88, he was traded to the Minnesota North Stars, and he later played with Pittsburgh and Ottawa before returning to Long Island to wrap up his career in 1994–95. Gord collected 106 points in 528 regular-season NHL games.

Paul Gillis was a second-round draft choice of the Quebec Nordiques in 1982, debuting with the team that season. Well into his ninth season with the Nordiques, he was traded to the Chicago Black Hawks in March 1991, then played for Hartford before retiring after the '92–93 season. He played 624 games in the NHL, contributing 242 points.

In his final season of Junior, Scott McLellan scored 43 goals and earned 101 points for the Peterborough Petes in 1982–83. Scott got a two-day look by the Boston Bruins that season.

After a sterling career with the Oshawa Generals, Tony Tanti was Chicago's first pick, 12th overall, in 1981. Just three games into his career as a Black Hawk, Tanti was traded to the Vancouver Canucks, where he established himself as a sniper. In his first full season in Vancouver (1983–84), he scored 45 goals, following that with seasons of 39, 39, 41, and 40. He also played in Pittsburgh and Buffalo. Tanti scored 287 goals and 273 assists for 560 points in 697 regular-season games.

The 1980–81 season brought a new coach to the St. Michael's Buzzers: Rick Cornacchia. "When I graduated from the Faculty of Education at the University of Toronto, I took a position with Father Henry Carr High School [in nearby Etobicoke]," recalls Cornacchia. "Then a job came available at St. Mike's and they asked me if I would like the position. I said yes, and there was also the coaching job, as Paul Gauthier was resigning to go to Niagara Falls. I taught math and physical and health education and was there from 1980 to 1983."

The coach was very proud of the 1980–81 team, which posted a record of 24 wins, 10 losses, and eight ties. "My first year, we had Kevin Dineen, who went to the NHL, and a bunch of guys who went to U.S. colleges, to Major Junior 'A', a few who went pro, and some guys who played in Europe."

Kevin Dineen, who followed his brother Gord on the Buzzers by one season, scored 15 goals and collected 28 points. Kevin remembers, "We had a well-coached, talented hockey team. I can't say enough about Rick Cornacchia and Bill Fifield. The two of them did a real solid job of steering the guys to land college scholarships, and you realize as you get later in life how important that education is. I think all of us had NHL dreams, but in reality, that school was as important as anything we've done. Just to be part of the tradition and the great things that have gone on at St. Mike's, it's an incredible thing to have been part of."

For three seasons beginning in 1980–81, Rick Cornacchia coached the Buzzers, and is credited with helping significantly develop the roster. He is immensely proud that a number of his players went on to U.S. and Canadian college hockey, Major Junior, European hockey, and several, including Gino Cavallini, Kevin Dineen, and Rick Tocchet, reached the NHL.

Kevin carried the lessons learned at St. Michael's with him through his life. "The curriculum of the school in Canada was a lot more advanced than I had been exposed to when I was in the States. It prepared me for a college level. On the hockey front, it was not too different than a professional schedule. We practised daily, had three games a week, and you learned to prioritize very well."

Kevin was drafted by the Hartford Whalers in 1982 and debuted with the team in 1984–85, scoring 25 goals as a rookie. In November 1991, he was traded to the Philadelphia Flyers, joining former Buzzer teammate Rick Tocchet. It was back to the Whalers in December 1995, and Kevin moved with the team when the franchise went to Carolina for the 1997–98 season. Signed as a free agent by Ottawa in 1999, he played one campaign with the Senators before finishing his NHL career with three seasons as a Columbus Blue Jacket. In 1,188 regular-season games, Dineen contributed 760 points, including 355 goals and 405 assists.

St. Michael's finished the 1980-81 season in first place in the Central Division, then went on to eliminate the Bramalea Blues and North York Flames to win the Metro championship.

Rick Tocchet spent most of the season with St. Mike's Midget team, but played five games and scored a goal as a Buzzer. He went on to a celebrated NHL career that lasted 18 seasons with Philadelphia, Pittsburgh (where he won a Stanley Cup championship in 1992), Los Angeles, Boston, Washington, and Phoenix. He scored 20 or more goals 11 times, amassing a total of 426. With 488 assists, Tocchet finished his 1,070-game NHL career with 914 points.

Netminder Doug Dadswell played 27 games over two seasons with the Calgary Flames.

"We had some outstanding players during my three years there," recalls Rick Cornacchia. Among them in 1981–82 were captain Jamie Wansborough and a feisty winger by the name of Gino Cavallini. The 22-goal scorer led the St. Michael's Buzzers to a second-place finish in the Metro Junior 'B' Hockey League with a sterling 22–7–6 record. The Buzzers won the league championship, then faced the Sarnia Bees for the provincial championship. Cavallini and the Buzzers edged the Bees four games to three to give St. Michael's its first Sutherland Cup since 1961.

Cavallini spent two years playing hockey at Bowling Green University in Ohio, then in May 1984, was signed as a free agent by the Calgary Flames. Through nine NHL seasons, Cavallini played with the Flames, St. Louis Blues, and Quebec Nordiques, earning 273 points in 593 regular season NHL contests.

In Rick Cornacchia's last season as Buzzers coach, they achieved a third-place finish in the newly created Fullan Division, winning 21, losing 13, and tying two through the 1982–83 season. Rick Mulligan, the team captain, was also the team MVP and a league All-Star, collecting 57 points for the Buzzers.

Moving into post-season play, St. Mike's eliminated Port Credit in the first round, then beat Wexford in the second. But it was the Henry Carr Crusaders, undefeated through the season, who went on to win the league championship and take home the Sutherland Cup.

Craig Duncanson went on to become a first-round selection of the Los Angeles Kings in 1985. He played parts of five seasons in California, followed by seasons with the Winnipeg Jets and New York Rangers. Between 1985–86 and 1992–93, Craig played 38 regular-season NHL games, in which he collected nine points.

Todd Elik scored 25 goals and 26 assists for St. Mike's in 1982–83. His inaugural NHL season was 1989–90, with the Los Angeles Kings. Elik later played with the Minnesota North Stars, Edmonton Oilers, San Jose Sharks, St. Louis Blues, and Boston Bruins. Over eight seasons and 448 games, Todd scored 110 goals and 219 assists for 329 points.

Defenceman John English earned 12 points for the Buzzers in 1982–83, and played three games with the Los Angeles Kings in 1987–88, earning four points.

"The students at St. Mike's were great, not only as hockey players, but as people," reflects Cornacchia. "Some of them went on to hockey careers, but many were successful in life because of the kinds of people they were — high achievers."

Rick Payne took over from Cornacchia as coach in 1983–84 and guided the squad to a third-place finish in the Fullan Division, recording 46 points. Henry Carr won the league championship.

Andy Pokupec was chosen as captain of the Buzzers, and was supported by two players who went on to NHL careers.

Born in Seoul, Korea, Jim Paek spent most of the 1983–84 season playing defence for the St. Mike's Midget team, but was brought up for five games with the Buzzers. While with the Oshawa Generals, Paek was chosen late in the 1985 NHL Entry Draft by the Pittsburgh Penguins. He made his entry into the NHL with three games as a Penguin in 1990–91, and has his name engraved on the Stanley Cup, as Pittsburgh took the championship that year. Jim made much more of a contribution to the Penguins' second title the following spring. He played three more NHL seasons, dressing for Los Angeles and Ottawa as well as the Penguins, and finished his NHL career with 217 games played, in which he totalled 34 points.

The netminder for the Buzzers was a commanding figure: six-foot, four-inch Sean Burke. Drafted by the New Jersey Devils in 1985, the much-travelled Burke played for New Jersey, Hartford, Carolina, Vancouver, Philadelphia, Florida, Phoenix, Tampa Bay, and Los Angeles during a stellar 18-season career. Burke retired after the 2006–07 season, with 324 wins, 341 losses, 101 ties, four overtime losses, and five shootout losses in 820 regular-season games. During the playoffs, he won 12 and lost 13 in 38 appearances. He participated in the NHL All-Star Game in 1989, 2001, and 2002.

The 1984–85 season was a disappointment for new Buzzer coach Bill Fifield, as St. Mike's finished a distant fifth in the Fullan Division and could only look on as the Bramalea Blues took the league championship.

Notable players in 1984–85 were captain Giancarlo Morrone, Bobby Babcock, Ted Mahovlich (son of Hall of Fame alumnus Frank), and goaltender Mike Rosati. Babcock was picked late in the NHL Entry Draft by the Washington Capitals and played single games with the NHL club in 1990–91 and 1992–93.

Rosati was drafted by the New York Rangers in 1988, but didn't make an NHL appearance for 10 years. After a sensational Junior career, he played in Europe for many years, most notably with the Bolzano Hockey Club, which he backstopped to two championships. He also competed with the Italian national team in the 1994 and 1998 Olympic Winter Games. In the summer of 1998, Mike was signed as a free agent by the Washington Capitals, where he served behind Olaf Kolzig and Craig Billington. Fate intervened, and after an injury to Billington, Rosati served as Kolzig's backup. On November 7, 1998, Kolzig was injured midway through a game against the Ottawa Senators and Rosati took his place in the crease. He played 28 minutes and did not surrender a goal as the Capitals dumped Ottawa 8–5. Rosati was credited with the win in what turned out to be his sole NHL appearance.

Coach Fifield had the benefit of some outstanding talent in 1985–86. Mike Rosati served as backup to Jason Muzzatti, and both would one day play in the NHL. The team finished with 40 points, 15 points better than the previous season, and were third in the Fullan Division. The Buzzers lost in the quarterfinal. It was the Pickering Panthers' turn to win the championship.

The Calgary Flames pinned big hopes on Muzzatti when they drafted him in the first round of the 1988 NHL Entry Draft. He first played with the Flames in 1993–94, and spent two seasons in Calgary. He played two more seasons with the Hartford Whalers, then in 1997–98 played six games with the New York Rangers and one with the San Jose Sharks. Heart surgery in September 1998 ended his NHL career, but not before he had made 62 appearances, with a record of 13 wins, 25 losses, and 10 ties.

Among the other Buzzers, defenceman Rob Cowie went on to become a U.S. College All-Star with Northeastern University, after which he signed with the Winnipeg Jets. But his NHL career would consist of two seasons with the Los Angeles Kings. Between 1994–95 and 1995–96, he played 78 games, scoring seven goals and assisting on 12 others.

Joe Day spent the 1985–86 season with St. Mike's after arriving from Chicago. He scored 23 goals for the Buzzers in 30 games and was selected by Hartford late in the 1987 Entry Draft. Joe played two seasons with the Whalers, beginning with 1991–92, then finished his NHL career by playing 1993–94 with the New York Islanders. In 72 NHL games, Joe had 11 points.

Chris Govedaris played just two games with the St. Michael's Buzzers, spending most of the 1985–86 season with the Toronto Young Nationals. After a strong Junior career with the Toronto Marlboros, he was drafted by the Hartford Whalers with their first pick in the 1998 NHL Entry Draft. Govedaris played three seasons in Hartford, finishing his NHL career with the Toronto Maple Leafs. In 45 NHL contests, Chris scored four goals and had 10 points.

The Buzzers won 21 games, losing 11 and tying five for a second-place Fullan Division finish in 1986–87, then were eliminated in the semifinal. The Henry Carr Crusaders took the league championship honours.

Jason Muzzatti split goaltending duties with Jeff Chisholm. Tom Auge was both the leading goal getter (29) and scoring leader, with 71 points. Captain Rob Cowie (25), Eric Klutke (25), and Jeff Harding (22) were other Buzzers to better the 20-goal mark.

The Philadelphia Flyers selected Jeff Harding in the 1987 draft and dressed him for 15 games between 1988–89 and 1989–90.

Jason Woolley was a good rushing defenceman with St. Mike's, using his talents to work his way to the National Hockey League. Debuting with the Washington Capitals in a single game in 1991–92, Woolley enjoyed a fine NHL career, playing with the Florida Panthers, Pittsburgh Penguins, Buffalo Sabres, and Detroit Red Wings, in addition to Washington. He played 718 games through 14 seasons, earning 314 points.

The St. Michael's Buzzers announced Scott McLellan as the new coach for 1987–88, and he proceeded to lead the team to a 51-point finish, good for third in the Fullan Division. Bill Konstantinou was captain of a squad that won 16, lost 14, and tied seven. It was the Buzzers' misfortune to meet the Bramalea Blues, the eventual champions, in the quarterfinals.

The Buzzers iced a powerhouse in 1988–89, winning the Fullan Division race handily with a record of 33 wins, five losses, and a tie for 67 points. After beating Kingston and Bramalea to win the Metro Junior 'B' championship, the Buzzers rolled over Sarnia, then faced the Niagara Falls Canucks for the Ontario championship. With a 5–3 win over the Canucks, St. Mike's took the series four games to one to claim the Sutherland Cup. It was the sixth Ontario Junior 'B' title for St. Michael's, and their first since 1982.

The goaltending tandem of Rich Shulmistra and Angelo Libertucci had the best goals-against average in the league. Shulmistra played two NHL games — one with the New Jersey Devils in 1997–98 and a second in 1999–2000 with the Florida Panthers.

Coach Scott McLellan was blessed with great offence as well. Steve Glugosh led the team with 90 points. Eric Lindros scored 24 goals and 43 assists for 67 points, Mike Thompson had 28 goals and 66 points, Mike Heaney collected 60 points, Rick Lacroix had 58 points (including 22 goals), captain Scott MacNair fired 20 goals with 56 points, and Jason Dexter had 24 goals and 50 points.

After one season on the Buzzers blue line, David Harlock joined the University of Michigan Wolverines for four years. Originally drafted by the New Jersey Devils in 1990, Harlock was signed as a free agent by the Toronto Maple Leafs in 1993 and joined the Leafs for parts of three seasons. He later played for the Washington Capitals, New York Islanders, and Atlanta Thrashers through his 212-game NHL career.

Eric Lindros's presence was dominating, both physically and in terms of offensive skill. In addition to his 67 points, he spent 193 minutes in the penalty box. In the playoffs, he shifted into high gear, scoring 23 goals and 25 assists in 27 contests, while being flagged for 155 playoff penalty minutes. A Memorial Cup champion with the Oshawa Generals in 1990, Lindros was tagged as a can't-miss superstar when, much to his chagrin, he was chosen first overall by the Quebec Nordiques in 1991. Refusing to play for the Nordiques, Eric was eventually traded to the Philadelphia Flyers in a massive and controversial deal (the Nordiques also traded Lindros to the New York Rangers on the same day). Lindros played eight seasons in Philadelphia, enjoying six 30-goal seasons and winning the Hart Trophy as the league's most valuable player. But injuries plagued Eric throughout his career. He missed the 2000–01 season in its entirety, then, after a trade, joined the New York Rangers for three seasons. He played 2005–06 with Toronto and ended his career with Dallas in 2006–07. Lindros retired with 865 points (372 goals and 493 assists) in 760 regular-season games (as well as 1,398 penalty minutes) and 57 points in 53 playoff contests.

Wes McCauley was recognized as one of the leaders on this squad. Drafted by Detroit in 1990, McCauley didn't play in the NHL, but followed his father, John, into officiating and became an NHL referee.

"If a championship was ever won by team effort and not by individual accomplishments, this one was and they all deserve congratulations," hailed *The Tower*, the school yearbook.

One of the standouts was defenceman Ken Klee. "I had lived in Indianapolis and I had some friends who talked about leaving home to play hockey in their last year of high school. They said that St. Mike's had given a bunch of guys scholarships, so I said I'd give them a call," recounts Klee.

Ken called the school and asked if he could try out for the team. "The coach said, 'If you want to pay your own way up, we'll take a look at you.' It was just a shot in the dark. I didn't know anything about St. Michael's. I was at a Jesuit high school at the time, so my parents were pleased that it was a good school. We went up in the spring and that was it. It was a stroke of luck."

Arriving in Toronto was a culture shock for the young American player. "Coming from Kansas City, where I had my own car to drive around and we lived in the southern suburbs, and then to live in a big city where I had to ride the subway every day was a big change. And with all the different languages and all of the different cultures that are in Toronto — it was quite an experience. They put me and Pat Rodgers, another American from Cleveland, with an older English lady, which was kind of like living with a grandma. She cooked dinners for us and it was great!"

Klee used the St. Michael's experience as a stepping-stone to a scholarship at a U.S. college. "I had to take eight classes so I could graduate, plus there is no question that I was getting looked at way more than I would have been on another team, just because we had so many other great players on the team."

Ken attended Bowling Green and was drafted by Washington in the 1990 Entry Draft. Joining the Capitals' defence corps in 1994–95, Klee played nine seasons in Washington, then joined the Toronto Maple Leafs, New Jersey Devils, Colorado Avalanche, and Atlanta Thrashers. "St. Mike's was the biggest boost to my hockey career I could ever imagine," he concludes. "To come from Kansas City, where they had two rinks for a town of two million people, to Toronto, where there were not only college scouts but pro scouts at the rink each game. And then you see the history when you go in the Old Boys' Room at the arena.

"I remember going to a dinner for Red Kelly and met the Mahovlich brothers. That's when it really clued into me that this was a hockey dynasty. I had had no idea when I moved up to Toronto."

In 1989, at an early-July meeting of the Metro Junior 'B' Hockey League, Buzzers coach Scott McLellan informed those assembled that there was a very distinct possibility that the Basilian Fathers would choose not to operate a team for the 1989–90 season. One of those in attendance, Terry Weir of the Henry Carr Crusaders, reported that there were three concerns outlined: "no money, no interest, and once St. Mike's dropped its minor [Metro Toronto Hockey League] program [in 1985], the writing was on the wall."

Eric Lindros's outstanding career was jumpstarted at St. Michael's College. After dominating as a Buzzer, he joined the Oshawa Generals and contributed to a Memorial Cup championship in 1990. His arrival in the NHL was heralded with the same anticipation that Wayne Gretzky and Mario Lemieux had once enjoyed.

The school had cancelled its MTHL program due to the small number of players on their teams that actually attended the school, while many of their students played in the league but for other teams.

McLellan acknowledged that the Buzzers lost money during the championship season in 1988–89, but stated that the Basilians had lost money in most of the 80 seasons they had operated a hockey program — and that, indeed, most Junior 'B' teams lose $50,000 to $70,000 each year.

On July 20, 1989, St. Michael's College School announced officially that would not ice a team. The decision left the school with no formal hockey program for the first time in more than 80 years. "It is always sad to see a long-standing tradition die," admitted Murray Costello, an alumnus who was serving as president of the Canadian Amateur Hockey Association at the time. "It has been an institution that has done a lot for young people. There are many out there who have benefited from what they were taught at St. Mike's."

Following a one-year leave of absence, the Buzzers merged with the Vaughan Raiders in 1990–91 but maintained the Buzzers name. The league they joined, known since the summer of 1989 as the Metro Junior Hockey League, was expelled from the OHA in June 1990, rendering it an independent or "renegade" league.

The team, coached by Greg Carrigan and featuring captain Dan Larmer, finished second in the Fullan Division, compiling 50 points on 22 wins, 16 losses, and six ties. The Wexford Raiders eventually went on to win the league championship, their first of four in a row.

Brad Brown spent most of the season with the Toronto Red Wings, but played two games with the Buzzers. The Montreal Canadiens chose the defenceman in the first round of the 1994 Entry Draft, and he joined them in 1996–97. Brad later played with the Chicago Black Hawks, New York Rangers, Minnesota Wild, and Buffalo Sabres.

Making an appearance in a single game (a precursor to becoming their regular goalie in 1991–92) was future NHLer Kevin Weekes. "My mom and dad were born in Barbados and came to Canada in the '70s. My dad didn't know much about hockey, but I saw my cousins playing and I wanted to play, too," smiles the affable Weekes. "I started to play hockey when I was six, and was a goalie right from the start. I was always fascinated with the equipment, so I never played any other position." Kevin laughs when he recounts early road hockey games. "I had an old 'Friday the 13th' mask, I used some foam I got from old sofa cushions for pads, and for a catcher, I had a margarine container attached to a glove. I couldn't catch the ball with it, but we sure had fun!"

Kevin was drafted by the Florida Panthers in 1993 and made his first NHL appearance with them in 1997–98. Since then, Weekes has played with the Vancouver Canucks, New York Islanders, Tampa Bay Lightning, Carolina Hurricanes, New York Rangers, and New Jersey Devils.

During the off-season, the Metro Junior Hockey League, already on the outs with the OHA, declared itself a Junior 'A' league. There had been no Tier II league in southern Ontario since the demise of the OHA's Provincial Junior 'A' league at the end of the 1986–87 season.

In 1991–92, with Kevin Weekes in goal and a team that included future NHLers Brett Lindros and David Ling, as well as captain Ben Davis, the St. Mike's Buzzers dropped to fourth in the Fullan Division. New coach Gord Davies led the team to 18 wins, 21 losses, and 5 ties, good for 41 points.

Hopes were set very high for Brett Lindros when he was selected by the New York Islanders with their first pick, the ninth overall, in the 1994 draft, but injuries prevented him from ever living up to expectations. In a game against the Los Angeles Kings on November 2, 1995, early in his second NHL season, Brett suffered a career-ending injury. He battled to return, but announced his retirement in May 1996, having played just 51 NHL games, collecting two goals and five assists.

After a sensational Junior career, David Ling was drafted by the Quebec Nordiques in 1993, but broke into the NHL with the Montreal Canadiens in 1996–97. He had also played with the Columbus Blue Jackets.

With an astounding 15 rookies in the lineup for the 1992–93 season, newly appointed coach Ken Moodie had his work cut out for him. Returning Buzzer Andrew Knott was named captain of the squad, and the young, hungry Buzzers, including John Jakopin and Craig Mills, battled hard and finished second in the Fullan Division, just two points behind the Muskoka Bears. The team won 24, lost 16, and tied six for 56 points. In the playoffs, St. Mike's swept Muskoka in four games, but lost to the Wexford Raiders in the final.

A six-foot, five-inch, 240-pound giant on the Buzzers' blue line, John Jakopin registered nine goals and 30 points for St. Mike's in 1992–93. Originally drafted by Detroit, Jakopin debuted with the Florida Panthers in 1997–98. He spent parts of three seasons in Florida, joined the Pittsburgh Penguins in 2001–02, and concluded his NHL career with the San Jose Sharks in 2002–03.

Craig Mills played one season with the St. Michael's Buzzers, scoring nine goals and collecting 30 points. The son of Dennis Mills, an alumnus instrumental in the subsequent return of the Majors to the OHL, Craig played three seasons with the Belleville Bulls and was named Canadian Major Junior Humanitarian of the Year in his final season. He debuted with the Winnipeg Jets in 1995–96, and was traded to the Chicago Blackhawks during the following summer. He played parts of two seasons in the Windy City. In 30 NHL regular-season games, Mills picked up five points.

Marc Moro attended St. Michael's College School between 1991 and 1993, although he played his minor hockey in Mississauga and never played for either the Buzzers or Majors. Still, Moro represented the school when he joined the Mighty Ducks of Anaheim for a single game in 1997–98. Moro played 27 games over three seasons with the Nashville Predators and two games with the Toronto Maple Leafs.

For a second straight season, the Buzzers finished with 56 points (25 wins, six ties, and 19 losses), although it landed them a third-place Fullan Division finish in 1993–94. Coach Dave Barrett named Ian McGonigal captain of the team, which also included Andy Sutton. St. Mike's lost out in the quarterfinal, and it was Wexford for a fourth season in a row that took the league championship.

At six feet, six inches and 245 pounds, Andy Sutton was an imposing figure on the St. Mike's blue line, and he chipped in with 17 goals and 40 points in his one season with the Buzzers. After starring with Michigan Tech, Sutton entered the NHL by way of the San Jose Sharks, playing two seasons there before moving to the Minnesota Wild, Atlanta Thrashers, and New York Islanders.

Coach Dave Barrett was behind the bench again as the Buzzers skated to a third-place finish in the Fullan Division, with a record of 26 wins, 18 losses, and six ties in 1994–95. The Caledon Canadians were dominant, finishing first and progressing to the Metro Junior 'A' Hockey League championship.

Scott Ludeviks captained the Buzzers in 1994–95, and one of his teammates had a noteworthy name: Syl Apps, a member of the third generation of outstanding hockey players in his family. Syl's father and grandfather (both also named Syl) played in the NHL. Syl's sister, Gillian, was part of the gold medal–winning Canadian Olympic hockey team in 2006.

Mark Moore spent most of the season playing with his brother Steve on the Senior Varsity team at St. Michael's, but was called up to play with the Buzzers during 1994–95. Mark is the oldest sibling of the remarkable hockey-playing Moore family that includes brothers Steve and Dominic, both of whom have made it to the NHL. All three played hockey at St. Michael's College and all three attended Harvard University, where they also starred on the hockey team (in 1999–2000, all three were regulars with the Crimson). Drafted by the Pittsburgh Penguins, Mark had his career ended by post-concussion syndrome during the 2002–03 season.

Along with the Bramalea Blues, Kingston Voyageurs, and Mississauga Chargers, the St. Michael's Buzzers left the Metro Junior Hockey League and joined the Ontario Provincial Junior 'A' Hockey League (OPJHL) for the 1995–96 season.

Coach Dave Barrett was behind the bench for his third and final season with St. Mike's, who were placed in the league's MacKenzie Division. Captain Chris Aishford and the Buzzers finished fifth in the six-team division, earning 47 points.

The 1992-93 version of the Buzzers included forward Craig Mills, whose father Dennis was instrumental in resuscitating the Majors franchise. Craig enjoyed a terrific Junior career before debuting in the NHL with the Winnipeg Jets in 1995-96.

The St. Mike's breeding ground spawned some outstanding talent in the late-1990s. Although the Buzzers were on hiatus, Jason Spezza and netminder Andy Chiodo played on the school's Senior Varsity squad.

Although the team's showing wasn't stellar, the number of players who would go on to the NHL confirmed St. Michael's standing as a superb training ground. Kip Brennan, an imposing forward, spent the 1995–96 season with the Buzzers. He joined Los Angeles in 2001–02 and spent three seasons with the Kings, followed by a year each with the Atlanta Thrashers in 2003–04 and the Mighty Ducks of Anaheim in 2005–06. Brennan was part of the New York Islanders organization in 2007–08, where he was made welcome by St. Michael's alumni Darryl Bootland, Rob Davison, Drew Fata, and Andy Sutton.

Drafted by the San Jose Sharks in 1998, Rob Davison joined the NHL team for the 2002–03 season and spent just over four seasons in the Bay Area. Early in 2007–08, he was dealt to the New York Islanders.

The Buffalo Sabres drafted Norm Milley in the second round of the 1998 NHL Entry Draft after he put up gigantic offensive numbers for the Sudbury Wolves. Milley spent three seasons with the Sabres, then moved to Tampa Bay for the 2005–06 season.

Steve Montador made the All-Rookie team with St. Mike's in 1995–96, his first of two seasons with the Buzzers. The Vancouver native was signed by the Calgary Flames as a free agent and joined the NHL squad in 2001–02. During the 2005–06 season, the defenceman was traded to the Florida Panthers.

Mike Futa took on the coaching chores for the Buzzers in 1996–97 and guided the team to fourth place in the MacKenzie Division, winning 26, losing 22, and tying three for 59 points. The Milton Merchants won the OPJHL championship that season. Returning stars included captain Dave Gallo and defenceman Rob Davison, who were joined by rising prospect Mike Glumac. After graduating from St. Mike's, Glumac attended Miami University in Ohio and was signed as a free agent by the St. Louis Blues. He made his debut with the Blues on January 3, 2006.

The Buzzers did not participate in the OPJHL for the 1997–98 and 1998–99 seasons. Although the Buzzers were on hiatus, the Majors were revived after a 36-year absence. And other school teams continued. The St. Mike's Senior Varsity team included team MVP Jason Spezza and goaltender Andy Chiodo.

The much-coveted Spezza was selected second overall in the 2001 NHL Entry Draft, the first pick of the Ottawa Senators. He didn't disappoint. Spezza is one of the NHL's most highly regarded stars, intelligent and talented, and is one of the cornerstones of the Ottawa club.

In the Buzzers' absence, the OPJHL had absorbed the failing Metro Junior 'A' league, resulting in an enormous league bulging at the seams with 37 teams playing in four divisions. The Buzzers were placed in the South Division and in 1999–2000, finished seventh under the guidance of first-year coach Chris DePiero, winning 18, losing 28, and tying three with no overtime losses. The Brampton Capitals took the league championship.

Drew Fata joined the New York Islanders in 2006–07. Also with the Buzzers in 1999–2000 were captain David Ovcjak and Matt Napier, the son of NHL and WHA star Mark Napier, who played one season with the Buzzers, then went on to write the best-selling children's book *Z Is for Zamboni*. Trainer Bobby Hastings later became one of the equipment managers of the Toronto Maple Leafs.

"In a season marked by many highs and lows, using dedication and guts, the Buzzers turned in a highly credible season," said *The Tower* of the 2000–01 season. The team finished sixth in the South Division, and collected 50 points on 23 wins, 22 losses, three ties, and an OT loss. The Thornhill Rattlers won the OPJHL championship and the Dudley Hewitt Cup, emblematic of the Junior 'A' championship of central Canada.

Mike McIsaac was captain of a team that included two future NHL stars, Geoff Platt and Anthony Stewart. Platt debuted with the Columbus Blue Jackets in 2005–06 and played two seasons there before joining the Anaheim Ducks in 2007–08. Stewart was a first-round pick of the Florida Panthers in 2003 and played his inaugural NHL contest in 2005–06.

St. Michael's College was on the verge of selling the Buzzers, citing financial concerns. "I got a call in the fall of 2001 and was informed that the Basilian Fathers were really struggling with the Buzzers and in order to keep them alive, the Buzzers had to find alternative funding," says Mike McCarron, who played goal for the Buzzers in 1978–79 and had become successful running a trucking company. "I was told Father Zorzi was selling the Buzzers to Harvey Shapiro and Peter Freedman with the Junior Canadiens. I had no problem with that, in fact, they're friends of mine. But the reality was, they didn't want the St. Mike's Buzzers. They wanted the Junior franchise. The thing that bothered me was that once the St. Mike's Buzzers were gone, they'd be gone forever."

McCarron spoke with Father Zorzi and tried to convince him to put the Buzzers on hiatus so that he could investigate ways in which to make the franchise viable. "I looked at what it was going to cost and said, 'Father, give me a chance. There's no question that I can make this work, but I can't do it now. I need a year.'"

After contacting the league, McCarron was told that since the team had already taken two sabbaticals, there was no way it would be allowed another. "'No sabbatical,' I was told. 'You get in this year or you're done.' Father Zorzi said, 'I've got to get rid of the Buzzers. I can't justify the cost. I'll make you a deal — I'll give it to you for a dollar.' I said, 'That's great, Father, but I can't really afford the $250,000 to $300,000 loss!'"

A Buzzers alumnus, Mike McCarron was approached about purchasing the team from St. Michael's in 2001. Today, he is very proudly the president of the St. Michael's Buzzers Hockey Club.

McCarron agreed to take on the team for a year. "It was only costing me a dollar and I had time to figure things out," he explains. "I said, 'I'll make you a deal. If the losses hit $300,000 — which is probably what the franchise was worth — I'm out of there.' I could cover some losses, but I couldn't justify writing cheques for $300,000 a year."

But a funny thing happened during that year. "I absolutely fell in love with it," McCarron laughs. "We changed a whole bunch of things, and we turned the [financial picture] around. The Buzzers are now quite successful and we're back in business using the same principles on which it was founded." Rightfully proud, he adds, "We have the lowest budget in the league. It's all volunteer. There's no hidden agenda. Our whole mandate to the players is, 'We're going to try our best to get you to the next level.' We've been very successful — 85 or 90% of our kids go on to the NCAA, the OHL, or OUAA.

"St. Michael's always meant a lot to me," he admits. "You tend to get measured by the Frank Mahovliches and the Dave Keons, but there are a hell of a lot more guys who found that the highlight of their hockey lives was putting on that 'M.' I know that myself. You talk about St. Mike's hockey and what it means to people, and it's incredible. It's not about the NHL, it's about what it did to guys like me in my life, and the skills and principles it taught me to carry on in the business world. I don't know if I really appreciated St. Mike's while I was going there, but there's a pride, a camaraderie and a discipline that you don't appreciate at the time.' Mike adds, "I was once told that you go into St. Mike's a boy and you leave as a man."

Finishing second in the South, just three points behind the Wexford Raiders, was a monumental accomplishment. The Buzzers won 34, lost 10, tied four, and had one overtime loss for a strong 73-point finish. Brampton went on to win the Buckland Trophy as OPJHL champions.

The team was greatly assisted by strong performances from several players, including captain Steve Dennis, 34-goal scorer Jonathan Lehun, Daniel Pegoraro, and Wojtek Wolski.

Wojtek Wolski's story is remarkable, all the more so when you realize that it was almost over before it began.

Born in Zabrze, Poland, Wojtek and his family moved first to East Germany, then, in 1990, to Canada. Wes and Zofia Wolski watched through their apartment window as children played hockey on outdoor rinks near their home, and they wanted their boys, Kordian and Wojtek, to feel included. They couldn't afford two pairs of skates, so the Wolski bothers shared a single pair, taking turns skating on the rink.

Wojtek wanted to play hockey, but the family was not in a position to buy the equipment and pay for the registration necessary to play. Then, one day, his father came home with second-hand equipment and indicated that Wojtek could now play organized hockey. It was the first step on a journey that would lead to the NHL.

While attending St. Michael's College, Wojtek was an excellent student. "We didn't have [Internet access] because it was too expensive," he told the *Rocky Mountain News*. "I was never on the computer. If I was, it was because I was doing homework."

After spending 2001–02 with the Buzzers, Wojtek saw his career soar during four seasons with the Brampton Battalion. Still able to live at home, he produced a 57-point season in 2002–03, 70 in 2003–04, and 73 in 2004–05, before exploding for 47 goals, 81 assists, and 128 points in 2005–06. The Battalion star was named the OHL's player of the month in December, January, February, *and* March, and by the conclusion of the season, Wolski had finished third in league scoring, been awarded the Red Tilson Trophy as the league's most valuable player, and earned the William Hanley Trophy as the most gentlemanly player.

Drafted in the first round of the 2004 NHL Entry Draft by the Colorado Avalanche, he got into nine games during 2005–06, making his mark with two goals and six points. More importantly, the Avalanche summoned him again for the playoffs — unheard of for a Junior-aged player. "It was a great experience," he says. "The intensity of the games was great. Even though we didn't advance, it gave us young guys a sense of how hard you have to work to win at that level."

What few knew was that during that incredible season, Wojtek's brother had been seriously injured in a car accident, a situation that would distract a lesser man. It only seemed to help Wolski put life in perspective. "There's always going to be ups and downs," he told ESPN's website. "I'm thankful for the positive things in my life. Sweating the small stuff just doesn't make much sense because at the drop of a hat, something bad can happen."

Although they finished third in the South Division in 2002–03, the Buzzers fell back in points, tumbling from 71 to 59 (25 wins, 15 losses, six ties, and three overtime losses). The Wellington Dukes were the cream of the league, taking both the OPJHL championship and Dudley Hewitt Cup.

Coach DePiero had several players who stood out, including captain Ryan Sullivan and Brian Ihnacak, as well as several who would provide the foundation for future Buzzers squads, including Jeff Kyrzakos and Peder Skinner. Ihnacak, the son of former NHL star Peter, scored 40 goals and 46 assists for 86 points to lead the Buzzers in scoring during his second season with the team.

The Buzzers posted a record of 33 wins, 13 losses, one tie, and two overtime losses to collect the South Division title in 2003–04. After sweeping both the Buffalo Lightning and Markham Waxers, the Buzzers defeated the North York Rangers in five games to win the division final. In the league semifinal versus the Bowmanville Eagles, St. Mike's triumphed again, this time in six games, but the Aurora Tigers, who had finished first overall in the OPJHL, took the league championship four games to two. After winning the Buckland Trophy as OPJHL champions, the Tigers proceeded to win the Dudley Hewitt Cup, emblematic of the central Canadian championship.

Peder Skinner led the team in scoring during the regular season with 83 points, including a team-best 34 goals. Rookie Andrew Cogliano finished with 26 goals and 72 points, and Jeff Kyrzakos had 25 goals and 55 points. The team employed several goalies through the campaign. Daniel Bellissimo shouldered much of the load, but Matthew Spezza (younger brother of Ottawa Senators star Jason) and Kain Tisi, who would play three strong seasons in goal for the Buzzers, were also in the mix during 2003–04.

In what was declared, quite fairly, as "one of the best seasons in the history of the Buzzers," the 2004–05 squad won 36, lost just seven, tied four, and suffered two overtime losses, putting them second, just behind the Wexford Raiders, in the competitive South Division and fifth overall in the OPJHL.

The scoring was led by Andrew Cogliano, a Toronto boy, who scored 36 goals and 66 assists to lead the league in scoring with 102 points.

The Buzzers swept the Thornhill Thunderbirds in the first round of the playoffs, then eliminated the North York Rangers in five games. The team won its second divisional championship in a row by defeating the Wexford Raiders in five games. The OHL semifinal against the Port Hope Predators went the full seven games, but the Buzzers took that series

Born in Poland, Wojtek Wolski joined the Buzzers in 2001–02, and after a brilliant stint with the Brampton Battalion, has starred in the NHL with the Colorado Avalanche since 2005–06.

and earned a berth in the championship final. They completed a victorious playoff run, one in which they won 20 games and lost just seven, by defeating Georgetown to win the Frank L. Buckland Trophy as champions of the Ontario Provincial Junior Hockey League.

Andrew Cogliano began attending St. Michael's College School in Grade 7 and spent seven years at the venerable institution. "I made a lot of great friends there," he says.

While attending the school, Cogliano played both hockey and soccer, but it was definitely the former that caught the attention of observers. "I knew pretty early on that I was going to go to [the University of] Michigan," he says, adding, "I committed to them in my Bantam year, when I was 15. I worked hard a lot of years to go to Michigan. I had been to Michigan and saw the school's setup and saw the atmosphere and I really enjoyed it, so I committed."

The St. Michael's Majors would have loved nothing more than to have had Andrew play for them, and even though they knew Cogliano had committed to a U.S. college, they selected him in the third round of the 2003 OHL draft. Cogliano held firm to his plan to attend Michigan, but while he prepared, he spent two years playing Junior 'A' with the Buzzers. Moving from Midget to Junior was expected to be quite a step for the young man. "Before the season started, my dad said I shouldn't expect to be the dominant player that I'd been at most levels." Wise advice, but ultimately unnecessary, as he set team records in assists and points in his second season, 2004–05, winning the OPJHL scoring crown in the process. That summer, Andrew was chosen by Edmonton in the first round of the NHL Entry Draft. It isn't common to be drafted directly out of Junior 'A,' and even more unusual to be taken 25th overall. Cogliano's coach with the Buzzers, Chris DePiero, called Andrew the best player of that age that he had ever coached. "I don't think I've ever seen a player at this level who's as quick and gets to top speed so quickly."

Andrew began attending the University of Michigan in September 2005, studying kinesiology. "I think it was the best possible hockey I could've been playing at my age," Andrew says. "Every night, I was playing against guys up to 26 years old. The hockey couldn't be better and the practising helped me a lot. I loved going to school."

After Cogliano attended a second training camp with the Oilers, general manager Kevin Lowe asked Andrew to turn pro and play with Edmonton in 2007–08. "It was obviously a good step for me, but it was a tough decision," he admits. "This is an opportunity that only comes once in a lifetime." Although he didn't finish his degree at the University of Michigan, he doesn't plan to abandon his schooling. "I did two years there. I will finish my education — maybe not at Michigan, but probably in Toronto."

During 2007–08, his NHL rookie season, Andrew set a league record by scoring overtime goals in three consecutive games. He went on to pot 18 goals and assist on 27 others while playing in all 82 games.

Reminiscing about St. Mike's, Cogliano says, "St. Michael's College School was an environment that enlightened my understanding about life and about dedication. This community gave me the opportunity to compete in both athletics and academics against the top competition in the province. St. Michael's truly made me a better person, allowing me to interact with unbelievable people on a daily basis and, most importantly, inscribing the 'Teach me goodness, discipline, and knowledge' motto in my life."

The Buzzers battled to a third straight first-place finish in the South Division, edging the Markham Waxers in 2005–06. St. Mike's won 29, lost 12, tied five, and had three overtime losses. Mike McKenzie led the team in scoring with 77 points, including 39 goals. Louie Caporusso followed with 73 points, 29 of which were goals.

Chris DePiero, in his seventh and final season as coach, guided the Buzzers to a league championship for the second consecutive season. The Buzzers defeated Oshawa, Wexford, and Markham to win their division, then dumped the Bowmanville Eagles four games to one in the league semifinal. It took six games, but St. Mike's triumphed over the Stouffville Spirit. Co-captains Mike McKenzie and Julian Zamparo accepted the Buckland Trophy on behalf of their teammates.

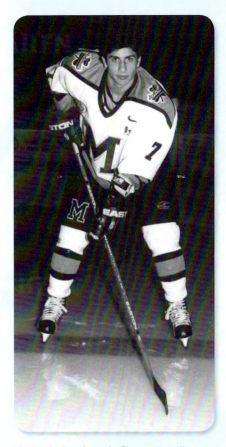

Making the leap from the Buzzers to college hockey, and then on to the NHL, Andrew Cogliano joined the Edmonton Oilers in 2007–08 and enjoyed an outstanding rookie season.

Nick D'Agostino and team captain Fred Cassiani, a St. Mike's student as well as a member of the Buzzers, celebrate a goal against the arch-rival Markham Waxers during the 2007–08 season.

Replacing long-term coach Chris DePiero in 2006–07 was Rich Ricci, who guided the Buzzers to a second-place finish, one point back of the Vaughan Raiders in the South Division. St. Michael's won 33, lost just nine, tied seven, and had no overtime losses. Louie Caporusso's 50 points placed him first on the team, followed by Fred Cassiani, whose 48 points included a team-best 25 goals. Mike Binnington and Cory Gershon divided goaltending duties for St. Mike's.

The Buzzers eliminated Ajax in the division quarterfinal, Markham in the semifinal, and Pickering in the South Division final, but were upset by Wellington in the league semifinal.

The Buzzers rode an exceptional 88-point season (43 wins, four losses, and two overtime losses) to first place in the South Division, two more than the Vaughan Raiders in 2007–08. The outstanding season, which included a remarkable 37-game unbeaten streak, gave the Buzzers first overall in the OPJHL. This edition of the team set club records for wins, points, fewest losses, and goals scored (291).

Fred Cassiani, a third-year Buzzer and captain of the team, led St. Mike's in scoring. His 32 goals and 57 assists gave him 89 points, third best in the OPJHL. Behind him was Richard Ryan with 81 points. Goal scoring wasn't a concern for St. Mike's, who got 30-goal seasons from Cassiani, Eric Rubino (41), Greg Miller (32), and Preston Cassidy. Cory Gershon was outstanding in goal.

The Buzzers got a bye into the South Division semifinal, where they dealt handily with the Toronto Junior Canadiens in six games, but fell to the Markham Waxers in a closely fought division final series, also in six. The Oakville Blades defeated the Waxers for the OPJHL championship.

38
Family Ties

The legacy of St. Michael's College School transcends generations, the experience of attending the school so profound that alumni often enroll their sons. So it is no coincidence that the list of those who have participated in hockey programs at St. Michael's College through the century reveal an unusual number of repeated surnames, and, upon further scrutiny, families that have shared the St. Michael's hockey experience.

From the Hall of Fame–inducted alumni alone, there are several such examples: Joe Primeau and his three sons; brothers Frank and Peter Mahovlich, as well as Frank's son Ted; brothers Bobby, Dave, and Frank Bauer, the first two of whom are Honoured Members of the HHOF; Les, Murray, and Jack Costello, brothers from the Timmins area; Dick and Les Duff, both of whom went on to professional hockey careers. Four generations of Kellys have attended St. Michael's College. "My father and my grandfather went to St. Mike's, so to go there was awesome," says Red Kelly. Red was the third generation of Kellys to attend St. Michael's College School, and a fourth generation has since been added, as both of Red's sons also attended the school.

There are many other families who have made St. Michael's and its hockey program a shared experience. Among the brother acts: Jack and Terry Caffery; Mike and Paul Gillis; Dave and Paul Gardner; Ray, Gord, and Pat Hannigan; Eric and Brett Lindros; Nick and Don Metz; and Jason and Matthew Spezza. Ed Harrison and Ed Sandford were cousins who starred first with the Buzzers, then the Majors, and later the Boston Bruins. Tod Sloan and David Keon are cousins who starred with the Majors and later with the Maple Leafs. Dennis Mills played while attending the school and was instrumental in bringing Major Junior hockey back to St. Michael's in 1997–98. His son Craig played with the Buzzers and graduated to the NHL.

Four of the more notable families to play hockey at St. Michael's College are the Costellos, Dineens, Drapers, and Moores.

Les Costello was born in 1928 and was recruited to play for the Majors in 1944. He played three seasons at St. Mike's and was an important factor in the team's Memorial Cup championships in 1945 and 1947, as well as their appearance in the 1946 final. His brother Murray, six years Les's junior, attended St. Michael's for grades 11, 12, and 13 and played with the Majors each of those three seasons — 1950–51, 1951–52, and 1952–53. Jack, born in 1939, attended St. Mike's in 1957–58 and 1958–59.

A good student, Murray was primarily at the school to play hockey, but benefited greatly from the lessons he took away from St. Michael's College. "While you were there, you didn't notice any of the overall education you were getting, but after leaving there and as the years go by, you look back and you see there was an awful lot of value," he explains.

"The priests who taught us and the priests who were working with the team really stressed the fact that you had to have something to fall back on and that you couldn't strictly rely on hockey. I've used that so many times in speeches as I crossed the country while I was with the Canadian Amateur Hockey Association. Of some 500,000 kids who lace on skates to play hockey across Canada every year, far less than 1% ever reach the point of being able to earn a living from the game. So you have to hedge your bets and have something to back it up, and education was the best thing to back it up with."

It was a lesson not lost on Murray. After chasing the brass ring of an NHL career, he returned to school and earned his law degree, then moved into a second career on the business side of hockey. Perhaps Murray's greatest hockey achievement was presiding over the Canadian Amateur Hockey Association, now known as Hockey Canada, from 1979 until 1998. He helped orchestrate the merger between Hockey Canada and the Canadian Hockey Association, which brought the entire Canadian development program into one stream. Costello can also take credit for nurturing the growth of women's hockey in Canada, first by creating a national women's team and then through the encouragement of its propagation. In 2005, Murray was inducted into the Builder category of the Hockey Hall of Fame.

While Les Costello found his calling in the priesthood, Murray found his in the hockey business and Jack in the field of education. All three would credit St. Michael's College for giving them a strong foundation upon which to build. "That message was instilled in us at St. Mike's and I think a lot of the guys went on from St. Mike's to U.S. colleges or went into post-graduate education and did very well," Murray adds. "That may be part of the reason we stay in touch with each other, too."

❖

Bill Dineen arrived at St. Michael's College from Ottawa in 1949 and joined the Majors that season. He was affectionately remembered by teammates as an outstanding player and a superb captain during his four seasons, in which he collected 182 points.

After graduating, Bill joined the Detroit Red Wings and was part of the team that won Stanley Cup championships in 1953–54 and 1954–55, his first two NHL seasons. During his fifth season, in December 1957, Dineen was traded to Chicago in an eight-player swap. His NHL career ended after that season, with 323 NHL games played, 51 goals scored, 44 assists, and 95 total points. "There were a lot of guys in those days, great hockey players, who never did get the opportunity of playing in the National Hockey League," states Bill. "I had the good fortune of being there."

But Bill's hockey career continued. He played six American Hockey League seasons with Buffalo, Cleveland, Rochester, and Quebec, then seven WHL seasons with Seattle and Denver.

While with the Denver Spurs, Bill began as a playing coach, easing into a full-time coaching career once he hung up his skates. When the World Hockey Association got off the ground in 1972, Dineen found a coaching position with the Houston Aeros, and during his six seasons with the Aeros, twice won the Avco Cup as WHA champions (1973–74 and 1974–75). In Houston, Bill was reunited with his old Detroit teammate Gordie Howe, and coached Gordie's sons Mark and Marty. The four were together again in 1978–79 with the New England Whalers.

After the WHA's demise, he returned to the AHL, this time coaching the Adirondack Red Wings from 1983–84 until 1988–89, winning two Calder Cup championships along the way. Dineen finally achieved his coaching dream when he was hired by the Philadelphia Flyers for the 1991–92 season. During his two seasons in Philadelphia, he coached two players he knew well: Mark Howe and his own son Kevin.

"Because my dad was a coach and a player, we lived in the United States pretty well until I moved and started going to St. Mike's," explains Kevin Dineen. Kevin knew about St. Michael's College through the stories told to him by his father. "You have this mystique about St. Michael's, kind of like Notre Dame has with football, and the tradition that went along with it. As children, we'd go up to Canada to visit relatives and inevitably, we'd run into one of Dad's friends who he went to St. Mike's with.

"Who knows how guys get nicknames, but my dad's name was 'Whipper.' The first time you ever hear your dad addressed as anything but 'Coach' or 'Dad' was weird. Somebody would say, 'Hey Whip, how're you doing?' It just left an incredible impression on me as a youngster to know that my dad was in this exclusive club."

Kevin, born in 1963, was the second of Bill's sons to attend St. Mike's — Gord, a year older, also played at the school. "When my brother started going to St. Mike's, he

Bill Dineen (standing behind the goaltender), the patriarch of the hockey-playing Dineens, starred the Majors for four seasons, beginning in 1949–50. Here, he assists his netminder in a contest against the Barrie Flyers.

inherited the name 'Whipper,'" laughs Kevin. "It was really neat, because we had patches that we wore on our blue blazers and my dad still had his, so it was really cool that we could go to school in the '80s with a patch from the '50s. It had some wear and tear on it, but we'd wear it with pride knowing that we were a second generation."

Gord joined the Buzzers in 1979–80, then played Major Junior with the Soo Greyhounds. Kevin was part of the Buzzers lineup in 1980–81. "We were so fortunate to have Rick Cornacchia as a coach, a guy who was such a stickler that the guys do well in school, and if the talent was there, they'd get a chance to go to Major Junior or college. He was a real believer in the college route, and that was good fortune for me that I was put in that direction." While brothers Peter and Gord took the Junior hockey route to the NHL, Kevin attended the University of Denver before being drafted by Hartford in 1982, joining the NHL squad in 1984–85. In 1,188 NHL regular-season games with Hartford, Philadelphia, Carolina, Ottawa, and Columbus, Kevin scored 355 goals and 405 assists for 760 points.

Gord, a defenceman, was selected by the New York Islanders and debuted with the team in 1982–83. He'd score 16 goals and 90 assists for 106 points in 528 NHL games played with the Islanders, Minnesota North Stars, Pittsburgh Penguins, and Ottawa Senators.

FAMILY TIES

The talented offspring of Bill Dineen — Kevin, Gord, Jerry, Peter, and Shawn – assisted at a hockey school in Penticton, British Columbia when this photo was taken in 1983.

Attending St. Michael's College helped launch the careers of both Dineen boys. "That was good for me, but to walk into the rink and know the history and to know your dad had been part of that history was always a nice feeling," smiles Kevin.

Mike Draper is the oldest of four brothers, three of whom starred on St. Michael's College hockey teams. "I was playing for Shopsy's and in those days [in the early 1950s] when you played for Shopsy's, [you were part of the Toronto Maple Leafs organization and] you either went to St. Mike's or you went to the Marlies. The majority of the guys I played with on Shopsy's went to the Marlies." But as a Roman Catholic, "it wasn't any decision at all for us" that he should attend St. Mike's. He began playing hockey at St. Michael's College while in Grade 9. "At that time, we [Mike and twin brothers Bruce and Dave] were on the Leafs' negotiation list. We didn't know about it until we were playing Junior 'B,' when we were offered $100 to sign a C-Form. It came as a complete surprise. My dad, Jack, had the foresight to ask why we would sign our lives away for a hundred dollars to be associated with the Toronto Maple Leafs."

Jack Draper was no stranger to either hockey or the Toronto Maple Leafs. He moved from Ottawa to Toronto in 1937 to play Senior with the Toronto Goodyears. During his three seasons with the team, Jack played with a number of future Leafs, including Hank Goldup, Red Heron, and Don Metz as well as Peanuts O'Flaherty, who would coach the St. Mike's Senior and Junior 'A' teams in the early 1950s, and Punch Imlach, the coach and GM of the Maple Leafs during their dynasty years in the 1960s.

"In those days, they gave out very few scholarships to St. Mike's, but we received scholarships from the school," continues Mike. "We didn't pay for tuition and we got our meals free. We were all born in Toronto and lived at home at the time, but in my second-last year of Junior, my dad was transferred back to Ottawa by Dow's Brewery, so that's when we started boarding at St. Mike's. And we got to practise in Maple Leaf Gardens, which was fantastic."

Mike began playing hockey at St. Mike's as a Minor Bantam in 1952–53. Twins Bruce and Dave joined the school's hockey program as Minor Midgets in 1955–56, and by 1957–58 were playing for Father Flanagan on the Buzzers. At that point, Mike was with the Majors, but he wasn't getting much ice time, so he asked to be assigned to the Buzzers. Father Flanagan placed Bruce at centre, Dave at right wing, and Mike at left wing, causing quite a sensation in the media and in the stands.

While all three brothers attended St. Michael's, they found it difficult to carry the scholastic load. "We were gifted hockey players; we weren't gifted students," Mike admits. "That was 100% because all we cared about was playing hockey. My mother and dad always used to say, 'If you had spent half as much time on your studies as you did on your hockey, you would have done all right.' But we did all right. We all graduated and got scholarships." Mike went to play with the University of Toronto in his last year, while Bruce and Dave moved up to the Majors, playing on a line with Larry Keenan in 1960–61, an explosive unit that carried the team to a Memorial Cup championship over the Edmonton Oil Kings.

On March 3, 1963, Bruce played with the Leafs in a 6–3 romp over the Boston Bruins, his only NHL game. "He was, by far, the best hockey player in our family," Mike says. "It was great for him to play that game. He definitely believed he had the talent to play in the NHL, and I do too, but they had quite the lineup at that time. Had Bruce arrived a couple of years earlier, I have no doubt in my mind that he would have excelled in the NHL for years."

While Bruce pursued a professional career, Mike and Dave elected to go to school, both accepting scholarships at Michigan Tech. "When I left to go to Michigan Tech, I was taken off the Leafs' list — unknown to me, just like I had no idea that I'd been put on it earlier on," laughs Mike. "Scotty Bowman contacted the coach at Michigan Tech, and he had wanted me to go to the Canadiens that fall. He had found out that Chicago had put me on their list." He played the 1963–64 season with Chicago's farm team, the St. Louis Braves, along with John Brenneman, Ray Cullen, and Phil Esposito. "I broke my hand in the last game of the year, so I missed the playoffs."

Mike's rights were traded to the Boston Bruins and he had a strong training camp in 1964. "I made the Bruins, but before the end of camp, I got mono and was sent home to Ottawa for three weeks to get my strength back," Draper says. "I went to Minneapolis, Boston's farm team, and Harry Sinden was the playing coach. I was there for a while, then I went to San Francisco and played there for a bit, and then they sent me to Greensboro." Finally, the head began to overrule the heart. "I had a degree and was playing in the minors and felt that I wasn't quite good enough to play on a regular basis in the NHL, so, during the summer, I saw an ad in the paper for a large company selling hospital supplies. I applied and got the job and I worked in the same job for the same company for 39 years."

Mike Draper stopped chasing the brass ring and played Senior hockey in Orillia, where he led the Terriers with 72 points and topped the league with 38 goals as part of an Allan Cup championship team in 1972–73. "We had a hell of a team," Mike says. "My buddy, Doug Kelcher, was playing coach. We had Grant Moore, Gary Milroy, Jimmy Keon, Claire Alexander, Tommy Polanic. The WHA had just started up and Gerry Cheevers went to Cleveland. He called and said he had a good deal for me to play with him in Cleveland. The money was pretty good, but I decided not to go. I didn't know if the league was going to last even one year. It's probably one of the best moves I ever made because I enjoyed my job and was able do well financially. I had three wonderful children, so am glad that I didn't go. It was certainly enticing, because we all love to play so much."

They called Dave Draper "Denny," and like his brothers, he was an excellent hockey player who was on the Leafs' negotiation list while playing at St. Michael's. After graduating in 1961, Dave attended Michigan Tech, where he played with brother Mike and former teammates from St. Michael's, including Bob Pallante and Gene Rebellato.

Dave stayed in hockey after retiring as a player. He coached OHL junior teams, starting with the Hamilton Fincups in 1977–78. He stayed with the team during phases

In 1957–58, Father Flanagan, coach of the Buzzers, placed all three Drapers on the same line. Mike, the eldest (right), and twins Bruce (centre) and Dave (left) all were members of the Majors. In fact, Bruce and Dave were key contributors to the 1961 Memorial Cup championship.

as the Brantford Alexanders (1978–79 to 1983–84) and Hamilton Steelhawks. Dave later turned to scouting. He joined the Quebec Nordiques in 1991 and stayed with the team through its move to Colorado (and a Stanley Cup in 1996) until 2000. Dave then joined the Phoenix Coyotes as vice-president and director of player personnel. "I enjoyed working with some great hockey minds and good people in Phoenix, from Wayne Gretzky to Cliff Fletcher to Mike Barnett on down," he says. "It was a great experience."

Just prior to the 2005–06 season, Draper was named to the Washington Capitals' scouting staff, and was with the Caps two seasons before retiring.

Bruce Draper joined the Buzzers in 1957–58 and appeared in two games with the Majors that season. By the following season, he had proven himself as one of the Majors' premier offensive talents, scoring 24 goals and 25 assists and tying for the team lead in points (49) with Jack Costello. Although his production fell in 1959–60, mostly due to injuries, he enjoyed a career-best season in 1960–61, capping a 44-goal, 33-assist regular season with the Memorial Cup. He was selected to the First All-Star Team and awarded the Max Kaminsky Trophy as the league's most sportsmanlike player.

Bruce turned professional with the Rochester Americans, Toronto's AHL farm team, in 1961–62 and scored 25 goals and 65 points. As he waited impatiently to crack the Leafs' lineup, Toronto was in the midst of winning three consecutive Stanley Cup championships. Coach/GM Punch Imlach favoured veterans, so few rookies were able to infiltrate the team. During 1962–63, Bruce toiled for the Americans as well as the Sudbury Wolves of the Eastern Professional Hockey League. Then, on March 3, 1963, he replaced Eddie Shack for a contest against the Bruins in Boston. Toronto doubled the Bruins 6–3 that evening. It was the only NHL game Bruce Draper would ever play.

After a season with Denver of the Western Hockey League, the Leafs traded Bruce to the Hershey Bears of the AHL to complete a transaction that brought Les Duff, another St. Mike's alumnus, into the Leafs organization. While playing with Hershey during the 1965–66 season, Bruce underwent surgery to have a malignant cyst removed from his lower abdomen. His weight plummeted from 175 pounds to 155 and he was diagnosed with leukemia. It appeared as though his hockey career was finished.

"Pat [the youngest of the four Draper brothers] and I were playing together in Greensboro in 1965–66 when we got a call from our dad that Bruce was going in for surgery. He had a great deal of pain in his abdomen," recalls Mike, finding the story difficult to recount. "I remember him telling us during the summertime that he went to the trainer in Hershey and said, 'My stomach is so hard,' and the trainer, Scotty Alexander, who was a great guy, said jokingly, 'Of course your stomach's hard. You've been playing hockey since September.' This was February and he went in and, unfortunately, he was diagnosed with cancer.

"Of course, it was devastating for all of us. My dad flew down and the surgeon said if it came back within five years it would be trouble."

The Drapers had made an annual summer ritual out of skating with other pro and semi-pro players at the Hull Arena to get ready for their respective training camps. "[One summer,] Bruce found a very tiny lump on one of his testicles. He went to the doctor and was told that it was nothing to worry about, training camp was a couple of weeks away, and to go and come back and see him next summer again. Next summer, he didn't go to see that doctor. The cancer had spread quite rapidly. Who knows, if they had diagnosed it at that point, whether they could have done anything anyway? We all felt that it would have given him seven months' headway."

Draper went through a long rehabilitation and by the summer of 1966 felt well enough to play 27 holes of golf a day. He rejoined Hershey in January 1967, but had lost the strength to play a regular shift and was released after two games. He reported to Hershey's training camp again in the fall of 1967, but was again released. He signed with Baltimore and played nine games before his health forced him to return to his wife, Judy, and two young children in Ottawa, where he died on January 26, 1968. He was 27 years old.

"Bruce left us at a very early age with a wonderful wife and two little girls," begins Mike, who then breaks into a broad smile. "He was one of the funniest guys you ever met in your life. He never had a worry in the world. He just loved life. He loved to play hockey and played it extremely well. In those days, with only six teams, it was pretty tough to break into that Leafs lineup. At centre, they had Red Kelly, Dave Keon, Bob Pulford, and Billy Harris. He played in the American Hockey League in 1961–62 and had an unbelievable year and was runner-up to Les Binkley by one vote for rookie of the year."

"I couldn't say enough about him," responded Father David Bauer, his coach during the Memorial Cup championship in 1960–61. "He was a tremendous boy from a tremendous family. He had a great devotion to hockey as a sport. I got caught in a snowstorm in Winnipeg and missed his funeral, and I always regretted it."

On April 19, 1969, more than 1,400 crowded into St. Michael's College Arena for the Bruce Draper Memorial Game, with proceeds channelled to Bruce's family. The game pitted the St. Mike's Old Boys against the Junior 'B' Buzzers. The Old Boys, coached by Father Flanagan, included Jack Caffery, Terry Clancy, Pete Conacher, Cal Gardner, Bob Goldham, Tim Horton, David Keon, Frank Mahovlich, and Johnny McCormack, as well as "funny antics from the one and only Father Les Costello," according to *The Globe*. The Old Boys beat the Buzzers 7–2, raising $5,500 along the way.

Today, the Draper legacy lives on in NHL circles. "We named our son Kristopher Bruce," says Mike. "Bruce was a great skater, and Kris skates like him." Born in 1971, hard-working, four-time Stanley Cup champion Kris Draper never knew his Uncle Bruce, but displays the heart and desire learned of at the feet of his dad and his uncle Dave.

❖

"St. Mike's is a Canadian hockey treasure," says Steve Moore. "I am not aware of any institution in the country, or the world, that has a deeper history in hockey than St. Michael's College School."

Steve is one of three brothers to attend St. Michael's College. What is even more extraordinary is that all three Moore boys graduated and attended Harvard University.

"We had heard from family friends, and others by way of reputation, that St Mike's was an excellent school, not just in regards to its historic hockey program, but also for

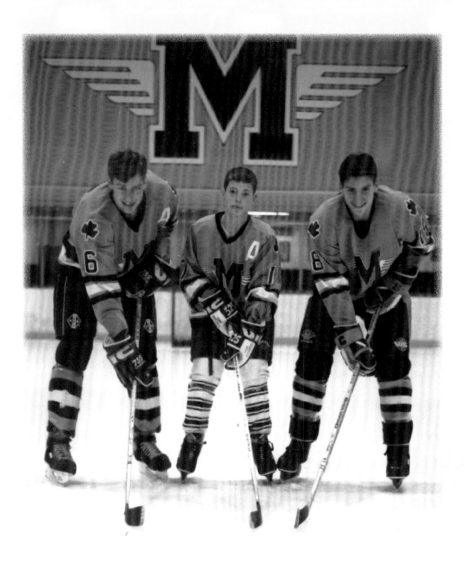

The Moore brothers (left to right: Mark, Dominic, and Steve) all played hockey while attending St. Michael's College School, then all went on to play for Harvard University. In 1999–2000, they played together on the Harvard Crimson.

its strong academics and its Catholic education," says Steve. "As I got older, I heard more and more about it, and became more and more hopeful that I would be able to attend there, especially as my older brother Mark started there, a couple years before me. I still remember the day I got the letter of acceptance, which was a huge thrill and relief!"

Mark, born in 1977, was the first of the brothers to wear the double blue. Steve, a year younger, followed next, and finally Dominic, born in 1980, attended the esteemed institution. There was no time at St. Mike's that all three played on the same team, but each participated on various school hockey teams. For example, during the 1993–94 season, Mark played on the Senior Varsity team while Steve was starring with the Junior Varsity Kerry Blues. In 1994–95, Mark and Steve played together on the Senior Varsity team, just as Dominic was arriving on the scene. Mark played with the Buzzers that season as well. In 1995–96, Mark and Steve played together with the Thornhill Islanders, and Steve and Dominic both played for the Islanders.

Mark was accepted at Harvard in 1996, and played defence for the Crimson for four years beginning in 1996–97 while earning a degree in mathematics. "He may just be the smartest hockey player ever to lace on skates," claims Michael Grange of *The Globe and Mail*. His Scholastic Aptitude Test (SAT) score was an almost perfect 1,590 out of 1,600.

After breaking the wrist on his writing hand, he learned to write with his other hand, but did so by writing everything backwards. His instructors agreed to grade his papers by using a mirror to read his work!

Steve Moore began attending Harvard in 1997 and joined brother Mark on the Crimson that season. He, too, attended the revered university for four years, playing hockey while he earned a degree in environmental science. Dominic entered Harvard to study sociology in 1999. That season, Dominic played with the Crimson as a freshman, Steve as a sophomore, and Mark in his graduating year. "It was special, having [Mark and Steve] there," Dominic told *Post Magazine*. It was the first time in Harvard's history that three brothers had ever played together on the school's hockey team, and just the sixth time in U.S. college hockey history.

Mark was drafted by the Pittsburgh Penguins in 1997, Steve by the Colorado Avalanche in 1998, and Dominic by the New York Rangers in 2000. Since then, Mark has been forced to retire due to post-concussion syndrome. "I was 26 years old, I had missed the last three-quarters of the previous season with a concussion, and I knew that this opportunity [with the Montreal Canadiens] was, in all probability, my last, best chance. The doctors wouldn't clear me to play, and the reality that was so hard to accept was that I couldn't anyway," writes Mark in his outstanding book *Saving the Game*.

Steve joined the Avalanche during the 2001–02 season. He was into his third season, and had played 69 games, earning 12 points, when he was involved in a well-documented incident involving Todd Bertuzzi of the Vancouver Canucks. In a game on March 8, 2004, Bertuzzi hit Steve from behind in a vicious attack that broke his neck and caused a serious concussion that has prevented him from returning to the game.

Dominic, meanwhile, made his NHL debut in 2003–04 with the New York Rangers. He joined the Rangers full time in 2005–06 and has since lent his speed and skill to the Pittsburgh Penguins, Minnesota Wild, and Toronto Maple Leafs.

"As kids, we played almost every sport out there, and like a lot of kids, took them pretty seriously. But when the time came that my brothers and I had to choose between sports, we all chose hockey," Mark mentions in his book. "There just wasn't anything that could come close to marching the fun and fulfillment of playing hockey. I don't mean any other sport, I mean anything. I never found anything so fulfilling as hockey, this activity that requires all of your physical, mental, and emotional powers."

The experience of attending St. Michael's College had a long-lasting effect on the Moore brothers. "St. Mike's was an influential place for us — the high standard of character-building there was very valuable," Dominic told *Post Magazine*. "We always took pride in our schoolwork and made sure we were as well-rounded as we could be."

Steve pays a wonderful tribute to his high school. "St. Mike's has had a very profound and positive influence on all areas of my life. And the long and proud history of the school, and the many great individuals that have attended over the years, including the many storied hockey players, was a constant inspiration for me. St. Mike's prepared me very well academically, athletically, and spiritually for my time at Harvard and beyond.

"St. Mike's, under the good and wise oversight of the Basilian Fathers, has the priorities right — to develop good character, knowledgeable students, disciplined individuals, and strong athletes."

39

St. Mike's First Superstar – Frank Rankin

Although better known today for its world-class theatrical productions, in the first decade of the twentieth century it would be difficult to dispute that Stratford, Ontario, was known most widely for its prodigious production of hockey talent. And foremost among local players were the young men of the Rankin family — Charlie, Gordon, Ramsay, Reg, and Frank.

Born in Stratford in 1889, Frank Rankin starred with his brothers on the local Stratford Hockey Club from 1904 until 1910. Frank, playing rover in the era of seven-person hockey, led his teams to Ontario Hockey Association championships in 1907, 1908, and 1909. As professionalism began to officially seep into hockey, Frank was lured to Toronto by the promise of cash to play for the Eaton Athletic Association's hockey club, and he was made captain of the team upon his arrival. Eaton's won the Ontario Hockey Association's Senior title in 1911 and 1912.

After two seasons, Rankin joined the St. Michael's Senior team, and in 1912–13, his first season with the school, dominated the scoring race by tallying 22 goals in eight games. He scored 10 goals in two games the following season.

Frank Rankin served in the Canadian army during the First World War, and when he returned to hockey, coached the Toronto Granites at an 11-day festival called the International Week of Winter Sports in Chamonix, France, in 1924. In 1926, this festival was retroactively deemed to be the first Winter Olympic Games. Hockey was immensely popular during the festival, and the Granites, representing Canada, were embraced by all as the dominant men's hockey team. Rankin's Canadian team overwhelmed the competition: 33–0 over Switzerland, 30–0 against Czechoslovakia, a 22–0 whitewash of Sweden, and a 19–2 triumph over Great Britain. With a 6–1 win against the United States in the final, Frank Rankin and the Toronto Granites had won a gold medal for Canada — the only one won by Canada that year.

For his outstanding service to hockey, in 1961, Frank Rankin was elected to the Hockey Hall of Fame.

Frank Rankin was the first St. Michael's alumnus to be honoured through induction into the Hockey Hall of Fame.

40
Noble Warrior – Reg Noble

After spending his Junior career playing for his hometown of Collingwood, Ontario, Reg Noble moved to Toronto for the 1915–16 campaign. With the Toronto Riversides, a Senior team, he led all scorers with six goals in four games to lead his team to the OHA championship. Once that season was completed, Noble was recruited to play for St. Michael's as they drove towards the Junior championship, and he promptly led the team with nine goals in six games.

Noble joined the National Hockey Association's Toronto Blueshirts in 1916–17. He was enjoying a superb season when the team folded. The Montreal Canadiens immediately picked up the talented goal scorer, who proceeded to collect four goals in six games, but was ruled ineligible to play with Montreal in the Stanley Cup final. That year, the Seattle Metropolitans made history by defeating the Canadiens to become the first U.S.–based team to claim the Stanley Cup.

In 1917–18, the National Hockey League was formed from the remnants of the NHA. Noble's rights were not retained by Montreal, and he was quickly signed by the Toronto Hockey Club. His 30 goals in 20 games during the NHL's inaugural season gave him third place in the scoring race. On March 30, 1918, the Toronto Hockey Club (widely known as the Arenas) defeated the Pacific Coast Hockey League champion Vancouver Millionaires to win the Stanley Cup.

The Toronto Arenas were sold and became the Toronto St. Patricks in 1919–20. Reg was extremely popular with the hometown crowds at the Arena Gardens, and one regular attendee was in the habit of winding up a siren every time he led a charge down the ice. He usually was flanked by Corb Denneny and Babe Dye, with whom he formed a very effective trio.

Prior to the start of the 1921–22 season, Reg was named the playing coach and captain of the St. Pats. On March 28, 1922, the St. Pats defeated the Vancouver Millionaires to win the best-of-five Stanley Cup final three games to two. It was Noble's second championship.

Finding the dual duties of playing and coaching too cumbersome, Reg relegated himself to strictly playing in 1922–23. In December 1924, Noble was dealt to the Montreal Maroons. During the 1925–26 season, he suffered a fractured skull in a game against Ottawa, but rejoined the Maroons after missing just four games. On April 6, 1926, Noble and the Maroons beat the Victoria Cougars 2–0 to win the best-of-five series three games to one and claim the Stanley Cup. Reg only played occasionally during the final, still recovering from his injury, but managed to contribute significantly to his third Stanley Cup championship.

In October 1927, Noble's former Toronto teammate, Jack Adams, acquired him for the Detroit Cougars. Through a name change (the Cougars were renamed the Falcons), Reg was a constant. Early in 1932–33, he was traded, this time back to the Maroons, and he concluded his NHL career after the season. At the time of his retirement, he was the last remaining player from the NHL's inaugural season.

Reg Noble played in the National Hockey League during its inaugural season (1917–18), and went on to play on three Stanley Cup winners.

Between the NHA and NHL, Noble played in 529 regular-season games. He scored 180 goals and 100 assists for 280 points. He died on January 19, 1962, and later that year was inducted posthumously into the Hockey Hall of Fame.

"Reg Noble ranks among the ten best forwards I have ever known," claimed Frank Selke in his autobiography, *Behind the Cheering*. Selke, recognized as an outstanding judge of talent through his long career involved in hockey, concluded: "He had an iron constitution and my players told me that every time they came into bodily contact with him, they were jarred from head to foot. It was not long before the hardest hitters in the professional game learned to give Noble a wide berth."

41

First-Class Champion – Joe Primeau

Although born in Lindsay, Ontario, Joe Primeau moved to Canada's west coast as a youngster. "I was raised in Victoria, B.C., where the winters are relatively mild. Most Canadian youngsters are on skates when they're five or six. When I first got on the ice, I was about 13," Joe told Stan and Shirley Fischler in *Heroes and History*. "I made my high school hockey team [at St. Michael's] and even though we only played about eight games all winter, we practised quite a lot. I was playing right wing then, and was one of the last ones to make the team. As the season went on, I improved and ended up playing centre." Primeau scored a goal and an assist during that season. "Eventually, I finished school and tried out for the Marlboros, a junior a team run by Frank Selke. I played two seasons with the Marlboros and then one year of Senior hockey."

Primeau joined the Toronto Maple Leafs during their first full season (1927–28), but he really hit his stride only when he was paired with Charlie Conacher and Harvey Jackson on what would become known as the Kid Line. In 1930–31, the trio assaulted opposing goaltenders — "Primeau made the bullets and Jackson and Conacher fired them," laughed Tommy Gaston in *A Fan for All Seasons*. A Maple Leaf season-ticket holder since the late 1920s, Gaston fondly remembered watching Primeau play. "'Gentleman Joe,' now there was a classy player! Boy, was he a smooth skater. And unselfish, too. He was happy to let Jackson and Conacher score the goals. He'd skate from his own blue line to the other team's blue line with the puck, then when the opposing team came at him, he would dish off to one of his linemates and they'd go in to score." That season, Primeau led the NHL in assists and Conacher led the league in goals. In 1931–32, Jackson won the NHL scoring title with 53 points, Primeau was second with 50, and Conacher was fourth with 48 — edged out of third by Howie Morenz's 49-point season. Their offensive heroics led the Leafs to a Stanley Cup championship.

A tenacious checker and great playmaker, Primeau earned the nickname "Gentleman Joe" designation because of his clean play. In 1931–32, he was awarded the Lady Byng Trophy for sportsmanship.

Primeau retired after the 1935–36 season, at the age of 30, and moved full time into his business interests as president of Joe Primeau Block (later known, via a merger, as Primeau Argo Block, with five plants across Canada). During his playing career, he accumulated 243 points in 310 NHL games, including 66 goals and 177 assists.

During the 1940s, Joe coached the Royal Canadian Air Force team, then was persuaded to helm the St. Michael's Majors. "We reached the Memorial Cup final three years in a row, winning it twice [1945 and 1947] and losing out in the last three minutes of the seventh game in the other series," Primeau recalled in *Heroes and Hockey*.

Joe Primeau starred as a player at St, Mike's, then returned to coach the Junior 'A' Majors. As a coach, he guided the Majors to the Memorial Cup championship, the Toronto Marlboros to an Allan Cup championship, and the Toronto Maple Leafs to a Stanley Cup championship.

On the basis of this success, Conn Smythe tapped Primeau to add the Toronto Marlboros Senior team to his coaching portfolio, and he joined the team in 1947–48. They lost the OHA Senior championship to Hamilton, but won the Allan Cup in 1950. Primeau graduated to the NHL as a coach in 1950–51, winning the Stanley Cup with the Toronto Maple Leafs in his first season. It gave Primeau the extraordinary distinction of winning the Memorial Cup, the Allan Cup, and the Stanley Cup as a coach, the only person in hockey history to accomplish that feat.

"He knew everything there was to know about the game," claimed Tim Horton, who touted Primeau as the finest coach he ever had. "We listened to every word he had to say, even though he never raised his voice. He got a great deal out of us because of his attitude. Actually, it would have been embarrassing for him to start shouting at us because we would have thought he had suddenly been taken ill."

In 1963, Joe Primeau was inducted into the Hockey Hall of Fame. He died on May 14, 1989, leaving behind an immense legacy as a gentleman and a champion.

42
Kitchener-Waterloo Warrior — Bobby Bauer

To fully understand the Bauer family's commitment to both religion and sports, it is important to understand the dedication of family patriarch Sir Edgar Bauer.

Edgar and Bertha Bauer, married in 1912, raised a family of 11 children in a large home across from the family business. Bauer Industries, started by Edgar's father in 1888 and originally a manufacturer of cotton felt and batts for horse-drawn carriages, today is one of the world's leading manufacturers of thermal and soundproofing materials for the automotive industry. Edgar became known as an excellent businessman and served, through the decades, as the firm's president, general manager, and chairman of the board.

But it wasn't all about work for Edgar. Every winter, he built a large rink behind the family home, and it became a natural gathering spot for the neighbourhood children. Of course, the Bauer children were already a team unto themselves. As his boys began to excel more and more in sports, Edgar took on various executive positions in Waterloo sporting organizations and the Waterloo Young Men's Club. He was also a separate school board trustee and a city councillor between 1922 and 1925.

A man of great faith, Edgar Bauer was also very involved in the spiritual activities in his community, including St. Louis Roman Catholic Church (his home parish), St. Jerome's College, the Knights of Columbus, the Holy Name Society, and the League of Sacred Heart, and was a key member of the committee that brought Carmelite nuns to the area. In 1957, Pope Pius XII made Bauer a Knight Commander of St. Sylvester to recognize his enormous contributions to the Church and its schools.

Given the role Edgar played as a community leader, the way his children followed in his footsteps should come as no surprise.

Bobby Bauer was born February 16, 1915, in Waterloo. After playing city hockey in the Kitchener-Waterloo area, 15-year-old Bobby headed to Toronto to attend St. Michael's College. In 1933–34, his final season with the Majors, Bobby collected six points in 10 games through the season and played an important role in helping his team win the Memorial Cup, scoring 10 goals and 15 points in 13 games. That squad included future NHL stars Reg Hamilton, Art Jackson, Pep Kelly, and Nick Metz. Bobby's younger brother, Frank, was a substitute on that team, and served as mayor of Waterloo in 1954–55.

In 1934–35, Bobby moved back to Kitchener and played a season of Junior with the Greenshirts. Also on that team were defenceman Woody Dumart and forward Milt Schmidt. All three were signed by the Boston Bruins, who placed them on a forward line together and sent them to their farm team, the Providence Reds, for seasoning in 1936–37. There, coach Albert "Battleship" Leduc dubbed them the "Sauerkrauts" because of their shared German heritage. That tag was shortened to the "Kraut Line." "We didn't mind," said Schmidt. "It was a name that kinda stuck to us."

Boston's Kraut Line was inseparable on and off the ice. Bobby Bauer, paired with linemates Milt Schmidt and Woody Dumart, led the Bruins to Stanley Cup championships in 1939 and 1941. In 1934, he led St. Michael's to its first Memorial Cup championship.

Bobby Bauer was called up to play his first NHL game on March 21, 1937, the Bruins' final game of the season. At 15:04 of the third period, he scored his first NHL goal. The Kraut Line debuted with Boston during the 1937–38 season. Bobby enjoyed a strong rookie season, leading the team in goals with 20 and finishing second on the team in points to Bill Cowley. The Bruins finished first in the NHL that season.

The Kraut Line helped the Bruins dominate the NHL during the late 1930s and early 1940s. Schmidt, the centre, was a tenacious worker, equally adept at scoring, checking, and leadership. Dumart, the left winger, owned a heavy shot. Bauer, small by NHL standards at five feet, six inches and 155 pounds, was the clever playmaker. "Bobby was the brains of the line," Dumart told reporters several years ago. "He was always thinking and a very clever playmaker. He had a knack of getting between the boards and the opposing winger and making a play. He had a good shot, was a good skater and stickhandler and had a way of finding holes. He and Milt would pass the puck back and forth. I got the garbage goals." Milt Schmidt added, "Bobby was our team. He was my right arm."

In 1938–39, the Bruins finished first and proceeded to win the Stanley Cup. Bauer was selected to the NHL's Second All-Star Team. The Bruins finished first again in 1939–40, with the Kraut Line finishing first, second and third in scoring — Schmidt collected 52 points, while Dumart and Bauer rolled up 43 each.

"There are several reasons why we had success that year," explains Schmidt. "The three of us roomed together. We had one big room, so that we were always together. After practices, we discussed things that we should work on. After a game, we'd say. 'Well, we did this wrong or did that wrong.' There was no nightlife or anything like that. We really worked at it and I think that had more to do with the success of our line than anything else. To finish one-two-three, I don't know of any other line that did that before us and we were quite proud of the fact." Schmidt was voted to the First All-Star Team, with Dumart and Bauer both selected to the Second All-Star Team. Bobby also picked up the Lady Byng Trophy as the NHL's most gentlemanly player.

For a fourth consecutive spring, the Boston Bruins finished on top of the seven-team NHL in 1940–41. Bill Cowley led the league in scoring with 62 points, while the Kraut Line remained hotter than July. Bauer collected 39 points and finished ninth in scoring, Schmidt was 12th and Dumart was 17th. For a third consecutive year, Bauer was chosen for the NHL's Second All-Star Team and for a second straight spring was awarded the Lady Byng Trophy. The Bruins swept the Red Wings in four straight in the Stanley Cup final. Bobby Bauer scored the Cup-winning goal at 8:43 of the second period in Game Four.

In February 1942, all three members of Boston's Kraut Line enlisted with the Royal Canadian Air Force. The three were among the first NHL players to join the military. On February 10, they played their last NHL game before heading off to Ottawa to await further instructions. That night, the Bruins easily dumped the Montreal Canadiens, 8–1. The Kraut Line combined for an astounding 22 points. At the final buzzer, an unusual and highly emotional event took place at the Boston Garden. "In spite of how tough we were playing against one another, after the game was over, both Montreal and Boston players hoisted us on their shoulders and carried us off the ice while the organist played 'Auld Lang Syne,'" recalls Milt Schmidt.

Bauer, Schmidt and Dumart played together as a unit for Ottawa's RCAF Flyers of the Quebec Senior Hockey League and helped the team win the Allan Cup before flying overseas.

In today's more sensitive environment, a nickname like the Kraut Line would never exist; and while no one gave it a second thought before the outbreak of World War II, it did become a bit of a touchy subject. "When we went into the service in 1942, they held contests in Boston to do away with the Kraut Line name," explains Schmidt. "The person who won called us the 'Buddy Line,' but it didn't last very long," he laughs. A newspaper tried to call the line the "Kitchener Kids," but that didn't last, either.

Although away from NHL action for almost four years, the Kraut Line showed upon its return that it hadn't lost a step. All three finished in the NHL's top 10 scorers in 1946–47, with Bauer enjoying a career year — 30 goals, 24 assists, and 54 points. He was elected to the Second All-Star Team again and won the Lady Byng for a third time. Then, seemingly at the peak of his hockey talents, Bobby ended his NHL career. He returned to the Kitchener area and entered the skate business, while coaching the Junior 'A' Guelph Biltmore Mad Hatters. Later that year, Bauer regained his amateur status and played Senior hockey with the Kitchener-Waterloo Dutchmen, leading the team to the finals in three consecutive springs between 1948 and 1950.

Bauer did return to the NHL for one final, celebrated contest. On March 18, 1952, he rejoined his mates on the Kraut Line for one last time. That night, the Boston Bruins honoured all three players by retiring their numbers. Early in the game, Bauer fed a pass to Dumart at centre ice, who skated in and fired a shot on goal. The save was made, but the rebound came out just outside the crease and Schmidt pounced on the puck and drove it into the net. Dumart immediately grabbed the puck and handed it to Schmidt. It was Milt's 200th career goal and, appropriately, earned with the linemates with whom he had enjoyed his most glorious moments. The Boston faithful roared like they hadn't done in years. Bauer later added a goal of his own.

Bobby Bauer's career statistics, though good, don't tell the whole story. In 327 regular-season NHL games, he scored 123 goals and assisted on 137 for 260 points. Fittingly, he was assessed just 36 penalty minutes during his career. But the story that sustains is his contribution to the Kraut Line, arguably one of the best lines in NHL history and a key reason why the Bruins dominated the NHL prior to World War II.

Bauer continued his involvement in hockey, coaching the Kitchener-Waterloo Dutchmen for a number of years. Beginning in 1952, he assumed the role of president, general manager, and coach of the team, and under his tutelage, they won two Allan Cup championships.

In 1956, the Allan Cup title earned the Dutchmen the right to represent Canada at the Olympic Winter Games. The Soviet Union was participating in the Winter Olympics for the first time and had a team entered in the hockey tournament. Olympic rules demanded that any athlete who had ever played as a professional was excluded from competition, so several former pros who had been reinstated as amateurs for OHA competition with the Dutchmen needed to be replaced. Bauer had no alternative but to drop former NHLers Clare Martin, Jackie Hamilton, and three others and replace them with Junior 'B' players. In that Olympic tournament in Cortina during 1956, the USSR took the gold medal, with the United States collecting silver and Bauer's Dutchmen claiming bronze. It was the worst showing in Canada's Olympic hockey history to that date. Nevertheless, the Dutchmen were greeted by 4,000 fans when they returned to Kitchener, and the city hosted a civic celebration in their honour.

The Dutchmen again represented Canada again at the 1960 Winter Olympics in Squaw Valley, California. This time, it wasn't because they were the Senior champions of Canada — in fact, the Whitby Dunlops had earned that title. But the Dunlops declined to take part in the Olympics, and the Dutchmen were invited to take their place.

Hall of Fame netminder Bill Durnan had coached the team in 1958–59 and had started the next season behind the bench, but resigned early in 1959–60. Bauer stepped in, and the Dutchmen had a strong tournament, earning the silver medal while the United States took the gold and the Soviet Union collected bronze.

Following the Olympic tournament, Bobby and Father David Bauer talked extensively about the Olympic experience, and it was these discussions that planted the seeds for the creation of a national team to represent Canada at international tournaments.

After retiring as coach, Bauer continued as president of the Dutchmen. He later was a director of the junior Kitchener Rangers and, with old pal Woody Dumart, was a partner in a hockey stick manufacturing company.

Then, while playing golf at Kitchener's Westmount Club, Bauer suffered a heart attack and died on September 16, 1964. He was just 49 years of age.

The Kraut Line was reunited, figuratively, once again in 1996, when Bobby Bauer was inducted posthumously into the Hockey Hall of Fame. Schmidt had been inducted in 1961, and Dumart in 1992.

43
Talent With Intensity — Ted Lindsay

Given that his father was an outstanding goaltender in the early decades of the 20th century, it is reasonable to assume that hockey talent was encoded in Ted Lindsay's DNA. Bert Lindsay was a netminder for the Renfrew Millionaires of the National Hockey Association (NHA), the Victoria Aristocrats of the Pacific Coast Hockey Association (PCHA), and the Montreal Wanderers, who straddled the last days of the NHA and the birth of the National Hockey League. Bert played his final season in 1918–19 with the Toronto Arenas.

But as fine a goalie as Bert was, his most memorable contribution to hockey will remain his son, Ted.

"My first pair of skates was given to me by a neighbour named Mrs. Brady, who gave me her husband's skates," smiles Ted, reminiscing about early winters in Kirkland Lake, Ontario. "They were naturally too big for me, but I put them on and in my little imagination, I would skate from one end of the rink to the other and across the rink in her backyard. When my dad saw that, he decided I would get a pair of skates of my own. At that time, a pair of skates would cost $4.75. You couldn't even afford $4.75 for a pair of skates, but my dad somehow found the money. Then I started playing. One year led to another year, but I still never dreamed of playing in the NHL, even though we used to listen to Foster Hewitt out of Toronto on Saturday nights.

"But I was not necessarily a Toronto fan. In Kirkland Lake on a clear, cold night, you could pick up a strong Detroit station called WJR, and in the mid-1930s we would listen to them and follow a couple of tough guys named Jack Stewart and Jimmy Orlando — both defencemen. They played my kind of hockey, and that's how I became a Red Wing fan, not ever thinking I'd play for them. I just liked those fellows."

Ted Lindsay earned Hall of Fame entry for an outstanding career as one of the premier left wingers of all time.

Ted ended up playing his Junior hockey with St. Michael's of the OHA. "I was going to go to St. Pat's in Ottawa. Gus Mortson and I had grown up together in Kirkland Lake and played for Holy Name Juveniles. We beat a very good Port Colborne hockey club, captained by Ted Kennedy. The next year, Gus and I decided to go to St. Mike's."

Lindsay's rights didn't belong to the Toronto Maple Leafs when he joined St. Mike's, and the club missed out on a chance to sign him through a misunderstanding. The story begins with a fluke injury Ted suffered in his St. Mike's debut against the Marlboros in 1943. "My calf got cut. Gus Mortson was playing defence and Jimmy Thomson [ironically, Mortson's future defence partner] was playing for the Marlboros. [Thomson] was going down the ice and Gus put his hip out. Jimmy was a big guy and was skating hard. He spun Gus around on one skate like he was a figure skater and the back of Gus's skate punctured my calf muscle just back of the shinpad. I ended up right on the ice with nothing but blood. They took me from there to the infirmary at St. Mike's. The doctor fixed it all up. I had to keep it elevated to keep the swelling out."

As it turned out, the father of Tom "Windy" O'Neill — a St. Mike's alumnus who was playing for the Leafs that season — had noticed Lindsay and decided to alert the Leaf front office. Without naming any names, he made it known that there was a promising young forward in the Majors' lineup. Intrigued by the tip, Frank Selke and Hap Day decided to attend the game at Maple Leaf Gardens.

Lindsay continues: "They went out, but I was on my back in the infirmary. There was a young guy named Joe Sadler on the team. He was a great skater and could put the puck in the net. He got a goal and a couple of assists, so it was natural for them to think this was the forward [Mr. O'Neill was] talking about. They put him on their [negotiation] list and forgot all about it. When I came back from my injury and went home for Christmas break, I think I had one assist. No one was looking at Lindsay to be a prospect in the NHL. But when I got home for Christmas, we had 10 days off and I skated as many hours as I could every day. When I came back after the New Year, things just fell into place. I was scoring goals, we were winning games and I was getting into fights and winning more than I was losing.

"One night, I came out of the old Barton Street Arena in Hamilton and a white-haired man in the intersection said, 'You Ted Lindsay?' I had my hockey bag over my shoulder and I said, 'Yes sir.' He said, 'I'm Carson Cooper, chief scout of the Detroit Red Wings.' He said, 'Did you ever think about playing pro?' My eyes went wide and I said, 'Yes sir. And as a matter of fact, Detroit is my favourite team.' He said, 'I'm going to put you on our list, but I have to check.'

"That's how I became a Red Wing and not a Maple Leaf. If I hadn't gotten injured, I probably would have wound up playing for the Maple Leafs. They had a pretty good hockey team at that time and Detroit was in the process of rebuilding. It gave me a better opportunity and worked out very well. I've often thought about it — I wonder how it would have changed my life. It would have changed my life family-wise, business-wise. I probably would have married a Canadian girl instead of an American girl. We just follow the path put in front of us."

After St. Mike's lost to the Oshawa Generals in the OHA Junior final that season, Oshawa added Lindsay, Mortson and David Bauer to their roster for the Memorial Cup final against the Trail Smoke Eaters. The Generals, coached by former Maple Leafs star Charlie Conacher, won the series. Mortson and Lindsay, of course, went on to fine NHL careers, while Bauer joined the seminary and, as Father David Bauer, coached St. Mike's to a Memorial Cup championship in 1961.

Lindsay joined the Detroit Red Wings for the 1944–45 season and scored 17 goals with 23 points in his rookie campaign. The fiery winger was soon placed on a line with veteran Sid Abel and newcomer Gordie Howe. The trio got tagged as the Production Line and was one of the highest-scoring trios of that era. In 1947–48, Ted led the NHL with 33 goals. But in 1949–50, the trio dominated more than usual, and Lindsay won the Art Ross Trophy as the NHL's leading scorer. "Winning the scoring championship was a team thing. In this case, it was actually a line thing. The Production Line of Sid at centre ice and Gordie on the right side and myself at left wing, we were one, two, three in scoring. I happened to be leading it so it was a wonderful thrill." But there was one thing more important than awards to Ted: "The only thing I was concerned about was winning."

During his first 13 seasons in Detroit, Ted was named to the NHL's First All-Star Team on eight occasions and to the Second Team, once. More importantly, the Red Wings won the Stanley Cup four times. "You're playing with the best hockey players in the world and you're playing against the best hockey players in the world. It was as great thrill."

While orchestrating a player's association that pre-dated the National Hockey League Players' Association (NHLPA) by 10 years, Ted was ostracized by Detroit's general manager, Jack Adams, and sent to the Chicago Black Hawks with Glenn Hall in July 1957 for Hank Bassen, Forbes Kennedy, Johnny Wilson, and a defence prospect named Ray Preston. Although he spent three seasons in Chicago, they were torturous years for Ted.

In spite of his star status in the NHL, Ted Lindsay never forgot his roots, and frequently returned to his alma mater.

"I went to Chicago for three years but I was never a Black Hawk. I was treated well by the fans and by management, but I had mediocre years. I still had a Red Wing on my forehead, on my backside, and over my heart. I was existing, nothing more. I was still a Red Wing at heart," he admits.

After retiring in 1960, Lindsay was coaxed out of retirement and played one final season with his beloved Red Wings in 1964–65. In 1,068 NHL games during the regular season, Ted Lindsay scored 379 goals and 472 assists for 851 points, making him the highest-scoring left winger to that date. Equally telling of his brand of play, though, are the 1,808 penalty minutes. During the playoffs, Ted scored 47 goals, added 49 assists, and totalled 96 points in 133 games.

In 1966, Ted was elected to the Hockey Hall of Fame. "I feel very honoured to have been voted into the Hall of Fame. It's something they can't take away from me."

44
A Dash of Red Mixed with Double Blue — Red Kelly

When Leonard Kelly arrived in the world on July 9, 1927, it was assumed that he would one day take over the family's Simcoe, Ontario, farm, following in the his father's footsteps. But the boy they called "Red" showed skills that set the course of his life in a different direction.

"We didn't have artificial ice," Red explains in regards to his earliest hockey memories. "They only had natural ice and open-air ponds, so you'd play hockey out on the ponds. You'd go out a few miles to the cedar swamp to play by the tracks.

"You'd play hockey in the arena at Port Dover and also in the arena at Simcoe. They usually wouldn't get ice there until just before Christmastime and it wouldn't last too long because the weather would get mild and the ice would thaw, so we wouldn't get a lot of skating.

"I think I played just three games of Midget because the ice melted and we didn't get a chance to play any more," he chuckles. "It's a little different today."

Red grew up a fan of the Toronto Maple Leafs, and recalls listening intently to Foster Hewitt's broadcasts. "I'd have my ear right up by the radio and listen to [the play of] Red Horner and [King] Clancy. You imagined yourself as a Leaf — Foster Hewitt made the games really great. Red Horner had red hair and I had red hair. I imagined myself being Red Horner, but I never played the game like him." Horner led the NHL in penalty minutes in eight consecutive seasons between 1932–33 and 1939–40, while Kelly won the Lady Byng Trophy as the NHL's most gentlemanly player on four occasions. "One time, I scored eight goals or some dang thing in one of the games and they nicknamed me. Because of the red hair, they started calling me 'Red.'"

Kelly might have realized his dream of playing with the Maple Leafs sooner than he eventually did. "There was a bird-dog scout up in Port Dover, Gerry Karges. He was originally out of the Kitchener area and he was working at our farm," Red recalls. "He said that he could get me into the Maple Leafs' training camp down at St. Catharines. We were working together out in the field and I got excited, but it didn't happen. At the last minute, he said he wasn't able to get me in there."

Although disappointed, the Kelly family, staunch Roman Catholics, encouraged Red to move to Toronto to continue his education. He was the third generation of Kellys to attend St. Michael's, and so wonderful was the experience for each one that later, Red's son Patrick enrolled at St. Mike's.

Kelly's hockey skills developed exponentially while at St. Mike's. "I got three times the skating there in one year that I would get back home," he says. "It was fantastic education-wise and hockey-wise and preparing you for life."

Playing left wing, Kelly was on the team that won the OHA's Midget championship in 1943–44. Most of that team advanced to the Buzzers the next year. "We won the 'B' championship with Father Flanagan," he recalls, and then a wide smile breaks out across Red's jovial face. "I think the greatest speech I ever had in the coach's room was at St. Mike's. The coach was Father Flanagan. We played awful in the first period. He came in, walked the length of the room, and everything was silent. Then, he turned and walked out again. All you could hear were the footsteps on the wooden floor and he slammed

Leonard "Red" Kelly played an integral role in a Sutherland Cup win with the Buzzers in 1945 and a Memorial Cup victory in 1947 with the Majors he followed that with an NHL career that included four Stanley Cup championships as a member of the Detroit Red Wings and another four with the Toronto Maple Leafs.

A studious looking Red Kelly (second row from the top, extreme left) poses for his 1945 class photograph. In the same form were teammates Ed Sandford (back row, fourth from left) and Les Costello (second row from bottom, fifth from left).

the door. He never said a word. Never said a word! But we got the message. We knew we had to move!"

The nucleus of the 1945 Memorial Cup champion St. Michael's team had turned professional by the time the 1945-46 season was about to commence, but the Buzzers moved up en masse and eliminated any concerns that the school wouldn't be able to ice a competitive Junior 'A' squad. Buzzer linemates Red Kelly, Ed Harrison, and Ed Sandford all became Majors, but didn't remain together through the entire Junior 'A' campaign.

Faced with a shortage of defencemen caused by the departure of Gus Mortson and Jim Thomson, coach Joe Primeau responded by converting Kelly to a blueliner. "Joe had seen how strong he was, how good with the stick and how smart in getting the puck out of the end zone," recalled Father Hugh Mallon in a September 1952 letter. Under the tutelage of Ted McLean, Kelly became an outstanding defenceman. On the Detroit blue line, he was part of four Stanley Cup championships and a Norris Trophy honoree; after a 1960 trade to Toronto, he was moved up to centre and played a role in four more championships.

The Majors returned to the Memorial Cup final in 1946, but lost a heartbreaking series to the Winnipeg Monarchs that went the full seven games. The *Ottawa Journal* noted that Kelly, playing with an injured leg, was the most popular player with the Gardens crowd. In 1947, the Majors went west to sweep Moose Jaw in four straight and reclaim the Memorial Cup.

Although many of his teammates were already property of the Toronto Maple Leafs, Kelly had not been signed by the team before he arrived at St. Mike's. Unbeknownst to him, one of Toronto's rivals had spotted him and put in a claim. "The first thing I knew anything was when I was playing Junior 'B,' I got a call from the principal, and he said there was a Detroit scout there, so would I come down, he'd like to meet with me. So I went down and Carson Cooper was there. He had me on the Detroit [negotiating] list, which I didn't even know, and he wanted me to sign so they could put me on the next list. I was tickled pink that anybody wanted me. I didn't hesitate about signing!"

After winning the Memorial Cup with St. Mike's, Detroit invited Kelly to their training camp in the fall of 1947. "The first training camp I ever went to was that first year. It was in Kitchener-Waterloo. They had put in new ice but were having problems with it, so instead of two practices a day, we would only skate early in the morning," Kelly told *The Hockey News*. While other Red Wing hopefuls pursued various activities to fill their time, Red drove home. "I lived in nearby Simcoe, so I'd go back every day and help on my father's farm."

Detroit was a powerhouse at the time, and it seemed unlikely that the young defenceman would make the team, which already boasted Doug McCaig, Bill Quackenbush, Leo Reise, and "Black Jack" Stewart, but the 20-year-old Kelly made the squad. "I was slated to go down to Indianapolis or Omaha — one of the farm teams. When training camp ended, they said I was going to Detroit as the fifth defenceman. When you were a fifth defenceman in those days, four played and the fifth one only got in occasionally."

But fate intervened. "At Christmastime, Doug McCaig broke his leg and I got to play on a regular basis. They thought I could do the job and when Doug got better, they traded him to Chicago. My partner was Bill Quackenbush. We roomed together on the road. I was the rookie, so I had to close the window in the morning when it was cold. But it was a great experience playing with those all-star defencemen. You learned a lot right off the bat."

Kelly laughs at one other memory. "Squib Walker [Toronto's head scout] bet Carson Cooper a hat that I wouldn't play 20 games in the NHL," he smirks. "I'm glad Cooper won the bet!"

The transition from Junior to the NHL was made easier with a solid grounding in hockey fundamentals. "You learn different things from each coach," explains Kelly. "Father Flanagan taught skating and speed, and Joe Primeau was more about handling the puck and passing and things like that. Tommy Ivan was quite similar to Joe Primeau in his manner. Gentleman Joe could really teach you. He taught me how to move from forward to defence and how to turn to take the guy coming down against you at 30 miles per hour when you're backing up at 10. He never shouted, never ranted and raved. He was very quiet. Tommy Ivan didn't teach me the things that Joe did, but Tommy Ivan's manner was much like Joe's — never shouted, never ranted and raved. Very quiet, but very authoritative, too. I was lucky. Tommy knew the systems and he trained you in those systems: how to play your position, where to play. I was lucky to have those kinds of coaches. I never had to play in the minors."

One of the lessons Primeau taught the future Lady Byng Trophy winner comes as a surprise. "I had a temper; I have red hair," laughs Red. "I was the welterweight boxing champ at St. Mike's. I could take care of myself. Joe Primeau taught me you don't win games in the penalty box. You've got to stay on the ice. Players would try to get you off the ice sometimes but you're more valuable to a team when you're on the ice."

Kelly broke in with a team that finished first in the NHL seven years in a row, and won the Stanley Cup in 1950, 1952, 1954, and 1955. He was named to the NHL's First All-Star Team six times and the Second Team twice during his time in Detroit. Feeling that Red's best days were behind him, Detroit GM Jack Adams traded him to the New York Rangers on February 5, 1960, but the deal was dissolved when he refused to report. "It was nothing against New York, I just didn't want to play there," explains Kelly. Instead, five days later, the Toronto Maple Leafs and Detroit Red Wings exchanged St. Michael's Majors alumni. In an act that the *Toronto Sun* recently described as "trading a rowboat for a battleship," Marc Reaume was sent to Detroit while Kelly arrived in Toronto. In fairness, Adams had little leverage at that point. He had admired Reaume, and knowing that Red Kelly was gone one way or another, accepted the trade.

Kelly discovered the Fountain of Youth in Toronto, playing centre for the Leafs until retiring at the end of the 1966–67 season. As a Leaf, he collected 20 or more goals three times and contributed to Stanley Cup championships in 1962, 1963, 1964, and 1967. Remarkably, at the same time, Kelly served three years as a member of Parliament, commuting between Toronto and Ottawa.

After the 1967 championship, Kelly moved into coaching, spending 10 seasons with Los Angeles, Pittsburgh, and Toronto.

In 1,316 regular-season games through 20 NHL seasons, Red Kelly scored 281 goals and added 542 assists for 823 points. Playoff activity added 33 more goals and 59 assists for 92 points in 164 games. He became an Honoured Member of the Hockey Hall of Fame in 1969.

45
Hockey's Hercules – Tim Horton

Amongst hockey fans and those just pulling into the drive-thru for a double-double and a cruller, few are aware that Tim was not Horton's given name. While awaiting his birth, his mother always referred to him by that name, but she was too ill to attend the christening and was later astonished to discover that her husband had named the baby Miles Gilbert Horton. "He was always Tim to relatives and friends, and later to his many fans," wrote Lori Horton. "Except for certain documents and the odd piece of official business, Tim's given names were never used."

Tim was bigger and stronger than the other neighbourhood boys in Cochrane, Ontario, and he bullied them over the years. "It was something Tim had a guilt complex about, even as an adult," explained his wife in *In Loving Memory: A Tribute to Tim Horton*. "He started going to church, all by himself, at age 12, in a conscious effort to change his ways. Even at that young age, he recognized that spirituality was a necessary part of a well-rounded life, and he continued to attend Sunday services throughout his life."

The Copper Cliff Redmen of 1946–47 featured two legends in the making: George Armstrong and Tim Horton. Armstrong had already signed a C-Form with the Toronto Maple Leafs and appeared to be headed to Toronto to attend Grade 12 at St. Michael's College the next season. But curiously, while still in Grade 11, Armstrong left Sudbury High School without finishing the school year. Instead of St. Mike's, Armstrong joined the Stratford Kroehlers of the OHA Junior 'A' loop for 1947–48.

Charlie Cerre, a St. Michael's Old Boy, had taken a teaching position at Sudbury High School after the Second World War. In addition, he coached football and hockey and ran intramural sports programs for the students. While in Toronto, he regularly visited St. Mike's, and whenever the opportunity presented itself, he recommended outstanding athletes from the Sudbury area to St. Michael's.

Such was the case with Tim Horton. When Armstrong decided not to attend St. Michael's, Cerre knew that there was a scholarship available at the school and worked diligently to persuade Tim to consider St. Mike's. Horton had also signed a C-form with the Leafs, so it all fit together well in principle.

In practice, there was a sticking point. In a letter to Cerre dated June 16, 1947, Father Mallon wrote, "You might tell him [Horton] that as far as the scholarship goes, I can look after that, but Father Bondy demurred somewhat over the fact that he is not a Catholic. Personally, I think it does us no harm to have a couple [of Protestant boys attending the school] as long as they are of good character and come well recommended, but I cannot always get others to agree with me."

But it wasn't just Horton's religious denomination that concerned Father Mallon. "Did [scout] Bob Wilson change his mind about him because of the glasses? We heard that the pro scouts lost interest in him as a prospect because of his eyes." While in the NHL, Horton admitted to being all but blind on the ice; he wore thick, Clark Kent–style eyeglasses off the ice.

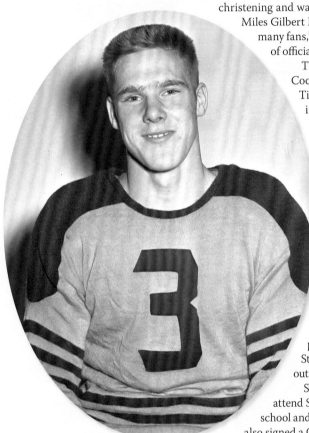

After starring at St. Mike's, Tim Horton spent parts of 24 seasons in the NHL, playing with the Toronto Maple Leafs, New York Rangers, Pittsburgh Penguins, and Buffalo Sabres before his death on February 21, 1974.

Classmates insist that Tim Horton was as hard-working in the classroom as he was on the ice. This yearbook photo shows Tim (middle row, far right) in 1948.

The obstacles were surmounted, however, and Horton was admitted to St. Michael's College School in the fall of 1947. If not always successful as a student, he was, if nothing else, diligent. "Tim's scholastic record is not that of a top-flight student, but it is that of a student taking every course he can, suiting up for every exam, passing some and flunking some," recalled Father O'Brien. Horton's St. Michael's roommate, Ted Carlton, stated: "For a hockey player, he tried hard. I met a lot of hockey players during my years at St. Mike's and some of them just did not give a damn about school and went through the motions."

Although Tim wasn't Roman Catholic, according to teammate and roommate (in 1948–49) Don Rope, he was infused with a great deal of faith and made a habit of studying the Bible. "It was a factor in his life and in his advice to others, without ever evangelizing," Rope is quoted as saying in *Open Ice*, Douglas Hunter's biography of Horton. "He was guided by it considerably." With the rest of the school, Tim went to Mass every morning, but on Sunday, chose to attend Metropolitan United Church.

The St. Michael's Majors had a tough year in 1947–48, finishing ninth in the 10-team league, but if there was one bright light, it was Horton. He scored six goals and seven assists that season, and led the OHA's Junior 'A' loop in penalty minutes with 137. That season, he was voted the team's most valuable player.

Although the Majors missed the playoffs for a second straight season, Horton was again voted team MVP with the Majors, and he was also selected the best defenceman in the OHA Junior 'A' loop in 1948–49. He had reined in (moderately) his time in the penalty box and had increased his production, scoring nine goals and 18 assists for 27 points.

Conn Smythe set his sights on stacking the Marlboros roster in hopes of winning the 1950 Memorial Cup. He had managed to convince George Armstrong to leave Stratford for the Marlies, and was relentless in his pursuit of Danny Lewicki of the Kroehlers, whom he finally landed. Smythe also wanted Tim to move from St. Mike's to the Marlboros, but Horton balked. He was a popular student and he especially appreciated coach Joe Primeau, a man he called "the greatest coach I ever played for."

Smythe countered with a pro contract. After calling his parents, Tim decided he would sign a contract and report to the Pittsburgh Hornets of the American Hockey League. When Hall of Fame defenceman Eddie Shore saw Horton playing in the AHL, he proclaimed, "He's the best-looking superstar I've seen in 10 years. He carries the puck, he stickhandles, there's nothing he can't do." On March 26, 1950, Horton was summoned from Pittsburgh to join the Maple Leafs for the last game of the NHL season, a 5–3 loss to the New York Rangers. Horton next appeared in the NHL in 1951–52, when he played four games, but by 1952–53, he was a full-time Maple Leaf.

While playing with the Leafs, Horton was the ringleader behind a lot of harmless shenanigans. "He liked to have fun," laughs Dave Keon. "He wanted everybody to be part of the fun and made sure that everybody was involved." Tim had a special affinity for the boys from St. Mike's, pranking Dick Duff, Keon, and Frank Mahovlich on a regular basis. "He was fun to be around," Keon adds. "He was a great player, teammate, and friend."

During his Toronto days, Horton was named to the NHL's First All-Star Team in 1964, 1968, and 1969, and to the Second Team in 1954, 1963, and 1967. Twice he was runner-up for the Norris Trophy as the NHL's best defenceman, finishing second to Pierre Pilote in 1964 and to Bobby Orr in 1969.

Punch Imlach had the highest regard for Tim Horton, who anchored the blue line as Toronto won the Stanley Cup in 1962, 1963, 1964, and 1967. "I have always had a special feeling for Tim Horton. When I took over in Toronto in 1958, he had already been a pro hockey player for nine years, and although he was known as the strongest man in the NHL, he didn't have a mean bone in his body," Imlach wrote in *Heaven and Hell in the NHL*. "He always called me George. 'Aw, George,' he'd say with that shy grin of his, on top of a neck that looked like part of a fire hydrant. "Don't worry, we'll win it for you.'"

But the two strong personalities occasionally butted heads, as Imlach explained in his earlier book, *Hockey Is a Battle*. "He never said much. Or listened much, for that matter. He's a stubborn so-and-so. The story with him is that he just keeps on getting better all the time, so naturally, he has faith in the way he does things."

Horton was traded to the New York Rangers in March 1970. The Pittsburgh Penguins claimed him in the 1971 Intra-League Draft. He played two seasons in Buffalo, beginning in 1972–73. In 1,446 regular-season NHL games. Tim scored 115 goals and 403 assists for 518 points. He added 11 goals and 39 assists for 50 points in 126 playoff contests.

On February 20, 1974, the Buffalo Sabres played the Maple Leafs at Maple Leaf Gardens. Horton, playing with a cracked jaw, played just the first two periods of the contest, a 4–2 Toronto win, but nevertheless was selected as the game's third star. On his drive back to Buffalo early the next morning, Tim's Ford Pantera went off the road. Tim Horton was dead, just 44 years old.

In the eulogy, delivered before hundreds of mourners at Oriole-York Mills United Church, family friend Gordon Griggs commented: "To Tim, life was a gift from God. He gave of himself in the game of hockey more than was required of any athlete. He shared the glory of a Stanley Cup with his family and friends. He accepted his gift of life, this brimming love that he possessed and shared with all those who could celebrate with him."

The pallbearers were George Armstrong, Bob Baun, Dick Duff, Billy Harris, Dave Keon, and Allan Stanley, six of his closest friends from the Maple Leafs' dynasty years.

"Everybody would have loved to see the guy around for a long, long time, just to enjoy his company," said Dick Duff. "He touched lots of people in different walks of life, and stayed the same through it all. He left his mark."

46
The Big M Wore the Big M — Frank Mahovlich

When most people think of Timmins, Ontario, two words spring to mind: gold and cold. Hockey fans know that there's more to the picture. And the town of Schumacher, located within the sprawling Timmins city limits, has sent an inordinate number of players to the National Hockey League, but none as celebrated as Frank Mahovlich.

"I was 12 years old and scouts had already started knocking on my door," smiles the distinguished St. Michael's College alumnus. One local scout who noticed the outstanding young Bantam hockey player on the local rink in Timmins was Archie Moynihan, who immediately notified the Detroit Red Wings, the team for which he scouted on a part-time basis. "I told them they better get a man up here in a hurry," Moynihan recalled in a 1968 interview with the *Toronto Daily Star*.

Too late. The early months of 1953 saw fierce competition for Frank Mahovlich's services. Every one of the NHL's six teams had a scout in the Timmins area, trying to convince the Mahovlich family that their boy should play for them.

Johnny Mitchell was the Red Wings' head scout. "He knocked on our door and was wearing a shirt and tie," Frank recalls. "Very seldom did anyone in Schumacher wear a shirt and tie.

"I had my face in a plate of spaghetti and my mom was downstairs. I was the only one in the kitchen. He [Mitchell] came to the door and said, 'Are your parents home, son?'" After Mitchell made his bid, other teams sent scouts, including the Montreal Canadiens and the Toronto Maple Leafs.

But it wasn't solely NHL teams that were clamouring to sign Frank. The St. Catharines TeePees, an unaffiliated Junior 'A' team (they had yet to be sponsored by the Chicago Black Hawks), saw Mahovlich as the answer to their prayers. A player of Frank's talent would elevate the team to the top of the OHA standings and draw full houses for each home game. Rudy Pilous, the team's owner and coach, offered the Mahovlich family a farm in the Niagara region if Frank would sign with the TeePees.

Amid the hysteria, Frank's father, Peter, sought the advice of managers in the mine where he toiled. Their verdict: Peter should insist on ensuring an education for his boy.

As fate would have it, on March 12, 1953, Father Faught sent a letter to the Mahovlich family on behalf of St. Michael's College. "We have been hearing down here that your son Frank is a pretty good hockey player. Would you be interested in having him continue his schooling at St. Michael's next year?"

The school was having a tryout during Easter week and invited Frank to come down to Toronto at the school's expense. "If Frank makes one of our teams for next year, he will be given a very generous spending allowance," wrote Father Faught. "We don't want Frank to come unless he is interested in the books and is willing to study. We believe that a Catholic school is the very best place for a young Catholic boy to learn his hockey, and besides, when every player on the team is going to school, it makes it a great deal easier for the boys to do well at the books."

The Toronto Maple Leafs' promise of a strong Roman Catholic education at St. Michael's College proved to be the deciding factor in Frank Mahovlich's signing with the Leafs after he was pursued relentlessly by NHL clubs.

Although not nearly as good as his mother's cooking, the cafeteria food served Frank well during his four years at St. Michael's (1953–54 to 1956–57). Mahovlich was recipient of the Albert "Red" Tilson Memorial Trophy as the Ontario Hockey League's most valuable player in 1956–57. Frank was the third Major to win the prestigious honour, following Tod Sloan in 1945–46 and Ed Sandford in 1946–47.

Meanwhile, the Red Wings thought they might have the inside track on young Frank. On March 24, head scout Johnny Mitchell wrote to fellow bird-dog Archie Moynihan: "I didn't hesitate to go to his house quietly and in a hurry. I was very impressed the way the family greeted me. I can still see his dad and I walking down to Mesich's [the family of prospect Matt Mesich, who, ironically, had played Senior hockey at St. Mike's with the Monarchs], and he gave me his promise. He looks like a gentleman who lives up to his word. You can tell him for me, Archie, that he won't regret doing any business with Mr. Adams and myself. We will be working in the best interest of his boy at all times, as this organization has in the past."

The Mahovliches were brought down to St. Catharines by the Toronto Maple Leafs, a development noted by Mitchell of Detroit. "I was able to talk with him [Peter Mahovlich Sr.] on several occasions at the arena. He promised me he hadn't made any deal with Toronto and was going to return the money they spent bringing him to St. Catharines," Mitchell wrote to Moynihan on April 17, 1953. "I had a long talk with Frank, too, and he told me he didn't know his father was coming to Toronto. He said he didn't want to play with the Maple Leafs or be connected with them in anyway. He would sooner play for Detroit and the Windsor Spitfires this coming winter."

The Red Wings could also promise Frank a quality education, according to Mitchell. "He could go to Assumption College [a Catholic school in Windsor run by the Basilian Fathers], receive his schooling and play for them [the school hockey team], forgetting about Junior 'A' hockey next winter and concentrating on his school work." Or, if he preferred, he could play for the Junior 'A' Spitfires. Either way, he would also receive $40 per week. "He [Frank] left me with the opinion he would like to play for us," Mitchell concluded.

Within months, however, Detroit moved its OHA Junior affiliate from Windsor to Hamilton. Whether the change had any bearing on the Mahovlich family's decision is unknown.

Meanwhile, at the insistence of Toronto's head scout, Bob Davidson, Father Flanagan was dispatched to Schumacher. "I remember him bringing up yearbooks," says Frank. "At that time, there were a couple of players playing with St. Mike's who were from northern Ontario. One fellow was Ronny Wallace and the other was Murray Costello. Murray ended up being a great friend of mine.

"My dad chose the Toronto Maple Leafs because of St. Michael's," states Frank. "Great tradition — Red Kelly, Tim Horton, although they had already left by the time I got there."

"The family never regretted the decision, although the reality of St. Michael's was somewhat different from the sales pitch they had been given," wrote Ted Mahovlich, Frank's son, in the biography *The Big M*. "The school lured hockey players to the Maple Leaf organization by pushing the educational benefits; however, there was a good reason why there weren't many schools with Junior 'A' teams. High school education and Junior 'A' hockey mixed like oil and water. The time commitment for Junior 'A' was demanding for any student. Even if a hockey player passed his courses, his marks were usually below what they should have been. For several years, the school looked the other way so that they, in partnership with the Maple Leafs, could reap handsome profits from the arrangement. In fairness to St. Mike's, they did offer a better chance at an education than most other scenarios. However, the bottom line was, Frank Mahovlich's scholarship was awarded so he could play hockey. If Frank, or any other player on scholarship, could benefit from the education being offered, all the better. But hockey always came first."

Frank played most of the 1953–54 season at home with the Juvenile Schumacher Lions, but played one game with the Majors, earning an assist and a minor penalty. The 15-year-old was brought in for the Majors' playoff run. "I felt I could do something right away, but I never got the chance," he admits. "In the playoffs that year against the St. Catharines TeePees, St. Mike's was playing the final game in St. Catharines. They had the lead but lost in overtime. They dressed me but I just sat on the bench. I felt that if I could have just got on that ice…"

By 1954–55, however, Frank was living in Toronto and attending St. Michael's College School. "Everything clicked right away," he says. In a pre-season exhibition game against Kitchener, Mahovlich scored three goals. "The coach at the time was Charlie Cerre. He was so amazed, he had me sit beside him on the bus on the way home and explain how I scored all those goals. I couldn't explain anything! It's just instinct!

"[Cerre] was a mathematics teacher," Frank adds. "He had systems and drew pennies on the board, but [hockey] just doesn't work that way." Although he missed half of the season with a knee injury, Mahovlich still collected 23 points in 25 contests in his first season of Junior 'A'.

In 1955–56, despite yet another knee injury, Frank still was able to connect for 24 goals and 26 assists in 30 games. In his final season of Junior, 1956–57, Mahovlich scored a league-best 52 goals plus 36 assists for 88 points in 49 games and was selected as the Red Tilson Memorial Award recipient as the league's outstanding player. "It was the highlight of my career to accept that from Joe Primeau," Frank says.

"The Toronto Maple Leafs wanted to make sure I had good coaching," he said of his years with the Majors, "so Conn Smythe asked Joe Primeau to help out." Primeau, who was occupied with running his own company, agreed to return to the school as a "coaching consultant." "Gentleman Joe was the best coach I ever had," continues Mahovlich. "He commanded respect without losing his cool, but when you made a mistake, you knew not to do it again. I learned more from him than any coach in the NHL."

Once Frank's final season of Junior had come to a conclusion, the Toronto Maple Leafs called him up for the last three games of their NHL season. Making his first NHL appearance on March 20, 1957 (a 2–1 loss to Montreal at Maple Leaf Gardens), the wide-eyed teenager realized he could play at that level. Wearing number 26, he scored a goal during his first foray into pro hockey, and by the next season, Frank was a full-time member of the Toronto Maple Leafs, winning the Calder Trophy as the NHL's best rookie.

Frank played parts of 11 seasons with Toronto, and along with fellow St. Mike's alumnus David Keon, helped lead the team from a playoff-missing squad to a dynasty. Mahovlich, now tagged "The Big M," led the Leafs in scoring in 1960–61 (84 points), 1961–62 (71), 1962–63 (73), 1964–65 (51) and 1965–66 (55 points). Eight times, he bettered the 20-goal plateau, including a 48-goal season in 1960–61. He was named to the NHL's First All-Star Team in 1961 and 1963, and to the Second Team in 1962, 1964, 1965, and 1966. During this period, Mahovlich and the Maple Leafs claimed the Stanley Cup on four occasions — 1962, 1963, 1964, and 1967.

It was no secret that the Leafs' GM/coach, Punch Imlach, didn't see eye-to-eye with his star winger, and Frank's health suffered as a result. Twice, he was hospitalized. After surprising everyone with a Stanley Cup championship in 1967, the Leafs, considered ancient in hockey terms, struggled through 1967–68. After a February cave-in that saw them lose 13 of 17 games and fall 13 points behind Boston for the fourth and final playoff berth, Leafs owner Stafford Smythe admitted defeat. "There's no point in talking trade now," he said, claiming that only the sixth-place Detroit Red Wings would have any interest in Toronto's players, but any deal between the two teams would be futile. Astonishingly, within 48 hours, Imlach pulled the trigger on a blockbuster that sent the 30-year-old Mahovlich, 24-year-old Peter Stemkowski, 20-year-old Garry Unger, and the rights to 29-year-old Carl Brewer (who had walked out on Imlach three years earlier and regained his amateur status) to the Red Wings for Floyd Smith and Norm Ullman, both 32, and Paul Henderson, who was 25 years old.

Although it was a relief for the beleaguered Mahovlich, the trade was disastrous for the Leafs, who had again sacrificed much of their youth for aging players. "That trade was all about the arrogance of Punch Imlach," Dave Keon stated in the book '67 by Damien Cox and Gord Stellick. "He traded for inferior players on another team because he was so arrogant, he felt he would make them better players. That proved not to be the case. To make matters worse, the guys from Detroit were being paid at a better rate than the Leaf guys, and that caused more resentment."

Frank Mahovlich (left) and Charlie Burns (right), both St. Mike's' alumni who went on to the NHL, thrill two young hockey hopefuls. The youngster on the left is Mike Murphy, who went on to play and coach in the NHL and is now the league's Vice-President of Hockey Operations. The boy on the right is Paul Cerre, who later played for the Buzzers, and who was the son of legendary St. Mike's player and coach Charlie Cerre.

Frank had three strong seasons in Detroit, including 1968–69, when he scored a career-best 49 goals. He was selected to the NHL's Second All-Star Team in both 1969 and 1970. But on January 13, 1971, Mahovlich was dealt to the Montreal Canadiens for Guy Charron, Billy Collins, and Mickey Redmond. In Montreal, Frank was reunited with Peter, his younger brother, for a second time. The two had enjoyed the opportunity of playing together while with the Red Wings as well. That spring, Frank was part of his fifth Stanley Cup championship. He would win a sixth in 1973.

In Montreal, Frank was playing on an offensively explosive team, and he fit in perfectly, leading the Canadiens in scoring with 96 points in 1971–72 and with 80 in 1973–74. He was a First Team All-Star selection in 1973.

When the World Hockey Association offered a great deal of money *and* the opportunity to return home to Toronto, he jumped to the Toros in 1974. When the franchise moved to Alabama as the Birmingham Bulls, Frank went with them and played out his career there.

In 1,181 regular-season NHL games over 17 seasons, Frank Mahovlich scored 533 goals and added 570 assists for 1,103 points. In 137 playoff contests, Frank added 51 goals and 67 assists for 118 points. During four WHA seasons, he played 237 more games and scored 89 goals, 143 assists, and 232 points in the regular season. In 15 WHA playoff games, he scored five goals and two assists.

Frank Mahovlich was elected to the Hockey Hall of Fame in 1981. In 1998, recognizing a career completed with class and passion, both on and off the ice, he was appointed to the Canadian Senate by Prime Minister Jean Chretien.

47
In a Class By Himself — Dick Duff

Just as prospectors combed the mineral-rich lands of northern Ontario for gold, nickel, copper and uranium, NHL scouts went north in the 1950s in search of hockey talent. And the Leafs struck the mother lode in Dick Duff. Born in Kirkland Lake in 1936, Dick came from a large Roman Catholic family. "I was one of 13 children," he says. Like most large families in northern Ontario, in the Duff household there were two things that took precedence over all others: the church and hockey, and not always in that order.

St. Michael's invited Dick and his older brother Les to an annual camp they held in Toronto during the Easter weekend. "The Leafs would pay for the ones that St. Mike's wanted and thought could play on their team," Dick says. With a laugh, he notes, "[The Majors] filled Maple Leaf Gardens for them with 15,000 people every Sunday afternoon, so they got more than paid back."

Having impressed the Leafs brass, Dick and Les were both offered the opportunity to move to Toronto to attend school — and become part of the Maple Leafs organization. "My mother was really happy when I went to St. Mike's. She knew I'd get good instruction there, which I did." Dick arrived at St. Michael's College School for Grade 10 in November 1951 and boarded at the school. "The school was an extension of my home life because my mother and father were strong Catholics," he adds.

For a 15-year-old, adapting to a new life in a new city was a challenge. "It wasn't easy when we first got here because we were young guys and it wasn't our choice to move 500 miles away from our friends and family members and board with people we didn't know." One of those who helped Dick was his coach with the Buzzers, Father Flanagan. "He had a good understanding of what the pros were going to want from me and he knew how the pro game was played." Duff clearly learned his lessons. By the next season, 1952–53, he was captain of the Buzzers and had been given a taste of Junior 'A' play with the Majors. During the regular season, Dick played in 16 games with the Majors and had five points. He also appeared in 16 playoff games, contributing 15 points.

By 1953–54, Dick was firmly established with the Majors, and went on to lead the team in both goals (35) and points (75). He led the team in scoring again in 1954–55, edging his brother with 53 points to Les's 51. On March 10, 1955, Duff played his first National Hockey League game — a scoreless tie between Toronto and Montreal.

During the 1940s and 1950s, Junior hockey was huge in Toronto, with 12,000 to 15,000 attending Saturday or Sunday afternoon games at Maple Leaf Gardens. "Junior hockey was a big part of people's entertainment in Toronto," Dick suggests. "It didn't cost a great deal of money to go and you could see the future pros play."

The school gave immense support to the Majors "The double blue and the big 'M' on the crest meant a lot," explains Duff. "The students were really behind the sports teams. We would have big pep rallies and it was a big deal to be a St. Mike's hockey player. People would save places for me to sit at lunch.

Dick Duff, playing on the Majors with his brother Les, terrorized opposing Junior netminders during the mid–1950s.

"We didn't disappoint them," he adds. "We gave them something to yell about."

There was added value in having both the St. Michael's Majors and the Toronto Marlboros play home games on the same rink as their NHL affiliate. "The guys who belonged to Detroit didn't play in the Olympia until they made it to Detroit. The guys who belonged to Chicago never saw Chicago Stadium until they went there as NHL guys. We grew up in [Maple Leaf Gardens], so we knew the feel of the building and who worked there and the reaction of the fans and how much hockey meant to them."

Like most boys who are talented hockey players, school comes a distinct second [or lower] in their lives, but Dick learned a very valuable lesson while attending St. Michael's College. "My first interest was sports and not school, but people at St. Mike's encouraged me to pursue my education," he admits. In fact, he was part of a wave of players that continued their education beyond high school. Both Dick and former teammate Murray Costello attended Assumption College, a Basilian facility in Windsor that later became the University of Windsor, where Dick earned his university degree. "We figured that by the time we were 30, we'd be out [of hockey] and we'd have to find something else to do. I thought that was great to get me away from hockey and become interested in other things."

Schooling had become a *cause célèbre* at St. Mike's in the 1950s, one that would later cause the school to withdraw from Junior 'A' competition. "Father Bauer became concerned that it was becoming harder and harder for some of the guys to finish their upper school in Grade 12 and 13. There were only a few of us that went on to play pro, so they had the obligation and responsibility to the other boys to enable them to finish Grade 12 and 13 and go on to something else."

Having earned the opportunity to play with the Maple Leafs, Dick surrendered his final season of Junior eligibility and signed with Toronto at the age of 19. He played eight full seasons for the Leafs and established himself as an exciting player who could put up points but who wouldn't back down from opponents. Duff was the Leafs' goal-scoring leader in three consecutive seasons (1956–57, 1957–58, and 1958–59), and also led Toronto in points in the latter two seasons.

With the Leafs in a slump going into the 1964 playoffs, the popular Duff was packaged with Arnie Brown, Bill Collins, Bob Nevin, and Rod Seiling and sent to the New York Rangers for Andy Bathgate and Don McKenney. Dick never fully forgave the Toronto Maple Leafs organization, but exacted a modicum of revenge when, after being traded to the Montreal Canadiens just before Christmas in 1964, he won four more Stanley Cup championships. Dick and the Canadiens won the Cup in 1965, 1966, 1968, and 1969.

In January 1970, Duff was moved to the Los Angeles Kings; then, in November, he was swapped to the expansion Buffalo Sabres, where he was reunited with Punch Imlach, his coach with the Leafs. Dick retired after eight games in the 1971–72 season, finishing with 283 goals and 289 assists for 572 points through 1,030 NHL regular-season contests. He also contributed 30 goals and 49 assists in 114 playoff games. After teaching for a handful of years, Duff returned to hockey and served as a scout, an assistant coach, and, in 1980–81, was head coach of the Maple Leafs for two games.

Elected to the Hockey Hall of Fame in 2006, Dick Duff is very proud to have spent formative years at St. Michael's College. "Whatever I needed to learn, I learned there. They helped me. They didn't care whether I was a hockey player. It was a good experience that went by quickly." He muses for a moment, then adds, "Whether it was Dave Keon or Frank Mahovlich that came after me, or Tim Horton who came before me, or Red Kelly that was ahead of him, these were all classic players. I'm quite happy to be put in their group. I thought that the NHL teams were very fortunate to get the kind of men that went to them from St. Mike's."

In his speech, delivered at the Hockey Hall of Fame at his Induction in 2006, Duff said, "St. Michael's is a special place in my journey. My years at St. Michael's are remembered fondly. Father Bauer's message was to challenge life with enthusiasm and to rely on the spirit within each of us. From a small town called Kirkland Lake to a great school called St. Michael's, and to my family and friends, thank you for caring and sharing this journey with me."

48
Smooth-Skating St. Mike's Centre – David Keon

When the Toronto Maple Leafs won the Stanley Cup in 1962, no fewer than 10 full-time members of the team had come from northern Ontario. Al Arbour, Eddie Shack, and George Armstrong came from the Sudbury area; Tim Horton, born in Cochrane, developed in the same region; Dick Duff and Larry Hillman were from Kirkland Lake; and Frank Mahovlich, Bob Nevin, and Allan Stanley were born and raised in and around Timmins. Finally, about an hour east of Kirkland Lake, on the Quebec side of the border, is Noranda, hometown of David Keon.

In 1955, Dave Keon was just 15 years of age, but his prodigious talent allowed him to play Juvenile. "I was under-age, so that meant I could go and play for whoever I wanted to, so I went and played for the Noranda Lions, who were not sponsored," explains Keon. "Prior to that, I had played for the Noranda Toilers, a Midget team sponsored by Detroit. They had a whole bunch of boys who went to play Junior in Hamilton (with the Red Wings' OHA Junior 'A' affiliate, the Tiger Cubs). The previous fall, before I started playing Juvenile, I went to Junior camp in Hamilton."

The Noranda Lions were coached by a gentleman who also did some scouting in the area for the Toronto Maple Leafs. Dave recalls the path that started him towards the National Hockey League. "The Leafs sponsored the team that year, so they had rights to everybody on the team, including Jacques Caron, who was the goaltender on that team, and myself. That's how I ended up going to Toronto."

Behind the scenes, the coach wrote an urgent letter to Toronto's chief scout, Bob Davidson, imploring the Maple Leafs to sign the young phenom. Davidson didn't waste any time, and although Detroit was also interested, Dave's parents were more receptive to Toronto's offer because of the opportunity for their son to further his education at St. Michael's College.

"St. Michael's was really one of the only places my parents felt comfortable in having me go, because I was going to live in residence. I was there with a lot of other guys who were away from home for the first time. We were all living in residence, so I think we more or less commiserated among ourselves. I do remember that the first month or so was very difficult because I had not been away from home before. It was a little bit frightening."

Dave's first cousin was Tod Sloan, who attended St. Michael's for two years beginning in 1944–45. Although there was not a great deal of conversation about the school between the cousins, Dave does remember Sloan giving him some sage advice: "Dave, whatever happens, no matter how bad things look, don't ever get discouraged."

That advice came in handy during Keon's first winter in Toronto. Arriving at St. Michael's for the 1956–57 school year, he was cut from the Junior 'A' Majors and assigned

In 1998, Dave Keon was ranked 69th on The Hockey News's *list of the top 100 NHL players of all time.*

The yearbook gives us a glimpse of a uniformed Keon in 1959, his Grade 12 year. Dave is in the back row, fourth from the left. Keon spent four seasons at St. Michael's College (1956–57 to 1959–60). His cousin Tod Sloan earlier attended the school and starred for the Majors.

to the Junior 'B' Buzzers. It prompted David to recognize that, although he was a very good offensive player, he was not yet a good professional prospect because of his inability, or disinterest, in playing the defensive parts of the game. "Two years ago, he thought he could get by on goals alone," stated Father David Bauer in a 1959 interview in *The Hockey News*. "Then, he made up his mind he'd have to learn to check in Junior hockey or spend two years in the American Hockey League learning it. He has applied himself and how he's a pretty good defensive player."

Although not alone in his praise of Father Bauer, the impact on Keon's hockey career by his mentor was especially profound. "Father Bauer had a certain idea how the game should be played and he emphasized that to the players at all times. He made the point to me that I was going to have to learn how to play the game without the puck, which meant I was going to have to check a little bit," admits David. "That was a two-and-a-half-year project for him. I was not too enamoured with that side of the game. He told me that if I figured I could score three goals a game every game I played, I wasn't going to have to learn to check.

"That was really the hallmark of all his teams, even when he was with Team Canada. There, they didn't have the greatest talent, but they worked very hard and they checked very well and most of the time, every game they played, they were in it. Those were the parameters. He impressed upon me the fact that how important it was going to be for me if I was going to play at the next level. Initially, I was not too interested in checking, but he persevered and he won out." In fact, observers of the NHL during Keon's career generally agree that he was the pre-eminent two-way forward of his era.

David played 1956–57 with the Buzzers. "The team had maybe three or four guys who were 18 or 19, but everybody else was either 15 or 16 and we ended up winning the Metro Junior 'B.' For whatever reason, we didn't continue on after we had won." That year, Father Flanagan and others at the school had decided that to play in the provincial semifinals would interfere with the players' studies, so the team the Buzzers defeated in the Metro final, the Dixie Beehives, represented the league in the all-Ontario playdowns.

After getting a brief taste of Junior 'A' play with the Majors in 1956–57, David spent three full seasons with the team, leading them in scoring in 1957–58 (50 points) and

1959–60 (71 points), and finishing just behind Jack Costello and Bruce Draper, who tied for the Majors' lead, in 1958–59. "My three years with the Majors was a good experience," says Keon. "We got to the OHA finals twice. We lost once in Peterborough and we lost in St. Catharines. Both of those teams went on to play for the Memorial Cup. Peterborough lost and St. Catharines won."

The Majors had a terrific foundation during Keon's tenure. "My first year of Junior 'A,' Gene Ubriaco, Lou Angotti, Bobby McKnight, Bob Savage, Cesare Maniago, and Darryl Sly were there, and then Larry Keenan and Bruce and Dave Draper came up [from Junior B], as did Terry O'Malley, Paul Jackson, and then Gerry Cheevers. We were fairly successful, but we never got over the hump of winning the OHA, which I had hoped for. Bob Goldham was our coach and did a good job, and Father Bauer was the general manager. Father Bauer would occasionally run practices when Bob wasn't there. And then the year after I left St. Mike's, Father Bauer became the coach and they did win the Memorial Cup.

"I always figured that once they got rid of me, they were fine!" he chuckles.

Keon, selected the best Toronto Maple Leaf ever in Mike Leonetti's *Maple Leafs Top 100: Toronto's Greatest Players of All Time*, played 1,296 regular-season games in 18 NHL seasons with the Maple Leafs and Hartford Whalers. Through that time, he scored 396 goals and an additional 590 assists for 986 points. In all that time, he served just 117 penalty minutes. In 92 NHL playoff games, David had 32 goals and 36 assists for 68 points, and had just six minutes in penalties.

Sandwiched between his terms with Toronto and Hartford, Keon spent four seasons in the rival World Hockey Association, playing with the Minnesota Fighting Saints, Indianapolis Racers, and New England Whalers. Dave played 301 regular-season WHA games and scored 102 goals and 189 assists for 291 points. He served just 20 minutes in penalties. In 36 playoff contests in the WHA, Dave scored 13 goals and 23 assists for 36 points, while serving eight minutes in the penalty box.

In 22 major-league seasons, Keon won a number of personal awards. He was the NHL's rookie of the year in 1961 and a Second Team NHL All-Star in 1962 and 1971. His gentlemanly play earned him the NHL's Lady Byng Trophy in 1962 and 1963 and the WHA's Paul Deneau Trophy in 1977 and 1978. His Toronto Maple Leafs won the Stanley Cup in 1962, 1963, 1964, and 1967, and Keon's contributions were so significant, specifically in the last Leafs championship, that he was awarded the Conn Smythe Trophy as the playoff MVP. Recognizing his extraordinary contributions to the game, Dave Keon was voted into the Hockey Hall of Fame in 1986.

"[Attending St. Michael's College] was one of the best times of my life," Keon recalls with fondness. "I wouldn't trade those years for anything. I was growing up, learning to play, living away from home, going to school — a combination of so many things.

"My parents were very strong and they had certain goals and ideas of what they wanted me to do," Dave concludes. "I was very fortunate. When I went to St. Mike's, there were a lot of priests there who were trying to mould men out of the clay that they had. There was always something to get done and they were pushing and prodding and making sure you got it done. I look back and realize I could probably have worked harder at school than I did. I did graduate Grade 12, but I could have got better marks. The discipline that we went through certainly helped, and so did the friendships among the priests, the teachers and all the people that I met who I remain friends with after all these years. Going to St. Mike's was a great experience for me, one I look back on as four of the best years of my life."

49
Instilling a Dream — Father David Bauer

Through a hundred-year hockey program that has produced an inordinate number of young men who have gone on to lead extraordinary lives, both on and off the ice, one man has risen above the rest as arguably the most exemplary representative of St. Michael's College's commitment to athletics and God.

Father David Bauer has been described as an inspirational coach, a caring educator, a master motivator, and a dreamer. He was devoted to the concept that education and hockey could mix. He viewed hockey as a means to develop a better person. He believed that building men came before building hockey players.

"We try to give our players a well-rounded education, not merely ice skills but mental and moral conditioning as well," he told reporters in 1961. "We can't help but be better off in the long run."

Dave was the third hockey-playing brother to attend St. Michael's College from the family home in Kitchener, Ontario. Bobby, nine years Dave's senior, was part of the school's first Memorial Cup championship in 1934 and went on to be inducted into the Hockey Hall of Fame after an outstanding career with the Boston Bruins. Another brother, Frank, was a spare player with the Majors in 1933–34.

On the advice of Bobby Bauer, the Boston Bruins had tried to sign Dave and have him join their newly launched Eastern Hockey League farm team, the Boston Olympics, in 1940–41, but Bauer instead chose to attend St. Michael's College School. The family patriarch, Sir Edgar Bauer, had instilled in his sons the idea that playing hockey was fine and good, but only after completing a proper education. Dave took the advice to heart and became a member of the St. Michael's Majors in 1942. A talented winger, Bauer was named team captain under Father Hugh Mallon, the team's coach, and scored 10 goals and added 11 assists for 21 points in 20 games that season.

The next year, Dave, captain of the team for a second year, scored 12 goals and 25 assists in 25 games. The Majors had an excellent team under new coach Paul McNamara, and through the playoffs, Bauer collected seven goals and five assists in 12 games, but it wasn't enough, as the Oshawa Generals eliminated St. Mike's. So impressed were the Generals with the young forward that, when they were allowed to add three players to their lineup for the Memorial Cup final against the Trail Smoke Eaters, they selected Bauer as well as teammates Ted Lindsay and Gus Mortson. Bauer scored four goals and nine points during the seven-game series to help the Generals to the championship.

Although he hoped to help his Majors win the Memorial Cup in 1945 (which they ultimately did), Bauer played but one game for St. Mike's that season. In the latter days of World War II, he enlisted instead and ended up playing hockey with the Windsor Junior Spitfires of the Windsor City Hockey League as well as the Ottawa Canadian Postal

David Bauer was a Memorial Cup champion as both a player and a coach, but his influence permeated hockey more significantly, earning him a berth in the Hockey Hall of Fame.

Corps of the Ottawa National Defence Hockey League. In 1945–46, having returned from military service, he played with the University of Toronto Blues. David then entered the novitiate of the Basilian Fathers to study for the priesthood.

"Dave Bauer was a class act all the way," states John McCormack, a teammate with the Majors. "He could've been a good one. He had more determination than Bobby. I played against Bobby, he was finesse. Dave was more grinding, He had all kinds of talent, and when it came to determination, no one was better. He would've made it to the NHL easily if he had wanted to."

Brian Conacher adds: "The interesting thing about Father Bauer was that he was a priest first and foremost, but I don't think a lot of people realize that he was also a terrific hockey player. He certainly could have gone on to play professional hockey and likely could have gone on to the NHL. He lived a little bit in the shadow of his brother Bobby, who was a big star with the Boston Bruins and the Kraut Line. But Father Dave chose the cloth and that was the direction he went."

David Bauer was ordained as a Basilian priest in 1953 and, a year later, joined St. Michael's College as both a teacher and a coach.

Father Neil Hibberd told CBC Radio what it was like to have Father Bauer as a teacher. "In Grade 9, he told us, 'I'll meet you after school on the field. You kick off to me. If you touch me before I return the ball to the goal line, you'll have a week off homework.' So we're thinking, 'Forty of us. We're smart. We're good athletes. Who's this old man?' So he's out there when we came out. He didn't even take his long cassock off. He just tucked the skirt into the belt. We kicked off to him and he ran through all 40 of us. Now, how are you going to turn down somebody like that, because he's also telling me about the love of God and how it is to live well, the same guy that can run through 40 of his young students? He left a mark on me that I'll never forget. What I wanted to do was to be anything even a little bit like that!"

Through the ensuing years, Father Bauer coached hockey at various levels for St. Mike's. He became manager of the Majors and in 1960, following the resignation of coach Bob Goldham, assumed the coaching duties himself. In an interview with Father William O'Brien from March 1987, Father Bauer reminisced about that year's team, which won the Memorial Cup. "We had two really good goal scorers, Bruce Draper and Larry Keenan. We had a very strong defence. We were quite a good checking team. We had a pretty good balance. We had a tremendous spirit of camaraderie amongst the players themselves which, in the final analysis, is really what wins or loses for you, along with a few breaks, no question about that.

In the Memorial Cup final, the Majors were pitted against the Edmonton Oil Kings. "Sonny Osborne scored the three goals for us [in Game Three] out in Edmonton. He was at the University of Toronto at the time and he missed the first two games. We had won the first two games, but Edmonton was sure they were going to catch up with us. We had a couple of players hurt so Sonny had finished his exams and flew out. They [Edmonton] couldn't believe it. This guy hadn't skated for a week and he scored the first three goals. We won 4–2. It was a bit of an accident, but in Edmonton, they thought we just had these players coming out of the wall. Unusual type of situation."

Citing the growing conflict between scholastics and the demands presented by long seasons and substantial travel, St. Michael's College decided to withdraw from the OHA Junior 'A' hockey program in 1961. Although it had been discussed for several years, few could believe the decision had actually been made, especially with the school basking in the spotlight after the Memorial Cup championship.

"Our General Council had talked about this for a long time and they talked to me about it," explained Father Bauer in his 1987 interview with Father O'Brien. "I suggested that some of our relationships may have been damaged a little bit if we left in a way that would sever our connection so abruptly. Hard feelings would arise from the league. At any rate, hockey as an institution has been poorer as a result of it but maybe that's because the entire world has become a marketplace. That spirit seems to be pervading everything.

"We [representatives of St. Michael's College School] were always trying to cut down on the violence, cut down on the length of schedules, cut down on the materialism of the whole thing. We regretted very much leaving because we knew that this [school] is a major recreational institution in this country. The 1961 season, I think we played 98 games. At that level and at that pressure, if you really look over the whole history of it, it's amazing the number of boys who did it and survived academically. It was amazing what could be done even with those difficult circumstances. You have to have mixed feelings about it. It would have been a good thing to remain to have that moderating influence on the sport, then to have the trickle-down effect and it permeates through. That seems to be absent but I don't know whether we could provide that if we were there today."

Although little was ever discussed publicly, it appears that Father Bauer accepted the decision begrudgingly, although it is likely no coincidence that the Basilian Fathers assigned him to St. Mark's College at the University of British Columbia in Vancouver in 1961. He served there as chaplain until 1988 and coached the UBC hockey team, the Thunderbirds, in 1962–63, taking them to the Canadian university final.

But Bauer had a vision for hockey in Canada. While attending the World Championship at Colorado Springs in 1962, he conceived of a permanent national hockey team. Canadian Amateur Hockey Association president Jack Roxborough encouraged Bauer to present his idea at the CAHA's annual meeting in Toronto that year.

To assure continuity from year to year, Father Bauer envisioned a team stocked primarily with university students, reinforced by a handful of players from the Senior ranks. (Olympic restrictions prevented players with experience in the National, American, Western, or Central hockey leagues from taking part in the World Championship or Olympic tournaments.) The plan was unanimously approved by the CAHA on August 26, 1962, and Bauer was provided with seed money. The CAHA also agreed to provide university fees and money towards room and board for the players, who would be based at UBC. Private donors, including Father Bauer's mother in Kitchener, contributed additional money.

In Jim Coleman's book *Hockey Is Our Game,* Canada's national team was called "the most nobly conceived of all Canadian hockey enterprises."

Father Bauer patterned the National Team after what he had observed at St. Michael's College in the late 1950s and early 1960s. By taking players with some natural ability and instilling good discipline and a strong comprehension of the fundamentals of the game, he felt, you could mould a team into a unit that was collectively much stronger than any one of its individual parts. "This was what Father Bauer did with the St. Michael's team when he coached it, and thus gained my respect, not only as a knowledgeable and capable teacher of hockey, but also as an astute, perceptive, and sensitive man," says Brian Conacher, a Stanley Cup champion with the Toronto Maple Leafs in 1967 who spent his entire life involved in various aspects of hockey.

In addition, Father Bauer studied the European teams of the late 1950s that had developed into strong contenders for the World Championship. He found that three nations in particular — Czechoslovakia, Sweden, and especially the Soviet Union — had progressed rapidly in the hockey world, while Canada was beginning to lose its grip on hockey supremacy. In 1959, the Belleville McFarlands represented Canada and won the gold medal. In 1960, the Kitchener-Waterloo Dutchmen, coached by Father Bauer's brother Bobby, represented Canada at the Olympic Winter Games, but the United States stunned the hockey world by working their first "Miracle on Ice." Canada took the silver medal.

The Trail Smoke Eaters won the World Championship in 1961, but in 1962 the Galt Terriers lost to Sweden, and in 1963 Trail lost to the Soviet Union. It became evident to the CAHA officials that the days had come to an end when Canada could send the Allan Cup champion to represent the country at the World Championship and expect to win.

"[Father Bauer] was enough of a hockey man to know that you do not build a team overnight," says Conacher. "His goals were to bring the World Championship back to Canada and to show that good hockey players can be good students, and that hockey can grow in conjunction with a continuing education. He saw hockey as an experience that could teach and develop men of character and fibre. Hockey as a game could help teach one how to play the game of life."

Father Bauer came up with about 40 players from across Canada, including several of his former players from St. Michael's College — Terry Clancy, Paul Conlin, Gary Dineen, Barry MacKenzie, Billy MacMillan, Terry O'Malley, and Rod Seiling. The Toronto Maple Leafs owned the rights to all, as well as Gary Begg, Ken Broderick, Brian Conacher and Ross Morrison. All had chosen to continue their education as opposed to turning professional at the end of their Junior careers. Roger Bourbonnais, whose rights belonged to the Detroit Red Wings, had been the captain of the Edmonton Oil Kings and was in law school.

"The thing that appealed to me the most about Father Bauer when I came in contact with him was that he was a teacher, and that's what I thought a coach should be," says Conacher, a passionate devotee to Bauer's instructional methods. "The coaches I had been exposed to, certainly in professional hockey, were guys like Punch Imlach and Joe Crozier, guys who were strategists but weren't teachers. I know that had I not played for Father Bauer, I would never have made it to the NHL. He taught me the discipline and the skills that were lacking. So many of the young players in that era played on natural ability. There were guys in the NHL when I played, forwards, who had trouble skating backwards. And they never had to. They avoided that situation.

"[Father Bauer] was a tough coach," Conacher continues. "He was very disciplined and very demanding, but you did it because you knew you were going to be better for it." Brian's experience with Punch Imlach stands in stark contrast. "One year with the Leafs, we had a bad game against Minnesota and lost, and the next day, Punch had us skating around for an hour or hour and a half for no purpose. Just mindless punishment. Father Bauer stimulated the players because there were new drills and he forced you to think about what you did on the ice. By the time I got to the Leafs, that was my value — I was a very useful utility player that could be used in a number of situations as opposed to being a one-dimensional left winger. In the first series of the 1967 playoffs against Chicago, I played right wing for George Armstrong, who was hurt. In the final against Montreal, I played left wing with Ronnie Ellis and Red Kelly. Had I not had that acquired skill, I would have been sitting on the bench."

"Father Bauer was very involved in the mental, physical and spiritual well-being of all his players. He truly was like a father to this whole group of guys. He was a very inspirational kind of coach. He left an indelible mark on every young man that he came in contact with through that program, from start to finish."

The "Nats" represented Canada at the 1964 Olympic Games in Innsbruck, Austria. The Soviet Union won all seven of their games while Canada, Czechoslovakia, and Sweden each finished with records of five wins and two losses. "Every player played his guts out and no one will ever be able to say that the 1964 Canadian Olympic Hockey team quit under pressure," maintains Conacher. "The hard fact was that we just didn't have the horses to do the job. The Russians were older, more experienced, and had more depth. And when you combined their situation with our inexperience, our youth, and our lack of depth, it was a tribute to the excellent coaching abilities of Father Bauer that we were as good a team as we were."

In an Olympic match against Sweden on January 30, a Swedish player broke his stick while cross-checking a Canadian player and, while tossing the broken shaft at the bench, caught Father Bauer in the forehead. Loyal Canadian team members were enraged, but as they were about to leave the bench to confront the Swede, Father Bauer issued a terse command that they remain on the bench, and tensions subsided. The next evening, Bauer invited the Swedish player to watch the Soviet–Czechoslovakia game with him. After the tournament was over, the Canadian coach was presented with a special gold medal for exemplary leadership.

The tournament was marred by a controversy that continues to rear its ugly head to this day. Brian Conacher tells the story. "While the final game was in progress, and it

In 1961, the Buzzers won the Junior 'B' championship of Ontario, while the Majors took the Memorial cup as national Junior 'A' champions. Here, Father Bill Conway, coach of the Buzzers (left) and Father David Bauer, the Majors' coach, hold the Memorial Cup in a parade to commemorate their victories.

Father Bauer's vision created a national hockey program that competed internationally, including at the 1964 Winter Olympic Games in Innsbruck, Austria.

Father Bauer (seated, fourth from right), included former Majors Terry O'Malley (back row, fourth from left), Gary Dineen (back row, second from right), Barry MacKenzie (middle row, second from left), Terry Clancy (middle row, sixth from left), and Paul Conlin (middle row, second from right) on his team.

became evident that there would be a three-way tie for the silver medal, Bunny Ahearne, president of the [International Ice Hockey Federation], decided to change the rules. He arbitrarily decided that [a tie in the] final standings would be [resolved] based on goals scored. As a result, Canada was shuffled out of the medals and finished fourth. After being robbed of a medal, Marshall Johnston turned to Father Bauer and said, 'It looks, Father, as if the shepherd and his flock have been fleeced!'"

Canada's National Team was transferred to Winnipeg from Vancouver in 1965. Father Bauer's role became that of an advisor while Gordon Simpson, the coach of the Allan Cup–winning Winnipeg Maroons, took over the coaching position. From 1966 to 1969, Jackie McLeod coached the Nats while Father Bauer served as manager. The team brought home the bronze medal at the Olympic Winter Games in Grenoble, France, in 1968, but was sadly outclassed by the Soviet and Czechoslovak teams, both of which were able to use their best available players. The IIHF had reneged on a promise to allow teams to use the best available players, professional or not, and because the vast improvement in the European hockey teams made it impossible to compete at the highest levels without the use of professionals, Canada withdrew from international competition on January 4, 1970, and did not return at the senior level until 1977.

That certainly didn't mean that Father Bauer was inactive. He continued to act as an advisor to UBC's hockey coaches and players, while also sharing his knowledge with fledgling hockey programs. During this 10-year period, Bauer travelled to Japan for six-week periods twice a year to instruct at hockey schools. It seems probable that Father Bauer's outlook on personal growth through hockey was particularly suited to a Japanese culture that valued discipline. In 1973, Bauer accepted an invitation from the Austrian Ice Hockey Federation to assist with their program.

Canada returned to the Olympics in 1980, and Father Bauer served as the team's managing director for the tournament in Lake Placid, New York.

"I travelled with Father Bauer and the National Team to Europe and Japan prior to the 1980 Olympic Games in Lake Placid, New York," wrote George Gross in the *Toronto Sun*. "We talked often about hockey principles, player behaviours, attitude, the concept of the National Team, the future of hockey in general and we usually ended the discussion in the wee hours of the next morning." Gross summed up the attributes of Father Bauer by stating, "Bauer instilled dignity in any discussion, whether it was sports, politics or religion. [He was] a man who preached dignity as a coach and, prior to that, as a player. Respect for your fellow man was another of his sermons."

Absence from international competition had severely damaged Canada's program, and the team finished sixth, well behind medallists USA, the Soviet Union, and Sweden. Father Bauer took particular pride in the participation of Terry O'Malley, who, at 39 years old, was the team's oldest member. O'Malley had been with Father Bauer since St. Michael's College in 1957–58, playing on the Memorial Cup champion Majors team of 1961 and the National Team from 1964 to 1970. Then, on the advice of Father Bauer, he played in Japan from 1971 to 1978.

In 1981, Father Bauer was appointed vice-president of Hockey Canada and chairman of the country's Olympic hockey program, and continued to teach at St. Mark's. He also continued to assist with the UBC hockey team.

Father David Bauer succumbed to cancer in Goderich, Ontario, on November 9, 1988, just a week after his 64th birthday. "Canada has lost a man who was extremely loyal to the ideals of amateur hockey," said Terry O'Malley.

In the years before his death, a multitude of honours had been bestowed on Bauer, acknowledging his importance to the game of hockey. He received the Order of Canada in 1967; had an arena in Calgary, which serves as the home base of Hockey Canada, named in his honour in 1986; and scholarships in his name are awarded at both St. Michael's College and at the University of British Columbia. In 1989, Father Bauer was posthumously inducted into the Hockey Hall of Fame in the Builders category, and he was added to the IIHF Wall of Honour in 1997.

But there can be no greater honour than the respect earned from the players whose lives he touched. "Father Bauer was a tremendous person and had a tremendous impact on my life," says Paul Conlin. "He made me see that while hockey was important, in the grand scheme of things, it wasn't the be-all and end-all. Getting an education and developing personally and being in a position to choose between playing hockey or pursuing some other vocation was important, and that was his vision for the National Team."

"Father Dave Bauer was an unbelievable guy," adds Mike Draper. "You talk about a guy who was a great motivator, not only on the ice, but in the classroom! Father Bauer was always so positive. He was always willing to help us out."

Rod Seiling reflects on his coach with both the Majors and the National Team. "He was well-versed in hockey and well-versed as a person. He had very strong views on how to play the game. Bauer had the ability to take the elements — checking, skating, shooting — and mold a team. It didn't have to be the most talented team to be very competitive because of his ability to take a team that worked very well together using those basics."

The accolades to an outstanding individual conclude with Jim Gregory. "Father Bauer put me on the hockey path and I am truly indebted to him. My dream was to be involved with Junior hockey and I never imagined that I would get to work in the NHL, much less be an Honoured Member of the Hockey Hall of Fame."

To Father David Bauer, it all came down to one sentence: "If you can improve the boy as a person, you will improve him as a hockey player."

50
Net Worth – Gerry Cheevers

In the days before the National Hockey League held an annual draft, teams sponsored entire networks of Junior and minor clubs, and their scouts travelled far and wide to sign up promising young players to play in these systems. Hall of Fame goaltender Gerry Cheevers was one of many who followed this route to the NHL. "My dad was a part-time Leaf scout," Cheevers explains, "so he suggested that St. Mike's might be a good place to go. When you decide to go to play hockey in a place sponsored by a National Hockey League team, you have your sights set on playing in the NHL."

Signing a contract to be part of the Leafs organization was a thrill for the young netminder. "When I was growing up, it was Leafs, Leafs, Leafs. My dad was assistant manager of the Garden City Arena, and the Leafs trained in St. Catharines. We got to know them. I didn't really have a player I followed. I liked [goaltender] Turk Broda, but I liked all of the Toronto Maple Leafs."

At St. Michael's, Gerry was tutored by some fine netminders. In 1956–57, having just turned 16, he played a single game with the Majors, while Bob Savage handled most of the netminding chores. The next season, Cesare Maniago was the principal goalie, with Savage playing a handful of contests and Cheevers again playing a single game. In 1958–59, he joined the team for six games, again serving as understudy to Maniago, but by 1959–60, Gerry was the Majors' regular netminder, leading the OHA in both shutouts (with five) and goals-against average (3.08). In 1960–61, his fourth season at the school, Gerry backstopped the St. Michael's Majors to the Memorial Cup championship.

After graduating from St. Michael's College, Cheevers turned pro in 1961–62. He dressed for the Pittsburgh Hornets of the American Hockey League for five games and the AHL's Rochester Americans for 19 contests, but spent most of the season with the Sault Ste. Marie Thunderbirds of the Eastern Professional Hockey League. He also saw his first NHL action, on December 2, 1961. "Johnny Bower was hurt and so was Donny Simmons, who was playing down in Rochester [the Leafs' AHL affiliate]. I got a call on Friday night and took the train down from the Soo. We played Chicago and it was a great thrill — no mask, Bobby Hull, scared to death. Billy Harris got three goals [the Leafs won 6–4]. Then we got on the train and played the next night in Detroit. We got beat 3–1. I'll never forget that night. Gordie Howe came down, shot what I thought was a routine wrist shot, and knocked the stick right out of my hands! I thought, 'Ooo, they're a little bit bigger and stronger up here!'"

Gerry then toiled in Rochester, where he led the AHL in wins in both 1963–64 and 1964–65. His goals-against average was the best in the league in the latter season, and

Gerry Cheevers played parts of five seasons with the Majors, leading the team to the Memorial Cup in his final season, 1960–61.

he earned a berth on the AHL's First All-Star Team. The Leafs, apparently believing they had a surplus of goaltending talent, left Cheevers exposed in the Intra-League Draft in June 1965. Boston claimed him, and he became part of the core, along with young OHA stars Bobby Orr and Derek Sanderson and the proceeds of a lopsided trade with Chicago — Phil Esposito, Ken Hodge, and Fred Stanfield — of a contending team that won the Stanley Cup in 1970 and 1972.

In the fall of 1972, Gerry leapt to the Cleveland Crusaders of the World Hockey Association. Although he won the Ben Hatskin Trophy as the league's best goaltender in 1973 and was named to All-Star teams in 1973, 1974, and 1975, he returned to the Bruins in January 1976 and finished his career with five more years in Boston.

Cheevers retired at the end of the 1979–80 season, and took over as the Bruins' coach from 1980-81 until he was relieved of his duties during the 1984–85 campaign. His goaltending statistics are spectacular: 230 wins, 102 losses, and 74 ties in 418 regular-season appearances in the NHL, to go with a sparkling career goals-against average of 2.89. He played in 88 NHL playoff games, winning 53 and losing 34. In the WHA, Gerry won 99, lost 78, and tied nine in 191 regular-season games.

When Gerry Cheevers was inducted into the Hockey Hall of Fame in 1985, it was all too appropriate that Father David Bauer, his coach with the 1961 Memorial Cup champions, was the person who introduced him.

Any NHL squad would have been ecstatic to have as fine a netminding tandem as the Junior 'B' Buzzers possessed in 1958–59. Gerry Cheevers (front row, left) shared his crease with Gary Smith (front row, far right).

51
A Lifetime Devoted to Hockey — Jim Gregory

After growing up in Dunnville, Ontario, Jim Gregory moved to Toronto to attend St. Michael's College in 1953, and there is nothing he would have loved more than to play hockey for the school. He tried out for the Junior 'B' Buzzers, but didn't make the team. "I thought I was pretty good," he shrugs. Instead, he was asked by his homeroom teacher, Father David Bauer, if he'd like to assist the Junior 'A' Majors. "I kept statistics and bought supplies for the team. By the time I finished school, I was the trainer and, later, the manager."

Jim got the opportunity to work with highly regarded Majors coaches Joe Primeau, Bob Goldham, and Father Bauer. In 1959, he was still with the Majors on a part-time basis while working for Colgate-Palmolive when Father Bauer introduced him to Stafford Smythe, co-owner of the Toronto Maple Leafs. "I had been making $65 a week, and Stafford asked me how much I was making," Jim chuckles. "I told him $95 a week. Stafford said, 'Okay, you can work full time at the sand pit [the Smythe family's sand and gravel business] in the summer and part time running the Junior team. In the winter, you'll work full time at hockey and part time at the pit. I'll pay you $65 a week for the full-time job and $30 for the part-time job.' I thought, 'Great! I just managed to get a $30 raise.'"

Prior to the start of the 1960–61 season, Bob Goldham resigned as coach of the St. Mike's Majors. Unable to find a suitable replacement, Father David Bauer took over at the helm of the team. The management team of Bauer and Gregory guided the Majors to a Memorial Cup championship in 1961, the school's first since 1947.

But it turned out to be a melancholy summer. The school made the decision to withdraw from the Ontario Hockey Association, and Father Bauer, Gregory's mentor, was assigned to St. Mark's College at the University of British Columbia.

Stafford Smythe promised the Basilian Fathers that he would alleviate their hockey concerns by creating a new league, one that would involve only Toronto-area teams and play a reduced schedule with less travel and lower overhead. The administration at St. Michael's College agreed to try the new league for one season.

The Metro Toronto Junior Hockey League was formed, and it included both St. Mike's and the Toronto Marlboros, as well as a handful of former Junior 'B' teams from the Toronto area. Jim Gregory assumed the dual role of manager and coach of the Majors. But after a single season, in which St. Michael's won the league championship, the school again found the situation unsatisfactory and withdrew from Junior 'A' competition completely.

After being cut as a player from St. Mike's, Jim Gregory rose through the ranks from stickboy to trainer to coach and manager before embarking on a Hall of Fame career in the NHL.

Gregory searched for a home for the team, and briefly considered moving the franchise to St. Jerome's College in Kitchener, but instead, went with another Toronto Catholic high school, Neil McNeil. With a roster composed primarily of Majors players from the previous year, Jim led the Maroons to the league championship in 1962–63.

Tony Fritz, who played on the Majors in 1961–62, fondly remembers his coach. "Jim Gregory was this little guy who couldn't skate, but he was an organizer, he was a politician, he was brilliant, and look at what he did with his career!"

Jim McKenny, a member of the Maroons, adds, "He was our coach and manager at Neil McNeil, but he was also our surrogate father."

The Metro Junior 'A' league disbanded after two years, and the Maple Leafs combined their two affiliates, the Maroons and the Marlies, into one outstanding team under the Toronto Marlboros banner. Gregory executed the merger and coached the Marlies to a Memorial Cup championship in 1964. The following season, he added the managing role as well. In 1965–66, Jim hired former Leafs star Gus Bodnar to coach the Marlboros, and the team won another Memorial Cup championship in 1967.

During that 1966–67 season, Punch Imlach got sick and King Clancy took over temporarily as coach of the Maple Leafs. Gregory filled in as interim manager, spending as much time with the Leafs as he did the Marlies. "I travelled with the team for about six weeks during the middle of the season. They gave me a Stanley Cup ring that year." The hard-working Gregory was also asked to become familiar with NHL players in anticipation of expansion. "My goal had always been to spend my career as the manager of the Junior team that supported the Toronto Maple Leafs," Jim states. "I got to work in scouting with Bob Davidson, the Maple Leafs' chief scout for 30 years. Conn Smythe loved Bob [who was captain of the 1945 Stanley Cup champion Leafs], and when Bob approved of me, Conn and I became close," Jim says, adding with a laugh, "Conn always called me 'Pope' because I was Catholic."

Jim joined Toronto's Western Hockey League affiliate, the Vancouver Canucks, as head coach in 1967–68. He spent the next season scouting for Toronto. But on April 6, 1969, Punch Imlach was fired and, at the age of 33, Jim Gregory became the general manager of the Toronto Maple Leafs.

At one point, Jim asked Stafford Smythe why he had been hired. Smythe replied, "I just had a feeling you were going to be a good hockey man. I watched you and made up my mind." He then added, "Oh, and by the way, I knew you were only making $65 when you were hired."

It was a tempestuous time in the Leafs' history. The team was owned by a triumvirate — Stafford Smythe, Harold Ballard and John W. Bassett. There were regular battles for control, and Jim routinely had to extinguish fires set by the owners. In his first year as general manager, Ballard and Smythe were charged with income tax evasion. Smythe died before he was jailed, but Jim made regular trips from Toronto to Kingston to discuss business with Ballard, who was incarcerated at the minimum-security Millhaven Institution from August 1972 to October 1973.

Gregory soldiered on, rebuilding a faded franchise around a core that included forwards Darryl Sittler, Lanny McDonald, Tiger Williams, and Ron Ellis, defencemen Borje Salming and Ian Turnbull, and netminder Mike Palmateer. An early advocate of adding skilled European players to the NHL rosters, Jim wishes he had ignored Ballard's advice and signed Anders Hedberg and Ulf Nilsson. "Harold didn't want to spend the money," he sighs. "Hedberg, especially, really wanted to play in Toronto. Those two would have added a goal and a half a game."

On July 4, 1979, after the Maple Leafs had been eliminated by the Montreal Canadiens in the quarterfinals, Ballard fired Jim and replaced him with Punch Imlach. The recycled GM proceeded to dismantle Gregory's team, alienating players and fans in the process, and dropping the team into an abyss from which it wouldn't recover for a dozen years. "I enjoyed all my time working at Maple Leaf Gardens for the Toronto Maple Leafs," states Gregory with pride. "I'm just sorry that it wasn't able to be more successful." During Gregory's 10-year tenure in Toronto, the Leafs made the playoffs eight times.

Celebrating the creation of a print by artist Les Tait depicting all-time greats throughout St. Michael's 100-year hockey history were several of the players included in the artwork. Left to right: former St. Mike's star Les Duff, Hall of Famer and alumnus Jim Gregory, Father James Murphy, longtime NHL scout Frank Bonello and alumnus and Hall of Fame member Dick Duff.

Jim wasn't unemployed long. He was hired as the director of Central Scouting by NHL president John Ziegler, and made the league's Central Scouting Bureau a cost-effective way for teams to evaluate hockey talent from around the world. In 1986, he was named executive director of hockey operations for the NHL. Most recently, Gregory was the NHL's senior vice-president of hockey operations. Under his management, a number of areas have been addressed, including rules, equipment, and the implementation of video review of disputed goals.

In spite of earning so many accolades, it wasn't difficult for Gregory to name a career highlight. "The high point was getting a job in hockey, and I can't say enough good things about the two guys who helped me, the late Father Dave Bauer and the late Stafford Smythe," says Jim. "Father Bauer put me on the hockey path and I am truly indebted to him. He taught me from the start about treating people fairly and keeping your priorities in life straight."

Jim Gregory was inducted into the Hockey Hall of Fame in the Builders category in 2007. In an emotional speech delivered at the induction ceremony, Jim said, "I did not have the skill to play the game, but I did have, and I still have, a great passion for the game. For a young guy who got cut from Junior hockey to wind up having a job with the Toronto Maple Leafs, let me tell you, in Canada, that was like winning the lottery and going to heaven in the same breath." He continued, "I consider what I have done as an honour and privilege. How often does someone get to live a dream?" Stopping for a moment, he added, "I did."

52
Hockey's Global Ambassador — Murray Costello

Although Murray Costello entered the Hockey Hall of Fame as a Builder, it would be a mistake to forget that, before he was a hockey executive, he was a very fine player.

Murray grew up in an athletic family in South Porcupine, Ontario. Rita, the oldest sibling, was followed by four rambunctious boys: Don, better known as "Moose," and three boys who would later star playing hockey at St. Michael's College. Les played with the Majors from 1944–45 to 1946–47, Murray from 1950–51 to 1952–53, and Jack from 1957–58 to 1958–59.

"Les set the tone and the attitude toward the game in our household," Murray says. "He taught us that we should enjoy hockey because it's only a game, play it to the fullest, and laugh as much as you can along the way." That philosophy served the Costellos well through their lives.

"When I was 16 years old, I had the opportunity to go to four or five different places from the north country," explains Murray. "Fortunately, I had an older brother who went to St. Mike's, and I tried to pin him down to ask him what he thought I should do. He avoided me a number of times and finally, I was a little bit upset and I said, 'Les, why wouldn't you talk to me about this? I just want to get your opinion from your experience.' He said, 'I don't want to tell you where you should go to play your hockey because, if I tell you and it doesn't work out, you'll hate me for the rest of your life.'

"I said, 'I'm not telling you to make the decision for me, but I should be able to trade on your experience. I want to know how you found leaving home and going to St. Mike's.' He said, 'When I had to make the decision you're making, somebody told me that if I chose to go to St. Mike's, I'd likely make friends that would remain with me the rest of my life. On the basis of that, I decided I should go there, too, and that's why I went to St. Mike's.'"

Murray found his first year in Toronto rather intimidating. "I came from a small school of less than 200 and suddenly, I was at St. Mike's, where there were 1,200 or more. The guys on the team were good, and the day students were very supportive of the hockey guys, and they helped out with my transition a lot."

After three seasons of Junior with St. Michael's College, years in which the six-foot, three-inch forward was consistently among the team's leading scorers, Murray made his debut with the Chicago Black Hawks during the 1953–54 season. He was traded to the Boston Bruins prior to the following season. Midway through the 1955–56 campaign, the Bruins sent Costello and Lorne Ferguson to Detroit in exchange for Real Chevrefils and Jerry Toppazzini. "It was nice to be among guys like Gordie Howe for the short time that I was, but there is no way any of us would've dreamed it would end up with being in the Hall of Fame. It was a thrill for a young guy to be able to play with those established stars."

Murray Costello, the second of three boys in his family to star at St. Michael's, went on to play in the NHL, but found his strength lay in administration and was rewarded with induction to the Hockey Hall of Fame for his hard work.

I lived with Red Kelly, Metro Prystai, and Bill Dineen at Ma Shaw's [boarding house]. That was a very special experience and one I will never forget."

After being sent to Edmonton of the Western Hockey League to finish the 1956–57 season, Murray was reinstated as an amateur and completed his playing career with the Windsor Bulldogs of the OHA Senior loop. In 162 regular-season NHL games, he collected 13 goals and 19 assists for 32 points.

Costello returned to school and earned his law degree, then moved into hockey's business side. As an executive with the Seattle Totems of the WHIL, Murray guided the team to back-to-back championships in 1967 and 1968. He was publicity director of the WHL before acting as arbitrator for the World Hockey Association Players' Association.

Perhaps his greatest accomplishment, though, was as president of the Canadian Amateur Hockey Association (now Hockey Canada) between 1979 and 1998. Among many accomplishments, Costello is recognized for making significant contributions to the merger of Hockey Canada and the Canadian Hockey Association, which brought Canada's entire developmental process into one stream. Murray also oversaw the formation of the Canadian women's team and, in turn, the rapid development of women's hockey.

As president of Hockey Canada, Costello always recognized the unsung heroes who help in the development of minor hockey in Canada. When he was elected to the Hockey Hall of Fame in 2005, his eloquent speech stated, "I can tell you that I understand that this is recognition of the amateur side of the game, and for the many thousands of volunteers who continue to make it happen year after year across Canada. I get to take the bow on their behalf because they do the work out there and our system is strong because of it."

Always an advocate of advancing the game of hockey throughout the world, Murray remains a member of the International Ice Hockey Federation council and is chairman of the IIHF's Medical and Technical/Arena committees. Previously, he had served on the IIHF's Statutes and Disciplinary committees and was its auditor for a number of years. "What's happening in the Koreas, Japan, and China is promising," he says. "Australia is doing quite well, things are developing in New Zealand, Israel is moving up, and I've had an interest in Mongolia. They're lacking funds. That's the main inhibitor of growth in a lot of countries. Some countries have so few arenas, and hockey is expensive compared to many other sports.

"Mexico, Ireland, Spain, and Iceland also have promising hockey programs. There are five or six arenas in Iceland, but only four with seating capacity," he explains. "They're looking to complete the fourth so they can get a league going and declare a national champion."

He comments that the inclusion of NHLers in the Olympics, beginning in 1998, was a boon to international hockey. "It's made a big difference," he states. "It really enhanced the appeal of the sport, playing best against best."

Murray Costello's love of the game grew and expanded to encompass both Canada and the four corners of this globe, and earned him entrance to the Hockey Hall of Fame.

53 Conclusion

When the St. Michael's Majors won the Memorial Cup championship in 1961, it gave the franchise a record for most Junior championships with four, an honour held until 1964 when the Toronto Marlboros, a team largely composed of former St. Mike's players, tied the record. The Marlies eclipsed the record with their championship in 1967, and ended up with seven titles before the team moved to Hamilton and then on to Guelph. The Majors are still second on the list, tied with the Oshawa Generals.

St. Michael's College had the finest Junior 'A' team in the country in 1934, 1945, 1947, and 1961, and was a Memorial Cup finalist in 1937 and 1946. In addition, the St. Michael's Buzzers can boast of having won the Sutherland Cup as the premier Junior 'B' team in Ontario in 1934, 1936, 1945, 1961, 1982, and 1989, and were runners-up in 1935 and 1948. Since moving up to Provincial Junior 'A' status, the Buzzers have also won the Frank L. Buckland Trophy as Ontario Provincial Junior Hockey League champions in 2005 and 2006. Although they haven't participated in a Senior league in decades, St. Michael's College has won the Allan Cup in 1910, and were OHA Senior champions in 1909.

Although the Buzzers and reborn Majors both bear the name of the school and a share of the glorious tradition of its 100-year hockey heritage, both teams are today privately owned. Happily, in both cases, the teams are owned by proud alumni of St. Michael's College School.

"We hope and pray that St. Michael's College can continue to be a guiding beacon to the game that is so central to our Canadian identity," says Father Joe Redican.

In the program commemorating St. Michael's 100-year hockey history, NHL commissioner Gary Bettman stated, "It is my distinct pleasure to recognize and commend St. Michael's for its commitment to instilling in young men the skills necessary to be successful athletes and good people."

Doce Me Bonitatem et Disciplinam et Scientiam
Teach me goodness, discipline, and knowledge

APPENDIX 1
All-Time St. Michael's Majors Regular-Season Scoring

1933-34

PLAYER	GP	G	A	PTS	PIM
Jackson, Art	12	23	13	36	16
Metz, Nick	12	18	15	33	10
Drouillard, Clare	11	14	11	25	42
Kelly, Pep	11	13	8	21	12
Acheson, John	11	10	10	20	2
Willson, Don	8	9	9	18	0
Bauer, Frank	7	7	3	10	2
Bauer, Bobby	10	4	2	6	0
Hamilton, Jack	12	3	0	3	10
Hamilton, Reg	5	2	1	3	12
Burke, Red	8	1	1	2	16
Regan, Bill	1	0	0	0	0

GOALIE	GP	GA	SO	GAA	
Teno, Harvey	11	30	1	2.73	
McLean, Leo	1	6	0	6.00	

1934-35

PLAYER	GP	G	A	PTS	PIM
O'Flaherty, Peanuts	12	10	6	16	10
Sheedy, Gene	11	6	7	13	0
Smith, Winkie	12	9	2	11	4
Corrigan, Chuck	12	5	4	9	4
Crawford, John	12	5	3	8	14
Conway, Eddie	12	5	1	6	4
Robinson,	12	3	3	6	16
Ryan,	11	2	4	6	8
Hamilton, Johnny	12	1	5	6	18
Orsini, Frank	1	0	0	0	0

GOALIE	GP	GA	SO	GAA	
Teno, Harvey	11	34	1	3.09	
McLean, Leo	1	3	0	3.00	

1935-36

PLAYER	GP	G	A	PTS	PIM
McCreavy, Pat	10	8	9	17	2
Mitchell, John	10	11	5	16	6
Benson, Bus	9	12	2	14	0
Metz, Don	10	9	4	13	5
Hunt, Fred	9	2	9	11	12
Convey, Eddie	8	6	1	7	4
Corrigan, Chuck	9	3	1	4	4
Jackson, Harold	8	2	1	3	4
Sheedy, Gene	7	1	1	2	2
McLean,	1	1	0	1	2
McNamara, George	9	0	0	0	6

GOALIE	GP	GA	SO	GAA	
Dunne, Tom	9	14	2	1.56	
Bernier, Raoul	1	2	0	2.00	

1936-37

PLAYER	GP	G	A	PTS	PIM
Inglis, John	11	16	6	22	6
McNamara, George	12	11	8	19	4
Sheedy, Gene	11	8	5	13	8
Hunt, Fred	12	5	5	10	16
Hunt, Ross	8	5	5	10	11
McNamara, Paul	12	5	4	9	0
Tonn, Ab	11	2	5	7	4
Morrison, Neil	9	4	2	6	2
Smith, Orval	11	3	3	6	10
Callahan, John	12	2	0	2	6
Lukasik, Bonik	10	1	1	2	4
Roach, Guy	1	0	0	0	0

GOALIE	GP	GA	SO	GAA	
Dunn, Tom	11	25	0	2.27	
Morrison, Claude	1	1	0	1.00	

1937-38

PLAYER	GP	G	A	PTS	PIM
Inglis, John	12	14	7	21	25
Sheedy, Gene	12	2	13	15	11
McNamara, George	12	8	5	13	2
McNamara, Paul	12	7	3	10	9
Schnurr, Louis	12	6	3	9	4
Roach, Guy	12	4	4	8	8
Smith, Orval	10	5	2	7	12
Callahan, John	12	3	3	6	8
Morrison, Neil	12	2	4	6	2
Sills,	12	1	0	1	2
Mulrooney,	1	0	0	0	0

GOALIE	GP	GA	SO	GAA	
Morrison, Claude	11	34	0	3.09	
Consaul, Art	1	4	0	4.00	

1938-39

PLAYER	GP	G	A	PTS	PIM
Dunbar, Don	14	7	14	21	4
McNamara, George	14	11	8	19	20
Sheedy, Gene	13	5	9	14	2
Regan, Frank	10	9	5	14	2
Morrison, Neil	11	8	3	11	2
Roach, Guy	12	5	4	9	6
Quigley, Jack	10	4	5	9	5
Callahan, John	12	6	1	7	14
Ralph, Fred	12	4	3	7	4
McNamara, Paul	6	4	1	5	0
Joplin, Jack	8	4	0	4	12
Quigley, F	3	2	2	4	0
Somers, Thomas	9	1	2	3	2
McKinnon, Dunc	5	0	0	0	0
McKay	1	0	0	0	0

GOALIE	GP	GA	SO	GAA	
Morrison, Claude	4	8	1	2.00	
Langille, Keith	9	32	0	3.56	
Hardy, Bill	1	2	0	2.00	

1941-42

PLAYER	GP	G	A	PTS	PIM
Bennett, Frank	17	9	11	20	10
Hickey, Jerry	14	11	5	16	6
Gregoire, Gerry	16	8	7	15	6
Dodd, George	18	6	9	15	7
O'Neill, Tom	18	6	6	12	28
Schmalz, Cec	17	6	5	11	5
Gallagher Farrell	9	4	5	9	6
Morrow, J.	14	5	2	7	0
Stanton, Bob	14	5	2	7	8
Lobraico, Bernie	16	2	3	5	2
Foley, Hugh	15	2	2	4	4
Rebstock, George	18	2	0	1	24
McCreavy, Don	2	1	0	1	2
Carter,	2	0	1	1	0
Midghall, Ernie	3	0	0	0	2
Spadoni	1	0	0	0	0
Irvine,	7	0	0	0	0
GOALIE	GP	GA	SO	GAA	
Cleary, Joe	14	98	1	7.00	
Marois, John	4	22	0	5.50	

1943-44

PLAYER	GP	G	A	PTS	PIM
Schnurr, Bob	25	33	27	60	10
Sadler, Joe	25	38	17	55	20
McCormack, John	24	18	30	48	6
Bauer, Dave	25	12	25	37	20
Lindsay, Ted	22	22	7	29	24
Dunlap, Frank	15	11	14	25	20
Melong, Frank	24	8	5	13	21
Mortson, Gus	25	5	6	11	16
Gregoire, Gerry	13	5	3	8	0
Marsalik, Joe	8	1	5	6	2
McLean, Ted	21	3	3	6	13
Thomson, Jim	22	2	2	4	40
Mulligan, Murray	6	1	0	1	2
Kane, Paul	1	0	1	1	0
Sadler, Maurice	17	0	0	0	0
Barrett,	1	0	0	0	0
GOALIE	GP	GA	SO	GAA	
Marois, John	14	44	1	3.14	
Boehmer, Pat	11	29	2	2.64	

1945-46

PLAYER	GP	G	A	PTS	PIM
Sloan, Tod	25	43	32	75	49
Mackell, Fleming	24	25	25	59	29
McKay, Roy	23	22	19	41	6
Paul, Bob	26	22	18	40	5
Costello, Les	24	17	23	40	17
Harrison, Ed	22	16	14	30	8
Blute, John	23	9	19	28	13
McLean, Ted	26	8	17	25	19
Kelly, Red	26	13	11	24	18
Sandford, Ed	26	10	9	19	28
Powers, Pat	24	3	9	12	40
Winslow, Warren	10	4	4	8	8
Muretich, Jack	6	1	3	4	2
Hannigan, Ray	2	1	0	1	0
Scholes, George	1	1	0	1	0
GOALIE	GP	GA	SO	GAA	
Boehmer, Pat	25 2/3	54	4	2.11	
DeCourcy, Bob	1/3	0	0	0.00	

1942-43

PLAYER	GP	G	A	PTS	PIM
Hickey, Gerry	19	15	12	27	8
Lynch, Bryan	19	17	7	24	19
Bauer, Dave	20	10	11	21	10
Carter, Greg	16	6	13	19	4
Schnarr, Bob	13	11	7	18	4
Schmalz, Cecil	20	10	7	17	10
Bennett, Frank	20	7	10	17	8
O'Neill, Tom	16	5	9	14	34
Dunlap, Frank	11	8	6	14	10
Dodd, George	18	4	4	8	27
McLean, Ted	1	1	0	1	4
Powers, Pat	1	1	0	1	2
GOALIE	GP	GA	SO	GAA	
Marois, John	20	99	0	4.95	

1944-45

PLAYER	GP	G	A	PTS	PIM
Gravelle, Leo	17	30	22	52	6
Blute, John	19	30	21	51	16
Sadler, Joe	18	21	21	42	11
McCormack, John	15	18	23	41	6
Sloan, Tod	19	21	16	37	14
Paul, Bob	16	12	15	27	9
Thomson, Jim	18	13	12	25	52
Turik, Frank	16	11	13	24	9
Costello, Les	17	11	8	19	4
Mortson, Gus	17	6	12	18	18
Arundel, John	10	3	5	8	10
McLean, Ted	11	4	4	8	0
Gray, Bob	8	1	1	2	13
Bauer, Dave	1	1	1	2	0
Samis, Phil	3	0	1	1	2
Harrison, Ed	1	1	0	1	0
Kelly, Red	1	0	0	0	0
McParland, Bill	1	0	0	0	0
GOALIE	GP	GA	SO	GAA	
Boehmer, Pat	20	94	0	2.58	

1946-47

PLAYER	GP	G	A	PTS	PIM
Mackell, Fleming	28	49	33	82	73
Sandford, Ed	27	30	37	67	40
Costello, Les	29	29	33	62	78
Harrison, Ed	28	30	25	55	27
Migay, Rudy	28	25	16	41	12
Kelly, Red	30	8	24	32	11
Winslow, Warren	26	15	14	29	21
Paul, Bob	25	12	14	26	17
McLellan, John	30	11	13	24	8
Hannigan, Ray	22	13	8	21	21
Woit, Ben	27	5	16	21	42
Psutka, Harry	29	5	12	17	77
Heathcott, Robert	1	0	2	2	0
Corcoran, Jack	1	0	2	2	0
DeCourcy, Joe	3	0	0	0	0
GOALIE	GP	GA	SO	GAA	
Harvey, Howie	30	57	9	1.90	

1947-48

PLAYER	GP	G	A	PTS	PIM
Barry, Ray	31	9	28	37	8
Hannigan, Gord	32	14	13	27	55
DeCourcy, Joe	31	12	8	20	45
McAllister, Brian	30	10	9	19	0
Horton, Tim	32	6	7	13	137
Whalen, Pete	31	9	4	13	9
Primeau, Joe Jr.	31	5	6	11	14
McNamara, Bill	31	4	6	10	28
Clune, Walter	32	3	5	8	37
Dunn, Bill	29	2	6	8	58
Fitzhenry, Jerry	31	1	4	5	21
Oberholtzer, Don	2	6	3	2	5
Valliquette, Murray	4	0	0	0	0
McDonagh, Bill	3	0	0	0	0
Jeanneau, Jean-Paul	2	0	0	0	0
Bellisle,	1	0	0	0	0
Flannigan,	2	0	0	0	0
Calox,	1	0	0	0	0
GOALIE	GP	GA	SO	GAA	
Shea, Tom	32	134	0	4.19	

1948-49

PLAYER	GP	G	A	PTS	PIM
Hannigan, Gord	32	21	13	34	59
Marshall, Willie	31	13	18	31	14
Rope, Don	31	16	13	29	6
Horton, Tim	32	9	18	27	95
Bonhomme, Connie	31	12	12	24	19
DeCourcy, Joe	29	10	3	13	38
Corcoran, Ray	28	4	7	11	12
McNamara, Bill	30	1	10	11	13
Clune, Wally	31	2	3	5	68
McCarthy, Tom	32	1	4	5	27
Corcoran, Norm	28	2	2	4	32
Sabourin, Bob	10	2	2	4	0
Whelan, Pete	13	3	0	3	2
Buchanan, Neil	26	0	1	1	26
Sandford, Fred	5	0	1	1	0
Roy, Gord	4	0	0	0	2
Buchanan, Mike	16	0	0	0	14
Mihilson, Joe	1	0	0	0	0
GOALIE	GP	GA	SO	GAA	
Shea, Tom	32	128	1	4.00	

1949-50

PLAYER	GP	G	A	PTS	PIM
Marshall, Willie	48	39	27	66	32
Labine, Leo	47	20	22	42	77
Ingoldsby, Joe	47	20	14	34	12
Dineen, Bill	44	15	19	34	43
Sabourin, Bob	47	21	11	32	38
Bonhomme, Connie	46	6	26	32	28
Alain, Paul	42	13	17	30	13
Roy, Rod	47	12	14	26	45
Sandford, Fred	38	8	9	17	36
Stanutz, Roy	39	4	10	14	102
Primeau, Bill	44	2	9	11	66
Plata, Ed	16	3	3	6	4
Marshall, Al	43	0	5	5	91
Buchanan, Neil	41	1	1	2	52
Nicoli, Derio	9	0	1	1	8
Ratchford, Mike	7	0	1	1	0
Peart, Don	3	0	0	0	0
Clune, Art	1	0	0	0	0
McNamara, Harold	1	0	0	0	0
Harrison, Gord	1	0	0	0	0
GOALIE	GP	GA	SO	GAA	
Howes, Lorne	47	203	1	4.32	
Young, Ed	1	10	0	10.00	

1950-51

PLAYER	GP	G	A	PTS	PIM
Marshall, Willie	43	29	30	59	20
Dineen, Bill	45	25	26	51	50
Wheldrake, Jack	52	20	29	49	17
Sabourin, Bob	54	25	18	43	54
McDonald, Dan	47	16	20	36	47
Costello, Murray	50	18	16	34	24
Ratchford, Mike	43	13	18	31	22
Lee, Bill	50	13	10	23	18
Sandford, Fred	25	9	12	21	29
Fyles, Tom	30	8	20	28	70
(incl. Marlboros)					
McNamara, Harold	48	6	13	19	116
Schiller, Bob	50	5	11	16	112
Buchanan, Neil	51	1	11	12	98
Clune, Art	35	4	7	11	55
Ingoldsby, Joe	19	4	4	8	4
Plata, Eddie	15	2	5	7	7
McCann, Joe	24	2	1	3	26
Sexton, Bill	7	0	2	2	2
Logan, Jim	2	1	0	1	0
McCarthy, Tom	2	1	0	1	0
Clark, John	2	0	1	1	0
Negladiuk, John	5	0	1	1	6
Schnurr, Joe	4	0	0	0	7
Reaume, Marc	5	0	0	0	2
Wolochatiuk, Walter	3	0	0	0	2
Harrison, Gord	3	0	0	0	0
Schneider,	1	0	0	0	0
Knox, Paul	2	0	0	0	0
Lamon, Paul	1	0	0	0	0
Caffery, Jack	1	0	0	0	0
GOALIE	GP	GA	SO	GAA	
Chadwick, Ed	39	148	2	3.78	
Boehmer, Pat	1	10	9	10.00	
Battaglia, Tom	6	27	0	4.45	
McDonald, A	2	14	0	7.00	
Young, Gerald	6	40	0	7.07	

1951-52

PLAYER	GP	G	A	PTS	PIM
Wallace, Ron	53	32	33	65	22
Sabourin, Bob	51	31	23	54	26
Logan, Jim	50	29	25	54	24
Dineen, Bill	47	21	30	51	37
Ratchford, Mike	48	20	26	46	41
Costello, Murray	51	16	27	43	18
Plata, Ed	47	19	16	35	41
Lee, Bill	42	14	17	31	22
Reaume, Marc	46	11	16	27	44
Knox, Paul	34	12	14	26	10
Schiller, Bob	51	4	18	22	130
Buchanan, Neil	43	5	9	14	86
Jacobi, Mike	39	2	11	13	66
Clune, Art	33	1	9	10	44
Watters, Lorne	16	1	6	7	16
Caffery, Jack	1	2	1	2	0
McDonald, Don	2	0	1	1	0
Knowles,	1	0	0	0	0
GOALIE	GP	GA	SO	GAA	
Chadwick, Ed	49	168	0	3.48	
McNamara, Gerry	5	20	0	4.26	

1952-53

PLAYER	GP	G	A	PTS	PIM
Caffery, Jack	56	37	39	76	38
Plata, Ed	55	29	33	62	105
Costello, Murray	51	30	28	58	38
Lee, Bill	56	20	38	58	31
Logan, John	56	23	29	52	24
Dineen, Bill	53	27	19	46	63
Ratchford, Mike	52	23	18	41	86
Knox, Paul	47	21	20	41	19
Toppazzini, Ted	51	8	18	26	63
Duff, Les	52	7	18	25	72
Reaume, Marc	41	5	16	21	75
Clune, Art	55	1	14	15	60
Linseman, Ken	27	2	7	9	17
Duff, Dick	16	3	2	5	6
Price, Noel	44	0	4	4	120
McGaffin, Paul	14	1	1	2	14
Retty, Jerry	3	0	1	1	0
Watt, Bob	6	0	0	0	0
Colvin, Billy	1	0	0	0	0
Cronin, Jerry	1	0	0	0	2
Pascht, John	6	0	0	0	6
Hope, Bill	1	0	0	0	2
Villemure, Andre	1	0	0	0	0
GOALIE	GP	GA	SO	GAA	
Chadwick, Ed	46	151	3	3.28	
McNamara, Gerry	10	30	0	3.00	

1953-54

PLAYER	GP	G	A	PTS	PIM
Duff, Dick	59	35	40	75	120
Knox, Paul	58	40	28	68	20
Logan, Jim	58	27	31	58	41
Caffery, Jack	47	25	32	57	40
Duff, Les	57	19	36	55	145
Gribbons, Ken	48	25	17	42	24
Colvin, Bill	50	22	20	42	10
Reaume, Marc	55	14	27	41	112
Linseman, Ken	55	13	21	34	47
Anderson, Brian	53	15	17	32	43
Toppazzini, Ted	59	4	23	27	78
Price, Noel	55	6	5	11	157
Pascht, John	54	1	6	7	24
Huggard, Pete	55	0	5	5	114
Hannigan, Pat	14	1	2	3	17
Butler, Bob	3	0	2	2	0
Holmes, Bob	1	1	0	1	2
Watt, Bob	7	0	1	1	8
Mahovlich, Frank	1	0	1	1	2
Robinson, Pete	1	0	1	1	0
Moroney, Des	1	0	1	1	0
Selby, John	1	0	1	1	0
Molinsky, Lorne	1	0	0	0	0
Comi, Angelo	1	0	0	0	0
Green,	1	0	0	0	0
August,	1	0	0	0	0
Vojtech, John	2	0	0	0	0
Bird, Darcy	1	0	0	0	0
Walsh, Joe	1	0	0	0	0
Hope, Bill	3	0	0	0	0
Gionna, Frank	3	0	0	0	0
Seymour, John	4	0	0	0	0
Cornett,	1	0	0	0	0
Kentish,	1	0	0	0	0
Annon,	1	0	0	0	0
Sheehan, Terry	1	0	0	0	0
Wadsworth,	1	0	0	0	0
Davenport,	1	0	0	0	0
Lowe,	1	0	0	0	0
GOALIE	GP	GA	SO	GAA	
McNamara, Gerry	57	205	2	3.59	
Dodds, Bob	2	6	0	3.00	

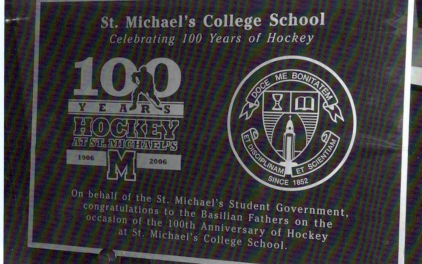

On January 13, 2007, St. Michael's College celebrated its 100-year hockey history as part of CBC-TV's 'Hockey Day in Canada.'

1954-55

PLAYER	GP	G	A	PTS	PIM
Duff, Dick	47	33	20	53	113
Duff, Les	41	13	38	51	112
Colvin, Bill	47	24	27	51	29
Gribbons, Ken	47	19	21	40	39
Linseman, Ken	47	21	17	38	57
Hannigan, Pat	44	13	19	32	40
Anderson, Brian	46	15	15	30	16
Mahovlich, Frank	25	12	11	23	18
Elik, Mike (incl. Marlboros)	43	4	11	15	48
Price, Noel	47	4	11	15	129
Buchmann, Peter	47	4	6	10	17
Pascht, John	47	1	7	8	59
Ubriaco, Gene	28	2	5	7	14
Meldrum, Tom	47	2	5	7	74
Gendron, Viger	47	2	4	6	70
Watt, Bob	47	4	0	4	26
Howarth, Frank	6	1	0	1	0
Selby, John	2	0	0	0	0
Begley, George	1	0	0	0	0
Devine, Hugh	1	0	0	0	0
Comi, Angelo	4	0	0	0	2
Gariepy,	1	0	0	0	0
GOALIE	GP	GA	SO	GAA	
McNamara, Gerry	45	149	2	3.24	

1955-56

PLAYER	GP	G	A	PTS	PIM
Hannigan, Pat	46	38	31	69	121
Mahovlich, Frank	30	24	26	50	55
Haworth, Frank	48	14	34	48	39
McKnight, Bob	48	20	26	46	17
Ubriaco, Gene	48	26	16	42	44
Price, Noel	46	10	22	32	84
Hook, Tim	48	9	13	22	22
Mattiussi, Dick	48	10	7	17	68
Watt, Bob	48	7	10	17	22
McMaster, Jack	17	4	10	15	2
Cushing, Pat	47	6	9	15	23
Foster, Norm	48	3	9	12	91
Angotti, Lou	48	6	6	12	29
Fleming, Reg	42	1	8	9	93
Selby, John	16	1	0	1	0
Gendron, Viger	11	0	1	1	10
Buchen, Steve	12	1	0	1	4
Bird, Darcy	1	0	0	0	2
Sonoski, Jim	3	0	0	0	0
Sullivan, Frank	3	0	0	0	0
Cosinato, Tony	10	0	0	0	7
O'Neill, Paul	48	0	0	0	15
Pallante, Bob	5	0	0	0	2
Draper, Mike	1	0	0	0	0
GOALIE	GP	GA	SO	GAA	
Savage, Bob	28	100	4	3.57	
Kelly, Tom	18	85	0	4.71	
Keenan, Don	2	10	0	5.00	

1956-57

PLAYER	GP	G	A	PTS	PIM
Mahovlich, Frank	49	52	36	88	122
Boucher, Bob	47	41	33	74	113
Ubriaco, Gene	51	22	32	54	49
McMaster, Jack	51	21	23	44	17
McKnight, Bob	52	12	31	43	8
Mattiusi, Dick	52	12	19	31	19
Angotti, Lou	51	11	17	28	28
Foster, Norm	49	2	21	23	127
Sly, Darryl	52	7	7	14	35
Hook, Tim	29	4	7	11	40
Sonosky, Jim	51	6	3	9	8
Rimstad, Dave	51	2	7	9	49
Pallante, Bob	48	0	8	8	63
Fuller, Bob	52	0	5	5	36
Disera, Fred	51	2	2	4	22
Keon, Dave	3	1	3	4	0
Odrowski, Gerry	42	0	1	1	4
Micallef, Tom	1	0	0	0	2
Wilson, Ted	28	0	0	0	30
Draper, Mike	16	0	0	0	7
O'Neill, Paul	8	0	0	0	4
GOALIE	GP	GA	SO	GAA	
Savage, Bob	51	185	1	3.63	
Cheevers, Gerry	1	4	0	4.00	

Through these doors has walked some outstanding hockey talent through the years.

1957-58

PLAYER	GP	G	A	PTS	PIM
Keon, Dave	45	23	27	50	29
Marczak, Henry	54	19	25	44	60
Angotti, Lou	52	23	19	42	72
Costello, Jack	52	19	21	40	27
Sly, Darryl	52	19	20	39	64
Ubriaco, Gene	39	19	18	37	43
Martin, Jack	50	11	15	26	32
McKnight, Bob	52	9	16	25	13
Kozak, Les	38	9	15	24	10
Mattiussi, Dick	51	9	15	24	98
Sonoski, Jim	52	5	13	18	8
Hook, Tim	30	6	10	16	57
Micallef, Tom	46	4	3	7	86
Pallante, Bob	50	3	3	6	41
Jackson, Paul	32	1	2	3	49
Draper, Mike	41	1	2	3	47
Keenan, Larry	3	0	1	1	2
Rebellato, Gene	1	0	1	1	0
Adair, Pat	6	0	1	1	0
O'Malley, Terry	17	0	1	1	2
Turnbull, Harvey	1	0	0	0	0
Baldwin, Pat	1	0	0	0	0
Young, Don	3	0	0	0	4
Draper, Dave	2	0	0	0	0
Draper, Bruce	2	0	0	0	2
Bell, Denny	1	0	0	0	0

GOALIE	GP	GA	SO	GAA
Maniago, Cesare	48	173	2	3.60
Savage, Bob	3	13	0	4.33
Cheevers, Gerry	1	3	0	3.00

1958-59

PLAYER	GP	G	A	PTS	PIM
Draper, Bruce	48	24	25	49	58
Costello, Jack	48	25	24	49	51
Keon, Dave	46	16	29	45	8
Rebelatto, Gene	46	13	23	36	50
Keenan, Larry	48	17	12	29	24
Draper, Dave	48	7	21	28	7
Sly, Darryl	48	8	16	24	58
Sonoski, Jim	46	13	9	22	8
Kozak, Les	43	10	8	18	18
Chambers, Dave	44	9	5	14	35
Jackson, Paul	48	0	13	13	82
Cole, Jack	21	3	7	10	8
O'Malley, Terry	46	1	9	10	84
Epp, Gord	48	1	8	9	52
Turnbull, Dave	15	0	2	2	0
Pallante, Bob	20	0	2	2	30
Cyr, Michael	24	2	0	2	8
Baldwin, Pat	15	0	1	1	4
Fowler, Jim	1	0	0	0	2
Chaczewski, Tom	2	0	0	0	0

GOALIE	GP	GA	SO	GAA
Maniago, Cesare	42	131	4	3.12
Cheevers, Gerry	6	28	0	4.67

1959-60

PLAYER	GP	G	A	PTS	PIM
Keon, Dave	47	33	38	71	31
Keenan, Larry	48	21	20	41	34
Draper, Bruce	38	16	22	38	23
Kozak, Les	42	18	17	35	23
Rebellato, Gene	41	18	8	26	29
Cole, Jack	43	14	7	21	40
Draper, Dave	30	8	11	19	5
Olah, George	48	7	11	18	8
Davidson, Bob	40	6	7	13	28
Cyr, Michael	48	2	10	12	31
Chambers, Dave	43	1	10	11	32
McDonald, Duncan	19	5	5	10	0
O'Malley, Terry	46	4	6	10	75
Jackson, Paul	48	1	9	10	79
Brown, Arnold	48	2	5	7	112
Fowler, Jim	45	2	6	8	33
Turnbull, Harvey	20	1	0	1	2
Champagne, Andre	1	0	0	0	0
MacMillan, Bill	2	0	0	0	0
Galipeau, Roger	2	0	0	0	2
Corbett, Mike	2	0	0	0	0

GOALIE	GP	GA	SO	GAA
Cheevers, Gerry	36	111	5	3.08
Dryden, Dave	12	39	1	3.25

Mike McCarron and his team of organizers created and executed an extraordinary celebration to commemorate 100 years of hockey being played at St. Michael's College. It was a full day of hockey memories for alumni and fans alike.

1960-61

PLAYER	GP	G	A	PTS	PIM
Draper, Bruce	46	44	33	77	46
Keenan, Larry	43	31	38	69	41
Draper, Dave	40	13	26	39	8
Jackson, Dave	48	9	15	24	114
Champagne, Andre	47	11	12	23	59
Cole, Jack	36	9	11	20	18
Osborne, Stan	27	8	11	19	2
MacMillan, Bill	46	7	12	19	31
Brown, Arnold	47	7	11	18	110
O'Malley, Terry	45	3	12	15	79
Conlin, Paul	46	4	10	14	8
Walsh, Brian	45	2	9	11	16
MacDonald, Duncan	47	5	5	10	11
Clancy, Terry	38	2	3	5	30
Galipeau, Roger	47	2	3	5	59
Noakes, Peter	33	2	2	4	10
Cheevers, Gerry	8	0	1	1	12
Corbett, Mike	2	0	1	1	0
Seiling, Rod	3	0	0	0	2
Polanic, Tom	11	0	0	0	8
Dineen, Gary	12	0	0	0	0

GOALIE	GP	GA	SO	GAA
Cheevers, Gerry	30	94	2	3.13
Dryden, Dave	18	66	1	3.67

1961-62

PLAYER	GP	G	A	PTS	PIM
Dineen, Gary	33	25	33	58	19
Corbett, Mike	31	19	33	52	44
Seiling, Rod	31	24	26	50	14
Champagne, Andre	29	14	18	32	79
MacMillan, Bill	28	13	15	28	11
Walton, Mike	29	14	12	26	12
McKendry, Jim	29	10	15	25	17
Conlin, Paul	21	13	8	21	14
Polanic, Tom	23	9	10	19	24
Clancy, Terry	32	3	15	18	16
Therien, Emile	27	7	8	15	67
Dupont, Ray	30	0	15	15	24
MacKenzie, Barry	18	5	9	14	58
Fritz, Tony	25	4	7	11	2
Watson, Barry	15	5	3	8	10
Kirley, Jim	3	0	3	3	0
McDonald, Barry	5	1	1	2	6
Cullen, Jim	4	1	0	1	2
Hutchison, Bill	3	0	1	1	2
Jacks, Barry	3	0	1	1	0
Mulholland, Mike	3	0	1	1	0
Gallant, Lloyd	4	0	0	0	10
Grace, Brian	3	0	0	0	0
Webb, Michael	6	0	0	0	0
Micaleff, Frank	2	0	0	0	0
Delvecchio, Rocky	1	0	0	0	0
Mosdell, Wayne	11	0	0	0	2

GOALIE	GP	GA	SO	GAA
Smith, Gary	31	83	3	2.68
McNabb, Bill	2	8	0	4.00

1997-98

PLAYER	GP	G	A	PTS	PIM
Zoryk, Steve	66	34	27	61	36
Terzo, Anthony	66	20	20	40	57
Stephens, Charlie	58	9	21	30	38
MacMillan, Jason	38	13	14	27	31
Katsuras, Sam	53	11	13	24	4
Cannon, Jason	66	6	18	24	103
Snita, Marcin	59	6	13	19	42
Corupe, Kenny	60	12	6	18	14
Gallace, Steve	39	6	11	17	51
Simpson, Brian	63	7	9	16	101
Dumonski, Steve	27	6	8	14	70
Sulc, Jan	34	3	10	13	11
Lakos, Andre	49	2	10	12	54
Robichaud, Ryan	64	6	6	12	138
Jefferson, Mike	18	4	6	10	77
Walsh, Ryan	50	1	6	7	51
Moriarty, Gerald	52	0	6	6	213
Cava, Chris	64	0	5	5	213
Turyk, Troy	53	1	4	5	152
Katavisto, Ari	41	2	2	4	20
Laceby, Mike	28	1	2	3	4
McKenzie, Scott	16	0	3	3	0
Murphy, Sean	57	1	2	3	115
Scanzano, Wesley	18	1	1	2	5
Stanfield, Rob	16	2	0	2	17
Biagini, Chris	15	0	1	1	23
Alvarez, Mauricio	1	0	0	0	0
Papageorge, Patrick	1	0	0	0	0
Scanzano, Shawn	15	0	0	0	9

GOALIE	GP	GA	SO	GAA
Amidovski, Bujar	48	153	0	3.40
Batten, Corey	25	97	1	4.69
Mehlenbacher, Chad	2	8	0	6.40

1998-99

PLAYER	GP	G	A	PTS	PIM
Keefe, Sheldon	38	37	37	74	80
Corupe, Kenny	68	22	33	55	24
Jefferson, Mike	27	18	22	40	121
Cannon, Jason	61	8	26	34	52
Nistas, George	57	9	24	33	14
Popovic, Mark	60	6	26	32	46
Cation, Shawn	36	9	21	30	129
Delaney, Keith	28	9	17	26	12
Barnes, Ryan	31	11	14	25	215
Boucher, Brock	35	6	18	24	17
Pinizzotto, Jason	64	10	14	24	28
Walsh, Ryan	66	10	10	20	36
Ellis, Matt	47	10	8	18	6
Bootland, Darryl	28	12	6	18	80
DeLeeuw, Adam	29	10	5	15	55
McAllister, Kyle	30	5	10	15	24
Simpson, Brian	60	6	6	12	105
Mulder, Brent	57	4	4	8	97
Gough, Mike	64	4	2	6	42
Stephens, Charlie	7	2	4	6	8
Hynes, Mark	64	1	5	6	66
Pierce, Brad	28	2	3	5	40
Cava, Chris	30	0	4	4	151
Boucher, Chris	55	1	1	2	49
Rasmussen, Ryan	39	0	2	2	30
Lakos, Phil	38	1	0	1	46
MacKenzie, Scott	6	1	0	1	0
Moriarty, Gerald	53	0	1	1	199
Leibel, Cody	3	0	0	0	0
Parfrey, Kevin	1	0	0	0	0
Ritskos, Jamie	1	0	0	0	0
Robichaud, Ryan	4	0	0	0	2
Turyk, Troy	1	0	0	0	2
GOALIE	GP	GA	SO	GAA	
Batten, Corey	13	48	0	3.80	
Dovigi, Patrick	39	143	0	4.28	
Bateman, Dwayne	24	100	0	5.09	
Thomson, Jeff	6	20	0	6.70	

1999-2000

PLAYER	GP	G	A	PTS	PIM
Delaney, Keith	67	24	38	62	60
Walsh, Ryan	68	21	34	55	66
Bootland, Darryl	65	24	30	54	166
Corupe, Kenny	40	22	24	46	47
Popovic, Mark	68	11	29	40	68
Ellis, Matt	59	15	20	35	20
DeLeeuw, Adam	45	11	19	30	107
Bannan, Matt	66	7	20	27	71
Doyle, Jeffrey	65	8	18	26	89
Woollard, Chad	26	13	10	23	31
Minard, Chris	28	5	14	19	6
Boucher, Chris	67	3	14	17	154
Csumrik, Dave	31	7	6	13	42
Gough, Michael	63	7	5	12	95
Mizzi, Greg	49	5	7	12	128
Misita, Lorne	21	6	4	10	33
Simpson, Brian	44	3	6	9	131
Nistas, George	22	1	8	9	8
Cook, Tyler	48	1	8	9	58
Pierce, Brad	40	3	5	8	47
Lakos, Philippe	56	1	7	8	107
Sellan, Mike	64	2	2	4	55
Farquharson, Steve	59	2	1	3	163
Kolarik, Michal	45	1	1	2	46
McAllister, Kyle	3	0	2	2	4
Budaj, Peter	34	0	2	2	6
Bateman, Dwayne	47	0	1	1	10
Rasmussen, Ryan	1	0	0	0	0
Delaney, Ryan	1	0	0	0	0
Mulder, Brent	2	0	0	0	7
Glaves, Rory	6	0	0	0	0
GOALIE	GP	GA	SO	GAA	
Bateman, Dwayne	47	160	0	3.96	
Budaj, Peter	34	112	1	4.01	

2000-01

PLAYER	GP	G	A	PTS	PIM
Walsh, Ryan	65	26	45	71	81
Bootland, Darryl	56	32	33	65	136
Lukes, Frank	61	23	33	56	37
Bannan, Matt	56	19	28	47	52
Ellis, Matt	68	21	24	45	19
Popovic, Mark	61	7	35	42	54
Misita, Lorne	52	16	23	39	52
Brent, Tim	64	9	19	28	31
DeLeeuw, Adam	54	11	14	25	122
Fata, Drew	58	5	15	20	134
Minard, Chris	40	11	8	19	28
Klein, Kevin	58	3	16	19	21
Plunkett, Lindsay	20	8	6	14	27
Gough, Michael	55	6	8	14	84
Doyle, Jeffrey	23	2	10	12	40
Boucher, Chris	68	0	12	12	100
Farquharson, Steve	58	7	4	11	133
Cook, Tyler	54	2	8	10	48
Bacon, Matt	35	3	6	9	44
Reynolds, T.J.	50	1	3	4	163
Robert, Ryan	27	1	1	2	4
Sellan, Mike	58	0	2	2	129
Mizzi, Greg	8	0	1	1	10
Talbot, Scott	2	0	0	0	0
Budaj, Peter	37	0	0	0	0
Chiodo, Andy	38	0	0	0	9
GOALIE	GP	GA	SO	GAA	
Chiodo, Andy	38	86	4	2.49	
Budaj, Peter	37	95	3	2.86	
Talbot, Scott	2	3	0	2.57	

2001-02

PLAYER	GP	G	A	PTS	PIM
Bootland, Darryl	61	41	56	97	137
Ellis, Matt	66	38	51	89	20
Lukes, Frank	63	27	37	64	50
Brent, Tim	61	19	40	59	52
Guenther, Joe	44	23	21	44	43
Popovic, Mark	58	12	29	41	42
Heffernan, Scott	68	4	26	30	93
Fata, Drew	67	7	21	28	175
Klein, Kevin	68	5	22	27	35
Boyce, Darryl	67	10	11	21	71
Bacon, Matt	67	8	9	17	79
Rorabeck, Ryan	61	8	6	14	10
Horvath, Scott	27	7	6	13	19
Knowles, Daryl	9	4	6	10	54
Freeland, Jordan	59	4	5	9	50
Gough, Michael	46	2	7	9	90
Smith, Jerrod	51	2	5	7	29
Patton, Geoff	65	1	6	7	110
Rawski, Steven	38	3	3	6	42
Spurr, Kyle	58	3	3	6	89
Seymour, Matthew	26	1	4	5	9
Bannan, Matt	8	1	2	3	13
Carlesimo, Mike	1	0	1	1	2
Reynolds, T. J.	8	0	1	1	27
Cook, Tyler	10	0	1	1	10
Gimblett, Tyson	29	0	1	1	38
Robert, Ryan	4	0	0	0	0
Talbot, Scott	1	0	0	0	0
Chiodo, Andy	33	0	0	0	9
Budaj, Peter	42	0	0	0	0

GOALIE	GP	GA	SO	GAA
Budaj, Peter	42	89	2	2.29
Chiodo, Andy	33	79	2	2.72
Talbot, Scott	1	4	0	4.00

2002-03

PLAYER	GP	G	A	PTS	PIM
Lukes, Frank	62	27	46	73	55
Brent, Tim	60	24	42	66	74
Klein, Kevin	67	11	33	44	88
Boyce, Darryl	64	16	21	37	119
Seymour, Matthew	68	13	20	33	65
Horvath, Scott	67	19	13	32	61
Peralta, Sal	53	17	15	32	20
Rorabeck, Ryan	55	11	19	30	20
Vitarelli, Cory	55	12	17	29	22
O'Brien, Shane	34	8	11	19	108
Fata, Drew	35	6	13	19	66
Foster, Craig	33	8	9	17	54
Rawski, Steven	42	7	8	15	53
McIver, Nathan	68	5	10	15	121
Bacon, Matt	49	7	7	14	107
Lehman, Scott	53	3	10	13	50
Cameron, Connor	50	4	7	11	45
Nolan, Alan	53	3	5	8	158
Mikhnov, Andrei	26	1	6	7	23
Knowles, Daryl	22	0	5	5	27
Spurr, Kyle	43	2	2	4	113
Rebernik, Chris	43	2	1	3	17
Perry, Ted	40	1	2	3	71
Cunningham, Chris	3	0	0	0	0
Karafiat, Martin	4	0	0	0	2
Patton, Geoff	8	0	0	0	6
Freeland, Jordan	14	0	0	0	6
Gimblett, Tyson	19	0	0	0	32
Onorati, Andrew	1	0	0	0	0
Peters, Justin	27	0	0	0	2
Chiodo, Andy	57	0	0	0	2

GOALIE	GP	GA	SO	GAA
Chiodo, Andy	57	154	3	3.01
Peters, Justin	23	55	0	3.12
Onorati, Andrew	1	1	0	5.45

2003-04

PLAYER	GP	G	A	PTS	PIM
Brent, Tim	53	26	41	67	105
Peralta, Sal	68	23	33	56	45
Rorabeck, Ryan	64	14	34	48	54
Vitarelli, Cory	66	29	18	47	32
Haskings, Tyler	54	17	24	41	30
Boyce, Darryl	64	13	24	37	110
Lehman, Scott	66	5	27	32	189
VanBallegooie, D.	44	7	23	30	40
Cameron, Connor	61	15	11	26	71
Wilson, Ryan	58	3	22	25	88
Kadatskiy, Evgeny	50	13	6	19	30
Good, Dale	42	7	10	17	88
Power, Colin	56	6	9	15	111
Nathan McIver	57	4	11	15	183
Waugh, Thomas	61	7	7	14	17
VanderVeeken, Jamie	48	5	6	11	33
Clutterbuck, Cal	60	4	7	11	112
Perry, Ted	57	0	6	6	137
Rand, Joe	35	2	3	5	25
Foster, Craig	12	4	0	4	12
Maracle, Ian	21	2	2	4	34
Cunningham, Chris	44	1	2	3	55
Peters, Justin	53	0	3	3	15
Pesek, Michal	8	1	1	2	7
McCaffrey, Chad	8	0	2	2	2
Small, Brent	26	0	2	2	2
Lavigne, Scott	6	1	0	1	4
Klein, Kevin	5	0	1	1	23
Spurr, Kyle	2	0	0	0	2
Rebernik, Chris	7	0	0	0	5
Ouzas, Michael	19	0	0	0	0

GOALIE	GP	GA	SO	GAA
Peters, Justin	53	139	4	2.65
Ouzas, Michael	19	47	0	2.91

2004–05

PLAYER	GP	G	A	PTS	PIM
Boyce, Darryl	67	15	35	50	152
Vitarelli, Cory	68	19	20	39	54
Wilson, Ryan	68	13	24	37	149
Power, Colin	53	12	19	31	123
Haskins, Tyler	62	12	20	32	64
Adams, John	55	15	15	30	31
McIver, Nathan	67	4	22	26	160
Donati, Justin	29	6	18	24	20
Ivanov, Alexei	42	11	10	21	31
Lehman, Scott	57	2	19	21	189
Good, Dale	60	4	16	20	106
Larsh, Jeff	35	9	10	19	19
Franchin, Peter	26	12	6	18	34
Donati, Tyler	28	9	8	17	12
Clutterbuck, Cal	38	10	6	16	55
VanderVeeken, Jamie	23	4	8	12	29
DiBenedetto, Justin	64	3	6	9	37
Elder, Travis	58	3	6	9	57
Rorabeck, Ryan	13	3	6	9	10
Halischuk, Matt	30	3	3	6	4
Cunningham, Chris	49	1	4	5	78
Lavigne, Scott	42	1	2	3	8
Montgomery, Craig	12	3	0	3	14
Mrazek, Jaroslav	57	0	2	2	54
Rand, Joe	48	2	0	2	29
Cameron, Connor	9	1	0	1	2
Preston, Cassidy	34	0	0	0	27
Whitely, Steven	30	0	0	0	26

GOALIE	GP	GA	SO	GAA
Peters, Justin	58	146	3	2.78
Savage, Wayne	24	47	1	2.85

2005–06

PLAYER	GP	G	A	PTS	PIM
Donati, Justin	62	46	63	109	50
Vitarelli, Cory	65	42	36	78	78
Haskins, Tyler	56	24	51	75	11
Donati, Tyler	68	36	36	72	50
Wilson, Ryan	64	12	49	61	145
Lehman, Scott	68	5	50	55	175
Caria, Matt	67	10	27	37	65
Halischuk, Matt	61	13	18	31	16
DiBenedetto, Justin	61	17	13	30	58
Larsh, Jeff	49	9	18	27	105
Horsky, Marek	58	6	17	23	44
Franchin, Peter	27	10	6	16	28
Haley, Michael	30	12	0	12	78
Kwiet, Rob	63	3	9	12	76
Mrazek, Jaroslav	61	0	12	12	84
Spade, Steve	38	4	4	8	61
Zamec, Adam	60	2	6	8	39
Lewis, Derek	47	1	5	6	28
Cunningham, Chris	27	0	6	6	40
Shennan, Andrew	21	1	3	4	52
Lavigne, Scott	19	1	2	3	16
Tapper, Anthony	7	1	2	3	4
Preston, Cassidy	17	0	3	3	10
Barletta, Jeff	53	0	2	2	16
Elder, Travis	18	0	2	2	15
Kemp, Eric	3	0	0	0	0
McGurk, Michael	10	0	0	0	6
Penney, Ryan	21	0	0	0	31

GOALIE	GP	GA	SO	GAA
Kubicz, Mark	4	7	0	2.85
Peters, Justin	20	75	0	3.83
Nie, Ryan	4	15	0	3.87
Savage, Wayne	45	174	1	4.05

2006–07

PLAYER	GP	G	A	PTS	PIM
Caria, Matt	59	33	42	75	114
Daugavins, Kaspars	61	18	42	60	64
Donati, Justin	35	26	30	56	24
Haley, Michael	68	30	24	54	174
Pelech, Michael	65	12	35	47	54
Cassidy, Jason	46	24	17	41	49
Kwiet, Rob	57	9	30	39	97
Piva, Matt	47	16	22	38	69
McCready, Matt	50	9	19	28	70
Preston, Cassidy	64	10	14	24	43
Messier, Jesse	24	9	14	23	14
Simich, Darryl	56	4	17	21	59
Elliott, Byron	58	6	10	16	50
Spade, Steve	44	2	10	12	72
Ekelman, Dustin	45	1	8	9	19
Grundmanis, Kriss	59	1	8	9	80
Billingsley, Tim	49	2	6	8	24
Allen, Tyler	50	3	3	6	12
O'Neil, Dylan	52	3	3	6	22
Tapper, Anthony	63	3	3	6	22
Barletta, Jeff	21	0	3	3	19
McGurk, Michael	68	0	3	3	113
Baker, Scott	18	0	2	2	8
Murray, Troy	20	0	2	2	46
Russo, Matt	7	1	0	1	4
Neuber, Kyle	26	0	1	1	70
Rinaldo, Zac	6	0	0	0	2

GOALIE	GP	GA	SO	GAA
Carrozzi, Chris	25	81	0	4.30
Kubicz, Mark	2	6	0	4.52
Savage, Wayne	54	229	1	4.72

2007-08

PLAYER	GP	G	A	PTS	PIM
Daugavins, Kaspars	62	40	34	74	42
Pelech, Michael	68	17	32	49	72
Messier, Jesse	64	21	22	43	72
Cizikas, Casey	62	18	23	41	41
Gaunce, Cameron	63	10	30	40	99
Sparre, Kris	56	22	13	35	33
Piva, Matt	47	16	19	35	40
Billingsley, Tim	68	5	22	27	95
Caria, Matt	20	8	14	22	35
Mayer, Jordan	32	6	11	17	12
Rinaldo, Zac	63	7	7	14	191
Larson, Justin	63	5	9	14	36
Kwiet, Rob	37	2	12	14	45
Tapper, Anthony	65	2	9	11	66
Allen, Tyler	64	6	4	10	25
McReady, Matt	36	1	9	10	47
Neuber, Kyle	54	4	4	8	133
McGurk, Michael	55	0	8	8	61
Barletta, Jeff	29	2	5	7	18
Russo, Matt	63	1	6	7	51
Parlett, Blake	28	0	7	7	53
Ekelman, Dustin	14	2	3	5	2
Elliott, Byron	13	2	2	4	6
Cassidy, Jason	9	1	0	1	18
O'Neil, Dylan	16	1	0	1	7
Bureau, Corey	3	0	1	1	0
Crawford, Bruce	1	0	0	0	0
Lopes, Ryan	1	0	0	0	2
Ciampini, Nick	2	0	0	0	16

GOALIE	GP	GA	SO	GAA
Carrozzi, Chris	47	115	4	2.75
Grieco, Anthony	24	85	0	4.00
Savage, Wayne	7	26	0	5.58
Sibley, Will	1	10	0	10.08

One of the highlights of St. Mike's celebration of "Hockey Day in Canada" on January 13, 2007, was a contest between the St. Mike's Alumni and the NHL Alumni. Performing the ceremonial faceoff between Rod Seiling of St. Mike's and Paul Coffey of the NHL were (left to right) Red Kelly, Harry Howell, Father Jerry Murphy, master of ceremonies (and alumnus) John Derringer of Toronto radio station Q107, and Dick Duff.

Terry Clancy attended the 100-year anniversary celebration and played on the St. Mike's Alumni team. Terry was part of the Majors' Memorial Cup championship in 1961.

APPENDIX 2
St. Michael's Buzzers — All-Time Roster

1933-34

Mike Cassidy
W.J. Cavanaugh
Eddie Conway
Johnny Crawford — NHL
John Faught
John Mitchell
Len Murphy
John "Peanuts" O'Flaherty — NHL
Frank Orsini
Gene Sheedy
Wilt Sheedy
Earl Smith
Dr. Jerry LaFlamme — coach

1934-35

Bus Benson
Bill Burkhart
Tom Dunne
J. Dutka
John Faught
L. Lacey
John LaRose
Bunky Lukasik
Harry McLean
George McNamara
Pat McReavy — NHL
John Mitchell
Frank Orsini
Billy Taylor — NHL
Dr. Jerry LaFlamme — coach

1935-36

Frenchy Alain
Francis Blackhall
Bill Burkhart
John Callahan
John Faught
Warren Heenan
Bunky Lukasik
Harry McLean
Tom McLean
Paul McNamara
Tony Meader
Monette
Bill Stukus
Billy Taylor — NHL
Ab Tonn
Dr. Jerry LaFlamme — coach

1939-40

Frank Bennett — NHL
Bill Callahan
Joe Cleary — captain
Lloyd Coburn
Joe Crothers
Rudy Desilets
Bill Doyle
J. Ferguson
Farrell Gallagher
Lionel McCauley
Brian McDonough
Ernie Midghall
J. Murphy
Cecil Zambri
Father Carter — coach

1940-41

Frank Bennett — NHL
Bill Callahan
Lloyd Coburn
Rudy Desilets
George Dodd
Wallace Finley
Farrell Gallagher — captain
Gerry Gregoire
Gerry Hickey
Barry Lobriaco
Jean Marois — NHL
Ernie Midghall
Tommy "Windy" O'Neill — NHL
Cecil Schmalz
Barry Sullivan
Father Mallon — coach

1941-42

Greg Carter
Bill Conway
Wallace Finley
Frank Imonti
J. Irwin
Jean Marois — NHL
John McReavy
Ernie Midghall
Gerald Midghall
Ray Midghall
Ed O'Reilly
William Silcox
R. Spadoni
L. Trushinski
Father Mallon — coach

1942-43

John Bennett
Hilliard Carter
Steve Coates
Pete D'Agostino
Jack Geary
Paul Kane
Joe Marzalik — captain
Doug McGillivray
Ted McLean
Ray Midghall
Pat Powers
Joe Sadler
Maurice Sadler
Father Whelan — coach

1943-44

John Blute
Hilliard Carter
Frank Clarke
Jack Geary
Gerry Hector
Barney L'Esperance
Doug McGillivray
Frank Murphy
Edmond Odette
Basil Orsini
Paul Pelow — captain
Ed Sandford — NHL
George Scholes
Warren Winslow
Father Flanagan — coach

1944-45

Ed Bury
Bob DeCourcy — NHL
Paul Dopp
Pat Gravelle
Gerry Hector
Ed Harrison — NHL
Leonard "Red" Kelly — NHL
Bill McNamara
Pete McParland
Paul Pelow
Bob Rafferty
Phil Samis — NHL
Ed Sandford — captain, NHL
George Scholes
Warren Winslow
Father Flanagan — coach

1945-46

Jack Donlevy
Bill Dunn
Ray Hannigan — NHL
Bill Holmes
Jim Kelly
Cam MacLellan
Gerald Macoretta
John McLellan — NHL
Pete McParland
Joe Primeau Jr.
George Scholes
Tom Selby
Father Flanagan — coach

1946-47

Jack Corcoran
Joe DeCourcy
Fred Grossi
Bob Heathcott
Jim Imonti
Jim Kelly
Brian McAllister
Ken McNally
Ray Oleksiuk
D'Arcy Prendergast
Joe Primeau Jr.
Tom Selby
Elwood Shell
Father Flanagan — coach

1947-48

Jean-Paul Belisle
Ed Brown
Bill Caswell
Jack Corcoran
Ray Corcoran
Bob Holland
Art Holmes
Jim Imonti
Bill McDonagh — NHL
Dennis Mooney
Bill Primeau
Rocco Volpe
Father Flanagan — coach

1948-49

Gerald Fitzhenry
Gord Harrison
Joe Ingoldsby
Don McDonald
Al McGillivray
Bob McLellan
Jim Michilson
Don Peart
Steve Posivy
Jim Primeau
Rod Roy
Bob Sabourin — NHL
Fred Sandford
Scanlon
Murray Skelton
Father Flanagan — coach

1949-50

Bev Bourke
Art Clune
John Clark
Gord Harrison
Bill Lee
Tom Lemon
Tom McCarthy — NHL
D'Arcy McDonald
Harold McNamara
Joe Michlisin
Ron O'Hearn
Don Peart
Mike "Butch" Ratchford
Joe Scanlon
Bill Tattersall
Mike Wadsworth
Walter Wolochatiuk
Gerry Young
Father Flanagan — coach

1950-51

Bev Bourke
Dino Boem
Jack Caffery — NHL
John Clark
Farrell Crook
Gene Cuccia
Gord Harrison — captain
Paul Knox — NHL
Walter Kruzel
Tom Lemon
Ken Linseman
Jim Logan
Alex MacDonald
Tom McCarthy — NHL
D'Arcy McDonald
Marc Reaume — NHL
Joe Schnurr
Bill Sexton
Father Flanagan — coach

1951-52

Charlie Burns — NHL
Jack Caffery — captain, NHL
Gene Cuccia
Jack Dockeray
Steve Dempsey
Bob Dodds
Dick Duff — NHL
Ray Hoffman
Ken Linseman
Paul Megaffin
John Pascht
Gary Schreider
Frank Zingrone
Father Flanagan — coach

1952-53

Bill Colvin
Gerry Cronin
Jack Dockeray
Bob Dodds
Dick Duff — captain, NHL
Dave Green
Pete Grossi
Bill Hope
Bryan Jones
Ken Linseman
John McRae
Des Moroney
John Pascht
Ed Ratza
Gene Scanlon
Andre Villemure
Frank Zingrone
Father Flanagan — coach

1953-54

Pete Buchmann
Paul Chase
Angelo Comi
Gerry Cronin
Hugh Devine
Jack Dockeray — captain
Frank Dumsha
Frank Glionna
Pat Hannigan — NHL
Frank Howarth
Frank Mahovlich — NHL
Lorne Molinski
John Selby
Father Flanagan — coach

1954-55

Jack Aldridge
Ian Anderson
Steve Bochen
George Begley
Pete Bourke
Tom Bourke
Angelo Comi
Pat Cushing
Hugh Devine
Jack Dockeray
Frank Dumsha
Bill Evon
Daniel Farrell
Thomas Hayes
Ken Hodgkinson
Frank Howarth — captain
Pete Kelly
Paul O'Neill
John Selby
Father Flanagan — coach

1955-56

Steve Bochen
D'Arcy Bird
Pete Bourke — captain
Tony Cusinato
Mike Draper
Bill Fernandez
Al Hinnegan
Don Jackson
Bob Keegan
Don Keenan — NHL
Merv McNamara
Bob Pallante
John Selby
Jim Sonoski
Frank Sullivan
Frank Thickett
Father Flanagan — coach

1956-57

Dave Bain
Bruce Draper — NHL
Dave Draper
Pat Flannery
Derek Holmes
Paul Jackson
David Keon — captain, NHL
Ed Low
Murray McGee
Merv McNamara
Tom Micallef
Terry O'Malley
Bill Sorensen
Frank Sullivan
Don Young
Father Flanagan — coach

1957-58

Bob Adamo
Pat Baldwin
Denny Bell
Larry Bowers
Gerry Cheevers — NHL
Bruce Cullen
Bruce Draper — NHL
Dave Draper
Larry Keenan — NHL
Bob Leger
Butch McGee
Jim McGinnis
George Olah
Terry O'Malley
Gene Rebellato
Harvey Turnbull
Don Young
Father Conway — coach

1958-59

Pat Baldwin
Arnie Brown — NHL
Tom Chasczewski
Gerry Cheevers — NHL
Bill Crawford
Michael Cyr
Roger Felesko
Jim Fowler
Roger Galipeau
Clem Giovanatti
Don Lillow
Duncan MacDonald
Billy MacMillan — NHL
Jim McInnis
Jerry Murphy
George Olah — captain
Jim Randle
Gary Smith — NHL
Wayne Taylor
Harvey Turnbull
Father Conway — coach

1960-61

Girard Albert	
Kevin Burkett	
Paul Cassidy	
Mike Corbett	NHL
Bill Crawford	
Gary Dineen	captain, NHL
Ray Dupont	
Barry Jacks	
Jim McKendry	
Mike McLellan	
Matt Oreskovich	
Tom Polanic	NHL
Mike Savage	
Rod Seiling	NHL
Gary Smith	NHL
Paul Sinclair	
Pete Speyer	
Wally Stanowski Jr.	
Emile Therien	
Father Conway	coach

1961-62

Mike Corrigan	NHL
Jim Cullen	
Rocky Delvecchio	
Bob Dunn	
Don Fraser	
John Gorman	
Brian Grace	
John Harris	
Barry Haywood	
Bert Holmes	
Bill Hutchinson	
Barry Jacks	
Jim Kerley	
Barry MacDonald	
John Mattachioni	
Jerry Merchant	
Frank Micallef	
Tom Morel	
Wayne Mosdell	
Michael Mulhall	
Don Sharpe	
Mike Webb	captain
Jim Young	
Father Volpe	coach

1962-63

Joe Brady	
Don Fraser	
Brian Grace	
Terry Gray	
John Harris	
John Henry	
John Jacquemain	
Frank Micallef	
Garry Monahan	captain, NHL
John Scandiffio	
Mike Sobeski	
Mike Sullivan	
Jim Young	
Father Volpe	coach

1963-64

John Bear	
Tim Belliveau	
Joe Brady	captain
Licio Cengarle	
Andy Culligan	
Tom Donovan	
Brian Dubeau	
Brian Dunn	
Frank Glionna	
Brian Grace	
Michael Grant	
Terry Gray	
John Henry	
John Jacquemain	
Peter McCarney	
Bill McNeill	
Frank Micallef	
Garry Monahan	NHL
Mike Sullivan	
Walter Winnik	
Father Volpe	coach

1964-65

Brock Armstrong	
John Bear	
Dave Cheravaty	
Licio Cengarle	
Grant Cole	
Andy Culligan	captain
Brian Dunn	
Mike Foley	
Don Fraser	
Brian Galbraith	
Paul McCann	
Bill McNeill	
Peter Meilleur	
Frank Micallef	
Pat Monahan	
Nick Slawson	
Bob Young	
Father Volpe	coach

1965-66

Dave Cheravaty	
Licio Cengarle	
Grant Cole	
Andy Culligan	
Bill Deluce	
Larry Fullan	NHL
Rick Fullan	
Brian Galbraith	
Steve Giuliani	
Shane Green	
Pat Killoran	
Paul McCann	
Bill McNeill	captain
Joe Meehan	
John Noble	
Paul Raino	
Nick Slawson	
Bob Young	
Ed Zuccato	
Gerry Marlborough	coach

1966-67

Did not ice a team

1967-68

Mike Boland	NHL
Phil Branston	
Grant Cole	
Larry Fullan	NHL
John Marks	
Sean McDonough	
Mark O'Hara	
John Noble	
Paul Noble	
Don Pagnutti	
Tom Sadler	
John Sher	
Peter Sullivan	NHL
Bob Tunstead	
Ed Zuccato	captain
Father Volpe	coach

1968-69

Phil Branston	captain
Dan Brennan	
Peter Breuer	
Don Ceci	
Daul Daly	
John Hirst	
David Hogg	
Sean McDonough	
Doug Merrit	
Steve Mitchell	
Mark O'Hara	
Paul Noble	
Don Pagnutti	
Doug Pettit	
Vic Sluce	coach

1969-70

Robin Ayers	
Dan Brennan	
Peter Breuer	
Brian Burkett	
Don Ceci	
Paul Cerre	
Dave Gardner	NHL
John Hirst	
David Hogg	
John Lee	
Doug Marrett	
Peter McCann	
Greg McGuire	
Steve Mitchell	captain
Don Pagnutti	
Paul Perras	
Doug Pettit	
Brian Rainey	
Vic Sluce	coach

1970-71

Robin Ayers	
Peter Breuer	
Paul Carpe	
John Cerre	
Gord Cowan	
Mike Dawe	
Dan Desmond	
David Dunn	
Dave Gouglas	
Steve Kelleher	
Neil Korzack	
Bill Low	
Peter McCann	
Dave Maloney	NHL
Paul O'Hara	
Dan O'Donohue	
Paul Perras	
Paul Wieczorek	captain
Vic Sluce	coach

1971-72

Robin Ayers	
Peter Breuer	
Michael Brown	
John Cerre	
Gord Cowan	captain
Greg Croke	
Mike Dawe	
Rick Graham	
Bill Low	
Dave Maloney	NHL
Mike Murray	
Tim O'Connell	
John Poce	
Sandy Santori	
Sam Taggart	
Peter Vandmark	
Vic Sluce	coach

1972-73

Michael Brown
Brian Cleary
Bill Cock
Greg Croke
Jamie Deluce
Danny Djakalovic
Mike Flynn
Rick Graham
Joe Haffey
Mike Murray
John Poce
Peter Ranieri
Greg Reeves — captain
Mike Stornik
Sam Taggart
Les Duff — coach

1973-74

Brian Anderson
Michael Carpe
Brian Cleary
Micha Fedorov
Kevin Fullan
Paul Gardner — NHL
Joe Haffey — captain
Ian MacLellan
John Maroney
Larry Muzzatti
Robbie Nicholls
John O'Hara
John Poce
Jim Ranieri
Peter Ranieri
Dwight Schofield — NHL
Mike Stornik
Phil Turner
Les Duff — coach

1974-75

Brian Anderson
Billy Carroll — NHL
Brian Cleary
Gerry Conroy
Mike Gillis — NHL
Ian MacLellan
John Maroney
Randy Maxwell
Loris Muzzatti
Peter Rajtek
Ray Scochelas
John Stornik — captain
Tim Vince
Mike Draper — coach

1975-76

Brian Anderson
Scott Burkart
Michael Carpe
Billy Carroll — NHL
Gerry Conroy
Phil Degerdon
Mike Ellwood
Dan Haffey
Ken Matwey
Randy Maxwell
Frank McCarthy
Loris Muzzatti — captain
Peter Rajtek
Ray Scochelas
Tim Vince
Mike Draper — coach

1976-77

Dan Batten
Scott Burkart
Gerry Conroy
Dan Duffy
Paul Fitzhenry
Joe Gagliardi
Joe Gallant
Pat Graham — NHL
Dan Haffey
Lauri Ihamaki
Dennis Krmec
Steve Latimer
Daryl Marchant
Ken Matwey
Wayne McDonald
Mike Norton
Mike Pikul
Rick Pikul
Peter Rajtek — captain
Mike Draper — coach

1977-78

Dan Batten
Steve Bice
Scott Burkart
Greg Britz
Dan Duffy
Mark Ellwood
Paul Fitzhenry
Joe Gagliardi
Joe Gallant
Dan Haffey — captain
Mike McCarron
Mike Norton
Peter Petcoff
Mike Pikul
Rick Pikul
Andy Sartor
Bill Yerex
Father Brady — coach

1978-79

Tom Anderson
Dan Batten — captain
Greg Britz — NHL
Tom Clune
Mike David
Mark Ellwood
Bernie Frith
Dick Gagliardi
Joe Gibbs
Rick Harris
Joe Jackman
Shayne Kukulowicz
Scott Magder
Craig Muni — NHL
Pat Murphy
Peter Petcoff
Mike Pikul
Tom Powers
Mike Rajtek
Howard Scruton — NHL
Mike Stothers — NHL
Ken Strong — NHL
Rick Zombo — NHL
George Volpe — coach

1979-80

Tom Anderson
Mark Barbara
Greg Beatty
Brent Chapman
Tom Clune
Wayne Deighton
Gord Dineen — NHL
Steve Feldcamp
Paul Gillis — NHL
John Godawa
John Hutchings
Joe Jackman
Shayne Kukulowicz
Scott Magder
Jeff McIntyre
Scott McLellan — NHL
Kevin O'Rahilly
Mike Pikul — captain
Rob Ricci
Tony Tanti — NHL
Dave Tetley
Brett Vance
Paul Gauthier — coach

1980-81

Mark Badali
Kevin Burden
Chris Callaghan
Nowel Catterall
Brent Chapman
Doug Clarke
Doug Dadswell — NHL
Grant Davidson
Wayne Deighton
Kevin Dineen — NHL
Steve Feldcamp
Mike Franchetto
John Godawa
Darren Gani
Mike Harvey
Joe Jackman
Patrick Kelly
J.J. Lyons
Scott Mader
Jeff McIntyre
Mike Pagnello
Tony Pallante
Tony Piselli
Rob Ricci — captain
George Spezza
Tom Takacs
Rick Tocchet — NHL
Mudge Tompsett
Carmine Vani
John Vechiarelli
Ken Vopni
Jamie Wansborough
Rick Cornacchia — coach

1981–82

Addison
Cliff Albrecht
Hugh Alcorn
Francesco Bazzochi
Chris Callaghan
Nowel Catterall
Gino Cavallini   NHL
Doug Clarke
Doug Dadswell   NHL
Steve Feldcamp
Mike Franchetto
Darren Gani
Rob Grossi
Mike Harvey
Peter Margie
Brian McDavid
Peter McLeod
Rick Mulligan
Mike Snell
Ken Stevens
Drake Turcotte
Ken Vopni
Lorne Wade
Jamie Wansborough   captain
Paul Wong
Norm Young
Frank Zakrajzek
Rick Cornacchia   coach

1982–83

Chris Callaghan
Kevin Carley
Al Carnes
Steve Catterall
Doug Clarke
Gord Cruikshank
Greg Dreschel
Craig Duncanson   NHL
Todd Elik   NHL
Clint Ellicott
John English   NHL
Mike Franchetto
Mark Johnstone
Ken Kingston
Peter Margie
John Marotta
Brian McDonald
Giancarlo Morrone
Rick Mulligan   captain
Joe Polino
Frank Schofield
Mike Snell
Drake Turcotte
Ken Vopni
Rick Cornacchia   coach

1983–84

Scott Bullock
Sean Burke   NHL
Kelly Cain
Chris Callaghan
Kevin Carley
Curtis Coyne
Gord Cruikshank
Junior Delbrocco
Gino DiGiacchino
Jerry Dineen
Greg Dreschel
Clint Ellicott
Steve Ewing
John Massara
Brian McDonald
Giancarlo Morrone
Eric Orschel
Jim Paek   NHL
Mike Pitcher
Andy Pokupec   captain
Phil Quenneville
Cole Sefc
Bryan Staal
Ken Stein
Rick Traugott
Rick Payne   coach

1984–85

Bobby Babcock   NHL
Jamie Baker
Martin Ball
Shawn Bowler
Kevin Carley
Ron Coristine
Curtis Coyne
Gino DiGiacchino
Jerry Dineen
Mike Flanagan
Jordan Flois
Ted Mahovlich
Jim Mandala
John Massara
John McDonald
Alex Moorehead
Giancarlo Morrone   captain
Quinn Moyer
John Murphy
Neil Paterson
Wil Payne
Andy Pokupec
Mike Polodziejczy
Tom Price
Phil Quenneville
Mike Rosati   NHL
Cole Sefc
Jeff Siliphant
Ed Sluga
Bill Teggart
Bill Fifield   coach

1985–86

Jamie Baker
Martin Ball
Frank Bartello
Rick Blakey
Rob Brown
Ron Buffa
Jon Burrows
Frank Canonaco
John Coppa
Phil Corradi
Rob Cowie   NHL
Joe Day   NHL
Bryan Deasley
Brian Denney
Grant Dickson
Chris Govedaris   NHL
Brendan Graham
Piero Greco
Tom Hill
Rick John
Jason Ketchell
Eric Klutke
John Massara
Andrew Matheson
Pierre Morin   captain
John Murphy
Jason Muzzatti   NHL
Dave Noseworthy
Neil Paterson
Mike Payer
Wil Payne
Steve Petricca
Mike Rosati
Vito Sarafini
Peter Schure
Vince Taglioni
Jeff Traill
Tom Wills
Bill Fifield   coach

1986–87

Tom Auge
Jamie Baker
Brad Baxter
Matt Brait
David Brown
Ron Buffa
Chris Caponi
Jeff Chisholm
Sandro Cioffi
Tom Corrigan
Rob Cowie   captain, NHL
Brian Denney
Luc Desrocher
S. Forest
Scott Gayle
Steve Glugosh
Richard Greer
Jeff Harding   NHL
Mike Heaney
Rick John
Steve Jolicoeur
Brad Jones
Eric Klutke
Bill Konstantinou
Mark Krys
Karl Lechowski
Scott MacNair
Jamie Mair
D. Murphy
Jason Muzzatti   NHL
Grant Nearing
Peter Schure
Vince Taglioni
Chris Venkus
Chris Wolanin
Jason Woolley   NHL
Greg Zona
Scott McLellan   coach

1987-88

Brad Baxter
G. Baxter
Ron Bilodeau
Shayne Bowle
Matt Brait
David Brown
Jeff Chisholm
Tom Corrigan
David D'Amico
William Davies
Andy Franklin
Steve Glugosh
Dino Grossi
Mike Heaney
Brad Jones
Bill Konstantinou — captain
Ted Kramer
Rick Lacroix
Gord Law
Angelo Libertucci
Scott MacNair
Jamie Mair
Paul McGuire
Jamie Meraw
Chris Mills
C. Norris
Tim Sebalj
C. Smith
Milton Smith
Vince Taglioni
Jason Woolley — NHL
Frank Zoccoli
Phil Zoccoli
Scott McLellan — coach

1988-89

Brad Baxter
Ron Bilodeau
Matt Brait
Allan Cox
Jason Dexter
Steve Glugosh
Dino Grossi
David Harlock — NHL
Mike Heaney
Brad Jones
Ken Klee — NHL
Perry Kotsopoulos
Rick Lacroix
Gord Law
Angelo Libertucci
Eric Lindros — NHL
Mike MacDougall
Scott MacNair — captain
Wes McCauley
Paul McGuire
Rich Perrie
Pat Rodgers
Rich Shulmistra — NHL
Michael Thompson
Phil Zoccoli
Scott McLellan — coach

1989-90

Did not ice a team

1990-91

Adrian Adams
Paul Alloway
David Barozzino
Shawn Betts
Jeff Bird
Todd Blackman
Brad Brown — NHL
Paul Cappizano
Alan Clarke
Ben Davis
Paolo Distasi
Mike Fabro
Bill Fry
Frank Gianfrido
Carmelo Giurleo
Jason Gladney
J. Gosselin
Justin Gray
Steve Grogan
Scott Harris
Jeff Harvey
Kevin Hastings
Scott Hay
J. Jaravis
Steve Kavanaugh
Chad Lang
Dan Larmer — captain
Greg Lonsdale
Derek Mann
Glen Martin
Mickey Mitrovic
Tony Patruno
Mike Peron
David Ranieri
Craig Reckin
Mark Sakala
Steve Thorpe
David Vililanti
Kevin Weekes — NHL
Greg Carrigan — coach

1991-92

David Barozzino
Pat Bellmore
Todd Blackman
Mike Bourne
Rob Boyko
Sonny Cardillo
Alan Clarke
Alfonso D'Allesio
Ben Davis — captain
Jamie Edwards
Brad Englehart
Mike Fabro
Bill Fry
Mike Haaksma
Ashlin Halfnight
Don Harris
Scott Harris
Scott Hay
Jim Hibbert
Sean Keck
Andrew Knott
J.P. Latreille
Brett Lindros — NHL
David Ling — NHL
Mark Luciuk
Dan Lupo
David Lylyk
Derek Mann
Ian McGonigal
Paul McInnis
Craig Reckin
Rob Shewchuk
Phil Simeon
Phil Sturock
Art Thomas
John Versteeg
Kevin Weekes — NHL
Tom Wilson
Adam Young
Gord Davies — coach

Although born in 1938, Gerry Odrowski still plays hockey on a regular basis. He was part of the game between St. Mike's Alumni and the NHL Alumni during the 100-year birthday celebration.

1992–93		1993–94		1994–95		1995–96	
Ryan Appel		Mike Cinelli		Chris Aishford		Chris Aishford	captain
Tom Basset		Kevin Crowe		Syl Apps III		Kip Brennan	NHL
Pat Bellmore		Matt Cumming		Steve Aquino		David Cinelli	
Dan Bellissimo		Ryan Davis		Mark Borg		Charlie Clark	
Jason Bertrand		John Day		Ryan Connolly		Rob Davison	NHL
James Boyd		John Direnzo		John Day		John Day	
Aaron Brand		Jamie Edwards		Jamie Edwards		Jamie Edwards	
Jason Couture		D.J. England		Jamie Evans		John Feeney	
Jamie Edwards		Steven Flynn		John Feeney		Chris Gallagher	
Bill Emra		Paul Gagne		Steven Flynn		David Gallo	
Ron Fleming		Erik Goldhar		Chris Gallucci		Trevor Grzybowkski	
Erik Goldhar		Don Harris		Don Harris		Mike Hurst	
Bill Govedaris		Erik Hartwig		Richard Irwin		Dean Jackson	
Ashlin Halfnight		Pavo Kekki		Bryan Kennedy		Darron Johnson	
Don Harris		Bryan Kennedy		Shane Killeen		J.C. Larocque	
John Jakopin	NHL	Shane Killeen		Rob Koh		Justin LeBlanc	
Scott Johnson		Andrew Knott		J.C. Larocque		Rob Ligas	
Pavo Kekki		Rob Koh		Justin LeBlanc		Scott MacDonald	
Bryan Kennedy		Andrew Lane		Rob Ligas		Ian McGonigal	
Andrew Knott	captain	Rob Ligas		Scott Ludeviks	captain	Jason Mikula	
Rob Koh		Scott Ludeviks		Ryan MacDonald		Martin Miljko	
Matt Langford		Jeff Marlow		Mark Moore		Norm Milley	NHL
Luciano Lossigio		Carl Marone		Al Nobes		Steve Montador	NHL
Scott Ludeviks		Craig McGillivray		D'Arcy O'Shea		Dan Nicoletti	
J. MacDonald		Ian McGonigal	captain	Ryan Poulton		Kevin O'Flaherty	
Ian McGonigal		Jeremy Miculinic		Brandon Sugden		Dan Passero	
Craig Mills	NHL	Fraser Morrison		Mark Szucs		Mike Piercey	
D. Morrison		Al Nobes		Matt Thomas		Matt Reda	
G. Moxey		D'Arcy O'Shea		Dave Barrett	coach	Pat Sills	
Rob Othman		Jason Payne-Cato				Casey Sinclair	
Claudio Peca		Paul Porcaro				Mike Spagnuolo	
Joe Ramani		Ryan Poulton				Peter Zavodny	
Craig Reckin		Dave Przeciszowski				Dave Barrett	coach
Vic Sharma		Rob Soja					
Phil Simeon		Andy Sutton	NHL				
Matt Thomas		Mark Szucs					
George Trakosas		Matt Thomas					
Ken Moodie	coach	Lui Vedovat					
Dave Barrett	coach	Bill Velliaris					
		Michael Wiseman					
		Dave Barrett	coach				

1996-97

Chris Aishford
Elliot Altberg
Nelson Avila
Matt Bannan
Mark Cappizano
David Cinelli
Elio D'Allesio
Rob Davison — NHL
Dmitri Deryabin
Danny DiMauro
Mike Dunsmuir
Anthony Dyriak
Adrano Fiacconi
Lou Foulidis
Chris Gallagher
David Gallo — captain
Mike Glumac — NHL
John Harper
Mike Hurst
Pujjuut Kusugac
Lawrence Longo
Peter McRae
George Nistas
Steve Nobili
Kevin O'Flaherty
John Osborne
Conor O'Shea
Matt Reda
Jim Sharpe
Pat Sills
Anton Strgacic
Kevin Tatum
Matt Thomas
Clarke Walford
Peter Zavodny
Mike Futa — coach

1997-98

Did not ice a team

1998-99

Did not ice a team

1999-2000

Rick Arnaldo
Patrick Barbieri
Vince Bellissimo
Stephen Dennis
Steve Direnzo
Pat Dovigi
Drew Fata — NHL
A.J. Greco
Andy Gillies
Rory Glaves
Adrian Henke
Adrian Kremblewski
Mark Lato
Jonathon Lehun
Michael McIsaac
Jordan Meloff
Colin Molloy
Matt Napier
Jan Olbrycht
Nick Onody
David Ovcjak — captain
Mike Prsa
Bryan Sand
Nick Small
David Williams
Michael Zuccan
Chris DePiero — coach

2000-01

Luciano Aquino
Patrick Barbieri
Chris Beckford-Tseu — NHL
Ron Berman
Vince Bellissimo
Stephen Dennis
Mark Anthony Franco
James Gadon
A.J. Greco
Daniel Greenbaum
Brady Jones
Adrian Kremblewski
Mark Lato
Jonathon Lehun
Michael McIsaac — captain
Nick Onody
Daniel Pegoraro
Geoff Platt — NHL
Mike Prsa
Chris Sgro
Nick Small
Anthony Stewart — NHL
Phil Turi
Chris DePiero — coach

2001-02

Mike Carlesimo
Joe Cooper
Stephen Dennis — captain
George Eliopolous
Mark Anthony Franco
James Gadon
Tyson Gimblett
Brian Ihnacak
Adrian Kremblewski
Jeff Kyrzakos
Jonathon Lehun
Matthew McIsaac
Drew Morrison
Michael Nicoletti
Nick Onody
Andrew Onorati
Daniel Pegoraro
Kevin Pickles
Nick Pomponio
Mike Prsa
Matt Seymour
Gord Simms
Tayler Simpson
Kyle Spurr
Mike Sullivan
Ryan Sullivan
Wojtek Wolski — NHL
Stefan Wonfor
Chris DePiero — coach

2002-03

Mike Alexiou
Charles Amodeo
Jacob Anderson
Trevor Battaglia
Ryan Berlingieri
Jamie Coghlan
Joe Cooper
Anthony Denino
Anthony Dinunzio
Michael Ella
Mike Fox-Higgins
Steve Henwood
Brian Ihnacak
Sean Kavanaugh
Jeff Kyrzakos
Scott Malcolm
Joe Milo
Chris Nugent
Kevin Pickles
Michael Potacco
Kevin Schmidt
Peder Skinner
Matthew Spezza
Ryan Sullivan — captain
Phil Turi
Daniel Vukovic
Stefan Wonfor
Chris DePiero — coach

2003-04

Jacob Anderson
Dan Bellissimmo
Corey Black
Tomek Budziakowski
Mike Carlesimo
Jamie Coghlan — captain
Andrew Cogliano — NHL
Sal Cutillo
Anthony Denino
Tony Dinunzio — captain
Brian Dunnigan
Matthew Ganas
Igor Gongalskyi
Steve Henwood
Matthew Kang
Jeff Kyrzakos
Jonathan Man
Matthew McIsaac
Egor Mironov
Derek Patskou
Michael Potacco
Kevin Schmidt
Patrick Sexton
Tayler Simpson
Peder Skinner
Jhase Sniderman
Matthew Spezza
Lee Swallow
Harrison Taylor
Kain Tisi
Phil Turi
Daniel Vukovic
Stefan Wonfor
Julian Zamparo
Chris DePiero — coach

2004–05

Paul Boissoneault
Chris Borges
Mike Binnington
Fred Cassiani
Matt Clune
Andrew Cogliano   NHL
John Costa
Aaron Dileo
Stephen Duffy
Mike Forgione
Ben Gazdic
Mike Gershon
Igor Gongalskyi
Matt Halischuk
Jeff Henderson
Steve Henwood
Brayden Irwin
Matthew Kang
Roger Kim
Mike Liambas
Daniel Lombardi
Mark Lozzi   captain
Jonathan Man
Brent McGrail
Mike McKenzie
Egor Mironov
Craig Montgomery
Michael Pelech
Michael Potacco
Zach Ray
Kevin Schmidt
Tyler Sgro
Dan Silva
Harrison Taylor
Jeff Taylor
Kain Tisi
Corey Wickett
Julian Zamparo
Chris DePiero   coach

2005–06

Angelo Asaro
Jeff Barletta
Mike Binnington
Louie Caporusso
Fred Cassiani
Aaron Dileo
Peter Drikos
Stephen Duffy
Mike Forgione
Mitch Goldenberg
Gilles Hickey
Mike Hossack
Brayden Irwin
Jonathan Man
Mike McKenzie   captain
Cassidy Preston
Lou Santelli
Brock Sawyer
John Scrymgeour
Tyler Sgro
Brendan Smith
Rory Smith
Mike Tansey
Harrison Taylor
Jeff Taylor
Julian Zamparo   captain
Chris DePiero   coach

2006–07

Angelo Asaro
Thomas Bark
Mike Binnington
Jeff Brown
Scott Burkhart
Brandon Burlon
Francesco Caporusso
Louie Caporusso
Fred Cassiani   captain
Matt Clune
Andrew Doyhenard
Stephen Duffy   captain
Nico Figliano
Sean Fontyn
Tyler Forbes
Mike Forgione
Cory Gershon
Tyler Kelloway   captain
Nikolai Knights
Greg Miller
Taylor Murphy
Kyle Neuber
Brian Potacco
Stefan Salituro
Brock Sawyer
Tyler Sgro
Brendan Smith
Rory Smith
Justin Troiani
Rich Ricci   coach

2007–08

J.P. Anderson
Erik Axell
Thomas Bark
Jeff Brown
Brandon Burlon
Fred Cassiani   captain
Daniel Ciampini
Nick Ciampini
Nick D'Agostino
Tyler Forbes
Cory Gershon
Sam Johnson
Jesse Juha
Eli Kim-Swallow
Adam Miceli
Greg Miller
Ben Morse
Louke Oakley
Kyle Pereira
Sean Perkins
David Porco
Brian Potacco
Cassidy Preston
Frank Salituro
Reilly Smith
Rory Smith
Dave Stevens
Justin Troiani
Rich Ricci   coach

Dick Duff finds his photograph on the St. Michael's College Wall of Fame.

St. Michael's Buzzers — All-Time Roster

APPENDIX 3

St. Michael's Alumni in National Hockey League

PLAYER	POSITION	YEARS	NHL DEBUT	SEASONS	NHL TEAM(S)
Reg Noble	forward/defence	1915–16	1917–18	16	Toronto, Montreal Maroons, Detroit
Stan Brown	defence	1917–18	1926–27	2	New York Rangers, Detroit
Art Gauthier	forward	1920–21	1926–27	1	Montreal Canadiens
Larry Aurie	forward	1921–22	1927–28	12	Detroit
Joe Primeau	forward	1924–27	1927–28	9	Toronto
Dave Trottier	forward	1923–24	1928–29	11	Montreal Maroons, Detroit
Bill Regan	defence	1925–29	1929–30	3	New York Rangers, New York Americans
Eddie Convey	forward	1927–29	1930–31	3	New York Americans
D'Arcy Coulson	defence	1927–29	1930–31	1	Philadelphia Quakers
Art Jackson	forward	1933–34	1934–35	11	Toronto, New York Americans, Boston
Pep Kelly	forward	1929–33	1934–35	8	Toronto, Chicago, Brooklyn
Nick Metz	forward	1930–34	1934–35	12	Toronto
Reg Hamilton	defence	1933–34	1935–36	12	Toronto, Chicago
Bobby Bauer	forward	1929–33	1936–37	9	Boston
Harold Jackson	defence	1935–36	1936–37	8	Chicago, Detroit
Chuck Corrigan	forward	1935–36	1937–38	2	Toronto, New York Americans
Johnny Crawford	defence	1933–35	1937–38	13	Boston
Clare Drouillard	forward	1933–34	1937–38	1	Detroit
Don Willson	forward	1933–34	1937–38	2	Montreal Canadiens
Pat McReavy	forward	1934–36	1938–39	4	Boston, Detroit
Harvey Teno	goaltender	1933–35	1938–39	1	Detroit
Don Metz	forward	1931–36	1939–40	7	Toronto
John O'Flaherty	forward	1932–35	1939–40	1	New York Americans
Billy Taylor	forward	1935–36	1939–40	7	Toronto, Detroit, Boston, New York Rangers
Frank Bennett	forward	1935–41	1940–41	1	Detroit
Frank Dunlap	forward	1935–38	1940–41	1	Toronto
Fred Hunt	forward	1935–37	1940–41	5	New York Americans, New York Rangers
Tommy O'Neill	forward	1939–42	1940–41	1	Toronto
John Marois	goaltender	1939–42	1943–44	2	Toronto, Chicago
Carl Smith	forward	1934–35	1943–44	1	Detroit
Ted Lindsay	forward	1943–45	1944–45	17	Detroit, Chicago
Leo Gravelle	forward	1944–45	1945–46	5	Montreal Canadiens, Detroit
Jim Thomson	defence	1943–45	1945–46	13	Toronto, Chicago
Gus Mortson	defence	1943–47	1946–47	13	Toronto, Chicago, Detroit
Bob DeCourcy	goaltender	1942–46	1947–48	1	New York Rangers
Ed Harrison	forward	1940–46	1947–48	4	Boston, New York Rangers
Red Kelly	defence/forward	1943–47	1947–48	20	Detroit, Toronto
Fleming Mackell	forward	1945–47	1947–48	12	Toronto, Boston
Johnny McCormack	forward	1943–44	1947–48	8	Toronto, Montreal Canadiens, Chicago
Ed Sandford	forward	1941–47	1947–48	9	Boston, Detroit, Chicago
Tod Sloan	forward	1944–46	1947–48	13	Toronto, Chicago
Les Costello	forward	1944–47	1948–49	2	Toronto
Ray Hannigan	forward	1945–47	1948–49	1	Toronto
John Arundel	defence	1944–45	1949–50	1	Toronto

PLAYER	POSITION	YEARS	NHL DEBUT	SEASONS	NHL TEAM(S)
Norm Corcoran	forward	1946–49	1949–50	4	Boston, Detroit, Chicago
Tim Horton	defence	1947–49	1949–50	25	Toronto, New York Rangers, Pittsburgh Penguins, Buffalo
Bill McDonagh	forward	1947–48	1949–50	1	New York Rangers
Rudy Migay	forward	1946–47	1949–50	10	Toronto
Phil Samis	defence	1944–45	1949–50	1	Toronto
Frank Sullivan	defence	1942–43	1949–50	4	Toronto, Chicago
Benny Woit	forward	1946–48	1950–51	7	Detroit, Chicago
Ray Barry	forward	1947–49	1951–52	1	Boston
Mike Buchanan	defence	1942–49	1951–52	1	Chicago
Leo Labine	forward	1949–50	1951–52	11	Boston, Detroit
John McLellan	forward	1945–46	1951–52	1	Toronto
Bob Sabourin	forward	1948–52	1951–52	1	Toronto
Gord Hannigan	forward	1947–49	1952–53	4	Toronto
Willie Marshall	forward	1949–50	1952–53	8	Toronto
Murray Costello	forward	1952–53	1953–54	4	Chicago, Boston, Detroit
Bill Dineen	forward	1949–53	1953–54	5	Detroit, Chicago
Jack Caffery	forward	1948–54	1954–55	3	Toronto, Boston
Dick Duff	forward	1951–55	1954–55	18	Toronto, New York Rangers, Montreal Canadiens, Los Angeles, Buffalo
Paul Knox	forward	1947–53	1954–55	1	Toronto
Marc Reaume	defence	1950–52	1954–55	17	Toronto, Detroit, Montreal Canadiens, Vancouver
Ed Chadwick	goaltender	1952–53	1955–56	6	Toronto, Boston
Wally Clune	defence	1946–48	1955–56	1	Montreal Canadiens
Frank Mahovlich	forward	1953–57	1956–57	22	Toronto, Detroit, Montreal Canadiens
Tom McCarthy	forward	1947–51	1956–57	4	Detroit, Boston
Noel Price	defence	1953–56	1957–58	14	Toronto, New York Rangers, Detroit, Montreal Canadiens, Pittsburgh Penguins, Los Angeles, Atlanta Flames
Charlie Burns	forward	1949–51	1958–59	11	Detroit, Boston, Oakland, Pittsburgh Penguins, Minnesota North Stars
Don Keenan	goaltender	1954–56	1958–59	1	Boston
Reg Fleming	forward	1955–56	1959–60	14	Montreal Canadiens, Chicago, Boston, New York Rangers, Philadelphia Flyers, Buffalo
Pat Hannigan	forward	1954–56	1959–60	5	Toronto, New York Rangers, Philadelphia Flyers
David Keon	forward	1956–60	1960–61	22	Toronto, Hartford
Cesare Maniago	goaltender	1957–59	1960–61	15	Toronto, Montreal Canadiens, New York Rangers, Minnesota North Stars, Vancouver
Jack Martin	forward	1957–58	1960–61	1	Toronto
Gerry McNamara	goaltender	1950–54	1960–61	2	Toronto
Gerry Odrowski	defence	1956–57	1960–61	10	Detroit, Oakland, St. Louis
Howie Young	defence	1951–52	1960–61	10	Detroit, Chicago, Vancouver
Arnie Brown	defence	1957–61	1961–62	13	Toronto, New York Rangers, Detroit, Atlanta Flames, Vancouver
Gerry Cheevers	goaltender	1955–60	1961–62	16	Toronto, Boston
Dave Dryden	goaltender	1960–61	1961–62	14	New York Rangers, Chicago, Buffalo, Edmonton
Larry Keenan	forward	1956–60	1961–62	6	Toronto, St. Louis, Buffalo, Philadelphia Flyers
Les Kozak	forward	1956–60	1961–62	1	Toronto
Andre Champagne	forward	1959–62	1962–63	1	Toronto
Bruce Draper	forward	1954–60	1962–63	1	Toronto
Rod Seiling	defence	1961–62	1962–63	17	Toronto, New York Rangers, Washington, St. Louis, Atlanta Flames
Lou Angotti	forward	1953–58	1964–65	11	New York Rangers, Chicago, Philadelphia Flyers, Pittsburgh Penguins, St. Louis
Peter Mahovlich	forward	1961–63	1965–66	16	Detroit, Montreal Canadiens, Pittsburgh Penguins
Darryl Sly	defence	1957–58	1965–66	4	Toronto, Minnesota North Stars, Vancouver
Gary Smith	goaltender	1959–63	1965–66	15	Toronto, Oakland, Chicago, Vancouver, Minnesota North Stars, Washington, Winnipeg
Mike Walton	forward	1960–62	1965–66	14	Toronto, Boston, Vancouver, St. Louis, Chicago

PLAYER	POSITION	YEARS	NHL DEBUT	SEASONS	NHL TEAM(S)
Terry Clancy	forward	1959–62	1967–68	4	Oakland, Toronto
Mike Corbett	forward	1956–62	1967–68	1	Los Angeles
Mike Corrigan	forward	1961–62	1967–68	10	Los Angeles, Vancouver, Pittsburgh
Dick Mattiussi	defence	1956–58	1967–68	4	Pittsburgh Penguins, California, Oakland
Garry Monahan	forward	1962–64	1967–68	12	Montreal Canadiens, Detroit, Los Angeles, Vancouver, Toronto
Gene Ubriaco	forward	1955–57	1967–68	3	Pittsburgh Penguins, California, Oakland, Chicago
Gary Dineen	forward	1960–62	1968–69	1	Minnesota North Stars
Barry MacKenzie	defence	1960–62	1968–69	1	Minnesota North Stars
Gerry Meehan	forward	1960–65	1968–69	10	Toronto, Philadelphia Flyers, Buffalo, Vancouver, Atlanta Flames, Washington
Terry Caffery	forward	1966–68	1969–70	5	Chicago, Minnesota North Stars
Tom Polanic	defence	1959–62	1969–70	2	Minnesota North Stars
Billy MacMillan	forward	1959–62	1970–71	7	Toronto, Atlanta Flames, New York Islanders
Dave Gardner	forward	1966–70	1972–73	7	Montreal Canadiens, St. Louis, California, Philadelphia Flyers, Washington
Mike Boland	forward	1966–68	1974–75	1	Philadelphia Flyers
Larry Fullan	forward	1962–67	1974–75	1	Washington
Dave Maloney	defence	1970–71	1974–75	11	New York Rangers, Buffalo
Paul Gardner	forward	1970–76	1976–77	7	Colorado Rockies, Toronto, Pittsburgh Penguins
Dwight Schofield	defence	1972–74	1976–77	12	Detroit, Montreal Canadiens, Washington, Pittsburgh Penguins, Winnipeg
Mike Kaszycki	forward	1971–72	1977–78	5	New York Islanders, Washington, Toronto
Mike Gillis	forward	1972–75	1978–79	6	Colorado Rockies, Boston
Peter Sullivan	forward	1967–68	1979–80	2	Winnipeg
Billy Carroll	forward	1974–76	1980–81	7	New York Islanders, Edmonton, Detroit
Paul Gillis	forward	1979–80	1980–81	12	Quebec, Chicago, Hartford
Tony Tanti	forward	1979–80	1980–81	12	Chicago, Vancouver, Pittsburgh Penguins, Buffalo
Pat Graham	forward	1975–79	1981–82	3	Pittsburgh Penguins, Toronto
Craig Muni	defence	1977–78	1981–82	16	Toronto, Edmonton, Chicago, Buffalo, Winnipeg, Pittsburgh Penguins, Dallas
Gord Dineen	defence	1979–80	1982–83	13	New York Islanders, Minnesota North Stars, Pittsburgh Penguins, Ottawa
Scott McLellan	forward	1977–80	1982–83	2	Boston
Howard Scruton	defence	1977–79	1982–83	1	Los Angeles
Ken Strong	forward	1978–79	1982–83	1	Toronto
Greg Britz	forward	1978–79	1983–84	4	Toronto, Hartford
Gino Cavallini	forward	1981–82	1984–85	9	Calgary, St. Louis, Quebec
Kevin Dineen	forward	1979–81	1984–85	18	Hartford, Philadelphia Flyers, Carolina, Ottawa
Mike Stothers	defence	1978–79	1984–85	4	Philadelphia Flyers, Toronto
Rick Tocchet	forward	1979–81	1984–85	18	Philadelphia Flyers, Pittsburgh Penguins, Los Angeles, Boston, Washington, Phoenix
Rick Zombo	defence	1979–80	1984–85	12	Detroit, St. Louis, Boston
Craig Duncanson	forward	1982–83	1985–86	7	Los Angeles, Winnipeg, New York Rangers
Doug Dadswell	goaltender	1979–80	1986–87	2	Calgary
Sean Burke	goaltender	1981–85	1987–88	18	New Jersey, Hartford, Carolina, Vancouver, Philadelphia Flyers, Florida, Phoenix, Tampa, Los Angeles
John English	defence	1982–83	1987–88	1	Los Angeles
Jeff Harding	forward	1986–87	1988–89	2	Philadelphia Flyers
Todd Elik	forward	1980–82	1989–90	8	Los Angeles, Minnesota North Stars, Edmonton, San Jose, St. Louis, Boston
Chris Govedaris	forward	1985–86	1989–90	4	Hartford, Toronto
Bob Babcock	defence	1983–84	1990–91	1	Washington
Jim Paek	defence	1983–84	1990–91	5	Pittsburgh Penguins, Los Angeles, Ottawa
Joe Day	forward	1985–86	1991–92	3	Hartford, New York Islanders
Jason Woolley	defence	1986–88	1991–92	14	Washington, Florida, Pittsburgh Penguins, Buffalo, Detroit
Eric Lindros	forward	1988–89	1992–93	13	Philadelphia Flyers, New York Rangers, Toronto, Dallas

PLAYER	POSITION	YEARS	NHL DEBUT	SEASONS	NHL TEAM(S)
David Harlock	defence	1988–89	1993–94	8	Toronto, Washington, New York Islanders, Atlanta Thrashers
Jason Muzzatti	goaltender	1985–87	1993–94	5	Calgary, Hartford, New York Rangers, San Jose
Rob Cowie	defence	1985–87	1994–95	2	Los Angeles
Ken Klee	defence	1988–89	1994–95	Active	Washington, Toronto, New Jersey, Colorado Avalanche, Atlanta Thrashers
Brett Lindros	forward	1991–92	1994–95	2	New York Islanders
Craig Mills	forward	1992–93	1995–96	3	Winnipeg, Chicago, Toronto
Brad Brown	defence	1990–91	1996–97	7	Montreal Canadiens, Chicago, New York Rangers, Minnesota Wild, Buffalo
David Ling	forward	1991–92	1996–97	5	Montreal Canadiens, Columbus
John Jakopin	defence	1989–93	1997–98	6	Florida, Pittsburgh Penguins, San Jose
Marc Moro	forward	1991–93	1997–98	4	Mighty Ducks of Anaheim, Nashville, Toronto
Rich Shulmistra	goaltender	1988–89	1997–98	3	New Jersey, Florida
Kevin Weekes	goaltender	1990–92	1997–98	Active	Florida, Vancouver, New York Islanders, Tampa, Carolina, New York Rangers, New Jersey
Mike Rosati	goaltender	1982–86	1998–99	1	Washington
Andy Sutton	defence	1993–94	1998–99	Active	San Jose, Minnesota, Atlanta Thrashers, New York Islanders
Mike (Jefferson) Danton	forward	1998–99	2000–01	3	New Jersey, St. Louis
Sheldon Keefe	forward	1998–99	2000–01	3	Tampa
Kip Brennan	forward	1995–96	2001–02	Active	Los Angeles, Atlanta Thrashers, Anaheim, New York Islanders
Norm Milley	forward	1995–96	2001–02	Active	Buffalo, Tampa
Steve Montador	defence	1995–96	2001–02	Active	Calgary, Florida, Anaheim
Steve Moore	forward	1992–97	2001–02	3	Colorado Avalanche
Rob Davison	defence	1996–97	2002–03	Active	San Jose, New York Islanders, Vancouver
Jason Spezza	forward	1997–98	2002–03	Active	Ottawa
Charlie Stephens	forward	1997–99	2002–03	2	Colorado Avalanche
Ryan Barnes	forward	1998–99	2003–04	1	Detroit
Darryl Bootland	forward	1998–2002	2003–04	Active	Detroit, New York Islanders
Andy Chiodo	goaltender	1997–2002	2003–04	1	Pittsburgh
Dominic Moore	forward	1994–99	2003–04	Active	New York Rangers, Pittsburgh Penguins, Minnesota Wild, Toronto
Mark Popovic	defence	1998–2000	2003–04	Active	Anaheim, Atlanta Thrashers
Peter Budaj	goaltender	1999–2002	2005–06	Active	Colorado Avalanche
Mike Glumac	forward	1996–97	2005–06	Active	St. Louis
Kevin Klein	defence	2000–03	2005–06	Active	Nashville
Geoff Platt	forward	2000–01	2005–06	Active	Columbus, Anaheim
Anthony Stewart	forward	2000–01	2005–06	Active	Florida
Wojtek Wolski	forward	2001–02	2005–06	Active	Colorado Avalanche
Tim Brent	forward	2000–04	2006–07	Active	Anaheim, Pittsburgh
Matt Ellis	forward	1998–02	2006–07	Active	Detroit, Los Angeles
Drew Fata	defence	2000–03	2006–07	Active	New York Islanders
Nathan McIver	defence	2002–05	2006–07	Active	Vancouver
Shane O'Brien	defence	2002–03	2006–07	Active	Anaheim, Tampa
Darryl Boyce	forward	2001–05	2007–08	Active	Toronto
Cal Clutterbuck	forward	2003–05	2007–08	Active	Minnesota Wild
Andrew Cogliano	forward	2003–05	2007–08	Active	Edmonton
Corey Locke	forward	1999–2000	2007–08	Active	Montreal, Anaheim
Chris Beckford-Tseu	goaltender	2000–01	2007–08	Active	St. Louis
Chris Minard	forward	1999–2001	2007–08	Active	Pittsburgh

APPENDIX 4
St. Michael's Alumni Who Have Coached in the NHL

COACH	TEAM(S)	Games	Wins	Losses	Ties	OT Losses
Lou Angotti						
1973–74 to 1974–75	St. Louis Blues	32	6	20	6	
1983–84	Pittsburgh Penguins	80	16	58	6	
Charlie Burns						
1969–70, 1974–75	Minnesota North Stars	86	22	50	14	
Gerry Cheevers						
1980–81 to 1984–85	Boston Bruins	376	204	126	46	
Bill Dineen						
1991–92 to 1992–93	Philadelphia Flyers	140	60	60	20	
Dick Duff						
1979–80	Toronto Maple Leafs	2	0	2	0	
Red Kelly						
1967–68 to 1968–69	Los Angeles Kings	150	55	75	20	
1969–70 to 1972–73	Pittsburgh Penguins	274	90	132	52	
1973–74 to 1976–77	Toronto Maple Leafs	318	133	123	62	
Ted Lindsay						
1979–80 to 1980–81	Detroit Red Wings	29	5	21	3	
Billy Macmillan						
1980–81	Colorado Rockies	80	22	45	13	
1982–83 to 1983–84	New Jersey Devils	100	19	67	14	
John McLellan						
1969–70 to 1972–73	Toronto Maple Leafs	310	126	139	45	
Joe Primeau						
1950–51 to 1952–53	Toronto Maple Leafs	210	97	71	42	
Pat Quinn						
1978–79 to 1981–82	Philadelphia Flyers	262	141	73	48	
1984–85 to 1986–87	Los Angeles Kings	202	75	101	26	
1990–91 to 1995–96	Vancouver Canucks	280	141	111	28	
1998–99 to 2005–06	Toronto Maple Leafs	574	300	196	52	26
Gene Ubriaco						
1988–89 to 1989–90	Pittsburgh Penguins	106	50	47	9	

Acknowledgements

This book would not have seen the light of day without the extraordinary help the authors received in compiling the material. First, without the permission and cooperation of Father Joseph Redican, C.S.B., President of St. Michael's College School, this book would not have been possible. We must acknowledge the remarkable assistance and boundless enthusiasm of Evelyn Collins, Archivist at the University of St. Michael's College, who was always there with her generous time and support.

The Office of Advancement at St. Michael's College School was most helpful, especially Director Kimberley Bailey and Communications Director Michael De Pellegrin. Richard McQuade, Director of Archives at St. Michael's College School, also gave generously of his time and counsel.

The Hockey Hall of Fame is second to none in providing information, images and encouragement. Special thanks to Phil Pritchard, Craig Campbell, Izak Westgate, Peter Jagla, Tyler Wolosewich and all of our other friends for their support and assistance.

Additional thanks must go to Dan Prendergast, SMCS's Alumni Affairs Officer, along with former vice-principals Jack Fenn and Hugh McDougall, and former English teacher (and current editor of the *Blue Banner*) Joe Younder. These gentlemen remain giants at the school and are always there to provide assistance.

Father Neil Hibberd, C.S.B. (Latin teacher extraordinaire and track and field coaching legend), SMCS alumni past president Peter Thurton (Class of '81) and Pal De Iuglio (Class of '69) encouraged this project in its infancy and gave us our initial boost to begin our journey. Also extraordinarily helpful were Father Daniel Zorzi, C.S.B., former president of St. Michael's College and M.J. (Mimi) Marrocco and Laurel-Ann Finn of Continuing Education of the University of St. Michael's College.

Great thanks are extended to Father Hugh Foley, C.S.B., whose memory and photographs contributed substantially to the St. Michael's manuscript. Peter Fillman, whose passion for all things St. Mike's is second to none, was a terrific resource, assisting with details as required. He and Father Michael Lehman, C.S.B., chaplain of the Buzzers, also assisted greatly with our list of all-time Majors and Buzzers.

Dan Nicholson, a retired St. Michael's College School teacher, generously shared his outstanding photo and artifact collections, as well as his encyclopedic knowledge of St. Michael's hockey, with the authors, and was tremendously cooperative and helpful.

Mike McCarron and the St. Michael's Buzzers Hockey Club are to be thanked for providing access to their photo archive.

The authors spoke to many whose stories form the common thread throughout the book, and thank the following for sharing their memories of St. Michael's College: Darryl Bootland, Darryl Boyce, Tim Brent, Arnie Brown, Peter Budaj, Ed Chadwick, Gerry Cheevers, Andrew Cogliano, Brian Conacher, Jack Conlin, Murray Costello, Kevin Dineen, Mike Draper, Dick Duff, Ron Ellis, Father Hugh Foley, C.S.B., Tony Fritz, Jim Gregory, Tyler Haskins, Red Kelly, David Keon, Ken Klee, Ted Lindsay, Madeleine MacGillivray (who shared the story of her mother-in-law, Marion Hayes), Barry MacKenzie, Frank Mahovlich, Cesare Maniago, Mike McCarron, John McCormack, Michael McGurk, Jim McKenny, Dennis Mills, Father Tom Mohan, C.S.B., Steve Moore, Mark Napier, Gerry Odrowski, Mark Popovic, Father Joe Redican, C.S.B., Phil Samis, Bob Schiller, Rod Seiling, Kevin Weekes, and Benny Woit.

In addition, there were a number of people who assisted greatly in securing interviews for this book, and we graciously thank Paul Bruno, Wendy Chamberlain-Davey (of the Mississauga St. Michael's Majors), Doug Kelcher, David Keon Jr., Ted Mahovlich, Steve McLean, Brad Morris, Parker Neale (formerly of the St. Michael's Majors), and Renee Weekes.

The authors met through a mutual love of hockey history as members of the Society for International Hockey Research (SIHR), and employed the vast knowledge provided by the society's website *www.sihrhockey.org*) and various members, most notably, Rick Cole, Ernie Fitzsimmons, Denis Gibbons, Len Kotylo, James Milks, the late John Paton, Larry Robertson, Jason Wilson, and Eric Zweig.

The authors wish to acknowledge the following for their knowledge and cooperation: Robert Tunney (Class of '81), arena manager of St. Michael's College School Arena, Andrij Harasymowycz (Class of '00), Jim Pantoleo (Class of '79) and Les Duff (Class of '54).

Kevin Shea wishes to acknowledge a long, successful relationship with Fenn Publishing. This being book number seven together, gratitude and a million thanks go to C. Jordan Fenn, whose vision has made this an outstanding relationship. Cheers! And to Sheila Evely, Steve St. Amant, and Laura Brunton, thank you for your contributions as well.

To Lloyd Davis, who superbly edited the book, and Michael Gray, who brilliantly designed the book you now hold, we send our deep appreciation.

Kevin Shea has a group of people who have supported him unconditionally through his dreams of becoming an author, and sends his love and continuing thanks to his partner Nancy Niklas, his parents Margaret and Gerry England, his brother Dale, Betty Shea and dear friends Maureen and Tim Burgess, Andrea Orlick, Steve Waxman, Kim Cooke, Anne Klisanich, Skip Crosby, Victoria Eves Adam, and Connie Atkinson.

Larry Colle sends his love and perennial thanks to Teresa, Stephen, and Alexander.

Paul Patskou expresses his eternal gratitude to his father, who took him to his first-ever St. Mike's game, and shared with him a passion for the game of hockey that has lasted a lifetime.

Finally, we acknowledge the faculty, staff, students, and alumni of both St. Michael's College School and the University of St. Michael's College, past and present, for making this hockey history well worth writing about.

Bibliography

'67: The Maple Leafs, Their Sensational Victory, and the End of an Empire, Damien Cox and Gord Stellick, (Toronto: Wiley and Sons, 2004)

100 Years of Dropping the Puck: A History of the OHA, Scott Young (Toronto: McClelland & Stewart, 1989)

Behind the Cheering, Frank Selke with Gordon Green (Toronto: McClelland & Stewart, 1962)

The Big M: The Frank Mahovlich Story, Ted Mahovlich (Toronto: HarperCollins, 1999)

The Bird: The Life and Times of Hockey Legend Wren Blair, Wren Blair with Ron Brown and Jill Blair (Kingston: Quarry Heritage Books, 2002)

Centre Ice: The Smythe Family, the Gardens and the Toronto Maple Leafs Hockey Club, Tom Smythe with Kevin Shea (Bolton: Fenn Publishing, 2000)

Dictionary of Basilian Biography: Lives of Members of the Congregation of the Priests of Saint Basil from its Origins in 1822 to 2002, P. Wallace Platt (Toronto: University of Toronto Press, 2005)

Doug: The Doug Harvey Story, William Brown (Montreal: Vehicule Press, 2002)

"John Elmsley and the Rise of Irish Catholic Social Action in Victorian Toronto," Murray Nicholson (CCHA Historical Studies 51 [1984], 46–66)

The Essential Blue & White Book, Andrew Podnieks (Vancouver: Greystone Books, 2001)

A Fan For All Seasons: Following the 75-Year History of Toronto's Maple Leafs through the Eyes of a Fan, Tom Gaston and Kevin Shea (Bolton: Fenn Publishing, 2001)

Gentle Eminence: A Life of Cardinal Flahiff, Philip Wallace Platt (Montreal: McGill-Queen's Press, 1999)

The Glory Years: Memories of a Decade, 1955–1965, Billy Harris (Toronto: Prentice-Hall Canada, 1989)

Heaven and Hell in the NHL, Punch Imlach with Scott Young (Toronto: McClelland and Stewart, 1982)

Henry Carr: Revolutionary, E.J. McCorkell (Toronto: Griffin House Press, 1969)

Heroes: Stars of Hockey's Golden Era, Frank Pagnucco (Toronto: Prentice-Hall Canada, 1985)

Heroes and History: Voices from the NHL's Past, Stan and Shirley Fischler (Toronto: McGraw-Hill, 1994)

A History of the Oshawa Generals, Babe Brown (Toronto: Chimo Publishing, 1978)

The Hockey Handbook, Lloyd Percival (Toronto: Random House, 1951)

Hockey in Canada: The Way It Is, Brian Conacher (Toronto: Gateway Press, 1970)

Hockey Is a Battle, Punch Imlach with Scott Young (Toronto: Macmillan of Canada, 1969)

In Loving Memory: A Tribute to Tim Horton, Lori Horton and Tim Griggs (Toronto: ECW Press, 1997)

Inside Maple Leaf Gardens: The Rise and Fall of the Toronto Maple Leafs, William Houston (Toronto: McGraw-Hill Ryerson, 1980)

Les Costello: Canada's Flying Father, Charlie Angus (Ottawa: Novalis, 2005)

Life After Hockey, Michael A. Smith (Cooper Publishing, 1996)

Lowering the Boom: The Bobby Baun Story, Bobby Baun with Anne Logan (Toronto: Stoddart Publishing, 2000)

Maple Leafs Top 100: Toronto's Greatest Players of All Time, Mike Leonett, (Vancouver: Raincoast Books, 2007)

The Memorial Cup: Canada's National Hockey Championship, Richard Lapp and Alec Macaulay (Madeira Park: Harbour Publishing, 1997)

Open Ice: The Tim Horton Story, Douglas Hunter (Toronto: Penguin Books, 1994)

Players: The Ultimate A-Z Guide of Everyone Who Has Ever Played in the NHL, Andrew Podnieks (Toronto: Doubleday, 2003)

Saving the Game: Pro Hockey's Quest to Raise Its Game from Crisis to New Heights, Mark Moore (Toronto: McClelland & Stewart, 2006)

The Rock, the Curse, and the Hub: A Random History of Boston Sports, edited by Randy Roberts (Boston: Harvard University Press, 2005)

Total Hockey: The Official Encyclopedia of the National Hockey League, Second Edition, edited by Dan Diamond, (Toronto: Total Sports Publishing, 2000)

War Games: Conn Smythe and Hockey's Fighting Men, Douglas Hunter (Toronto: Penguin Books, 1996)

The authors also made extensive use of school yearbooks from the University of St. Michael's College (1910–1949 and 1969–1999) and St. Michael's College (1950–2008).

In addition, the authors made use of archived newspaper articles from *The Hockey News*, *The Globe and Mail*, the *Toronto (Daily) Star*, the *Toronto Sun*, and the Toronto *Telegram*, as well as the *Edmonton Journal*, *Regina Leader-Post*, and *Summerside Journal-Pioneer*.

Index

Note to readers:
Page numbers in *italics* refer to a photograph.

Abel, Sid, 131, 239
Acheson, John, 38, 39, 42
Adams, Erik, 168
Adams, Jack, 32, 35, 63, 123, 239
Ahearne, Bunny, 260
Aishford, Chris, 215
Alain, Paul, 83
Albert, Girard, 204
Alexander, Claire, 225
Alexander, Scotty, 227
Alexander Cup, 91–92
Allan, Bill, 204
Allan, Sir Montagu, 18
Allan Cup, 18, 19–20
Amidovski, Bujar, 169–70, 172
Anderson, Brian, 106
Angotti, Lou, 107–8, *108*, 113, 116, *117*, 255
Angus, Charlie, 70
Antipov, Vladimir, 168
Apps, Gillian, 215
Apps, Syl III, 215
Arena Gardens, 15
Armstrong, George, *83*, 244, 245, 246
Arundel, Johnny, 56, 65, 89, 91, 92, 135
Ashbee, Barry, 201
Ashworth, Frank, 61, 62
Auge, Tom, 212
Aurie, Larry, 27

Babando, Pete, 59
Babcock, Bobby, 211
Baker, Hobey, 23–24
Baker, Scott, 185
Baldwin, Pat, 201
Ballard, Harold, 93, 106, 144, 152–53, 164, 265
Barilko, Bill, 85
Barlow, Hugh, 103
Barnes, Ryan, 172, 173
Barrett, Dave, 215
Barrie Colts, 173, 175
Barrie Flyers, 84, 94
Barry, Ray, 80, 81
Bassen, Hank, 239
Bassett, John W., 265
Bassin, Sherry, 164
Bateman, Dwayne, 172, 175
Bathgate, Andy, 37, 127, 252
Battaglia, Tom, 85
Batten, Corey, 168, 172
Batten, Dan, 208
Bauer, Bertha, 235, 258
Bauer, Bobby, 38, 39, 40, 42, 52, 89, *235*, 235–37, 256, 257

Bauer, Father David, 51, *52, 53*, 53–54, 55, 64, 68, 111, *117*, 118, 121, 126, 128–35, 137–45, *139*, 157, 189, 204, 227, 237, 239, 252, 254–61, *256, 259, 260*, 263, 264, 266
Bauer, Frank, 38, 42, 235, 256
Bauer, Sir Edgar, 235, 256
Baumgarten, Trent, 168
Baun, Bob, 35, 37, 112, 246
Bear, John, 206
Begg, Gary, 259
Bellisle, Father Henry, 27
Bellissimo, Daniel, 218
Bendo, Lou, 99
Bennett, Frank, 50, 51, *52*, 193
Benson, Bus, 44
Bentley, Bev, 61, 77
Bentley, Reg, 91
Bentley, Roy, 61
Bertuzzi, Todd, 229
Bettman, Gary, 269
Biagini, Chris, 168
Billington, Craig, 211
Binkley, Les, 100
Binnington, Mike, 220
Bird, D'Arcy, 199
Bitove, Tom, 188
Blair, Dusty, 89, 92
Blair, Wren, 156, 157
Blake, Hector "Toe," 91, 92
Blom, Buddy, 150
Blute, Johnny, 56–59, 61, 62, 65, 194
Bobbie, Len, 148
Bochen, Steve, 199
Bodnar, Gus, 129, 130, 131, 265
Boehmer, Pat, 52, 56, 59–62, 65
Boland, Mike, *167*, 206
Bonello, Frank, 164, *266*
Bonhomme, Connie, 82, 83
Bootland, Darryl, 172, 173, 175, 178
Boston Hockey Club, 23
Boucher, Bobby, 34, 113
Boudrias, Andre, 147
Bougie, Georges, 92
Bourbonnais, Roger, 259
Bourke, Peter, 199
Bourke, Tom, 199
Bower, Johnny, 88, 190
Bowman, Scotty, 113, 116, 121, 206
Boyce, Darryl, 178, 181–84
Bradley, Brian, 146
Brady, Father Joe, 208
Brampton 7-Ups, 145, 146
Branch, David, 164, 166, 190
Branston, Phil, 206
Brantford Lions, 50, 51

Brayshaw, Russ "Buster," 136, 137, 138
Brennan, Kip, 216
Brenneman, John, 130, 131
Brent, Tim, 175, 178–82, *179*
Brewer, Carl, 35, 37, 112, *112*, 153, 249
Britz, Greg, 208
Brockville Hockey Club, 24
Broda, Walter "Turk," 39–40, 111, 147, 149
Broderick, Ken, 146, 147, 259
Brown, Arnie, 37, 111, *125*, 125–27, 129, 131, 132, 135–38, 145, 189, 201–2, 252
Brown, Brad, 214
Brown, Jerry, 128
Brown, Stan, 22
Bruyea, Leo, 29
Buchanan, Mike, 83
Buchanan, Neil, 83, 85, 86
Buchanan, Ron, 156
Buchmann, Pete, *197*, 198, 199
Buckland, Frank, 201
Budaj, Peter, 175–76, 178–79, *179*
Burgess, Tom, 137, 138
Burke, Bill, 188
Burke, Jim, 38
Burke, Sean, 211
Burkett, Kevin, 204
Burnett, Kenny, 60
Burns, Charlie, 198, *250*
Bury, Ed, 195, 196
Bush, Eddie, 128, 132, 133, 150
Byles, Joe, 168

Caffery, Jack, 97–100, 103, 104, 189, 197–98, 227
Callahan, Bill, 193
Callahan, John, 45, 49
Cameron, Connor, 185
Cameron, Dave, 175, 180, 183, *188*, 189
Canadian Amateur Hockey Association (CAHA), 77
Canadian Hockey Association (CHA), 18
Canadian National Team, 142, 151, 237, 258–61, *260*
Cannon, Jason, 168
Cannon, Jimmy, 201
Caporusso, Louie, 220
Caria, Matt, 186
Carleton, Wayne, 146
Carlton, Ted, 245
Carnegie, Chuck, 148
Caron, Jacques, 253
Carr, Father Henry, 13–14, 16, 17, 18, 22, *22*, 55
Carrigan, Greg, 214

Carroll, Billy, 207, 208
Carse, Bill, 40
Carter, Cardinal Emmett, *166*
Carter, Father, 192
Carter, Greg, *50*
Caruso, Jim, 168
Casa El Norte, 109
Cashman, Wayne, 156
Cassiani, Fred, 220, *220*
Cassidy, Jason, 186
Cassidy, Paul, 204
Cassidy, Preston, 220
Cation, Shawn, 172, 173, 174
Cava, Chris, 168
Cavallini, Gino, 210
Cengarle, Licio, 206
Ceresino, Ray, 73
Cerre, Charlie, 29, 30, 94, 97–99, 101, 102, 103, 105, *105*, 106–7, 244, 249
Cerre, Paul, 105, 207, *250*
Chabot, Lorne, 30
Chadwick, Ed, 85–88, 94, 97–101, *111*, 112, 189
Champagne, Andre, 128, 132, 134–38, 145, 147–50, 154, 157–61, 189
Charbonnel, Bishop Armand-François-Marie de, 11–12, 13
Charron, Guy, 250
Chasczewski, Tom, 202
Cheevers, Gerry, 113, 117, 121, 124, 129, 131, 133, 134, 135, 137, 138, 141, 145, 189, *198*, 200, 201, 225, 255, *262*, 262–63, *263*
Chenier, John, 60, 61
Cherry, Don, 100, 190
Chevrefils, Real, 84, 267
Child, Art, 90
Chiodo, Andy, 175–76, 178, *179*, 181, 216, *216*
Chisholm, Jeff, 212
Chiz, Don, 137
Cities Service Oilers, 40
Cizikas, Casey, 190
Clancy, Francis "King," 30, 39, 43, *43*, 63, 118, 129, 147, *153*, 154, 265
Clancy, Jack, 130
Clancy, Terry, 129, 130, 137, 142, 145, 146, 148–51, *167*, 189, 227, 259, *260*
Cleary, Joe, 50, 192–93
Clune, Art, 98–101
Clune, Wally, 80, 82, 83, 85
Clutterbuck, Cal, 182, 185
Coburn, Lloyd, 193
Cogliano, Andrew, 218–19, *219*
Cole, Grant, 206
Cole, Jack, 121, 130, 134, 137, 138, 140, 145, 189

Coleman, Jim, 258
Collins, Bill, 37, 127, 146, 148, 250, 252
Colville, Neil, 40
Colvin, Billy, 98, 103, 106, 198, 199
Conacher, Alex "Rollie," 28, 32
Conacher, Bert, 93
Conacher, Brian, 110, 111, 145, 146, 257, 258–60
Conacher, Charlie, 30, 32, 34, 43, 67, 233
Conacher, Pete, 227
Conacher, Roy, 93
Conlin, Paul, 128, 131, 134, 137, 138, 142, 145, 147, 148, 149, 154, 156, 159, 189, 259, *260*, 261
Convey, Eddie, 29, 30, *30*, 34
Conway, Father Bill, *51*, 54, 126, 141, 162, 189, *193*, 194, 201–4, *204*, 259
Cook, Bill, 43
Cooper, Carson, 239, 242, 243
Cooper, Cliff, 35
Copper Cliff Redmen, 46, 244
Corbeau, Bert, 34
Corbett, Mike, 131, 145, 146, 147, 149, 150, 151, 156–60, 203–4, 205
Corcoran, Jack, 196
Corcoran, Norm, 83
Corcoran, Ray, 83
Cormier, Emery "The Cat," 134, 135
Cornacchia, Rick, 209, 210, *210*, 211
Corrigan, Chuck, 44
Corrigan, Mike, 156, 159, 205
Corriveau, Andre, 91
Corupe, Kenny, 168, 172
Costello, Bruce, 255
Costello, Father Les, 54, 56, *58*, 58–62, 65–75, 66, *72*, 77, 80, 147, 189, 221, 222, 227, *242*, 267
Costello, Jack, 116, *117*, 119, 121, 222, 226, 267
Costello, Murray, 69–70, 85, 86, 94–99, 101, 110, 221–22, 248, 252, *267*, 267–68
Cotton, Harold "Baldy," 43, 134–35, 201
Coulson, D'Arcy, 28
Couture, Doc, 61
Cowan, Gord, 207
Cowie, Rob, 211–12
Crain, Jason, 168
Crawford, Bill, 204
Crawford, Johnny, 44, 48, *48*, 93, 191
Crisp, Terry, 160
Cronin, D., 27

INDEX

299

Cronin, Jerry, 98
Crook, Farrell, 197
Crowdis, Lou, 72, 73
Crowley, Father John, 106–7, 114
Crozier, Roger, 129, 130, 131, 135
Cullen, Father Ronald, 95, 96
Cullen, Jim, 148
Cullen, Ray, 124–25, 130–31
Culligan, Andy, 206
Cunningham, Bob, 134
Curik, Bill, 59
Curik, Leo, 73
Cusinato, Tony, 199
Cyclic, George, 101

Dadswell, Doug, 210
D'Agostino, Nick, *220*
Daly, Tim, 43
Danton, Mike. *See* Jefferson, Mike
Daugavins, Kaspars, 186, 190
Davidson, Bob, 115, 125, 126, 129, 145, 155, 248, 253, 265
Davidson, Bob Jr., 129
Davie, Ivan, 149
Davis, Ben, 214
Davison, Rob, 216
Day, Hap, 43, 90, 93, 118, 239
Day, Joe, 212
De La Salle Oaklands, 27
De Paolis, Lorne, 53
DeCourcy, Bob, 65, 80, 195
DeCourcy, Joe, 80, 82, 196
DeJordy, Denis, 200
Delaney, Keith, 172, 173, 175
DeLeeuw, Adam, 172, 173, 175
Delvecchio, Rocky, 205
Dennis, Steve, 217
DePiero, Chris, 216, 219
Desilets, Rudy, 193
Deslauriers, Jacques, 91
Detroit Red Wings, 32, 247–48
Development and Peace, 109
Dewsbury, Al, 59
Dillabough, Bob, 131
Dineen, Bill, 83, 85, 86, 94, 95, 97–101, 150, 189, 222, *223*, 268
Dineen, Gary, *112*, 131, 142, 145, 146, 148, 150, 151, 156–59, 161, *202*, 203–4, *204*, 205, 259, *260*
Dineen, Gord, 209, 222–23, *224*
Dineen, Jerry, *224*
Dineen, Kevin, 209–10, 222–24, *224*
Dineen, Peter, 209, *224*
Dineen, Shawn, *224*
Dissette, Frank, 17
Dissette, Jimmy, 17, 23
Dixie Beehives, 200–201
Dockeray, Jack, 199

Dodd, George, 50
Doheny, Clarence, 17
Doiron, Phillip, 134
Donati, Corinne, 185
Donati, Justin, 184, 185, *185*
Donati, Tyler, 183, 184, 185, *185*
Donlevy, jack, 73
Dopp, Paul, 195
Doran, Mike, 156, 158, 159
Doraty, Ken, 43, 74, 76
Dornhoefer, Gary, 160
Douglas, Kent, 37
Dovigi, Patrick, 172
Dowell, Hanson, 77
Doyle, Bill, 193
Draper, Bruce, 116, 121, *121*, 124, 128–33, 136, 137, 138, 140, 141, 145, 189, *198*, 200, 201, *202*, 224–25, *226*, 255, 257
Draper, Dave, 116, 121, *121*, 131, 132, 133, 136, 141, 145, 147, 189, *198*, 200, 201, 224–25, *226*, 255
Draper, Jack, 93, 224
Draper, Kris, 227
Draper, Mike, 113, 116, *117*, 199, 200–201, 207, 208, 224–25, *226*, 227, 261
Draper, Pat, 227
Drillon, Gordie, 81
Drouillard, Clare, 38, 39, 40, 42
Dryden, Dave, 110, 124, 129, 135, 141, 145, 146, 149, 189
Duff, Dick, 36, *36*, 37, 97, 98, 100, 103, 106, *107*, 111–12, 127, 147, 153, *167*, 177, 189, 197, 198, 199, 246, *251*, 251–52, *266*
Duff, Les, 97, 98, 103, 106, *107*, 189, 207, *266*
Duff, Less, *104*
Dumart, Woody, 42, 235, 236, 237
Dunbar, Don, 47
Duncanson, Clarke, 168
Duncanson, Craig, 210
Dunlap, Frank, 51, 52, *52*, 53, *53*
Dunlap, Jake, 51
Dunn, Bill, 80
Dunn, Bob, 205
Dunn, Brian, 206
Dunn, Vic, 24
Dunne, Tommy, 44, 45, 46
Dunne, V., 27
Dupont, Ray, 148, 150, 156, 157, 160, 204

Eaton Hockey Club, 20–21
Eddie Powers Memorial Trophy, 57, 67
Edmonton Athletic Club Roamers, 39–40
Edmonton Oil Kings, 135–39, 257

Edwards, Marv, 101, 103, *104*
Elik, Todd, 210
Ellis, Matt, 178
Ellis, Ron, 145, 149, 161
Elmsley, John, 12–13
Emms, Hap, 100, 101, 107, 144–45, 156, 161
English, John, 210

Fata, Drew, 175, 178, 181, 216
Faught, Father Don, 96, 97, 99, 103, 247
Felesko, Roger, 201
Fenn, Jack, 176
Ferguson, Lorne, 267
Fifield, Bill, 209
Fischler, Stan, 63
Fitkin, Ed, 43
Fitness Institute, 102
Fitzgerald, Armand, *50*
Fitzgerald, J.P., 16
Fitzhenry, Jerry, 80
Fitzpatrick, Father Norman, 164
Flahill, Cardinal George, 54
Flanagan, Father Ted, 32, 54, 85, 94, 96, 119, 145, *146*, 147, 149, 150, 189, 194, 200, 201, 227, 241–42, 248, 251
Flannery, Pat, 200
Fleming, Reg, 107, 108, *108*, 189
Fletcher, Brian, 148
Fleury, Lionel, 135
Flying Fathers, 70
Fogolin, Lee, 59
Foley, Father Hugh, 50, *50*, 54–55
Foley, Vincent, 54, 55
Forgione, Mario, 188
Forth, Neil, 132
Foss, Roy, 166, 167
Foster, Craig, 185
14th Regiment (Kingston), 17
Fowler, Spencer, 168
Fowler, Tom, 89, 91
Francis, Emile, 128, 134
Freedman, Peter, 217
Fritz, Tony, 145, 147, *153*, 153–55, 265
Frost, David, 173–74
Frost, Harry, 39
Fullan, Larry, 206
Fullan, Rick, 206
Fulton, Father Patrick, 16
Futa, Mike, 167, 171, 172, 175, 177, 216
Fyles, Tommy, 86

Galipeau, Roger, 138, 140–41, 145, 189, 202
Gallace, Steve, 168
Gallagher, Farrell, 50, *50*, 193
Gallinger, Don, 192
Gallo, Dave, 216
Galt Red Wings, 59, 73
Gardner, Cal, 227

Gardner, Dave, 207
Gardner, George, 160
Gardner, Paul, 207
Gaston, Tommy, 233
Gaudet, Oscar, 135
Gaudet, Ron, 134–35
Gaunce, Cameron, 190
Gauthier, Art, 27
Gauthier, Paul, 165, 209
Geer, Terry, 179
Gershon, Cory, 220
Gibson, Andrew, 168
Gilbert, Rod, 133, 134
Gillis, Mike, 207–8
Gillis, Paul, 209
Gimblett, Tyson, 185
Glover, Fred, 73
Glugosh, Steve, 212
Glumac, Michael, 168, 216
Goldham, Bob, 116, *117*, 122, 128, 227, 255, 264
Good, Dale, 183
Goodenow, Joe, 173
Govedaris, Chris, 212
Graham, Pat, 208
Grant, Benny, 52
Grant, Michael, 204
Gravelle, Leo, 57–63
Gravelle, Pat, 195
Gray, Bobby, 61, 65
Green, Tommy, 199
Gregoire, Father Gerry, 50, *53*, 54, 64
Gregory, Jim, *117*, 128, 132, 141, 145, 146, 147, *149*, 156, 158, *160*, 161, 189, 261, *264*, 264–66, *266*
Gribbons, Ken, 103
Griggs, Gordon, 246
Gross, George, 261
Gross, Lloyd, 32, 34
Gruhl, Cec, 59
Guelph Royals, 133–34

Haffey, Joe, 207
Hainsworth, George, 43
Hale, Larry, 136, 137
Haley, Michael, 186
Hall, Glenn, 239
Hall, Murray, 130
Halloran, F., 27
Hamilton, John, 38, 42, 44
Hamilton, Reg, 38, 40, 42
Hamilton Red Wings, 131–33, 149–50
Hamilton Tiger Cubs, 123
Hamilton Tigers, 24
Hannigan, Father Ray, 54, 59, 68, 71, 72, 73, 75, 78, 80, 82, 135
Hannigan, Gord, 80–83, 89–92, 135
Hannigan, Pat, 68, 69, 73, 83, 90, 107, *108*, 109, *109*, 135, 189, *197*, 198, 199
Hannigan, Ray, 196
Harding, Jeff, 212

Harlock, David, 212
Harmer, Gary, 160
Harrington, BIll, 101
Harris, Billy, 35, 98, 153, 246, 262
Harris, Ron, 131
Harrison, Ed, 63, 65, 66, 71–75, 80, 147, 194, 195, 196, 242
Harrison, Gord, 196, 197
Harvey, Doug, 59, 60, 61
Harvey, Howie, 59, 60, 61, 71, 74, *76*, 77, 80
Haskins, Tyler, 182, *182*, 184
Hastings, Bobby, 216
Hauck, Lou, 61, 62
Hay, Bill, 153
Hayes, Marion, 25, *25*
Head, Don, 85
Heaney, Mike, 212
Hector, Gerry, 194, 195
Henderson, Bill, 158
Henderson, John, 85, 101
Henderson, Paul, 150, 249
Heron, Red, 93
Hershey Centre, 188, 189
Hewitt, Jack, 133
Hewitt, W.A., 17, 20, 47, *60*, 62, 63, 64
Hextall, Bryan, 136, 137, 138
Hibberd, Father Neil, 257
Hickey, Gerry, 50, 51
Higgins, Jack, 101
Hillman, Larry, 37
Hinnegan, Al, 199
Hodge, Charlie, 101
Holleran, Jim, 141
Hollett, Flash, 89–90
Holmes, Father Art, 54
Holt, Punk, 29
Horner, Red, 32, 34, 43, 241
Horton, Lori, 244
Horton, Tim, *36*, 37, 80–83, *81*, 105, 112, 147, 189, 227, 234, *244*, 244–46, *245*
Houle, Buck, 35
House, Matthew, 168
Howarth, Frank, 199
Howe, Gordie, 154, 239, 262
Howes, Lorne, *83*, 84, 85, 94
Hudson, Steven, 166, 167
Hughes, Phil, 89, 90, 91
Humphreys, Jack, 133
Hunt, Fred "Fritz," 44, 45, 46
Hunt, Ross, 45, 46
Hunt, Vic, 85
Hunter, Douglas, 49
Hunter, Ken, 91

Ihnacak, Brian, 218
Imlach, George "Punch," 37, 93, 119, 121, 122, 126, 127, 128, 157–58, 226, 246, 249, 259, 265
Imonti, Frank, 194
Imonti, Jim, 196
Inglis, Johnny, 45, 46, 47

Ingoldsby, Joe, 83, 196
Ironstone, Joe, 32
Irvin, Dick, 24, 97
Irvine, Joe, 194
Ivan, Tommy, 243

J. Ross Robertson Cup, 20
Jack Gatecliffe Arena, 188
Jacks, Barry, 204
Jackson, Art, 38, 39, 40, *42*, 42–43
Jackson, Don, 199
Jackson, Hal, 44, 45
Jackson, Harvey "Busher," 30, 32, 34, 233
Jackson, Paul, 121, 133, 135, 141, 145, 189, 255
Jakopin, John, 215
James, Art, 27
James, Gerry, 99
James, Jessie, 29
Jarrett, Doug, 127, 130
Jarrett, Gary, 145, 148, 149
Jauernig, Daniel, 167
Jefferson, Mike, 170, 172, *173*, 173–74, 175
Jeffrey, Larry, 131, 132
Jennings, Bill, 93
Jessiman, Harvey, 58, 59
Joannette, Rosario "Kitoute," 91
Johnston, Marshall, 260
Jones, Bob, 180
Jordan, Dennis, 133, 134

Kaminsky, Max, 124, 129, 139
Karges, Gerry, 241
Kassian, Dennis, 138
Kaszycki, Mike, 207
Katavisto, Ari, 168
Kazarian, Harry, 59
Kealey, Greg, 168
Keating, Bernie, 134
Keefe, Sheldon, 172–75
Keegan, Bob, 199
Keenan, Don, 107, 199
Keenan, Larry, 121, *121*, 122, 124, 128–31, 133, 134, 136, 137, 138, 140, 145, 189, 201, 255, 257
Keenan, Mike, 169
Kehoe, Wilf, 29, 30
Kelcher, Doug, 146, 225
Kellough, Howie, 131
Kelly, Dave, 159
Kelly, Father P.J., 16
Kelly, Leonard "Red," *36*, 65–66, *66*, 71, *72*, 73, 74, *76*, 80, 147, 177, 189, 195, 197, *241*, 241–43, *242*, 268
Kelly, Regis "Pep," 38, 39, 40, *42*, 43
Kelly, Tom, 107
Kelly, Tommy, 199
Kendall, Larry, 200, 201
Kennedy, Forbes, 239
Kennedy, Sam, 89, 90, 91

Kennedy, Ted, 121
Keon, David, 36, 37, 110–11, *112*, 113, 116, *116*, *117*, 119, 121, 124, 147, 189, *198*, 200, 201, 227, 246, 249, *253*, 253–55, *254*
Keon, Jimmy, 154, 156, 160, 225
Killen, Jack, 27
King, Darcy, 168
Kitchener-Waterloo Dutchmen, 89, 121, 237
Klee, Ken, 213
Klein, Kevin, 175, 178, 181, 182
Klutke, Eric, 212
Knott, Andrew, 214–15
Knox, Charlie, 137
Knox, Paul, 95, 98, 99, 100, 103, *104*, 197
Kolzig, Olaf, 211
Koneczny, Chester, 86
Konstantinou, Bill, 212
Kosterewa, Mike, 168
Kowalski, Julian, 148
Kozak, Les, 119, 122
Kraut Line, 42, 235–37
Kucher, Frank, 168
Kwong, Larry, 91
Kyrzakos, Jeff, 218

Labine, Leo, 83, 84, *84*, 85, 94
Lach, Elmer, 49
Lacroix, Rick, 212
LaFlamme, Dr. Jerry, 17, 18, 19, 21, 23, 24, 38, 39, 44, 45, 46, 191
LaFlamme, William, *17*
Lamoriello, Lou, 174
Laperriere, Jacques, 147
Lapp, Richard, 53
Larmer, Dan, 214
Leach, Jay, 168
LeBrun, Al, 133, 134
Lecompte, Louis, 92
Leduc, Albert "Battleship," 42, 235
Lee, Bill, 95, 99, 101, 196
Legge, O., 27
Lehman, Scott, 182, 183, 184
Lehun, Jonathan, 217
Levinsky, Alex, 32, 34
Lewicki, Danny, *83*, 245
Leyden, Matt, 149
Libertucci, Angelo, 212
Lindros, Brett, 214
Lindros, Eric, 212, *212*, 212–13
Lindsay, Bert, 238
Lindsay, Ted, 52, *53*, 53–54, 63, 189, *238*, 238–40, *240*, 256
Ling, David, 214
Linseman, Ken, 197, 198, 199
Lobriaco, Bernie, 50
Lockhart, Don, 85
Logan, Jim, 94, 99, 101, 103

Long, Bill, 159
Loranger, V., 27
Lordon, John, 134
Los Angeles Monarchs, 89
Loveday, Gord, 107
Lowes, Art, 17
Lowrey, Gerry, 32
Ludeviks, Scott, 215
Lukasik, Bonik "Bunky," 45
Lukes, Frantisek, 175, 181
Lumley, Harry, 88
Lund, Larry, 138
Lundquist, Vic, 75
Lynch, Brian, 51
Lynch, Father, 39
Lynch, Jack, 27

Macaulay, Alec, 53
MacDonald, Barry, 149, 205
MacDonald, Duncan, 137, 141, 145, 149, 189
MacDonald, Lowell, 150
MacGillivray, Madeleine, 25
MacGillivray, Marion (Hayes), 25, *25*
Mackay, Calum, 72
Mackell, Fleming, *58*, 59, 60, 66, *66*, 68, 71–74, *72*, *75*, 77, 78, 80, 147, 169
Mackell, Jack, 78
MacKenzie, Barry, 131, 132, 133, 141–42, *142*, 146, 148–51, *151*, 154, 157, 259, *260*
Mackie, Norm, 141
MacMillan, Billy, 134, 137, 138, 145, 147–50, 156–60, 189, 202, 259
MacMillan, Ken, 134
MacNair, Scott, 212
MacNeil, Al, 35
Mahovlich, Frank, 36, *36*, 37, 106, 107, *107*, *108*, *112*, 113, *114*, 147, *167*, 169, 189, *197*, 198–99, 227, *247*, 247–50, *248*, *250*
Mahovlich, Peter, 37, 161, 205–6, 250
Mahovlich, Peter Sr., 247–48
Mahovlich, Ted, 211, 248
Mailley, Owen, 136
Mallon, Father Hugh, 49, 51, *52*, 54, 62, 63, 77, 193, 195, 242, 244
Malone, Cliff, 60, 61
Maloney, Dave, 207
Maniago, Cesare, 117–20, *118*, 121, 255, 262
Mantha, Moe, 100
Mantha, Moe Jr., 188
Maple Leaf Gardens, 15, 189, 252
Maple Leaf Sports and Entertainment, 189
Marks, Jack, 125
Marlborough, Gerry, 206
Marois, Jean, 50–53, *53*, 193, 194

Marquess, Mark, 53, 61, 62
Marshall, Al, 83
Marshall, Willie, 82–86, 90, 94
Martin, Jack, 113, 200, 201
Martin, Pit, 150
Marzalik, Joe, 194
Matthews, Herb, 18, 19, 23
Matthews, Ron, 58
Matthias, Shawn, 186
Mattiussi, Dick, 107, *108*, 113, 189
Maxner, Wayne, 159, 160
Maxwell, Randy, 208
McAllister, Brian, 80, 196
McAtee, Red, 46
McBride, Dean, 73
McBurney, Eugene, 166
McCaig, Doug, 242
McCallion, Hazel, 190
McCann, Joe, 85, 86
McCarnet, Chris, 27
McCarron, Mike, 208, 216–17, *217*
McCarthy, Frank, 208
McCarthy, Red, 82
McCauley, Wes, 213
McComber, W., 27
McCormack, Johnny, 52, 53, *53*, 56–59, 61, 62, 64, *64*, 65, 68, 135, 147, 156, 227, 257
McCown, Bob, 167
McCracken, Billy, 89–92
McCullough, Chuck, 91
McCurry, Dr. Duke, 40
McDonagh, Bill, 196
McDonald, Bucko, 115
McGonigal, Ian, 215
McGurk, Michael, 190, *190*
McIntyre, Pete, 118
McIsaac, Mike, 216
McIver, Nathan, 182, 183
McKay, Baldy, 121
McKay, Roy, 65, 66
McKechnie, Walt, 37, 161
McKee, Father Brian, 70
McKendry, Jim, 131, 145, 147, 150, 156, 157, 160, *161*, 162, 203, 204, 205
McKenney, Don, 37, 100, 101, 127, 252
McKenny, Jim, 37, 156, 159, 161, 163, 265
McKenzie, Mike, 219
McKenzie, Scott, 168
McKnight, Bob, 113, 116, *117*, 189, 255
McLean, Father Ted, 42, *51*, 52, *53*, 54, 56, 59, *60*, 61, 62, 64, 65, 67, 68, 242
McLean, Hugh, 133
McLean, Tom, 191
McLellan, John, 71, *72*, 73, 80, 82, 196
McLellan, Mike, 204
McLellan, Scott, 209, 212, 213–14

McLeod, Jackie, 260
McMahon, Mike, 133
McMaster, Jack, 113, 199
McMillan, Ken, 204
McMullan, Brian, 188
McNabb, Bill, 147, 149–50
McNamara, Bill, 80, 82, 195
McNamara, George, 44–47, 49, 98
McNamara, Gerry, 94, 95, 100, 103, 106, *107*, 189
McNamara, Hal, 85, 86, 94
McNamara, Merv, 199
McNamara, Paul, 45, 47, 49, 52, 56, 63
McNeill, Bill, 206
McParland, Pete, 196
McReavy, Pat, 44, 45, 46, 191
Meehan, Gerry, 37, 156, 158, 161, *167*, *167*, 204, 206
Megaffin, Paul, 98, 99
Mehlenbacher, Chad, 168
Meisenheimer, Harvey, 132
Meldrum, Jack "Gabby," 89, 91, 92
Melnyk, Eugene, 176, *176*, 185, 188, 189
Memorial Cup, 26–27, *27*
Menard, Howie, 150
Mesich, Matt, 89, 90, 92
Messier, Jesse, 185, 190
Metro Junior 'A' Hockey League, 145–52, 156–61
Metro Junior 'B' Hockey League, 199–200
Metro Junior Hockey League, 214
Metz, Don, 44, 45
Metz, Nick, 38, 40, *42*, 43
Micallef, Tom, 113, 206
Midghall, Ernie, 193, 194
Midghall, Gerry, 194
Midghall, Ray, 194
Migay, Rudy, 68, 71, 75, 76, 78, 80, 189
Miley, Siss, 16
Millan, Jack, 27
Miller, Greg, 220
Miller, Jack, 62
Milley, Norm, 216
Mills, Craig, 166, 215, *215*
Mills, Dennis, 165–68, *166*, 176, 204, 215
Milroy, Gary, 149, 225
Mississauga IceDogs, 188
Mississauga St. Michael's Majors. *See* St. Michael's Majors
Miszuk, John, 131, 132
Mitchell, Johnny, 44, 247, 248
Mitchell, Steve, 207
Mitchell, Vera, 25
Mohan, Father Thomas, 165–68, *166*, 171, 176
Mohns, Doug, 100
Monahan, Garry, 37, 161, 204–6

INDEX

301

Moncton Beavers, 134–35
Moncton Hawks, 40
Monson, Walter, 67
Montador, Steve, 216
Monteith, Steve, 159
Montreal Royals, 59–61
Montreal Victorias, 18
Moodie, Ken, 214
Mooney, Dennis, 196
Moore, Dominic, 215, 228, 228, 229
Moore, Grant, 225
Moore, Mark, 215, *228*, 228–29
Moore, Steve, 215, 227–28, *228*, 229
Moose Jaw Canucks, 61–62, 74–78
Morenz, Howie, 46, 233
Moriarty, Gerald, 168
Moro, Marc, 215
Morrison, Claude, 47
Morrison, Neil, 49
Morrison, Ross, 259
Morrone, Giancarlo, 211
Mortson, Gus, 52, 53–54, 56, *57*, 58, 59, 61, 62, 65, 68, 147, 189, 238, 242, 256
Mosdell, Kenny, 129
Mosdell, Wayne, 129, 147, 148, 156, 205
Mousseau, Win, 59
Moynihan, Archie, 247, 248
Mullen, Riley, 91
Mulligan, Eddie, 89, 90, 92
Mullins, Ken, 75
Muloin, Wayne, 137
Muni, Craig, 208
Munroe, Herb, 27
Murchie, Jim, 110
Murphy, Father James, 266
Murphy, Jeff, 168
Murphy, Jimmy, 17, *17*, 18, 24
Murphy, Joe, 27
Murphy, Mike, *250*
Murphy, Sean, 168
Muzzatti, Jason, 211, 212
Muzzatti, Loris, 208

Napier, Mark, 167, 169–72, *170*, *171*, 177, 179, 180
Napier, Matt, 171, 216
National Hockey Association (NHA), 18
National Hockey League (NHL)
Amateur Draft, 36–37, 161
sponsorship of Junior clubs, 31–37
National Sports Institute, 189
Nattrass, Jack, 62
Neale, Harry, 35
Neil McNeil Maroons, 154–60, *160*, 265
Nesterenko, Eric, 98
Nevin, Bob, 35, 37, 127, 153, 252

New Jersey Devils, 173–74
New York Athletic Club, 23
New York Rangers, 31
Niagara Falls Flyers, 159–60, 164–65
Nichol, Peter, 167
Noakes, Peter, 135, 141, 145, 189
Noble, Reg, 21–22, *231*, 231–32
Noonan, Ricky, 141
North Toronto Red Devils Track Club, 102
Northey, William, 18

Oakley, Jack, 29
Oberholtzer, Don, 80
O'Brien, Father William, 32, 33, 143, 245, 257
O'Brien, Shane, 181
O'Connor, G., 27
O'Connor, Jim, 59, 61
Odrowski, Gerry, 113, 115, *115*
O'Flaherty, Bill, 93
O'Flaherty, Gerry, 93
O'Flaherty, John "Peanuts," 44, 85, 86, 89–94, *93*, 157, 191
Olah, George, 201
O'Leary, Father, 189
Olmstead, Bert, 61, 62
O'Malley, Terry, 121, 128, 130, 133, 135, 137, 138, 141, 142, 189, *198*, 201, *202*, 255, 259, *260*, 261
O'Neill, Paul, 199
O'Neill, Tommy "Windy," 50, 51, *52*, 193
Ontario Hockey Association (OHA), 16, 19–20
Junior leagues reorganized, 26, 191
Prep School league, 16–17
Senior league, 89–90, 92
Ontario Hockey League (OHL), 26
Ontario Provincial Junior 'A' Hockey League (OPJHL), 215
Ontkean, Michael, 204
Oreskovich, Matt, 204
Orillia Terriers, 225
Orlando, Jimmy, 91
Orr, Bobby, 156, 157, 158, 169
Orsini, Father Frank, 54
Osborne, Mark, 172, 179, 180
Osborne, Stan "Sonny," 110, 131, 135, 137, 257
Oshawa Generals, 47, 53–54, 72–73, 103, 156, 161, 239, 256
Ottawa Cliffsides, 18
Ottawa-Hull Canadiens, 116
Ovcjak, David, 216

Pacific Coast Hockey League, 89
Paek, Jim, 211
Pallante, Bob, 107, 113, 199
Pallett, Howard, 201
Papadakos, Andy, 167
Papageorge, Patrick, 168
Park, Brad, 37
Parkdale Canoe Club, 18, 20
Pascht, John, 98
Patterson, George, 32
Paul, Bob, 57–61, 65, *72*, 73–77, 80
Pavelich, Marty, 59
Payne, Rick, 211
Peart, Don, 196
Pegoraro, Daniel, 217
Pelech, Michael, 186, 190
Pelow, Paul, 194
Peralta, Sal, 182
Perani, Bob, 135, 146, 148, 149
Percival, Lloyd, 97, 100, 102, 103, 202
Pereyma, Jack, 29
Perry, Ted, 182
Peterborough Petes, 121
Peters, Justin, 182, 184
Phillips, Nathan, 141, 204
Pickard, Al, 76, 77
Pierce, Brad, 172, 173, 175
Pikul, Mike, 209
Pilous, Rudy, 58, 103, 124, 130, 247
Pirie, Stu, 59
Plager, Bob, 133, 134
Plata, Ed, 83, 99, 101
Platt, Geoff, 216
Platt, Phillip Wallace, 54
Plumley, Andrew, 168
Pogue, Eric, 72
Pokupec, Andy, 211
Polanic, Tom, 145, 148, 150, 151, 189, 203, 204, 225
Pollock, Lloyd, 150
Pollock, Sam, 98, 113
Popovic, Mark, 172, 175, 177, *177*, 178
Porcupine Combines, 59, 73–74
Porter, Doug, 196
Poti, Tom, 184
Power, Bishop Michael, 11
Power, Colin, 182, 183
Powers, Pat, *50*, 51, 65, 67
Pratt, Stan, 92
Prendergast, Danny, 176
Preston, Ray, 239
Price, Noel, 98, 103, 104, 107, *108*
Primeau, Bill, 196
Primeau, Jim (brother of Joe), 29, 196
Primeau, Jim (son of Joe), 83
Primeau, Joe, 28, 32, 34, 39, 43, 56, *57*, 58, 60, 62, 65, *66*, 67, 72, *72*, 73, 77, 82, 85, 97, 100, 106, 114, 141, 189, 233–34, 242, 243, 245, 249

Primeau, Joe Jr., 80, 196
Prystai, Metro, 61, 62, 75, 79, 268
Psutka, Harry, 73, 80, 89, 90
Pulford, Bob, 35, 153

Quackenbush, Bill, 242
Quebec Junior Hockey League, 98
Queen's University, 18–19, 24
Quinn, Frank, 70
Quinn, Pat, 123, *123*
Quinn, Reg, 164–67

Rafferty, Bob, 195
Rajtek, Peter, 208
Rankin, Charlie, 17
Rankin, Frank, 20–21, 230, *230*
Ratchford, Mike "Butch," 94, 99
Ratelle, Jean, 128, 133, 134
Reaume, Marc, 94, 97, 98, 99, 103, 197, 243
Rebellato, Gene, 201
Rebstock, George, 50
Redding, George "Shorty," 89, 90, 91
Reddoch, Bill, 73
Redican, Father Joe, 187, *187*, 269
Redmond, Mickey, 250
Reeves, Greg, 207
Regan, Bill, 29
Regan, Father, 87
Reid, Dave, 98
Reise, Leo, 242
Retty, Jerry, 98
Ricci, Rich, 220
Rice, Steve, 27
Richard, Maurice, 147, 201
Richardson, Dave, 136, 138
Richardson, William "Dutchy," 17, 23
Ridley, Frank, 149
Rimstad, Dave, 118
Riordan, Barry, 96
Rivers, Wayne, 154
Roach, Guy, 47
Robertson, George, 67
Robertson, John Ross, 20
Robichaud, Ryan, 168
Robinson, Doug, 130–31
Roche, C.E., 17
Rocque, W., 27
Rooney, Jim, 166
Rope, Don, 82, 189, 245
Rosati, Mike, 211
Roxborough, Jack, 258
Roy, Rod, 83, 196
Royal Bank Cup, 26
Rubino, Eric, 220
Sabourin, Bob, 85, 86, 94–97, 196
Sadler, Joe, 52, 56, 58–62, 65, 194, 239
St. Andrew's College, 16, 27

St. Catharines Falcons, 58–59
St. Catharines TeePees, 124–25, 128, 129–31, 247
St. Jerome's College, 145, 156
Saint John Beavers, 92
St. Joseph's College, 25
St. Mark's University, 145, 258
St. Michael's Buzzers, 63, 187, 191–217, *192*
1961 Memorial Cup championship, 257
hiatus from Jr. 'B' play, 213–14
move up to Tier II Jr. 'A', 214
refuse to play in OHA playoffs, 200–201
sold to McCarron, 216–17
win Buckland Trophy, 218–19
win Sutherland Cup, 39, 191, 192, 195–96, 203–4, *204*, 210, 212
St. Michael's College School
campus moved to Bathurst and St. Clair, 15
campus moved to Bay and Bloor, 13–15
drops MTHL hockey program, 213–14
established, 12–13
St. Michael's College School Arena, 15, 169, 180, *186*, 187, 189
St. Michael's College women's team, 25, *25*
St. Michael's Juniors (Prep School League), 16–17, *18*, *19*, 20, *21*, 27–29
St. Michael's Majors, *52*, *53*, *151*, *152*, *165*
1934 Memorial Cup championship, 38–43, *41*
1945 Memorial Cup championship, 56–63, *0*, 68
1947 Memorial Cup championship, 71–78, *5*, *76*
1961 Memorial Cup championship, 128–41, *139*, *140*
granted OHL expansion franchise, 164–68
hiatus from OHA Junior 'A' league, 49
join Metro Jr. 'A' league, 145–52
move to Mississauga, 188–90
rivalry with Marlboros, 110–12
sold to Melnyk, 176
sponsorship agreement with Maple Leafs, 32–33
withdraw from Junior 'A' hockey, 152–53, 162, 264
withdraw from OHA Jr. 'A' league, 143–45, 257–58, 264
St. Michael's Monarchs, 89–92, 93
St. Michael's Seniors, *17*, 17–20, 21, 23–24

St. Nicholas Hockey Club, 23–24
Samis, Phil, 61, 63, 65, 72, 195
Sampson, Gord, 202
Sandford, Ed, 63, 65, 66, 68, 71–74, *72*, *75*, 77, 79, *79*, 80, 195, 196, 242, *242*
Sandford, Fred, 196
Saskatoon Quakers, 91
Saunders, Robert, 63, 77
Savage, Bob, 107, 113, 255, 262
Savage, Mike, 204
Savage, Wayne, 184
Sawchuk, Terry, 73, 83
Scherer, Punch, 89
Schiller, Bob, 85, 86, 94, 95–96, 101
Schmalz, Cecil, 50, 193
Schmidt, Jack, 91
Schmidt, Milt, 42, 48, 235, 236, 237
Schnurr, Bob "Snuffy," 51, 52, 53
Schock, Ron, 160
Schofield, Dwight, 207
Scholes, George, 194, 195, 196
Scott, Bill, 73
Scruton, Howard, 208
Scully, Father, 68
Scurrah, Roy, 74
Seiling, Rod, 37, 127, 131, 142, *144*, 145–50, 156–59, 161–62, *167*, 171, 203–4, 205, 252, 259, 261
Selby, Brit, 145, 159
Selby, John, 199
Selby, Tom, 196
Selke, Frank, 27, 30, 34, *34*, 232, 239
Senick, George, 91
Sexsmith, Paul, 136, 137, 138
Shack, Eddie, 113
Shapiro, Harvey, 217
Shea, Tom, 80, 82
Shearer, Pete, 148
Sheedy, Father Matthew, 54, 127, 143, 144
Sheedy, Gene, 39, 45–46, 47, 49
Sheffield, Bob, 202
Sherbrooke Hockey Club, 19
Shillington, Clare, 90
Shore, Eddie, 246
Shouldice, Hap, 92
Shulmistra, Rich, 212
Silverman, Max, 46
Simpson, Brian, 168
Simpson, Cliff, 146
Simpson, Gordon, 260
Sinclair, Paul, 204
Sittler, Darryl, 208

Skinner, Peder, 218
Sloan, Tod, 56, *58*, 58–62, 65–68, 147, 189, 253
Slota, Frank, 160
Sluce, Vic, 206
Sly, Darryl, 113, 116, 121, 189, 255
Smith, Art, 32
Smith, Bill (Majors director), 167
Smith, Bill (Whitby player), 146, 148
Smith, Carl "Winky," 191
Smith, Des, 129
Smith, Floyd, 249
Smith, Frank, 63
Smith, Gary, 129, 145–50, 156, 159, 160, 161, *202*, 202–5, *263*
Smith, Orville, 45, 47
Smith, Sid, 59
Smith, Tommy, 135
Smith, Tomy, *136*
Smythe, Conn, 31, *31*, 32–35, 49, 68, 83, 109, 144, 153, 245–46, 265
Smythe, Dorothea, 33
Smythe, Stafford, 33, 35–36, 97, 98, 101, 145, 146, 152–53, 161, 249, 264, 265, 266
Smythe, Tommy, 33
Snita, Marcin, 168
Somers, Tom, 49
Sonoski, Jim, 199
Southwell, Jason, 168
Speyer, Peter, 204
Spezza, Jason, 216
Spezza, Matthew, 218
Sportsmen's Patriotic Association (SPA) Trophy, 27–28, 38
Spratt, Father Jack, *20*, 23, 24, 28–29, 54
Spratt, Peter, 18, 23
Spurr, Kyle, 185
Stanfield, Rob, 168
Stanley, Allan, 37, 246
Stanley Cup, 18
Stanowski, Wally Jr., 129, 204
Stanton, Bob, 50
Stanutz, George, 94
Stefanski, Bud, 183, 184, 186
Stein, Harvey, 77
Stemkowski, Peter, 249
Stephens, Charlie, 168, 170, 172
Stephenson, Ken, 136, 137
Stewart, Anthony, 216
Stewart, Black Jack, 243
Stewart, Ron, *111*
Stornik, John, 207
Stothers, Mike, 208
Stratford Juniors, 16, 17

Stratford Kroehlers, 51, 71, 94
Stratford Midgets, 46
Stratford Seniors, 18
Strong, Ken, 208
Stukus, Bill, 191
Sulc, Jan, 168
Sullivan, Barry, 58, 59
Sullivan, Frank, 89, 90, 199
Sullivan, Jimmy, 29
Sullivan, Peter, 206
Sullivan, Ryan, 218
Sutherland, Capt. James T., 63
Sutherland Cup, 26, 191
Sutton, Andy, 215
Sweeney, Bill, 113

Taggart, Jack, 58
Tanti, Tony, 209
Tarasov, Anatoli, 97, 102
Taylor, Billy, 46, 47, 191–92
Taylor, Billy Jr., 133
Taylor, Harry, 67
Teal, Skip, 100
Teal, Vic, 129
Ted Reeve Arena, 15
Teno, Harvey, *39*, 40, 42, 44
Terzo, Anthony, 168, 170
Tessier, Orval, 100
Therien, Emile, 147, 148, 203, 204
Thompson, Mike, 212
Thompson, Winnett, 17, 23
Thomson, Jeff, 172
Thomson, Jimmy, 52, 53, *53*, 54, 56–59, *57*, 61, 62, 65, 68, 147, 238, 242
Timmons, Jules, 17
Tisi, Kain, 218
Tocchet, Rick, 210
Tonn, Ab "Two Ton," 45, 191
Toppazzini, Jerry, 267
Toppazzini, Ted, 96, 98, 99, 101, 103
Toronto Argonauts, 18
Toronto Beaches Hockey League, 21
Toronto Falcons. *See* Toronto Ravinas
Toronto Granites, 230
Toronto Junior Hockey League, 16
Toronto Lions, 44, 47
Toronto Maple Leafs, 31–37, 85
Toronto Marlboros, 28, 29, 30, 32, 34, 35–36, 51, 57, 85–86, 145, 161
rivalry with Majors, 110–12
Toronto Native Sons, 50
Toronto Ravinas, 32, 34
Toronto Rugby and Athletic Association (TR&AA), 21
Toronto St. Mary's, 34

Toronto St. Michael's Majors. *See* St. Michael's Majors
Toronto Senior Marlboros, 82, 89–90, 92, 234
Toronto Victorias, 21
Toronto Young Rangers, 49, 50, 51, 81
Tourvieille, Pierre, 11
Trail Smoke Eaters (junior), 53–54
Trail Smoke Eaters (senior), 121
Tripp, Bob, 148
Trottier, Dave, 27–28
Turik, Frank, 53, 56, 59–62
Turnbull, Harvey, 201
Turyk, Troy, 168
Tyrell, Ross, 167

Ubriaco, Gene, *108*, 113, 116–17, 189, 255
Ubriaco, Johnny, 89, 91, 92
Ullman, Norm, 249
Unger, Garry, 249
Unionville Seaforths, 145, 146
University of British Columbia Thunderbirds, 258
University of Prince Edward Island Panthers, 185
University of Toronto, 13
University of Toronto Schools (UTS), 27
University of Toronto Varsity Grads, 28, 31
Upper Canada College, 16

Vaive, Justin, 185
Valleyfield Braves, 91–92
Valliquette, Murray, 80
Vaughan Raiders, 214
Vis, John, 168
Vitale, Phil, 129
Vitarelli, Cory, 182–85
Volpe, Father Rocco, 54, *112*, 194, 196, 205, 206
Volpe, George, 208
Voss, Carl, 32

Walker, Squib, 34, 243
Wall, Bob, 131, 132, 150
Wallace, Ron, 94, 248
Wallner, John, 31
Walsh, Ryan, 168, 175, *180*
Walton, Bobby, 151
Walton, Mike, 145, *147*, 148, 150, 151–52, 154, 156, 159, 160, 161, *167*, 204
Wansborough, Jamie, 210
Waterloo Hurricanes, 85
Watson, Barry, 129, 146
Watson, Harry, 129
Watson, Ken, 89, 91, 92
Watt, Bob, 107

Watt, Gordon, 40
Waugh, Tom, 185
Webb, Mike, 204, 205
Weekes, Kevin, 214
Weir, Terry, 213
West Toronto Nationals, 44–45, 93
Whaley, Reg, 133
Whelan, Father Maurice, 29, 54, 194
Wheldrake, Jack, 85
Whitby Dunlops, 121, 237
Whitby Mohawks, 145, 146
White, Jack, 84, 147
White, Tex, 24
White, Tom, 199
Wieczorek, Paul, 207
Wildey, Ed, 50, 81
Wilkey, Doug, 168
Williams, Joe, *72*, 80
Willson, Don, 38, 39, 43
Wilson, Bob, 75, 244
Wilson, Father, 119
Wilson, Johnny, 239
Wilson, Pat, 89
Wilson, Rick, 208
Wilson, Ryan, 183, 184
Windsor Spitfires, 71
Winnipeg Monarchs, 67
Winnipeg Victorias, 19–20
Winslow, Warren, 194, 195
Wiseman, Lyall, 60
Woit, Benny, 71, 73, 78, 80
Wolfe, Trevor, 168
Wolski, Wojtek, 217–18, *218*
women's hockey, 25, *25*
Woolley, Jason, 212
Wren, Dr. Hank, 132, 141
Wright, Bob, 147

Yale University, 24
Young, Don, 201
Young, Gerry, 86, 196
Young, Howie, 199

Zamparo, Julian, 219
Zeidel, Larry, 91
Ziliotto, Larry, 131
Zombo, Rick, 208–9
Zoryk, Steve, 170
Zorzi, Father Daniel, 171, 176, *188*, 217
Zuccato, Ed, 206

Photo Credits

St. Michael's College School Archives: pages 36, 42, 58, 76, 102, 104, 105, 107, 108, 114 (top and bottom), 117 (top), 118, 121, 123, 138, 140, 142, 144, 146, 147, 149, 152, 162, 166, 176, 182, 186, 187, 197, 198, 202, 204, 205, 220, 223, 224, 233, 254, 259, 260, 263, 264

University of St. Michael's College Archives: pages 10, 12, 13, 14, 17, 18, 19, 20, 21, 22, 24, 25, 27, 28, 30, 39, 41, 51 (top and bottom), 52, 53, 57, 60, 66, 68, 72, 75, 79, 81, 83, 192, 193, 194, 242, 245, 256

St. Michael's Buzzers Hockey Club: pages: 171, 215, 217, 273, 274, 275, 280 (top and bottom), 288, 290

Hockey Hall of Fame
Hockey Hall of Fame Archives: pages 230, 231
Imperial Oil-Turofsky/HHOF: pages 8, 31, 34, 43, 48, 64, 84, 87, 93, 100, 109, 111, 112, 115, 125, 136, 139, 160, 163, 235, 238, 240, 241, 244, 247, 248, 251, 253, 262, 267
Michael Burns Sr./HHOF: pages 116, 117 (bottom), 151

Paul Cerre Family Collection: page 250

Mike Draper: page 226

Father Hugh Foley, C.S.B.: pages 50, 54

Tony Fritz: page 153

Markham Waxers Hockey Club: page 210

Dan Nicholson: pages 165, 167, 170, 173, 177, 179 (top and bottom), 180, 184, 185, 188, 190, 213, 216, 218, 219, 228, 266

Bob Schiller: page 96

Every effort has been made to properly credit the owner of each photograph. Should readers discover discrepancies, please contact the authors through the publisher.